MIGRANTS, WORK, AND THE WELFARE STATE

MIGRANTS, WORK, AND THE WELFARE STATE

edited by Torben Tranæs and Klaus F. Zimmermann

*with contributions by Thomas Bauer, Amelie Constant, Horst Entorf,
Christer Gerdes, Claus Larsen, Poul Chr. Matthiessen,
Niels-Kenneth Nielsen, Marie Louise Schultz-Nielsen,
and Eskil Wadensjö*

University Press of Southern Denmark
and The Rockwool Foundation Research Unit

Migrants, Work, and the Welfare State
© The authors and University Press of Southern Denmark 2004

Printed by Narayana Press

ISBN 87 7838 774 4

Cover design by
Klaus Bjerager, Designco

Linguistic advisor: Tim Caudery

Published with support from:
The Rockwool Foundation

University Press of Southern Denmark
Campusvej 55
DK-5230 Odense M
Phone: +45 6615 7999
Fax: +45 6615 8126
E-mail: Press@forlag.sdu.dk
www.universitypress.dk

Distribution in the United States and Canada:
International Specialized Book Services
5804 NE Hassalo Street
Portland, OR 97213-3644 USA
Phone: +1-800-944-6190
www.isbs.com

Contents

Preface		11
CHAPTER 1	Migrants, Work, and the Welfare State: An Introduction	15
	By Torben Tranæs and Klaus F. Zimmermann	
	1.1 The Lisbon Process and Economic Growth	16
	1.2 How Migrants Do, and What They Do	20
	1.3 The Genesis of the Project	22
	1.4 An Overview of the Book	26
	References	27
CHAPTER 2	Immigration Policy and Danish and German Immigration	31
	By Thomas Bauer, Claus Larsen, and Poul Chr. Matthiessen	
	2.1 Introduction	31
	2.2 Immigration Policy	32
	2.2.1 Denmark	32
	2.2.2 Germany	36
	2.2.3 Migration Policy in Europe	40
	2.3 Migration to Denmark and Germany	41
	2.3.1 Net Migration	41
	2.3.2 Asylum Seekers and Refugees	47
	2.3.3 Temporary Immigration	53
	2.4 The Demographic Characteristics of Immigrants in Germany and Denmark	57
	2.4.1 Source Countries	57
	2.4.2 Sex and Age Distributions	59
	2.4.3 Regional Distribution	62
	2.5 Summary	64
	References	65
CHAPTER 3	The Educational Background and Human Capital Attainment of Immigrants	75
	By Amelie Constant and Claus Larsen	
	3.1 Introduction	75
	3.2 The Educational Level of Foreigners – A Descriptive Analysis	76
	3.2.1 The Schooling Systems and School-to-Work Transition in Denmark and Germany	76
	3.2.1.1 Denmark	76

3.2.1.2	Germany	78
3.2.1.3	Differences and Similarities between Denmark and Germany	80
3.2.2	Measurement Issues	81
3.2.3	The Human Capital of Foreigners in Denmark and Germany	82
3.2.3.1	Education Obtained in the Home Country	83
3.2.3.2	Education Obtained in the Receiving Country	86
3.3	Determinants of Human Capital Formation	95
3.3.1	Previous Studies of the Educational Attainment of Immigrants in the Host Country	95
3.3.2	Modeling of Educational Levels: Methods, Data, and Variables	98
3.3.2.1	Data	98
3.3.2.2	Variables	98
3.3.2.3	Methods and Hypotheses	102
3.3.3	Estimation Results	104
3.3.3.1	Multinomial Logit Results on Primary/Lower Secondary Schooling and Gymnasium/University Education	105
3.3.3.2	Binomial Logit Results for Vocational Training and No Vocational Training	111
3.4	Summary and Conclusions	115
	References	117

CHAPTER 4 Employment Trends for Immigrants and Natives 119
By Marie Louise Schultz-Nielsen and Amelie Constant

4.1	Introduction	119
4.1.1	Immigrant Employment in Denmark and Germany	120
4.1.2	Importing Manpower, Providing a Safe Haven, or …?	121
4.2	Employment Trends for Immigrants and Natives	123
4.2.1	Why are Immigrants more often Employed in Germany than in Denmark?	126
4.2.2	Why has Immigrant Employment Fallen over Time?	131
4.2.3	Why is Immigrant Employment so Sensitive to the Business Cycle?	135
4.3	German Unification	136
4.4	Long Run Integration: From First to Second Generation Immigrants	137
4.5	Occupational Sorting by Country of Origin	139
4.6	Summary and Conclusion	143
	References	145

Contents

CHAPTER 5	Labor Force Participation and Unemployment: Incentives and Preferences		147
	By Amelie Constant and Marie Louise Schultz-Nielsen		
	5.1	Introduction	147
	5.2	The Monetary Incentives: Does it Pay for Immigrants to Work?	149
	5.3	Are the Unemployed Available to the Labor Market? . .	155
	5.4	Who Joins the Labor Force?	159
	5.5	Employment Chances	169
	5.6	Immigrants and the Job Hierarchy	175
	5.7	Summary and Conclusions	181
	References:		184
CHAPTER 6	Immigrant Selection and Earnings		187
	By Amelie Constant and Marie Louise Schultz-Nielsen		
	6.1	Introduction	187
	6.2	The Anatomy of the Guest worker System	189
	6.2.1	Germany's Immigrants	189
	6.2.2	Denmark's Immigrants	190
	6.3	Method and Data	191
	6.3.1	Description of the Data Set	191
	6.3.2	Analysis and Variables	192
	6.4	Characteristics of the Sample Population	195
	6.5	Empirical Results	199
	6.5.1	Selection-Adjusted Earnings Profiles	199
	6.5.2	Counterfactual Analysis of the Immigrant Earnings Profiles	203
	6.6	Recapitulation and Concluding Remarks	208
	References		210
CHAPTER 7	Immigrant Self-Employment and Economic Performance		213
	By Amelie Constant and Marie Louise Schultz-Nielsen		
	7.1	Introduction	213
	7.2	Labor Market Institutions, Policies, and Cyclical Dynamics	215
	7.2.1	The German Realities: Emphasis on Immigrants	215
	7.2.2	The Danish Realities: Emphasis on Immigrants	217
	7.3	Modeling of Self-employment: Methods and Hypotheses	219
	7.3.1	Self-Employment probabilities	219
	7.3.2	Economic Returns to Self-employment	223
	7.3.3	Data	223

	7.4	Characteristics of the Sample Populations	224
	7.4.1	Self-Employed Versus Salaried Workers	224
	7.4.2	Self-Employed Ethnic Groups	229
	7.5	Estimation Results	233
	7.5.1	Proclivity for Self-Employment. Binomial Logit Results	233
	7.5.2	The Returns to Self-Employment	236
	7.5.3	A Country or an Immigrant Effect?	239
	7.6	Conclusions	241
		References	243

CHAPTER 8 Social Transfers to Immigrants in Germany and Denmark 245
By Niels-Kenneth Nielsen

	8.1	Introduction	245
	8.2	Formal Access Condition to Social Security Benefits in Germany and Denmark	246
	8.2.1	Unemployment Insurance	247
	8.2.2	Social Assistance	249
	8.2.3	Old-age Pension	251
	8.2.4	Disability Pension	254
	8.2.5	Housing Benefit	255
	8.2.6	Child Benefit	256
	8.2.7	Rules of Access to Social Security Systems: Summary	257
	8.3	Who Receives Benefits in Denmark and Germany?	258
	8.3.1	Unemployment Insurance	259
	8.3.2	Social Assistance	263
	8.3.3	Old-age and Disability Pension	265
	8.4	Probability of Receiving Benefits	269
	8.4.1	Germany	270
	8.4.2	Denmark	275
	8.4.3	Comparison of Germany and Denmark	279
	8.5	Summary and Conclusions	280
		References	282

CHAPTER 9 Immigration and Crime in Germany and Denmark 285
By Horst Entorf and Claus Larsen

	9.1	Introduction	285
	9.2	Immigration and Crime in Germany: Descriptive Evidence	286
	9.3	Immigration and Crime in Denmark: Descriptive Evidence	293
	9.3.1	Criminality Rates Among Immigrants, Descendants, and Danes – Convictions	295
	9.3.2	Trends in Crime Levels Measured with Danish Data Adjusted to German Statistics	301

	9.4	Comparison of Descriptive Evidence from Germany and Denmark	306
	9.5	Prevention of Immigrant Crime: Education and Other Factors	308
	9.6	Conclusions, Future Research	314
	References		315

CHAPTER 10 Immigrants and the Public Sector in Denmark and Germany . . . 319

By Eskil Wadensjö and Christer Gerdes

	10.1	Immigration, the Public Sector and the Economy – the Starting Point	319
	10.2	Immigration and its Fiscal Impact: Theory	319
	10.3	Data	322
	10.3.1	Denmark	322
	10.3.2	Germany	324
	10.4	The Fiscal Impact of Immigration in Denmark, 1991-2000	327
	10.5	The Fiscal Impact of Immigration in Germany 2002 . . .	331
	10.6	Which Factors Influence the Individual Net Transfers to the Public Sector in Denmark and in Germany?	332
	10.6.1	Denmark	332
	10.6.2	Germany	342
	10.6.3	A Comparison	350
	10.7	Summary and Conclusions	353
	References		355

CHAPTER 11 Some Socioeconomic Consequences of Immigration 357

By Eskil Wadensjö and Christer Gerdes

	11.1	Immigration, Wages and Unemployment	357
	11.2	Immigration, Employment and Incomes in Denmark . .	358
	11.3	The Impact of Immigration on the Native Wage Rate . .	367
	11.4	Self-employed Immigrants in Denmark	371
	11.5	Immigration and Unemployment among Native Workers in Denmark	374
	11.6	Income Distribution among Immigrants and Natives . .	377
	11.7	Summary and Conclusions	384
	References		385

CHAPTER 12 Migrants, Work, and the Welfare State: Summary and Conclusions 391

By Torben Tranæs and Klaus F. Zimmermann

	12.1	Migration and the Policy Stand	391
	12.2	Educational Attainment and Training	392

	12.3	Employment Trends	*394*
	12.4	Employment Incentives	*395*
	12.5	Earnings Dispersion	*396*
	12.6	Immigrant Self-employment	*397*
	12.7	Welfare take-up	*399*
	12.8	Crime	*400*
	12.9	The Public Coffers	*400*
	12.10	Socio-economic Consequences	*401*
	12.11	The Findings in Brief	*402*
APPENDIX		Data Description	*405*
	By Thomas Bauer and Niels-Kenneth Nielsen		
	A.1	Introduction	*405*
	A.2	Data Sources for Denmark	*405*
	A.2.1	The Rockwool Foundation Migration Survey – Denmark (RFMS-D)	*405*
	A.2.2	Sample Design	*406*
	A.2.3	Response Rate	*408*
	A.2.4	Representativeness in the Danish Survey	*409*
	A.2.5	Weighting of the Danish Data	*411*
	A.2.6	Survey among Danes	*412*
	A.3	Danish Register Data	*413*
	A.4	German Data	*414*
	A.4.1	Arrangement of the German Survey	*415*
	A.4.2	Sample Design	*415*
	A.4.3	Response Rate	*417*
	A.4.4	Item Non-response	*418*
	A.4.5	Representativeness of the RFMS-G	*419*
	A.4.6	Weighting in the German Data Set	*422*
	A.5	References	*427*

Index *429*

The Rockwool Foundation Research Unit: Publications in English *435*

Preface

During much of the nineteenth and first half of the twentieth century Europe was a continent of net emigration, as millions left to seek their fortunes in the New World and elsewhere. This pattern changed radically in the second half of the twentieth century. In the 1950s, faced with massive labor shortages for its rapidly expanding economy, Germany became the first European country to open its borders to migrant workers who were not from its former colonies. One by one other European countries, including Denmark, followed suit. But while immigration did ease the pressures of the labor shortage, it also brought problems of social integration, and by the end of the twentieth century immigration and immigrant populations were issues that featured on the political agendas of countries throughout Europe.

Now, at the opening of the twenty-first century, Europe once again has a need for an increase in the workforce, because European populations are ageing. The proportion of the retired among the population is increasing, while the workforce itself is actually shrinking. One partial solution to these demographic problems might once again be found in immigration. Fortunately for Europe, the continent can offer a greater potential for employing labor productively than can some neighboring countries to the south and south-east. This means that workers should be able to raise their standard of living by moving to Europe, while Europe could benefit from their work output. It seems that everyone might have something to gain.

So far, however, it is by no means clear that mass migration to Europe has brought much economic advantage either to the receiving nations or to the immigrants themselves. For both parties, the primary precondition for a mutually beneficial arrangement is that immigrants should be successfully integrated into the labor market. This does not just mean that immigrants should be able to find work. It is important what types of employment they can obtain, and how much they are paid for their work. If, for example, it is the case that immigrants systematically earn less than natives then there is cause for concern, because such a pattern would indicate a return to the class-divided societies of the past, but this time with the division based on ethnicity.

It is concerns such as these, as well as the potential solutions to demographic problems that immigration may offer, that have motivated the research that forms the basis of this book. By examining the effects of immigration to date on both the immigrants and the societies to which they have migrated, it may be possible to see whether and how future immigration can be handled to the benefit of all.

The research presented here is based on a comparative approach. Such an approach can reveal much of interest. However, comparisons involving several nations are difficult, and consequently often restricted in scope. This research focuses on two nations only: Germany and Denmark. These two countries have different social institutions and traditions, but share similar goals. Detailed comparisons between the two countries are possible for many parameters, allowing the researchers to produce a number of findings of relevance for the general consideration of the effects of immigration. In this book the authors consider demographic trends, educational and labor market factors, and immigrants' use of the social services in Denmark and Germany, all from a comparative perspective. The issues of crime and the effects of immigration on salaries and employment for the host population are also analyzed and discussed. Finally, the book considers the question of the financial sustainability of the welfare state. What impact does immigration have on the public purse, in both the first and subsequent generations?

The research presented in the book is the result of collaboration between the Institute for the Study of Labor (IZA) in Germany and the Rockwool Foundation Research Unit (RFF) in Denmark. Both these organizations were engaged before in research on the areas of immigration and integration, and they formed natural partners for this new project. Most of the data used for analysis come from two major surveys carried out specifically for the project, the Rockwool Foundation Migration Survey – Denmark (RFMS-D) and the Rockwool Foundation Migration Survey – Germany (RFMS-G). The results of this major research effort are now presented here to the international research community, to politicians, to those working in the field with immigration issues, and to the general public.

Acknowledgments. The editors wish to express their great gratitude to the many people who have contributed to the research project and to the production of this book. The project itself was initiated by Gunnar Viby Mogensen, the former Head of Research at the Rockwool Foundation Research Unit. We owe him much for his contributions both to this specific project and to migration research in general over many years.

The Board of the Rockwool Foundation, who had previously shown a great interest in and commitment to research into integration in Denmark, enthusiastically adopted the idea of a comparative study between Denmark and Germany and generously provided the necessary funds. The project has been particularly expensive because it required the collection of representative survey data for both Denmark and Germany. Our gratitude therefore goes to the entire Board of the Rockwool Foundation and its chairman, Tom Kähler, as well as its Managing Director, Poul Erik Pedersen, both for giving us the opportunity to work on this project and for their helpful assistance all the way through it.

Next, we wish to thank the members of the actual research team: Thomas Bauer, Amelie Constant, Horst Entorf, Christer Gerdes, Claus Larsen, Poul Christian Matthiessen, Niels-Kenneth Nielsen, Marie Louise Schultz-Nielsen, and Eskil Wadensjö. They organized the collection of the data in Germany and Denmark, carried out the subsequent analysis of the material, and wrote the chapters in this book.

We thank Bent Jensen and Hanne Lykke from the Rockwool Foundation Research Unit in Copenhagen for preparing the final manuscript and supervising it through production; Georgios Tassoukis, the data bank manager of IZA, for his invaluable help with the preparation of the data; and the student assistants at the Rockwool Foundation Research Unit in Copenhagen, Mark Gervasini Nielsen, Christian Scheuer, Esben Anton Schultz, and Kåre Steffen Valgreen, for their assistance with the compilation of the data.

We also thank the entire management staff at Statistics Denmark, under the leadership of state statistician Jan Plovsing, for their interest in and work on this book, and also the interview department and the staff of the excellent library. Our thanks go too to Harald Bielenski and Gabriella Fischer of Infratest Sozialforschung, Germany, for their involvement in our project. Likewise we owe the Danish Ministry of Finance our gratitude for their very positive attitude to independent research based on the "The Law Model", and we thank Frederik Hansen in particular for his assistance with the data and for his many helpful comments. Finally we wish to thank Lilo Locher, Regina Riphahn, Phil Savage, and Arne Uhlendorff for their help, comments and excellent advice during the project.

June 2004, Copenhagen and Bonn

Torben Tranæs
Research Director
The Rockwool Foundation
Research Unit (RFF)

Klaus F. Zimmermann
Director
The Institute for the Study of Labor (IZA)

CHAPTER 1

Migrants, Work, and the Welfare State: An Introduction

By Torben Tranæs and Klaus F. Zimmermann

Migration has become a global phenomenon. Currently, about 2.9 percent or 175 million people worldwide are international migrants (IOM, 2003). This estimate captures, among other types of migrants, people moving for purposes of family reunification, refugees, and displaced persons. Relatively few are economic migrants, at least at a formal level. The estimate does not include illegal migrants. Europe has a stock of 56 million migrants in the population; the next largest stocks are in Asia, with 50 million migrants, and North America, with 41 million.[1] Although North America is placed only third in these terms, by far the greatest part of international economics research into migration has dealt with the situation there. A rapidly growing literature for Europe is beginning to cope with this deficit, but reliable research findings are still missing for many countries and issues.

In contrast, the need for additional knowledge concerning migrants in Europe has increased as a result of the effects of globalization, the internally-created demographic burden, and the sluggish European economic development. Migration seems to be at the same time both a threat and a solution in relation to many issues. Globalization of information and production calls for a higher speed of adjustment. The increasing importance of human capital in the production of goods and services around the world is linked to a decline in the demand for unskilled labor.[2] This generates migratory moves away from two adverse situations. On the one hand, there is excess demand and hence global competition for high-skilled workers. These workers have the opportunity to engage in flexible work and to move from one country to another throughout their working lives. On the other hand, low-skilled workers face excess supply on their labor markets. They become forced migrants who need to move in order to obtain an adequate income.

---

1 For more recent detailed migration figures for the OECD countries see SOPEMI 2003 (2004).
2 See Zimmermann, Bauer, Bonin, Fahr, and Hinte (2002) for a long-term evaluation of this problem for Germany.

For the European Union as a whole and its member countries in particular, there are four important challenges[3]:

- There is an increasing pressure from people from all parts of the less developed world to be allowed to enter the European Union to work and take up welfare services and benefits.
- High-skilled labor is becoming both more mobile and more in demand. Europe is being forced to enter into world-wide competition in order to obtain a fair share in this market.
- Trade is one source of virtual labor imports: imported goods carry labor. But the ultimate challenge is the Internet, which allows for a more and more effective virtual immigration of labor.
- Over the medium term future, Eastern enlargement of the European Union will soon create more open labor markets and potential needs for adjustment.

European Union member countries like Denmark and Germany will soon have to decide how to meet these challenges. Is a continuation of the current policy – what in the media is often referred to as the "Fortress Europe" policy – appropriate, or does the European Union need a labor immigration policy that is more "rational" in the sense that it considers economic interests? In order to develop an appropriate policy it is necessary to learn more about the way immigrants currently fare in European member countries, and how they affect the economic well-being of the native populations and public sector finances. It is furthermore important to understand how policy measures have contributed to the current migration situation. This book presents the results of a comprehensive comparative study between Denmark and Germany and provides new evidence for this purpose, hence contributing to the development of better policies.

1.1 The Lisbon Process and Economic Growth

There is much concern about the economic prospects of the European Union (see Sapir Report, 2004). In response to low growth, high inflation, and low levels of employment, the European Community has been implementing various political strategies in order to overcome these deficiencies. Among recent initiatives have been the *Lisbon Agenda*, which aims at making Europe the most competitive and dynamic knowledge-based economy in the world, capable of sustainable economic growth, with more and better jobs and greater social cohesion, by 2010; and *Eastern enlarge-*

---

[3] A more general outline of the European migration problem is contained in Zimmermann (1995).

ment, the aim of which is to rapidly raise living standards in the new member states and to improve economic conditions in the European Union in general.

Both initiatives have implications for migration and integration strategies. The Eastern enlargement process has caused debates about additional immigration from the East, since all labor markets will eventually have to open up to workers from the new member states. The newly agreed European Constitution also suggests that the social security systems of the host countries take care of citizens of the EU member states, which has created concerns about "country hopping" and "welfare shopping". The Lisbon Agenda states that employment and economic policies should aim at a rise of the overall employment rate in Europe to as close as possible to 70 percent of the population aged 15-64, and an increase in the employment rate for women to more than 60 percent (Lisbon targets). The Stockholm European Council of 2001 sets intermediate targets for the employment rates in the EU in 2005 of 67 percent of the total working-age population and 57 percent for females (Stockholm targets). In order to achieve these goals, the labor market implications of immigration have to be taken into account.

In June 2003, the European Commission adopted a *Communication on Immigration, Integration, and Employment* that studied immigration in the context of demographic change and proposed a strategy to promote a better integration of immigrants and to prepare for attracting more immigrants in the medium-term future. The need for such initiatives is suggested by the fact that even if the Lisbon targets are achieved by 2010, employment in Europe will start to fall significantly afterwards, due to the aging of the population as a result of demographic changes. Achieving sustained economic growth would require a greater increase in productivity than can probably be achieved. It is, therefore, important to mobilize the current stock of migrants to enter the labor market, and to prepare for new immigration by implementing better integration strategies.

How far is the Lisbon Agenda on its way, and to what extent are its goals likely to be achieved for immigrants as well as others? Table 1.1 provides some insights into these questions for the European Union in total, and for its member states Denmark and Germany. The employment rates presented for 2002 suggest that the European Union is still far from reaching these goals. While Germany is doing somewhat better and Denmark is already significantly above the required levels, it seems as though it will be difficult to achieve the Lisbon goals by 2010 at the EU level. Increases of about 6 percentage points for the total EU employment rate and about 4 percentage points for the female EU employment rate have to take place for the targets to be achieved. EU-national immigrants exhibit higher overall employment rates, and are hence closer to the employment goals. This also suggests that their moves between countries are more often determined by the motive to work in the receiving country.

Table 1.1. Employment and Unemployment Rates 2002 (percent)

	Denmark	Germany	European Union
Employment, total	75.9	65.3	64.3
EU nationals	77.2	66.5	66.4
Non-EU nationals	49.8	51.2	52.6
Low-skilled	60.4	43.6	49.4
Medium-skilled	80.6	69.8	70.5
High-skilled	87.0	83.0	82.8
Employment, females	71.7	58.8	55.6
EU nationals	73.5	60.3	58.8
Non-EU nationals	42.7	39.8	41.2
Unemployment, total	4.3	8.6	7.7
EU nationals	4.2	8.1	7.1
Non-EU nationals	13.0	16.2	15.8
Low-skilled	6.7	13.5	10.8
Medium-skilled	3.6	8.7	7.3
High-skilled	3.7	4.3	4.6

Source: European Communities (2003).

Notes: Employment rates defined as the proportion of persons aged 15-64 in employment as a percentage of the population of the same age group. Unemployment rates are defined as unemployment among persons aged 15-64 as a percentage of the labor force of the same age group. The European Union refers to the 15 member states. Only the rows "EU nationals" and "Non-EU nationals" refer to foreigners. All other figures include foreigners and natives. Lisbon targets: Employment rates 70 percent of the total, and more than 60 percent for females, in 2010. Stockholm targets: Employment rates 67 percent of the total and more than 57 percent for females in 2005.

Non-EU-national immigrants have exceedingly low employment rates. Unlike EU nationals, they are not well integrated into the labor markets. The employment rates are around 50 percent for the whole non-EU immigrant population, and around 40 percent for the female subgroup. Denmark performs surprisingly poorly, being worse than Germany and the EU average on the overall measure, and only ahead of Germany and the EU average by a small margin for the female group. There is a substantial integration problem with respect to non-EU nationals in labor markets across Europe, but it is most severe in Denmark. Non-EU nationals in Denmark have a total employment rate that is 26 percentage points below the overall rate, and females are even 29 percentage points below this rate. This difference is less severe in Germany, being 14 percentage points overall, and 19 percentage points for females; the differences at the European level are 12 and 14 percentage points respectively.

One caveat should be mentioned, though, namely that the group "foreign nationals" does not coincide with the group "immigrants", because some immigrants have adopted the nationality of the host country. Since there are different patterns of naturalization behavior across countries and across immigrant nationalities within a country, the size and distribution of groups of foreign nationals can provide an incomplete picture of the sizes of the various groups of immigrants.

Another marginalized group in Europe are the low-skilled. Their employment rate in the EU is only 49 percent overall. While Germany is worse than the average in that it employs only 44 percent of this group, Denmark manages to employ over 60 percent of the low-skilled, a remarkable result. However, the good Danish situation highlights again the integration problem which non-EU nationals face in that country in relation to the generally high levels of attachment to the labor market. Low-skilled natives and non-EU nationals may compete for jobs. It is interesting to determine whether the findings for Denmark in terms of the very low employment rates of non-EU nationals in comparison to the low-skilled, which are contrary to the findings for Germany and the EU as a whole, are the consequences of particularly policy measures, low human capital upon arrival, or a particularly unfortunate combination of the two.

Table 1.1 also contains some facts about the differences in the unemployment rates. Again, Denmark performs best by having the lowest rates, and Germany exhibits the largest unemployment problem. EU nationals are again not a problem; their unemployment rates are the same as the overall rates. Non-EU nationals have the highest unemployment rates, about 2 to 3 times larger than the overall rates, the factor being 3 in the case of Denmark. Although a large proportion of the low-skilled workers are active in the Danish labor force, they are not relatively more unemployed than low-skilled Germans. This mirrors the point made above about the labor market integration of non-EU nationals in Denmark: the larger presence of low-skilled natives in the work force there does not hurt their relatively good performance, probably at the expense of the immigrants.

For both Denmark and Germany, and for the European Union in general, the unemployment rates for the low-skilled are substantially above the total rates, but not as high as the rates for the non-EU nationals. The unemployment rates for the medium-skilled are compatible with the general rates. Only the high-skilled have significantly lower levels of unemployment rates in Germany and in the European Union as a whole. In Denmark, the unemployment rate for this group remains at around 4 percent.

This analysis has identified two important issues. (i) The success of the Lisbon Agenda will depend mainly on the ability to provide jobs to the low-skilled. As Table 1.1 demonstrates, the 70 percent rule for the general employment rate has already been achieved for the medium-skilled and the high-skilled in the EU in general; this is also the case for Denmark, and almost so for Germany. It would help to get more females into work, but the deficits with respect to the Lisbon goals are much smaller than for the low-skilled. (ii) Non-EU nationals are largely underemployed, especially in Denmark. This integration problem is very probably not socially sustainable, but is also not economically rational. If more is done to attract the low-skilled population in general to entering employment, this may also help the non-EU nationals since they are largely low-skilled. In the face of the larger predicted deficits in skilled workers in the medium term, an active labor-market integration policy for immigrants with early training measures should also prove beneficial.

1.2 How Migrants Do, and What They Do

Economic research has investigated the migration issue in four major research areas:

- the determinants of mobility,
- the economic integration and adjustment of migrants to the labor market of the host country,
- the impact immigrants have on the natives, and
- the effects of immigration on government policies and the development of immigration policies.

A number of recent books deal with these issues. The series of articles contained in the four volumes on the *Economics of Migration* selected by Zimmermann and Bauer (2002) within the frameworks of four areas has placed particular focus on work relevant to the European economies. The book *Migration,* edited by Faini, de Melo, and Zimmermann (1999), has dealt with the interactions between migration, trade, and development. The book *Immigration Policy and the Welfare System* edited by Boeri, Hanson, and McCormick (2002) provides a recent update and an overview of migration data and policy issues for Europe and the United States. A more detailed evaluation of the European situation is contained in Brücker, Epstein, McCormick, Saint-Paul, Venturini, and Zimmermann (2002).

The book *How Labor Migrants Fare,* edited by Zimmermann and Constant (2004), presents recent research on the issue of immigrant adjustment to the labor market of the host country, and studies how immigrants perform in society. Trends in earnings, employment, unemployment, self-employment, occupational choices and educational attainment after migration are investigated. The role of language in labor market integration and the situation of illegal, legalized, and unwilling migrants is also examined. Some policy effects are studied; among those are the effects various criteria for the selection of immigrants have on their labor market success and on the public sector budget of the receiving country.

There is still a substantial lack of empirical evidence for the European countries. The book edited by Zimmermann (2004) on *European Migration: What Do We Know?* complements the literature by filling this gap, and provides a major source of reference. It collects original country chapters for all major European countries and contrasts the European evidence with experiences from most of the traditional immigration countries. This book provides for the first time complete evidence for Europe on questions such as: How do migrants fare and assimilate on the labor markets of the host country? And how do they affect the economic conditions of the native labor force? The evolution of migration policies and migration flows is studied and contrasted with the evidence from traditional immigration countries.

The lessons one can draw so far from the literature are these: in the past, the labor market integration of migrants has been slow, but steady. The impact of immigrants on the native population has not been very strong, but mostly beneficial. However, with globalization, the special pressure on low-skilled workers, and the increased demands on high-skilled people, the nature of the game seems to be changing. The economic position of the new immigrants has become weaker. From this perspective, it seems to be even more important than before to discuss a selective immigration policy. The successful Canadian experience is quite supportive of such a position. The limits of the Canadian model, however, have been shown recently by the failure of New Zealand to implement it successfully. The development of a European framework should benefit from these lessons.

Bauer, Dietz, Zimmermann, and Zwintz (2004) have summarized the findings of the rich literature on immigration for Germany. They find that in the 1950s and 1960s, migration was largely linked to labor market activities. Since the 1970s and early 1980s this turned into a phase of family migration. The 1980s and later periods were finally dominated by refugee migration. This all means that since the 1970s, most immigrants have not been members of the labor force, and furthermore that this trend has been on the increase. Policy measures like the halt to the guest-worker system in 1973, and the uncontrolled inflow of non-economic migration afterwards, are responsible for this development. The available earnings studies suggest that there is no clear-cut assimilation picture for the guest-worker generation. Ethnic Germans were generally found to assimilate, although at a slow rate. Individuals with foreign passports are more likely to be unemployed. However, this is largely the consequence of occupational status, and not of behavior. Ethnic Germans largely behave in a way similar to the natives. Self-employment is a channel that helps immigrants to integrate into the host society and often to obtain a salaried job later. Finally, there are not many indications that immigrants depress the wages of native workers. Mostly, the effects are small or insignificant, or even positive, a fact which can be interpreted as meaning that immigrants are complements to natives.

Pedersen (2004) provides a survey of migration research in Denmark. The Danish literature lacks a larger number of studies investigating the process of assimilation of immigrants and the impact of immigration on the labor market success of natives. As in Germany, guest workers were hired mainly from Yugoslavia and Turkey until the legislation stopping this programme was passed in 1973. Afterwards, there have been three different kinds of immigration flow, namely family reunifications, immigration from other OECD countries (mainly from the Nordic and other EU countries), and an inflow of refugees during the 1980s and 1990s. The process of labor market integration of immigrants from less developed countries and refugees has not been very successful. Their participation rates are low, especially for refugees, and the corresponding unemployment rates have remained high. Integration problems are caused by de facto high minimum wages, and lack of language skills and educational qualifications among the immigrants.

1.3 The Genesis of the Project

Research on the degree of success for the integration of non-Western immigrants into the Danish labor market has grown considerably since the first comprehensive study was delivered by Hummelgaard et al. (1995). This study was based on national administrative registers and, due to the comparatively easy access to these registers, has inspired a number of studies like Dahl et al. (1998), Wadensjö (1999), Husted et al. (2001), Rosholm et al. (2001a), Rosholm et al. (2001b), Wadensjö and Orrje (2002), and Nielsen et al. (2003). However, the registers contain no information about such potentially important factors as language proficiency, perceived job discrimination, or educational attainment in the home country.[4]

It can therefore be considered as something like a breakthrough for Nordic research in this area that recently Norwegian and Swedish researchers have combined in collaboration with national statistical offices extensive questionnaire surveys of both living conditions, language skills, and discrimination variables among non-Western immigrants with register information on the respondents' labor market characteristics. For such studies see Blom (1998) for Norway, and Swedish National Board of Health and Welfare (1999) for Sweden.

In Denmark, the Rockwool Foundation Research Unit established a similar collaboration with Statistics Denmark in 1999 to prepare a survey of living conditions among non-Western immigrants. The main results based on this investigation are reported in Mogensen and Matthiessen (2000) and Schultz-Nielsen et al. (2001). In 2001 a new survey was produced, and the results are summarized in Mogensen and Matthiessen (2002). The analysis showed that the likelihood of an immigrant being in employment depends largely on age, health, language proficiency, education, length of stay in Denmark, contact with Danes, and the presence of small children in the family; but also that measures of discrimination and economic incentives to work seem to play a role.

Given the many structural similarities between Denmark and Germany, and the existing body of literature in both countries, one would not expect the present comparative study to find many different determinants of integration success in the two countries. Nevertheless, the integration process as such might have progressed a little further in Germany than in Denmark. One reason for this might be that Germany received many more immigrants much earlier than Denmark, which leaves German

---

4 Information on home country educational attainment was made available from the Danish registers from 2002.

immigrants with more years in the host country than Danish immigrants. Second, German asylum policy was tightened up earlier than in Denmark (see Mogensen and Matthiessen, 2002). Third, the fact that immigrants have had easier access to social security benefits in Denmark than in Germany, at least until access conditions were recently changed, might have been an incentive for some immigrants to choose Denmark rather than Germany (see Hansen et al., 2002).

As Table 1.1 showed, the treatment and behavior of the non-EU nationals is crucial for the fulfillment of the employment goals of the countries concerned and for the integration of migrants into the labor market of the host country. The possibility of carrying out a similar survey on the living conditions of immigrants in both Denmark and Germany was innovative and promising. For the purpose of the investigation in the survey approach chosen, the group "non-EU nationals" was substituted by "non-Western nationals". Western countries are the EU countries before the enlargement in 2004, Iceland, Liechtenstein, Norway, Switzerland, North America, Australia, and New Zealand; all other countries are labelled non-Western, although some of them are now EU members.

One of the main reasons for the focus on non-Western countries is obviously that immigrants from these areas may face serious language impediments and a strong cultural diversity in relation to the host country. Therefore, they also have relatively large problems in integrating into the labor market of the host country. Furthermore, it is immigration from non-Western countries in particular that has been growing most rapidly in the last few decades, especially since the end of the 1960s.

There were 686,000 foreign nationals in Germany back in 1960, corresponding to 1.2 percent of the population. This increased to 2,381,000 in 1969, and continued to increase until the ban on immigration in 1973, when the number of foreign nationals reached 3,966,000, or 6.4 percent of the population. Immigration more or less stagnated for the remainder of the decade, and then began to move up again in the 1980s, with the number of immigrants in the population reaching 4,846,000 in 1989. Since then, numbers have increased considerably, and at the end of 2001 totalled 7,319,000 persons, or 8.9 percent of the population as a whole.

The pattern of immigration to Denmark has been somewhat different. In 1960, there were only just over 40,000 foreign nationals in Denmark, corresponding to less than 1 percent of the population. This increased only slowly throughout the 1960s, reaching 60,000 in 1969, but then grew to over 83,000 over the next three years. While immigration slowed somewhat up to the mid-1980s, recent years have again seen a strong rise, to 267,000 in 2002, or 5.0 percent of the population.

As soon as an immigrant acquires the nationality of the host country ("naturalization"), it may become impossible to distinguish him/her from the natives in some countries, including Germany. More and more of the immigrants who have come to Denmark since the end of the 1960s have become naturalized. This has happened more often in Denmark than in Germany. The naturalization rate calculated as average number of acquisitions of citizenship for 1995-2000 divided by the stock of third country nationals in 2000 from European Communities (2003: 189) is 6.7 percent for Denmark and 2 percent for Germany. This means that a growing number of any immigrant cohort disappears from official statistics year by year if one looks only at citizenship.

Moreover, since there are different patterns of naturalization behavior across nationalities, as mentioned above, the size and distribution of groups of foreign nationals may provide an incomplete picture not only of the total size but also of the relative size of the various ethnic groups. At first sight, this seems less of a problem for Germany, where there have been relatively fewer naturalizations. However, many ethnic Germans from Eastern Europe have emmigrated to Germany over recent decades. By law they are treated as Germans from the day of entry, and hence they also disappear from the immigration statistics. All these problems of the official statistics can be avoided by using specially-designed surveys that measure the process appropriately.

Furthermore the acquisition of citizenship does not automatically imply integration into society. An alternative definition of the immigrant population has therefore been introduced in the official Danish statistics. According to this alternative definition, the immigrant population consists of immigrants and descendants. The two groups are defined as follows:

- An *immigrant* is defined as a person born outside Denmark whose parents are both (or one of them if there is no available information on the other parent) foreign citizens or born abroad. If there is no available information on either of the parents and the person was born abroad, the person is also defined as an immigrant.
- A *descendant* is defined as a person born in Denmark to parents neither of whom are Danish citizens born in Denmark. If there is no available information on either of the parents and the person is a foreign citizen, the person is defined as a descendant.

In 2002, immigrants and descendants made up 7.7 percent of the population in Denmark, and of these three-quarters were from non-Western countries. The remaining 92 percent of the population are "persons where at least one of the parents is of Danish nationality and born in Denmark" (Schultz-Nielsen et al., 2001), who in the official Danish statistics are termed "Other". In this book, the more idiomatic term "Danes" is used, which follows the practice in the official statistics in the other Nordic countries. It is not possible to break down the population in Germany in quite the same way on the basis of the available register data.

The core part of this book uses data collected specifically for this project that consist of the results of two surveys carried out among the same groups of immigrants and descendants in Denmark and Germany respectively. In this book, these surveys are referred to as the *Rockwool Foundation Migration Survey – Denmark* (RFMS-D) and the *Rockwool Foundation Migration Survey – Germany* (RFMS-G). Both surveys are based on similar questionnaires, enabling the researchers to perform a real comparative analysis of the socio-economic characteristics and the living and working conditions of immigrants in Denmark and Germany. The interviews for the Danish survey were carried out by Statistics Denmark in Copenhagen, while Infratest Sozialforschung in Munich collected the German data. An extensive presentation and discussion of the data set is contained in the Appendix chapter.

In general, the Danish survey collected for the present study consists of two main parts, namely a questionnaire part and a register part. The following describes register data and the questionnaire data respectively. The register data cover all non-Western immigrants and descendants, together with representative samples of 25 percent of Western immigrants and descendants and 2 percent of the Danish population as a whole (including immigrants and descendants) in the 16-70 age group on January 1st for each year in the period 1984-2002 and on July 1st in 1998 and 2000. In the two samples from July 1, 1998 and 2000, family members of the sample population are also included. The register data are from Statistics Denmark, and include information about demographic variables, labor market characteristics, housing, income, crime, social benefits, and education.

The register data have been supplemented by interview surveys of representative samples of eight of the largest non-Western immigrant groups in Denmark. These surveys were carried out in 1999 and 2001 among immigrants and descendants with a minimum of two years' residence originating from the former Yugoslavia, Iran, Lebanon, Pakistan, Poland, Somalia, Turkey, and Vietnam. These groups together make up about two-thirds of all non-Western immigrants and descendants in Denmark. The 1999 survey involved 3,615 persons, of whom 2,431 were foreign nationals, while the 2001 survey involved 3,262 persons, of whom 1,769 were foreign nationals. Almost three-quarters of the interviews in the Danish 2001 survey were re-interviews of persons who also participated in the 1999 survey, allowing the researchers to determine whether the respondents' situations and qualifications had changed over time. For comparative reasons selected questions from these surveys in Denmark were also included in interviews of representative samples of the Danish population as a whole in Statistics Denmark's regular omnibus surveys. The 1999 sample consisted of nearly 1,000 persons, and the 2001 sample of nearly 3,000.

The German data consists of an interview survey of 5,569 foreign nationals from the former Yugoslavia, Iran, Lebanon, Poland, and Turkey. These five nationalities together make up two-thirds of all foreign citizens from non-Western countries living in Germany. The interviews were collected by Infratest Sozialforschung from a sample of foreign nationals taken from the AZR (Auslaenderzentralregister – the central register for foreign nationals) in the 100 largest cities in West Germany and the three largest in East Germany.

In order to compare immigrants in Denmark and Germany as closely as possible, the German questionnaire was based on the Danish questionnaire, though there are a number of minor differences between the two. First, there are institutional differences between the two countries, which made it necessary to modify the questions on education and the labor market characteristics in particular. Second, the possibility for researchers of using register data is nearly non-existent in Germany, which meant that it was necessary to ask respondents in Germany questions about information which was available in Denmark from the registers, especially information on income and social transfers.

According to the analysis in this chapter, a key challenge for migration research is the identification of the trends and determinants of work participation. Integration into society in an economic sense does not imply cultural or behavioral assimilation but a successful participation in the labor market. Hence, the project had to investigate employment, unemployment, self-employment, and the respective earnings. It is further important to understand differences in the endowment of human capital upon arrival and the driving forces behind educational attainment and vocational training in the host country. These issues, which form the core of the project, are analyzed by use of the micro data from the *Rockwool Foundation Migration Survey*, applying advanced econometric techniques and the Law Model developed by the Danish Ministry of Finance. The data analysis requires a proper understanding of the institutional settings in both countries, from social security systems to the educational and training systems. Finally, a few issues connected with immigration that often concern the public are dealt with: take-up of welfare benefits, crime, the burden on the public purse, and immigrant effects on the labor market outcomes for natives are all studied in order to obtain a complete picture of the immigration challenge.

1.4 An Overview of the Book

The book carefully summarizes the institutional settings, the policy concepts, and the migration pressures for both Denmark and Germany. It provides ten chapters of new research that deepen the knowledge available on the performance of immigrants and their host countries. The comparative nature of the approach makes it possible to achieve more clear-cut findings.

In Chapter 2, on "Immigration policy and Danish and German immigration", Thomas Bauer, Claus Larsen, and Poul Chr. Matthiessen provide a review of the institutional migratory settings, the immigration pressures over the past decades, and the immigration policies in both countries. Then Amelie Constant and Claus Larsen outline the educational systems in Denmark and Germany in Chapter 3. This contribution on "The educational background and human capital attainment of immigrants" investigates the educational and training activities of immigrants before and after arrival in the host countries. The key question is how immigrants get to work, and employment developments are studied in Chapter 4 by Marie Louise Schultz-Nielsen and Amelie Constant writing on "Employment trends for immigrants and natives". The role of work incentives for employment and unemployment are evaluated in Chapter 5 by Amelie Constant and Marie Louise Schultz-Nielsen writing on "Labor force participation and unemployment: Incentives and preferences". Chapter 6, on "Immigrant selection and earnings" by Amelie Constant and Marie Louise Schultz-Nielsen, examines the key qualitative variable of any objective evaluation of immigrant performance, namely earnings.

Self-employment is a further route to success, but research evidence on this is still very scarce. Amelie Constant and Marie Louise Schultz-Nielsen study this important issue in Chapter 7 on "Immigrant self-employment and economic performance". The significant take-up of welfare benefits by immigrants and their involvement in crime are matters of broad concern. They are addressed by Niels-Kenneth Nielsen in his Chapter 8 on "Social transfers to immigrants in Germany and Denmark" and by Horst Entorf and Claus Larsen in their Chapter 9 on "Immigration and crime in Germany and Denmark". Do migrants generate a surplus or a deficit for the public purse? This question is addressed in Chapter 10, written by Eskil Wadensjö and Christer Gerdes on "Immigrants and the public sector in Denmark and Germany". A further investigation by Eskil Wadensjö and Christer Gerdes on "Some socio-economic consequences of immigration" in Chapter 11 deals with the differences in labor market performance of immigrants in comparison with natives in terms of wages and unemployment, examines how immigrants affect the performance of natives, and studies the redistribution of income.

Which country is more attractive for workers and entrepreneurs? What incentives have the welfare state to offer in terms of education and job possibilities? A final evaluation of all of the research findings in the book in Chapter 12 ("Migrants, work, and the welfare state: Summary and conclusions") by Torben Tranæs and Klaus F. Zimmermann points out the highlights of the research results and sets them in perspective for researchers and policy-makers.

References

Bauer, Thomas, Barbara Dietz, Klaus F. Zimmermann, and Eric Zwintz. 2004. "German Migration: Development, Assimilation and Labor Market Effects," in Klaus F. Zimmermann (ed.): *European Migration: What Do We Know?* Oxford: Oxford University Press.

Blom, Svein. 1998. *Levekår blant ikke-vestlige innvandrere i Norge (Living Conditions among Non-Western Immigrants in Norway)*. Oslo.

Boeri, Tito, Gordon Hanson, and Barry McCormick (eds): *Immigration Policy and the Welfare System*. Oxford: Oxford University Press.

Brücker, Herbert, Gil S. Epstein, Barry McCormick, Gilles Saint-Paul, Alessandra Venturini, and Klaus F. Zimmermann. 2002. "Managing Migration in the

European Welfare State," in Tito Boeri, Gordon Hanson, and Barry McCormick (eds): *Immigration Policy and the Welfare System*. Oxford: Oxford University Press, 1-167.

Coleman, David and Eskil Wadensjö with contributions by Bent Jensen and Søren Pedersen. 1999. *Immigration to Denmark. International and National Perspectives*. Aarhus: Aarhus University Press.

Dahl, Jeanette E., Vibeke Jacobsen, and Ruth Emerek. 1998. *Indvandrere og arbejdsmarkedet (Immigrants and the Labour Market)*. Aalborg.

European Communities. 2003. *Employment in Europe 2003. Recent Trends and Prospects*. Luxembourg: Office for Official Publications of the European Communities.

Faini, Riccardo, Jaime de Melo, and Klaus F. Zimmermann. 1999. *Migration. The Controversies and the Evidence*. Cambridge: Cambridge University Press.

Hansen, Hans, Helle Cwarzko Jensen, Claus Larsen and Niels-Kenneth Nielsen. 2002. *Social Security Benefits in Denmark and Germany – With a Focus on Access Conditions for Refugees and Immigrants. A Comparative Study*. Copenhagen: Rockwool Foundation Research Unit.

Hummelgaard, Hans, Leif Husted, Anders Holm, Mikkel Baadsgaard, and Benedicte Olrik. 1995. *Etniske minoriteter, integration og mobilitet (Ethnic Minorities, Integration and Mobility)*. Copenhagen: AFK (Amternes og Kommunernes Forskningsinstitut).

Husted, Leif, Helena Skyt Nielsen, Michael Rosholm, and Nina Smith. 2001. "Employment and Wage Assimilation of Male First Generation Immigrants in Denmark," *International Journal of Manpower* 22 (1/2), 39-68.

IOM. 2003. *World Migration 2003. Managing Migration – Challenges and Responses for People on the Move*. Geneva: International Organization for Migration.

Mogensen, Gunnar Viby and Poul Chr. Matthiessen (eds.) with contributions by Olaf Ingerslev, Claus Larsen, Hans Jørgen Nielsen, Niels-Kenneth Nielsen, Søren Pedersen, Marie Louise Schultz-Nielsen and Eskil Wadensjö. 2000. *Integration i Danmark omkring årtusindskiftet*. Aarhus: Aarhus University Press. An English version of the core chapters is published as Schultz-Nielsen et al. (2001).

Mogensen, Gunnar Viby and Poul Chr. Matthiessen (eds.) with contributions by Claus Larsen, Niels-Kenneth Nielsen, Marie Louise Schultz-Nielsen, Eskil Wadensjö, Ritt Bjerregaard, and Bertel Haarder. 2002. *Indvandrerne og arbejdsmarkedet (Immigrants and the Labour Market)*. Copenhagen: Spektrum.

Nielsen, Helena Skyt, Michael Rosholm, Nina Smith, and Leif Husted. 2003. "Integrational Transmissions and the School-to-Work Transition of 2nd Generation Immigrants," *Journal of Population Economics* 16 (4), 755-786.

Pedersen, Peder J. 2004. "Immigration in a Scandinavian Welfare State: The Recent Danish Experience," in Klaus F. Zimmermann (ed.): *European Migration: What Do We Know?* Oxford: Oxford University Press.

Rosholm, Michael, Kirk Scott, and Leif Husted. 2001a. "The Times They are A-changin': Organizational Change and Immigrant Employment Opportunities in Scandinavia," *IZA Discussion Paper no. 258*. Bonn: IZA.

Rosholm, Michael, Helena Skyt Nielsen, Nina Smith, and Leif Husted. 2001b. "Qualifications, Discrimination, or Assimilation? An Extended Framework for Analysing Immigrant Wage Gaps," *IZA Discussion Paper no. 365*. Bonn: IZA.

Sapir Report. 2004. André Sapir, Philippe Aghion, Giuseppe Bertola, Martin Hellwig, Jean Pisani-Ferry, Dariusz Rosati, José Vinals, Helen Wallace. *An Agenda for a Growing Europe*. Oxford: Oxford University Press.

Schultz-Nielsen, Marie Louise with contributions by Olaf Ingerslev, Claus Larsen, Gunnar Viby Mogensen, Niels-Kenneth Nielsen, Søren Pedersen, and Eskil Wadensjö. 2001. *The Integration of Non-Western Immigrants in a Scandinavian Labour Market: The Danish Experience*. Copenhagen: Rockwool Foundation Research Unit.

SOPEMI 2003. 2004. *Trends in International Migration*. Paris: OECD.

Swedish National Board of Health and Welfare. 1999. *Social och ekonomisk förankring bland indvandrare från Chile, Iran, Polen och Turkiet (Social and Economic Foundation among Immigrants from Chile, Iran, Poland and Turkey)*. Stockholm.

Wadensjö, Eskil. 1999. "Economic Effects of Immigration," Chapter 7 in *Immigration to Denmark. International and National Perspectives*. Aarhus: Aarhus University Press.

Wadensjö, Eskil and Helena Orrje. 2002. *Immigration and the Public Sector in Denmark*. Aarhus: Aarhus University Press.

Zimmermann, Klaus F. 1995. "Tackling the European Migration Problem," *Journal of Economic Perspectives* 9 (2), 45-62.

Zimmermann, Klaus F. and Thomas Bauer. 2002. *The Economics of Migration*. Vol. I-IV. Cheltenham: Edward Elgar Publishing Ltd.

Zimmermann, Klaus F., Thomas Bauer, Holger Bonin, René Fahr, and Holger Hinte. 2002. *Arbeitskräftebedarf bei hoher Arbeitslosigkeit. Ein ökonomisches Zuwanderungskonzept für Deutschland*. Berlin, et al.: Springer-Verlag.

Zimmermann, Klaus F. and Amelie Constant. 2004. *How Labor Migrants Fare*. Berlin, et al.: Springer-Verlag.

Zimmermann, Klaus F. 2004. *European Migration: What Do We Know?* Oxford: Oxford University Press.

CHAPTER 2

Immigration Policy and Danish and German Immigration*

By Thomas Bauer, Claus Larsen, and Poul Chr. Matthiessen

2.1 Introduction

The main purpose of this chapter is to set the stage for the empirical analyses in the remaining chapters of this book by describing the main institutional features of Danish and German immigration policies and the historical development of immigration in both countries. The chapter will further discuss some central characteristics of the foreign populations in Denmark and Germany.

The first section after the introduction provides a short historical overview of Danish and German legislation regulating access for foreigners to the respective countries and to their labor markets as well as the regulations with regard to residence permits and naturalization. In both countries, immigrants are defined as foreign citizens with some sort of permission to be resident. Note that – apart from some consideration of the Danish Integration Act – this section will not discuss specific legislation concerning the living conditions of immigrants, such as regulations that are aimed at foreigners with the purpose of facilitating their integration into the economy or society. These regulations will be discussed in more detail in other chapters of this book for which they are more relevant.

Section 2.3 briefly describes the migration experiences of Denmark and Germany. In the first subsection we will outline the overall pattern of immigration and emigration in both countries since World War II, including the wave of guest worker immigration, which ended in 1973, and family reunification, which has been the single most important cause of permanent immigration during the past three decades. For a more detailed description we refer to Bauer et al. (2004) and Larsen and Matthiessen (2002). The next two subsections will describe more recent migration patterns of the 1980s and 1990s: the inflow of asylum seekers and refugees, which has increased substantially since the mid-1980s, and the inflow of temporary workers, which played an important role in the 1990s, especially in Germany.

---

* We wish to thank Jens Vedsted-Hansen, professor at the School of Law, University of Aarhus, for his helpful comments, and also Georgios Tassoukis, Database Manager at IZA.

Section 2.4 aims to provide a description of some central demographic characteristics of the foreign populations of Germany and Denmark. The first subsection discusses differences in the composition of the foreign populations with respect to the countries of origin. The second subsection provides a description of the sex and age distributions of the foreigners, while the third subsection presents some descriptive statistics for the regional distribution of foreigners in both countries. The chapter concludes with a short summary.

2.2 Immigration Policy

2.2.1 Denmark

Legislation regarding foreigners in Denmark comprises several different laws, including the Aliens Act (*Udlændingeloven*) regulating the access of foreigners to the country and the duration of residence and work permits, the Nationality Law (*Indfødsretsloven*) regulating who can obtain Danish citizenship, and other laws regulating the terms of repatriation (*Repatrieringsloven*) and the integration of new immigrants (*Integrationsloven*). In the following, we provide a brief overview of important elements of the legislation of the last 50 years which have had direct effects on immigrants to Denmark.

Up until 1983, immigration to Denmark was regulated by the Aliens Act of 1952. According to this law, foreigners could enter the country relatively freely to seek work. As early as 1969, however, there were administrative attempts to restrict immigration, because of increasing social problems caused by a large increase in the number of job-seeking foreigners. These attempts peaked in November 1973 with a total ban on immigration because of the employment situation and fears of a recession as a consequence of the first oil crisis. After 1973, residence permits for employment or business reasons could only be granted in exceptional circumstances (to experts, specialists, au pairs, etc.). Recently, a so-called "Job Card" has been introduced aimed at making the bureaucracy more flexible for people with qualifications which are in short supply in Denmark. Note that the ban does not apply to citizens of the Nordic countries or the European Union (EU), who are free to enter the country, take up residence, and look for a job.

Despite these restrictions, foreigners continued to enter Denmark between 1973 and 1983, but now through the process of family reunification and, to a lesser extent, as asylum seekers. In 1983, a new Aliens Act was passed in order to improve and protect the legal rights of people entering the country through these two processes. A *legal* right to family reunification involving children, spouses and parents was introduced. Family migrants, however, had to meet certain conditions. For example, parents brought to Denmark under family reunification had to be older than 60 years. Family reunification could also be made conditional on the person living in

Denmark being able to support the parents who applied for a residence permit. The maintenance aspect and its implementation through administrative practice gradually became of increasing importance. In 1992 an amendment to the Aliens Act tightened up these rules (Vedsted-Hansen, 1997); this reduced the number of residence permits granted for family reunification from about 8,000 a year to 5,000 in 1993. After 1993, the immigration of family members gradually increased again (Larsen and Matthiessen, 2002). It is important to note that *in practice* the maintenance condition was not applied to refugees or to Danish or Nordic nationals in the case of family reunification with a spouse or cohabitant.[1] For immigrants from other countries of origin, the amendment to the Aliens Act applied "unless exceptional reasons made it inappropriate". For example, the condition would not be imposed in the case of family reunification with children who were still minors, while it would be in the case of family reunification with parents – irrespective of the nationality of the person living in Denmark.

The new Aliens Act of 1983 further established the group of "de facto refugees" *legally*,[2] which gave asylum seekers who did not meet the conditions defined in the UN Refugee Convention the possibility of obtaining asylum for "other similar or otherwise compelling" reasons involving a well-founded fear of persecution or similar violation.[3] In addition, it was made more difficult for the authorities to return asylum seekers, and a process of appeal was introduced through a new Refugee Board (*Flygtningenævnet*) against any negative decision (rejection). Finally, a Danish Immigration Service was established to administer the law, this having been formerly the responsibility of the Commissioner of Police (von Eyben et al., 1996). Internationally, the 1983 Aliens Act gave Denmark a reputation as a country with a particularly humanitarian refugee policy (Kjær, 1995).

A sharp rise in the number of asylum applications followed, and legislation with regard to asylum seekers has been tightened several times since. This tightening reflects growing concerns about the social and economic effects of an increased inflow of refugees, suspicions that some asylum seekers have applied more than once or in more than one country, and increasingly serious attempts to ensure that those asylum seekers who have been rejected actually leave the country. In December 1985, an accelerated "manifestly unfounded" procedure was introduced, allowing the Immigration Service to reject an application administratively without access to appeal when it was evident that the outcome would be a rejection. If the Danish Refugee Council – a non-governmental organization which interviews each asylum

---

1 The maintenance condition was abolished for Danish citizens in 1998, but reintroduced in 2002.
2 Abolished in 2002. In Denmark it meant a rather secure status with a "residence permit with the purpose of permanent residence" (possible after 3 years), whereas Germany offers "de facto refugees" temporary protection, cf. *Duldung* (Appendix Table 2.3).
3 The last part was added in 1998 to indicate more precisely that the asylum seeker had to be at risk as an *individual* (Lassen, 2000).

seeker – agrees with the decision, the asylum seeker must leave the country. In 1986, the principle that asylum seekers could enter the country and be admitted to the formal asylum procedure without having a valid passport and visa was abolished, and a system was introduced whereby asylum seekers could be turned back at the border if they had traveled through a safe third country. The "manifestly unfounded" procedure and "safe third country returns" were later adopted within the EEC, cf. the Dublin Convention (1990) and the London Resolutions (1992). Denmark ratified the Dublin Convention in 1991 and the Schengen Convention in 1997 (Kjær, 2000), but "as a result of the Danish referenda on the Maastricht Treaty in 1992 and 1993, Denmark has a number of exemptions from the EU... Denmark participates in the intergovernmental co-operation on justice and home affairs, ..., but is not involved in the supranational co-operation in this field" (Danish Ministry of Foreign Affairs, 2003). Denmark entered the Schengen co-operation in 2001.

In 1992, a special law granted temporary residence permits to certain refugees from the former Yugoslavia on conditions which suspended the normal asylum procedure.[4] Most of these refugees, however, had received permanent residence permits by the mid-1990s. In 1999, a similar law was passed granting temporary residence permits to refugees from Kosovo. Laws passed in 1993 and the following years offered financial and advisory repatriation assistance to those willing to return to their home countries.[5] An actual Act on Repatriation was passed in 1999 gathering the different provisions regarding repatriation under one law (Vedsted-Hansen, 2000).

Major changes in immigration legislation have taken place since 1998. Both refugees and family members reunited with immigrants already living in Denmark who have been granted a residence permit after January 1, 1999 must take part in a 3-year "introduction program" managed by the local municipalities.[6] It includes an introductory course to Danish society, language courses, labor market training, and other educational activities. Participation is compulsory for those who are not self-supporting or supported by others. Participants may receive an "introduction allowance".[7] For refugees there are strict provisions as to place of residence. Immigrants not participating fully, refugees moving without permission, etc. may lose their introduction allowance (Vedsted-Hansen, 2000).

---

4 Also in 1992 – following intense political and media attention – a special law gave permanent residence permits to a number of stateless Palestinians from Lebanon.
5 For certain groups, this includes the possibility of changing their mind about the repatriation decision and returning to Denmark.
6 Before 1999 an introduction program – then managed by the Danish Refugee Council – lasted 18 months.
7 Lower than the ordinary social security transfer payments, which can only be obtained by persons who have stayed in Denmark for a total of at least 7 of the previous 8 years. However, the introduction allowance may be supplemented if necessary (see also Chapter 8 of this book).

Amendments to the Aliens Act since 1998 – and especially in 2002 – have tightened conditions of entry to Denmark. Among other things, immigrants must now have had an unlimited residence permit for at least 3 years before spouses or partners can be brought to Denmark, and parents can no longer be reunited with their adult children living in Denmark. Legislation has also been aimed at preventing pro forma and forced marriages, e.g. by abolishing the legal right to family reunification with spouses for young people under the age of 24. Furthermore, it must be substantiated that the married couple's aggregate ties with Denmark are stronger than with any other country.[8] Conditions also include the proof of the availability of suitable accommodation for at least 3 years beyond the date of application. The person living in Denmark must prove that he or she can support the spouse or partner, must furnish a guarantee of DKK 53,096 (approx. EUR 7,000) for possible future social security payments, and must not have received social security benefits for a period of 1 year before the time of the application and until a residence permit is granted.[9] As mentioned above, "de facto refugee" status has been abolished and replaced by a "protective" status. It is no longer possible to apply for asylum at a Danish agency abroad (Danish Ministry of the Interior, 2000; Danish Ministry of Refugee, Immigration and Integration Affairs, 2002a).

Permission to enter the Danish labor market is closely connected to the residence permit. Asylum seekers are not allowed to work, unless they already have a residence permit when they apply for asylum. As a general rule, a residence permit carries with it the right to work in Denmark. The first residence permit will always be time-limited but issued "with the purpose of" either *permanent* or *temporary* residence. If not intrinsically limited by its nature (e.g. permits for students, specialists, and au pairs) it may become unlimited after a certain amount of time. By July 1, 2002, the required length of legal residence before a permanent residence permit could be issued was raised from 3 to 7 years. A criminal record may hinder the issuance of a permanent residence permit, as may the failure to complete the introduction program or similar program. Further conditions are that the alien must have passed a test in the Danish language and have no overdue debts to public authorities.

Since the present Danish nationality law came into force in 1950, a number of amendments have been passed. In recent years, these amendments have predominantly tightened the rules for obtaining Danish citizenship. A child acquires Danish citizenship at birth if the father *or* – since 1979 – the mother is Danish. Danish citizenship thus depends on the nationality of the parents rather than on place of

---

8 Subsequently, this "attachment requirement" has been relaxed and does not apply if the person residing in Denmark either (1) has had Danish citizenship for more than 28 years or (2) was born or brought up in Denmark and has resided legally in the country for more than 28 years.

9 These conditions normally also apply to Danish citizens and refugees. Historically, refugees have been treated in the same way as Danish citizens once they were granted asylum.

birth. When Danish citizenship is not acquired at birth it is the general rule that it is granted by an Act of Parliament. A criminal record may prevent or delay naturalization, as may public debt. Furthermore, citizens of the Nordic countries must have lived legally and continuously in Denmark for at least 2 years, other nationals for at least 9 years – though the period is only 8 years for refugees and stateless persons. Marriage to a Danish citizen shortens the required length of residence. After 3 years of marriage, a minimum of 6 years' continuous residence is required. 7 years of continuous residence is required after 2 years of marriage and 8 years if the marriage has lasted only 1 year.[10] Finally, the applicant must prove to have sufficient command of the Danish language and knowledge of Danish society, history, and culture. A foreign citizen who has lived in Denmark for at least a total of 10 years, and at least a total of 5 of the last 6 years, and – since 2000 – has no criminal record, can, after reaching the age of 18, but before reaching 23, obtain Danish citizenship by declaration.[11]

2.2.2 Germany

Germany's migration experience after World War II can be described as consisting of two parallel flows. This necessitates differentiation between two basic groups of immigrants: (i) immigrants of German descent or former citizenship, and (ii) foreigners with no German ancestry, including foreign workers and their families, refugees, and asylum seekers. In the past five decades, immigration legislation directed towards these two groups has been changed several times. Since the German data set used in this book does not enable the study of ethnic German immigrants, the following description of Germany's migration regulations concentrates on those for foreigners.[12]

An immigration policy on foreigners began in Germany in the second half of the 1950s. Because of rapid economic growth, the German labor market experienced an increasing shortage of low-skilled workers. The need could no longer be satisfied by the inflow of ethnic Germans from Eastern Europe, forcing the German government to introduce a guest worker program. This program was based on bilateral recruitment agreements signed first with Italy in 1955, then Spain and Greece in 1960, Turkey in 1961, Morocco in 1963, Portugal in 1964, Tunisia in 1965, and finally with Yugoslavia in 1968. These agreements regulated the recruitment of unskilled

---

10 Before July 2002, the required length of residence was 2 years less, except for citizens of the Nordic countries.
11 Old rules are described in Danish Ministry of Justice (1999); new rules in Danish Ministry of Refugee, Immigration and Integration Affairs (2002b).
12 A detailed description of the legislation concerning ethnic German migrants is given by Bauer et al. (2004) and Schmidt (1997).

guest workers, predominantly males, for the industrial sector.[13] In general, work and residence permits were given for one to two years. After this period, the guest workers were required to return home in order to keep immigration temporary.

In the face of increasing social tensions and fears of a recession following the first oil price shock, the active recruitment policy was terminated on November 23, 1973. This recruitment halt started a period of consolidation in German immigration policy. After the cessation of recruitment, the possibility of legal migration to Germany was restricted to a few groups of individuals, including the dependants of foreigners living in Germany, citizens of other EU countries, ethnic Germans, asylum seekers and refugees, seasonal and contract workers, managers of international corporations, scientists, and individuals with special occupations (Münz and Ulrich, 1996).

After the halt in recruitment, a discussion began about how to encourage return migration. Already in 1972, Germany had signed a bilateral treaty with Turkey to create incentives for return migration, which included special aid for returning individuals such as education, financial consultancy, and investment support for migrants to help them establish businesses in their home countries (Frey, 1986). However, it took almost ten years before the new conservative German government passed a law in 1983 which initiated a program that included financial incentives, measures to reduce mobility barriers, and guidance to foreigners who intended to re-migrate. Provided they were unemployed or in short-term employment, foreigners from countries with a recruitment treaty were eligible for this program, but overall the program turned out to be rather unsuccessful, as the number of foreigners using it fell short of the government's expectations (Dustmann, 1996).

The political changes in Eastern Europe that started in the late 1980s initiated a number of changes in the German immigration policy. Several factors caused an increase in the stream of asylum seekers and family migrants from Europe: the political confusion in the former socialist states of Eastern Europe induced by the fall of the Iron Curtain; the war in former Yugoslavia; and the clashes between Turks and Kurds in the south-east of Turkey. The heavy increase in the inflow of asylum seekers and refugees between 1988 and 1992, which will be described in more detail below, resulted in a change in the right to asylum in the Constitutional Law (*Grundgesetz*) in 1993. Under the new regulations, deportation proceedings were speeded up, and the possibilities of applying for asylum were restricted. This restriction has been brought about mainly through the implementation of the "third country rule". In a similar manner to Denmark, Germany immediately sends back all asylum seekers who have traveled through member states of the European Union or other so-called "secure countries" as defined by the law. The fact that Germany is surrounded by these secure countries limits the possibility of immigration by asylum

---

13 Bauer et al. (2004) provide a detailed description of the process of recruitment.

seekers to Germany to arrival via air or sea. In addition, Germany signed treaties with Romania and Poland in 1993, Switzerland in 1994, and Bulgaria and the Czech Republic in 1995 regarding the return of asylum seekers.[14]

The economic boom after German reunification, however, caused some pull migration. Germany signed several bilateral agreements with Central and Eastern European Countries (CEEC) concerning the immigration of temporary workers: these have been used mainly by Polish and Czech workers.[15] The following goals were at the core of these bilateral agreements: (i) to bring the CEEC countries up to Western European standards; (ii) to provide solidarity with CEEC countries; (iii) to mediate skills in the use of modern technology to Eastern European firms and workers in order to foster economic development in the countries of origin; (iv) to decrease immigration pressure from these countries; and (v) to promote economic co-operation with them. A more detailed description of this form of temporary immigration will be provided in Section 2.3.3 (see also Appendix Table 2.4).

The current German regulations concerning the possibilities for entry, residence and employment in Germany are very complicated, spreading over numerous different laws and amendments to these laws, including, for example, the Aliens Act (*Ausländergesetz*), the EEC Residence Act (*Aufenthaltsgesetz/EWG*), the Asylum Procedure Act (*Asylverfahrensgesetz*), the Act on the Central Aliens Register (*das Gesetz über das Ausländerzentralregister*), the Nationality Law (*Staatsangehörigkeitsgesetz*), the Federal Expellees Act (*Bundesvertriebenengesetz*), the Act on Benefits for Asylum Seekers (*Asylbewerberleistungsgesetz*) and other laws. Because a detailed description of these laws would go far beyond the scope of this chapter, we will refer only to the most important characteristics of the current regulations.[16] Leaving aside ethnic Germans, the German immigration policy differentiates between citizens of other EU countries, family members of foreigners already residing in Germany, asylum seekers and refugees, and all other foreigners not covered by the former groups. In accordance with this detailed differentiation of immigrants, the German migration regulations differentiate between numerous different residence and work permits.

---

14 See Bauer et al. (2004) and Münch (1993) for a more detailed description of the changes in the asylum regulations.

15 These agreements regulated the immigration of so-called *Werkvertragsarbeitnehmer*, i.e. workers of Eastern European firms working in Germany under project-linked work arrangements co-ordinated under contracts with German firms; *Guest workers*, who had immigrated under a program that aimed to improve the professional and linguistic skills of the participants; and seasonal workers. An exhaustive description of these different programs can be found in Bauer et al. (2004).

16 A detailed description of the German regulations concerning the admission of foreigners, residence and work permits, and the right to apply for asylum is provided by Bauer (1998), Bauer et al. (2004), and Velling (1995). The regulations can also be downloaded from the homepage of the German representative for migration, asylum, and integration: http://www.integrationsbeauftragte.de.

(A detailed description of the different residence and work permits is provided in Appendix Tables 2.1 and 2.2; Appendix Table 2.3 further summarizes the most important groups of immigrants in Germany.)

Together with members of the ethnic German groups outside Germany, mainly in Eastern Europe, it is relatively easy for citizens of other EU countries to migrate to and work in Germany. Because of their freedom to choose their workplace within the European community, citizens of EU countries are entitled to a special EU residence permit (*Aufenthaltserlaubnis-EG*), which gives them a right to stay in Germany for an indefinite period. Furthermore, citizens of other EU countries do not require work permits. All other immigrants are allocated different types of residence permits, which are determined by the German authority for the affairs of foreigners (*Ausländerbehörde*). These different types of residence permits range from the so-called *Aufenthaltsgestattung*, which is usually given to asylum seekers whose application is being processed and which gives the asylum seekers no freedom to choose the place of residence themselves and which allows the German authorities the possibility of deporting the asylum seekers, to the most secure residence status, the *Aufenthaltsberechtigung*, which gives a foreigner the rights to stay in Germany for an unlimited time and work without a work permit. Among other requirements, a foreigner has to stay in Germany for at least eight years before he/she can apply for an *Aufenthaltsberechtigung*. With the exception of citizens of other EU countries and foreigners with an *Aufenthaltsberechtigung* or an *unbefristete Aufenthaltserlaubnis*, all immigrants need a work permit in order to be allowed to enter the German labor market (see Appendix Table 2.1). Work permits are issued by the German Labour Office, which is required to investigate whether the job of an applicant for a work permit could not be taken over by an unemployed German, EU citizen, or foreigner with an unlimited residence permit. As with the residence permits, Germany differentiates between different types of work permits (see Appendix Table 2.2) that differ with regard to the restrictions on the types of job the foreigner may have and the duration of the permits.

Since the coalition of Social Democrats and the Green Party came to power in 1998, several changes in the regulations regarding immigrants have taken place. Most importantly, the new government passed a new nationality law in 2000. According to this law, a child born in Germany automatically receives German citizenship if one of the parents has legally resided in Germany for at least eight years. Such children are also allowed to hold the citizenship of their parents. If they hold two citizenships, however, they have to decide at the age of 23 which one of them to retain. In addition, in 2000, the German government introduced the so-called "Green Card" in order to meet the demands of the German labor market for qualified information technology experts. Under this program, a total of 20,000 IT specialists could enter Germany between 2000 and 2003 for a maximum of 5 years. Foreign students who have obtained a university degree in information technology at a German University can stay and work in Germany under this program rather than being forced to leave the country.

The introduction of the "Green Card" started a debate about the necessity for an immigration law that would integrate the various regulations existing in numerous laws, improve the integration of foreigners, and increase the opportunities for high-skilled workers to come to Germany. In the light of this debate, the German government appointed a commission to work out a proposal for an immigration and integration law. The report of the commission was delivered in July 2001. On the basis of this report, the German Minister for the Interior prepared an immigration law that passed both chambers of parliament and was signed by the German president in September 2002. In December 2002, however, the German Supreme Court blocked the new immigration law by ruling in favor of a group of conservative-led states, which had argued that the bill had passed through the upper house of the parliament illegally. Six of Germany's federal states that are governed by the conservative parties claimed that one disputed vote in favor of the law in the upper house of parliament should not have counted when the bill was passed in March 2002.[17]

After nearly four years of negotiations, the German government and the opposition agreed upon a new immigration law, which passed the German Federal Council (Bundesrat) in July 2004. The law allows legal immigration of workers only in the case of highly qualified foreigners, such as engineers, computer specialists, and scientists. In addition, self-employed people who offer a certain number of jobs to natives will be allowed to immigrate. Furthermore, the law makes it easier for the responsible officials to deport "hate preachers" and terror suspects.

2.2.3 Migration Policy in Europe

The asylum policies of Denmark and Germany must be interpreted in relation to the joint migration policy of the European Union. EU migration policy since 1988 has been marked by two different developments. First, since the original Treaty of Rome of 1957, internal migration within the EU has been liberalized steadily, reaching its conclusion in Article 8a of the Single European Act. This Act required that the free movement of people, capital, goods, and services should be achieved by January 1, 1993, which implied the abolition of controls at the interior borders of the EU. Second, with respect to immigration from outside the EU, there have been increasing efforts to establish a collective and more restrictive policy.[18] The plan for a common

---

17 The contested vote from Brandenburg was counted by the president of the upper house as a "yes", even though there was a 50-50 split between the state's four representatives.
18 See Zimmermann (1994, 1995) for a comprehensive discussion of the immigration policies of the EU and its single members.

European market necessitated a common policy on migration, as giving up interior border controls results in each member state being dependent on the immigration policy of the other states. Progress towards a joint EU migration policy started with the Schengen Accords of June 1985 (Schengen I) and June 1990 (Schengen II) and with the Dublin Accord of June 1990, and continued with the Maastricht Treaty of February 1992.

The main objectives of these initiatives have been the elimination of internal border controls, consistent and tighter external border controls, a unified visa policy, and the co-ordination of different national asylum policies. For the time being, the final step can be found in the Treaty of Amsterdam from 1997. Concerning migration policy, Article 63 of the treaty suggests

- closer co-operation to prevent illegal immigration,
- the elaboration of joint norms regarding the acceptance of asylum seekers and the prerequisites for the immigration and residence of persons from countries outside the EU,
- the alignment of the rights and conditions by which immigrants to one EU member country can reside in another member country.

The Treaty of Amsterdam explicitly states, however, that there is no specific time schedule for the implementation of the measures listed above to create a joint migration policy.

2.3 Migration to Denmark and Germany

2.3.1 Net Migration

Figure 2.1 shows the net migration flows of individuals to Germany and Denmark since World War II. Even though migration to and from these countries occurred on very different scales, the cyclical pattern appears to be very similar. The migration experience of Germany and Denmark can roughly be divided into four different phases: war adjustment, manpower recruitment, consolidation or restricted migration, and the dissolution of Communism and its aftermath.

In Germany, the period of war adjustment was characterized by a huge inflow of ethnic Germans from Eastern Europe (and hence does not show up in the numbers depicted in Figure 2.1). Between the end of World War II and the mid-1950s, 11.5 million Germans left Eastern Europe, of whom about 8 million went to the Federal Republic of Germany (Schmidt and Zimmermann, 1992). Between 1950 and the construction of the Berlin Wall in 1961, about 2.6 million Germans moved from East to West Germany. Unlike Germany, Denmark experienced net emigration in almost

Figure 2.1. Net migration to Denmark and Germany, 1946-2001 (thousands).

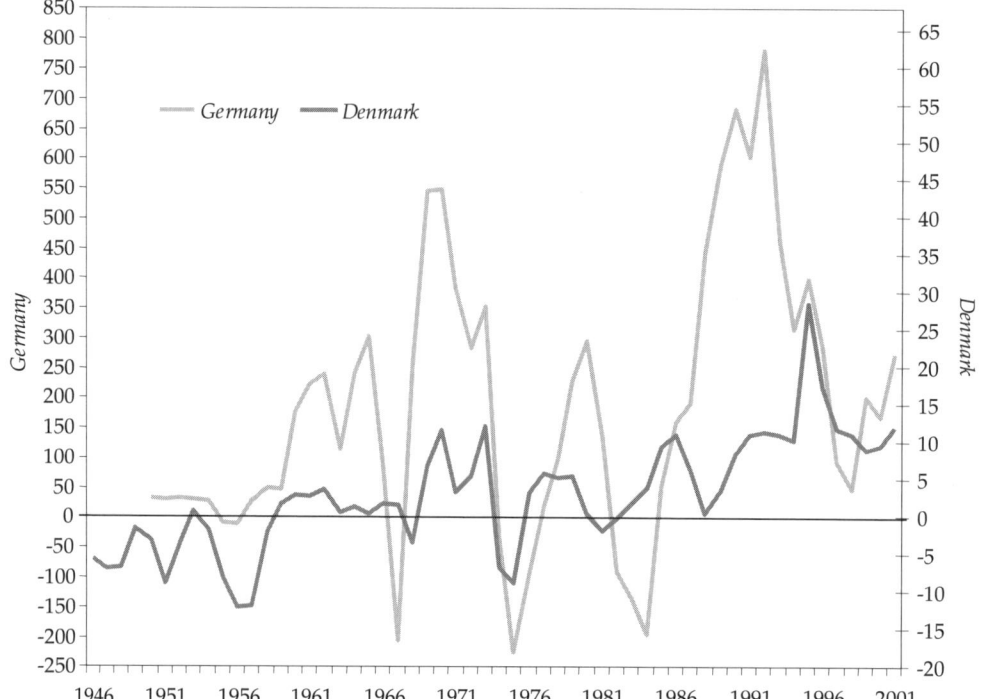

Sources: Statistics Denmark, *Befolkningens bevægelser* 1994, 2000, *Nyt fra Danmarks Statistik* 58/2002 and Federal Statistical Office Germany, *Statistisches Jahrbuch*, several volumes.

every year of this period. Until the mid-1960s, immigrants to Denmark came mostly from Norway, Sweden, Finland, Germany, and the USA – the same countries which were the most frequent destinations for emigrants. In many cases, the immigrants were Danish expatriates returning home, while emigrants went back to their respective homelands after a stay in Denmark.

The phase of manpower recruitment, which started in the mid-1950s in Germany and about ten years later in Denmark and ended in 1973 in both countries, can be seen as a period of labor migration. In this period, both countries experienced an increasing net immigration flow that was only interrupted by an economic recession in 1967 in Germany and in 1968 in Denmark. In 1970, for example, Germany experienced a net inflow of almost 550,000 persons and Denmark about 12,000 individuals.

Like some other European countries (e.g. France), Germany and Denmark faced a shortage of low-skilled labor, which induced the establishment of an active recruitment policy. As already mentioned, the German guest worker system was based on recruitment treaties with Italy, Spain, Greece, Turkey, Morocco, Portugal, Tunisia, and Yugoslavia. Between 1955 and 1968 recruitment offices were opened in these countries, soon attracting thousands of migrants.[19] In Denmark, immigrants have increasingly come from non-Western[20] countries since the 1960s, consisting mainly of guest workers from Turkey, Yugoslavia, and Pakistan. As in Germany, the guest workers in Denmark predominantly had low-skilled jobs in the manufacturing industry. In Denmark, most of the guest workers came on their own initiative, with only a small proportion of the labor migration being based on Danish firms' recruitment through employment offices in, for example, Yugoslavia and Turkey. Some of the guest workers had formerly worked in Germany, but moved on to Denmark at the onset of economic recession in Germany (Matthiessen, 2000).

Starting in 1973, a period of restraint on migration began all over Western Europe, lasting until the late 1980s, except for a sudden inflow of asylum seekers to Germany in 1979-81 and to Denmark in 1984-86. In the face of increasing social tensions and fears of a recession following the first oil price shock, active labor recruitment came to a halt. Hence, net immigration to both countries decreased. For example, whereas Denmark experienced a total net inflow of more than 51,000 individuals between 1958 and 1973, this number fell to 36,000 in the following period of fifteen years between 1974 and 1988. Between 1958 and 1973, Germany experienced a net inflow of more than 3.6 million persons. This figure decreased to a total net inflow of about 860,000 between 1974 and 1988. These numbers indicate, however, that total net migration to both countries remained positive despite the immigration restrictions introduced in 1973. Immigration after 1973 was mainly based on the family reunification policy of both countries. Furthermore, it turned out to be rather difficult to induce return migration. Because of a high fertility rate in the foreign population and the admission of refugees, there was a further increase in the size of the foreign population living in Denmark and Germany.

Family reunification involving children, spouses, and parents has been the single most important source of permanent immigration for the three decades since 1973. The reunification of spouses can either involve spouses who were already married before migration or the formation of new families where immigrants and descendants find spouses in the country of origin.

Despite its quantitative importance, reliable data on the number of persons immigrating to Germany as family members exist only since 1996. Existing estimates indicate that more than half of the immigration flow in the 1970s and 1980s was due to family reunification (Unabhängige Kommission Zuwanderung, 2001). Since 1996, statistics on the number of immigration permits granted to spouses and minor children of persons residing in Germany have been collected by the Ministry of Foreign Affairs. Note, however, that these statistics do not include

---

19 The organization of the recruitment of guest workers in Germany is described in more detail in Bauer and Zimmermann (1997a, 1997b).
20 EU countries before the enlargement in 2004, Iceland, Liechtenstein, Norway, Switzerland, USA, Canada, Australia, and New Zealand are here termed "Western", all other "non-Western".

other family members and persons immigrating on tourist visas and getting married in Germany. According to the statistics of the Ministry of Foreign Affairs, 75,888 individuals received immigration permits based on the regulations for family reunification in the year 2000, of whom 17,699 were minor children and 58,189 spouses of persons residing in Germany. Among the foreign spouses who received immigration permits, 34 percent were the partners of foreign males and 13 percent the partners of foreign females already residing in Germany. 53 percent of the visas were issued to foreign partners of Germans. In addition to these visas to spouses and minor children, 28,196 immigration permits were granted to other family members of persons residing in Germany (Unabhängige Kommission Zuwanderung, 2001).[21] Hence, 104,084 individuals immigrated to Germany under the family reunification regulations in 2000, which was about 12 percent of the total gross immigration to Germany in this year.

For Denmark, figures on the number of residence permits granted for family reunification have been published since 1988. In 1988, the Danish Immigration Service and the Refugee Board granted 6,996 residence permits for family reunification, a number which increased to 9,480 in 1999, after a decrease in 1993 following the tightening of the rules in 1992 mentioned earlier. In 2000 and 2001 the figures were 12,571 and 13,187 respectively. However, the increases from 1999 to 2000 and again to 2001 were mostly technical in nature, since from May 2000 onward all children of foreigners were required to have separate residence permits. Before this change in May 2000, between two thirds and three quarters of all cases of family reunification involved spouses and cohabitants, and family reunification as such accounted for about one third of all residence permits granted.

In 2000, nine out of ten of all married or cohabiting immigrants and descendants from the former Yugoslavia, Pakistan, Somalia, Turkey and Vietnam were married to someone from their own country of origin, compared with about 75 percent for all non-Western immigrants and only about 13 percent for Western immigrants and descendants.

Taking the immigrant population as a whole, high proportions married to or cohabiting with a person of the same national origin are not unexpected, since many will have been reunited with a spouse to whom they were already married when they came to Denmark. But many young persons who grew up in Denmark also find spouses in the home countries of their parents. In 1998, among 18- to 25-year-old married immigrants with at least 10 years of residence in Denmark and descendants without Danish citizenship, this was the case for around 70 percent of both men and women from the former Yugoslavia and Pakistan, 90 and 80 percent of young Turkish men and women respectively, and around 80 and 70 percent of all male and female non-Western immigrants and descendants. As indicated earlier, more women than men get married to a fellow countryman already living in Denmark.

---

21 Note, however, that this figure is not considered to be reliable.

The proportions of spousal reunifications representing the reunion of spouses and the creation of new families respectively can be estimated on the basis of the time of the marriage. If the time limits for the cases which are to be considered as creating new families are set at marriages taking place less than a year before or less than six months after the time of immigration, then in 1998 almost 30 percent of married non-Western men and nearly 50 percent of women can be defined as coming to Denmark in connection with the creation of new families. Reunification of existing marriages accounts for 33 and 36 percent of cases respectively (Larsen and Matthiessen, 2002). The remaining marriages took place more than six months after arrival in Denmark.

The tightening of the Aliens Act, which took effect from July 1, 2002 is reflected both by the number of applications and the number of positive decisions relating to family reunification in Denmark. Ignoring children born to foreigners in Denmark, the number of applications fell from 15,370 in 2001 to 11,250 in 2002 and 6,413 in 2003. The number of positive decisions on family reunification – i.e. residence permits granted – fell from 10,950 in 2001 to 8,151 in 2002 and 4,796 in 2003. Of these residence permits, the numbers granted to spouses and cohabitants were 6,499 in 2001, 4,880 in 2002 and 2,544 in 2003 (Danish Immigration Service, 2004).

Starting in the late 1980s, several factors caused a sharp increase in migration towards Western Europe. Most importantly, the fall of the Iron Curtain and the war in the former Yugoslavia induced an increasing inflow of asylum seekers and refugees. These events further increased family reunification, since many foreigners from the endangered areas brought their relatives to Germany and Denmark. Germany further experienced a sharp increase in the inflow of ethnic Germans from Central and Eastern European countries.

In 1992, when immigration to Germany reached its historical peak, Germany received 1.5 million new immigrants; net immigration was 782,000 (see Figure 2.1). In order to understand the magnitude of this inflow, consider the fact that U.S. immigration inflow in the first decade of the 20th century was large enough to increase the population in 1900 by 1.2 percent per year. In relative terms, this is the largest immigration stream in U.S. history. The inflows to Germany have been above this level. Gross immigration to Germany divided by the beginning-of-the-period population size reached an average annual rate of 1.4 percent from 1962-1973, 0.9 percent from 1974-1988, 2.5 percent in 1989, and 1.8 percent for each year from 1990-1992 (Schmidt and Zimmermann, 1992). As described in the last section, the increased inflow of migrants led Germany to tighten its asylum regulations. In addition, Germany introduced some restrictions on the possibilities for ethnic Germans to immigrate. These policy changes led to a sharp decrease in net immigration. Immigration decreased from about 1.5 million people in 1992 to about 800,000 immigrants in 1998, and increased again slightly to 880,000 immigrants in 2001. During the period 1993-1997, gross immigration divided by the population size at the beginning of the year gradually decreased to about 1.0 percent in 1997 and remained at that level from 1998-2001. Net immigration decreased to about 50,000 immigrants in 1998 and increased again to 272,000 immigrants in 2001 (see Figure 2.1).

A somewhat similar development could be observed in Denmark. After the sudden increase in the number of asylum applications in 1984-86 and the resulting increase in the number of residence permits during the following years, net immigration fell to almost zero in 1988, only to increase sharply again from 1989 onward. As in Germany, this inflow consisted to a large extent of refugees.[22] With 63,000 new immigrants and a net inflow of more than 28,000, immigration to Denmark peaked in 1995, when a large number of refugees from the former Yugoslavia, who till then had been covered by a special law, received residence permits. Reflecting a smaller immigration potential from the former Yugoslavia, immigration fell to slightly more than 50,000 individuals in 1999; net immigration in this year amounted to 8,896 persons. In 2001, almost 56,000 migrants entered and 44,000 left Denmark, resulting in a net immigration of 12,000 persons (see Figure 2.1). Gross immigration to Denmark measured as a percentage of the beginning-of-the-period population size has fluctuated less than has been the case in Germany. It came to an average annual rate of 0.6 percent from 1962-1968, 0.7 percent from 1969-1974, 0.6 percent from 1974-1984, 0.7 percent from 1985-1989, then increased to slightly more than 0.8 percent from 1990-1994, until a peak was reached at 1.2 percent in 1995; from 1996-2001 the average annual rate has remained constant at 1.0 percent.

Figure 2.2 shows the proportions of foreigners in the total populations of Denmark and Germany for the period from 1980 to 2002. The figure reflects the changes shown in Figure 2.1. Whereas the proportion of foreigners in the total German population remained largely constant at around 6 percent in the 1980s, it increased from 5.7 percent in 1988 to 9.0 percent in 1997 and stayed relatively constant at that level thereafter. Until 1985, the proportion of foreigners in the total population in Denmark stayed roughly constant at 2 percent and then increased on average by about 0.2 percentage points per year to 5.0 percent in 2002. Instead of foreign citizens, however, Statistics Denmark normally bases its figures on the concept of immigrants and descendants (see Appendix Figure 2.1).[23] Measured in this way (the dotted line in Figure 2.2), the proportion of the total population with a foreign background also increased by an average of 0.2 percentage points per year from a stable level of about 3 percent in the first half of the 1980s to 5.3 percent in 1995. From 1995 to 1996, when many refugees from the former Yugoslavia received residence permits, the proportion increased by 0.6 percentage points to 5.9 percent. Since then the annual increase has been 0.3 percentage points. In 2002, 7.7 percent of the Danish population belonged to the group of immigrants and descendants.

22 Asylum seekers whose applications are still being processed or have been rejected are not included in the Danish population statistics – only refugees with residence permits.
23 Immigrant: Person born abroad to parents who are both either non-Danish citizens or born abroad. Descendant: Person born in Denmark to parents neither of whom is both a Danish citizen and born in Denmark (see, for example, Larsen and Matthiessen, 2002). More detailed definitions are included in the notes to Appendix Figure 2.1.

Figure 2.2. Foreign populations in Denmark and Germany, 1980-2002 (in percent of total populations).

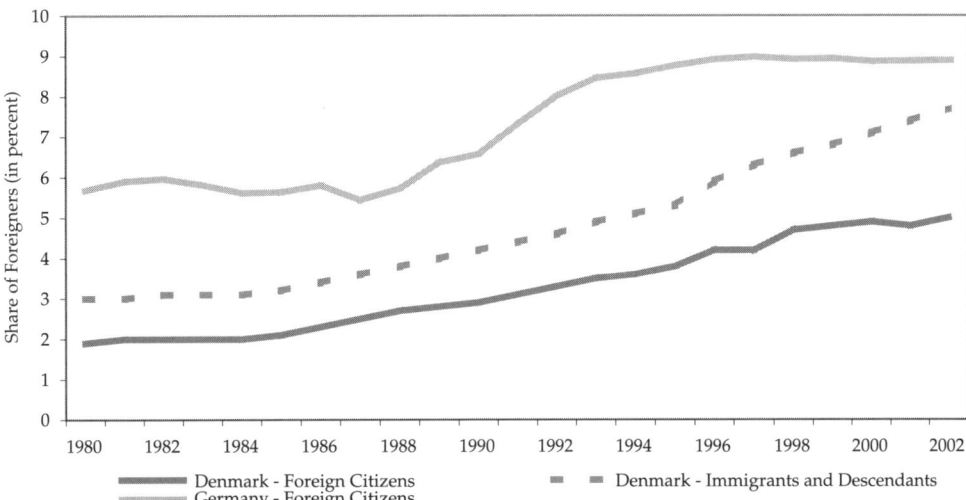

Note: See the text and Appendix Figure 2.1 for definitions of "immigrants" and "descendants".

Sources: Statistics Denmark, unpublished material, *Statistiske Efterretninger (Befolkning og valg)* 1997:16, 2000:4, 2001:4, 2002:5, *Statistisk tiårsoversigt* 1998 and Federal Statistical Office Germany, *Statistisches Jahrbuch*, several volumes.

The more rapid increase in the number of immigrants and descendants in recent years compared with the number of foreign citizens is due to an increasing number of naturalizations. The naturalization rate differs among different nationalities, and in general the composition of the foreign population has changed from a majority with a Western background, characterized by few naturalizations and a high rate of return migration, to a majority with a non-Western background, characterized by higher naturalization rates and low return migration (Larsen and Matthiessen, 2002).

2.3.2 Asylum Seekers and Refugees

The situation with regard to asylum seekers and refugees is to a large extent determined by external (push-) factors. Consequently, there are many similarities between the Danish and the German experiences. Differences in the inflow of asylum seekers to each country – and possible pull-factors – stem from differences in legislation, administrative practice, geography, and history.

Ignoring ethnic German immigrants from Eastern Europe and the former GDR, both countries received relatively few refugees in the period from the end of World War II up until the late 1970s. From 1953 to 1978, Germany experienced an average annual inflow of a little more than 7,000 asylum seekers (Münz, Seifert, and Ulrich, 1999). From 1956 to 1979, Denmark granted asylum to slightly more than 400 persons each year (Matthiessen, 2000; Dansk Flygtningehjælp, 1997).[24] The uprising in Hungary in 1956 and the "Prague Spring" in 1968 resulted in increased numbers of refugees moving to Western Europe, as did an anti-Semitic wave in Poland the year after. In the 1970s, refugees fled from the military coup in Chile, the Communist takeover in South Vietnam, and from the unrest during the years of Idi Amin's rule in Uganda. In the beginning of the 1980s, more than 50 percent of the refugees who were granted asylum in Denmark came from Vietnam. In 1979-1981, the situation in Turkey leading to a military coup in 1980, and the protests in Poland first leading to the formation of the free trade union *Solidarity* in 1980 and later to martial law being imposed in 1981, resulted in 200,000 asylum applications being submitted in Germany in these 3 years, over 20,000 more than the total for the previous 25 years. This dramatic increase led to measures being taken to reduce the numbers of asylum seekers. The immediate results of these measures can be seen in Figure 2.3, which shows the number of asylum applications in Germany and Denmark since 1980. The figure also illustrates the effects of the 1993 amendment to the German Constitutional Law and – as far as Denmark is concerned – of the rather liberal Aliens Act of 1983 and the subsequent tightening of the regulations in 1985-1986 and again from 2000.

Note that for the period up until 1998 only asylum applications lodged *and* processed in the country are included in the Danish data, while so-called Dublin/safe third country returns, etc. are not. As noted by the UNHCR (2000),[25] data should, if possible, refer to persons rather than cases. For Germany, such data are only available since 1995. Before 1995 some persons were counted more than once through reopened cases and appeals. The Danish figures only include initial (first instance) applications. Up to 2002 it was possible to apply for asylum at a Danish agency abroad, and many asylum seekers used this possibility between 1987 and 1996 (UNHCR, 2000), but only a negligible number of these applications lead to asylum (Matthiessen, 2000). Therefore, applications submitted abroad are not included in Figure 2.3.[26]

In the 1980s, Iranian and Polish refugees made up major groups in both countries. This picture changed gradually, as Tamils fled from the civil war in Sri Lanka, and

---

24 A comparison of the number of asylum seekers (in Germany) with the number of residence permits granted to asylum seekers (in Denmark) seems reasonable in this case, partly because of the rather limited number of refugees created by isolated events, and partly because of the liberal German asylum policy at the time. Since the 1970s the situation has become increasingly more complex.
25 These data and similar statistics (1980-1999) for other selected countries can also be found in UNHCR (2000).
26 Other reservations as to comparability are mentioned in the notes to the table.

Figure 2.3. Asylum applications lodged in Denmark and Germany, 1980-2002 (thousands).

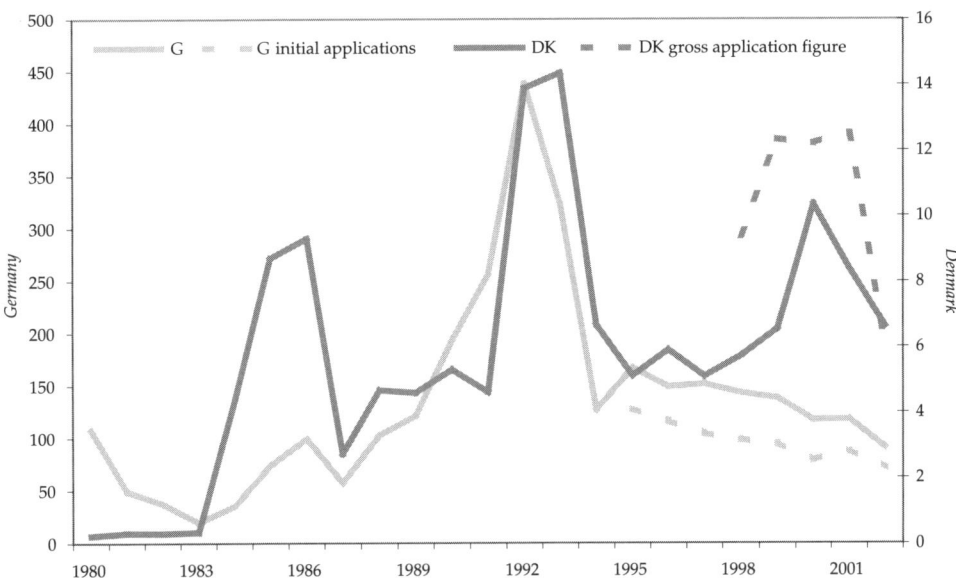

Notes: G/G initial applications: Germany: Until 1995, initial applications and reopened cases and appeals were not registered separately in the German asylum statistics, which means that some persons appear more than once in the German figures. The German data include asylum seekers who were sent back to another EU country or other safe third country as well as disappearances, but not withdrawals. DK/DK gross application figure: Denmark: Until 1998 only asylum applications lodged *and* actually processed in the country were included in the Danish data (the processing figure). Figures which included Dublin/safe third country returns and disappearances and withdrawals, etc. before the formal asylum procedure were not available until that year. The figures for Denmark do not include those covered by the above-mentioned special law, which granted temporary residence permits to certain refugees from former Yugoslavia on conditions that suspended the normal asylum procedure; these refugees later received permanent residence permits. Applications submitted abroad are not included and none of the figures include quota refugees.

Sources: Danish Ministry of the Interior (1994), Statistics Denmark, *Statistiske Efterretninger (Befolkning og valg)* 1998:11, 2002:7, *Nyt fra Danmarks Statistik* 83/1989, 46/1990, 51/2003, 213/2003 and Federal Statistical Office Germany, *Statistisches Jahrbuch*, several volumes.

others from Iraq and civil wars in Lebanon, Somalia and the former Yugoslavia. In recent years Afghans have become one of the largest groups. A general overview of the composition of the inflow of asylum seekers as measured by the numerically most important groups in the two countries since the middle of the 1980s shows that Iraqis have been one of the largest groups in Denmark during the entire period. In Germany, this has only been the case since 1995. Afghans have come to both countries in the second half of the 1990s, but most markedly to Denmark. Stateless persons (mainly Palestinians) have been one of the five largest groups in Denmark during most of the period, as have Somalis in the 1990s, while this has not been the case in Germany. In Germany, Turkey has been the predominant country of origin since 1979. Refugees have to a large extent come from the Kurdish minority in Turkey. Some of the refugees from Iran and Iraq belong to the Kurdish minorities of these two countries. In the second half of the 1980s – i.e. earlier than in Denmark – Germany was already experiencing an inflow of asylum seekers from (the former) Yugoslavia. From 1990 to 1994, Romanians ranked between first and third among the largest nationalities, and from 1991 to 1993 Bulgarians made up one of the largest groups.[27] The rather parallel developments in Denmark and Germany, with a heavy increase in the inflow of asylum seekers and refugees between 1988 and 1992/1993, are replaced by a decrease in the number of initial applications to Germany since 1993, a development which did not occur in Denmark until 2001. This divergence can mainly be explained by the changes in the German legislation on asylum seekers that occurred in 1993 (see Section 2.2.2).

Except for the relatively few quota refugees (not included here), who are admitted under a special arrangement with the UNHCR or for other reasons, a formal asylum procedure decides whether an asylum seeker can stay or not and under what conditions. As indicated by the description of the legislation in Section 2.2 and by the inflow of asylum seekers, comparable recognition rates are difficult to calculate on the basis of single calendar year statistics for asylum applications and residence permits granted in asylum cases. This is especially true when it comes to using data for comparisons between countries, but there are problems even for making comparisons within the same country over a period. A case may not be finalized in the same year that the application is lodged; cases may be reopened and decisions appealed against; and some nationalities may have better chances of being considered in need of protection than others. Furthermore, there are differences in legislation, types of residence permits and administrative and statistical practices as well as changes over time. However, annual statistics can give an indication of the size of the acceptance rate and whether it is high or low in relation to other countries. Table 2.1 depicts the most recent and most comparable figures for Denmark and Germany, showing initial applications and residence permits in asylum cases per 1,000 inhabitants for the period from 1995 to 2002.

As already mentioned, 1995 and 1996 are not representative as far as residence permits in asylum cases in Denmark are concerned. Ignoring these two years, the

---

27 Citizens from the former Soviet Union and other Eastern European countries have also been among the asylum seekers in Denmark, but in most cases they have been sent back without having their applications processed in the formal asylum procedure. *Sources*: Statistics Denmark, *Statistiske Efterretninger (Befolkning og valg)* 1992:11, 1994:10, 2002:7, *Nyt fra Danmarks Statistik* 83/1989, 46/1990, StatBank Denmark, and Bundesamt für die Anerkennung ausländischer Flüchtlinge, homepage http://www.bafl.de/template/index_asylstatistik.htm.

Table 2.1. Asylum applications and residence permits granted to asylum seekers in Denmark and Germany, number of persons and number per 1,000 inhabitants, 1995-2002.

Year	1995	1996	1997	1998	1999	2000	2001	2002
				Denmark				
Total population (thousands)	5,216	5,251	5,275	5,295	5,314	5,330	5,349	5,368
No. of applications								
Applications, initial[1]	5,104	5,893	5,092	5,702	6,530	10,347	8,385	6,621
Applications, initial[2]				9,370	12,331	12,200	12,512	6,068
Residence permits	20,347	8,717	5,925	4,758	4,443	5,156	6,264	4,067
– refugee status	19,931	6,387	4,940	4,442	4,223	4,388	5,742	3,486
– other reasons	416	2,330	985	316	220	768	522	581
Per 1,000 inhabitants								
Applications, initial[1]	0.98	1.12	0.97	1.08	1.23	1.94	1.57	1.23
Applications, initial[2]				1.77	2.32	2.29	2.34	1.13
Residence permits	3.90	1.66	1.12	0.90	0.84	0.97	1.17	0.76
– refugee status	3.82	1.22	0.94	0.84	0.79	0.82	1.07	0.65
– other reasons	0.08	0.44	0.19	0.06	0.04	0.14	0.10	0.11
				Germany				
Total population (thousands)	81,538	81,817	82,012	82,038	82,028	82,145	82,260	82,435
No. of applications								
Applications, initial	127,937	116,367	104,353	98,644	95,113	78,564	88,287	71,127
Residence permits	27,099	26,082	20,990	13,857	12,361	13,043	26,102	8,107
– refugee status	23,468	24,000	18,222	11,320	10,261	11,446	22,719	6,509
– other reasons	3,631	2,082	2,768	2,537	2,100	1,597	3,383	1,598
Per 1,000 inhabitants								
Applications, initial	1.57	1.42	1.27	1.20	1.16	0.96	1.07	0.86
Residence permits	0.33	0.32	0.26	0.17	0.15	0.16	0.32	0.10
– refugee status	0.29	0.29	0.22	0.14	0.13	0.14	0.28	0.08
– other reasons	0.04	0.03	0.03	0.03	0.03	0.02	0.04	0.02

Notes: See notes to Figure 2.3. 1) Processing figure. 2) Gross application figure, which is more comparable with the German statistics and usually larger than the processing figure. It may be smaller due to a time lag between the lodging of and the decision to process the asylum application. This was the case in 2002.

Sources: The Danish Immigration Service, Statistics Denmark and Bundesamt für Migration und Flüchtlinge.

general picture still seems to be that, relative to the size of the population, more asylum applications have been lodged in Denmark than in Germany. This difference was increasing up until 2002, when there was a significant decrease in Denmark, reflecting amendments to the Aliens Act. Furthermore, relative to the size of the population, the number of residence permits – especially with (convention or other) refugee status – has been significantly higher in Denmark. Also, a recent comprehensive study showed that over the decade from 1992 to 2001, Denmark had the highest recognition rate among all industrialized countries – namely almost 70 percent or 6 to 7 times the level in Germany and about 3 times the EU average (OECD, 2003).

From the point of view of comparability, the most appropriate way to compile asylum statistics would be to follow *cohorts* of asylum seekers from the time they submitted their applications to the final decision, using identical guidelines in each country and with asylum seekers broken down by nationality. The Danish Immigration Service (2003) has published such statistics (though not broken down by nationality), following cohorts of asylum seekers for each year from 1998 to 2001 and for the first half of 2002.[28] Unfortunately, there is not much material on cohort analyses available from other countries, but the Danish Immigration Service and the corresponding German institution, Bundesamt für Migration und Flüchtlinge, have given permission to compare unpublished material for three selected countries – Afghanistan, Iraq and Sri Lanka – belonging to the 1998 cohort.

A preliminary overview at the end of 2000 showed that practically all asylum cases had been processed by Denmark, while between 21 and 31 percent of the cases were still pending in Germany. Denmark had granted residence permits with convention status to about 44 percent of the Afghans, 5 percent of the asylum seekers from Iraq and 2 percent of the asylum seekers from Sri Lanka. Residence permits with "de facto refugee" status, which – in Denmark – were comparable in practice with convention status, have been given to 23 percent of the asylum seekers from Afghanistan, 61 percent of the asylum seekers from Iraq, and 21 percent of the asylum seekers from Sri Lanka. In total, then, in Denmark, about two thirds of the asylum seekers from both Afghanistan and Iraq and one quarter of the asylum seekers from Sri Lanka received residence permits with either convention or "de facto" status. The figures for Germany are 2 percent for asylum seekers from Afghanistan, 45 percent for asylum seekers from Iraq, and 9 percent for asylum seekers from Sri Lanka (convention status). In Germany, about 30 percent of the asylum seekers from Afghanistan have received the temporary and less secure asylum status; the comparable numbers for asylum seekers from Iraq and Sri Lanka are less than 1 percent.

Overall, together with the above description of legislations and practices, the statistics presented in this section seem to support the view that the Danish asylum

---

28 Data are presented according to a format agreed upon by the member states of the IGC – Intergovernmental Consultations on Asylum, Refugees and Migration in Europe, USA, Canada, and Australia.

system has been more liberal than the German system, or at least that it was so until 2002.

2.3.3 Temporary Immigration

Most of the immigration flows in the late 1980s and the 1990s were caused by push-factors. The boom period after German reunification, however, also caused some pull migration of temporary workers that was based on agreements between Germany and a number of Central and Eastern European Countries (CEEC) and on the introduction of the "Green Card" in 2001, which has been described in more detail in the previous section. In this subsection we want to give a short description of these special arrangements and the resulting inflow of migrants.

In the 1990s, Germany signed bilateral agreements with some CEEC countries concerning temporary immigration of workers. Germany's aim was to bring the CEEC countries up to Western European standards, to demonstrate solidarity with these countries, to train Eastern European workers in using modern technologies to foster economic development in the countries of origin, to decrease the immigration pressure from these countries, and to promote economic co-operation with them. In accordance with these goals Germany created three different categories under which workers from CEEC countries could temporarily work in Germany: *Werkvertragsarbeitnehmer, Gastarbeitnehmer* (not the same as guest workers), and seasonal workers. Appendix Table 2.4 provides detailed descriptions of the definitions of these three categories of temporary foreign workers.

In the program for *Werkvertragsarbeitnehmer,* Eastern European firms are allowed to employ their own workers in project-linked work arrangements co-ordinated under contracts with German firms. The workers immigrating under this category are allowed to stay for a maximum of three years. After a worker has stayed in Germany as a *Werkvertragsarbeitnehmer,* he must leave Germany for at least as long as he has been there, before he is allowed to come back again. The wages of the *Werkvertragsarbeitnehmer* must be the same as those of similar German workers; the social security contributions for these workers are, however, paid by their firm in the country of origin according to the rules of that country. Due to this arrangement, the wage costs of *Werkvertragsarbeitnehmer* are in general lower than those of comparable Germans. The number of workers who can work under these treaties is limited by country quotas, and these are adjusted each year according to the labor market situation in Germany. Furthermore, work permits are not granted for jobs in districts in which unemployment is significantly higher than the national average. The employment of *Werkvertragsarbeitnehmer* increased sharply from 14,500 in 1988 to 95,000 in 1992. Due to a steady reduction in the quotas, this number decreased to about 46,000 in 1996. In 2002, on average 45,000 *Werkvertragsarbeitnehmer* were living in Germany at any one time, of whom about 13,000 were working in the construction sector. In most years, Polish *Werkvertragsarbeitnehmer* constituted almost 50 percent of all workers employed in Germany under these bilateral agreements, followed by workers from Hungary, Romania, and the former Yugoslavia.

In addition to the *Werkvertragsarbeitnehmer*, Germany initiated programs for so-called *Gastarbeitnehmer* with several CEECs. The aim of this type of program is to improve the professional and linguistic skills of the participants. The 18- to 40-year-old participants must have completed a vocational training course and have a basic knowledge of the German language. These *Gastarbeitnehmer* can stay in Germany for a maximum of 18 months. They need a work permit, even though the programs are not dependent on the labor market situation in Germany. They must be paid the same wages as similar German workers. In contrast to the *Werkvertragsarbeitnehmer*, their social security payment requirements follow the German standards. From 1991 to 1993 the number of *Gastarbeitnehmer* increased from 1,570 to 5,771 and decreased thereafter to 1,926 in 2002. Most of them came from the Czech Republic, Hungary, Poland, Romania, and Slovakia.

On the basis of bilateral agreements between Germany and several CEEC countries, foreign seasonal workers have been able to obtain German work permits for a maximum of three months since 1991. These seasonal workers are only allowed to work in agriculture, hotels, restaurants, and as showmen. They must be employed under the same wage and working conditions as German workers, and their employment requires the payment of social security contributions according to German standards. In addition, the employer has to provide seasonal workers with accommodation. In general, there is no quota restriction on this type of employment. However, the German Labour Office has to check whether similar unemployed native workers are available. From 1992 to 1999 the number of seasonal workers employed ranged between 130,000 and a maximum of 246,000 per year. After 1999 the number of seasonal workers increased steadily, reaching almost 300,000 in 2002 and about 263,000 in the first half of 2003. Most of the seasonal workers come from Poland; in 2002, for example, Poles constituted almost 85 percent of all seasonal workers.

As noted in Section 2.2.2, the introduction of the "Green Card" for foreign IT specialists started a heated debate about the necessity for an immigration law for Germany. Under this "Green Card" program, a total of 20,000 IT specialists were allowed to enter Germany between 2000 and 2003 for a maximum of 5 years. Table 2.2 shows that only 14,144 temporary work permits (71 percent of the total quota) have been issued by the German Labour Office to foreign IT specialists. This number is far below the prior expectations of the German government. There may be various reasons for this. First, several characteristics of the "Green Card" program are not particularly attractive to either the German firms or potential IT specialists. For example, applicants without a formal degree in a subject related to IT have to be paid a minimum annual wage of EUR 51,000. The work permit for the foreign IT specialists is restricted to a maximum of five years, and their partners are not allowed to work in Germany for the first two years. In addition, problems in the

Table 2.2. Work permits for foreign IT specialists in Germany, August 2000-April 2003.

Nationality	Total		Males	Females	Immigrated from a foreign country	Foreigners finishing a German university degree	Firm size		
							<101	101-500	>500
	No. of persons	In percent of total	In percent of (1)						
	(1)	(2)	(3)	(4)	(5)	(6)	(7)	(8)	(9)
Bulgaria	418	2.96	80.14	19.86	84.45	15.55	68.18	10.77	21.05
Former Yugoslavia	719	5.08	82.06	17.94	84.28	15.72	56.47	14.33	29.21
Romania	1,017	7.19	84.76	15.24	94.20	5.80	60.67	18.19	21.14
Hungary	500	3.54	91.40	8.60	92.80	7.20	63.60	15.40	21.00
Czech/Slovak Republic	961	6.79	94.69	5.31	95.94	4.06	67.33	15.09	17.59
Former USSR	1,836	12.98	87.85	12.15	90.96	9.04	65.85	14.54	19.61
India	3,533	24.98	92.33	7.67	94.62	5.38	62.24	21.60	16.16
Pakistan	201	1.42	98.01	1.99	81.59	18.41	63.68	10.45	25.87
Algeria, Morocco, Tunisia	424	3.00	92.22	7.78	34.91	65.09	52.12	16.98	30.90
South America	373	2.64	77.48	22.52	82.04	17.96	46.38	17.43	36.19
Others	4,162	29.43	84.05	15.95	73.38	26.62	51.11	16.00	32.89
Total	**14,144**	**100.00**	**87.70**	**12.30**	**84.76**	**15.24**	**58.89**	**17.03**	**24.07**

Source: Bundesanstalt für Arbeit, own calculations.

so-called *new economy* occurring shortly after the introduction of the "Green Card" program reduced the demand for IT specialists in Germany.

Table 2.2 further shows that the biggest group of IT specialists that have received "Green Cards" come from India (25 percent), followed by IT specialists from countries of the former USSR (13 percent), Romania (7 percent) and, the former Yugoslavia (5 percent). Almost 88 percent of all temporary work permits in this program have been issued to males, and most of them immigrated from foreign countries rather than being foreign students at a German university. Finally, more than half of the foreign IT specialists are working in small firms with less than 101 employees.

In Denmark, temporary immigration in connection with work or studies has continued to take place even after the total ban on immigration in 1973. As mentioned in Section 2.2.1, however, residence permits for employment or business reasons can only be granted in exceptional cases. The ban has never applied to citizens of the Nordic countries, who do not need a permit to enter and work in Denmark, or to citizens of the EC/EU. Unlike Germany, Denmark has not signed any bilateral agreements of the kind described above.

From the late 1980s to 1995, on average 2,800 residence permits per year were granted in EC/EEA cases, a figure which increased to 6,000 from 1996 onward (Larsen and Matthiessen, 2002; Danish Immigration Service, 2003). As far as non-Nordic, non-EU/EEA nationals are concerned, from 1988 to 2000 a little more than 2,700 residence permits for employment reasons were granted each year on average. This number decreased in the first half of the 1990s, but increased again from 1996 onwards, reaching 5,000 permits in 2001 and 2002. Finally, between 4,000 and 5,500 residence permits given for exceptional reasons, of which education and work as au pair were the most important, were issued between 1988 and 1995, increasing to between 6,000 and 8,000 from 1996 to 2001 and to 9,612 in 2002.

Conditions for residence permits for employment given to non-Nordic, non-EU/EEA nationals are that there should be no Dane or foreigner living in Denmark who could undertake the job, and that wage and other working conditions are in accordance with Danish standards. Furthermore, the job must be of a special character – i.e. not normal skilled or unskilled work. In some cases an authorization is needed. Trade organizations are consulted to help the Danish Immigration Service to decide whether there is a lack of local labor available for a job. The "Job Card" arrangement introduced in 2002 suspends this consulting process for persons with certain qualifications on a continuously updated "positive list" – i.e. which are in short supply. Examples are certain engineers and scientists in the natural sciences and technology sector, doctors, and nurses. Finally, special access conditions exist for experts and specialists, scientists, and managers, and – but on different terms – for interns and trainees, students, and au pairs. Self-employed and owners of businesses must prove that the financial foundation of their businesses is sound, that Danish commercial interests will benefit from the business, and that the person's presence in Denmark is necessary. Normally it will not be possible to obtain a residence (and work) permit to open a restaurant or a retail shop.

Experts and specialists, etc. and persons on the "positive list" may receive a residence permit for up to three years, with the possibility of prolongation; others may receive a permit for up to one year, with the possibility of prolongation.

To summarize, despite the halt on immigration for foreign workers introduced in 1973, both Germany and Denmark experienced a considerable inflow of temporary workers who immigrated on the basis of special bilateral agreements, special programs, or exceptions to the usual restrictive immigration laws for workers with specialized skills.

2.4 The Demographic Characteristics of Immigrants in Germany and Denmark

2.4.1 Source Countries

Even though Denmark and Germany have a rather similar history of immigration (see Section 2.3), they differ remarkably with regard to the source countries of the immigrants. Table 2.3 shows the composition of the foreign populations by citizenship in both countries for the period from 1987 to 2001. Column 2 of Table 2.3 again reflects the different levels of immigration to Denmark and Germany. Between 1987 and 2001, the foreign population in Denmark grew by more than 100 percent from 128,255 to 258,629 persons. In the same period, the foreign population in Germany increased by almost 73 percent from 4.2 to 7.3 million people. As already outlined in Section 2.3.1, this amounts to about 5 percent[29] of the total population in Denmark and about 9 percent of the total population in Germany.

Compared to Germany, Denmark has a high proportion of foreigners from the other Nordic countries, which can be largely explained by the historically liberal immigration policy that Denmark has towards people from Finland, Iceland, Norway, and Sweden. Reflecting the increasing immigration of asylum seekers and refugees in the 1990s, the proportion of foreigners from other EU countries of the total population of foreigners decreased in both countries, even though between 1987 and 2001 the number of foreigners from other EU countries increased from about 26,500 to 41,500 in Denmark and from 1.2 to almost 1.9 million in Germany.

The proportion made up of persons from the former Yugoslavia increased sharply at the beginning of the 1990s in both countries, which is largely a reflection of the increased inflow of refugees following the civil war in this region. Whereas the number of foreigners from the former Yugoslavia increased steadily to about 35,000 persons in Denmark, the number of persons from this region decreased from about 1.3 to slightly over 1.0 million in Germany. This can primarily be explained by the different policies towards refugees from the former Yugoslavia. Whereas Germany followed a policy of sending refugees back after the end of the civil war, many refugees from the former Yugoslavia in Denmark received permanent residence permits (see Sections 2.2 and 2.3).

Immigration from Turkey plays a much more important role in Germany than in Denmark. Since 1993, there has been a population of about 2 million persons of Turkish origin, making Turkey by far the most important source country for immigrants in Germany. In Denmark, however, the Turkish population has been only

---

29 As mentioned in Section 2.3.1, the broader concepts of immigrants and descendants specific to Denmark, which cannot be applied to Germany, result in an increase in the proportion of the population with a foreign background from about 3 percent in the first half of the 1980s to 7.7 percent in 2002.

Table 2.3. Foreign population in Denmark and Germany by citizenship, 1987-2001.

				Third countries				
Year	Total	Nordic countries and North America	EU countries	Former Yugoslavia	Turkey	Pakistan	Others	Total third countries
				Denmark				
1987	128,255	22.37	20.75	6.51	17.40	5.14	27.84	56.88
1988	136,177	20.82	19.74	6.46	17.93	4.77	30.28	59.44
1989	142,016	19.76	18.71	6.44	18.36	4.54	32.18	61.53
1990	150,644	18.65	17.79	6.33	18.54	4.17	34.52	63.56
1991	160,641	17.89	17.34	6.25	18.48	3.88	36.16	64.76
1992	169,525	17.02	16.77	6.32	18.89	3.59	37.42	66.21
1993	180,103	16.29	16.43	6.28	18.69	3.48	38.84	67.27
1994	189,014	15.87	16.53	6.15	18.34	3.37	39.74	67.59
1995	196,705	15.89	17.14	5.76	17.78	3.25	40.18	66.97
1996	222,746	14.90	15.68	12.61	16.04	2.94	37.83	69.42
1997	237,695	14.67	15.74	13.54	15.50	2.83	37.71	69.58
1998	249,628	14.52	15.89	13.59	15.03	2.78	38.20	69.60
1999	256,276	14.46	15.86	13.44	14.85	2.78	38.60	69.68
2000	259,361	14.59	15.77	13.52	14.10	2.74	39.27	69.63
2001	258,629	14.80	16.00	13.52	13.62	2.73	39.32	69.20
				Germany				
1987	4,240,532	2.06	29.25	13.01	34.28	0.37	21.04	68.69
1988	4,489,105	2.04	28.42	12.90	33.94	0.38	22.32	69.54
1989	4,845,882	2.04	27.35	12.60	33.28	0.41	24.33	70.61
1990	5,342,532	2.00	26.93	12.40	31.72	0.46	26.48	71.06
1991	5,882,267	1.96	25.28	13.18	30.25	0.48	28.85	72.76
1992	6,495,792	1.86	23.20	15.67	28.56	0.50	30.21	74.94
1993	6,878,117	1.82	22.33	17.77	27.89	0.50	29.70	75.86
1994	6,990,510	1.81	22.38	18.03	28.12	0.49	29.17	75.81
1995	7,173,866	1.76	22.24	18.11	28.08	0.51	29.29	75.99
1996	7,314,046	1.75	22.18	17.73	28.02	0.52	29.80	76.07
1997	7,365,833	1.75	25.12	16.41	28.61	0.52	27.59	73.13
1998	7,319,593	1.77	25.33	15.28	28.83	0.52	28.26	72.89
1999	7,343,591	1.79	25.31	15.24	27.96	0.52	29.18	72.90
2000	7,296,817	1.83	25.66	14.19	27.39	0.51	30.42	72.51
2001	7,318,628	1.83	25.55	13.81	26.62	0.48	31.72	72.62

Notes: East Germany was included under EU countries from January 1, 1991, and Austria from January 1, 1995. Sweden and Finland, like Austria EU members since 1995, are included under the Nordic countries throughout the period.

Sources: Matthiessen (2002) and Federal Statistical Office Germany, *Statistisches Jahrbuch*, several volumes.

slightly higher than the population from the former Yugoslavia, at least since the mid-1990s. Foreign citizens from Pakistan in Denmark constitute a considerable proportion of the total population of foreigners, which can be explained by the recruitment of guest workers from Pakistan in the 1960s and early 1970s. Even though the total number of Pakistanis living in Germany in 2001 is about five times bigger than that in Denmark, they make up only a small proportion of the total foreign population.

2.4.2 Sex and Age Distributions

Table 2.4 shows the age and sex distributions in the populations of Western and non-Western immigrants and of natives, and also in the total populations of Denmark and Germany. In general, the foreign population is younger than the respective native populations. There is a higher proportion of male foreigners than male natives in both countries in all age groups up to the 40- to 44-year-olds, and the same is true of female foreigners in comparison to the native population in Denmark. In Germany, there are greater proportions of the population for foreign females than native females in all age groups up to the 30- to 34-year-olds. This pattern occurs in almost all countries with a substantial immigrant population, and can be explained primarily by the higher migration incentives for younger individuals as well as the higher fertility rates among immigrants compared to natives.

The overall picture, however, conceals significant differences in the age structures for migrants of different origins. In both countries and for both males and females, foreigners originating from Western countries appear to be slightly older than natives, whereas foreigners from non-Western countries are significantly younger than natives. These differences probably reflect the different situations under which persons in the respective groups have migrated to Denmark and Germany as well as the immigration history of the two host countries. In Germany, for example, many immigrants from Western countries originate from Italy, Portugal, Spain, and Greece. The immigration of these groups was initiated during the guest worker recruitment phase in the 1960s and early 1970s, and hence many of these immigrants are now in their fifties.

In Denmark, the distribution by sex is roughly the same in all groups, namely about 50 percent males and 50 percent females. However, there is a difference between Western and non-Western immigrants; of the Western immigrant population 53 percent are males and 47 percent females, while among non-Western immigrants there is a larger percentage of females than males – 52 and 48 percent respectively. Among the population as a whole, there is a slightly greater proportion of males up to the age of 55, which is to be expected since a few more boys are born than girls. The picture is slightly different in the immigrant population, however. Among non-Western foreigners, there is a greater number of boys up to the age of 20, after which women are in the majority. Finally, among Western immigrants there is

Table 2.4. Sex and age structure of the populations of Western and non-Western foreign populations, of the native populations and of the total populations of Denmark and Germany (in percent of the total populations in the respective groups), 2002.

Denmark[1)]

	Males					Females				
	Foreign population					Foreign population				
Age	Western	Non-Western	Total	Danes	Total	Western	Non-Western	Total	Danes	Total
0-4	2.1	4.8	4.0	3.2	3.2	1.9	4.6	3.8	3.0	3.0
5-9	2.1	4.4	3.7	3.3	3.4	1.9	4.2	3.5	3.2	3.2
10-14	1.9	4.4	3.6	3.0	3.0	1.8	4.0	3.3	2.8	2.9
15-19	1.6	3.8	3.1	2.7	2.7	1.8	3.7	3.1	2.5	2.6
20-24	3.9	3.8	3.8	2.9	3.0	5.0	4.8	4.9	2.8	2.9
25-29	5.8	5.0	5.2	3.5	3.5	5.3	6.8	6.3	3.3	3.5
30-34	6.7	5.7	6.0	3.6	3.7	5.1	6.7	6.2	3.4	3.6
35-39	6.6	4.9	5.4	4.0	4.1	4.7	5.4	5.2	3.8	3.9
40-44	5.4	3.4	4.1	3.6	3.6	3.9	3.7	3.8	3.4	3.5
45-49	4.6	2.3	3.0	3.5	3.5	3.4	2.6	2.9	3.4	3.4
50-54	4.0	1.5	2.3	3.6	3.5	3.3	1.8	2.3	3.5	3.5
55-59	3.3	1.2	1.8	3.6	3.6	3.1	1.1	1.8	3.6	3.5
60-64	2.2	0.8	1.3	2.6	2.5	2.1	1.0	1.3	2.6	2.6
65-69	1.1	0.7	0.8	2.0	2.0	1.4	0.8	1.0	2.2	2.2
70-74	0.7	0.5	0.6	1.7	1.6	1.1	0.7	0.8	2.0	1.9
75-79	0.5	0.2	0.3	1.3	1.3	0.7	0.3	0.4	1.8	1.8
80-84	0.2	0.1	0.1	0.8	0.8	0.3	0.1	0.2	1.4	1.4
85-89	0.1	0.0	0.0	0.4	0.4	0.1	0.1	0.1	0.9	0.8
90+	0.0	0.0	0.0	0.2	0.1	0.1	0.0	0.0	0.5	0.5
65+	2.7	1.5	1.9	6.4	2.0	0.0	0.0	2.5	8.9	0.0
Total	44,065	87,310	131,375	2,522,771	2,654,146	39,271	96,083	135,354	2,578,854	2,714,208

	Germany[2]									
	Males					**Females**				
	Foreign population					Foreign population				
Age	Western[3]	Non-Western[4]	Total	Germans	Total	Western[3]	Non-Western[4]	Total	Germans	Total
0-5	2.0	3.6	3.2	2.9	2.9	1.9	3.5	3.0	2.7	2.8
6-9	1.5	2.9	2.5	2.0	2.0	1.5	2.8	2.4	1.9	1.9
10-14	2.0	3.8	3.3	2.9	2.9	1.9	3.6	3.1	2.7	2.8
15-17	1.2	2.2	1.9	1.7	1.7	1.1	1.9	1.7	1.6	1.6
18-20	1.5	2.5	2.2	1.7	1.8	1.5	2.3	2.1	1.6	1.7
21-24	3.1	4.1	3.8	2.2	2.3	3.0	4.2	3.8	2.1	2.3
25-29	5.5	6.3	6.0	2.6	2.9	4.8	5.9	5.6	2.6	2.8
30-34	6.5	6.1	6.2	3.8	4.0	5.2	5.3	5.3	3.6	3.8
35-39	6.0	5.3	5.6	4.4	4.5	4.6	4.1	4.2	4.3	4.3
40-44	5.3	3.6	4.1	4.1	4.1	3.8	3.1	3.3	4.0	3.9
45-49	4.4	2.8	3.3	3.6	3.6	3.6	2.9	3.1	3.5	3.5
50-54	4.5	2.7	3.2	3.2	3.2	3.7	2.8	3.1	3.2	3.2
55-59	4.0	2.3	2.7	2.7	2.7	2.8	1.9	2.1	2.8	2.7
60-64	3.3	1.9	2.3	3.6	3.5	1.9	1.4	1.6	3.8	3.6
65+	4.5	2.0	2.7	7.1	6.7	3.4	2.2	2.5	11.1	10.4
Total (1,000)	1,135.0	2,746.0	3,881.0	36,393.6	40,274.6	916.3	2,520.9	3,437.2	38,728.4	42,165.6

Notes: The sum of a column shows the sex distribution. 1) Figures for Denmark refer to December 31, 2001. 2) Figures for Germany refer to January 1, 2002. 3) Without New Zealand. 4) With New Zealand.

Sources: StatBank Denmark (Statistics Denmark), Federal Statistical Office Germany, own calculations.

a small majority of males up to the age of 14, a majority of females among the 15- to 24-year-olds, and a (falling) majority of men in the 25-64 age group. Here, too, there are more women than men in the older age groups.

The picture is significantly different in Germany. Whereas the proportions of males and females are roughly equal among Germans, there are far more males than females for both Western and non-Western foreigners. Among Germans, there is again a small majority of males up to the age of 50. As a result of deaths in World War II, the predominance of women in the older age groups is more pronounced in Germany than in Denmark. Among Western foreigners, there is a roughly equal distribution of males and females up to the age of 24, after which men are in the majority. Again this may be interpreted against the background of the German recruitment policy in the 1960s and early 1970s. Westerners under the age of 24 are mainly second generation immigrants, but the greater number of males in the older age groups can be explained by the fact that Germany recruited predominantly male guest workers. For non-Western immigrants the sex distribution is much more equal, with a small majority of males in almost all age groups. In this group, several different factors are at work. Whereas Turkish migrants, whose immigration was also initiated during the guest worker recruitment phase, could be expected to show a similar sex distribution across age groups to that of the Western foreigners, asylum seekers and refugees in general could be expected to be distributed much more equally across gender and to be younger than the average population.

2.4.3 Regional Distribution

As in most immigration countries, immigrants and their descendants in Denmark and Germany cluster in specific regions and in urban areas. This clustering has to be kept in mind when interpreting the empirical results given in the following chapters.

Table 2.5 shows the distribution of natives, foreigners, and the total population in Germany by federal states and by city size. Compared to the German population, immigrants and their descendants are over-represented in North Rhine-Westphalia, Baden-Württemberg, and Hesse. This clustering can partly be explained historically, because these regions are characterized by strong manufacturing sectors and hence received many guest workers during the guest worker recruitment phase in the 1960s and early 1970s. Table 2.5 further shows that very few foreigners are living in the new federal states in the east of Germany. Again, this can partly be explained historically, since the former GDR hardly experienced any immigration from other countries. Another explanation for the lack of foreigners in East Germany is the severe economic problems of these regions. Finally, the table shows a clustering of foreigners in urban areas. More than 75 percent of all foreigners but only 56 percent of all Germans live in cities with at least 20,000 inhabitants.

Table 2.5. Regional distribution of natives and foreigners in Germany (in percent of respective total populations), 1997.

	Germans	Foreigners	Total
Regions:			
Schleswig-Holstein	3.48	2.10	3.35
Hamburg	1.93	3.55	2.08
Lower Saxony	9.74	7.52	9.53
Bremen	0.77	1.35	0.83
North Rhine-Westphalia	21.27	27.78	21.89
Hesse	7.05	10.18	7.35
Rhineland-Palatinate	4.93	4.42	4.89
Baden-Württemberg	12.06	18.31	12.66
Bavaria	14.54	16.16	14.70
Saarland	1.32	1.32	1.32
Berlin	4.02	6.00	4.21
Brandenburg	3.41	0.35	3.12
Mecklenburg-Western Pomerania	2.44	0.10	2.22
Saxony	6.07	0.44	5.53
Saxony-Anhalt	3.63	0.29	3.31
Thuringia	3.33	0.14	3.03
City size:			
<20,000	44.13	24.32	42.25
20,000-500,000	42.45	48.38	43.01
>500,000	13.42	27.30	14.74

Sources: Mikrozensus 1997, own calculations.

The regional distribution of natives, foreigners, and the total population in Denmark by county[30] and city size is shown in Table 2.6. In Denmark, too, immigrants and descendants cluster in specific areas. More than 40 percent live in the metropolitan area.

The proportion living in the metropolitan area is even higher if the concepts of immigrants and descendants (see above and Appendix Figure 2.1) are applied instead of nationality; it was 53 percent in 1999 according to Statistics Denmark (1999), and 22 percent of all immigrants and descendants live in the municipality of Copenhagen. Immigrants from less developed countries[31] in particular cluster in the metropolitan area and in other counties with large cities such as Odense and Århus.

---

30 Denmark is divided into 14 counties and a number of municipalities. The municipalities of Copenhagen and Frederiksberg in the metropolitan area do not belong to any county but form their own local authorities and function both as municipalities and as counties.
31 As defined by the United Nations.

Table 2.6. Regional distribution of natives and foreigners in Denmark (in percent of respective total populations), 2002.

	Danes	Foreigners	Total
Regions:			
Copenhagen and Frederiksberg municipalities	10.34	24.07	11.02
Copenhagen county	11.28	15.62	11.50
Frederiksborg county	6.91	6.74	6.90
Roskilde county	4.42	3.55	4.37
West Zealand county	5.64	4.04	5.56
Storstrøm county	4.94	3.21	4.85
Bornholm county	0.84	0.53	0.82
Funen county	8.89	7.11	8.80
South Jutland county	4.74	4.18	4.72
Ribe county	4.23	3.15	4.18
Vejle county	6.61	5.22	6.54
Ringkøbing county	5.19	3.53	5.11
Århus county	12.08	10.73	12.01
Viborg county	4.47	2.39	4.36
North Jutland county	9.40	5.95	9.23
City size:			
<20,000	42.91	24.62	42.00
20,000-500,000	31.84	31.71	31.83
>500,000 (Metropolitan area)	25.25	43.66	26.16

Source: StatBank Denmark (Statistics Denmark), own calculations.

Immigrants and descendants from more developed countries are more evenly distributed across the country, including rural districts and small towns. As in the case of Germany, the regional clustering of non-Western immigrants and descendants in certain urban areas may be explained historically, as it may be traced back to the phase of guest worker immigration.

2.5 Summary

This chapter has shown many similarities between Denmark and Germany with regard to their current legislation regulating the possibilities which foreigners have of immigrating and the access of immigrants to the respective labor markets. Apart from different names for residence permits and ways of obtaining a work permit, especially for workers from Central and Eastern European Countries (CEEC) and for asylum seekers, the differences between Denmark and Germany are mainly historical, with Denmark following a more liberal immigration policy towards immigrants from the Nordic countries and – until recently – asylum seekers.

Except that the sizes of the inflows have always been larger in Germany in terms of both total numbers and per capita, the two countries have shown very similar patterns of net immigration since the 1960s. In the 1960s and early 1970s both countries recruited foreign guest workers. After stopping the recruitment of foreign workers in 1973, both countries experienced sizeable levels of immigration that consisted mainly of family members of guest workers who had immigrated before 1973. In the late 1980s Denmark and Germany experienced a sharp increase in the inflow of asylum seekers and refugees, leading to a tightening of the asylum legislation in both countries in the mid-1990s. Unlike Denmark, however, Germany has experienced in addition an increased inflow of temporary workers from Eastern Europe since the early 1990s.

Even though Germany and Denmark share some similarities with regard to the historical trends in immigration, there are some differences with regard to the demographic characteristics of the foreign populations in the two countries. These differences with respect to the source countries, and also with respect to the age and sex distributions of the populations, have to a large degree a historical explanation. Unlike Denmark, for example, Germany also recruited guest workers from Southern European countries like Greece and Italy in the 1960s and early 1970s. As in most immigration countries, immigrants and their descendants in Denmark and Germany cluster in metropolitan areas.

References

Bauer, Thomas K. 1998. *Arbeitsmarkteffekte der Migration und Einwanderungspolitik: Eine Analyse für die Bundesrepublik Deutschland.* Heidelberg: Physika-Verlag.

Bauer, Thomas K., Barbara Dietz, Klaus F. Zimmermann, and Eric Zwintz. 2004. "German Migration: Development, Assimilation and Labor Market Effects," in K. F. Zimmermann (ed.): *European Migration: What Do We Know?*, forthcoming 2004. Oxford: Oxford University Press.

Bauer, Thomas K. and Klaus F. Zimmermann. 1997a. "Unemployment and Wages of Ethnic Germans," *Quarterly Review of Economics and Statistics* 37, 361-377.

Bauer, Thomas K. and Klaus F. Zimmermann. 1997b. "Integrating the East: The Labor Market Effects of Immigration," in Stanley W. Black (ed.): *Europe's Economy Looks East – Implications for Germany and the European Union.* Cambridge: Cambridge University Press, 269-306.

Bauer, Thomas K. and Klaus F. Zimmermann. 1999. "Assessment of Possible Migration Pressure and its Labour Market Impact Following EU Enlargement to Central and Eastern Europe," *IZA Research Report* No. 3. Bonn: IZA.

Christensen, Lone B., Niels-Erik Hansen, Gunnar Homann, Ellen Brinch Jørgensen, Kim U. Kjær, Morten Kjærum, Ida Elisabeth Koch, Nina Lassen, Jens Vedsted-Hansen, and Lene Wendland. 2000. *Udlændingeret*, 2nd ed. Copenhagen: Jurist- og Økonomforbundets Forlag.
Danish Immigration Service. 2003. *Statistical Overview 2002*. Copenhagen.
Danish Immigration Service. 2004. *Applications for family reunification, Figures on family reunification*. Copenhagen. http://www.udlst.dk/english/Statistics/Default.htm.
Danish Ministry of Foreign Affairs. 2003. *Denmark and the EU*. Copenhagen. http://www.um.dk/english/fp/dkandeu.asp.
Danish Ministry of the Interior. 1994. *Statistik om udlændinge 1994*. Copenhagen.
Danish Ministry of the Interior. 2000. *Udlændinge 2000*. Copenhagen.
Danish Ministry of Justice. 1999. *Cirkulære om dansk indfødsret ved naturalisation* No. 90 of June 16, 1999. Copenhagen.
Danish Ministry of Refugee, Immigration and Integration Affairs. 2002a. *Årbog om udlændinge i Danmark 2002*. Copenhagen.
Danish Ministry of Refugee, Immigration and Integration Affairs. 2002b. *Cirkulæreskrivelse om nye retningslinier for optagelse på lovforslag om indfødsrets meddelelse* No. 55 of June 12, 2002. Copenhagen.
Dansk Flygtningehjælp. 1997. *Flygtninge i tal*. Copenhagen.
Dustmann, Christian. 1996. "The Social Assimilation of Immigrants," *Journal of Population Economics* 9, 37-54.
von Eyben, Bo, Jørgen Nørgaard, and W.E. von Eyben. 1996. *Karnovs lovsamling* 14th ed., Vol. 5. Copenhagen: Karnovs Forlag, 7428.
Federal Statistical Office Germany. Various years. *Statistical Yearbook*, several volumes. Wiesbaden.
Frey, M. 1986. "Direkte und indirekte Rückkehrförderung seitens der Aufnahmeländer – Überblick," in H. Körner and U. Mehrländer (eds.): *Die neue Ausländerpolitik in Europa*. Bonn: Verlag Neue Gesellschaft.
Kjær, Kim U. 1995. "Historik: Oversigt over udviklingen i den danske asylprocedure," in Lone B. Christensen et al. (2000), 237-241.
Kjær, Kim U. 2000. "Afvisning af asylansøgere, Dublin-proceduren, Åbenbart grundløs-proceduren," in Lone B. Christensen et al. (2000), 97-133, 135-190, 429-469.
Larsen, Claus and Poul Chr. Matthiessen. 2002. "Indvandrerbefolkningens sammensætning og udvikling i Danmark," in G. Viby Mogensen, and Poul Chr. Matthiessen (eds.): *Indvandrerne og arbejdsmarkedet*. Copenhagen: Spektrum, 25-79.
Lassen, Nina. 2000. "Flygtningekonventionen og udlændingelovens flygtningebegreber," in Lone B. Christensen et al. (2000), 309-404.
Matthiessen, Poul Chr. 2000. "Indvandringen til Danmark i det 20. århundrede," *Nationaløkonomisk Tidsskrift* 138 (2000), 79-94.
Matthiessen, Poul Chr. 2002. *Befolkning og samfund*, 7th ed. Copenhagen: Handelshøjskolens Forlag.

Münch, U. (1993). *Asylpolitik in der Bundesrepublik Deutschland. Entwicklungen und Alternativen*, 2. Auflage. Opladen: Leske & Budrich.

Münz, R. and R. Ulrich. 1996. "Internationale Wanderungen von und nach Deutschland, 1945-1994, Demographische, politische und gesellschaftliche Aspekte räumlicher Mobilität," *Allgemeines Statistisches Archiv* 80(1), 5-35.

Münz, R., W. Seifert, and R. Ulrich. 1999. *Zuwanderung nach Deutschland. Strukturen, Wirkungen, Perspektiven*, 2., aktualisierte und erweiterte Auflage. Frankfurt/New York: Campus Verlag.

OECD. 2003. *Economic Survey of Denmark* May. Paris.

Schmidt, Christoph M. 1997. "Immigrant Performance in Germany: Labor Earnings of Ethnic German Migrants and Foreign Guest-Workers," *Quarterly Review of Economics and Statistics* 37, 379-397.

Schmidt, Christoph M. and Klaus F. Zimmermann. 1992. "Migration Pressure in Germany: Past and Future," in Klaus F. Zimmermann (ed.): *Migration and Development*. Berlin: Springer-Verlag, 207-236.

Statistics Denmark. Various years. *Befolkningens bevægelser*, several volumes. Copenhagen.

Statistics Denmark. Various years. *Nyt fra Danmarks Statistik* 83/1989, 46/1990, 58/2002 51/2003, 213/2003. Copenhagen.

Statistics Denmark. Various years. *Statistiske Efterretninger (Befokning og valg)* 1992:11, 1994:10, 1997:16, 1998:11, 2000:4, 2001:4, 2002:5, 2002:7. Copenhagen.

Statistics Denmark. 1998. *Statistisk tiårsoversigt 1998*. Copenhagen.

Statistics Denmark. 1999. *Statistisk tiårsoversigt 1999*. Copenhagen.

Statistics Denmark. 2001. *Befolkningens bevægelser 2000*. Copenhagen.

Think Tank on Integration in Denmark. 2002. *Befolkningsudviklingen 2001-2021 – mulige udviklingsforløb*. Copenhagen.

Unabhängige Kommission Zuwanderung. 2001. *Bericht der Unabhängigen Kommission Zuwanderung*. Berlin.

UNHCR. 2000. *Refugees and Others of Concern to UNHCR. 1999 Statistical Overview*. Geneva: United Nations High Commissioner for Refugees.

Vedsted-Hansen, Jens. 1997. *Opholdsret og forsørgelse*. Copenhagen: Jurist- og Økonomforbundets Forlag.

Vedsted-Hansen, Jens. 2000. "Grundbegreber og hovedsondringer i udlændingeretten, Bortfald og inddragelse af opholdstilladelser," in Lone B. Christensen et al. (2000), 3-10, 513-530, 577-603.

Velling, Johannes. 1995. *Immigration und Arbeitsmarkt. Eine empirische Analyse für die Bundesrepublik Deutschland*. Baden-Baden: Nomos-Verlagsgesellschaft.

Zimmermann, Klaus F. 1994. "The Labour Market Impact of Immigration," in S. Spencer (ed.): *Immigration as an Economic Asset: The German Experience*. Stoke-on-Trent: Trentham Books.

Zimmermann, Klaus F. 1995. "Tackling the European Migration Problem," *Journal of Economic Perspectives* 9 (2), 45-62.

Appendix Figure 2.1. Rules for defining a person as either an immigrant, a descendant of immigrants or a Dane (the group "Other") in the population register of Statistics Denmark.

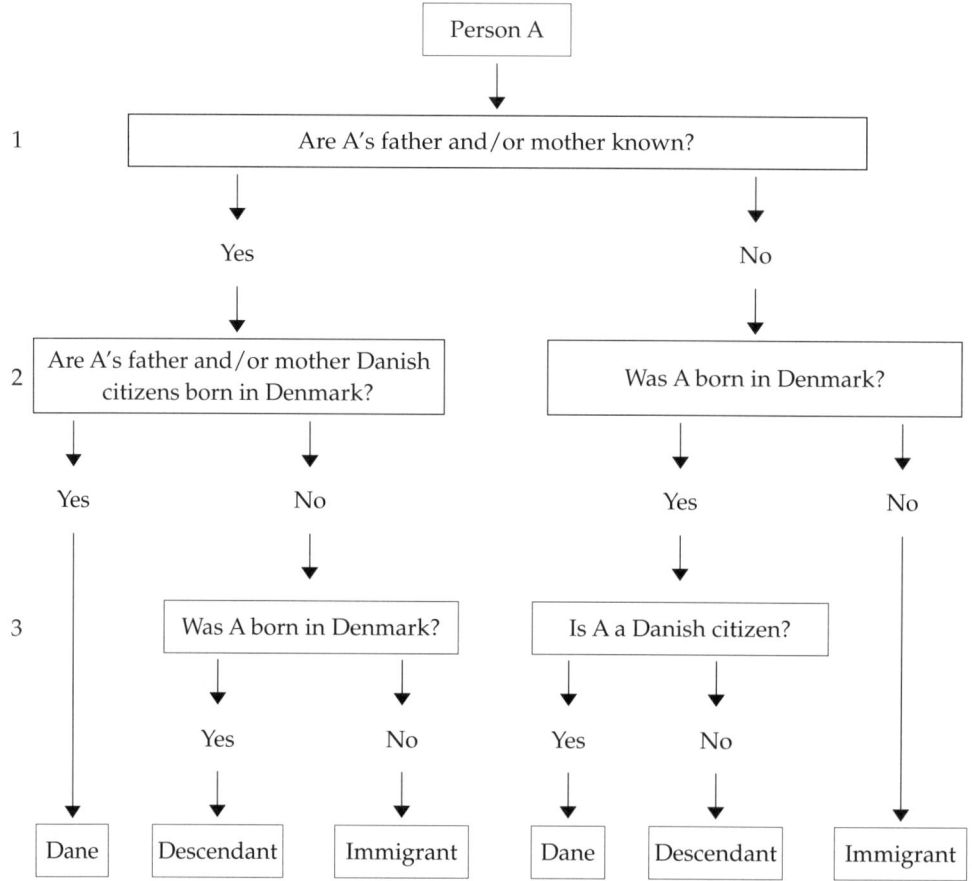

Immigrant	A person born abroad whose parents are both (or one of them if there is no available information on the other parent) either foreign citizens or born abroad. If there is no available information on either of the parents and the person was born abroad, the person is also defined as an immigrant.
Descendant	A descendant is defined as a person born in Denmark whose parents are both (or one of them if there is no available information on the other parent) either foreign citizens or born abroad. If there is no available information on either of the parents and the person in question is a foreign citizen, the person is also defined as a descendant.

Sources: Statistics Denmark (2001) and the Think Tank on Integration in Denmark (2002).

Appendix Table 2.1. Residence permits in Germany.

Name	Description
Aufenthaltserlaubnis-EG (residence permit for EU/EEA citizens and their family members)	EU/EEA citizens and their family members enjoy the right of free movement and residence within the EU/EEA area. Receiving a residence permit is a formality and is not regulated by the Aliens Act. Only if the person concerned proves unable to support himself or herself over an extended period of time will the residence permit be withdrawn. A work permit is not required for holders of an *Aufenthaltserlaubnis-EG*.
Aufenthaltsbewilligung (residence permit for specific purposes)	Entitles a foreigner to stay in Germany for a specific purpose (e.g. students, holders of work contracts). The holder of the permit must leave the country when the purpose of the stay has been achieved. A work permit is required.
Aufenthaltserlaubnis, befristet (limited residence permit)	This permit may be prolonged and is the basis for permanent residence, which can be obtained through obtaining first an *unbefristete Aufenthaltserlaubnis* and next an *Aufenthaltsberechtigung*. A work permit is required.
Aufenthaltserlaubnis, unbefristet (unlimited residence permit)	The first step towards permanent residence status. Holders of a *befristete Aufenthaltserlaubnis* can apply for this residence permit after five years provided they satisfy certain other criteria. No work permit is required.
Aufenthaltsberechtigung (right of unlimited residence)	The best and most secure residence status under the Aliens Act. Holders of a *befristete Aufenthaltserlaubnis* or an *unbefristete Aufenthaltserlaubnis* can apply for an *Aufenthaltsberechtigung* after eight years provided they satisfy certain other criteria. No work permit is required.
Aufenthaltsbefugnis (residence permit for exceptional purposes)	Has existed since 1991. Usually granted on humanitarian grounds and in practice mostly to civil war refugees on application. It can only be renewed if the humanitarian grounds for its issue still obtain, though holders may apply for an *unbefristete Aufenthaltserlaubnis* after eight years. There may be restrictions on the place of residence. A work permit is required.
Types of residence status that are not considered to be residence permits	
Duldung (temporary suspension of deportation)	The government abstains from deporting the person concerned. It may be granted on application when a foreigner is legally obliged to leave the country but there are legal or factual reasons against deportation. There are restrictions on where holders of a *Duldung* may live. A work permit is required.
Aufenthaltsgestattung (a permission to reside)	Status accorded to an asylum seeker whose application is being processed. There are restrictions on where holders of an *Aufenthaltsgestattung* may live. A work permit is required.

Appendix Table 2.2. Work permits in Germany

Name	Description
Arbeitsgenehmigungen	Foreigners are in general required to have a work permit to have employment in Germany. There are exemptions: 1) Citizens from EU/EEA countries; 2) Foreigners with an unlimited residence permit (*unbefristete Aufenthaltserlaubnis* or *Aufenthaltsberechtigung*); and 3) Foreigners from other countries when there is a bilateral agreement or other legislative basis. The work permit will have the form of an *Arbeitserlaubnis* if there is no legal claim for an *Arbeitsberechtigung*.
Arbeitserlaubnis	This permit can be granted when: 1) There are no "negative effects" for the labor market or the regional structure of employment related to granting the permit as assessed by the German Labour Office; 2) When Germans and foreigners with the same legal position are not available; and 3) The work conditions are not inferior to conditions for Germans in similar jobs. This work permit can be given with a time limit and for specific job types.
Arbeitsberechtigung	This permit can be granted when: 1) The foreigner has a *befristete Aufenthaltserlaubnis* or an *Aufenthaltsbefugnis* and (i) has had 5 years of social security contribution history in relation to work or (ii) has lived in the country for a continuous 6-year period; and 2) The work conditions are not inferior to those of Germans in similar jobs.

Appendix Table 2.3. Immigrant groups in Germany

1. Workers and students

Guest workers	Arrived from the traditional guest worker countries outside the present EU/EEA area before the recruitment stop in 1973. Currently this group of immigrants usually have a *befristete Aufenthaltserlaubnis*, an *unbefristete Aufenthaltserlaubnis*, or an *Aufenthaltsberechtigung*. A work permit may or may not be required depending on type of residence permit.
Experts and specialists	Today the only labor immigration allowed in Germany. Only persons with special qualifications (e.g. "Green Card") or jobs, such as scientists, people in leading/executive positions, artists, and staff to care for the sick and the elderly. They usually receive a *befristete Aufenthaltserlaubnis* and a work permit is required.

Students and trainees	Stay in Germany is for a specific purpose and they must leave the country when the purpose of the stay has been achieved. An *Aufenthaltsbewilligung* is granted on the basis of studies or employment which have been arranged before the person arrives in Germany. There are special bilateral agreements based on quotas between Germany and a number of Eastern European countries about *Gastarbeitnehmer*. A work permit is required for trainees.
Temporary immigrants and commuters	*Werkvertragsarbeitnehmer* are granted an *Aufenthaltsbewilligung*. *Saisonarbeitnehmer* (seasonal workers) do not need a residence permit, as they are not allowed to work in Germany for more than three months per year. Both temporary immigrants and commuters are subject to special bilateral agreements between Germany and a number of Eastern European countries. The system is based on quotas. A work permit is required.

2. Family members

Family reunification (incl. marriage migration)	Foreigners living in Germany may have the right to bring family members to Germany. Family members obtain a *befristete Aufenthaltserlaubnis* or an *Aufenthaltsbefugnis*, depending on the residence status of the person already living in Germany. A work permit is required.
Foreign children	Foreign children are granted an *unbefristete Aufenthaltserlaubnis* provided that they satisfy certain criteria concerning, among other things, length of stay. A work permit is required if they do not have an unlimited residence permit.
Young foreigners who have lived in Germany as minors	Young foreigners who have lived legally in Germany as minors are granted a *befristete Aufenthaltserlaubnis* provided that they satisfy certain criteria. A work permit is required.
Descendants born in Germany	Descendants born in Germany are guaranteed the right to stay in the country and have a legal claim for German citizenship if they apply for it provided that they satisfy certain criteria concerning, among other things, length of stay. They obtain an *unbefristete Aufenthaltserlaubnis*. A work permit is not required.

3. Asylum seekers and refugees

Asylberechtigte (persons entitled to asylum)	Recognized victims of *political persecution* under article 16a of the Basic Law receive an *unbefristete Aufenthaltserlaubnis*. They need to prove that they are victims of persecution *directed specifically at their persons by organs of the state* in the entire territory of their country of origin. People who have entered or wish to enter the country from a "safe third country" cannot rely on article 16a of the Basic Law. Persons entitled to asylum have the right to bring their family members to Germany. A work permit is not required.

Konventionsflüchtlinge (convention refugees)	According to the Geneva Convention on the Legal Status of Refugees of July 28, 1951, convention refugees are defined as persons who, because of their membership of a particular political or social group, religion, race, or nationality, cannot or will not return to their own country for fear of serious persecution. Convention refugees receive an *Aufenthaltsbefugnis*. Convention refugees have the right to bring their family members to Germany under certain conditions. A work permit is required.
Kontingentflüchtlinge (quota refugees)	Quota refugees are accepted in the course of humanitarian aid campaigns. They are granted a permanent right to stay in Germany without first having to apply for asylum. They receive an *unbefristete Aufenthaltserlaubnis*. A work permit is not required.
Kriegs- und Bürgerkriegsflüchtlinge (refugees from war or civil war)	Refugees from war or civil war have the possibility for provisional acceptance without separate evaluation of each case under § 32a (effective since July 1, 1993) of the Aliens Act. The war refugee status is conditional upon no application for asylum having been made or refused, and such refugees cannot demand to live in a specific place or state in Germany. These persons are granted an *Aufenthaltsbefugnis*. Note that many of the refugees from the republics of the former Yugoslavia (especially from Bosnia and Herzegovina) are not subject to § 32a but are staying in the country because their deportation has been temporarily suspended (*Duldung*). A work permit is required.
De facto Flüchtlinge (de facto refugees)	The largest refugee group in Germany, comprising those who have not applied for asylum or whose application has been refused. Their deportation is deferred because they face serious, real danger to their lives or freedom in their home countries, or because urgent humanitarian or personal grounds dictate that they should be allowed to remain in Germany for the time being (*Duldung*). A work permit is required.
Asylum seekers	Permission to reside (*Aufenthaltsgestattung*) is the status accorded to an asylum seeker whose application is being processed. A work permit is required.

Appendix Table 2.4. Bilateral agreements between Germany and CEEC countries concerning temporary immigration.

Categories	Countries	Conditions	Quotas	Length of stay
Workers employed under a contract for services (*Werkvertragsarbeitnehmer*)	Bosnia-Herzegovina, Bulgaria, Croatia, Czech Republic, Hungary, Latvia, Lithuania, Poland, Republic of Macedonia, Romania, Russian Federation, Slovakia, Slovenia, Turkey, Former Yugoslavia	• Restrictions on activity • No possibility of family reunification • No possibility of changing status • Seconded by employer in the country of origin • Work permit (except for workers carrying out maintenance, repair or installation of machines furnished by a foreign company if they stay less than 3 months)	• By economic sector and by country • Adjusted annually according to the labor market situation in Germany	• 2 years • 3 years in exceptional cases
Guest workers (*Gastarbeitnehmer*)	Albania, Bulgaria, Czech Republic, Estonia, Hungary, Latvia, Lithuania, Poland, Romania, Russian Federation, Slovakia, Switzerland	• Restrictions on activity • No possibility of family reunification • No possibility of changing status • Age limit: 18 – 40 years	• By country	• 12-18 months
Seasonal workers	Bulgaria, Croatia, Czech Republic, Hungary, Poland, Romania, Slovakia, Slovenia	• Restrictions on activity • No possibility of family reunification • No possibility of changing status • Availability of other resident workers is ground for refusal • Request must be made by German employer • Minimum Age: 18 years	• None. Verification necessary of whether similarly qualified unemployed natives are available	• 3 months

Source: Bauer and Zimmermann (1999).

CHAPTER 3

The Educational Background and Human Capital Attainment of Immigrants*

By Amelie Constant and Claus Larsen

3.1 Introduction

It has been well documented by many studies that in economics human capital is of paramount importance. Most research on immigrants has focused on the labor market outcomes of immigrants in the host country. Previous research has established a strong positive link between human capital investment and earnings or occupations. Surprisingly, little research has been devoted to the analysis of post-migration human capital investment *per se*. In this chapter we focus on post-migration human capital investment by immigrants and their descendants. Proficiency in the language of the receiving country is also included under this heading. Human capital formation is a vital element in individual advancement, in improving living standards, in economic growth and development, and in reducing inequality. Such a study can significantly contribute to the understanding of the process of integration and can explain the often puzzling non-assimilation results for immigrant earnings. In this chapter we research immigrants' educational attainment in the host country as well as the factors determining their levels of educational attainment.

In Section 3.2 we describe the educational systems in Germany and Denmark and evaluate how they have affected and influenced the post-migration human capital formation of immigrants. We also look at the educational backgrounds and current trends in immigrants' educational attainment at different levels of education, and compare these with trends in the total population. We present differences in pre- and post-migration human capital by sex and ethnicity, comparing similar ethnic groups in the two countries under study. In Section 3.3 we investigate the determinants of human capital accumulation in the host country. We aim at evaluating the impingement that several economic, social, personal, family, and envi-

---

* We wish to thank Thomas Bauer and Holger Bonin for stimulating discussions on an earlier draft of this chapter. Constant would also like to acknowledge Pascal Arnds' able student assistance.

ronmental factors have on the probabilities of attaining different educational levels in the host country, exploiting the unique features of our Danish-German surveys (RFMS-D and RFMS-G) conducted for this project. Vocational training is common in both countries, and we study the determinants of finishing vocational training separately. In the last section we summarize and draw our conclusions, comparing the human capital accomplishments of the same immigrant groups in Denmark and Germany.

3.2 The Educational Level of Foreigners – A Descriptive Analysis

The aim of this section is to describe the educational background of foreigners – in terms of education obtained in both the home and the receiving countries – and to compare it with that of the total population. Starting with an overview of the educational systems in Denmark and Germany, we proceed with a descriptive analysis of the pre- and post-migration human capital of immigrants, including proficiency in the language of the receiving country.

For comparative purposes the study presented in this chapter is centered on our interview surveys and, therefore, the main sources of information about education and language proficiency are the immigrants themselves. The reason for this is that only in Denmark is it possible to combine administrative registers from the national statistical office with interview data.

3.2.1 The Schooling Systems and School-to-Work Transition in Denmark and Germany

This subsection provides a description of the schooling systems in Denmark and Germany, setting up the institutional frameworks within which comparisons are made. It also shows how the transition from school to the world of work takes place.

The descriptions of the main features of the schooling system and school-to-work transition in Denmark are taken from a text in English published by The Danish Centre for Assessment of Foreign Qualifications (CVUU, 2003), a center within the Danish Ministry of Education. Descriptions in English of the German system are provided by Riphahn (2001, 2002). Other sources of information used in this chapter are the Bundesanstalt für Arbeit (2003) and Statistics Germany (2002, 2003).

3.2.1.1 Denmark

In Denmark, according to law all children between the age of 7 and 16 must receive education – either in the publicly provided municipal school system, in a private school, or at home. Education in the Danish *Folkeskole* is free. It combines *primary* and *lower secondary school* and comprises 9 years of compulsory schooling and an optional 10th year. Teaching takes place in classes and the students remain together for the entire period of compulsory school. Differentiation, i.e. ability grouping in certain subjects, takes place within the framework of the class. Lower secondary education may also be completed in continuation schools (*efterskoler*), which are boarding schools offering education at the 8th to 10th class levels.

General upper secondary school is academically oriented and qualifies students for higher education. The 3-year *gymnasium* is attended by students who come directly from lower secondary school, while the 2-year *higher preparatory examination* called *hf* is directed mainly at young people and adults who wish to return to the education system. Both schools qualify students for higher education. *Technical and commercial upper secondary school programs* called *htx* and *hhx* are offered at technical and business colleges respectively and qualify students for employment in trade and industry, usually in training positions, as well as for higher education. Like the gymnasium, the htx and the hhx are 3-year programs attended by students who come directly from lower secondary school. One- and two-year hhx programs are directed at students who have already completed other upper secondary level education or training. For those going directly from lower secondary school to either the gymnasium or hhx/htx, the final school examination (*Folkeskolens afgangsprøve*) is required in certain subjects and at certain levels and also, in some cases, a recommendation from the previous school.

Vocational education and training programs (VET) at technical and business schools or colleges qualify students to enter the labor market as skilled blue- or white-collar workers. In many cases VET also allow students to directly access certain professional higher education levels. These programs have taken various forms over the years and are made up of periods of practical training, most often on-the-job (apprenticeship), alternating and complementing training with courses at school or college. The first years may be school-based, and if no work placement can be found, on-the-job training can be replaced by college-based practical training. Typically, to receive a certificate of completed apprenticeship, a training of 3½ to 4 years is required. Social and health care colleges offer *basic social and health education (SOSU)* of 1 to 2½ years' duration, and a number of *other programs*, mainly within the primary sector, lead to the qualifications of, for example, skilled farmer and able seaman.

The *higher education* system in Denmark consists of the university sector, offering research-based teaching, and a wide range of other institutions offering professionally-oriented programs. Generally, admission to higher education requires 12 years of prior schooling or training, i.e. upper secondary school or VET, and there may be specific requirements as to the combination and/or level of subjects taken, grades obtained, and work experience. Access to a number of study programs is restricted.

The *university sector* comprises multifaculty universities as well as institutions specialized in fields such as engineering, education, and business studies, and specialist university-level institutions in architecture, music, etc. A Bachelor's degree (first level) requires the successful completion of 3 to 3½ years of study, and a Master's degree (second level) usually 5 years of study, while the Ph.D. degree (third level) normally requires 8 years of higher education and research.[1] *Short-cycle professional higher education programs* normally take 2 (up to 3) years and "qualify the student for performing practical, vocational tasks on an analytical basis". Examples are laboratory technicians and policemen. *Medium-cycle programs* require 3 to 4 years of study and "provide students with theoretical knowledge as well as knowledge of its application to professions and industries". Examples are schoolteachers, nurses, and certain bachelors of Science in engineering. A number of Civil Service educations and also education within the armed forces, financing and insurance and shipping are internal and organized by the service or sector itself.

3.2.1.2 Germany

In Germany, schooling policy is the responsibility of the individual states (Bundesländer). In general, schooling is mandatory from the age of 6 to 14, and it is free in public state-run schools. Initially, all children enter the same program of primary schooling (*Grundschule*).[2] In contrast to Denmark, the German school system is divided into different tracks. As early as 4th grade, or around the age of 10, students must begin to follow one of the following four types of schools. The track that they enter is based on their grades and performance, and determines which type of school they can next enter, and finally, whether they will go to a university or enter a technical field or trade. *Hauptschule* (general secondary school) is the basic level or lowest track of education and a preparation for blue-collar occupations. Individuals leave after 5 or 6 years of secondary school. *Realschule* (intermediate school) provides middle level education and prepares students for mid-level white-collar jobs. It offers 6 years of secondary schooling and, based on grades, it is possible to transfer to the highest track, the *Gymnasium*, which prepares students (and is a precondition) to enter a university. Gymnasium provides a total of 9 years of secondary schooling and leads to the *Abitur*. *Gesamtschule* (comprehensive school) offers all three tracks, but normally the different tracks are offered at different schools. *Abschluss der polytechnischen Oberschule* refers to the final examination of the 10-year comprehensive school of the former German Democratic Republic (GDR) and is

---

1 The traditional Danish doctoral degree requires a minimum of 5-8 years of individual and original research and public defense of a dissertation.
2 In the state of Bavaria, this is called *Volksschule*. There is also the *Sonderschule* (special school) that was originally designed for students with special needs but has become more popular among students with general difficulties.

here grouped together with *Realschule*. Differences exist between the German states as to the organization of the educational system and names of education, training, and courses.[3] It is possible for schools to depart from the general rule of (early) differentiation, but the final examinations are the same. Nine or ten years of full-time school attendance and a further 2 or 3 years of part-time education in the form of labor market introductory courses are compulsory in Germany.

Transition from school to working life depends on the track chosen, but as compulsory school attendance extends beyond the 9 or 10 years of primary and lower secondary school, those who leave school with a Hauptschulabschluss (*Berufsreife*) or a Realschulabschluss (*mittlere Reife*) must participate in some sort of vocational training scheme afterwards. Those who go to the Gymnasium and leave school with *Abitur* (*allgemeine Hochschulreife*) have, by then, met the requirements with respect to compulsory school attendance.

Like in Denmark, the most common form of *vocational education and training* is an apprenticeship. There are two subcategories: the dual system, and the stand-alone vocational schools that offer complete vocational training. This system provides the missing link between the general educational system and the labor market. In Germany, apprenticeships last 2 to 4 years in a combination of practical on-the-job training (at privately- or state-owned businesses) and formal education at vocational schools (*Berufsschule*, financed and operated by the state). Another similarity between the two countries is that vocational schools offer training programs to those not able to find an apprenticeship. The training schemes mentioned above also comprise *Berufsvorbereitungsjahr*, which is a 1-year "vocational preparation" for those not qualified for an apprenticeship. This scheme overlaps with basic school as the students can complete *Hauptschule* at the same time. *Berufsgrundbildungsjahr* is also a 1-year scheme, but builds on completed basic school and teaches students elementary, occupation-specific vocational skills, which will allow them to finish an apprenticeship in a shorter time than usual. *Berufsfachschule* is directed at individuals who have completed compulsory full-time school, but have no prior vocational training, and offers both 1-year vocational preparation courses and actual vocational training. After 2 years of full-time studies, participants can take an examination – *Fachschulreife* – which is at the same level as *Realschulabschluss*. Persons with (some) prior vocational training may achieve *Fachschulreife* at *Berufsaufbauschule*.

Fachgymnasium is vocationally orientated and can be compared with the Danish hhx/htx. It is a 3-year program, and *fachgebundene Hochschulreife* qualifies students for university and other higher education in the same way as Gymnasium. Admission requires *Realschulabschluss*. Other ways to qualify for higher education are through

---

3 The names of the schools also differ from one state to the other. We find the *Mittelschule* in Saxony, the *erweiterte Realschule* in Saarland, the *integrierte Haupt- und Realschule* in Hamburg, and *regionale Schule* in Rhineland-Palatinate, to name a few.

Fachoberschule, which leads to *Fachhochschulreife*, or through *Berufs- und Technische Oberschule*, which leads to *fachgebundene Hochschulreife* and, if an additional exam is passed, *allgemeine Hochschulreife (Abitur)*. *Realschulabschluss* is required to enter these last-mentioned programs, which may be completed in shorter time than *Fachgymnasium* due to the students' prior vocational training and working experience. Students who finish *Realschule* with the special *Fachabitur* diploma can proceed to university education.

Higher education takes place at universities and university-like institutions (*Hochschulen*) and at the more practically-orientated *Fachhochschulen*. *Gesamthochschulen* comprise both kinds. University-like institutions may be found within the fields of pedagogy, theology, and art. *Fachhochschulen* offer a wide range of study programs within, for example, engineering, the social sector, design, and informatics. *Verwaltungshochschulen* are institutions within the public sector offering education in public administration to public employees. Education and training in the health sector – nurse, midwife, etc. – takes place at special *Schulen des Gesundheitswesens*. Study programs at institutions outside the university sector are normally of shorter duration than programs within the university sector. Recently, Bachelor's and Master's degrees were introduced at the universities, replacing the former *Diplom(U)*- or *Staatsprüfungen* and making degrees more directly comparable with those of other countries. Studies at other institutions lead to, for example, *Fachhochschulabschluss*.

3.2.1.3 Differences and Similarities between Denmark and Germany

There are thus many similarities between the two educational systems with regard to structure, years of education, and length of various programs. Major differences are the early differentiation of the German school system, as opposed to the comprehensive principle applied in Denmark, and the extension in Germany of compulsory education beyond primary and lower secondary school to include an introduction into vocational training for those individuals who do not follow the Gymnasium track.

The above only outlines the basic features of the two publicly administered systems, which set the standards any institution in the field must live up to. In both countries, teaching at primary and secondary level can be obtained through other arrangements than these. It is possible, for example, for adults to complement previous schooling by following evening classes, and children may be taught in private schools. While in Denmark children can be home-schooled by their parents, this is not allowed in Germany. In Denmark, private schools, including *free schools* based on different religious or ideological convictions, educational priciples, etc., are attended by more than 10 percent of all compulsory-school-age pupils. Teaching of children under private management is, however, subsidized and controlled by the state, which covers approximately 85 percent of the operating costs of private schools. While the organization of the teaching is less restrictive, private education must measure up to that of the municipal schools. A number of possibilities exist for adults to supplement their vocational or professional qualifications through short courses or longer training programs. In Germany, private schools for general education are in the form of *Ersatzschulen*. These schools receive financial assistance from the federal states, so they can keep their fees low enough to be accessible to everybody. Some schools (especially Catholic schools) do not charge schooling fees at all, since they receive compensatory payments from the church or a supporting association. In 2001, there were about 2,400 of these private schools, or less than 5 percent of the total.

Finally, and especially relevant in the context of this book, immigrant children who have the host country language as their second language may be offered *extra language teaching* (including mother-tongue teaching) from pre-school age onward.[4] A whole range of host country language courses, some of which are compulsory, are offered to adult immigrants as well.

3.2.2 Measurement Issues

No general statistics exist for immigrants' and descendants' proficiency in the language of the receiving countries. For the purposes of analysis, this information – and a number of other facts of relevance to the analysis of integration – must be obtained by questionnaire surveys or similar techniques.

Information about both Danish *and* foreign schooling, education, and training can be obtained from the records of Statistics Denmark. This is the result of a large-scale questionnaire survey carried out in 1999 among immigrants without completed Danish vocational training, university, or other education qualifying them to enter the labor market in specific occupations. The response rate was 50 percent and seems, not surprisingly, to have been highest among the better qualified immigrants. Consequently, information about education for the other 50 percent was based on imputations. The register is being continuously updated and new immigrants to Denmark are asked about completed training and education, which is then reported to Statistics Denmark, reducing the proportion of returns based on imputations. In the short run, however, the official statistics seem to overestimate the educational level of immigrants to a certain extent. Comprehensive documentation (in Danish) of the survey can be found in Mørkeberg (2000).

Unfortunately, the possibility of combining register with interview data does not exist in the case of Germany, and comparisons between the two countries will be based entirely on interviews (RFMS-D and RFMS-G). Register data will only be used to describe the educational level of the total population.

---

[4] A negligible number of "foreign schools" exist in both countries. In Germany, these cater to foreign children who are staying in the host country temporarily. These schools follow the home country's educational system and teach in the home country's language. For example, Greek schools in Germany offer a "Greek Abitur". In Denmark, such schools are almost entirely restricted to schools for the German minority living permanently in the south of the country.

It is known that self-reporting and non-response are sources of uncertainty in telephone and face-to-face interviews as well as in questionnaire surveys. These issues can potentially lead to a certain overestimation. However, both surveys employed here were conducted by experienced and highly professional agencies that minimize the margin of error. With regard to the questions about command of the language of the host country, a check was possible by asking the interviewers to assess the respondents' language skills by trying to carry out as much of the interview as possible in Danish/German.[5] In our analyses, we use the interviewer's assessment of the language fluency of the respondent, thus avoiding the self-reported measurement error inherent in similar studies.

The German sample for this comparative study was drawn from among foreign nationals, while the Danish sample was drawn from among "immigrants and descendants" according to definitions now predominant in official Danish statistics and based primarily on the nationality and place of birth of the parents rather than of the person in question (see Chapter 2). This has resulted in a large number of Danish citizens being included, while the only German citizens are those who have become naturalized after the sample was drawn. In this chapter, all Danish/German citizens are put together in one group irrespective of national origin. Forty-six percent of the respondents in the Danish sample are Danish citizens, while German citizens make up about 6 percent of the German sample.

3.2.3 The Human Capital of Foreigners in Denmark and Germany

Human capital obtained in the home country and human capital obtained in the receiving country will be discussed separately. In many cases, however, it makes sense to construct a combined measure of education, which includes both, in order to get the total picture of a person's qualifications. Such combined measures have been constructed earlier for immigrants in the Danish surveys (see Larsen, 2002). In Denmark, the CVUU referred to above, and in Germany, the *Zentralstelle für ausländisches Bildungswesen* (Central Office for Foreign Education) are commissioned to assess the level of foreign qualifications and their usefulness in the context of the receiving country.

In the analysis below, German educational statistics are the point of departure for defining "vocational" training (including programs which in Denmark are referred to as short-cycle professional higher education, as well as most of those termed medium-cycle) and "university" education. In Denmark, engineers may graduate from medium-cycle as well as from university-like institutions, but in this analysis they are all placed in the university group. Certain lower secondary level schoolteachers are placed in the university group in the German sample but in the vocational group in the Danish sample.

---

5 For a full description of these surveys see the Appendix Chapter "Data Description".

3.2.3.1 Education Obtained in the Home Country

Only immigrants aged 13 and over at the time of immigration were asked about completed foreign education and training. Statistics in this subsection refer to this group. Immigrants who arrived at a younger age were asked if they had attended school before immigration, and for how many years. That group is studied together with descendants under the heading "second generation immigrants" in the subsection about education and training obtained in the host country.

In the German survey, immigrants were asked about both (a) primary and secondary schooling and (b) vocational training and university education, while no detailed questions about schooling were asked in the Danish survey if the respondent had completed education or training qualifying for the skilled labor market. Therefore, if it is not only the highest level of education or training that is of interest, schooling must be assigned according to some specified rule to those in the Danish survey who have also completed vocational training or university. Persons with education at university level, for example, are assumed to have completed upper secondary school. Persons with vocational training are assumed to have completed upper secondary school, if access to similar training or education in Denmark would normally require that, and lower secondary school otherwise.

In the following subsections, emphasis is placed on the five countries of origin that are included in both the Danish and the German surveys, namely: Turkey, former Yugoslavia, Poland, Iran, and Lebanon.

(a) Primary and Secondary Schooling

Table 3.1 shows three levels of schooling completed before immigration by ethnicity and gender, along with age at entrance: (1) no primary or secondary schooling completed, (2) primary or lower secondary schooling completed, and (3) upper secondary schooling completed. The most striking finding in this table is the large difference between Denmark and Germany in the "no primary or secondary schooling completed" category.

Clearly, a higher percentage of male and female immigrants in Denmark had no schooling completed upon arrival. In both countries, the highest shares with no schooling completed are found among immigrants from Turkey and Lebanon, while the lowest shares are found among immigrants from Iran (in Germany) and Poland (in both Germany and Denmark). Among immigrants in Germany with no schooling completed, 50 percent had not attended school at all in their home country, while the corresponding figures for immigrants in Denmark are significantly lower, ranging from 2 percent among men from the former Yugoslavia to 31 percent among Iranian women.

Comparing immigrants in Denmark to immigrants in Germany, Table 3.1 shows that a larger percentage of immigrants in Germany had completed primary or upper

Table 3.1. Primary and secondary schooling completed before immigration to Denmark/Germany, first generation immigrants, year 2001/2002, percent of all.

Nationality	DK[1,2]	G	DK[1,2]	G	DK[1,2]	G	DK	G	DK	G
	No primary or secondary schooling		Primary or lower secondary		Upper secondary		Average age at entrance		No. of persons	
	------------------ Percent -------------------									
Men										
Former Yugoslavia	48	17	38	64	14	20	32	27	205	434
Iran	54	13	26	19	20	68	28	29	57	468
Lebanon	89	33	9	37	2	27	24	26	54	419
Poland	25	13	52	55	23	31	27	29	27	321
Turkey	87	33	10	54	4	13	22	25	132	465
Naturalized[3]	54	20	24	46	22	38	23	25	403	101
Women										
Former Yugoslavia	46	33	33	49	21	18	32	28	190	366
Iran	58	15	12	19	31	66	30	30	62	367
Lebanon	86	49	9	30	5	20	26	26	65	332
Poland	13	8	46	35	42	57	30	28	142	623
Turkey	91	47	7	43	1	11	22	25	133	468
Naturalized[3]	48	14	20	46	26	34	24	24	253	89

Notes: Education completed by immigrants 13 years and older on arrival. 1) No information about primary and secondary schooling in the Danish survey, if the respondent had also completed vocational training or university education. Primary or secondary schooling is, therefore, assigned in accordance with the level of vocational training or university education (see the text). 2) A weight has been constructed for the Danish survey to take into account a certain over-representation of individuals with a stronger link to the labor market among those interviewed in comparison with those who declined to participate and other non-respondents. 3) A weight has been constructed to take into account the five nationalities' actual shares of the populations.

Source: Own calculations based on the RFMS-D and RFMS-G.

secondary school before arrival. In Denmark, men and women from Lebanon and Turkey have the lowest levels of education in these categories. In Germany, it is the men and women from Iran who have the lowest percentages of education completed in primary/lower secondary school and the men and women from Turkey who have the lowest percentages of education completed in upper secondary school. While the Poles dominate the upper secondary category in Denmark, it is the Iranians who dominate this category in Germany. The naturalized in both countries fall in between in all categories of schooling before migration. On average, with the exception of the nationals of former Yugoslavia, immigrants to Denmark are slightly younger than immigrants to Germany upon arrival. Excluding people from the former Yugoslavia, the average age at entrance is about 25.5 years in Germany and 24 years in Denmark.

(b) Vocational Training and University Education Qualifying for Entering the Skilled Labor Market

The shares with completed vocational training and university education from the home country are shown in Table 3.2.

Table 3.2. Vocational training and university education completed before immigration to Denmark/Germany, first generation immigrants, year 2001/2002, percent of all.

Country of origin	DK[1,2]	G	DK[1,2]	G	DK[1,2]	G	DK	G	DK	G
	No vocational training or university education		Vocational training		University education		Average age at entrance		No. of persons	
	---------- Percent ----------									
	Men									
Former Yugoslavia	54	53	36	42	10	5	32	27	205	434
Iran	69	65	23	22	8	13	28	29	57	468
Lebanon	91	77	9	20	0	3	24	26	54	419
Poland	29	43	61	47	10	10	27	29	27	321
Turkey	93	74	5	23	2	3	22	25	132	465
Naturalized[3]	70	73	20	24	10	3	23	25	403	101
	Women									
Former Yugoslavia	62	76	30	21	8	3	32	28	190	366
Iran	70	59	20	26	10	15	30	30	62	367
Lebanon	93	87	5	10	2	3	26	26	65	332
Poland	29	41	52	44	19	15	30	28	142	623
Turkey	97	89	3	9	0	2	22	25	133	468
Naturalized[3]	72	73	21	22	7	5	24	24	253	89

Notes: Education completed by immigrants 13 years and older on arrival. 1) No information about primary and secondary schooling in the Danish survey, if the respondent had also completed vocational training or university education. Primary or secondary schooling is, therefore, assigned in accordance with the level of vocational training or university education (see the text). 2) A weight has been constructed for the Danish survey to take into account a certain over-representation of individuals with a stronger link to the labor market among those interviewed in comparison with those who declined to participate and other non-respondents. 3) A weight has been constructed to take into account the five nationalities' actual shares of the populations.

Source: Own calculations based on the RFMS-D and RFMS-G.

The picture of the shares of immigrants with training or higher education (who qualify, in principle, to enter the skilled labor market) is much more mixed, and the differences between Denmark and Germany are much smaller. Polish men have, on average, more vocational training and university education upon arrival than any other immigrant group. Polish women are at the same high levels, while women in general have completed training or higher education before arrival to a lesser extent than men, except for those who have become naturalized, and Iranian women.

However, it is not obvious from Tables 3.1 and 3.2 that there is a clear correlation between pre-immigration education and naturalization.

3.2.3.2 Education Obtained in the Receiving Country

In this subsection, as in Subsection 3.2.3.1, first generation immigrants are defined as those who were 13 years or older on arrival, while immigrants who arrived at the age of 12 or younger and persons born in the receiving country (descendants) are defined as second generation immigrants.

While the Danish and German educational systems have many similarities, one of the differences is the early differentiation which takes place in Germany at primary school level. In the following descriptive analysis this difference is illustrated by an extra column for primary school in Germany in Tables 3.3 and 3.6.

(a) First Generation Immigrants

Primary and Secondary Schooling

Table 3.3 shows that relatively few immigrants have completed schooling in the receiving country. This is to be expected, given their older age at entrance. However, with Turkish men as the only exception, markedly higher shares of immigrants with host country schooling are found in Denmark than in Germany. This indicates that immigrants in Denmark invest in post-migration schooling more than immigrants in Germany. The corresponding shares for the total population are included in the table as well, but as immigrants in this subsection have not grown up in the receiving country, their schooling is predominantly from their home countries. It also has to be kept in mind that immigrants and descendants differ from the total population with regard to age as well as gender distribution. This is even more pronounced as far as the second generation is concerned, as it is a particularly young group compared with the native or total population.

The highest shares of people with post-migration schooling are found among naturalized men in both countries, but only among naturalized women in Denmark. Women as well as men from Iran stand out in both countries for hav-

Table 3.3. Primary and secondary school completed in Denmark/Germany, first generation immigrants, year 2001/2002, percent of all.

Country of origin	DK[1]	G	G	DK[1]	G	DK[1]	G	DK	G
	No primary or secondary schooling/ not stated		Primary	Lower secondary		Upper secondary		No. of persons (total pop. in millions)	
	------------------ Percent ------------------								
Men									
Former Yugoslavia	88	95	5	9	0	3	0	205	434
Iran	74	90	2	14	1	12	7	57	468
Lebanon	80	97	2	9	0	11	1	54	419
Poland	82	94	4	11	1	7	1	27	321
Turkey	93	89	9	5	1	2	1	132	465
Naturalized[2]	69	84	14	16	1	15	1	403	101
Total population	0	8	39	78	28	22	24	1.91	27.93
Women									
Former Yugoslavia	83	96	2	12	1	5	1	190	366
Iran	88	93	1	6	2	6	4	62	367
Lebanon	91	96	2	3	1	6	1	65	332
Poland	86	95	2	8	2	6	1	142	623
Turkey	91	95	4	8	1	1	0	133	468
Naturalized[2]	71	92	2	19	5	10	1	253	89
Total population	0	8	36	73	34	27	21	1.88	27.30

Notes: Immigrants 16 years and older on arrival, 16-70 years. Total population DK: 15-69 years, G: 15-64 years. Average age at entrance and average number of years since migration, see Table 3.4. No early differentiation like that of the German school system into Hauptschule (primary), Realschule (lower secondary), and Gymnasium (upper secondary) takes place in the Danish school system. Two-three percent not stated are included under "DK: Lower secondary" as far as the total population is concerned. 1) A weight has been constructed for the Danish survey to take into account a certain over-representation of individuals with a stronger link to the labor market among those interviewed in comparison with those who declined to participate and other non-respondents. 2) A weight has been constructed to take into account the five nationalities' actual shares of the population.

Sources: Own calculations based on the RFMS-D and RFMS-G, Statistics Germany (2003: 373-374), and Statistics Denmark (2002: 107).

ing completed upper secondary school, followed in Denmark by Lebanese men and also, but at a lower level, by Polish male immigrants. Turks, both men and women, have the lowest share for finishing upper secondary school in either country. Compared to the total population, these statistics on immigrants' post-migration schooling are extremely low in both countries.

Vocational Training and University Education Qualifying Holders to Enter the Skilled Labor Market

Table 3.4 refers to the same groups and shows the shares with completed vocational training or university education in the receiving country.

Immigrants from Iran, Poland, and those naturalized stand out even more than in Table 3.3 as having higher shares of vocational training and in particular university education. More immigrants from Turkey complete training or education in Germany than in Denmark. In general, the percentage of this first generation immigrant group with university education is quite low, ranging from 0 to 13 percent for men and from 0 to 6 percent for women. Compared to the total population, this table shows that, in general, first generation immigrants lag behind.

Immigrants in Germany, and especially those from the former Yugoslavia, have generally spent a longer time in the country than immigrants in Denmark, and with the exception of those from the former Yugoslavia, they arrived at an older age, at least as far as male immigrants are concerned.

Danish/German Language Proficiency

The levels of proficiency in the language of the receiving country of immigrants who were born and raised abroad are shown in Table 3.5. This information is based on the, in all probability, more objective assessment of the interviewer and not on the self-assessed answer of the respondents. In the case of both countries, it is clear that the majority of naturalized male and female immigrants speak the host country's language well. Among men, the Iranians have the highest percentage with good language proficiency, followed by the Poles. Among women, people from the former Yugoslavia stand out in Denmark, and the Poles stand out in Germany. While the Turks have been in the host countries the longest, they score among the lowest in language proficiency.

(b) Second Generation Immigrants

This subsection pertains to the immigrants who migrated at an age younger than 13 and descendants. As was mentioned above, the samples are drawn from foreign

Table 3.4. Vocational training and university education completed in Denmark/Germany, first generation immigrants, year 2001/2002, percent of all.

Country of origin	DK[1]	G	DK[1]	G	DK[1]	G	DK	G	DK	G
	No vocational training or university education/not stated		Vocational		University		Average age at entrance		Years since migration, average	
	------------------ Percent ------------------									
Men										
Former Yugoslavia	95	92	5	7	0	1	32	27	8	17
Iran	67	77	22	11	11	12	28	29	11	15
Lebanon	95	92	5	7	0	1	24	26	11	12
Poland	81	89	6	9	13	2	27	29	13	12
Turkey	98	89	1	9	1	2	22	25	19	20
Naturalized[2]	66	83	23	14	11	3	23	28	17	21
Total population	44	28	46	58	10	14	/	/	/	/
Women										
Former Yugoslavia	95	93	5	6	0	1	32	28	7	17
Iran	85	88	15	8	0	4	30	30	8	12
Lebanon	97	93	3	7	0	0	26	26	10	12
Poland	82	89	15	9	2	2	30	28	11	11
Turkey	99	92	1	6	0	2	22	25	16	19
Naturalized[2]	70	90	24	5	6	5	24	26	18	19
Total population	49	35	45	56	5	9	/	/	/	/

Notes: Immigrants 16 years and older on arrival, 16-70 years. Total population DK: 15-69 years, G: 15-64 years. Number of persons: Total population DK is a sample consisting of 37,059 men and 36,469 women; for other groups, see Table 3.3. 1) A weight has been constructed for the Danish survey to take into account a certain over-representation of individuals with a stronger link to the labor market among those interviewed in comparison with those who declined to participate and other non-respondents. 2) A weight has been constructed to take into account the five nationalities' actual shares of the population.

Sources: Own calculations based on register data from Statistics Denmark, the RFMS-D and RFMS-G, and Statistics Germany (2003: 373-374).

nationals in Germany and from immigrants/descendants irrespective of citizenship in Denmark. In the Danish sample, as opposed to the German sample, almost everybody is a Danish citizen. A weight has been applied to the "naturalized" group to take into account the actual shares of the total population, which the respective groups make up.

Table 3.5. Proficiency in Danish/German language, first generation immigrants, year 2001/2002, percent of all.

Country of origin	DK[1]	G	DK[1]	G	DK[1]	G	DK[1]	G	DK	G
	Speaks well		Speaks with average skill		Speaks poorly		Years since migration, average		No. of students[3]	
	------------------ Percent ------------------									
Men										
Former Yugoslavia	39	55	29	29	32	15	8	17	21	5
Iran	64	65	31	19	6	16	11	15	6	15
Lebanon	50	44	35	32	15	23	11	12	2	15
Poland	52	60	31	24	17	16	13	12	2	13
Turkey	28	44	41	34	31	22	18	20	2	9
Naturalized[2]	72	71	23	27	5	2	18	21	22	1
Women										
Former Yugoslavia	49	51	22	21	28	28	7	17	38	3
Iran	32	51	40	25	28	24	7	12	15	19
Lebanon	21	21	52	28	26	51	10	12	2	2
Poland	40	66	39	22	20	12	11	11	16	32
Turkey	20	20	32	29	48	51	15	19	4	4
Naturalized[2]	62	69	31	21	7	10	18	19	17	4

Notes: Immigrants 16 years and older on arrival, 16-70 years. Number of persons, see Table 3.3. 1) A weight has been constructed for the Danish survey to take into account a certain over-representation of individuals with a stronger link to the labor market among those interviewed in comparison with those who declined to participate and other non-respondents. 2) A weight has been constructed to take into account the five nationalities' actual shares of the population. 3) Students are omitted in Section 3.3.

Source: Own calculations based on the RFMS-D and RFMS-G.

Primary and Secondary Schooling

As can be seen from the "Age, average" column in Table 3.7, immigrants and descendants in this subsection are, on average, younger than the total population. This is especially so in Denmark. On the basis of age alone, then, one would expect a higher level of schooling among the younger groups, i.e. among immigrants and descendants, due to a general rise in the level of education compared to that of older generations. Comparing Table 3.6 to Table 3.3, we see that in both countries fewer

Table 3.6. Primary and secondary school completed in Denmark/Germany, second generation immigrants and descendants, year 2001/2002, percent of all.

Country of origin	DK[1]	G	G	DK[1]	G	DK[1]	G	DK	G
	No primary or secondary schooling/not stated		Primary	Lower secondary		Upper secondary		No. of persons (total pop. in millions)	
Percent									
Men									
Former Yugoslavia	28	25	44	65	19	7	12	11	98
Iran	52	30	11	26	23	22	36	4	53
Lebanon	0	40	37	71	18	29	5	10	79
Poland	4	21	48	76	23	20	8	15	71
Turkey	17	17	47	77	27	6	9	29	251
Naturalized[2]	13	7	39	59	21	28	33	182	46
Total population	0	8	39	78	28	22	24	1.91	27.93
Women									
Former Yugoslavia	1	29	29	89	30	10	12	13	84
Iran	60	40	13	40	26	0	21	5	38
Lebanon	10	48	33	70	18	20	1	10	84
Poland	0	22	42	70	25	30	11	7	76
Turkey	14	14	45	74	31	12	10	26	214
Naturalized[2]	14	14	45	48	35	38	6	168	85
Total population	0	8	36	73	34	27	21	1.88	27.30

Notes: Second generation includes immigrants 12 years and younger on arrival and descendants born in Denmark/Germany, 16-70 years. Total population DK: 15-69 years, G: 15-64 years. Average age, see Table 3.7. No early differentiation like that of the German school system into Hauptschule (primary), Realschule (lower secondary), and Gymnasium (upper secondary) takes place in the Danish school system. Two-three percent not stated are included under "DK: lower secondary" as far as the total population is concerned. 1) A weight has been constructed for the Danish survey to take into account a certain over-representation of individuals with a stronger link to the labor market among those interviewed in comparison with those who declined to participate and other non-respondents. 2) A weight has been constructed to take into account the five nationalities' actual shares of the population.

Sources: Own calculations based on the RFMS-D and RFMS-G, Statistics Germany (2003: 373-374), and Statistics Denmark (2002: 107).

Table 3.7. Vocational training and university education completed in Denmark/Germany, second generation immigrants, year 2001/2002, percent of all.

Country of origin	DK[1]	G	DK[1]	G	DK[1]	G	DK	G	DK	G
	No vocational training or university education/not stated		Vocational		University		Age, average		No. of persons (total pop. in millions)	
	---------------- Percent ------------------									
Men										
Former Yugoslavia	93	65	7	32	0	3	18	27	11	98
Iran	100	87	0	11	0	2	19	27	4	53
Lebanon	91	84	9	15	0	1	18	24	10	79
Poland	68	66	28	34	4	0	20	35	15	71
Turkey	79	67	18	31	3	2	23	28	29	251
Naturalized[2]	77	66	18	34	5	0	23	29	182	46
Total population	44	28	46	58	10	14	39	40	0.04	27.93
Women										
Former Yugoslavia	95	75	5	24	0	1	18	28	13	84
Iran	100	76	0	13	0	11	17	25	5	38
Lebanon	100	90	0	10	0	0	19	24	10	84
Poland	88	70	12	30	0	0	19	36	7	76
Turkey	84	69	16	30	0	1	23	27	26	214
Naturalized[2]	73	68	25	27	2	5	24	29	168	85
Total population	49	35	45	56	5	9	40	40	0.04	27.30

Notes: Second generation includes immigrants 12 years and younger on arrival and descendants born in Denmark/Germany, 16-70 years. Total population DK: 15-69 years, G: 15-64 years. Number of persons: Total population DK is a sample consisting of 37,059 men and 36,469 women. 1) A weight has been constructed for the Danish survey to take into account a certain over-representation of individuals with a stronger link to the labor market among those interviewed in comparison with those who declined to participate and other non-respondents. 2) A weight has been constructed to take into account the five nationalities' actual shares of the population.

Sources: Own calculations based on register data from Statistics Denmark, the RFMS-D and RFMS-G, and Statistics Germany (2003: 373-374).

immigrants and descendants are in the "no school" category in the former, and that the shares of immigrants and descendants with lower or upper secondary school diploma are considerably higher for both countries. Lebanese men and Polish women in Denmark show a high level of achievement of upper secondary school, and Iranian men and women stand out as frequently achieving an *Abitur* diploma in Germany. Naturalized men in Germany, like naturalized men and women in Denmark, fare par-

Table 3.8. Proficiency in Danish/German, second generation immigrants, year 2001/2002, percent of all.

Country of origin	DK[1]	G	DK[1]	G	DK[1]	G	DK	G
	Speaks well		Speaks with average skill		Speaks poorly		No. of students[3]	
	Percent							
Men								
Former Yugoslavia	93	87	7	12	0	1	5	14
Iran	100	91	0	9	0	0	2	20
Lebanon	89	90	11	10	0	0	8	15
Poland	100	86	0	8	0	6	8	13
Turkey	91	91	6	8	3	0	8	39
Naturalized[2]	99	100	1	2	0	0	69	10
Women								
Former Yugoslavia	100	89	0	6	0	5	6	19
Iran	80	100	20	0	0	0	4	16
Lebanon	100	80	0	14	0	6	6	20
Poland	100	75	0	16	0	9	3	9
Turkey	85	92	11	7	4	1	8	32
Naturalized[2]	96	92	4	5	0	3	63	12

Notes: Second-generation includes immigrants 12 years and younger on arrival and descendants born in Denmark/Germany, 16-70 years. 1) A weight has been constructed for the Danish survey to take into account a certain over-representation of individuals with a stronger link to the labor market among those interviewed in comparison with those who declined to participate and other non-respondents. 2) A weight has been constructed to take into account the five nationalities' actual shares of the population. 3) Students are omitted in Section 3.3.

Source: Own calculations based on the RFMS-D and RFMS-G.

ticularly well with regard to post-migration upper secondary schooling. For Germany, the number of immigrants completing primary schooling is dramatically higher.

Vocational Training and University Education Qualifying Holders to Enter the Skilled Labor Market

Table 3.7 parallels the analysis of Table 3.4 for the second generation immigrants. As can be seen from this table the second generation group is, on average, much younger in Denmark than in Germany. This table shows that more of the second generation immigrants in Germany than in Denmark invest in vocational training, whereas the rate of achievement of a university degree is very low in both countries. In Denmark, there are practically no women with university degrees. This is likely to reflect the younger age of the group. Overall this table shows that, compared to the total population, second generation immigrants have a large gap to traverse.

Danish/German Language Proficiency

Table 3.8 shows levels of proficiency in the host country language for the second generation immigrants. As expected, immigrants who grew up in the host country speak that country's language very well, and we hardly find any immigrants in the "speaks poorly" category.

To sum up, this section has provided an overview of the educational systems in Denmark and Germany, and presented the pre- and post-migration human capital of immigrants in the two countries. Based on our surveys, in general, we found that the majority of immigrants who migrated to Denmark after the age of 13 had not completed primary or secondary schooling in the home country, while only a minority had vocational training or university degrees from their home countries. Overall, there is some ethnic variation, with Poles standing out among the most educated, and the Lebanese and Turks being the least educated. In Germany, the percentage of immigrants without completed pre-migration schooling is lower. While the Iranians and Poles are the most educated immigrants, Turks are the least.

With regard to post-migration education it is important to differentiate between first and second generation immigrants. Our descriptive analysis showed that among the first generation immigrants few have invested in lower levels of schooling, and this is most probably linked to their older age on arrival. However, the percentage of immigrants in Denmark who managed to obtain post-migration schooling is larger than that of immigrants in Germany. Within this group of immigrants quite a few have also invested in vocational training and university education; the naturalized, the Iranians, and the Poles stand out for their achievement in both countries, but immigrants in these groups still lag behind the total populations. Turks are at the bottom with regard to post-migration educational achievement.

The naturalized immigrants also stand out for their proficiency in the host country's language, followed by the Iranians and the Poles. Turks in the two countries score the lowest in language proficiency, although they have on average been in the countries the longest since migration. As expected, a high percentage of the second generation immigrants have completed primary and secondary schooling in the host countries. In this category of schooling we find that the second generation immigrants have managed to narrow the educational gap between them and the total population. Some second generation immigrants have also completed vocational training – although more in Germany than in Denmark. However, all immigrant groups lag behind the total population when it comes to vocational training and university degrees. Finally, the second generation immigrants in both countries have mastered the host country's language very well.

This descriptive analysis shows that immigrants in Denmark invest more in post-migration primary and secondary schooling than immigrants in Germany. Among the second generation immigrants, a much larger share of immigrants in Germany, who are also, on average, older, have completed vocational training than is the case for second generation immigrants in Denmark. However, there is considerable variation by national origin in both countries. Invariably, Iranians and the naturalized acquire more human capital than other groups, while Turks acquire less human capital than others.

In the next section we investigate the determinants of post-migration schooling among immigrant men and women in Denmark and Germany, and try to explain the above statistics within each country. The results from this analytical exercise can help us obtain some insights as to why some immigrant groups fare better than others in the host country, and how the intergenerational transmission process operates.

3.3 Determinants of Human Capital Formation

The purpose of this section is to determine which characteristics have an impact on the educational attainment of immigrants in Denmark and Germany. We measure educational attainment as the highest level of education completed in the respective countries. To put it another way, in this section we aim at evaluating the effects that several economic, social, personal, family, and environmental factors have on the probabilities of achieving different educational levels in the host country. We conduct two separate analyses. First, we estimate the proclivity to obtain an educational qualification (primary, secondary, or university) and second, the proclivity to choose a vocational training qualification. The results from this analytical exercise can help us obtain some insights as to why some immigrant groups fare better than others in the host country, why there are often persistent wage differentials between immigrants and natives, and how the intergenerational transmission process operates. These results can also offer an insight into how unskilled workers can be transformed into skilled workers, and may have policy implications by shedding light on the effects that different policy measures have on educational attainment.

The rest of this section is structured as follows: in Section 3.3.1 we briefly review the relevant economics literature on immigrants' post-migration human capital investments; in Section 3.3.2 we present the model, the hypotheses, and the variables employed; and in Section 3.3.3 we present and discuss the econometric results.

3.3.1 Previous Studies of the Educational Attainment of Immigrants in the Host Country

First formulated by Mincer (1958) and later elaborated by Becker (1993), the concept of "human capital" occupies an essential role in the literature. Education is the basic form of human capital; it is an investment that can produce enormous returns in the future if properly promoted. Chiswick's (1978) seminal work on the integration of immigrants argues that immigrants suffer an initial disadvantage mainly because they are not able to completely transfer their human capital to the host country. However, they invest more in post-migration human capital, and thus achieve more rapid wage growth than comparable natives. The literature on the immigrant education for various countries shows that the educational outcomes for immigrants are largely determined by age at entrance, years since migration, migration motives, ethnicity, sex, and parental and family background (Chiswick and Miller, 1994). By studying the educational attainment of immigrants in Australia, Chiswick and Miller (1994) found a positive relationship between pre- and post-migration schooling. Schaafsma and Sweetman (2001) also studied the educational attainment of immigrants in Canada. They found the age at entrance to be the most important determinant, since return to schooling was very similar to that of natives for immigrants who migrated as children. Other researchers, however, have found a negative relationship (Borjas, 1982).

The level of post-migration schooling and the health of immigrants have been studied by Schultz (1984). Focusing on second generation immigrants in the US and comparing them to natives, he found a process of convergence between these two groups. While children suffered an initial period of disadvantage, on average, they overranked the children of native parents within a decade. Cohen et al. (1997) found that the level of schooling attained by immigrants in the US increased in the 1980s among all immigrants except Mexicans and immigrants from Latin America. For Asians, the level of schooling achieved was even higher than that of natives; for Europeans and Canadians, the level of schooling was the same as that of natives; for Central and South American immigrants, the level of schooling was lower than that of the native born. Khan (1997) found that refugee immigrants invest more in post-migration schooling than non-refugee immigrants, and that naturalized immigrants acquire more schooling than the non-naturalized.

Evaluating the association between immigrant status and academic achievement, Kao and Tienda (1995) found that parental immigrant status is more important than the immigrant status of the young. Immigrant children consistently perform at the level of or higher than their native counterparts. They concluded that "The second generation immigrant is best positioned for scholastic success by having foreign-born parents and the language fluency conferred by native birth in the United States" (p. 17). Cobb-Clark et al. (2001) undertook the study of post-migration human capital investment in a family context. They found that the probability of post-migration school enrolment in Australia is higher for immigrants who have high education levels upon arrival. Which partner makes the schooling investment is dictated by gender roles. Besides human capital, social capital is also of paramount importance for high school completion. Indeed, social capital can counterbalance the effects of years since migration, ethnicity, and lower socioeconomic status (White and Kaufman, 1997).

Studies of the educational attainment of immigrant children in Germany are usually based on the GSOEP. Alba et al. (1994) found considerable differences between German and foreign children with regard to finishing school. Haisken-DeNew et al. (1997) found that foreign children in Germany have a significantly higher probability of attaining only the minimum level of education (*Hauptschule*). However, parental ability or income preference clearly increase the children's probability of completing *Gymnasium*. While they found ethnic differences, they did not find gender differences. In contrast, Gang and Zimmermann's (2000) results show that for Germans, the father's education has a large impact on the educational outcomes for the children, but parental background has no differential effect on the educational outcomes of the children of immigrants. Constant and Zimmermann (2003) found that Germans are more likely to choose occupations similar to their father's occupation when their father's is in the white-collar or professional category. In stark contrast, the immigrants' occupational choice is more influenced by their mother's education and not by their father's occupation.

Riphahn (2003) also dealt with intergenerational issues of education. Using various Mikrozensus surveys between 1989 and 1996 for Germany she found that the schooling success of German-born children of immigrants still lags substantially behind that of natives even after controlling for characteristics such as demographic variables, immigrant assimilation variables, parental human capital indicators, country of origin, regional effects, and yearly fixed effects. The alarming evidence is that the achievement gap seems to be increasing, and there is no tendency for assimilation towards native standards in educational attainment across generations. While the educational attainment of natives has improved greatly over recent decades, current second generation immigrants do not achieve higher levels of education than those of a few decades earlier. This seems to point to a major problem for German integration policy and calls for strong reforms in national educational policies.

In a study focusing on the educational achievement of children of guest workers in Denmark, Jakobsen and Smith (2003) also found that these young second generation immigrants from Turkey, Pakistan, and the former Yugoslavia are lagging behind young native Danes and that there are large differences between the three ethnic minority groups. Especially young Turks have a low probability of completing education. As part of the explanation of this and the high drop-out rates are mentioned language problems, age at first marriage, and parental capital in the form of mothers' education; but for young women the effect may stem from different cultural factors related to marriage behavior and religion, rather than marriage itself. Furthermore, the attitude of the parents concerning the importance of education is mentioned as a very important factor. Jakobsen and Smith (2003) conclude, however, that the lower educational achievement is mainly due to unfavorable background characteristics and not that second generation immigrants have a lower level of preference for education than young native Danes.

3.3.2 Modeling of Educational Levels: Methods, Data, and Variables

3.3.2.1 Data

In order to empirically study the post-migration investment in human capital we use data from our surveys referred to above about immigrants in Germany and in Denmark (RFMS-G and RFMS-D). These data sets have several comparative advantages, in that they contain information on the pre-migration experiences of immigrants, including family background, social and environmental settings, and visa status at migration. The data sets also provide rich information on post-migration schooling investments and labor market experiences, including actual years of labor market experience and actual years since migration for both uninterrupted residence and for residence interrupted by return or frequent remigration. One thing that is especially important about these surveys is that we can avoid some measurement error because we have actual information on schooling and we do not need to estimate it, and we use the interviewers' assessed language fluency of the respondents. As in Section 3.2, in this section we look both at men and women in Denmark and Germany from the following countries of origin: Turkey, former Yugoslavia, Poland, Iran, and Lebanon. In contrast to the procedure described in Section 3.2, the samples we select for our analyses here exclude those individuals who are enrolled in school. Further, we select only respondents with no missing values in the pertinent variables.[6] Our final sample size for the Danish analysis is 1,866 observations of persons aged between 16 and 72 and for the German analysis 5,291 observations of persons aged between 17 and 87.

3.3.2.2 Variables

The dependent variables in our analyses are: (1) completion of levels of schooling, namely *Haupt-/Realschule* or *Folkeskole*, and upper secondary school or university, and (2) completion of vocational training. For the first exercise – levels of schooling in the host country – the dependent variable is carefully constructed to represent distinct educational levels in line with the German and Danish educational systems. *Haupt-/Realschule* represents a different educational track from *Gymnasium* or university. Both the number of years of schooling required for the *Realschule* option and the level of education obtained from this type of schooling are different from the *Gymnasium* option. In Germany, it is also very rare that an individual who graduates from this track ever goes on to *Gymnasium* or university, whereas in Denmark, the *Folkeskole* is a prerequisite for continuing to upper secondary school level (see Section 3.2). In the following, "Gymnasium" is used to designate upper secondary

---

6 In the German sample, we lost 37 observations. In the Danish sample we lost 6 observations.

school. Because we are primarily interested in the differential sorting into educational tracks, we construct this variable as a trichotomous variable that takes the value of zero if an individual has no schooling in the host country, the value of one if an individual has finished *Haupt-/Realschule* or *Folkeskole*, and the value of two if the individual has finished Gymnasium or university. These levels of schooling are recorded as the highest level obtained by the respondent.

Vocational or professional training is a complementary feature of the educational system in both countries that deserves special attention and warrants separate analysis. Graduates from both *Haupt-/Realschule* or *Folkeskole* and from the Gymnasium can go on to vocational training (see Section 3.2.1 for a description of the educational systems). The dependent variable "vocational training" is a dummy variable that takes the value of one if the individual has finished vocational training in the host country and the value of zero otherwise.

The choice of the independent variables is based on economic theory. These variables are expected to have an impact on the individual's probability of investing in further post-migration education or in vocational training. The explanatory variables used in this section include human capital variables, family background variables, social and cultural variables from the individual's upbringing, and other control variables (ethnicity and gender). Table 3.9 shows the coding of the variables.

The vector of human capital variables includes age at entrance into the host country, years since migration, schooling completed in the home country, vocational training completed in the home country, pre-migration labor market experience, and health status. Education in the home country is depicted by dummy variables representing the following educational levels: (1) no schooling, (2) lower secondary education, (3) upper secondary education, and (4) university degree. Finishing lower secondary education is the reference category. Completion of vocational training is kept as a separate dummy variable. Pre-migration experience in the home country is another variable that captures additional human capital due to exposure to the labor market. It includes on-the-job training, and reflects how one values education. It often happens that individuals who join the labor market decide to go back to school and acquire additional education, aiming at higher job prospects. It could also be the case that immigrants decide to migrate in order to take advantage of the host country's educational system. Health is a vital component of human wealth, and the health status of an individual has been long acknowledged in the literature as another facet of human capital. To capture the health status of an individual we construct a dummy variable from their self-reported disability status. This variable takes the value of one if the individual is disabled, chronically ill, or handicapped, and zero otherwise.

Age at entrance and years since migration are the chief determinants of post-migration investment in human capital. The variable "years since migration" is constructed from the immigration year and from additional information on the self-reported number of years living in Germany. The number of years in Denmark is

Table 3.9. Descriptive statistics of the dependent and explanatory variables.

Variable	Description	Denmark Mean	Denmark St. Error	Germany Mean	Germany St. Error
Dependent variables					
Completed primary or lower secondary school in DK/G		16.83	37.42	17.50	38.00
Completed upper secondary school/university in DK/G		15.97	36.64	5.29	22.39
Completed vocational training in DK/G		16.29	36.94	12.53	33.11
Explanatory variables					
Age at Entrance	Age upon arrival in years	23.50	12.71	22.98	12.39
Years Since Migration	Number of years since arrival	15.09	8.03	17.12	11.12
Disability	Chronically ill/handicapped (0/1)	0.17	0.37	0.18	0.38
Primary/Lower Secondary Home (omitted)	Schooling, vocational training, and university education obtained in the home country (0/1)	0.22	0.41	0.34	0.47
Upper Secondary Home		0.17	0.38	0.27	0.45
University Home		0.07	0.26	0.06	0.24
Vocational Training Home		0.21	0.41	0.23	0.42
No Degree Home		0.61	0.49	0.38	0.49
Work Home	Work in home country (0/1)	0.49	0.50	0.51	0.50
Father No School (omitted)	Father's level of education (0/1)	0.26	0.44	0.23	0.42
Father Elementary		0.32	0.47	0.41	0.49
Father Secondary		0.12	0.33	0.19	0.39
Father High		0.31	0.46	0.18	0.38
Father Blue-collar/ Unskilled (omitted)	Father's occupation (0/1)	0.27	0.44	0.37	0.48
Father Blue-Collar/Skilled		0.14	0.34	0.17	0.37
Father Lower White-collar		0.12	0.32	0.07	0.26
Father Upper White-collar		0.11	0.31	0.10	0.30
Father Farmer		0.10	0.30	0.09	0.29
Father Self-employed		0.13	0.33	0.11	0.32
Father Professional		0.05	0.22	0.03	0.16
Father other		0.08	0.27	0.06	0.23
Large City Home (omitted)	City where the person grew up if in the home country (0/1)	0.27	0.45	0.21	0.41
Average City Home		0.42	0.49	0.37	0.48
Small City Home		0.14	0.35	0.29	0.45
Large City DK/G (omitted)	City where the person grew up if in the receiving country (0/1)	0.06	0.23	0.04	0.19
Average City DK/G		0.08	0.27	0.13	0.33
Small City DK/G		0.02	0.13	0.02	0.12
Religion	Raised religious (0/1)	0.84	0.36	0.85	0.36
Born in DK/G	Born in the host country (0/1)	0.06	0.23	0.09	0.29
Turkish (omitted)	Citizenship (0/1)	0.16	0.37	0.25	0.43
From former Yugoslavia		0.19	0.39	0.18	0.38
Polish		0.09	0.28	0.19	0.40
Iranian		0.05	0.23	0.16	0.37
Lebanese/Stateless		0.06	0.24	0.16	0.37
Danish/German		0.45	0.50	0.06	0.23
Male	Male (0/1)	0.52	0.50	0.50	0.50
Number of Observations		1,866		5,291	

Note: In this calculation we have excluded those currently enrolled in primary or secondary school or participating in vocational training or higher education.

Source: Own calculations based on RFSM-D and RFSM-G.

based on information from Statistics Denmark's population register. Age at entrance is in turn calculated from age and years since migration. These are continuous variables and measure the time and quality of exposure to the Danish or German environments. They also reflect familiarity with the culture of the host country, and knowledge of the institutional factors that affect the demand for education. Because in our sample we include both the first and second generation immigrants, the "age at entrance to the host country" variable is crucial for capturing these differences. Immigrants who migrate before the age of 16, for example, are obliged by law to go to school.[7]

Family background, environmental factors, and cultural and religious mores are essential determinants of a person's educational choices. We therefore include the following variables in the regressions. Father's education and occupation are entered as dummy regressors to capture the individual's family background. The father having no education and the father being in an unskilled job are the reference categories for these. The city where one grew up also affects the demand for education. Our data sets give us the opportunity to control for the size of the city in the home or host countries. We differentiate among small (less than 10,000 inhabitants), average, and large (in Germany with at least 1 million inhabitants and in Denmark the Copenhagen metropolitan area) city sizes. Large city size is the reference category. Lastly, we construct a dummy variable for whether an individual was raised in a particular religious belief. "Raised religious" includes upbringing in the Muslim, Christian, or Jewish faiths.

The final set of regressors control for gender and ethnicity. Besides the five nationalities in our samples, we control for Danish/German citizenship and whether an individual was born in Denmark/Germany. Immigrants to Germany, even those who were born in Germany, are not automatically German citizens. Although the laws on acquiring citizenship have been less stringent since the 1990s, many immigrants choose not to become German citizens. In Denmark, descendants of immigrants are not automatically Danish citizens at birth either, but, in contrast to the situation in Germany, laws on acquiring citizenship have been tightened in recent years. As in Germany, many immigrants in Denmark choose not to become naturalized citizens. However, during the 1990s – especially during the period 1998-2000 – the number of naturalizations increased. In constructing the citizenship variable, we omitted from every ethnic group those who had become naturalized and issued with a passport of the host country, and grouped them together. For the nationality dummies, Turks are the omitted category.

---

7 However, the law does not require a person to obtain a school leaving certificate. It is thus possible – for both immigrants and natives – to leave school after the required grades or age without having completed school.

3.3.2.3 Methods and Hypotheses

The question we seek to answer in this section is: what is the probability that immigrants will choose a given level of education in the host country? To model the educational choice we estimate reduced form models. Empirically, the unit of analysis is the individual. We assume that individual agents in the host country can choose among three distinct educational levels: (1) no schooling in the host country, (2) *Haupt-/Realschule* or *Folkeskole*, and (3) Gymnasium/university. Individual agents maximize utility gained from the attributes of that choice. Such behavior is described in probabilistic terms. This probability is not directly observed. The estimating equation is a multinomial logit that estimates the probability of choosing *Haupt-/Realschule* or *Folkeskole* as opposed to choosing no schooling in the host country, and the probability of choosing Gymnasium/university as opposed to choosing no schooling in the host country. Because of the specific role and importance that vocational training occupies in Denmark and Germany, we also estimate the impact of the independent variables on the probability of choosing vocational training. For this exercise we employ a separate binomial logit.

Our hypotheses are derived from human capital theory. We expect that more years since migration will increase the probability of acquiring education and that this relationship is non-linear, so that demand for education increases at a decreasing rate.[8] The "age at entrance" variable, while it complements the "years since migration" variable, specifically captures the generational effect. The younger one was on arrival, the higher the probability of going to school after immigration, and the higher the probability of finishing a higher level of schooling. The rationale here is that the younger the age on arrival, the higher the degree of assimilation or integration. Immigrants in that group are more likely to resemble and behave like natives. Conversely, we expect that as age at entrance increases, the probability of going to school and acquiring a qualification decreases, and at an increasing rate. Older immigrants will have higher opportunity costs of investment in education, and less time to recoup the benefits of education.

On the basis of the persistence hypothesis, we suggest that individuals who have acquired some schooling in their home country will be more likely to invest in further schooling after immigration. In principle, there are two types of pre-migration schooling: a higher level of schooling and a lower level of schooling. We expect that it will be easier for individuals with higher levels of schooling to invest in additional schooling after migration because it will be easier for them to get their qualifications recognized and because such additional schooling can augment and enrich their

---

8 For a full explanation on the mechanism of YSM see Chiswick and Miller (1994). They argue that although "annual propensities to invest would be expected to diminish with duration, the cumulative effect would be an increase with duration (but at a decreasing rate) in the probability of having acquired a qualification" (p. 167).

previous education. Besides, additional schooling in the host country may render their pre-migration human capital more portable. Individuals who have already attended school and have acquired high-level qualifications value education more and are more dedicated to investing in human capital. Their demand for post-migration schooling will, thus, be higher.

On the other hand, individuals with lower levels of schooling would also have a higher tendency to acquire education, seeing the host country as providing a golden opportunity to go to school and advance their educational level. Immigrants with a low level of education on arrival may find themselves with education that is inferior and has no value in the host country. In this case, the incentives to invest will be higher. Immigrants would want to take advantage of the educational system in Germany or Denmark and improve their marketability in the host country, or abroad if they should emigrate.

We expect individuals whose fathers are educated to have a higher probability of investing in human capital. Similarly, individuals whose fathers are in a white-collar or professional occupation will be more likely to choose Gymnasium or university. Intergenerational effects may operate here (following in one's father's footsteps, positive role models, advantageous upbringing, social connections, etc.), and more educated parents will also push their children towards higher education (because they value education more, or even as a matter of social prestige). On the other hand, individuals whose fathers are in blue-collar or craft occupations will be more likely to choose vocational training. We further expect that individuals who grew up in small cities will have a lower probability of going to school or acquiring higher education. It is often the case that small cities do not offer the right opportunities for education. Small cities may not offer all educational tracks. Children who want to go to Gymnasium may need to commute to the next bigger city. This may increase the cost and lower the probability of graduating from the Gymnasium. A larger city, on the other hand, can offer additional incentives and opportunities for acquiring education.

With regard to religion, we seek to investigate how a religious upbringing can influence the choice of educational level. We expect that those individuals who are raised in a religious belief will have a higher probability of going to school and acquiring higher qualifications. In principle, religion teaches stronger ethics and ascribes a value to education, and it also instills discipline and solid work ethics, which are invaluable for acquiring education and becoming a well-rounded person.[9] Association with a congregation can also provide a comfortable social circle, with incentives and opportunities that further one's education. A congregation can make a difference especially when the parents are uneducated or unskilled by offering sound guidance, so that individuals can make informed decisions. Chiswick (1993)

---

9 It is often for these reasons that in the US, for example, even non-religious parents send their children to Catholic schools. The relevant literature shows that children in these schools perform better than children in public schools.

found that Jews have substantially higher levels of schooling and earnings than other groups. However, when the distinction is between religious fundamentalists or more conventional religious groups, research finds a strong negative effect of religion on educational achievement (Darnell and Sherkat, 1997).

Just as ethnic identity is an indicator of cultural distance between immigrants and natives, it also reflects the cultural distance among the different immigrant groups. We expect that the chances of acquiring educational qualifications after arrival are significantly different among the different ethnic groups. We conjecture that those immigrants who are born in Germany and Denmark and have German/Danish passports will be more likely to acquire educational qualifications and complete higher education. Lastly, we expect that there would not be significant differences between men and women in their attainment of post-migration education, because in principle, both Denmark and Germany offer equal chances to both sexes.

3.3.3 Estimation Results

In Table 3.9 we presented the average characteristics of our immigrant samples in both countries. Compared to the tables in Section 3.2, this table is based on the immigrants who are not students. Though on average the immigrants in our sample entered either Denmark or Germany in their early 20s, immigrants in Denmark nevertheless entered at a slightly older age than immigrants in Germany. The immigrants in Denmark also had fewer years since migration and a larger percentage of them had no completed schooling from their home country. In both countries, 50 percent of the immigrants in the samples were male, and 50 percent had pre-migration work experience. While the majority of immigrants in both countries had fathers with elementary school only, more immigrants in Denmark than in Germany had a father with a high school education. Similarly, the majority of the immigrants' fathers were blue-collar or unskilled workers. However, more immigrants had a blue-collar father in Germany than in Denmark.

Table 3.9 further shows that immigrants in both countries grew up in an average-sized city setting, whether in the home or the host country. The overwhelming majority (85 percent) of immigrants in Denmark and Germany were raised religious. One considerable difference between the immigrants in Denmark and Germany was that almost half of the former were Danish citizens, while only 6 percent of the immigrants in Germany were German citizens. In contrast, only 6 percent of the immigrants in Denmark were Danish-born, while 9 percent of the immigrants in Germany were German-born. Looking at the five national groups that composed our immigrant samples, we see that in Denmark, the largest immigrant group was from the former Yugoslavia, followed by the Turks and the Poles. In Germany, a third of the immigrants in the sample were Turkish, followed by the Poles and the people from the former Yugoslavia.

3.3.3.1 Multinomial Logit Results on Primary/Lower Secondary Schooling and Gymnasium/University Education

Tables 3.10 and 3.11 present the results of the multinomial logit estimated on the Danish and German data respectively. The reference outcome is the probability of not having completed any education in Denmark/Germany. These tables show how the different characteristics of the immigrants affect the log-odds of acquiring specific levels or types of schooling in Denmark/Germany. We present the coefficient estimates, the standard errors, and the marginal effects – evaluated at the mean of all covariates. An asterisk denotes significance at the 5 percent level.

(a) Immigrants and Descendants in Denmark

Results of the estimations for the immigrant population in Denmark show that age at entrance has the expected significant impact on the probability of acquiring education. For each additional year older the immigrant is on arrival, the probability of finishing *Folkeskole* or Gymnasium/university decreases, and at an increasing rate. Years since migration are significant only for the choice of entry to Gymnasium/university. Additional years since migration increase the probability of completing Gymnasium or university education, but at a decreasing rate. The disability effect is also significant for the Gymnasium/university outcome only. Immigrants with disabilities are less likely to finish higher education in Denmark.

As expected, immigrants who have upper secondary schooling in their home country have a higher probability of finishing higher education in Denmark, compared to those who only have lower secondary/primary schooling. This indicates that those who arrive with some education are more likely to continue investing in education and pursue a higher qualification than the one they have from home – following the persistence hypothesis. Immigrants who have no school qualification from their home countries are significantly less likely to finish *Folkeskole*. We suspect that these are the first generation immigrants who arrived as unskilled guest workers and never went to school in Denmark. Understandably, those immigrants with a university degree from their home country also have a low probability of finishing *Folkeskole*. Contrary to our predictions, the effect of work experience in the home country is negative and significant for both outcomes. That is, those immigrants who were working before migration are less likely to obtain any educational qualification, all else being equal. This indicates that immigrants with pre-migration experience migrate purely for labor market reasons and have no intentions of taking advantage of the educational opportunities in the host country.

The effect of father's education is significantly positive only on the probability

Table 3.10. Multinomial logit results for the probabilities of educational attainment in Denmark. Reference outcome is the probability of not having completed any education or training in Denmark.

Variable	Probability of completing Folkeskole			Probability of completing Gymnasium/university		
	Coefficient	St. Error	Marginal Effects	Coefficient	St. Error	Marginal Effects
Age at Entrance	-0.231*	0.035	-0.026	-0.171*	0.040	-0.011
Age at Entrance²	0.002*	0.001	0.0003	0.001	0.001	0.0001
Years Since Migration	-0.009	0.041	-0.004	0.238*	0.057	0.020
Years Since Migration²	-0.001	0.001	-0.0001	-0.006*	0.001	-0.0005
Disability	-0.119	0.257	-0.008	-0.657*	0.292	-0.044
Upper Secondary Home	0.185	0.335	0.007	0.927*	0.351	0.093
University Home	-1.263*	0.501	-0.104	-0.367	0.358	-0.018
Vocational Training Home	-0.437	0.330	-0.049	-0.027	0.363	0.003
No Degree Home	-0.748*	0.315	-0.100	0.156	0.378	0.022
Work Home	-0.457*	0.219	-0.049	-0.558*	0.221	-0.040
Father Elementary	0.363	0.205	0.040	0.444	0.246	0.033
Father Secondary	-0.068	0.292	-0.018	0.630*	0.310	0.064
Father High	-0.188	0.262	-0.035	0.902*	0.266	0.089
Father Craft	0.159	0.271	0.025	-0.377	0.334	-0.029
Father Lower White-collar	0.650*	0.270	0.082	0.600	0.309	0.045
Father Upper White-collar	0.193	0.330	0.017	0.479	0.320	0.042
Father Farmer	-0.169	0.351	-0.028	0.595	0.357	0.062
Father Self-employed	0.223	0.283	0.018	0.621*	0.298	0.057
Father Professional	0.244	0.419	0.034	-0.070	0.413	-0.009
Father Other	0.362	0.323	0.037	0.631	0.338	0.056
Average City Home	-0.464*	0.199	-0.053	-0.202	0.191	-0.011
Small City Home	-0.501	0.279	-0.046	-1.068*	0.418	-0.062
Average City Denmark	0.554	0.387	0.077	0.179	0.420	0.006
Small City Denmark	0.541	0.544	0.085	-0.322	0.667	-0.030
Religion	-0.276	0.249	-0.022	-0.768*	0.231	-0.072
Born in Denmark	0.412	0.649	0.033	1.022	0.679	0.108
From former Yugoslavia	0.222	0.370	0.005	1.212*	0.545	0.130
Polish	1.076*	0.389	0.049	2.572*	0.501	0.375
Iranian	0.947*	0.420	0.035	2.444*	0.527	0.367
Lebanese	-0.391	0.444	-0.071	1.657*	0.532	0.247
Danish citizen	1.239*	0.249	0.107	2.546*	0.392	0.225
Male	0.330*	0.163	0.031	0.713*	0.175	0.054
Intercept	2.721*	0.779		-2.984*	0.985	
Log likelihood function				-1093.2		
χ²				1023.0		
Number of Observations				1866		

Note: * denotes 5 percent significance level in a 2-tailed test.

of completing Gymnasium or university. Immigrants whose father had secondary or higher school qualifications also have a higher probability of finishing Gymnasium/university in Denmark, which points to an intergenerational link, but for the upper end of the spectrum only. With regard to father's occupation, we also find some significant effects. When their father is in a low white-collar job (as opposed to being in a blue-collar job) immigrants are more likely to finish *Folkeskole* than not to finish any level of schooling at all. It is interesting that when the father is self-employed the probability of choosing Gymnasium or university is highly significant.

The effect of growing up in a city of average or small size in the home country (as opposed to growing up in a large city) is negative. Specifically, those who grew up in an average sized city have a 5.3 percentage point lower probability of finishing *Folkeskole*, and those who grew up in a small city have a 6.2 percentage point lower probability of completing Gymnasium/university in Denmark in comparison with not finishing school at all. Clearly, a small city of upbringing in the home country has a negative impact on higher education. Also negative is the effect of religion, but is significant for the Gymnasium/university outcome only. It appears that religiosity lowers the probability of finishing higher education in Denmark by 7.2 percentage points.

Poles and Iranians have significantly higher probabilities of finishing education or training in Denmark rather than not finishing any education or training. Compared to Turks, these immigrants have a 3.5 to 37.5 percentage point higher probability of finishing *Folkeskole* or Gymnasium/university respectively. Similarly, Danish citizens are highly likely to complete either qualification in Denmark, as opposed to not finishing any at all. Compared to Turks, people from the former Yugoslavia and the Lebanese have a higher probability of finishing Gymnasium/university. This finding points to the fact that, everything else being constant, all other ethnic groups have a higher proclivity to acquire an educational qualification in Denmark than the Turks.

Finally, we find that men have a higher probability of finishing either *Folkeskole* or Gymnasium/university than women, indicating strong gender roles among the immigrants.

Comparing the two outcomes, the positive effects from additional years since migration and family background are more important for the choice between Gymnasium/university and no schooling at all than for the choice between *Folkeskole* and no schooling at all. This is also true for ethnicity. All ethnic groups are more likely to finish Gymnasium/university than to obtain no schooling at all, compared to Turks.

Table 3.11. Multinomial logit results for the probabilities of educational attainment in Germany. Reference outcome is the probability of not having completed any education or training in Germany.

Variable	Probability of completing Haupt-/Realschule			Probability of completing Gymnasium/university		
	Coefficient	St. Error	Marginal Effects	Coefficient	St. Error	Marginal Effects
Age at Entrance	-0.333*	0.028	-0.017	-0.206*	0.033	-0.005
Age at Entrance^2	0.004*	0.0005	0.0002	0.002*	0.001	0.0001
Years Since Migration	0.037*	0.016	0.002	0.181*	0.028	0.005
Years Since Migration^2	-0.001*	0.0003	-0.0001	-0.004*	0.001	-0.0001
Disability	-0.106	0.179	-0.005	-0.427*	0.216	-0.010
Upper Secondary Home	-0.518*	0.254	-0.027	1.542*	0.279	0.063
University Home	0.015	0.556	0.001	-0.277	0.282	-0.007
Vocational Training Home	-0.042	0.261	-0.001	-0.507*	0.246	-0.012
No Degree Home	0.942*	0.184	0.052	0.994*	0.303	0.029
Work Home	-0.771*	0.199	-0.041	-0.075	0.200	-0.001
Father Elementary	0.077	0.156	0.004	0.223	0.237	0.006
Father Secondary	0.502*	0.189	0.029	0.514*	0.259	0.015
Father High	0.273	0.221	0.013	0.877*	0.262	0.031
Father Craft	0.290	0.167	0.016	0.076	0.248	0.002
Father Lower White-collar	0.494*	0.219	0.032	-0.354	0.342	-0.009
Father Upper White-collar	0.026	0.259	0.001	-0.072	0.271	-0.002
Father Farmer	-0.129	0.249	0.007	0.144	0.329	0.004
Father self-employed	0.465*	0.215	0.028	0.082	0.253	0.001
Father Professional	-0.333	0.488	-0.016	0.810*	0.329	0.033
Father Other	0.354	0.260	0.021	-0.138	0.352	-0.004
Average City Home	0.101	0.180	0.006	-0.311	0.181	-0.008
Small City Home	0.149	0.194	0.009	-0.450	0.262	-0.011
Average City Germany	0.376*	0.191	0.022	0.170	0.283	0.004
Small City Germany	-0.712*	0.339	-0.027	-2.455*	1.065	-0.026
Religion	-0.286	0.154	-0.015	-0.529*	0.166	-0.016
Born in Germany	-2.069*	0.297	-0.056	-1.165*	0.400	-0.020
From former Yugoslavia	-0.538*	0.183	-0.024	-0.184	0.284	-0.004
Polish	0.290	0.199	0.015	0.412	0.285	0.012
Iranian	-0.294	0.244	-0.016	1.215*	0.265	0.051
Lebanese	-1.305*	0.197	-0.047	-0.975*	0.337	-0.019
German citizen	0.847*	0.245	0.054	1.366*	0.292	0.063
Male	0.504*	0.117	0.025	0.621*	0.146	0.017
Intercept	2.495*	0.514		-2.445*	0.703	
Log likelihood function				-1826.663		
χ^2				3333.789		
Number of Observations				5291		

Note: * denotes 5 percent significance level in a 2-tailed test.

(b) Immigrants in Germany

The results of the corresponding multinomial logit performed on the German data are presented in Table 3.11. The results for the human capital model are as predicted by the theory. Specifically, we find that the older one is on arrival in Germany the lower is the probability of acquiring any level of education, and it decreases at a decreasing rate. In addition, we find that the more years since migration one has in Germany, the higher is the probability of acquiring any level of schooling or education/training in Germany, but this probability increases at a decreasing rate. As expected, but in sharp contrast to the Danish results, immigrants who have no qualification from their home countries (compared to those with lower secondary schooling) are more likely to acquire any level of schooling in Germany. This is in line with the "seizing the opportunity" hypothesis, whereby uneducated immigrants find the opportunity to finish school in the host country, and seize it. Those who finish upper secondary schooling in their home country, as opposed to lower secondary schooling, have a lower probability of acquiring *mittlere Reife* (understandably, since they already have this qualification from home), but a higher probability of acquiring *Abitur* or a diploma. In this case, pre-migration schooling acts as a complement to schooling in Germany and plays a pivotal role in the transferability of skills. Clearly, immigrants in Germany – both those who have pre-migration schooling and those who do not – are more likely to finish school. This pre-migration human capital complements and pushes immigrants into further educational investment in the host country. In accordance with the persistence hypothesis, early investments in human capital boost and encourage later investment.

Pre-migration vocational training has a negative effect on the odds of acquiring higher education in Germany. Understandably, having such training means that these immigrants have already completed their education in the home country by choosing a specific track and do not need to go to school in Germany. They migrate purely for economic reasons. Hence, they may not want to invest in additional human capital in the host country. Another explanation could be that vocational training in the home country may not be transferable, thus making access to higher education impossible. Though age has been controlled for by including age at entrance and years since migration, pre-migration work experience has a negative effect on finishing *Haupt-/Realschule*. As predicted, and in the same way as for Denmark, our results also show that immigrants with disabilities have a lower probability of going to Gymnasium or university, while disability is not relevant for finishing *Haupt-/Realschule*.

The coefficients from the father's education dummies show that there is a clear link between the father's education and the children's level of schooling. If the father has secondary education, as opposed to no education at all, the children are more likely to choose either *Haupt-/Realschule* or *Gymnasium/university* rather than no schooling at all. When the father has higher education, the children are significantly more likely to choose to finish high school or university. The father's occupation also verifies this strong intergenerational link. As predicted, when the father is in a professional job, such as lawyer or doctor, we find that the individual is more likely to choose Gymnasium or university. Moreover, immigrants whose fathers are in low white-collar jobs or self-employed have a higher probability of finishing secondary education in Germany.

While the city size in the country of origin has no significant effect on the probabilities of choosing a certain level of school attainment in Germany, growing up in a small city in Germany has a clear negative effect on the probability of choosing either level of schooling in Germany. In fact, growing up in a small German city as opposed to growing up in a large German city decreases the chances of acquiring *Haupt-/Realschule* by 2.7 percentage points, and the chances of acquiring Gymnasium or university education 2.6 percentage points. As in the Danish case, a religious background has a pronounced negative effect on higher educational attainment. Those immigrants who were raised under a particular religious belief (Catholic, Protestant, Orthodox, or Muslim) are 1.6 percentage points less likely to finish Gymnasium or university in relation to not having obtained an educational qualification a degree in Germany. Although it is often the case that less educated people are more religious, we believe that there may be other factors that can explain this result.

While German citizenship clearly increases the chances for acquiring and finishing education in Germany – as was the case in Denmark – being born in Germany does not. In fact, those who were born in Germany have a 5.6 percentage point lower probability of finishing *Haupt-/Realschule* and a 2.0 percentage point lower probability of finishing Gymnasium/university than those born abroad. This puzzling finding is, however, also found in studies by Riphahn (2001) and Gang and Zimmermann (2000). One explanation could be that some kind of selection takes place here. These are second generation immigrants, who are likely to be disadvantaged because their parents migrated as guest workers and are not integrated enough to be able to guide them properly. Moreover, if second generation immigrants are born in Germany, but grow up in enclaves and poor areas where they struggle to make ends meet, finishing school may not be a priority for them. Unaware of the higher future economic returns of education, these second generation immigrants might prefer to join the labor market as unskilled workers rather than investing in costly education. Furthermore, second generation immigrants who are born in Germany and grow up in a rich developed country might become more complacent, less ambitious, and take things for granted, compared to those who come from abroad and value the new country's opportunities more. At the same time, for these second generation immigrants the high level of socioeconomic contrast between them and the natives might give them a feeling of hopelessness, paralyze them, and render them unwilling to seek a better future through education. Another explanation could be that there has never been a German integration policy for second generation immigrants. The German educational system can often leave immigrant youth isolated and vulnerable to dropping out.

With respect to ethnicity we find that, in contrast to Denmark, there are significant differences among the different nationalities. While the Turks are still at the bottom, not all nationalities perform well. The odds of choosing to finish *Gymnasium* or university are highest for Iranians – compared to Turks, who are the reference group – and the lowest for Lebanese. The Lebanese, along with those from former Yugoslavia, are also less likely to finish *Haupt-/Realschule* than the Turks. As with the results for immigrants in Denmark, we find that males have a higher probability of completing either type of schooling: *Haupt-/Realschule*, or Gymnasium/university. In fact, the male coefficient is larger in Germany, indicating that females are in a more critical plight in Germany than in Denmark. It could be that women, as a group, are subjected to gender-role pressures. It could also be that the German system is not very successful in integrating women and equipping them with a qualification. It is still puzzling, however, that immigrant women in highly industrialized countries have lower chances of finishing schooling than men.

3.3.3.2 Binomial Logit Results for Vocational Training and No Vocational Training

In Tables 3.12 and 3.13 we present the results for the choices between vocational training and no vocational training at all for Denmark and Germany respectively. While the results for the vocational training choice in Denmark are slightly different from the results for the schooling choice in Denmark, the results for vocational training in Germany are qualitatively similar to the results for schooling and converge to the same substantive conclusions.

(a) Immigrants and Descendants in Denmark

Table 3.12 shows that age at entrance impacts significantly on the choice of vocational training in Denmark, but here, the older one is on arrival in Denmark, the greater the probability of finishing vocational training, although at a decreasing rate. As expected, the older immigrants value training more and realize that this extra education can help them find a better job with higher remuneration. Likewise, and in accordance with the persistence hypothesis referred to above, which assumes that individuals who have acquired some education or training in their home country will be more likely to invest in further education after migration, those who have finished upper secondary schooling or vocational training in their home countries are more likely to finish vocational training in the host country.

While father's education plays no role, father's occupation is positively significant only when the father is in an upper white-collar job. As with the schooling choices, growing up in an average or small-size city in the home country – as opposed to growing up in a large city – lowers the probability of finishing vocational training.

Table 3.12. Binomial logit results for the probabilities of finishing vocational training. Reference outcome is the probability of not having finished vocational training in Denmark.

Variable	Probability of finishing vocational training in Denmark		
	Coefficient	St. Error	Marginal Effects
Age at Entrance	0.037	0.030	0.004
Age at Entrance^2	-0.001*	0.001	-0.0001
Years Since Migration	0.067	0.042	0.007
Years Since Migration^2	-0.002	0.001	-0.0001
Disability	-0.440	0.228	-0.040
Upper Secondary Home	0.670*	0.277	0.081
University Home	-0.633	0.344	-0.052
Vocational Training Home	0.608*	0.298	0.071
No Degree Home	0.410	0.317	0.040
Work Home	0.001	0.190	0.0001
Father Elementary	0.228	0.195	0.024
Father Secondary	0.200	0.246	0.022
Father High	-0.084	0.222	-0.008
Father Craft	-0.195	0.254	-0.019
Father lower white-collar	0.315	0.243	0.035
Father upper white-collar	0.551*	0.258	0.066
Father farmer	-0.152	0.313	-0.015
Father Self-employed	0.034	0.248	0.004
Father Professional	0.044	0.344	0.005
Father other	0.208	0.276	0.023
Average City Home	-0.354*	0.169	-0.035
Small City Home	-0.701*	0.300	-0.059
Average City Denmark	0.093	0.274	0.010
Small City Denmark	0.396	0.444	0.047
Religion	-0.502*	0.191	-0.058
Born in Denmark	0.345	0.358	0.039
From former Yugoslavia	0.609	0.418	0.072
Polish	1.528*	0.384	0.242
Iranian	1.706*	0.407	0.289
Lebanese	0.119	0.516	0.013
Danish citizen	1.593*	0.297	0.179
Male	-0.068	0.142	-0.007
Intercept	-3.434*	0.768	
Log likelihood function		-720.4	
χ^2		218.0	
Number of Observations		1866	

Note: * denotes 5 percent significance level in a 2-tailed test.

The Educational Background and Human Capital Attainment of Immigrants 113

Likewise, the effect of religion is negative. Evidently, religiosity lowers the chances of immigrants pursuing a training that could help them professionally. With regard to ethnicity, we find that immigrants from Iran and Poland consistently do better than Turks. Being Iranian or Polish increases the possibility of having finished vocational training in Denmark in relation to being Turkish, while people from the former Yugoslavia and Lebanese do not significantly differ from Turks. Being a Danish citizen increases the chances of finishing vocational training by 17.9 percentage points, while gender does not have a significant effect on finishing vocational training.

(b) Immigrants in Germany

In Table 3.13 we present the results for the vocational training choice for the German immigrants. In sharp contrast to the results for Denmark, but similar to the results for the levels of schooling in Germany, we find that age at entrance decreases the chances of finishing vocational training, and at an increasing rate, while years since migration increases the chances of finishing vocational training at a decreasing rate. Both those immigrants with pre-migration upper secondary schooling and those with no school qualification are more likely to finish vocational training, compared to those with lower/primary schooling. Evidently, both the persistence and the seizing the opportunity hypotheses are operating in the German case. Something about the vocational training in Germany operates in a favorable way for immigrants. The father's education and profession play a positive role only when the father has a high school diploma and a lower white-collar job. This result confirms a powerful intergenerational dynamic for immigrants in Germany.

Second generation immigrants who were born in Germany are, once again, less likely to finish vocational training, while those who have been naturalized are more likely to do so. Still, we find significant ethnic differences. Polish immigrants are now more likely than Turks to finish vocational training in Germany, while Lebanese immigrants are still less likely to finish vocational training than Turks. In this analysis we also consistently find that male immigrants have a higher probability of finishing vocational training than females.

To sum up, in this section we investigated the determinants of post-migration investment in schooling and vocational training in Denmark and Germany. Overall, our results show that there are notable differences between the two countries in post-migration human capital investment. Specifically, there are more differences in the choice between *Haupt-/Realschule* or *Folkeskole* and no schooling at all than between the choice of Gymnasium/university and no schooling at all. Within the first outcome, the differences between the two countries center upon the years since migration, no pre-migration schooling, family background, city size in Germany, born in Germany, and nationality. It is particularly interesting to find that those immigrants who have no schooling in the home country are more likely to finish

Table 3.13. Binomial logit results for the probabilities of finishing vocational training. Reference outcome is the probability of not having finished vocational training in Germany.

Variable	Probability of finishing vocational training in Germany		
	Coefficient	St. Error	Marginal Effects
Age at Entrance	-0.085*	0.020	-0.007
Age at Entrance^2	0.0008*	0.0004	0.0001
Years Since Migration	0.102*	0.016	0.009
Years Since Migration^2	-0.002*	0.0003	-0.0002
Disability	-0.166	0.135	-0.013
Upper Secondary Home	0.527*	0.154	0.049
University Home	-0.258	0.244	-0.020
Vocational Training Home	-0.303	0.159	-0.024
No Degree Home	0.493*	0.154	0.043
Work Home	-0.102	0.136	-0.009
Father Elementary	0.025	0.129	0.002
Father Secondary	0.244	0.148	0.022
Father High	0.376*	0.167	0.035
Father Craft	0.228	0.131	0.020
Father lower white-collar	0.436*	0.167	0.042
Father upper white-collar	0.341	0.180	0.032
Father farmer	-0.198	0.202	-0.016
Father Self-employed	0.163	0.166	0.014
Father Professional	-0.043	0.305	-0.004
Father other	0.040	0.214	0.003
Average City Home	0.068	0.134	0.006
Small City Home	0.175	0.153	0.015
Average City Germany	-0.088	0.154	-0.007
Small City Germany	-0.173	0.314	-0.014
Religion	-0.137	0.119	-0.012
Born in Germany	-0.443*	0.199	-0.032
From former Yugoslavia	-0.152	0.147	-0.012
Polish	0.368*	0.152	0.034
Iranian	-0.081	0.179	-0.007
Lebanese	-0.378*	0.164	-0.029
German Citizen	0.414*	0.178	0.040
Male	0.279*	0.092	0.023
Intercept	-2.273*	0.398	
Log likelihood function		-1733.642	
χ^2		526.0184	
Number of Observations		5291	

Note: * denotes 5 percent significance level in a 2-tailed test.

school in Germany than they are to do so in Denmark. The intergenerational link is also stronger in the case of Germany than in Denmark, where the link exists only for the choice of Gymnasium/university. It is interesting that, in both countries, self-employed fathers have a significantly positive effect on their children's education. However, it is of concern that immigrants who are born in Germany and women have lower probabilities of finishing schooling in Germany.

With regard to vocational training, noteworthy differences exist with respect to age at entrance and years since migration. While in Denmark the probability of finishing vocational training is higher for those who are older when they arrive, the opposite is true for Germany. Moreover, a longer period of residence in Germany increases the likelihood of finishing vocational training, but this factor is not significant in Denmark. Immigrants with no school qualification from the home country are more likely to finish vocational training in Germany, but this characteristic is of no significant importance in Denmark. Average city size in the home country and religiosity are deterrents to vocational training education in Denmark but have no effect in Germany. Lastly, German-born second generation immigrants have a significantly lower probability of finishing vocational training. Overall, for both countries and both models, women fare significantly worse than men and Lebanese worse than Turks. All other nationalities fare better than the Turks. Both analytical models, for both countries, underscore the importance of religiosity as a negative determinant of educational attainment.

3.4 Summary and Conclusions

This chapter's goal was to provide a portrait of the post-migration human capital achievement of the same five groups of immigrants in Denmark and Germany. These groups share similar reasons for migration to Denmark/Germany. They arrived under the guest worker policy, under the family reunification policy, or as refugees. Reviewing the educational systems in Denmark and Germany, we saw that while there are similarities in their educational systems, there is a significant difference related to the schooling tracks in Germany. The analysis of raw data in Section 3.2.3 showed that immigrants in Denmark are less educated upon arrival, but they acquire more schooling once they are in Denmark, compared to immigrants in Germany. This could be related to a more intense and effectively applied integration policy in Denmark. Whether second generation immigrants fare better than the first generation is not possible to tell from the tables of Section 3.2. Obviously, with regard to host country primary and secondary schooling, they have narrowed the gap between them and the total population. With regard to finishing vocational training, more immigrants in Germany finish vocational training than in Denmark. This indicates that there is something in the German vocational system that attracts immigrants to it. As expected, we also found significant differences in the educational attainment among nationalities. Consistently, Poles and Iranians acquire more human capital in Denmark than other groups, while the Lebanese and the Turks rank the lowest. In Germany, the Iranians stand out for their high level of attainment, and the Turks are at the bottom.

In Section 3.3 we analyzed the levels of post-migration educational and professional attainment for immigrants in Germany and Denmark. We experimented with both a multinomial (for the choice of educational levels of schooling) and binomial (for the choice of vocational training) logit. The empirical results for Denmark are not very similar between the two models. The empirical results for Germany are qualitatively similar between the two models, and they are in line with other studies (Chiswick and Miller, 1994). Overall, our analysis of the educational levels in Denmark showed that younger, healthier males from Poland and Iran, or those who have acquired a Danish passport and have a more educated father, have higher probabilities of finishing *Folkeskole* or Gymnasium/university. Pre-migration work experience, religiosity, and small size city or non-urban area act as barriers to finishing schooling, however. For the choice of vocational training in Denmark, we found that the older immigrants with pre-migration education who have acquired a Danish passport and foreign nationals who come from Poland or Iran and whose fathers are upper white-collar employees have higher chances of finishing vocational training, irrespective of gender. Apparently the incentive structure in Denmark does not seem to encourage those with low skills to take advantage of the Danish educational system.

Our analysis of the educational levels in Germany indicated that those male immigrants who are healthier, who arrive in Germany at a younger age, who have lived in Germany for a long time, who have no pre-migration schooling and who have an educated father have a higher probability of completing *Haupt-/Realschule* or Gymnasium/university as opposed to the option of not going to school in Germany. Most importantly, our results show that there is intergenerational transmission of human capital. Still, the educational attainment of immigrants in Germany is dependent on gender and ethnicity. While German citizens have higher probabilities of finishing schooling in Germany, it is of concern that immigrants who are born in Germany have lower probabilities of finishing schooling in Germany. There are more ethnic differences in Germany than in Denmark. However, the Iranians consistently fare better than the Turks and the Lebanese fare worse than the Turks.

With regard to vocational training, we reached the same conclusions. Younger age at entrance, more years since migration, some or no pre-migration education, family background, and citizenship are all significant positive determinants for finishing vocational training. Ethnic differences show that the Poles have higher chances of finishing vocational training and the Lebanese lower, compared to Turks. Immigrant women and second generation immigrants born in Germany invariably have lower chances. Gender differences in the vocational training system in Germany may be the putative causes for the differences in career paths and the occupational sex segregation of women.

References

Alba, R. D., J. Handl, and W. Müller. 1994. "Ethnische Ungleichheit im Deutschen Bildungssystem," *Kölner Zeitschrift für Soziologie und Sozialpsychologie* 46, 209-237.

Becker, G.S. 1993. *Human Capital: A Theoretical and Empirical Analysis with Special Reference to Education*, 3rd Edition. Chicago: University of Chicago Press.

Borjas, G. 1982. "The Earnings of Male Hispanic Immigrants in the United States," *Industrial and Labor Relations Review* 35, 343-353.

Bundesanstalt für Arbeit. 2003. *Berufs- und Studienwahl*. Nürnberg. http://www.arbeitsamt.de/hst/services/bsw/information/index.html.

Chiswick, B.R. 1993. "The Skills and Economic Status of American Jewry: Trends over the last Half-century," *Journal of Labor Economics* 11 (1), 229-242.

Chiswick, B.R. 1978. "The Effect of Americanization on the Earnings of Foreign-Born Men," *Journal of Political Economy* 86 (5), 897-922.

Chiswick, B.R. and P. W. Miller. 1994. "The Determinants of Post-immigration Investments in Education," *Economics of Education Review* 13 (2), 163-177.

Cobb-Clark, D., M.D. Connolly, and C. Worswick. 2001. "The Job Search and Education Investments of Immigrant Families," *IZA Discussion Paper* 290.

Cohen, Y., T. Zach, and B.R. Chiswick. 1997. "The Educational Attainment of Immigrants: Changes over Time," *Quarterly Review of Economic and Finance* 37 (Special Issue), 229-243.

Constant, A. and K.F. Zimmermann. 2003. "Occupational Choice across Generations," *Applied Economics Quarterly* 49 (4), 299-317.

CVUU (The Danish Centre for Assessment of Foreign Qualifications). 2003. *The Danish Education System*. Copenhagen. http://cvuu.uvm.dk/en/education/education.htm?menuid=5520.

Darnell, A. and D.E. Sherkat. 1997. "The Impact of Protestant Fundamentalism on Educational Attainment," *American Sociological Review* 62 (2), 306-315.

Gang, I. N. and K.F. Zimmermann. 2000. "Is Child like Parent? Educational Attainment and Ethnic Origin," *Journal of Human Resources* 35 (3), 550-569.

Haisken-DeNew, J., F. Buechel, and G.G. Wagner. 1997. "Assimilation and Other Determinants of School Attainment in Germany: Do Immigrant Children Perform as Well as Germans?" *Vierteljahrshefte zur Wirtschaftsforschung – Quarterly Journal of Economic Research (Special Issue)* 66 (1), 169-179.

Jakobsen, Vibeke and Nina Smith. 2003. "The Educational Attainment of the Children of Danish 'Guest Worker' Immigrants," *IZA Discussion Paper* 749.

Kao, G. and M. Tienda. 1995. "Optimism and Achievement: The Educational Performance of Immigrant Youth," *Social Science Quarterly* 76 (1), 1-19.

Khan, A. 1997. "Post-Migration Investment in Education by Immigrants in the United States," *Quarterly Review of Economics and Finance* 37 (Special Issue), 285-313.

Larsen, Claus. 2002. "Education and Danish Language Skills," *News from the Rockwool Foundation Research Unit* December 2002, 11-12.

Mincer, J. 1958. "Investment in Human Capital and Personal Income Distribution," *Journal of Political Economy* 56, 281-302.

Mørkeberg, Henrik. 2000. *Indvandrernes uddannelse*. Copenhagen: Statistics Denmark.

Riphahn, R. T. 2001. "Dissimilation? The Educational Attainment of Second-Generation Immigrants," *CEPR Discussion Paper* No. 2903.

Riphahn, R. T. 2002. "Residential Location and Youth Unemployment: The Economic Geography of School-to-work Transitions," *Journal of Population Economics* 15 (1), 115-135.

Riphahn, R. T. 2003. "Cohort Effects in the Educational Attainment of Second Generation Immigrants in Germany: An Analysis of Census Data," *Journal of Population Economics* 16 (4), 711-737.

Schaafsma, T. and A. Sweetman. 2001. "Immigrant Earnings: Age at Migration Matters," *Canadian Journal of Economics* 34 (4), 1066-1099.

Schultz, T. P. 1984. "The Schooling and Health of Children of US Immigrants and Natives," *Research in Population Economics* 5, 251-288.

Statistics Denmark. 2002. *Statistisk Årbog 2002*. Copenhagen.

Statistics Germany. 2002. *Statistisches Jahrbuch 2002 für die Bundesrepublik Deutschland*. Wiesbaden.

Statistics Germany. 2003. *Statistisches Jahrbuch 2003 für die Bundesrepublik Deutschland*. Wiesbaden.

White, M. T. and G. Kaufman. 1997. "Language Usage, Social Capital, and School Completion among Immigrants and Native-Born Ethnic Groups," *Social Science Quarterly* 78 (2), 385-398.

Chapter 4

Employment Trends for Immigrants and Natives

By Marie Louise Schultz-Nielsen and Amelie Constant

4.1 Introduction

This chapter provides an overview of the general employment trends in Germany and Denmark for both immigrants and natives. We look at some important dynamic aspects of the employment situation. More specifically we discuss changes in the labor market attachment of immigrants as measured by the employment rate, both as it interacts with the business cycles and with respect to its more structural trend. In this way, the chapter also sets the stage for the more disaggregated analysis to follow by providing numbers for the recent trends in one of the main aggregate measures of interest for integration in general, namely the employment rate.

Integration is more than employment. Yet in countries like Denmark and Germany, with large public sectors financed primarily through taxation of work income, employment is of central importance when it comes to the integration of newcomers. The institutions behind social and labor market insurance, pensions, health, education, and other public services were set up simultaneously with the formation of our work and employment traditions. The resulting division of labor between family, the market place, civil institutions (e.g. the church), and the public sector is thus a complex social situation which has developed over time. The amount of paid work relative to non-paid work that is done in society is an important piece of machinery in this social construction, and if a new generation, or a significant wave of new immigrants, introduce a very different pattern of work, other elements of the social construction will have to change as well. Fewer things can be financed by taxes on earned income, for instance, if the newcomers take up paid work less frequently than the indigenous population; this would mean less finance for public services, for example, which would have consequences for health care, education, children's care, care of the elderly, etc. which would again influence the trade-off between various family models (more or less extended families, one or two breadwinners, etc.). Thus, any drop in the average employment rate would have a domino effect, and many norms and institutions in society would have to change as well.

Hence, the higher the employment rate is for newcomers, the less need there is for reform, though that need might be great for other reasons – an aging population, for example, or a rigid labor market. Another advantage of high immigrant employment is that it provides an opportunity for immigrants to meet and interact with natives. Contacts at the workplace between natives and immigrants are very important for mutual understanding of the different cultures, and they mitigate the polarization of society which can otherwise occur, with all the problems and conflicts this may cause.

Before we take a closer look at the employment trends for immigrants in Denmark and Germany, we first summarize the current employment situation and also sketch the recent history of immigration to get an idea about the origin of its composition as it is today. Apart from using our main data source, the two new surveys RFMS-G and RFMS-D conducted specifically for this project, the present chapter will use data from Statistisches Bundesamt, Statistics Denmark, and Eurostat.

Finally, whenever we in this chapter use German data alone, or use German data in comparison with Danish data, then an immigrant or a foreigner is, if not explicitly stated otherwise, defined to be an individual with foreign citizenship living in the country in question. The individual may or may not have been born in the host country.

4.1.1 Immigrant Employment in Denmark and Germany

Immigrants make up some 8 percent of the German labor force (immigrant men 5 percent) and 4 percent of the Danish labor force (immigrant men 2 percent). These fractions have been increasing over recent decades and will increase further, as predicted in Chapter 2 of this volume. Thus, there are good reasons for studying the labor market for immigrants as a macro economic phenomenon; it is of a significant size and its importance is on the increase.

The focus of this chapter is on the employment rate and not the unemployment rate. This is because the latter approach overlooks possible hidden unemployment. It would, for instance, ignore the fact that a high rate of early retirement could indicate some involuntarily exclusion from the labor market. In Denmark, immigrants who receive cash benefits are not registered as unemployed if they are attending one of the government's language courses or other government training programs. In the following, we therefore consider employment among *everybody* of the working age, though where relevant, analyses based solely on persons in the labor force are also presented.

The main feature of employment among non-Western immigrants is that they are under-employed compared to natives in both Denmark and Germany. The main difference between the two countries is that immigrants in Denmark are more under-employed than immigrants in Germany. In Denmark the immigrant employment rate is 50 percent lower than the rate for natives, the rates being 38 and 76 percent respectively. This has to be compared to there being "only" 25 percent under-employment of immigrants in Germany, where the rates for immigrants and natives are 49 and 65 percent respectively. These contrasts are particularly striking because native Danes, both men and women, have a higher employment rate than native Germans. As we shall see below, there has not always been this big a difference between immigrant and native employment, in particular not in Germany.

There are some institutional issues to be aware of. There is no statutory minimum wage in Germany or Denmark. But the labor markets are characterized by the presence of strong trade unions with collective labor contracts covering some 69 percent of the market in Denmark and 92 percent in Germany (OECD, 1997). The German labor market is more regulated than the Danish one. In Germany it is expensive to fire employees, whereas Denmark is the cheapest of countries within OECD to lay off people in. Unemployment insurance benefits are somewhat higher in Denmark. For the core labor force and in the short term, German and Danish Unemployment Insurance (UI) replacement rates are about the same; but in the long term and for low-skilled workers, the replacement rate in Denmark is significantly higher than in Germany (see Hansen, 2002). So even though there is no statutory minimum wage, the social safety net in Denmark provides a higher effective wage floor.

4.1.2 Importing Manpower, Providing a Safe Haven, or …?

Immigration to North-Western Europe has both fluctuated in quantity and changed in characteristics several times since the Second World War. From the mid 1950s, when the migration aftermath of the war ended, both Germany and the Scandinavian countries (including Denmark) started to import labor – Germany first, and more intensively. This period of "manpower recruitment", as Schmidt and Zimmermann (1992) have termed it, ended only when the international economic crises began around 1973.[1]

The period was characterized as "manpower recruitment" because the increasing demand for labor resulting from the boom in these years was to a large extent met by importing guest workers. These were mostly younger unskilled men from Southern Europe (Italy, Spain, Portugal, and Greece), but subsequently also from countries such as Turkey, Morocco, Tunisia, and the former Yugoslavia. The population of foreigners in West Germany rose from 0.9 percent in 1955 to 6.4 percent in 1972 (Bauer et al., 2004). In 1972, Italians constituted the largest group of guest

---

1 For an excellent outline of the migration phases and labor market issues of the European migration see Zimmermann 1995.

workers in Germany, making up 30 percent of the foreigners, but return migration has since then been more intensive for immigrants from the (Southern) EU countries than for non-EU people like Yugoslavs and Turks (Constant and Massey, 2003). In Denmark, guest workers started arriving in significant numbers only at the end of the 1960s. These were also young men; they came mainly from Turkey, Yugoslavia, and Pakistan. In 1972 the share of foreigners in Denmark was still only 1.8 percent of the population.

After both Denmark and Germany stopped the recruiting of immigrants in 1973, the inflow of foreigners dropped as expected. This meant that the size of the foreign population increased relatively modestly up until 1988, at which point in Germany it constituted 7.3 percent of the population and in Denmark 2.7 percent. In the coming period the level and composition of the immigrant populations in both countries nevertheless still underwent changes, primarily due to family reunifications (which also included family creation), the inflow of new refugees, and a higher fertility among some of the immigrant groups. The result was that the proportion of immigrants from third countries[2], who in 1974 made up 57 percent of the foreign population in Germany, increased to 70 percent in 1988 and 73 percent in 2001. In Denmark the figures were 44 percent in 1974 and 59 percent in 1988, rising to 70 percent in 2001. So both Germany and Denmark have experienced a shift towards immigrants from third countries, but the shift happened earlier in Germany.

As shown in Bauer et al. (2004), the proportion of foreigners among all employed workers in Germany fell from 10.0 percent in 1974 to 7.6 percent in 1988. The immigrants in fact had a higher employment rate than Germans in the beginning of the period, when they largely consisted of guest workers, but around the mid-1980s immigrants and native Germans had roughly the same employment rates. In Denmark the only available data are participation rates from 1981 and onwards. These figures show that the participation rate of foreigners fell from 1981 to 1985, especially among people from the former Yugoslavia, Pakistan, and Turkey (Pedersen, 1999). But in the period before, Denmark had also experienced a structural shift from guest workers towards reunified families and refugees. It is, therefore, very likely that the decline in the participation rate for immigrants that can be detected from 1981 to 1985 actually started as early as the 1970s. Later we shall take a closer look at the employment rate in the period from 1985 to 2002.

The first wave of non-Western refugees came to Denmark primarily from Eastern Europe during the years after the end of the Second World War. Poles started applying for asylum from the 1960s onward, while Hungarians started to come after the

---

2 Third countries are almost equivalent to non-Western countries, since they include all countries except the EU, North America and the Nordic countries, cf. also Table 2.3 in chapter 2.

1956 uprising, and Czechs in 1968, (Pedersen, 1999). This situation changed around 1980, when refugees from further afield started finding their way to Denmark. The 1973 ban on immigration did not apply to refugees. Before 1980 Denmark received only a relatively modest number of refugees; besides those from Eastern Europe, these refugees came from countries such as Chile and Uganda. Then around 1980 the origin of refugees shifted to primarily countries outside Europe, such as Iran, Iraq, Sri Lanka, Palestine, the former Yugoslavia and Somalia. The first to come were the Vietnamese, followed in short order by Iranians, Iraqis, Sri-Lankans, and stateless persons (especially Palestinians, but also Lebanese and Kurds).

In Germany, the right to asylum as it existed up to mid-1993 was included in the constitution, and was worded very generously. This law became effectively an instrument for allowing uncontrolled migration to Germany, with serious economic repercussions. The Asylum Procedure Act was comprehensively amended in 1987, 1988, 1990, and 1991. In June 1993 the Act to Amend the Basic Law took effect to prevent foreigners from abusing the law. Naturally, the number of foreigners began to decrease thereafter. In 1999 the main countries of refugee origin were the former Yugoslavia, Turkey, Iraq, Afghanistan, and Iran.

The background for the present composition of the immigrant populations is that the number of non-Western immigrants in both Denmark and Germany has increased dramatically over the last 30 years, while the number of Western immigrants has remained fairly constant. Coleman (1999) suggests that the relatively stable and identical economic, demographic, and political development in Western countries during the period is the reason for this. But this can also be explained by the fact that non-Western immigrants have displayed much less of a tendency to re-emigrate than Western immigrants, many of whom are living abroad for education and not with plans for permanent migration.

4.2 Employment Trends for Immigrants and Natives

In order to be able to separate and evaluate both the structural trends and the business cycle components of employment in the two countries, we examine employment data from the mid-1980s to the present. This period is of considerable interest, due to the high inflow of immigrants to both Denmark and Germany.

Figure 4.1 shows the development in the employment rates over time for natives and immigrants from non-Western countries in both Denmark and Germany.

The German figures are from Eurostat's Labour Force Survey, collected as part of the German Microcensus.[3] In the period 1985-90, the figures are for West

---

3 The German Microcensus is an annual interview survey of 1 percent of the population of Germany.

Figure 4.1. Employment rates for nationals and non-nationals from non-Western countries in the 16-66 age group in Denmark and Germany.

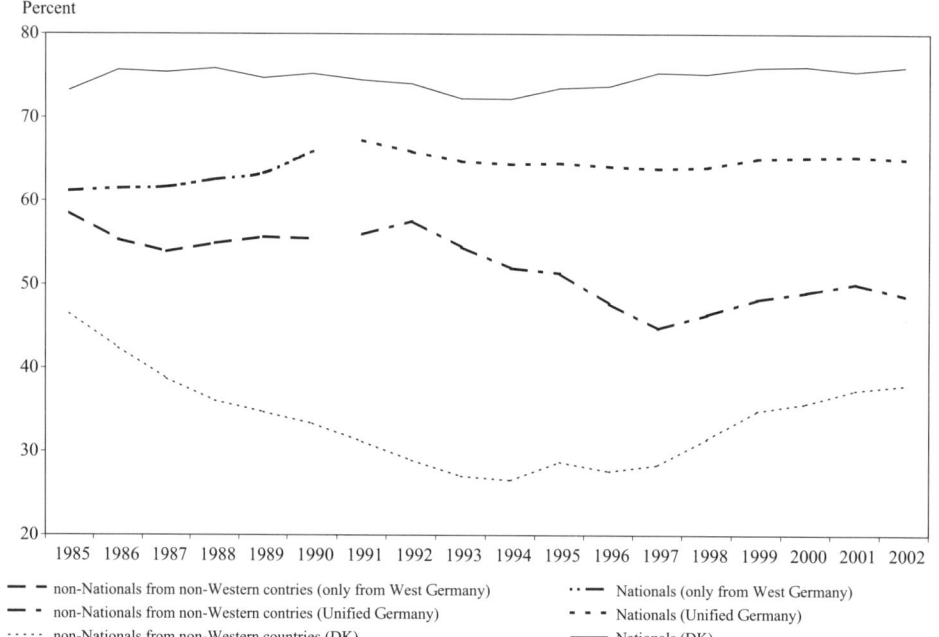

Source: Eurostat (special data inquiry) and own calculations, based on register data from Statistics Denmark.

Germany only, and for the reunited Germany thereafter. The figures for Danish citizens also come from Eurostat's Labour Force Survey, while the figures for foreign citizens in Denmark are a total count from Statistics Denmark's registers.[4] The Eurostat survey simply included too few citizens of non-Western countries living in Denmark to be usable. We are confident about mixing these two

---

4 In practice, the employment rate is calculated as the participation rate times one minus the average unemployment rate. The participation rate is based on official labor force statistics in November of the previous year, while unemployment figures are based on the present year's average unemployment rate in CRAM (Central Register for Labor Market Statistics). Both figures are based on Statistics Denmark's calculation methods. It should be noted, however, that the figures for the labor force can be slightly underestimated, to the extent that attachment to the labor market among immigrants improves with length of residence and economic conditions in general have a positive effect on the size of the labor force. The former will not apply to Danes, of course, since there is no comparable influx of new persons to this group. But in recent years, the employment rate for immigrants would have been 3 percentage points higher if figures for the labor force had been based on data for one year later. That newer data is not used because it would break with the traditional calculation method of Statistics Denmark and that information for part of the population would be lacking.

Figure 4.2. General unemployment rates in Germany and Denmark.

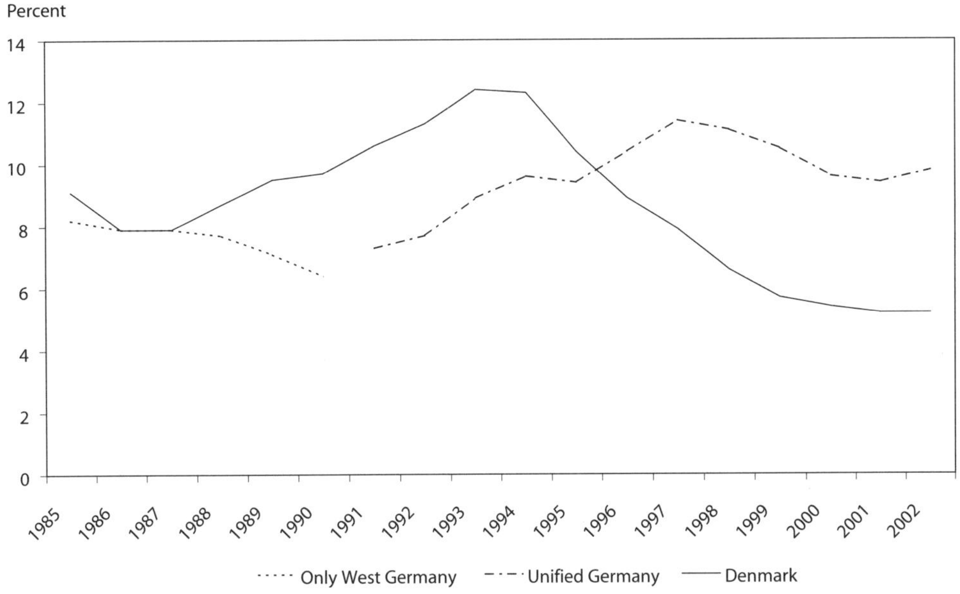

····· Only West Germany   –·– Unified Germany   —— Denmark

Source: Germany: Statistisches Bundesamt, Denmark: Statistics Denmark.

independent data sources, as their results coincide almost entirely with respect to the employment rate for Danish citizens.

As Figure 4.1 shows, there are both important similarities and differences in the recent employment history of natives and immigrants in Denmark and Germany. Immigrants are under-employed compared to natives. But the differences between the employment rates of natives and immigrants have increased over time in both Denmark and Germany. The employment rate has increased a little for natives, while it has fallen for immigrants in both countries. In Germany, however, the under-employment of immigrants is much less than in Denmark, and we need only to go back to the mid-1980s to find no under-employment of immigrants in Germany. Recently, the employment rates for foreigners have increased somewhat, first in Denmark and then also in Germany.

Apart from the decline in employment in both countries, one can also observe a similar pattern of high sensitivity of immigrants' employment to general economic conditions as represented, for instance, by the overall unemployment rate of the economy. As it can be seen in Figure 4.2, the general Danish unemployment rate increased rapidly until 1993-94 and then dropped even faster afterwards to a level of around 5 percent in 2001. This trend is matched by decreasing employment of immigrants until 1994 and increasing employment throughout the rest of the period. The upswing in immigrant employment is rather modest compared to the previous fall, and thus, in total, there is an overall drop in the immigrant employment rate from 47 percent in 1985 to 38 percent in 2002. The employment rate of native Danes exhibits the same variations qualitatively, but the movements are much smaller and the trend is slightly upwards.

The general picture is the same for Germany: the employment of immigrants is more sensitive to the business cycle than the employment of natives. Overall, unemployment decreased in (West) Germany until 1991-92, increased until 1997, and then dropped to a little more than 9 percent in 2001. Apart from a fall in employment between 1985 and 1987, the employment rate of immigrants follows the trend in the overall employment opportunities as measured by the aggregate unemployment rate. Immigrant employment increased until 1992, then fell until 1997, and finally increased in the period up until 2001. It even fell a little between 2001 and 2002, when unemployment in Germany also increased. Over the period as a whole the employment rate of immigrants from non-Western countries fell from 59 percent in 1985 to 49 percent in 2002. The business cycle variations in the employment rate for native Germans are scarcely visible, but the trend is slightly upward, as it was for the native Danes.

Hence, the overall picture is that immigrants are under-employed compared to natives and that the gap is widening over time, as immigrant employment is falling; that immigrant employment is more sensitive to the business cycle than native employment; and that immigrants are more often employed in Germany than in Denmark. What are the determining factors behind this picture? These will be discussed in the following sections. There are, of course, a number of potential explanations: institutional differences, differences in employee characteristics, the macro-economic performance, etc.

4.2.1 Why are Immigrants more often Employed in Germany than in Denmark?

There are basically two possible explanations: either the Danish immigrants are harder to employ, or Denmark is simply not as efficient as Germany at employing immigrants, assuming that both countries have the same goal of attaining high immigrant employment. Below, we will first compare the composition of the immigrant populations in both countries. We then discuss the social safety net and other possible explanations as to why immigrants are less integrated into the labor market in Denmark.

The Composition of the Immigrant Population and the Differences in Employment Patterns
The compositions of the foreign populations in Denmark and Germany with respect to country of origin are depicted in Table 4.1. We will examine some of the largest groups of immigrants from non-Western countries in both Germany and Denmark.

Turks constitute 37 percent of the non-Western immigrants in Germany and are by far the largest group of immigrants in Germany, followed by immigrants from

Table 4.1. The composition of the immigrant population. Percentages of all non-Western immigrants.

	Germany (2002)	Denmark (2001)	
	Non-nationals	Non-nationals	All immigrants and descendants[1]
Former Yugoslavia	20	15	14
Iran	2	5	4
Lebanon	1	5	7
Poland	6	5	4
Turkey	37	13	17
All 5 nationalities	66	43	46
All 8 nationalities[2]	–	57	61
No. of Observations	5,216,228	226,621	308,588

Notes: 1) An immigrant is defined as a person born abroad to parents who are both either foreign citizens or born abroad, while descendants are persons born in Denmark to parents neither of whom are both Danish citizens and born in Denmark. 2) Includes the five nationalities mentioned above plus Pakistan, Somalia and Vietnam.

Source: Germany: Statistisches Bundesamt, Denmark: Statistics Denmark.

the former Yugoslavia and Poland, while Iranians and Lebanese are rather small groups. Together these groups constitute 66 percent of the non-nationals from non-Western countries. In Denmark, the biggest groups are Turks and people from the former Yugoslavia, though the Turkish group is smaller in Denmark than the one in Germany. Other immigrant groups – from Iran and Lebanon, but also from Pakistan, Somalia, and Vietnam – are large in Denmark. These groups constitute 57-61 percent of the non-Western immigrants in Denmark, depending on whether one considers the non-nationals only or all immigrants and descendants (including those with Danish citizenship).

These differences between Denmark and Germany in the composition of the immigrant populations may or may not be important with respect to employment. What matters is whether the different groups also take up employment at different rates. This is revealed in Table 4.2, where the employment rates for Germany and Denmark are shown for the main groups of foreigners in the two countries.

As can be seen from Table 4.2, the German immigrants have an average employment rate of 54 percent, which is slightly above the level for all foreign citizens from non-Western countries appearing in Figure 4.1. The difference can primarily be attributed to differences between the countries and (partly) age, since the employment measures used in our two immigrant surveys, RFMS-G and RFMS-D, are closely related to the employment definition in the Eurostat Labour Force Survey.

It is striking how much the employment rate varies by nationality, with Polish

Table 4.2. Employment rates for immigrants by country of origin. Percent.

	Germany (2002)	Denmark (2001)	
	Non-nationals	Non-nationals	All immigrants and descendants[1]
Former Yugoslavia	53	47	51
Iran	57	37	53
Lebanon	34	20	32
Poland	64	56	64
Turkey	52	50	54
All 5 nationalities[2]	54	46	51
All 8 nationalities[3]	-	43	50
No. of Observations	5,453	1,721	3,200

Notes: 1) An immigrant is defined as a person born abroad to parents who are both either foreign citizens or born abroad, while descendants are persons born in Denmark to parents neither of whom are both Danish citizens and born in Denmark. 2) Weighted according to the actual size of the relevant immigrant groups in Germany and Denmark respectively. 3) Includes the five nationalities mentioned above plus Pakistan, Somalia and Vietnam. Weighted according to the actual size of the relevant immigrant groups in Denmark.

Source: RFMS-G and RFMS-D. All respondents 16-65 years old.

immigrants ranking the highest and the Lebanese immigrants ranking the lowest – in both Denmark and Germany.

Our survey for Denmark (RFMS-D) includes interviews with both immigrants and descendants from all eight nationalities. For this entire group the employment rate was 50 percent in 2001[5] – some 7 percentage points higher than for the foreign citizens alone. It is not possible to calculate the number of immigrants and descendants in Germany. As mentioned in chapter 2 of this book, the proportion of naturalized immigrants can be expected to be lower in Germany than in Denmark and, consequently, one would expect a smaller dispersion in the employment measures for foreign citizens and all immigrants in Germany than in Denmark. One would also expect the employment rate in Germany to be higher for the whole group of immigrants and descendants than among the non-nationals alone, as we see for Denmark. However, since the level of employment for non-nationals in Germany is generally also above that for all immigrants and descendants in Denmark, this merely underlines the fact that immigrants seem to be better integrated into the German labor market than into the Danish – irrespective of the choice of definition used for measurement.

---

5 The average employment rate for all non-Western immigrants and descendants in Denmark, not just the 8 countries included in RFMS-D, was 46 in 2001.

If we ignore the differences in the level, then there are some similarities between the employment figures for the same immigrant groups in the two countries. Poles have the highest employment rate in both countries, while persons from Lebanon have the lowest. People from Iran, Turkey and the former Yugoslavia are in between. Among these, Turks are the most frequently employed group in Denmark, while in Germany it is the Iranians.[6]

Thus, population composition differences could explain some of the weak labor market performance of immigrants in Denmark. However, Table 4.2 suggests that integration generally fails in Denmark in comparison to Germany: the employment rates are higher in Germany than in Denmark for all the immigrant groups, even though the employment rate for Danes is higher than the rate for Germans.

Another relevant difference between Denmark and Germany is the employment rate for women. One might expect that immigrant women would have a relatively weaker employment record in Germany, in line with the low employment rates for German women, and a stronger record in Denmark, in line with the higher employment rate of Danish women. As can be seen from Table 4.3, these expectations clearly do not hold. This issue will be discussed below in more detail. For a thorough discussion of the differences in labor market attachment and wages among German women and guest worker women see Constant (1998) and Dustmann and Schmidt (2000).

Table 4.3 first shows that, as expected, the employment rate for German women (60 percent) is lower than that for Danish women (72 percent). It is somewhat surprising that this is also the case for men, although at a considerably lesser difference of 8 percentage points. However, an age-distributed employment rate for men (not shown here) shows that the employment rate for men is lower especially among the younger and the older age groups, while it is higher (90 percent) for the core labor force between 25 and 49, both in Germany and Denmark (Eurostat, 2001). One obvious explanation for the older group is the earlier retirement in Germany, which is encouraged by the rather generous early retirement incentive schemes existing for the past decade.

These findings may lead us to expect that there would also be relatively more women in employment among foreigners in Denmark than in Germany. Yet the reverse is true, at least for the immigrants from the five countries considered. Thus, while 45 percent of the women and 62 percent of the men in Germany are employed, the proportions for Denmark are 37 and 57 percent respectively. In Denmark, employment among immigrant males is 1.5 times higher than for women, while the corresponding figure for Germany is less than 1.4. So one can say with certainty that the integration of women has not been better in Denmark than in

---

6 It is not surprising that it is the Poles who do relatively well considering that, as mentioned in the introduction to the chapter, they are a group that have been in Western Europe a long time, they have a reasonably good educational background, and they are otherwise culturally close to the host countries. How important such factors are for the probability of being in employment will be examined in the following chapter.

Table 4.3. Employment rates by gender and citizenship. Percent.

	Germany (2002)		Denmark (2001)	
	Nationals[1]	Non-nationals[2]	Nationals	Non-nationals[2]
Men	73	62	81	57
Women	60	45	72	37
All	67	54	76	46
No. of Observations	201,878	5,453	10,200	1,172

Notes: 1) The numbers for nationals in Germany are from 2001. 2) The figures for Non-nationals refer to immigrants from the five countries of origin in the survey.

Source: Nationals in Germany and Denmark: Eurostat Labour Force Survey 2001. Non-Nationals: RFMS-G and RFMS-D. All respondents 16-65 years old.

Germany – contrary to expectations. Part of the Danish integration problem, thus, seems to be the lack of success in getting women into the labor market. It is fair to say that there are no signs of assimilation in this respect, in Denmark.

Labor Market Institutions, Attitudes, and Self-selection
Attitudes and motivations are not observable to us, at least not in our data set. We cannot rule out the possibility that immigrants are self-selected, and that those motivated to work choose Germany, while the others decide more often to migrate to Denmark. Another question concerns the difficulty of integrating into the culture of the respective labor markets: is it more difficult to be a foreigner in the Danish labor market than in the German? Are the employment barriers higher in Denmark? These are interesting questions, but they are difficult to investigate with our data.

It is, nevertheless, important to describe the relevant labor market institutions in both countries and the way they work to facilitate the employment integration of immigrants. The work incentives for the unskilled in Denmark are considerably weaker than in Germany. In fact, the net compensation rate for a significant proportion of unskilled labor in Denmark is close to 100 percent.[7] This weakens the motivation to work, because the high benefits effectively become a high wage floor. There are simply no jobs in Denmark that pay wages as low as the initial qualifications of many immigrants would require, at least not in the formal sector.

Because individuals with no work experience whatsoever still receive high benefits in Denmark, it can be expected that the incentive problem will be much larger in Denmark than in Germany. This, of course, does not rule out other explanations

---

[7] More detailed analysis of this issue is provided in Chapter 5 of this book.

as to why immigrant employment is lower in Denmark; explanations such as the organization of the integration process, discrimination, and self-selection. It simply suggests that weak work incentives are a deterrent to immigrant employment – both directly and indirectly.

4.2.2 Why has Immigrant Employment Fallen over Time?

The recent history of immigration to Denmark and Germany began with significant waves of guest workers arriving with the sole purpose of taking jobs in their new country. When this pattern changed in 1973, a period of family unification followed. Spouses, children, and parents of the guest workers arrived. A decade later refugees from non-Western countries came in increasing numbers. It is not surprising that family reunification, when it was the main purpose of moving to Germany or Denmark, did not foster the labor market integration of immigrants. Thus, in a historical comparison one would initially expect a high employment rate, with a falling trend over time. Actually, immigrants had a very high employment rate initially in the early period of the guest-worker regime; in Germany the rate was even higher for immigrants than for natives. The rate declined thereafter until it reached a lower level that accounted for the families of the immigrants and the general conditions in the labor markets of the receiving countries. These conditions include skill compatibility, minimum wages, discrimination, etc.

The falling employment trend seems to represent an "immigrant adjustment effect" in the transition from a guest-worker regime to a regime with more non-employment immigration. This adjustment, however, will be disguised by a change in the structure of the immigrant flow, the "population composition effect". If the characteristics of the immigrants change over time, this is likely to affect the employment rates. To understand the different impacts of the adjustment effect and the composition effect it is useful to investigate the employment experience on the basis of years since immigration for different immigration cohorts. To study all immigrants, even if they change citizenship, we again include all immigrants and descendants in Denmark, with and without foreign citizenship. We then separate the effects of changes in the characteristics of immigrants and the falling trend in employment. The following section pertains to the Danish case only as there are no similar data available for Germany.

Cohort and Composition Effects
The integration of immigrants into the host country's labor market was the topic of a now classical discussion between Chiswick (1978) and Borjas (1985). According to this literature, the empirical studies on cross-sectional data in the US generally show a higher degree of earnings assimilation over time than those examining also the cohort effects.

Figure 4.3 shows the participation rate for non-Western men by year of arrival in

Denmark and thus decomposes the total changes in participation into a time effect and a cohort effect. The results of similar calculations for non-Western women are also discussed below. We study the participation rates rather than the employment rates, because the latter are highly sensitive to economic fluctuations.

In Figure 4.3 we use data for the period 1985-2002 for all individuals who were between 16 and 66 years in the year in question. For those immigrants who arrived in the period from 1973-75, we have calculated the participation rates for the 10th to the 29th years after arrival in Denmark. Similar calculations have been carried out for those who arrived from 1978-80 for the 5th to the 24th years after arrival, etc. People who arrived before 1973 are not included in this calculation, because the date of entry was not systematically recorded before 1973.

As can be seen from Figure 4.3, those non-Western men who arrived in the period 1973-75 have a high, albeit slightly declining, participation rate from the 10th to the 29th years of residence. This fall may be age-determined, as the average age in the 16-66 age group rose from 33 years at the beginning of the period to 45 years at the end.

Men who arrived in 1978-80 also have a high participation rate. However, if we allow for the duration of residence, the participation rate for the same length of residence is generally slightly lower than for immigrants who arrived 3-7 years earlier in the period 1973-75. This could be the immigration adjustment effect, which was then relatively small.

The participation rates for non-Western male immigrants who came to Denmark between 1983 and 1985 differ significantly from those of earlier arrivals. While non-Western men who arrived between 1978 and 1980 had a high participation rate only five years after arrival, those who came between 1983 and 1985 needed considerably more time to integrate into the labor market. Their participation rate had only reached about 70 percent after nine years in Denmark, although after the 15th year it was only slightly lower than among those who arrived in 1978-80.

The same pattern applies more or less to non-Western men who arrived between 1988 and 1990. For those years it has been possible to obtain data for 13 years after arrival. The participation rate of this group was even lower than for men who arrived in 1978-80. Note that the years of arrival 1996-98 follow directly after those of the earlier group 1993-95; there is no three-year gap, as there was between the earlier cohorts. The fact that the observations for both cohorts are so close to each other makes it harder to determine whether there has been a shift in the participation rate in between the two cohorts.[8]

A decreasing level that fades out from the 1983-85 arrivals to the 1996-98 arrivals could be assumed to be the adjustment effect. However, the effect is small relative to

---

8 We have, nonetheless, chosen to include recent arrivals, because it is only by doing so that one can see the extent to which attempts to improve the integration of immigrants into the labor market have succeeded. This has been a controversial issue in the Danish debate in recent years, not least after the introduction of the Integration Act in January 1999, the aim of which was precisely to improve immigrants' integration into the labor market.

Figure 4.3. Participation rates for 16 to 66-year-old men from non-Western countries, by time of arrival and length of residence.

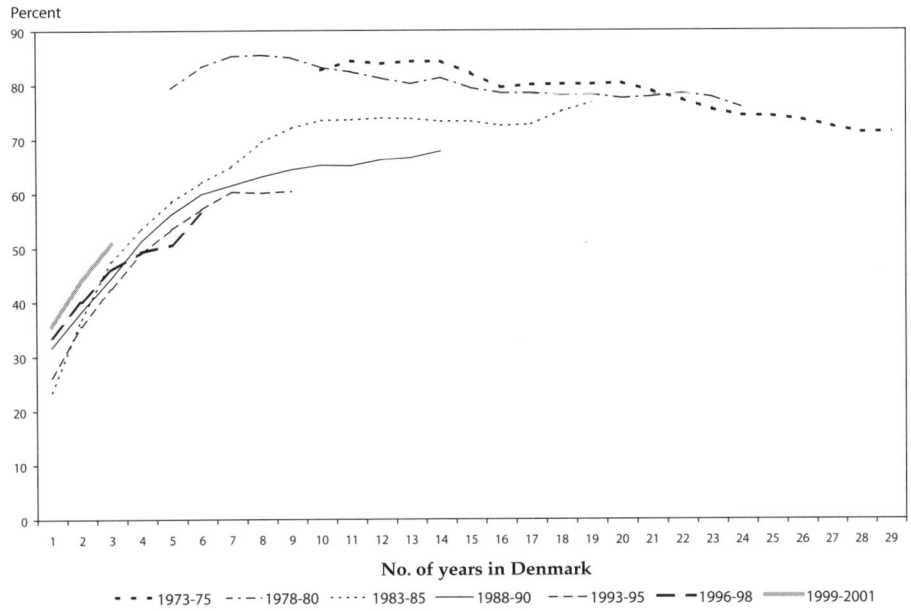

Source: Own calculations based on register data from Statistics Denmark.

the trend break for immigrant men between the 1978-80 and the 1983-85 cohorts, and again with the latest arrivals.[9] Before 1980 the inflow of non-Western immigrants consisted of family reunifications and a relatively modest number of refugees, primarily from Eastern Europe. But around that time there was a shift towards a larger number of refugees, especially in the period from 1984 to 1986, where many Iranians arrived. For a long time these refugees had a rather low labor market participation rate, and this partly explains the "trend break". At the same time the new cohorts of other immigrants had a lower participation rate than their countrymen arriving earlier. And this explains why the participation rate continued to fall even in periods where the number of refugees was smaller. A decomposition of the non-Western immigrants into immigrants from developed and less developed countries shows that the share of non-Western immigrants coming from less developed countries did not rise, but that the fall in the participation rate was considerably larger for this group.

Although it is still too early to conclude that the long run trend of decreasing participation rates for new arrivals has finally stopped, it is possible that the 1999-2001 arrivals mark a reversal of the trend. As can be seen from Figure 4.3, the newly

---

9 Among women from non-Western countries the participation rate is also higher for the immigrants who arrived earlier, but the falling participation rate from cohort to cohort is a more gradual transition, with less of a trend break in the beginning of the 1980's.

arrived men have a higher participation rate than those from previous years. Corresponding calculations for non-Western women show that the participation rate is highest for the women who came to Denmark the earliest, but generally lower for women than for men (Schultz-Nielsen, 2001).

The conclusion from the cohort analysis in Denmark is that both factors – the immigration adjustment effect and the changing composition effect – are likely to have contributed to the declining participation rates of immigrants. However, the changing composition seems to be the main contributoring factor.

It should be noted that a high participation rate does not imply a high employment rate. If a large proportion of the earliest arrivals to Denmark are more often unemployed, then the lower participation rate of the new arrivals is perhaps of less importance. This is not the case in general, as the unemployment rate for non-Western immigrants in the period 1985-87 is at a lower level than in 1997-98. But, as mentioned above, the long economic upswing in Denmark has also had a positive effect on unemployment among immigrants. Thus, in the last four years for which data is available, the unemployment rate for non-Western immigrants was lower than during the whole preceding period.

It is possible that the increased number of non-Western immigrants and the decreasing average level of education within the total group of immigrants have been contributing factors to the falling employment trend. However, the aggregate picture for Denmark does not support this view, as the over-representation of the less educated among the unemployed has been fairly constant over the last two decades. It seems that the relatively lower demand for unskilled labor has been accommodated partly by the general rise in the educational level and partly by the increasing number of people on income transfers other than unemployment compensation.

As the immigrants from non-Western countries are less educated than natives and the demand for unskilled labor in Denmark seems to be diminishing, we should expect to find a lower employment rate for foreigners over time. For this effect to occur there is no need that the absolute skill level of immigrants should decrease. If the relative skill level has fallen, this is likely to have contributed to a weaker employment performance. This said, the most crucial characteristic of non-Western immigrants' attachment to the labor market in Denmark is that, in the period 1985-97, the proportion of 16 to 66-year-olds in the labor force declined from 70 percent to 49 percent. Since then this figure has increased slightly, but the result of the long decline in the participation rate for non-Western immigrants is that the employment rate for Danes in 2002 was 1.7 times higher than that for non-Western immigrants. In 1985 this factor of over-employment was only 1.4.

The Immigrant Employment Trend in Sweden
The problem of declining employment also exists in other countries. The findings for Denmark are in line with the findings in Ekberg and Gustafsson (1995) on immigrants' relative earned income in Sweden according to length of residence and date

of entry. Their study shows that those immigrants who came to Sweden in 1968-70 had a relatively higher earned income after ten years' residence than those who came in 1973-75, who in turn had a relatively higher income than those who arrived in 1978-80 and later.

These findings were replicated by Ekberg and Hammarstedt (2002) under the title "20 years worsening integration of immigrants". The worsening situation in Sweden, especially from 1980 and onwards, is explained partly by the increasing importance of the service related functions in the Swedish economy, and by the increasing demands on immigrants for expertise in written Swedish and knowledge of social conditions. Another possible explanation is the increased inflow of immigrants from other countries of origin, whose educational systems are less compatible with the Swedish one. Finally, there are also the possible weaknesses in the Swedish integration policy in the 1990s: an example of a weak integration measure was the distribution of refugees throughout the country, which was determined more by the housing situation than by the employment situation.

The first two explanations, which are of a more structural nature, could also apply to Denmark, Germany, and other Western European countries. A trend in favor of jobs that require special training and country-specific knowledge must be expected to generate a competitive pressure on non-Western migrants. This is of particular importance for a very small language area, such as Denmark, where immigrants cannot be expected to know the language before they arrive in the country.

4.2.3 Why is Immigrant Employment so Sensitive to the Business Cycle?

Initially, there could be some doubt that immigrant employment is in fact highly sensitive to business cycle fluctuations. First, the variations in employment could again be due to a changing population composition with respect to immigrants' characteristics such as age, education, country of origin, etc. But the fact that immigrant employment correlates well, and negatively, with the trend in overall unemployment in both countries suggests some support for our conjecture. We do have the opportunity to control for the age composition in Denmark. We can compute employment rates by age groups for the immigrants and then weight the age groups according to the age composition in the native population. This reveals that the change in age distribution cannot explain the sharp fall in employment among non-Western immigrants from 1985 to 1994 nor the subsequent rise until 2002.

Second, congestion in immigrant entries, related to the speed of the inflow of immigrants, could generate variations in aggregate employment. It is difficult to assess precisely how much of the employment fluctuation was due to the inflow of new immigrants. But the huge inflow of refugees around 1991 in particular must have had a negative impact on employment, as newcomers must be expected to exhibit a lower employment rate than immigrants who have been in the country for a while. Furthermore, some of the improvements after 1998 could also be due to the decline in the number of immigrants. But again, this is not sufficient to explain the overall co-variation with the business cycle.

To illustrate further how sensitive the immigrants' employment situation is to economic fluctuations we will quote some unemployment figures from Statistics Denmark. Unemployment increased in Denmark between 1986 and 1994 from 8 to 12 percent, but for immigrants the increase was from 24 to 41 percent. In 2002 the overall unemployment rate was at a low 5 percent level, while immigrant unemployment was down to 14 percent. Thus, the fluctuations in unemployment are also larger for immigrants than for Danes, a fact which underlines the higher business cycle sensitivity.

So either non-Western immigrants are employed in industries with a particularly fluctuating labor demand, or they are systematically being hired last and fired first.

As we will examine below in further detail, immigrant employment in Germany and Denmark is more concentrated in industries like manufacturing, and in Germany also construction, and less in the public sector and in finance. But we cannot rule out the other hypothesis that immigrants are at the end of the job queue compared to natives, which would also contribute to explaining the lower employment level. Is it really the case? And if so, is it because of discrimination, or because immigrants are less skilled? Research in this volume suggests that immigrants do indeed have considerably weaker labor market skills than natives in both Denmark and Germany, and also that the weaker qualifications in terms of experience, language, and education do contribute to higher unemployment risk. But so does ethnicity, and therefore we cannot rule out discrimination as an explanation.

4.3 German Unification

Above we discussed the employment rates of both natives and foreigners (from non-Western countries) in Germany in the period 1985-2001 (see Figure 4.1). The most conspicuous feature of this period remains the reunification of East and West Germany in 1990. In Figure 4.4 data from the Federal Statistical Office in Germany is used to decompose unemployment into its East and West components. These are simply employment rates by regions so that we can show employment in both the reunited Germany for the period 1991-2001 and for the former West Germany from 1985-2001. The numbers cover all foreigners and natives for the age group 14-66 (both years inclusive). As is clear from the figure, decomposing the employment for both Germans and foreigners into figures for all Germans and West Germans does not change the conclusion we reached in Section 4.2 that new immigrants to Germany have been employed steadily less and less over a period where the employment level has been rising for Germans.

Figure 4.4. Employment rates for nationals and non-nationals in the former West Germany and in Germany, 14 to 66-year-olds.

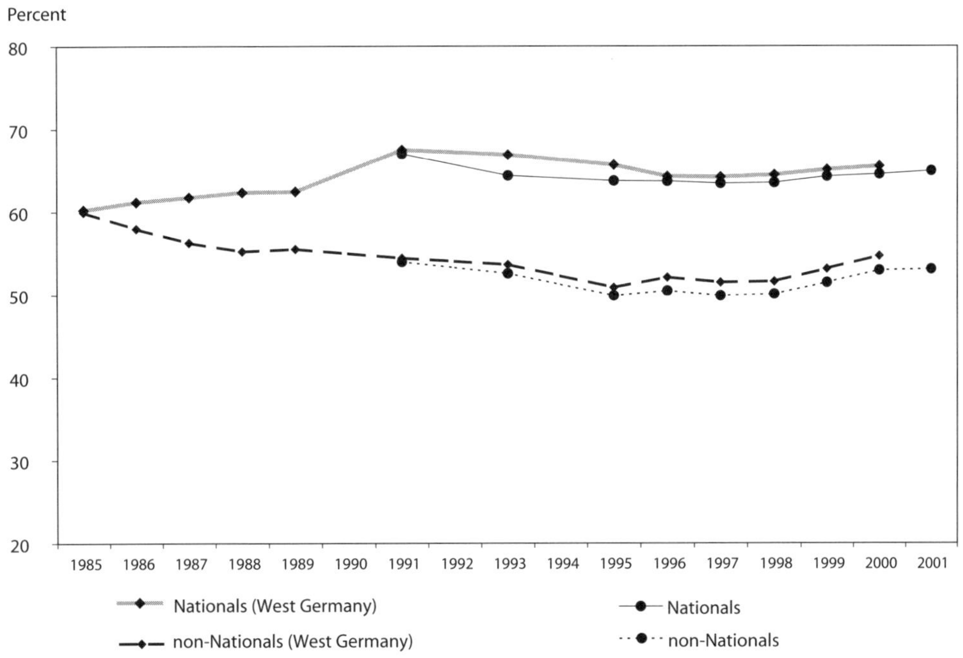

[Figure: Line graph showing employment rates (Percent, y-axis from 20 to 80) from 1985 to 2001. Four series: Nationals (West Germany), non-Nationals (West Germany), Nationals, non-Nationals. Nationals remain around 60-68%, while non-Nationals decline from ~60% in 1985 to around 50-55% in later years.]

Source: Statistisches Bundesamt, own calculations.

4.4 Long Run Integration: From First to Second Generation Immigrants

An obvious question to be asked is whether the employment problems of immigrants will reproduce themselves among second generation immigrants and maybe continue with the next generations to come. We investigate this by using a decomposition of newcomers into immigrants and descendants, where immigrants are the first generation, and descendants the second generation. Immigrants are defined as foreign-born to parents who are either foreign citizens or born abroad, while descendants are defined as persons born in the host country to parents neither of whom are Danish citizens or born in Denmark. In Figure 4.5 we show employment rates for Danes and for immigrants and descendants from both Western and non-Western countries according to this definition. The analysis is based on register data for all non-Western immigrants and descendants, a 25 percent sample of Western immigrants and descendants, and a 2 percent sample of Danes. These definitions of immigrants and descendants are often used in Nordic statistics, and differ from citizenship, which was used in the previous section. The main difference is that naturalized persons are also included in the immigrant population, though their children are not, if they were born in Denmark and have Danish citizenship. The employment picture for Danes is the same as the one we saw in Figure 4.1. That the rate is not much higher in 2002 than in 1987 is due to the fact that the participation rate is a little lower in 2002, namely 79 percent, compared to 81 percent in 1987.

The employment rate for Western immigrants more or less follows the same trend as that for Danes, albeit at a lower level. At the same time, the gap between Danes and Western immigrants' employment widened somewhat between 1985 and 2002, to 14 percentage points in 2002 against 10 in 1985. The employment rate for Western descendants is higher than for Western immigrants, but still lower than that for Danes.

The same pattern applies to non-Western descendants, although their employment rate has varied a lot more compared to all other groups. The excess variation can largely be attributed to a fall in the participation rate between 1987 and 1994 and a subsequent increase, combined with a particularly sharp drop in unemployment for non-Western descendants, which fell to 7 percent in 2002 from 19 percent in 1994.

The changes in the participation rate for non-Western descendants over time are to a large extent due to the fact that the average age of descendants has fallen, that the number of 16 to 20-year-old non-Western descendants rose strongly from the late 1980s onward, and that this young group has only started to enter the labor market in large numbers in recent years.

Thus, if we calculate the employment rate for immigrants and descendants as though they had the same age distribution as Danes, the trend in the employment rate for non-Western descendants will be more or less the same as for Western descendants, albeit at a slightly lower rate in the period 1989-94. Standardizing age does not markedly change the trend in the employment rate for the other groups, the Western descendants and the Western and non-Western immigrants.

The higher employment rate for descendants is probably due to the fact that they are linguistically and culturally closer to Denmark than first generation immigrants, many of whom came here as adults. The only problem with the calculation described above is that there are relatively few descendants over 30 years old, and this makes the calculation more uncertain than for immigrants.

Nevertheless, we find that the second generation non-Western immigrants do much better on the labor market than the first generation. Moreover, they seem to catch up to a large extent even with descendants from Western countries. Thus, employment integration makes progress, but the improvements seem to be more between generations than within generations. An important issue is therefore whether the descendants will in the future continue to marry new immigrants arriving from their home countries.[10] If not, the long-run consequences of immigration

---

10 A Danish calculation dating from 1998 showed that among young (18-25 years old) married non-nationals with more than 10 years' stay in Denmark, 80 percent of the men and 69 percent of the women were married to newly arrived immigrants, while only 12 and 20 percent were married to countrymen already living in Denmark. For both men and women, 2 percent were married to Danes, and around 6 percent to non-nationals from a country other than their own home country (Pedersen, 2000).

Figure 4.5. Employment rates for immigrants and descendants in the 16-66 age group (inclusive) from Western and non-Western countries.

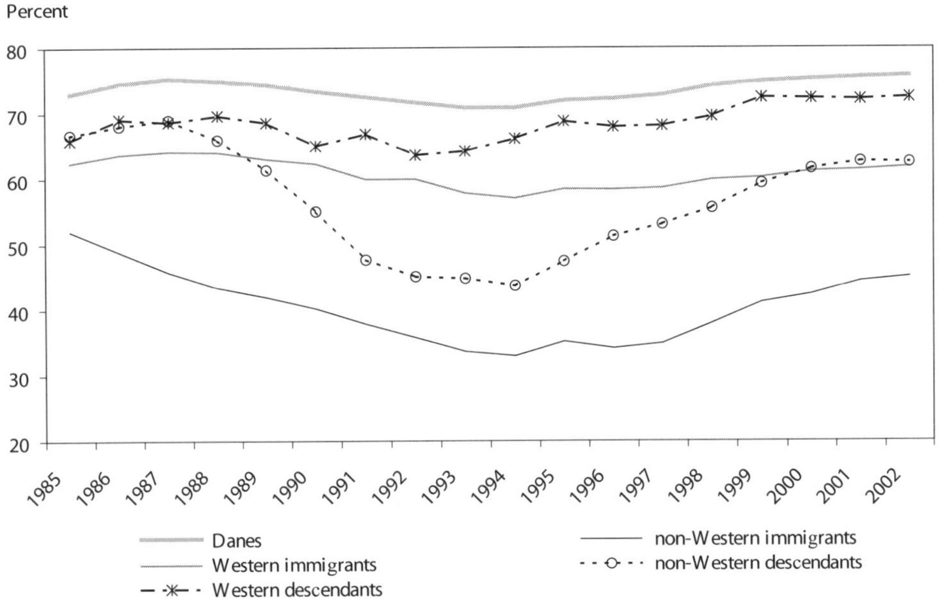

Source: Own calculations based on register data from Statistics Denmark.

might have more to do with earnings and thus with educational and occupational traditions than with employment *per se*.[11]

4.5 Occupational Sorting by Country of Origin

Although immigrants from non-Western countries have a weak attachment to the labor market in both Germany and Denmark, many do have jobs. In the following, we will take a brief look at the characteristics of the employed immigrants in Germany and Denmark. Table 4.4 shows the age distribution for natives in Germany and Denmark and for immigrants from the five countries of origin considered. Here, the numbers of the employed include both employees, the self-employed and spouses who assist the self-employed.

---

11 In general, the educational level (in both Germany and Denmark) is lower among the young generation from non-Western countries than among natives of the same age and those from Western countries. Furthermore, a recent study shows that even among the second generation from non-Western countries who receive a higher education in Denmark, the probability of using it is relatively low, especially for the young women (Jacobsen and Smith, 2003).

Employed immigrants clearly have a younger age profile than employed natives in both Denmark and Germany. This is the reason why immigration from less developed countries has often been seen as the solution to the European aging problem.

Until now, we have looked at whether people have jobs, but not at how many hours they work. Table 4.5 shows the average working hours per week for the four relevant population groups. The working hours are about the same, with Germans working one hour longer than Danes and natives working one hour longer than immigrants. The frequency of part-time work is more or less the same for Danes and Germans. The histories behind these pictures, however, are very different. The frequency of part-time work has been on the rise for the last 20 years in Germany, as more women have entered the labor market. In Denmark, in contrast, it has been falling, because the younger generation of women are increasingly opting for full-time employment, rather than the part-time jobs preferred by their mothers. Part-timers in Germany are often women; in Denmark they consist also of a relatively higher proportion of students – of both sexes (Hoffmann and Walwei, 2000). In Germany, 85 percent of the part-timers are women; in Denmark it is only 73 percent. Among the immigrants, the frequency of part-time work is higher than among natives in both Germany and Denmark.[12]

Another interesting aspect of employment is the distribution of workers by industry. If, for example, immigrants work particularly in cyclical industries, it would help to explain the relatively stronger fluctuations in employment among immigrants over the business cycle that we saw in Figure 4.2.

With few exceptions, the pattern of employment for both natives and immigrants is similar in the two countries (see Table 4.5). Significant differences are found, nevertheless between immigrants and natives within the two countries. For instance, around 30 percent of the immigrants in both countries work in the service industry, especially in cleaning, which is twice as high a proportion as for natives. There are also many immigrants employed in manufacturing. And there are substantially fewer immigrants working in public services, especially in Germany. One of the few country differences is that large numbers of immigrants work in construction in Germany, which is not the case in Denmark. Given the similarity in the structure of vocational training in the two countries (see Chapter 3), it is striking how few immigrants are employed in this industry in Denmark.

With regard to the business cycle sensitivity, Table 4.5 indicates a clear overrepresentation of immigrants in cyclical industries, which could explain some of the fluctuations in immigrant employment.

---

12 This should be interpreted with some caution with regard to non-nationals in Germany, however, because the survey only asked about typical working hours, and not whether respondents were in full-time or part-time jobs. In Germany, the number of hours in a full-time job can vary from 35 to 40 hours, depending on the labor contract. People typically work slightly longer hours in the former East Germany than in West Germany. In table 4.5, full-time work for non-nationals means a 37-hour working week. This is also the official working week in Denmark.

Table 4.4. Age distribution of employed 16- to 65-year-olds. Percent.

	Germany (2002)		Denmark (2001)	
	Nationals	Non-Nationals	Nationals	Non-Nationals
Age:				
16-19 years old	4	2	5	8
20-29 years old	16	28	20	25
30-49 years old	57	52	49	58
50-59 years old	19	15	22	8
60-65 years old	4	3	4	0
All	100	100	100	100
No. of Observations	133,639	2,840	7,557	564

Note: The figures for Non-nationals refer to immigrants from the five countries of origin in the survey.

Source: Nationals in Germany and Denmark: Eurostat Labour Force Survey 2001. Non-nationals: RFMS-G and RFMS-D.

Turning to the type of occupation, there are again clear similarities between immigrants in Germany and Denmark, and large differences between immigrants and natives. With respect to the distribution over the various occupations, immigrants and natives differ very significantly in both countries, and in the same manner. Immigrants are concentrated further down the job hierarchy than natives. They are, for instance, poorly represented among legislators and managers, professionals, technicians and clerical workers.

Immigrants are employed in service industries and manufacturing to a greater extent than nationals, and are less well represented in jobs in other industries, many of which require higher qualifications. Finally, both Germans and Danes are not very frequently self-employed, and here immigrants are not different from the natives.[13]

The future implications of this occupational profile of immigrants are somewhat disturbing. If immigrants are over represented in unskilled jobs, then in the future they will face unemployment or low wages, or even both to a greater extent than natives. This represents a substantial challenge to the German and Danish labor markets and societies in general.

---

13 As self-employment can vary a lot by nationality, the picture might look a little different if all immigrants are included. In Denmark the self-employed constituted 11 percent of all employed immigrants and descendants (including those with Danish citizenship) from non-Western countries in 2001 (Schultz-Nielsen, 2002).

Table 4.5. Proportions of 16- to 65-year-old persons in employment, by sector and occupation.

	Germany (2002)		Denmark (2001)	
	Nationals[1]	Non-nationals	Nationals	Non-nationals[2]
Working hours[3]:				
Full-time work	80	66	81	74
Part-time work	20	32	19	26
Not stated	0	2	0	0
Average hours worked	36.9	35.9	36.1	35.4
Industries:				
Agriculture, fishing and forestry	3	1	3	1
Extracting raw materials, energy and water supply	1	1	1	0
Manufacturing	23	26	18	28
Construction	8	9	7	2
Sales and repairs	14	15	14	11
Transport, post and communication	6	3	7	7
Financial intermediation etc.	4	1	3	1
Service industries	16	33	17	30
Public services	25	10	30	17
Not stated	0	1	0	4
All	100	100	100	100
Occupation[4]:				
Self-employed and assist. spouse	11	10	8	9
Legislators and managers	3	2	4	1
Professionals	11	3	13	5
Technicians	20	9	19	6
Clerical workers	13	6	11	3
Service and sales workers	11	13	15	16
Agriculture/fishery workers	1	1	1	1
Craft/related workers	15	20	10	10
Plant and machine operators	7	9	7	17
Elementary operators	7	28	11	32
Military forces	1	0	0	0
No answer	1	-	0	-
All	100	100	100	100
No. of Observations	133,639	2,840	7,557	564

Notes: 1) The number for nationals in Germany is from 2001. 2) The figures refer to immigrants from the five countries of origin in the survey. 3) For non-nationals, full-time work is defined as 37 hours a week or more. Nationals were asked directly whether they had full-time or part-time jobs. 4) Based on ISCO-88.

Source: Nationals in Germany and Denmark: Eurostat Labour Force Survey 2001. Non-nationals: RFMS-G and RFMS-D.

4.6 Summary and Conclusion

This chapter has discussed the labor market situation for immigrants, first from a more historical perspective, and then with a focus on the structural conditions which apply today.

There are a number of differences in the employment performance of immigrants in Germany and Denmark recorded over the past few decades, but there are even more similarities. An important common feature is the under-employment of immigrants in both countries: only 54 percent of immigrants from non-Western countries in the German survey were in employment, as opposed to 67 percent of the native Germans. In Denmark, 46 percent from the same non-Western countries were in employment, compared to 76 percent of the native Danes. Apart from showing the under-employment problem shared by Germany and Denmark, these figures demonstrate the main difference between the employment integration in the two countries: both in absolute and in relative terms, the employment rate is lower for non-Western foreigners in Denmark than it is in Germany. Employment of immigrants has simply been more successful in Germany. Explanations of this difference are likely to be found both in the different composition of the two immigrant populations with respect to education and work culture and in the difference in institutional settings. In particular, work incentives for newcomers without seniority in the host countries' labor markets have been much weaker in Denmark than in Germany. However, we cannot rule out other explanations such as differences in attitudes (e.g. discrimination) and in the way the integration is organized.

The fact that Germany is more successful than Denmark in employment participation does not indicate that the country does not have a problem with the low employment rates of immigrants. Germany has experienced a downward trend in employment rates since the mid-1980s, a phenomenon that can be traced back to the beginning of the 1970s.

This trend has a clear parallel in Denmark. In the case of Denmark, where we have cohort data, it seems that a very important contributing factor to the declining employment trend for non-Western immigrants has been that the new cohorts of immigrants who arrived after the 1970s had a very different employment pattern, initially and over the course of the first decade in Denmark.

Another notable feature shared by immigrants in Denmark and Germany is that employment among immigrants is highly sensitive to the general employment situation measured by the aggregate unemployment rate. It seems that immigrant labor incurs a disproportionately high share of the adjustment costs of the total economy. To some extent, this can be explained by the fact that immigrant employment is relatively concentrated in industries with business cycle fluctuations. It is also a possibility that immigrants are simply at the end of the job queue due to skills, attitudes, discrimination, or other factors.

Despite the difference in employment levels for foreign citizens in Germany and Denmark, the pattern of employment for the various nationalities is fairly similar across the two countries. Poles have the highest level of employment in both countries, while employment levels are the lowest for persons from Lebanon, who in fact are often stateless Palestinians. The relative employment rate for male and female immigrants is also more or less the same in Denmark and Germany. Thus, the generally higher employment among women in Denmark does not seem to have influenced the immigrants coming to Denmark.

The weak labor market attachment among immigrants is not only a problem for the immigrants themselves, it is also a problem for the German and the Danish welfare states. Both countries will be faced with an increasing maintenance burden in coming years, due to the aging of their populations. This increases the urgency to integrate immigrants far better than today. The good news here is that between generations the employment integration works much better. So if the continuous inflow of new immigrants is not too high, the consequences of immigration in the very long run might have more to do with earnings and occupational traditions than with employment *per se*.

In terms of occupations we saw some striking differences within the two countries between immigrants and natives, and similarities between the countries: the immigrants' job profiles are very similar in Denmark and Germany, as are the job profiles for natives. Immigrants are concentrated at the lower end of the job hierarchy.

So immigrants are generally less frequently employed than natives, and many of those who are employed do not have the best jobs. It is, therefore, important to understand more precisely what the decisive factors are for the labor market situation of immigrants when controlling for all the observed individual characteristics we have information on from our survey.

Such knowledge is important in order to make integration succeed. The advantage of a comparative study such as this, of course, is that the importance of institutional factors can be included to a far greater extent than would otherwise be possible. It enables one to focus on why attachment to the labor market is better for foreigners in Germany than in Denmark. Similarly, by focusing on persons from the same countries of origin, we can gain an insight into how the same immigrant groups fare in different countries.[14]

In the following chapters, therefore, based on our two large-scale immigrant surveys in Germany and Denmark, we examine factors of importance for the success of integration, with a special focus on the most important groups of immigrants in

---

14 Of course, just because two countries have taken in immigrants from the same country, it does not mean that those immigrants have the same characteristics. They may have emigrated at different times, for different reasons, and come from more or less urban areas. All these are factors which may distinguish one group of immigrants from other groups of their fellow-countrymen.

the two countries. Success is defined here both in the sense of getting oneself a job, or of becoming self-employed and creating one's own and others' employment, and also in the sense of receiving a wage corresponding both to one's qualifications and to the wage levels of natives.

References

Bauer, Thomas K., Barbara Dietz, Klaus F. Zimmermann and Eric Zwintz. 2004. "German Migration: Development, Assimilation and Labor Market Effects," in K. F. Zimmermann (ed.), *European Migration: What Do We know?* forthcoming 2004. Oxford: Oxford University Press.

Borjas, George J. 1985. "Assimilation, Changes in Cohort Quality, and the Earnings of Immigrants," *Journal of Labor Economics* 3, 463-89.

Chiswick, Barry R. 1978. "The Effect of Americanization on the Earnings of Foreign-Born Men," *Journal of Political Economy* 86, October, 897-921.

Coleman, David. 1999. "International Migration in the Context of Global Demographic Change," in D. Coleman and E. Wadensjö: *Immigration to Denmark: International and National Aspects.* Aarhus.

Constant, Amelie. 1998. "The Earnings of Male and Female Guestworkers and Their Assimilation into the German Labor Market: A Panel Study 1984-1993." Ph. D. Dissertation, Vanderbilt University.

Constant, Amelie and Douglas S. Massey. 2003. "Self-selection, Earnings, and Out-Migration: A Longitudinal Study of Immigrants to Germany," *Journal of Population Economics* 16, 631-693.

Dustmann, Christian and Christoph M. Schmidt. 2000. "The Wage Performance of Immigrant Women: Full-Time Jobs, Part-Time jobs, and the Role of Selection." *IZA Discussion Paper* No. 233.

Ekberg, Jan and Björn Gustafsson. 1995. *Invandrare på arbetsmarknaden.* Stockholm.

Ekberg, Jan og Mats Hammarstedt. 2002. "20 år med allt sämre arbetsmarknadsintegrering för invandrare" (20 years worsening integration for immigrants). *Ekonomisk debatt* 4, 2002.

Eurostat. 2001. *European Social Statistics – Labour Force Survey Results 2001.* Luxembourg.

Hansen, Hans. 2002. *Elements of Social Security, 9th edition.* Copenhagen.

Hoffmann, Edeltraud and Ulrich Walwei. 2000. *The Change in Work Arrangements in Denmark and Germany: Erosion or Renaissance of Standards?* Paper from conference on Nonstandard Work Arrangements in Japan, Europe and the United States.

Jacobsen, Vibeke and Nina Smith. 2003. "The Educational Attainment of the Children of the Danish 'Guest Worker' Immigrants." *IZA Discussion Paper* No. 749.

OECD. 1997. *Employment outlook 1997.* Paris.

Pedersen, Søren. 1999. "Migration to and from Denmark during the period 1960-97," in D. Coleman and E. Wadensjö: *Immigration to Denmark: International and National Aspects*. Aarhus.

Pedersen, Søren. 2000. "Indvandrernes demografiske forhold". In G. V. Mogensen and P. C. Matthiessen: *Integration i Danmark omkring årtusindskiftet*. Copenhagen.

Schmidt, Christoph M. and Klaus F. Zimmermann. 1992. "Migration Pressure in Germany: Past and Future," in K. F. Zimmermann (ed.): *Migration and Economic Development*. Berlin. Springer-Verlag.

Schultz-Nielsen, Marie Louise. 2001. *The Integration of Non-Western immigrants in a Scandinavian Labour Market: The Danish experience*. Copenhagen.

Schultz-Nielsen, Marie Louise. 2002. "Indvandrernes tilknytning til arbejdsmarkedet 1985-2001," in G. V. Mogensen and P. C. Matthiessen (eds): *Indvandrerne og arbejdsmarkedet* (Immigrants and the Labor market). Copenhagen.

Zimmermann, Klaus F. 1995. "Tackling the European Migration Problem," *Journal of Economic Perspectives* 9 (2), 45-62.

CHAPTER 5

Labor Force Participation and Unemployment: Incentives and Preferences*

By Amelie Constant and Marie Louise Schultz-Nielsen

5.1 Introduction

Despite an improvement in the employment situation for non-Western immigrants in recent years in both Germany and Denmark, the general trend over the last two decades has been a weakening of their attachment to the labor market. Today the labor force participation is much lower and the unemployment rate much higher for immigrants than for natives, as we saw in the previous chapter, and this was not always the situation. We also saw that this tendency is much more widespread in Denmark than in Germany.

In this chapter, we will discuss what could be the reasons for the weak labor market attachment of immigrants. Causes come from both the demand side and the supply side. According to human capital theories, one would expect to find that the "well endowed" are particularly in demand by firms; well educated workers who are not too close to retirement, who are in good health, and who do not have small children who might cause them to take time off are the most marketable. In addition, one would also expect good language skills to be important for labor market participation. The lack of language skills is a factor that can be a particular barrier for immigrants coming to a small language area like Denmark, because there is little opportunity (or incentive) to learn the language prior to immigrating. Similarly, most immigrants to Germany are not familiar with the German language before migrating.

---

* We would like to thank Holger Bonin for many helpful suggestions on an ealier version of the model used to make the incentive calculations for Germany in section 5.2. We would also like to thank Peder J. Pedersen for his good comments on an ealier draft of the regressions in Sections 5.4 and 5.5.

Demand for well educated workers could be expected to be especially noticeable in regulated labor markets where the wage floor[1] is relatively high and the wage spread relatively small, conditions that are characteristics of both the German and Danish labor markets and contrary to the USA, for example. Low immigrant employment could also be due to lack of demand for foreign labor as a result of discrimination, or lack of knowledge about the existence of this labor resource, either because immigrants do not have contact with native networks, or because the immigrants do not actively seek work. Active job-searching, of course, depends upon the individual actually wanting a job. In turn, willingness to work is influenced by reservation wages, and is expected to depend upon both taste for work and the financial incentives to work.

In the following, the importance of these factors will be examined more closely. Besides the usual culprits of weak employment attachment – disrupted period after migration, initial adjustment period, period of investment in skills, and possible non-transferability of skills – one possible explanation for the low labor market integration of immigrants could be that the economic incentives in the host country are weak. In Section 5.2 we examine this by looking at the extent to which it "pays to work". Furthermore, the individuals' preferences for leisure or "taste for work" could be a factor as well. In Section 5.3 we approach this question by looking at the "availability" for work of the unemployed. Availability will be judged according to the standard ILO (International Labour Organization) criteria, and thus our data are only indirect evidence of "taste for work". We will return to this last point later when we also discuss the relationship between availability and economic incentives. A more general picture of the factors that are important for immigrants' participation in the labor market is presented in Section 5.4, while Section 5.5 analyses what differentiates the employed workers from the unemployed workers. In this analysis we cannot encompass all relevant factors as our cross sectional data do not allow this. In order to use the availability information, for instance, we would need a panel or at least observations from two different dates or periods, because availability is only measured for the unemployed workers. Concerning the financial incentives, we face a similar problem; we would need a panel in order to approach the problem of missing variables and ideally also some decent instruments to deal with endogeneity. A more in-depth analysis of the employment situation of immigrants that includes availability and financial incentives will have to await further studies.

We conclude the chapter by looking at the occupations of immigrants; how are the immigrants distributed across the job hierarchy? Gaining employment is one thing; a different question is what type of employment. In Section 5.6, we present a detailed picture of the observable characteristics of immigrants in Germany and Denmark at different levels of the job ladder.

---

1 Neither in Germany nor in Denmark is there an official statutory minimum wage. But due to the collective agreements many sectors have defined a lowest acceptable wage.

5.2 The Monetary Incentives: Does it Pay for Immigrants to Work?

One important factor that influences labor market participation is the reservation wage. Reservation wages are influenced in turn by non-labor market incomes, tastes for leisure, for consumption, etc. Non-labor market income includes accumulated wealth, other assets, unemployment compensation, and all sorts of welfare payments. For immigrants, reservation wages also depend on their pre-migration labor force participation and work experience. In this chapter, we incorporate the idea of reservation wages into the rubric "financial incentives to work". Our question is whether working is financially worthwhile compared to staying on welfare. In this section we present computations of the difference in disposable income between a full time job and unemployment. The method used is briefly outlined below.[2]

The main difference with respect to employment between immigrants and natives is the very low employment rate of immigrants, as the number of hours worked is more or less the same for employed immigrants and natives (see Chapter 4 of this volume). Therefore, in this chapter we focus on the financial reward of full time work compared to unemployment (the extensive margin), and not the marginal reward from one extra hour of work (the intensive margin).

The aggregate picture in Hansen (2002) shows that for a single person with unemployment insurance and with an income of 75 percent of the average production worker, the net replacement rate in the case of unemployment is lower in West Germany than in Denmark. In 1999, the replacement ratio was 59 percent in Germany and 79 percent in Denmark. For a worker who earns 125 percent of an average production worker, the West-German net replacement ratio is the higher of the two. This situation arises primarily because unemployment benefits in Denmark reflect a high compensation rate (proportion of the previous income), but with a relatively low upper cap, whereas in Germany the upper cap is high and the compensation rate relatively low.

For individuals not resembling the "average production worker", this aggregate picture is not accurate and this is a particular problem when it comes to immigrants. Therefore, using information on the respondents from our surveys RFMS-G and RFMS-D, and on the basis of the applicable tax rules and transfer income,[3] we compute for each individual the difference, GAP, between the monthly disposable incomes as full time employed and as full time unemployed:

GAP = (Annual disposable income from full time employment – annual disposable income from full time unemployment)/12.

---

2 For a more complete description the reader will have to contact the authors. A description in Danish can be found in Pedersen and Smith (2003) and Pedersen et al. (2003).
3 The surveys were conducted in Germany in 2002 and in Denmark in 2001 and the rules that applied in these years respectively are used in the estimations.

We begin with the employed individuals. The income from employment for this group is known, as is the extent to which they are eligible to receive benefits, and the rates are well defined. The disposable income of full time workers is estimated using the hourly wages stated by the respondents in the survey. To this amount, child benefits and rent assistance are added and income tax, social insurance, transport expenses between home and work, and the cost of child minding are subtracted.

Some amounts, like rent assistance, are household related and are therefore divided between spouses. But the entire marginal change in the amounts caused by a specific person in the household changing their status from employed to unemployed is included in the disposable income calculations.

The annual unemployment benefit is the starting point for computing the disposable income of the unemployed. To this amount, child benefits and rent assistance are added, while any tax paid is subtracted.

Note that the transfer income included in the computation is unemployment benefits, that is, "Arbeitslosengeld" in Germany and "arbejdsløshedsdagpenge" in Denmark. These benefits are not accessible to everyone, and they can only be received for a limited period of time. In Denmark, only members of an UI fund (*A-kasse*) are eligible and then normally only after a certain qualifying period as employed. In Germany, unemployment insurance contributions are compulsory for everyone who is employed over 15 hours a week or who earns over a certain income threshold. In practice, this means that the computations will cover all the full time employed in Germany as long as they meet the "qualifying period" criteria. In Denmark the calculations only include those who are insured, which is almost 80 percent of the labor force, employed and unemployed. We will return to this issue later.

Whether or not the costs of child care should be included in the estimations is debatable because, in principle, one is not available to the labor market if one is caring for small children. On the other hand, the estimations show that for immigrants in the Danish survey, the costs of child care were higher among the employed than the unemployed individuals, which supports inclusion of this expense in the calculations. Therefore, in the following, the estimations are carried out both with and without the costs of child care.

The results of the computations are presented in Table 5.1. It can be seen that the proportion of the employed aged 25-55 years whose additional disposable income from employment as compared to unemployment is under €100 is 17 percent in Germany and 35 percent in Denmark when the cost of child care is excluded.

When the cost of child care is included, the figures increase to 18 percent and 41 percent respectively. The inclusion of the cost of child care has a far greater importance in Denmark than in Germany, and this is primarily because expenditure on child care by employed immigrants in Germany is on a modest level compared to Denmark, whereas the use of state subsidized child care is very widespread.

Table 5.1. Economic incentives: The fraction of employed immigrants for whom the net gain from employment per month, the GAP, is smaller than €0 or €100.

	Germany			Denmark		
	< €0	< €100	No. of Observations	< €0	< €100	No. of Observations
Excl. child care costs:						
Men	5	17	726	13	27	476
Women	3	16	509	23	47	321
All	4	17	1,235	17	35	797
Incl. child care costs:						
Men	5	18	717	21	33	476
Women	4	17	501	33	52	321
All	5	18	1,218	26	41	797

Remark: The computations cover those 25-55 years old.

Regardless of whether the cost of child care is included or not, there are clearly greater financial incentives for UI insured immigrants to work in Germany than in Denmark. This is first and foremost because the drop in income following the shift from employment to unemployment is much larger for immigrants in Germany than in Denmark.

A decomposition by gender shows that, in particular, immigrant women in Denmark have a small or negative GAP. This is primarily because they are lower paid than men in general. They also generally have slightly higher expenses for child care than men, but this last aspect is more than outweighed by the fact that men have higher work related transport costs.[4]

Since immigrant women in Germany also have lower wages than immigrant men, it is surprising to see that almost the same rate of women and men in Germany have a negative or a very small GAP. The main reason is that women are typically secondary wage earners in Germany; men are more often sole wage earners. Therefore, the effect on the household's net subsidy (e.g. housing subsidy) is smaller for women than for men; on average, if a woman becomes unemployed the housing subsidy for instance increases less than when a man becomes unemployed.

---

[4] This is possible to see as we make the calculation for each of the respondents between 25 and 55 years old, who are employed or unemployed. When we calculate the annual disposable income from full time employment and full time unemployment we estimate the following factors: Income before tax, income tax, social insurance, child benefits, rent assistance, transport expenses between home and work and the cost of child care. Except from transport expenses and child care all elements are calculated twice for each respondent, first if we assume they are full time employed and second if we assume that they are full time unemployed. As the calculation is made for each respondent we can group them the way we want by gender or low vs. high incomes etc.

As mentioned earlier, the results for employed immigrants in Denmark only include the members of the UI fund, who on the other hand make up almost 80 percent of the employed in RFMS-D. The uninsured can obtain social assistance, which is means tested against the household income, not just the individual's income. Social assistance is generally up to 80 percent of the unemployment benefit if one has children or up to 60 percent of the unemployment benefit when there are no children in the household.[5] However, those with many children can obtain a significantly higher extra amount in rent assistance. On the other hand, those who are cohabitants and whose spouse has earnings above a certain level will have their social assistance reduced accordingly. Immigrants, who on average have more children and lower household incomes than native Danes, would therefore be expected to receive a larger amount in social assistance than Danes.

A computation (excluding costs of child care) undertaken on the basis of the rules for social assistance benefits mentioned above shows that 14 percent of the uninsured in Denmark would, if they became unemployed, have a negative GAP, while 25 percent would have less than €100 a month extra from full time work compared to being unemployed. With the inclusion of the uninsured in the Danish estimations 33 percent have less than €100 a month extra. As the corresponding figure for Germany is 17 percent there is no doubt that the economic incentives to work, at least in the shorter term, are smaller in Denmark than in Germany.

In both Germany and Denmark one can only receive unemployment benefit for a limited period of time. In Denmark this period is four years, including an "activation period".[6] In Germany the duration of benefits depends on age and previous length of employment, but the period is generally much shorter than in Denmark. When unemployment benefits run out, unemployment assistance *(Arbeitslosenhilfe)* is available, and this provides a somewhat lower level of compensation than unemployment benefits *(Arbeitslosengeld)* but continues indefinitely. Finally, it is possible to obtain social assistance if the total household income is below a certain amount, but this level is significantly lower than the level of Danish social assistance.

Up to this point the computations have focused on the employed workers. This is of interest because the economic incentives could influence whether the employed want to stay employed in the longer term.

Obviously, it is also interesting to measure the economic incentives of the unemployed, especially for the immigrant group, which has a particularly high unemployment problem. In the following, a parallel analysis of the unemployed immigrants is carried out. We do not know, of course, what the expenses for child care and transport would be for this group of unemployed workers, were they to find a job.

---

5 Since the 1st of July 2002, new immigrants who have not resided in Denmark for 7 out of the last 8 years, have only been able to receive lower welfare benefits, but neither the respondents in RFMS-D nor by far the majority of immigrants in Denmark fit into this category.

6 The unemployed join an education program or work in a private or public workplace.

Therefore, the computations exclude child care costs, while transport costs are set as the average transport costs of employed men and women in the respective countries. Naturally, the income from employment is not known either, but it is assumed that the unemployed would be paid in accordance with their wage expectations, in case they found a job.

At first glance it would appear to be a simple task to determine unemployed immigrants' income by adding up the amounts they actually have received. However, a complication arises because these amounts are based on unemployment assistance received by an unemployed person throughout a year, and the respondents have often received several different types of benefits, sometimes in the same periods. Therefore, the expected hourly wage rate is used as the basis for these computations. From this, the amount of benefits that the unemployed persons would be eligible for, if they had obtained that particular hourly rate, is calculated. This method is also used in Pedersen and Smith (2003) and Pedersen et al. (2003).

Two different methods are used to calculate the results presented in Table 5.2. In the first method unemployment benefits are distributed according to the same principles as were applied to the insured employed in Table 5.1 above. Thus, an impression can be gained of what the economic incentives for the unemployed would have been if they had had the same access to unemployment benefits as the insured employed (method 1).

It can be seen that, in this case, approximately 1 percent of the unemployed immigrants in Germany would have a negative GAP, while approximately 24 percent would have a GAP of less than €100. For the unemployed immigrants in Denmark, the corresponding figures are significantly higher, at 20 percent and 54 percent respectively.

It is perhaps surprising that the proportion of the unemployed with a negative GAP in Germany is lower than was the case for the employed in Table 5.1, considering that their expected wages are generally below the actual wages of the employed. The explanation, however, is that here transport costs are distributed as the average cost of transport instead of varying with actual costs. This is particularly important for those who have a negative GAP in Germany, because here there are many who lie just above the €0 margin. In a control estimation where transport costs are allowed to vary, the proportion of the unemployed with a negative GAP becomes greater than for the employed. The proportion under the €100 limit is not affected very much. Overall, the unemployed would have greater incentive problems than the employed if they were eligible for unemployment benefits.

Computations based upon the actual types of assistance received show, not surprisingly, that the proportion with less economic incentive falls, particularly, of course, among those who do not receive unemployment benefits. In Germany, the proportion with a GAP under €100 is estimated to be 18 percent when applying method 2 compared to 24 percent when all unemployed are assumed to be eligible for UI benefits.

Table 5.2. Economic incentives: The percentage of unemployed immigrants for whom the net gain to employment per month, the GAP, is smaller than €0 or €100.

	Germany			Denmark		
	< 0 €	< 100 €	No. of Observations	< 0 €	< 100 €	No. of Observations
Method 1:						
All	1	24	341	20	54	279
Method 2:						
Unemployment benefits	0	20	126	17	49	143
Unemployment assistance	3	19	128	-	-	-
Social assistance	3	10	48	6	15	136
All	1	18	302[1]	12	35	279

Remark: The computation covers those 25-55 years old.
Note 1) 4 more respondents say that they have not received any of the 3 above mentioned benefits, and 35 respondents do not know.

In Denmark the difference between the proportion with a small and negative GAP seems to be considerably greater, depending on benefit types. For those who receive social assistance, the proportion with a small or negative GAP is 15 percent, compared to 49 percent of those who are eligible to receive unemployment benefits. The percentage is slightly lower than the 54 percent in the estimations using method 1, because those on social assistance generally have a lower labor market attachment than those on unemployment benefits, and they also have a lower expected future wage.

As mentioned, the analysis is hampered by the uncertainty about the situation of the unemployed, particularly those who receive social assistance. Despite this, there is no doubt that unemployed immigrants in Denmark clearly have lower financial incentives to work than those in Germany. Table 5.2 shows that 18 percent of the unemployed immigrants in Germany have less than €100 extra a month when unemployed, compared to 35 percent in Denmark.

In the aggregate, almost the same percentages of employed and unemployed immigrants have weak financial incentives to work; in Denmark a higher share of the unemployed have weak incentives. In Germany around 1/6 and in Denmark around 2/5 of the labor force has little or no financial incentives to work in the short run. Whether the difference is significant when other explanatory variables are included will be discussed in Section 5.5.

The analysis in this section documented that economic incentives to work cover many more immigrants in Germany than in Denmark. For this reason one would expect that the lack of economic incentives is considerably less of a barrier to immigrant employment in Germany than in Denmark. This is also in accordance with the higher employment rate of immigrants in Germany compared to Denmark that we found in Chapter 4.

5.3 Are the Unemployed Available to the Labor Market?

An individual's active labor supply is of course also determined by his or her taste for work, together with financial incentives and possibly demand barriers. An individual who dislikes working might need a very big financial reward in order to be induced to join the labor market, compared to an individual who likes working a lot. As long as we cannot control for "pure preferences", availability and incentives to work need not be correlated. Individuals with the same financial incentives could have any degree of availability due to variations in taste for working. Given that we do not have any direct measure of the individual's tastes, it is interesting – as second best – to see to what extent the unemployed workers are available for work. Put differently, the issue is: are individuals involuntarily unemployed? Availability is a factor that is expected to influence very directly whether or not an unemployed worker eventually finds a job. Unlike tastes, availability has been measured by us.

According to the ILO, a person is defined as being (involuntarily) unemployed if he/she does not have a job, has been actively seeking a job in the recent past, and would be able to take up a job offer quickly. The EU statistics office, Eurostat, has interpreted these criteria as, seeking a job within the last 4 weeks, and being able to take up a new job within 2 weeks. The requirements for active job-seeking and availability to take up a job within 2 weeks are waived if the person has already found a new job or has been promised reemployment by the previous employer.

In our surveys RFMS-G and RFMS-D, a range of questions were asked to determine availability according to this definition. Table 5.3 shows the percentages of unemployed immigrants in Germany and Denmark who met the ILO's availability criteria by gender.

The estimations are based on the responses of the 563 persons in RFMS-G and 294 persons in RFMS-D who describe themselves as being unemployed, who have received unemployment benefits,[7] and who are not currently studying or covered by an employment scheme. Out of these respondents, 12 percent in Germany and 21 percent in Denmark state that they would not take a job. In the case of Denmark, this is a remarkable jump compared with 1999, when this percentage was approximately the same as that for Germany. Part of the explanation could be that unemployment in 2001 was lower than in 1999 and presumably, few of the unemployed individuals who report that they do not want a job, or that they were not searching for one, actually got a job between 1999 and 2001. It could thus be that this group of "voluntarily" unemployed comprises a higher fraction of the general small group of unemployed in 2001 compared to 1999.

---

[7] In Denmark, unemployment benefits *(dagpenge)* or social assistance *(kontanthjælp)*. In Germany, unemployment benefits *(Arbeitslosengeld)*, unemployment assistance *(Arbeitslosenhilfe)* or social assistance *(Sozialhilfe)*.

Table 5.3. Proportion of unemployed[1] immigrants in Germany and Denmark who meet ILO's availability criteria by gender.

	Germany			Denmark			
	Foreign citizens (weighted)			Immigrants and descendants (weighted)			
	2002			2001			1999
	Men	Women	All	Men	Women	All	All
Persons, total	439	124	563	127	167	294	239
Total percentage	100	100	100	100	100	100	100
Of whom:							
• Do not want a job (-)	13	12	12	15	24	21	12
• Not looked for a job for the last 4 weeks (-)	22	25	22	32	29	30	25
• Not looked for a job, but expect reemployment or to have a new job (+)	2	0	2	7	3	5	5
• Have looked for a job, but cannot start for at least 2 weeks (-)	7	6	7	3	4	3	17
ILO definition of unemployed	61	57	60	57	46	51	50

Note: 1) The table includes solely people who receive unemployment benefits or social assistance for the unemployed and who are not studying or covered by an employment scheme.

In both Germany and Denmark a significant proportion of the unemployed immigrants, namely 22 percent and 30 percent, respectively, have not looked for a job within the previous 4 weeks. In Denmark this figure was 25 percent in 1999. Some have a good reason for this, in that they have already found a new job or are temporarily laid off, and these people therefore belong to the group that meets the ILO's availability criteria. While those who have looked for a job within the previous 4 weeks but cannot start within two weeks do not meet the criteria. In 2001, 7 percent of the immigrants in Germany and 3 percent in Denmark fell into this category. There has been a large improvement in availability in this category in Denmark since 1999, when 17 percent did not meet the criteria.

Overall, 40 percent of the unemployed immigrants in Germany did not meet the availability criteria in 2002 compared to 49 percent and 50 percent in Denmark in 2001 and 1999 respectively.[8]

---

8 The corresponding proportion of all unemployed (including natives) who met the availability criteria in Denmark in 2002 was higher, namely 66 percent, according to Statistics Denmark (2002).

When decomposed by gender, there are relatively few observations (particularly for Denmark) and one should, therefore, interpret the figures with caution. Keeping this in mind, the decomposition by gender shows that immigrant women in Denmark are less available for work than men, in that 46 percent of women compared to 57 percent of men meet the ILO's availability criteria. Native unemployed women are also less likely to be available to work than native unemployed men in Denmark (see Schultz-Nielsen, 2001).

The gender difference in availability of the unemployed immigrants in Germany is significantly smaller than in Denmark. This is in accordance with the gender differences with respect to the GAP between the two countries. It could also reflect the differences between the two types of welfare states: one where one earns the right to the good benefits, the German system, and one where benefits are more or less universal. In Germany, one is less likely to receive high unemployed benefits without an employment record if one does not want a job. In the Danish system, individuals have the opportunity of receiving a compensating income even without ever having a job, simply by announcing that they would want to have a job.

In Table 5.4 the percentages of those who are available to the labor market are presented according to the type of benefits received. As it can be seen from the table, the percentage of immigrants in Germany who are available to the labor market depends only to a small extent on the type of benefits received.

Among the immigrants in Denmark there is a markedly greater difference in availability depending on the benefit type. While the availability proportion of those receiving unemployment benefits is 62 percent, the proportion of those receiving social assistance is down to 30 percent. Over a third of this group responded that they did not want a job and a similar number responded that they had not sought a job in the previous four weeks.

The reasons for not meeting the ILO criteria can be manifold, as mentioned above. The lack of financial incentives to work is one possibility. As we discussed earlier, there need not be any correlation between availability and financial incentives as long as we cannot control for taste for work. However, when looking at the difference between both incentives and availability in Denmark and Germany Table 5.4 suggests that there is a correlation, so that weak incentives are correlated with low availability. A supplementary logistic regression[9] on the relationship between the ILO-availability and a range of personal characteristics points in this direction although the effect is not significant. Whether this is due to a very small number of observations (less than 300) or it is a more basic phenomenon possibly related to missing variables is too early to say.

---

9 This and other regressions mentioned but not shown in the chapter are available from the authors on request.

Table 5.4. Proportion of unemployed[1] immigrants in Germany and Denmark who meet ILO's availability criteria by transfer income.

	Germany				Denmark			
	Foreign citizens (weighted)				Immigrants and descendants (weighted)			
	2002				2001			
	Unempl. Benefits	Unempl. Assistance	Social Assistance	All	Unempl. Benefits	Social Assistance	All	
Persons, total	239	224	100	563	127	167	294
Proportion total	100	100	100	100	100	100	100
Of whom:							
• Do not want a job (-)	13	14	6	12	12	36	21
• Not looked for a job for the last 4 weeks (-)	20	26	21	22	27	36	30
• Not looked for a job, but expect reemployment or have a new job (+)	2	2	0	2	5	4	5
• Have looked for a job, but cannot start for at least 2 weeks (-)	6	7	10	7	4	2	3
ILO definition of Unemployed	63	55	63	60	62	30	51

Note: 1) The table includes solely people who receive unemployment benefits or social assistance for the unemployed and who are not studying or covered by an employment scheme.

In line with this chapter's main theme, namely the factors that influence immigrants' integration into the labor market, the ultimate question is whether the unemployed immigrants' lack of availability leads, in the longer term, to a lower likelihood of being employed. This is a question which, due to its nature, can only be answered with time. As far as Germany is concerned, all the respondents whose availability is included in the survey, were unemployed at the time of the survey. To answer our question we would need to re-interview them in a follow-up study to find out. For Denmark, we interviewed the RFMS-D individuals in 2001, but also in 1999. We will return to availability and employment chances in Section 5.5.

In relation to immigrants' labor market integration in Denmark it is striking that only approximately half of unemployed immigrants meet the availability criteria. In Germany, 60 percent of the unemployed immigrants meet the criteria, a percentage that is not impressive either. This might be an important factor behind the poor employment integration of immigrants in Denmark and Germany in general and in Denmark in particular.

5.4 Who Joins the Labor Force?

Up until now we have tried to uncover some of the factors that can be particularly contributory to whether or not an immigrant obtains work. In the following, we investigate more closely, for both Denmark and Germany, what differentiates immigrants who participate in the labor force from those who do not. The aim is to gain a better understanding of the factors that contribute to the low labor market participation of immigrants. In the subsequent chapter, the factors that determine the wage level among the employed, including the extent to which immigrants' pay improves with duration of residency, will be examined.

Earnings assimilation is a topic that has gained a prominent place in the immigration literature, not least due to the seminal work of Chiswick (1978), who identified the importance of duration of residency on the immigrants' earnings, as well as the later cohort-effect of Borjas (1985).

Among the existing studies of immigrants' integration into the labor market in Germany, relatively more work has been done on immigrants' earnings assimilation than on what determines whether immigrants are employed or unemployed (see Constant, 1998 and Bauer et al., 2004).

In labor markets that differ from the US market, in that they are more highly regulated, have minimum wages at a considerably higher level and a much smaller wage spread, it is not certain that immigrants can enter the labor market at all. This is shown to be the case in Australia (see Antecol et al., 2003). As both the German and the Danish labor markets are characterized by these forms of regulation, one will expect to find lower employment rates among immigrants, precisely as emerged in Chapter 4.

Most of the German studies that investigate employment and unemployment of immigrants, compared to natives look at the situation for *"Aussiedler"* and *"Übersiedler"*, which is not the focus here. However, the studies by Cramer (1984), Bender and Karr (1993), and Winkelmann and Zimmermann (1993) cover guestworkers, who certainly constitute a subset of the respondents included in RFMS-G and RFMS-D.

Among the existing Danish studies on labor market attachment, earnings assimilation is also a common subject. A study that examines the labor market integration of immigrants in two steps was carried out by the Ministry for Refugees, Immigration, and Integration (2002). The first step is participation in the labor market and later, in the second step one obtains a job. The analysis shows that the likelihood of participating in the labor market is highest for immigrants who come from more developed countries, have immigrated at a younger age, are educated, are married, and who reside in a smaller municipality. For women, the presence of children lowers their likelihood of participating in the labor market, but for men, this factor is insignificant. The studies mentioned above are all undertaken on the basis of registers and therefore do not include information on ability to speak Danish. While Schultz-Nielsen (2001) and Schultz-Nielsen (2002) uses this information they only examine whether one is employed or not. Similar to the Ministry for Refugees, Immigration, and Integration study (2002), she does not include estimations for Danes. Her results are similar to the findings in this chapter.

Based on our surveys RFMS-G and RFMS-D, Table 5.5 presents selected summary statistics of the respondents in Germany and Denmark aged 18-59 by their employment status. While the Danish survey includes immigrants and descendants from eight non-Western countries, the German survey includes foreign nationals from five non-Western countries only.[10] These five groups are, however, totally comparable. Table 5.5 shows that, on average, the German respondents are slightly older than the Danish respondents, have slightly longer residency duration, and, to a greater extent, education from their home country. They also have slightly more frequent contact with the natives. However, the fluctuations in the individual variables in relationship to labor market attachment of immigrants are, to a large extent, similar in the two countries.

In sum, these characteristics show that there are clear differences between the employed and unemployed. Namely, the employed immigrants speak better German/Danish, have more years since arrival, and are better educated than their unemployed counterparts. A larger percentage of the employed have also become citizens, and do not live in enclaves.

In the following, these findings are investigated more closely through a multivariate analysis presented in Table 5.6 and 5.7. Following economic theory, we employ a range of variables that are important for the immigrants' employment in Germany and Denmark. The dependent variable is whether one participates in the labor market or not. The analysis is limited to persons between 18 and 59 years of age who are not registered as students. Individuals close to retirement age are omitted, since we do not have the necessary information to model this participation decision. To better evaluate what effect the inclusion of certain variables has on the estimations, the regressions are carried out in three steps.

The first step includes only gender and pure human capital factors, i.e. age, years since migration, state of health, and education acquired in the home country and in Germany/Denmark.

In the second step language skills are included as they are also an important measure of human capital. Because language skills may be correlated with education it is useful to include this variable in the second step so as to assess its effect on the education variable. Furthermore, the following range of explanatory variables is added; country of origin, basis of residency, unemployment rate in the local area, and citizenship.

---

10 See the Appendix of this book for a description of the two surveys.

Table 5.5. Selected summary statistics on employed, unemployed and persons not in the workforce in Germany and Denmark. All respondents 18-59 years old, excluding students.

Variables description		Germany Employed Mean	Std. Dev.	Germany Unemployed Mean	Std. Dev.	Germany Not in Workforce Mean	Std. Dev.	Denmark Employed Mean	Std. Dev.	Denmark Unemployed Mean	Std. Dev.	Denmark Not in Workforce Mean	Std. Dev.
Gender and small children	Women with children	0.089	0.285	0.051	0.220	0.347	0.476	0.133	0.340	0.318	0.466	0.240	0.427
	Women without children	0.332	0.471	0.220	0.415	0.417	0.493	0.273	0.446	0.260	0.439	0.361	0.481
	Men with children	0.157	0.364	0.246	0.431	0.043	0.202	0.223	0.417	0.225	0.418	0.117	0.322
	Men without children	0.422	0.494	0.483	0.500	0.193	0.395	0.371	0.483	0.197	0.398	0.282	0.450
Age		37	11	38	10	38	10	36	10	35	9	41	11
Years Since Migration		17	10	16	9	14	10	16	8	14	7	14	9
Bad health		0.033	0.179	0.151	0.359	0.126	0.332	0.019	0.138	0.063	0.242	0.355	0.479
Employment in Home Country		0.419	0.493	0.500	0.500	0.393	0.489	0.405	0.491	0.389	0.488	0.508	0.500
Education in Home Country		0.630	0.483	0.592	0.492	0.582	0.493	0.341	0.474	0.252	0.435	0.319	0.466
Education in host country	Primary and lower Secondary	0.228	0.420	0.181	0.386	0.112	0.315	0.198	0.399	0.184	0.388	0.103	0.305
	Upper secondary	0.039	0.193	0.014	0.116	0.009	0.096	0.145	0.352	0.074	0.262	0.046	0.209
	University	0.038	0.191	0.022	0.147	0.013	0.112	0.078	0.268	0.014	0.116	0.007	0.083
	No education	0.695	0.460	0.783	0.413	0.866	0.341	0.579	0.494	0.729	0.445	0.844	0.363
Vocational Training		0.177	0.382	0.098	0.298	0.067	0.249	0.216	0.411	0.088	0.283	0.068	0.252
Language	Speaks fluently	0.381	0.486	0.239	0.427	0.141	0.348	0.354	0.478	0.115	0.320	0.091	0.288
	Speaks average/well	0.524	0.500	0.575	0.495	0.466	0.499	0.557	0.497	0.707	0.456	0.506	0.500
	Speaks poorly/very poorly	0.095	0.293	0.186	0.390	0.393	0.489	0.088	0.284	0.178	0.383	0.403	0.491
Land of origin	Former Yugoslavia	0.180	0.385	0.153	0.360	0.178	0.383	0.156	0.363	0.055	0.228	0.224	0.417
	Iran	0.183	0.387	0.166	0.372	0.155	0.362	0.104	0.306	0.060	0.238	0.107	0.309
	Lebanon	0.116	0.320	0.275	0.447	0.263	0.440	0.064	0.244	0.345	0.476	0.105	0.307
	Pakistan	-	-	-	-	-	-	0.104	0.306	0.049	0.217	0.151	0.358
	Poland	0.267	0.442	0.146	0.353	0.159	0.366	0.189	0.392	0.099	0.299	0.074	0.261
	Somalia	-	-	-	-	-	-	0.059	0.236	0.126	0.332	0.095	0.293
	Turkey	0.254	0.435	0.261	0.440	0.245	0.430	0.186	0.389	0.233	0.423	0.138	0.346
	Vietnam	-	-	-	-	-	-	0.138	0.345	0.033	0.179	0.107	0.309
Refugee (Yes vs. no)		0.250	0.433	0.431	0.496	0.410	0.492	0.380	0.486	0.373	0.484	0.429	0.495
Unemployment in region (in percent)		8.967	2.837	10.158	3.592	9.646	3.113	5.022	1.059	5.045	1.062	5.057	1.004
Citizen		0.044	0.204	0.024	0.152	0.013	0.115	0.533	0.499	0.392	0.489	0.287	0.453
Contact with Natives (much vs. less)		0.966	0.181	0.917	0.276	0.854	0.353	0.864	0.343	0.619	0.486	0.648	0.478
Religion	Strong faith, Muslim	0.274	0.446	0.432	0.496	0.538	0.499	0.423	0.494	0.751	0.433	0.583	0.493
	Little faith, Muslim	0.201	0.401	0.202	0.402	0.089	0.284	0.103	0.305	0.049	0.217	0.086	0,280
	Strong faith, not Muslim	0.104	0.306	0.049	0.216	0.089	0.285	0.087	0.282	0.066	0.248	0.058	0.234
	Little faith, not Muslim	0.421	0.494	0.317	0.466	0.284	0.451	0.387	0.487	0.134	0.341	0.273	0.446
Live in Enclaves		0.386	0.487	0.508	0.500	0.472	0.499	0.234	0.424	0.458	0.499	0.391	0.488
No. of Observations		2,727		590		1,501		1,460		365		571	

The third and final step includes variables that are certainly expected to affect labor market attachment, but for which there is a risk that these particular variables may be endogenous. Despite this problem, these variables are included first of all in order to see their correlation with participation, and secondly in order to see whether inclusion affects the estimates.

To save space, the individual regressions for men and women are not presented, but differences between the two genders will be commented on along the way. Not surprisingly, the presence of small children gives the largest difference in the estimates for men's and women's labor supply. Therefore, gender and children are included as an interaction in the model. Besides the dummy for whether the respondent is a man or a woman, two extra dummies are included, one for men with small children between 0 and 6 years of age and one for women with small children. As expected, for both Germany and Denmark, there is a significantly greater likelihood that men are in the labor force than women, and the likelihood of being in the labor force is lowest for women with small children. In Germany, immigrant men with children have a significantly higher likelihood of being in the work force than the reference group "others", which is not the case in Denmark. The estimation results are only slightly affected by the inclusion of additional variables. Compared to a regression for Danes,[11] immigrant females (especially in Germany) both with and without children have lower odds of being in the labor force.

Age is specified as a quadratic form in the model, and age is significant in model 2 for Denmark and in models 2 and 3 for Germany. The estimation results show, as expected, that the likelihood of being in the labor market is lower for the youngest, but particularly for the oldest compared to those in the middle age group. The somewhat limited importance of age on participation is due to the age delimitation (18-59 years), as we look at immigrants at an age where retirement for most people is not an option. A control regression shows that if all immigrants between 16 and 66 years were to be included, the age variable would be significant in all three models both in Germany and in Denmark. For the estimates on the other variables such a change has only a very limited effect.

---

11 The analysis uses register information, which on the one hand gives access to a large sample, that is 54,655 persons equivalent to two percent of all Danes (18-59 years old), but on the other hand, only a limited amount of information is available. In the model, fewer variables are included for determining the likelihood of labor market participation compared to Tables 5.6 and 5.7. The analysis shows that compared to women, the odds of participating in the labor market are 40 percent higher for men. For women with small children the odds are 30 percent lower than for others, however, men with small children are more than twice as likely to be in the labor market. The youngest, and particularly the oldest, are less likely to participate in the labor market, just as those with a limited education are also less likely to participate – particularly compared to university graduates, but also compared to those who have vocational training or have completed upper secondary school. Furthermore, Danes who live in areas with high unemployment are slightly less likely to participate in the labor market.

Total years since immigration also enters the models as a quadratic equation. For the respondents who were born in Germany or Denmark, years since immigration is just their age. By including both age and years since immigration, age at immigration is implicitly included. Furthermore, this can be an important indicator of how well one settles into the surrounding community. The years since migration variable is significant in all three models for both Germany and Denmark. The variable for years since immigration shows an increasing likelihood of participating in the labor force during the first years after arrival, subsequently, the pace of the increase declines and eventually becomes negative. But it continues to be better to have been in the country for a long period than not at all.

Poor health is synonymous with respondents stating that they have a chronic health condition that restricts their daily life. As would be expected, the state of health, for obvious reasons, plays an important role on whether or not an individual participates in the labor force in both Germany and Denmark. For immigrants in Germany, the odds of being in the labor force are reduced by around 70 percent when one suffers from poor health. In Denmark, the odds are reduced by 94 percent. A decomposition by gender shows that this difference is quite large, given that the estimation on the labor supply of immigrant women in Germany is less dependent on health.

In Germany, having had a job in the home country has a clearly positive influence on the likelihood of labor market participation in the first model. A special regression (not reported here) showed that with the inclusion of language skills, the importance of "job in the home country" is reduced, which is also suggested by Table 5.6 model 2, where the effect disappears completely. In Denmark, the pre-migration experience variable is insignificant in all three models. It is surprising that employment qualifications attained in the home country do not have a greater impact than is actually the case. This could be due to the difficulty of transferring these "foreign" qualifications to a German/Danish job.

Whether one has completed an education in the home country is represented by the dummy variable "education from home country". Generally, educational qualifications would be expected to have a positive influence on the likelihood of participating in the labor force. It is of no surprise that this variable is significant in all three models for Germany. However, while in the first model home country education doubles the chance of participating in the labor force, its effect is reduced in the second model where home country education only increases the chance of labor force participation by 43 percent. In Denmark this variable is positive but only significant in the first model. The explanation for this might be found in the differences between the composition and backgrounds of immigrants in Germany and Denmark. As it can be seen from Table 5.5, relatively fewer immigrants who come to Denmark have a home country education.

Educational attainment in Germany/Denmark is specified by two variables. The first is based on the level of school education attained, the second is an independent dummy variable for whether or not one has vocational training. Level of schooling

Table 5.6. Binomial logistic regressions. Probability of being in workforce in Germany. All respondents 18-59 years old, excluding students.

		Model 1			Model 2			Model 3		
		Estimate	St. Error	OddsRatio	Estimate	St. Error	OddsRatio	Estimate	St. Error	OddsRatio
Constant		-1.226*	0.544	-	-1.718*	0.585	-	-1.483*	0.618	-
Gender and small children	Male	1.099*	0.095	3.001	1.325*	0.103	3.764	1.278*	0.104	3.591
	Male with children	0.452*	0.161	1.571	0.610*	0.167	1.841	0.654*	0.169	1.924
	Female with children	-1.373*	0.105	0.253	-1.356*	0.111	0.258	-1.336*	0.112	0.263
Age		0.025	0.029	1.025	0.065*	0.031	1.067	0.056	0.031	1.058
Age^2		-0.001*	0.0004	0.999	-0.001*	0.0004	0.999	-0.001*	0.0004	0.999
Years Since Migration		0.127*	0.013	1.136	0.104*	0.015	1.109	0.102*	0.015	1.107
Years Since Migration^2		-0.002*	0.0003	0.998	-0.002*	0.0003	0.998	-0.002*	0.0003	0.998
Bad health		-1.255*	0.136	0.285	-1.145*	0.144	0.318	-1.138*	0.145	0.320
Employment in Home Country		0.292*	0.091	1.340	0.080	0.096	1.084	0.055	0.097	1.056
Education in Home Country		0.827*	0.096	2.286	0.357*	0.105	1.429	0.334*	0.106	1.397
Education in Germany	Primary and lower secondary	0.623*	0.143	1.864	0.125	0.153	1.134	0.097	0.154	1.102
	Upper secondary	1.162*	0.319	3.197	0.474	0.331	1.606	0.350	0.332	1.419
	University	1.018*	0.313	2.768	0.527*	0.320	1.694	0.417	0.323	1.517
Vocational Training in Germany		0.650*	0.140	1.915	0.467*	0.147	1.596	0.448*	0.148	1.564
Language	Speaks average/well				0.959*	0.104	2.608	0.825*	0.109	2.281
	Speaks fluently				1.454*	0.142	4.280	1.268*	0.147	3.553
Land of Origin	Former Yugoslavia				-0.050	0.132	0.951	-0.216	0.148	0.806
	Iran				0.005	0.147	1.005	-0.115	0.152	0.892
	Lebanon				-0.446*	0.139	0.640	-0.435*	0.141	0.647
	Pakistan				-	-	-	-	-	-
	Poland				0.521*	0.133	1.683	0.341*	0.167	1.406
	Somalia				-	-	-	-	-	-
	Vietnam				-	-	-	-	-	-
Refugee (Yes vs. no)					-0.475*	0.106	0.622	-0.439*	0.107	0.645
Unemployment in region (in percent)					-0.046*	0.013	0.955	-0.049*	0.013	0.952
German citizen					0.796*	0.291	2.217	0.780*	0.289	2.181
Contact with Natives (much vs. less)								0.394*	0.154	1.483
Religion	Strong faith, Muslim							-0.384*	0.122	0.681
	Little faith, Muslim							0.265	0.150	1.304
	Strong faith, not Muslim							-0.136	0.146	0.873
Live in Enclaves								-0.067	0.081	0.935
AIC (Intercept and covariates)		4,312.3			4,011.1			3,975.9		
Likelihood ratio		1,172.9			1,492.1			1,528.8		
No. of Observations		4,414			4,414			4,409		

*= Significant at 5 percent-level.

Table 5.7. Binomial logistic regressions. Probability of being in workforce in Denmark. All respondents 18-59 years old, excluding students.

		Model 1			Model 2			Model 3		
		Estimate	St. Error	OddsRatio	Estimate	St. Error	OddsRatio	Estimate	St. Error	OddsRatio
Constant		-1.047	0.855	-	-2.472*	0.975	-	-1.947	1.017	-
Gender and small children	Male	0.329*	0.163	1.389	0.569*	0.175	1.766	0.519*	0.178	1.681
	Male with children	0.114	0.205	1.120	0.108	0.214	1.114	0.171	0.217	1.187
	Female with children	-0.706*	0.174	0.494	-0.522*	0.185	0.593	-0.502*	0.186	0.605
Age		0.090	0.046	1.094	0.142*	0.049	1.152	0.142*	0.049	1.152
Age²		-0.002*	0.001	0.998	-0.002*	0.001	0.998	-0.002*	0.001	0.998
Years Since Migration		0.181*	0.029	1.198	0.144*	0.036	1.155	0.144*	0.036	1.154
Years Since Migration²		-0.004*	0.001	0.996	-0.004*	0.001	0.996	-0.004*	0.001	0.996
Bad health		-2.763*	0.191	0.063	-2.684*	0.201	0.068	-2.657*	0.202	0.070
Employment in Home Country		0.165	0.154	1.179	-0.042	0.163	0.959	-0.070	0.164	0.932
Education in Home Country		0.530*	0.150	1.699	0.154	0.165	1.167	0.135	0.165	1.144
Education in Denmark	Primary and lower secondary	0.174	0.202	1.190	-0.085	0.211	0.919	-0.081	0.213	0.922
	Upper secondary	0.311	0.272	1.365	0.076	0.292	1.078	0.049	0.294	1.050
	University	1.995*	0.627	7.351	1.629*	0.660	5.098	1.587*	0.657	4.889
Vocational Training in Denmark		0.609*	0.216	1.839	0.486*	0.232	1.625	0.453	0.233	1.572
Language	Speaks average/well				0.972*	0.157	2.644	0.968*	0.162	2.632
	Speaks fluently				1.474*	0.264	4.365	1.398*	0.270	4.047
Land of Origin	Former Yugoslavia				-0.056	0.278	0.946	-0.370	0.316	0.691
	Iran				-0.697*	0.310	0.498	-0.955*	0.340	0.385
	Lebanon				-0.219	0.265	0.804	-0.195	0.266	0.823
	Pakistan				-0.948*	0.244	0.387	-1.056*	0.247	0.348
	Poland				0.900*	0.305	2.459	0.472	0.386	1.604
	Somalia				-0.346	0.293	0.707	-0.441	0.297	0.643
	Vietnam				0.028	0.293	1.029	-0.339	0.386	0.712
Refugee (Yes vs. no)					-0.197	0.171	0.821	-0.179	0.173	0.836
Unemployment in region (in percent)					0.024	0.064	1.024	0.017	0.065	1.017
Danish citizen					0.146	0.180	1.158	0.114	0.182	1.121
Contact with Natives (much vs. less)								0.165	0.151	1.180
Religion	Strong faith, Muslim							-0.272	0.258	0.762
	Little faith, Muslim							-0.044	0.305	0.957
	Strong faith, not Muslim							-0.041	0.302	0.960
Live in Enclaves								-0.488*	0.137	0.614
AIC (Intercept and covariates)		1,804.8			1,717.6			1,710.9		
Likelihood ratio		580.2			690.9			707.1		
No. of Observations		2,228			2,227			2,226		

*= Significant at 5 percent-level.

is reported for three levels in both Germany and Denmark. The reference category of the regression is that one has not completed an education in Germany/Denmark. As can be seen from the first model for Germany, the chances of participating in the labor force are higher for persons who have completed a school education (particularly an upper secondary school education) or a university degree. Moreover, having completed vocational training also has a significantly positive influence. The inclusion of the language variable in model 2 reduces the effect of education because the two variables, to a certain extent, are correlated, in that, as a rule, the better educated also have better language skills. For Danish immigrants the importance of education is also reduced by the inclusion of the other explanatory variables in model 2, but the estimations are more robust. The likelihood of being in the labor force is markedly higher for those who have vocational training and particularly university qualifications. In Germany, only vocational training counts – not university – when language and the other extra controls are included.

Overall, the analysis has thus far shown that human capital has a positive and differential effect upon the labor force participation decision.

Information for the variable, language skills, i.e. how well one speaks German/Danish, is given by the interviewer's evaluation of the respondents' language (see Chapter 3 of this volume). Unlike other studies, this gives us an advantage of employing an objective variable. Good language skills can reduce employer's discrimination in the hiring process, and can make migrants more marketable. The variable, language skills, is, for both Germany and Denmark, clearly significant whenever it is included, indicating that good language skills increase labor force participation. The odds of participating in the labor force are 3.5 to 4 times higher in both Germany and Denmark if one speaks the respective language fluently as opposed to speaking it poorly or very poorly.

The country of origin is included in models 2 and 3 and can be interpreted as a country specific term which is not otherwise included in the model. The reference category is Turkey in the regressions for both Germany and Denmark, while, as mentioned earlier, only the Danish study includes interviews with people of Pakistani, Somali, and Vietnamese origin. As can be seen in Table 5.6, the likelihood of being in the labor force in Germany is significantly higher for Poles than Turks, whereas the likelihood is significantly lower for the Lebanese. People from the former Yugoslavia as well as people from Iran have the same likelihood of being in the labor force as the Turks, all else being equal. This result is unchanged by the inclusion of extra variables in the model. In the case of Denmark, people from Poland also have a higher likelihood of being in the labor force than Turks, but here it is the Pakistanis and Iranians in particular who have a lower likelihood of participation. This could be because the Iranians, who often have university degrees from their home country, have to use more time in updating their qualifications, while Pakistani women in particular, for cultural reasons, are often housewives, who stay at home. A breakdown by gender shows that the Pakistani women stand out "negatively" in this respect.

The basis of residency is broken down into whether one has residency as a refugee or not. Refugees in Germany are shown to have a significantly lower chance of participating in the labor market than others. A similar tendency is also seen in Denmark but here the effect is not significant. There may be many reasons for the lower chances of refugees being in the labor force; they can be affected by traumatic experiences, they have not primarily come to seek employment (unlike guest workers), their networks in the recipient country might be weaker than, in particular, family reunion immigrants, and administrative conditions can prevent them from labor force participation. In Germany, there are limits on how long people with refugee status can remain with assurance in the country. There are also restrictions on which jobs they can take. In Denmark, until now, anyone being granted refugee status was entitled to remain in the country permanently, and there have not been any employment restrictions. Therefore it is not surprising that particularly German refugees have a lower likelihood of participating in the labor force.

The regional unemployment is also included in models 2 and 3 to give an indication of the extent to which the general job possibilities in the area affect participation in the labor force. This variable is significant for Germany and indicates that the higher the unemployment rate is in a region, the lower is the labor force participation. Local unemployment is not significant for Denmark.

The dummy for citizenship is positive and significant for immigrants in Germany but not in Denmark. In Germany, citizenship is positively correlated with participation, even when taking account of the other variables. In fact, labor force participation doubles for the immigrants who have become German citizens, all things equal. This result does not change with the inclusion of additional variables in model 3. On the face of it, it may seem surprising that citizenship does not play any role in participation in the labor force in Denmark, when, as shown in chapter 4, there is clearly greater labor market attachment generally among the naturalized Danes. The explanation, however, is that those who are naturalized have also held long term residency in Denmark and have better language skills etc., and when we control for this in the regression the importance of citizenship disappears. In the German case it is probably different because it has traditionally been difficult to become a German citizen and it is only in recent years that larger numbers have been naturalized.

The rest of the variables included in the model are, as mentioned by way of introduction: contact with natives, importance of religion, and the enclaves indication. The estimations have so far only revealed small changes when the variables are included in model 3 compared to model 2. It is particularly the estimates of country of origin, language skills and education that change a little following inclusion of the additional variables. Contact with natives is a dummy variable that has the value of zero if the respondent only greets or never speaks to natives and the value one if the respondent regularly speaks to or associates with natives. For the German immigrants the correlation is significantly positive. For Danes, the correlation is also positive but insignificant.

The variable capturing the importance of religion is based on the respondents' information about which religion they grew up in and whether they themselves hold religious beliefs. This latter point is measured in the first instance by whether the respondent goes to religious services regularly. Since many practicing Muslims (especially women) do not attend religious services, the importance of religion is also measured by whether the respondents keep religious rules, indicated by whether they state that they never drink beer, wine or spirits. The importance of religion for labor supply could be ambiguous. On the one hand, one would expect that religious people observe existing moral norms, including participation in the labor force. On the other hand, some religious people can, to a certain extent, be reluctant to accept the "modernity" of the surrounding society, and this will prompt lower labor force participation. Religious attachment is shown to be important for the German Muslim immigrants' likelihood of being in the labor force, in that those who hold stricter religious beliefs have a lower likelihood of being in the labor force. For the Danish immigrants the religion variables are not significant.

The variable, enclave, indicates whether the neighborhood has high or low immigrant density. It is a dummy variable that takes the value of 1 if the respondent states that approximately half or more of residents in the suburb are immigrants, otherwise the variable takes the value of zero. In model 3 for Germany, there is no significant relationship between being in the labor force and living in a suburb with a high concentration of immigrants. This is in contrast to the situation in Denmark, where immigrants who live in such a suburb have a lower likelihood of being in the labor force.

In summary, the analysis shows that the likelihood of participating in the labor market is greater for immigrants who are between 25 and 45 years of age, have good health and have lived in the country for a reasonable period of time. In general, women, especially those with small children, have a lower likelihood of participating in the labor force than men. All else being equal, immigrant women in Germany are relatively less likely to participate in the labor force than immigrant women in Denmark. To have qualifications from the home country in the form of education and work experience seems to play a greater role for the immigrant labor force participation in Germany than in Denmark. Education or training completed in Germany/Denmark clearly plays a positive role in both countries, as does language proficiency. However, citizenship, religious background, the local unemployment rate, and contact with natives only seem to be significant for labor force participation in Germany, whereas the negative effect of refugee status is greatest here. Lastly, only in Denmark is living in a suburb with many immigrants having a negative impact on the labor force participation.

5.5 Employment Chances

Having analyzed the importance of several variables for labor force participation of immigrants in Germany and Denmark, it is natural to ask who actually has a job. Put differently, the question we seek to answer here is, given that one is in the labor force, what is the probability that one works, as opposed to being unemployed. Employment status is determined from survey data information about whether the respondents stated that they were employed or unemployed at the time of the interview. Thus, the analysis here differs from that of the Ministry for Refugees, Immigration, and Integration (2002), where it is the average unemployment rate during the year that is analyzed. The method used here also differs from Winkelmann and Zimmermann (1993), who study the frequency of unemployment spells of natives and guest workers in Germany and Cramer (1984) and Bender and Karr (1993), who investigate the unemployment rates, controlling for differences in characteristics between natives and guest workers.

The analysis is based on immigrants between 18 and 59 years of age (both years included) who participate in the labor market. As in the previous section, students are excluded from the analysis. Using a logistic regression, the factors that are important for whether one is employed or not are examined. The response variable takes a value of 1 if the respondent is employed and 0 if the respondent is unemployed (and in the labor force). The estimation results for immigrants in Germany and Denmark are presented in Tables 5.8 and 5.9. As was the case in the previous section, the variables are included in the model in 3 steps.

In Table 5.8 we see that immigrant women in Germany have a significantly higher likelihood of being employed compared to immigrant men, given that they are part of the labor force. Having small children negatively affects the likelihood of being employed for men. However, when other variables are added in models 2 and 3, only the general effect of women having a higher likelihood of being employed than men stays significant.

For immigrants in Denmark the picture is the other way round. In the first model women have a lower likelihood of being employed than men. A control regression of 2 percent of all Danes confirms that the pattern is the same for this group, but the effect is less strong.[12] Having small children affects the likelihood of being employed negatively for both immigrant men and women. When the additional variables are included in models 2 and 3, the differences between the likelihoods of

---

12 For Danish men the odds of having a job are 12 percent higher than for women. The odds of having a job are reduced by 48 percent for women with small children. On the other hand, the odds of being employed are 59 percent higher for men with children. To have a university degree increases the chances most, namely by a factor of 4, but the chances also increase for those who have completed upper secondary school or vocational training. Age is significant and the likelihood of being employed is sligthly reduced for the youngest and oldest. The likelihood is also reduced when living in an area with high unemployment.

being employed, for both men with children and women with children, are reduced. However, women still have a significantly higher likelihood of not being employed. The reasons for these rather different patterns are most likely linked to the different labor force participation patterns. As mentioned earlier in the chapter, the German welfare state is largely based upon the family with the mother and housewife at its centre. In Denmark, the role of housewives as unpaid workers in the home has largely disappeared. Some of those who would otherwise find themselves in this category receive welfare benefits instead regardless of whether or not they are in the labor force. It was shown in Section 5.3 that a large proportion of the immigrant women in Denmark who were registered as unemployed did not want a job. The relatively lower likelihood of immigrant women being employed in Denmark compared to Germany is likely to be a reflection of this.

Age, which was shown to be of some importance for whether or not one participated in the labor force, seems to be less important for determining whether or not one actually has a job, given that one is in the labor force. For both Germany and Denmark the variable is insignificant in all models. The number of years-since-migration does not seem to be important for the employment of immigrants either.

State of health is, however, very influential on whether one has a job or not, just as it was very important for labor force participation. Whereas in Germany poor health reduces the chances of immigrants being employed by 82 percent, in Denmark this decrease is a little smaller, namely, approximately 72 percent. The estimates are robust and significant in all three models for immigrants in both Germany and Denmark.

Employment in the home country, which for immigrants in Germany had a positive effect on the likelihood of being in the labor force, has a negative effect on the likelihood of those in the labor force being employed. This is unexpected, but one explanation could be that although home-country experience may give formal access to the labor force, in reality it is hard to use it to further one's employment chances. Immigrants could also be slightly less inclined to take just any job, given that they have a specific experience (it increases their reservation wages). In addition, there may be transferability barriers. For Denmark, the variable is insignificant.

As expected, having an education from the home country increases the likelihood of being employed in both countries. As was the case in the previous section, the Danish estimates are less robust than the German estimates when the additional variables are included in models 2 and 3. Correspondingly, one would expect that education or training acquired in Germany/Denmark would also increase the likelihood of being employed. In contrast to Table 5.8, only upper secondary education in Germany increases the chances of having a job. Compared to immigrants with no education in Germany, the chances are 3 times higher. Controlling for language, origin, and other covariates in models 2 and 3 this effect disappears. In Denmark, on the other hand, a university degree increases the likelihood significantly, by 7 times. However, when the additional variables are included in models 2 and 3, this effect disappears again. The effect of having vocational training in Germany or Denmark stays significant in all models for both countries. This indicates that vocational training is a valuable asset in the respective labor markets, and having it increases the chances of having a job.

Language skills also have a clearly positive influence on the likelihood of being employed. In Germany, the odds of being in employment are 2 to 3 times higher if one speaks the language fluently. In Denmark, the odds of being in employment are 3 to 4 times higher if one speaks the language fluently compared to if one speaks the language poorly or very poorly.

Nationalities that generally had the highest likelihood of labor force participation in Section 5.4 also have the highest likelihood of being employed. In Germany, immigrants from Poland have a significantly higher likelihood of being in employment compared to immigrants from Turkey. This pattern is not the same for immigrants in Denmark. As can be seen from Table 5.9, it is particularly immigrants from Vietnam, Poland, the former Yugoslavia, and Pakistan who have the highest likelihood of employment, while those from Lebanon and Somalia have the lowest likelihood of employment compared to immigrants from Turkey. For Yugoslavs, Pakistanis and Poles the country of origin effect becomes insignificant in model 3, when we control for unemployment in region, contact with natives, citizenship, enclaves, and religion.

Refugee status, which was shown to have a negative effect on labor supply, particularly in Germany, is also shown to have a negative effect on the likelihood of employment in Germany. The refugee effect, although not significant, is the opposite for Denmark. As mentioned earlier, the work restrictions placed on refugees in Germany can partly explain this difference. However, as the basis of residency plays such a limited role in the case of Denmark, the difference could also be due to a shift in the definition of a refugee, which means that, as noted by Coleman (1999), a proportion of those who previously came as guest workers are today forced to come as refugees, or they would not be granted residency visas.

As was the case for the labor supply decision, high regional unemployment has a negative effect on the likelihood of having a job in Germany, while the effect is insignificant in Denmark. Surprisingly, citizenship plays no significant role on the likelihood of employment in either Germany or Denmark. As mentioned in the previous section, the moderate influence of citizenship should be seen as implying that the variables that are important for employment and for which there is divergence between those with foreign and those with German/Danish citizenship, are already included in the model and, thus, it is not citizenship per se that is influential in whether one is employed or not.

Model 3 shows that for immigrants in Denmark, there is a clear relationship between the likelihood of employment and the immigrants' contact with natives. We recognize that there may be a risk of endogeneity because, to a certain extent,

Table 5.8. Binomial logistic regressions. Probability of being employed in Germany for 18-59-year-old immigrants in workforce, excluding students.

		Model 1			Model 2			Model 3		
		Estimate	St. Error	OddsRatio	Estimate	St. Error	OddsRatio	Estimate	St. Error	OddsRatio
Constant		1.743*	0.746	-	1.918*	0.788	-	2.105*	0.837	-
Gender and small children	Male	-0.615*	0.128	0.541	-0.429*	0.134	0.651	-0.449*	0.136	0.638
	Male with children	-0.286*	0.133	0.751	-0.132	0.138	0.877	-0.110	0.140	0.896
	Female with children	-0.079	0.227	0.924	-0.048	0.233	0.953	-0.072	0.235	0.931
Age		-0.007	0.040	0.993	0.030	0.041	1.031	0.027	0.041	1.028
Age^2		-0.0004	0.001	1.000	-0.0005	0.001	1.000	-0.0004	0.001	1.000
Years Since Migration		0.008	0.020	1.008	0.005	0.022	1.005	0.004	0.022	1.004
Years Since Migration^2		0.0003	0.0005	1.000	0.00001	0.0005	1.000	0.0001	0.0005	1.000
Bad health		-1.715*	0.179	0.180	-1.683*	0.185	0.186	-1.682*	0.187	0.186
Employment in Home Country		-0.230	0.125	0.794	-0.268*	0.130	0.765	-0.293*	0.131	0.746
Education in Home Country		0.731*	0.134	2.078	0.458*	0.142	1.581	0.461*	0.143	1.585
Education in Germany	Primary and lower secondary	0.130	0.183	1.139	-0.232	0.193	0.793	-0.215	0.194	0.806
	Upper secondary	1.073*	0.413	2.924	0.427	0.423	1.532	0.410	0.425	1.507
	University	0.473	0.312	1.604	0.104	0.328	1.110	0.041	0.331	1.042
Vocational Training in Germany		0.571*	0.172	1.770	0.429*	0.177	1.535	0.395*	0.177	1.485
Language	Speaks average/well				0.431*	0.157	1.539	0.303	0.168	1.354
	Speaks fluently				0.911*	0.195	2.486	0.725*	0.206	2.065
Land of Origin	Former Yugoslavia				0.207	0.174	1.230	0.053	0.189	1.054
	Iran				0.132	0.187	1.141	0.014	0.192	1.014
	Lebanon				-0.309	0.172	0.734	-0.314	0.173	0.731
	Pakistan				-	-	-	-	-	-
	Poland				0.423*	0.177	1.527	0.213	0.216	1.238
	Somalia				-	-	-	-	-	-
	Vietnam				-	-	-	-	-	-
Refugee (Yes vs. no)					-0.484*	0.134	0.616	-0.460*	0.135	0.631
Unemployment in region (in percent)					-0.111*	0.016	0.895	-0.110*	0.016	0.896
German citizen					0.246	0.307	1.279	0.204	0.308	1.226
Contact with Natives (much vs. less)								0.411	0.231	1.508
Religion	Strong faith, Muslim							-0.239	0.155	0.787
	Little faith, Muslim							-0.110	0.165	0.895
	Strong faith, not Muslim							0.250	0.236	1.283
Live in Enclaves								-0.425*	0.105	0.654
AIC (Intercept and covariates)		2,632.4			2,512.8			2,492.4		
Likelihood ratio		209.2			346.8			373.3		
No. of Observations		3,052			3,052			3,050		

*= Significant at 5 percent-level.

Table 5.9. Binomial logistic regressions. Probability of being employed in Denmark for 18-59-year-old immigrants in workforce, excl. students.

		Model 1			Model 2			Model 3		
		Estimate	St. Error	OddsRatio	Estimate	St. Error	OddsRatio	Estimate	St. Error	OddsRatio
Constant		3.194*	0.967	-	1.542	1.114	-	1.814	1.206	-
Gender and small children	Male	0.584*	0.181	1.792	0.833*	0.203	2.299	0.755*	0.206	2.127
	Male with children	-0.450*	0.193	0.638	-0.049	0.212	0.952	0.000	0.216	1.000
	Female with children	-0.749*	0.186	0.473	-0.269	0.207	0.764	-0.229	0.211	0.796
Age		-0.100	0.054	0.905	-0.048	0.058	0.953	-0.054	0.060	0.948
Age^2		0.001	0.001	1.001	0.001	0.001	1.001	0.001	0.001	1.001
Years Since Migration		-0.078	0.042	0.925	-0.067	0.051	0.935	-0.065	0.051	0.937
Years Since Migration^2		0.003*	0.001	1.003	0.001	0.001	1.001	0.001	0.001	1.001
Bad health		-1.115*	0.321	0.328	-1.311*	0.345	0.269	-1.339*	0.361	0.262
Employment in Home Country		0.068	0.165	1.070	-0.278	0.181	0.758	-0.296	0.184	0.744
Education in Home Country		0.588*	0.168	1.800	0.185	0.193	1.203	0.169	0.196	1.184
Education in Denmark	Primary and lower secondary	-0.065	0.193	0.937	-0.332	0.213	0.717	-0.371	0.217	0.690
	Upper secondary	0.254	0.259	1.289	-0.287	0.292	0.750	-0.317	0.293	0.728
	University	1.964*	0.523	7.128	1.026	0.559	2.789	0.939	0.558	2.558
Vocational Training in Denmark		0.964*	0.216	2.622	0.648*	0.239	1.913	0.618*	0.244	1.854
Language	Speaks average/well				0.528*	0.207	1.695	0.470*	0.215	1.599
	Speaks fluently				1.397*	0.305	4.044	1.183*	0.315	3.263
Land of Origin	Former Yugoslavia				0.938*	0.331	2.555	0.603	0.387	1.827
	Iran				0.022	0.350	1.022	-0.292	0.392	0.747
	Lebanon				-1.726*	0.259	0.178	-1.728*	0.263	0.178
	Pakistan				0.694*	0.328	2.002	0.555	0.334	1.742
	Poland				0.734*	0.292	2.083	0.484	0.426	1.622
	Somalia				-0.786*	0.314	0.456	-0.972*	0.320	0.378
	Vietnam				1.477*	0.378	4.378	1.457*	0.505	4.294
Refugee (Yes vs. no)					0.237	0.194	1.268	0.234	0.198	1.263
Unemployment in region (in percent)					0.010	0.069	1.010	-0.004	0.070	0.996
Danish citizen					0.236	0.188	1.266	0.192	0.192	1.211
Contact with Natives (much vs. Less)								0.658*	0.166	1.931
Religion	Strong faith, Muslim							-0.137	0.334	0.872
	Little faith, Muslim							0.113	0.386	1.120
	Strong faith, not Muslim							-0.771*	0.315	0.462
Live in Enclaves								-0.427*	0.152	0.652
AIC (Intercept and covariates)		1,589.3			1,411.1			1,389.4		
Likelihood ratio		190.9			392.7			423.8		
No. of Observations		1,735			1,734			1,733		

*= Significant at 5 percent-level.

immigrants who are employed would be expected to meet natives in their workplaces. However, immigrants are often in jobs that do not offer much contact with natives (i.e. assembly lines etc). Evidence in favor of the opposite relationship is that 10 to 12 percent of the employed immigrants state that German/Danish friends or acquaintances found their current jobs for them.

The importance of religion is also included in model 3. The impact of religion is only significant for Denmark, where the religious (particularly non-Muslims) have a lower likelihood of being employed than others. While to some extent religion is of importance for whether one is employed or not in Denmark, the previous section showed that it was more important for labor force participation in Germany than in Denmark.

In both Germany and Denmark the likelihood of employment is negatively related to living in a suburb with a high ethnic concentration. The odds of being employed are reduced by 33 percent in Germany and 40 percent in Denmark if one lives in a suburb where half or more of the residents are immigrants, compared to living in a suburb where the ethnic concentration is lower.

As mentioned in Section 5.2, the economic incentives to work could be expected to influence the choice between working and not working. An alternative regression where the economic incentives are added to the explanatory variables in Tables 5.8 and 5.9 shows that the economic incentives in a cross-sectional analysis, like this one, have only a significant effect on the employment chances in Germany, when we control for the type of benefits received (UI benefits versus social assistance) together with the extra variables of models 2 and 3. The endogenity problems might simply be too severe in Denmark for a cross-sectional approach to work.

It has been shown many times that incentives are important for the individual's employment record. The endogenity problem can be somewhat reduced by lagging the replacement rate and adding other lagged independent variables, e.g. lagged observed characteristics like the unemployment history. Lately, Pedersen et al. (2003) take this approach and show that for Denmark, those immigrants who had clear economic incentives to have a job in 1999 were, two years later, generally employed to a greater extent than those who had lower economic incentives. In the appendix we present the result of a similar analysis but there we only include individuals who were unemployed in 1999. Unlike Pedersen et al. (2003) we also include availability in 1999 and control for the experience of unemployment in 1999. These results confirm once again that financial incentives matter for the employment chances.

In the regression shown in the appendix we include availability, as mentioned, in order to see whether the unemployed immigrants' lack of availability can lower the likelihood of being employed in the future. The results are as expected: the unemployed workers who met the ILO's availability criteria in 1999 had a significantly higher likelihood than others of being employed in 2001, when controlling for gender, age, education, the replacement rate, and the presence of children. It is not possible to carry out a similar estimation for immigrants in Germany as we have data for only one year, 2002.

Overall the analysis here shows that, in particular, good health, a strong educational background from the home country or even better, vocational education (– not university) – from Germany/Denmark, and good language skills have a positive influence on the likelihood of being employed for those in the labor force. Similarly, there is a positive relationship between being employed and being in contact with natives and/or living in a suburb with relatively few immigrants. Of those who participate in the labor force in Germany, the likelihood of being employed is higher for women, and, to a certain extent, for immigrants from Poland. The likelihood is also higher if one is not a refugee and had no employment in the home country. In Denmark, immigrant women (especially those with children) and people from Lebanon and Somalia have a lower likelihood of being employed. However, for all immigrants who participate in the labor market, there are no significant employment effects of either age or years since migration. Neither in Germany nor in Denmark does citizenship affect the chances for employment once the individuals are in the labor market.

These factors are also, to a large extent, the ones that characterized immigrants who are in the labor force. The difference is, among other things, that while men in Germany have a higher likelihood of participating in the labor market than women, those who are in the labor force have a lower likelihood of being, employed and the same seems to apply to those with work experience in their home countries. Similarly, Iranians and Pakistanis in Denmark are relatively less likely to participate in the labor force, given their other characteristics; however, they are clearly more likely to be employed than Lebanese and Somalis.

5.6 Immigrants and the Job Hierarchy

So far this chapter has focused on whether immigrants participate in the labor force and have a job. In Chapter 4 it was shown that immigrants not only differ from natives in that there are fewer of them in employment, but also that the types of jobs they perform when they are employed generally require fewer qualifications. In this section, the differences between immigrants with jobs requiring high qualifications and those with lower level jobs will be examined more closely. The aim here is to identify the factors that are important for whether immigrants succeed in acquiring jobs that require high qualifications. The analysis concentrates on employed wage earners and assisting spouses aged 18-59, regardless of incomes. Unemployed immigrants and immigrants out of the labor force are omitted.

Immigrants are over-represented in the lowest level jobs (see Table 4.4), where 28 percent of foreign citizens in Germany and 32 percent in Denmark are "Elementary operators", the lowest job classification. In sharp contrast, 7 percent of the natives in Germany and 11 percent in Denmark are in this classification. On the other hand, the proportion with professional jobs was higher among natives, with 11 percent in

Germany and 13 percent in Denmark, as opposed to only 3 percent and 5 percent of those with foreign citizenship in Germany and Denmark, respectively.

The relatively limited number of immigrants in jobs requiring high qualifications makes it necessary to split up the general job categories. To do this, wage and salary earners are divided into three groups:[13] "Upper/middle level wage and salary earners", "Lower level wage and salary earners" and "Elementary operators", who make up the lowest classification.

In line with the previous sections, in order to increase the number of observations in the Danish part of the analysis, all immigrants from the 8 non-Western countries, regardless of citizenship, are included. To preserve space, unlike in the two previous sections, the variables are included in one step.

Using the three job categories defined above, the variable for job type is a response variable in a multinomial logit regression, where job type is explained by a range of personal characteristics. As in the two previous sections, it is expected that human capital factors play an important role. Hence, the differences in job types are expected to be related to acquisition of the required qualifications and language skills, and employment in higher level jobs is expected to be positively correlated with longer residency period, age (to the extent that one has an education), and the family situation. As the previous section showed, the presence of children increases the labor supply of males and decreases the labor supply of females. A corresponding effect could be expected to be found for professional ambition.

Similarly, one could expect that immigrants from near-neighboring countries, such as Poland, would find it easier to get a higher level job than those from Turkey or perhaps Somalia. A higher level job might also be expected to be related to German/Danish citizenship, contact with natives, and living in suburbs with lower ethnic concentrations. The effect of religion can be ambiguous, stricter religious beliefs are expected to give either a higher work ethic or a negative attitude towards the surrounding modern society.

The results for Germany are shown in Table 5.10 and for Denmark in Table 5.11. The model includes gender, small children, age, years since migration, health, education both from Germany/Denmark and from the home country, and employment in the home country, language skills, sector, country of origin, citizenship, refugee status, contact with natives, religion and ethnic concentration in the surrounding suburb.

The overall impression from these estimates is that immigrants in Germany have a greater likelihood of being employed at the upper/middle level than being "Elementary operators" if they have completed a university degree, vocational qualifica-

---

13 The following categories from Table 4.4 are combined to make up three job categories. "Legislators and managers" and "Professionals and technicians" make up the upper/middle wage and salary level. "Clerks", "Service and sales workers", "Agricultural/fishery workers", "Craft related workers", and "Plant and machinery operators" make up the lower level, while "Elementary operators" are a separate group.

tion or upper secondary school in Germany, have qualifications or work experience from the home country, speak good German, are from Iran, are not refugees, live in an area that does not have a high ethnic concentration and work in "Financial intermediation" or "Public sector".

In Denmark, the likelihood of an employed immigrant holding a job at the upper/middle level rather than being an "Elementary operator" also increases if one has completed a university degree, vocational qualification or upper secondary school in Denmark, or if one has an education from the home country, speaks good Danish, is from Somalia, lives in an area that does not have a high ethnic concentration and is employed within the "Public sector". However, the results also show that having Danish citizenship, and not being a practicing Muslim are decisive in having an upper/middle level job. In contrast to Germany refugee status does not seem to be crucial.

In Germany, lower level wage and salary earners differ from "Elementary operators", in that they are more often men, are slightly younger, have completed vocational training in Germany or have an education from the home country, speak fairly good German, are more often Iranian and work in "Construction", but less often in "Service sector" and "Public services". In Denmark, lower level wage and salary earners more often also have vocational training or secondary education than is the case for "Elementary operators". Likewise, they are also less often employed in the "Service sector". However, only in Denmark do the lower level group have longer periods of residency and have more often had employment experience in the home country and less often are women with children.

Tables 5.10 and 5.11 also show that education, training and language skills are among the variables that seem to have the most importance for what type of employment immigrants have in both countries. Immigrants in Germany who speak German fluently are 0.22 times more likely to be employed in an upper/middle level job compared to being employed as an "Elementary Operator". For immigrants in Denmark who speak fluent Danish, the likelihood increases to 0.42 times. In Germany, immigrants with average/good language skills are also significantly more likely to be employed on the lower level rather than as an "Elementary operator". In Denmark, this effect is insignificant.

Similarly, immigrants who have obtained a university degree in Germany have a 0.76 times higher likelihood of being employed on the upper/middle level compared to the reference category, while the corresponding figure in Denmark is 0.65. As mentioned, vocational training also has a positive effect on the likelihood of having a job on a higher or a lower level in both countries. However, only in Denmark does completion of secondary education have a positive influence on the likelihood of being employed on the lower level.

There could be several reasons why completion of secondary education has a positive effect in Denmark, despite it being a preparation for further tertiary study rather than a job qualification. First, some portion of the employed will also be con-

Table 5.10. Multinomial logit results on the probabilities of employment on upper/middle level and lower level in Germany. Reference outcome is the probability of being employed on elementary level, excluding students.

		Probability of employment on Upper/middle level			Probability of employment on Lower level		
		Coefficient	St. Error	Marginal Effects	Coefficient	St. Error	Marginal Effects
Constant		-3.326*	1.463	-	1.317*	0.908	-
Gender and small children	Male	0.187	0.211	-0.025	0.565*	0.153	0.120
	Male with children	0.199	0.276	0.019	0.071	0.184	0.000
	Female with children	-0.124	0.267	-0.008	-0.081	0.208	-0.009
Age		-0.045	0.067	0.006	-0.130*	0.046	-0.027
Age^2		0.0003	0.001	0.0001	0.002*	0.001	0.000
Years Since Migration		-0.003	0.032	-0.002	0.021	0.022	0.005
Years Since Migration^2		-0.0002	0.001	0.00001	-0.0005	0.0005	0.0001
Bad health		-0.384	0.502	-0.056	0.252	0.314	0.085
Employment in Home Country		0.555*	0.218	0.052	0.191	0.148	-0.002
Education in Home Country		0.724*	0.281	0.052	0.404*	0.170	0.039
Education in Germany	Primary and lower secondary	0.522	0.317	0.058	0.112	0.219	-0.021
	Upper secondary	1.375*	0.426	0.251	-0.035	0.384	-0.180
	University	4.763*	1.035	0.760	0.993	1.084	-0.505
Vocational Training in Germany		1.623*	0.259	0.048	1.599*	0.218	0.189
Language	Speaks average/well	1.216*	0.401	0.094	0.611*	0.197	0.046
	Speaks fluently	2.439*	0.426	0.224	1.133*	0.235	0.020
German citizen		0.343	0.388	0.014	0.320	0.318	0.044
Land of origin	Former Yugoslavia	0.088	0.306	0.010	0.015	0.207	-0.004
	Iran	1.044*	0.316	0.070	0.716*	0.231	0.061
	Lebanon	0.217	0.341	0.032	-0.047	0.221	-0.031
	Poland	0.427	0.319	0.026	0.312	0.229	0.037
Refugee (Yes vs. no)		-0.491*	0.231	-0.048	-0.086	0.160	0.017
Industry	Primary sector	-0.770	0.858	-0.043	-0.564	0.409	-0.087
	Construction	0.564	0.398	0.020	0.547*	0.249	0.074
	Sales and Repairs	0.599	0.311	0.041	0.392	0.202	0.036
	Transport, post and comm.	-0.239	0.654	-0.053	0.393	0.405	0.107
	Financial intermediation etc.	2.352*	0.936	0.529	-0.259	0.983	-0.388
	Service sector	0.169	0.256	0.073	-0.594*	0.164	-0.159
	Public sector	1.828*	0.298	0.402	-0.463	0.238	-0.336
	Not stated	0.003	0.666	0.141	-1.783*	0.593	-0.400
Contact with Natives (much vs. less)		0.776	0.764	0.069	0.058	0.299	-0.037
Religion	Strong faith, Muslim	-0.483	0.268	-0.050	-0.053	0.185	0.025
	Little faith, Muslim	-0.266	0.273	-0.042	0.152	0.196	0.057
	Strong faith, not Muslim	-0.303	0.263	-0.010	-0.324	0.200	-0.055
Live in Enclaves		-0.441*	0.169	-0.044	-0.099	0.118	0.012

Log likelihood value	-1,579.1
X^2	835.9
No. of Observations	1,977

*= Significant at 5 percent-level.

Table 5.11. Multinomial logit results on the probabilities of employment on upper/middle level and lower level in Denmark. Reference outcome is the probability of being employed on elementary level, excluding students.

		Probability of employment on Upper/middle level			Probability of employment on Lower level		
		Coefficient	St. Error	Marginal Effects	Coefficient	St. Error	Marginal Effects
Constant		-4.601*	1.672	-	0.914	1.242	-
Gender and small children	Male	-0.022	0.264	0.026	-0.222	0.219	-0.050
	Male with children	-0.023	0.304	0.001	-0.038	0.241	-0.006
	Female with children	-0.534	0.331	-0.019	-0.566*	0.263	-0.070
Age		0.040	0.076	0.017	-0.070	0.062	-0.022
Age^2		-0.0002	0.001	0.0002	0.001	0.001	0.0003
Years Since Migration		0.072	0.060	-0.002	0.110*	0.049	0.017
Years Since Migration^2		-0.003	0.001	0.00003	-0.003*	0.001	0.0004
Bad health		-0.363	0.829	-0.074	0.156	0.578	0.079
Employment in Home Country		0.073	0.290	-0.053	0.491*	0.225	0.106
Education in Home Country		0.671*	0.290	0.118	0.042	0.232	-0.086
Education in Denmark	Primary and lower secondary	-0.092	0.340	-0.071	0.432	0.264	0.111
	Upper secondary	1.709*	0.404	0.128	1.247*	0.370	0.018
	University	3.568*	0.666	0.647	0.591	0.738	-0.485
Vocational Training in Denmark		1.950*	0.343	0.168	1.307*	0.323	-0.008
Language	Speaks average/good	1.794*	0.637	0.278	0.199	0.261	-0.191
	Speaks fluently	2.581*	0.682	0.417	0.463	0.341	-0.275
Danish citizen		0.663*	0.293	0.096	0.131	0.233	-0.058
Land of origin	Former Yugoslavia	-0.415	0.510	-0.064	-0.019	0.392	0.048
	Iran	0.565	0.586	-0.022	0.838	0.511	0.110
	Lebanon	0.869	0.562	0.036	0.805	0.454	0.055
	Pakistan	0.217	0.418	0.119	-0.522	0.326	-0.160
	Poland	-0.690	0.546	-0.094	-0.114	0.453	0.057
	Somalia	1.181*	0.550	0.115	0.724	0.430	-0.020
	Vietnam	-0.630	0.593	-0.106	0.099	0.475	0.097
Refugee (Yes vs. no)		0.014	0.279	0.037	-0.253	0.227	-0.063
Industry	Primary sector	-1.152	1.160	-0.101	-0.601	0.539	-0.026
	Construction	0.720	0.954	-0.046	1.173	0.771	0.153
	Sales and Repairs	0.618	0.421	0.096	0.151	0.323	-0.057
	Transport, post and comm.	0.296	0.484	-0.040	0.655	0.359	0.108
	Financial intermediation etc.	0.828	1.216	0.397	-1.451	1.274	-0.435
	Service sector	-0.481	0.311	0.126	-1.710*	0.233	-0.348
	Public sector	1.232*	0.323	0.297	-0.312	0.264	-0.266
	Not stated	0.357	0.455	0.197	-0.825*	0.359	-0.255
Contact with Natives (much vs. less)		0.258	0.344	0.013	0.236	0.230	0.023
Religion	Strong faith, muslim	-0.888*	0.445	-0.154	0.045	0.360	0.126
	Little faith, muslim	0.091	0.456	0.056	-0.281	0.393	-0.081
	Strong faith, not muslim	0.373	0.383	0.069	0.009	0.324	-0.052
Live in Enclaves		-0.574*	0.261	-0.093	0.014	0.194	0.074

Log likelihood value	-985.1
X^2	686.8
No. of Observations	1,290

*= Significant at 5 percent-level.

tinuing with tertiary studies. Second, a large percentage of students never gain any qualifications and drop out of tertiary education, and this tendency is generally greater among immigrants than others (see Jacobsen and Smith, 2003).

As expected, having an education from the home country also has a positive influence on job type. In both Germany and Denmark, there is a significantly higher likelihood of being an "upper/middle level wage and salary earner" if one has an education from the home country. For "lower level wage and salary earners", this is only the case for immigrants in Germany. Employment in the home country has a particularly positive effect in Germany on the likelihood of being an "upper/middle wage and salary earner", while in Denmark it only has a positive influence on the likelihood of being a "lower level wage and salary earner".

Skills from the home country in the form of work experience or education, therefore, generally seem to be of greater significance in Germany than in Denmark. On the other hand, in both Germany and Denmark there seems to be a positive effect of increasing periods of residency for "lower level wage and salary earners". This relationship can be encouraging in that, following relatively short retraining, immigrants can bring their qualifications up to the lower wage and salary level, while achieving employment on an upper/middle level will imply a longer retraining period. The significance of the period of residency can also imply that there is on-the-job-training in the workplace.

The age variable is not significant in Denmark. However, it is significant for immigrants in Germany. All else being equal, the jobs requiring higher qualifications are held by those who are slightly younger. This is surprising because qualification levels would be expected to increase with age. In relation to immigration, one would, at the same time, expect that a proportion of the assimilation process will occur over generations, such that first-generation immigrants undertake relatively low level jobs in the expectation that their children will attain something better. This relationship would be expected to be of greater importance in Germany than in Denmark because immigration in Germany has, to a greater extent and from earlier on, been dominated by guest workers who were recruited for unskilled jobs.

In Germany, it can be seen that women have a lower likelihood of being employed on the lower level as compared to being employed as "Elementary operators". In Denmark, this is only the case for women with children. The reason seems to be that many immigrant women are employed in jobs that do not, over time, provide career development leading to jobs on the lower level. If one is a cleaner one probably stays a cleaner, while unskilled workers in industrial production, for example, can improve their qualifications by undertaking courses. For employment on the upper/middle level, gender and children have only limited effects. As demonstrated earlier, formal education and training is vital for higher level employment, and hence, only women who have a higher level of education and are in the labor force will be eligible for such jobs. Therefore, the barrier for women is, to a larger extent, not having the relevant education.

There is no significant difference in the states of health of immigrants employed in the different types of jobs either in Denmark or in Germany.

Among the relatively few immigrants from Somalia who have a job in Denmark, surprisingly many have employment on the upper/middle level. But the effect of country of origin on immigrants in Denmark is in general small. In Germany, Iranian immigrants have a significantly higher likelihood of being "upper/middle level wage and salary earners" than of being "lower level wage and salary earners".

Overall, the analysis in this section has shown that education and training as well as language skills appear to be crucial for which type of jobs immigrants hold. It is, however, reassuring in the sense that these are well-founded qualification requirements which the individual has the opportunity to influence.

These estimations do not provide much evidence on the extent to which immigrants make use of their qualifications on an equal basis with natives. The numbers available for Denmark imply that immigrants do not, to the same degree as Danes, get the full benefits of their educational qualifications, especially from the education obtained in their home country. Uncertainty with regard to the value of educational qualifications is likely to have an important role in this situation, but discrimination cannot be excluded as an explanation. In any case only few of the immigrants in Germany and Denmark, who could not utilize their education and training from the home country, stated that they believed this was due to discrimination.

5.7 Summary and Conclusions

This chapter has examined the possible explanations for why immigrants generally have a lower labor market attachment than natives, particularly in Denmark.

One of the reasons could be that the financial incentives to work are low. A computation of the immigrants' financial rewards from working compared to being unemployed, the GAP, shows that the proportion of immigrants in the labor force between 25-55 years old who have less than €100 extra per month from working was between 17-18 percent in Germany and between 33-41 percent in Denmark.

The financial incentives to work are lower in Denmark primarily because the unemployment benefit system pays a higher replacement rate to the low paid groups, which include many immigrants. In Germany, the lowest paid receive relatively lower benefits than in Denmark, and the middle and high earners relatively more.

With the cross-section data at hand we have not been able to analyze whether the financial incentives, represented by the replacement rate, influence the individuals' future employment situations. In our cross sectional analysis the replacement rate is only significant in Germany when we control for the type of benefits received (UI benefits or social assistance). We know, nevertheless, from studies in Denmark alone (where we do have two waves, 1999 and 2001) that financial incentives have a significant effect on the employment prospects both for immigrants and for natives (see also Pedersen et al., 2003).

The lack of availability to the labor market among immigrants has, as expected, a negative influence on immigrants' future employment chances (again tested only on Danish data). Therefore, it is striking that the proportion of unemployed immigrants who meet the ILO's availability criteria is 60 percent in Germany and 51 percent in Denmark, compared to 66 percent of the unemployed workers in general in Denmark in 2002. In Denmark, immigrants (and natives) receiving social assistance are less likely to meet the availability criteria, whereas in Germany this does not vary much with the type of compensation. Correspondingly, the availability among female immigrants is lower than male immigrants in Denmark, while the difference is less pronounced in Germany. This is largely due to the differences between the welfare systems in the two countries, where the Danish model, to a much greater extent, encourages women to join the labor force independently of their employment chances and aspirations. Apparently, the consequence of this is that fewer immigrant women in Germany take care of the home and at the same time receive unemployment compensation than in Denmark.

The analysis on which factors are decisive for whether immigrants participate in the labor force shows that female immigrants, all else being equal, are relatively less likely to be in the labor force in Germany than in Denmark, whereas female immigrants in Germany have a relatively (compared to men) better chance of being employed, once they participate in the labor force.

The analysis also shows that human capital factors are important for the immigrants' labor market attachment in both Germany and Denmark. Hence, the likelihood both of participating in the labor force and of being employed are positively related to good health, good language skills, and a good educational background, either from the home country or, even better, from Germany/Denmark. Generally, educational qualifications acquired in the home country play a greater role on the immigrants' labor market attachment in Germany than in Denmark.

Vocational training seems to have a positive effect on labor market attachment in general in both countries, whereas the benefits of having a university degree are less clear. Employment seems to be higher for immigrants with a university degree solely because it increases labor force participation, whereas the employment chances for these immigrants are not better than for immigrants with no education. There are traces of a positive effect on unemployment in Denmark for university degree immigrants, but this is not beyond what good language skills do to reduce the unemployment risk. In fact, the employment chances for immigrants with vocational training are higher than for immigrants with a university degree in both countries. Fortunately, a university degree significantly increases the chance that an immigrant will get a job at the upper or middle occupational level.

Being around 25 to 45 years old and having a longer period of residency are also decisive factors for immigrants' participation in the labor force, both in Germany and in Denmark. On the other hand, these factors are not decisive for the subsequent employment chance, only for participation.

The importance of other variables differs between the two countries. For example, refugees and those who live in areas of high unemployment have a significantly lower likelihood of participating in the labor force or being employed in Germany, while this is not the case in Denmark. The analysis also shows that Polish immigrants, all else being equal, have the highest likelihood of participating in the labor force and of being employed in both Denmark and Germany. On the other hand, Lebanese immigrants have the lowest likelihood of participating in the labor market in Germany. While in Denmark, Lebanese immigrants (and to the same extent Somali immigrants) are particularly poorly represented among the employed, Iranians and Pakistanis have the lowest likelihood of participating in the labor force.

The variables for religious background and contact with natives are not decisive for the above results. The estimates on these variables suggest that contact with natives is generally positively related to employment; in Germany by increasing labor force participation and in Denmark by furthering the employment chances for the labor-force participants. The opposite applies to living in areas that have a high ethnic concentration, except that this also seems to reduce participation in Denmark. Having a strong religious faith decreases employment probabilities, although this effect is not significant for Muslims in Denmark and non-Muslims in Germany. As with the variable "contact with natives", the influence is via participation in Germany and via employment chances for the participants in Denmark.

Among the immigrants who are employed, the human capital variables are shown to be of central importance in determining what types of jobs they hold. Here the educational and language qualifications are particularly decisive. This finding suggests that well founded qualification requirements determine employment. This is a positive result in that these are job requirements that the individual immigrant has the ability to influence.

References:

Antecol, Heather, Peter Kuhn and Stephen J. Trejo. 2003. "Assimilation via Prices or Quantities? Labor Market Institutions and Immigrant Earnings Growth in Australia, Canada and the United States." *IZA Discussion Paper* No. 802. Bonn.

Bauer, Thomas K., Barbara Dietz, Klaus F. Zimmermann and Eric Zwintz. 2004. German Migration: "Development, Assimilation and Labor Market Effects," in K. F. Zimmermann (ed.): *European Migration: What Do We know?*, forthcoming 2004. Oxford: Oxford University Press.

Bender, Stefan and Werner Karr. 1993. "Arbeitslosigkeit von ausländischen Arbeitnehmern: Ein Versuch, nationalitätenspezifische Arbeitslosenquoten zu erklären," *Mitteilungen aus der Arbeitsmarkt- und Berufsforschung*, 2, 192-206.

Borjas, George J. 1985. "Assimilation, Changes in Cohort Quality, and the Earnings of Immigrants," *Journal of Labor Economics* 3, 463-89.

Chiswick, Barry R. 1978. "The Effect of Americanization on the Earnings of Foreign-Born Men," *Journal of Political Economy* 86, October, 897-921.

Coleman, David. 1999. "International Migration in the context of global demographic change," in D. Coleman and E. Wadensjö: *Immigration to Denmark: International and National Aspects*. Aarhus: Aarhus University Press, 13-45.

Constant, Amelie. 1998. *The Earnings of Male and Female Guestworkers and Their Assimilation into the German Labor Market: A Panel Study 1984-1993*. Ph. D. Dissertation, Vanderbilt University.

Cramer. 1984. "Multivariate Analyse von Arbeitslosenquoten," *Mitteilungen aus der Arbeitsmarkt- und Berufsforschung* 3, 330-335.

Hansen, Hans. 2002. *Elements of Social Security, 9th edition*. Copenhagen.

Jacobsen, Vibeke and Nina Smith. 2003. "The Educational Attainment of the Children of the Danish 'Guest Worker' Immigrants." *IZA Discussion Paper* No. 749. Bonn.

Ministry for Refugees, Immigration, and Integration. 2002. *Yearbook of Foreigners in Denmark 2002*. Copenhagen.

Pedersen, Søren and Nina Smith. 2003. "Kan det betale sig at arbejde – Nye beregninger 2001" (Does it pay to work? – New calculations from 2001). Chapter 3 in *Fra mangel på arbejde til mangel på arbejdskraft* (From lack of work to lack of labor) by N. Smith, P. J. Pedersen, S. Pedersen and M. L. Schultz-Nielsen. Copenhagen.

Pedersen, Peder J., Søren Pedersen and Marie Louise Schultz-Nielsen. 2003. "Indvandrernes incitamenter" (Immigrants' incentives). Chapter 4 in *Fra mangel på arbejde til mangel på arbejdskraft* (From lack of work to lack of labor) by N. Smith, P. J. Pedersen, S. Pedersen and M. L. Schultz-Nielsen. Copenhagen.

Schultz-Nielsen, Marie Louise. 2001. *The Integration of Non-Western Immigrants in a Scandinavian Labour Market: The Danish experience*. Copenhagen.

Schultz-Nielsen, Marie Louise. 2002. "Hvorfor er så mange indvandrere uden beskæftigelse?". Chapter 3 in Gunnar Viby Mogensen og Poul Chr. Matthiessen (eds): *Indvandrerne og arbejdsmarkedet*. København.

Statistics Denmark. 2002. Statistiske Efterretninger, Arbejdsmarkedet. Kvartalsvise opgørelser fra arbejdskraftundersøgelsen. (The labor force survey, quarterly editions). Copenhagen.

Winkelmann, Rainer and Klaus F. Zimmermann. 1993. "Ageing, migration and labor mobility," in P. Johnson and K.F. Zimmermann (eds): *Labour Markets in an Ageing Europe.* Cambridge: Cambridge University Press, 255-282.

Appendixtable 5.1. Binomial logistic regression. Employment chances in 2001 for unemployed immigrants in 1999, Denmark.

		Estimate	St. Error	OddsRatio
Constant		12.833	8.497	–
Met availability criteria in 1999		0.484*	0.190	0.380
Gender and children 0-6 years old	Female	0.424	0.289	2.334
	Male with children	-0.007	0.257	1.015
	Female with children	-0.551	0.319	3.008
	Male/female without children	Ref.		
Age		0.275	0.167	1.317
Age^2		-0.004	0.002	0.996
Education	Primary and secondary school	-0.099	0.340	2.429
	Vocational Training	1.085*	0.463	7.933
	University	Ref.		
Long_unempl* Log(net compensation rate in 1999)		1.224	2.004	
Long_unempl[1])		-23.011	11.811	
Short_unempl* Log(net compensation rate in 1999)		-3.756*	1.727	
AIC (Intercept and covariates)		215.2		
Likelihood ratio		191.2		
No. of Observations		159		

*= Significant at 5 percent-level

Note 1) Unemployed more than half of the time from 1997 to 1999.

CHAPTER 6

Immigrant Selection and Earnings*

Amelie Constant and Marie Louise Schultz-Nielsen

6.1 Introduction

A good measure of the individual worker's labor market performance is earnings. The monetary success of native and immigrant workers is welcomed in any country, since it not only benefits the individuals concerned but also leads to higher tax revenues and lower welfare payments for the state. Moreover, if we assume that the level of earnings reflects productivity, then greater monetary success of native and immigrant workers is an indication of higher productivity, which is very desirable for any country.

The legal immigrant population of Germany in 2002 comprised 9 percent of the total population. While guest-workers made up the largest group of immigrants, the numbers of Poles, Vietnamese, and Lebanese were also high. In the same year, the immigrant population in Denmark (including descendants) amounted to 8 percent of the Danish population.

In contrast to the situation in the US, immigrants in welfare states such as Germany and Denmark enjoy considerable employment protection and sizable unemployment benefits. They tend to be highly concentrated within the host countries, both geographically and in terms of occupation. In Germany the strong employment protection regulations, coupled with high severance payments and comparatively low welfare benefits, encourage more workers to join the labor force. Once workers find a job (natives and immigrants alike), they usually stay in that job for a very long time. While employment protection is not as rigid in Denmark, welfare benefits are higher. In particular, immigrants who arrived in Denmark before 07.01.2002 enjoy very generous unemployment and welfare benefits, and this implicitly may lead to a lower level of job search activity. Consequently, we would expect that immigrants who gain employment in Denmark should fare better than immigrants in Germany, at least in terms of their earnings.[1]

---

* Constant deeply appreciates the conversations and witty remarks of Spyros Konstantopoulos. She is also indebted to Constantine Katsinis for his unflagging support and encouragement, to carry this research through.
1 In general, Danish workers earn more than German workers. In 2002, the average gross weekly earnings of an average production worker amounted to €790 in Denmark and €639 in Germany (OECD, 2003). This does not necessarily imply that it is cheaper to hire employees for German employers, primarily because employers' social contributions are higher in Germany. When

→

The earnings assimilation of immigrants has been the subject of many studies in many countries. Typical results for the US, for example, show that immigrants can approach and reach the earnings of natives with additional years of residence in the US (Chiswick, 1978), although the speed of this earnings assimilation can be slow if one adjusts for cohort effects and takes ethnicity into account (Borjas, 1985). Previous literature on the situation in Germany has shown that immigrants are not well integrated; their earnings are far below those of the natives, and there are no prospects of assimilation (Licht and Steiner, 1994, and Constant, 1998). These studies are mostly based on the traditional guest worker groups. For Denmark, however, studies have shown that there is some earnings assimilation, suggesting that certain immigrant groups in Denmark are doing well (Husted et al., 2001, and Nielsen et al., 2001).

The central aim of this chapter is to study the earnings of immigrants in Germany and Denmark based on our RFMS-G (2002) and RFMS-D (2001) surveys, and gauge any earnings dispersion among the immigrant groups within each country and across countries in a bi-national comparison. Our innovation in this chapter is that we employ the actual years of work experience in the host country, along with age and age at entry, and use the quatric specification of years of labor market experience as a better approximation than a quadratic equation. In addition, by taking advantage of our surveys we are able to disentangle work experience in the host country from years of residence in the host country. We are, furthermore, able to employ an objective measure of host country language proficiency, and we create a "pure" nationality variable by extracting the immigrants who ascend to citizenship from their corresponding nationalities. Finally in this chapter, we compare the corresponding immigrant groups in the surveys of each country.

Our economic analysis is based primarily on the human capital theory, which posits that the young and the better-educated are more likely to migrate and that migration yields higher returns to the more able and the more highly motivated. Migrants with higher levels of human capital will command higher wages in the labor market, since investment in human capital raises their productivity. Our econometric analysis of the earnings of the immigrants in Germany and Denmark uses the Heckman two-stage technique that controls for selection in the labor force. We lastly correct the errors for possible heteroscedasticity.

The chapter is organized as follows. Section 6.2 presents a brief overview of the immigration policies, laws, and "guest worker" systems of Germany and Denmark. Section 6.3 outlines the methodology and the predictions to be tested. Section 6.4 describes our immigrant samples. Section 6.5 presents the econometric findings and

→ this is taken into account the total labor costs are at almost the same level in Denmark and Germany. For instance, in the Industry and Service sectors the total labor cost per hour in 2000 was €27.10 in Denmark and €26.54 in Germany (Eurostat, 2003). Furthermore, the consumption value of earnings seems to be on the same level in the two countries, as both income taxes and prices are higher in Denmark (OECD, 2003, and OECD, 2004).

the counterfactual analysis of the earnings performance of immigrants were they to move to the other country. We conclude with a recapitulation of the main points of the chapter in Section 6.6.

6.2 The Anatomy of the Guest worker System

The German and Danish immigration systems share many features and histories, and parallels can be drawn between them. Both countries have high rates of immigration, have used the guest worker system, have not had overt and consistent immigration policies for a long time, and have experienced a shift in the composition of their immigrant populations. At the same time there are also some differences. For example, Denmark has been more liberal with its refugees and more generous with its welfare payments. In this section we review the immigration systems in both countries. We concentrate on the groups of immigrants who are closer related to our sample in the RFMS-G and RFMS-D.[2]

6.2.1 Germany's Immigrants

From the second half of the 1950s until the early 1970s Germany initiated and experienced the "guest worker migration" – demand-driven immigration. The term *guest workers* reflects the notion that workers were invited to work in Germany but were not expected to stay permanently. They were to work temporarily in Germany and help alleviate the post-war labor shortages. The *"Rotationprinzip"*, or the idea that immigrants can be employed in rotation as they are needed in the labor market, provided an excuse to the German government not to take an open position *vis à vis* an overt and consistent immigration policy. In other words, immigrants could come and go as part of a labor market scheme and not as part of an immigration policy.

The guest workers were a subgroup of economic migrants in Germany who came from Turkey and certain countries in southern Europe, namely Italy, Greece, Spain, Portugal, and Yugoslavia. Under the auspices of the Federal Labor Institute (FLI) and in cooperation with labor unions and local authorities, German employers actively recruited foreign workers, without any quota limits being imposed by the government. According to the German law, immigrants were to be recruited into identical jobs at identical wages to Germans, and only when native Germans were not available.

These immigrants were recruited to fill a need in unskilled jobs. Since the ban on recruitment in 1973, migration to Germany has been mostly supply driven. The ban excludes immigrants from other EU member countries. The composition of the immigrant groups has shifted from young males to women and children who have arrived in Germany to join their husbands and fathers, creating a strong second gen-

---

[2] For a more thorough presentation, see Chapters 2 and 4 of this volume, and Zimmermann (1995).

eration of immigrants. Various geopolitical reasons have contributed to a still changing composition of immigrant groups to Germany. The number of asylum seekers skyrocketed in Germany in the 1980s and early 1990s. Iranians made up a large percentage of this group.[3] The high numbers of refugees and asylum seekers resulted in a more restrictive asylum law. The designation of safe countries of origin, among other measures, led to a decrease in the number of asylum seekers in Germany.[4]

After the fall of the iron curtain, Germany gave preferential treatment in the late 1980s and early 1990s to some countries from Eastern Europe, namely Yugoslavia and Poland. Under temporary contracts tied to specific projects and seasonal work, Germany allowed many Poles and people from former Yugoslavia to immigrate. By the year 2000, almost 9 percent of the German population were immigrants. Taking a pioneering stance, the German government introduced the Immigration Act (*Zuwanderungsgesetz*) in 2001, a reduced version of which passsed in July 2004 and will come into effect on January 1, 2005.

6.2.2 Denmark's Immigrants

Denmark experienced an economic upswing in the 1960s, with excess demand for labor. A version of a guest worker system was put into practice in Denmark as well. Immigrants were mainly from Yugoslavia and Turkey, while Pakistanis were also recruited to a limited extent. The inflow of immigrants from non-Western countries has been increasing since the 1960s. In a nutshell, every person who could provide for themselves had free entry to Denmark. Guest workers were mainly absorbed into unskilled jobs.

In 1973, following other European countries, Denmark enforced a ban on immigration. This ban excluded immigrants from other EU members and Nordic countries. As happened in Germany, the number of immigrants continued to rise, but now merely through family reunification, and the effect of the ban on the total number of immigrants is unclear. From the mid-1980s Denmark experienced another upsurge of immigration in the form of refugees and asylum seekers. The Danish liberal and humanitarian laws were the main cause of the high refugee inflows. The main countries of origin were Poland, Iran, Iraq, Lebanon, and Sri Lanka (Pedersen and Smith, 2001). For further discussion, see Chapter 2.

Global turbulence, especially unstable political circumstances in various nations, led to another wave of refugees coming to Denmark in the 1990s. These immigrants were mainly from the former Yugoslavia and Somalia. In 2002, the immigrant population in Denmark amounted to 8 percent of the Danish population. In recent years new measures have been enforced in an attempt to curb immigration flows. Impor-

---

3 The numbers of Vietnamese and Chinese immigrants were also on the high side.
4 One undesirable consequence was the increase in illegal immigrants to Germany.

tant changes include the abolition of the "de-facto refugee" status, the imposition of a "24-year rule", which means that both spouses have to be 24 years old or more before they can be eligible for family reunification in Denmark, and the "attachment-rule", which states that the two spouses all in all must have greater attachment to Denmark than to another country.

Similar to Germany and other countries with migration experiences, Denmark has not applied a consistent immigration policy. Denmark's liberal laws on refugees have attracted not only refugees but also other immigrants who try to label themselves as refugees in order to enter the country and enjoy the high welfare benefits provided. The social legislation is more favorable to refugees than to labor migrants. For example, refugees do not need to provide evidence of being able to support themselves and their family members, and have almost the same rights as Danish citizens to welfare programs.[5] For labor migrants there are restrictions on the size of state pensions that they can receive which are related to the number of years of residence in Denmark.

The 1998 immigration law was drafted with the integration of both immigrants and refugees in mind. Both groups have access to special 3-year programs where they can learn the language and participate in other training courses.

6.3 Method and Data

6.3.1 Description of the Data Set

The sample we use in our estimation is extracted from our surveys, the RFMS-G and RFMS-D. For compatibility and comparison purposes, the sample includes the same five immigrant nationalities in both countries: people from former Yugoslavia, Poles, Iranians, Lebanese, and Turks.[6] Here we focus on male and female respondents between the ages of 18 and 59 who are not students, in training/apprenticeship, or in self-employment. We include the second generation immigrants – those born in Germany/Denmark or those migrating as children – and those who have acquired German/Danish citizenship. Using these selection criteria, the German sample is reduced to 4,473 observations and the Danish sample to 1,623 observations. The final sample of individuals, based on those who reported positive earnings, hours of work, and years of experience (adjusted for outliers), is further reduced to the following figures: 1,998 German immigrants and 879 Danish immigrants.

---

5 See Chapter 8 of this volume for an extensive discussion on welfare state issues.
6 The Danish sample includes 3 more nationalities: Pakistanis, Somalis, and Vietnamese.

6.3.2 Analysis and Variables

We follow the standard analysis of the earnings literature. Our model specification is an augmented version of the Mincerian model (Mincer, 1974). Because workers might differ from non-workers in unobservable ways we adjust the mean of earnings for possible non-random selection of workers (Heckman, 1979). Earnings are a function of the same socio-economic characteristics of all five groups of immigrants, specified in the following structural equation:

$$\ln W = \alpha + X'\beta + A\gamma_1 + A^2\gamma_2 + Z\delta_1 + Z^2\delta_2 + E\xi_1 + E^2\xi_2 + E^3\xi_3 + E^4\xi_4 + c\lambda + v$$

The dependent variable is the natural logarithm of the gross weekly wages as reported in the surveys (in Euros). The vector of socio-economic characteristics, X, includes human capital, demographics, and labor market structures. The variables A and Z stand for age and age at date of entry in the host country. To capture the non-linear effect of these variables on earnings, A^2 and Z^2 are entered as additional regressors. The coefficient γ_2 measures the rate at which the earnings of the immigrants increase with age, and δ_2 measures the rate at which earnings change as age of arrival increases. We expect to find that earnings increase with age, but at a decreasing rate.

With respect to the age at date of entry, intuition suggests that the earnings of immigrants who arrived as children are likely to differ from the earnings of immigrants who arrived as adults and be similar to the earnings of natives or of those of the second generation (Piore, 1979). In line with other studies (Wilkins, 2003),[7] we conjecture that earnings increase with each year older an immigrant was on arrival, although at a discounting rate. Our rationale is that immigrants who were older on arrival had acquired more pre-migration human capital and accumulated more pre-migration experience. Even taking into account the non-perfect transferability of these assets, they are valuable assets that contribute to increased productivity and are expected to be rewarded in the labor market.

The years of actual labor market experience in the host country (E) is entered as a separate variable. The number of years the immigrant has accumulated in the host country's labor market is expected to be the most important variable in our estimation of immigrant earnings. This variable measures specific host country training and human capital acquired on the job, and includes seniority on the job. The quatric algebraic specification of this variable allows for a better approximation of the effect of experience, a higher degree of flexibility, and a more in-depth analysis of its non-linear impact on earnings (Murphy and Welch, 1990). The experience coefficients in ξ measure the rate at which earnings change over the productive life of the worker with additional years of labor market experience, above and beyond any

---

7 On the basis of Australian data, Wilkins (2003) found that initial immigrant wages increase with increased age on arrival but that the rate of wage growth decreases with age on arrival.

age or cohort effects. For example, earnings can increase or decrease at an increasing or decreasing rate for certain ranges of labor market experience. We expect to find that post-migration labor market experience is a powerful predictor of earnings.

According to economic theory, the following independent variables in the vector X are expected to exert an impact on earnings. The first set of dummy variables pertains to pre- and post-migration education, language capability, health, and pre-migration employment. We expect to find that the better-educated immigrants who are healthy and speak the host country's language well will command higher wages in the labor market. We also expect that immigrants who have experience before migration will be rewarded in the host country's labor market. In principle, labor productivity is determined by pre-migration investments in human capital, and this should be reflected in higher earnings in the host country, irrespective of whether these investments are formally recognized or not.

The second group of variables in X refers to labor market structures. Including the variable "working in a small company of less than 200 employees" tests the hypothesis that large firms pay more than small firms (Schmidt and Zimmermann, 1991). We expect a negative coefficient for this variable. Hours of work per week is a continuous variable that captures the idea that immigrant earnings are tied to the number of hours they work. The type of job that immigrants are in reflects their hourly remuneration. We expect that immigrants who work more hours will earn more money. The type of industry that immigrants are in is also an important determinant of their earnings. Immigrants are often concentrated in occupations that do not require intellectual skills and the exercise of authority. We expect different returns to industry types and lower returns when immigrants are in "immigrant-intensive" industries, as immigrants are more frequently employed in sectors with strong business cycle fluctuations (see Chapter 4). We also expect higher earnings in private sector jobs, because the public sector offers more job security.

The next set of dummy variables refers to ethnicity. The five nationality variables in both data sets are constructed in such a way that they do not include naturalized immigrants. Turkish nationality is the reference category. We expect to find significant variations in earnings according to nationality. The citizenship variable includes people of all nationalities who have acquired host country citizenship. Our goal here is to test the hypothesis that immigrants who are willing to adhere to the host country's political system and are granted citizenship are rewarded in the labor market. The variable "being born in the host country" is also included in order to capture additional acculturation and integration effects. We expect these variables to have a positive sign.

The last independent variables to be included in X are gender and lambda. The gender variable takes the value of 1 when the immigrant is a man and zero when the immigrant is a woman. We expect that men earn significantly more than women in both countries. The selection term lambda is included to adjust the mean of earnings from non-random labor force participation of workers. A significant coefficient

Table 6.1. Selected labor market and other characteristics.

Characteristics	Germany Mean	Germany St.Dev.	Denmark Mean	Denmark St.Dev.
Average Gross Weekly Wages, Euro[1]	378.65	239.03	572.55	265.56
Working Hours per Week[1]	34.33	12.51	35.68	6.99
Years of Work Experience in Host Country[1]	9.39	8.08	4.97	5.11
Years since Migration	15.71	9.86	14.88	7.92
Age	37.40	10.20	37.45	10.12
Age at Entry	21.69	11.37	22.58	11.54
Male	0.47	0.50	0.51	0.50
Labor Force Participation	0.67	0.47	0.76	0.43
Employed	0.51	0.50	0.57	0.50
Registered as Unemployed	0.14	0.35	0.19	0.39
Not Employed	0.33	0.47	0.24	0.43
Working in a Small Company	0.83	0.38	0.85	0.35
Working in Service, Banking, or Insurance Industries[2]	0.19	0.39	0.13	0.34
Working in Commerce, Maintenance, or Repair Industries[2]	0.08	0.27	0.05	0.22
Working in Government or Non-Profit Industries[2]	0.07	0.25	0.16	0.37
Working in Manufacturing[2]	0.12	0.33	0.14	0.35
Working in Construction or Mining[2]	0.05	0.22	0.02	0.13
Working in Other Industries[2]	0.03	0.17	0.08	0.28
Primary/Secondary School in Host Country	0.19	0.30	0.17	0.37
Abitur/University in Host Country	0.05	0.21	0.17	0.37
No education in Host Country	0.76	0.42	0.67	0.47
Vocational Training in Host Country	0.13	0.34	0.17	0.37
Speak Host Country Language Well	0.55	0.50	0.56	0.50
Disability	0.15	0.36	0.16	0.37
Pre-Migration Education	0.76	0.43	0.84	0.37
Pre-Migration Employment	0.49	0.50	0.49	0.50
Non-Wage Assets	0.60	0.49	0.65	0.48
Married	0.74	0.44	0.77	0.42
Children under 14 at Home	0.50	0.50	0.51	0.50
Live in Enclaves	0.44	0.50	0.32	0.46
Gained Residence on basis of Employment Status	0.12	0.33	0.06	0.23
Gained Residence on basis of Family Reunion Status	0.35	0.48	0.39	0.49
Gained Residence on basis of Refugee/Asylum Status	0.33	0.47	0.41	0.49
Gained Residence on basis of Other Status	0.10	0.30	0.07	0.25
Gained Residence on basis of being Born in Host Country	0.10	0.29	0.07	0.25
Born in Host Country	0.10	0.29	0.06	0.25
Citizen of Host Country	0.05	0.23	0.44	0.50
Citizen of Former Yugoslavia	0.17	0.38	0.19	0.39
Polish	0.20	0.40	0.09	0.29
Iranian	0.15	0.35	0.05	0.22
Lebanese	0.18	0.38	0.07	0.25
Turkish	0.25	0.43	0.16	0.37
Number of Observations		4,473		1,622

Notes: 1) Based only on individuals with positive wages and working hours. N=2,020 for Germany. N=886 for Denmark. 2) Based on observations of workers.

would indicate that our wage earners are not a random sample of workers, and that a correction was therefore necessary. The error term v captures all other factors that affect earnings; we adjust for heteroscedasticity of errors.

6.4 Characteristics of the Sample Population

In this section we present and contrast the characteristics of the German and Danish immigrants as indicated by the "raw" data[8] in order to obtain a better picture of our sample. Selected labor market and various demographic and human capital characteristics are presented in Tables 6.1 and 6.2 for both German and Danish immigrants.

The first row of Table 6.1 shows that, on average, immigrants in Germany earn considerably less (approximately 34 precent less) than Danish immigrants. Put differently, Danish immigrant workers earn €200 more per week than the German immigrant workers. German immigrant workers have almost twice as many years of labor market experience in Germany as Danish immigrant workers have in Denmark. Nonetheless, they work fewer hours per week.

In general, immigrants in Germany have accumulated more years of residence in Germany than the immigrants in Denmark. The statistics presented in Table 6.1 also reveal that immigrants in Germany are of the same average age as the Danish immigrants but they migrated at a younger age: the average age at entry is 22 years. This younger age could be due to the larger proportion of second generation immigrants in Germany. In the Danish immigrant sample 51 percent are males, while in the German immigrant sample 47 percent are males.

The following rows of Table 6.1 show that in comparison to the Danish sample, our sample group of immigrants in Germany have a lower labor force participation rate, a lower percentage of them are employed, and a lower percentage of them are registered as unemployed. This shows that in the sub-sample used in this Chapter, immigrants in Denmark have a higher attachment to the labor market.[9] Statistics on the composition of the immigrant population by industrial category show that the most important sector in terms of employment for immigrant workers in Germany is the Service, Banking and Insurance sectors, while in Denmark it is the Government and Non-Profit sectors. This could be linked to the higher citizenship rates for immigrants in Denmark, which gives them access to public sector jobs. The manufacturing industry is the next largest employer of immigrants in both countries.

With respect to human capital variables, German immigrants as a group have less pre- and post-migration education than observationally equivalent Danish immigrants. For example, 76 percent of the German immigrants do not have an

---

8 These summary statistics are not weighted.
9 The average labor market attachment for the entire immigrant population in Denmark is low by international standards and markedly lower than in Germany, as we saw in Chapter 4.

education from the host country, as opposed to 67 percent of the Danish immigrants. This educational deficit is partially compensated for, however, by the greater amount of work experience among the German immigrants. While more German immigrants have primary/secondary schooling in Germany (19 percent), Danish immigrants have more upper level schooling in Denmark (17 percent are high school graduates or have a university degree). Danish immigrants also have had more vocational training in Denmark than the German immigrants have had in Germany. Similarly, when we look at their pre-migration human capital, we find that a smaller percentage of the German immigrants have pre-migration schooling. However, the same proportions of immigrants to each of the two countries worked before migration.

Statistics for their wealth show that over 60 percent of our sample of immigrants in both countries do have non-wage assets. The spatial distribution of immigrants shows that a larger percentage of the German immigrants live in neighborhoods with more than 50 percent ethnic make-up than is the case for Danish immigrants (44 percent live in enclaves in Germany, versus 32 percent in Denmark). These average statistics provide evidence that employed immigrants in Germany are not as well adjusted and spatially integrated as the employed immigrants in Denmark. A smaller proportion of immigrants in Germany are married than is the case for immigrants in Denmark. However, in both countries more than half of the immigrants have children under 14 years of age living at home, testifying to a degree of permanency in the immigrant population.

The next rows of Table 6.1, which are based on self-report, show the basis for obtaining a residence permit in the host country. It is clear that in Germany, immigrants have most frequently acquired residence through family reunification. However, a large percentage of them gained their right of residence through their refugee status. The opposite is the case for immigrants in Denmark, where immigrants have most frequently gained residence through refugee status. There is a noticeable difference in the proportions who have gained right of residence through employment status; twice as many immigrants in Germany have gained residence rights through their employment status as is the case for immigrants in Denmark, and a larger percentage have gained residence through being born in the host country.

The ethnic composition of the German immigrant sample shows that Turks make up the largest share (25 percent) of immigrants. Poles and people from former Yugoslavia are the next largest groups in the sample. In the Danish sample, immigrants from the former Yugoslavia rank first, followed by the Turks. While more immigrants in Germany were born in Germany (indicating a larger second generation), it is the immigrants in Denmark who have most frequently become Danish citizens. There is a remarkable gap in citizenship between the 2 countries; 5 percent versus

44 percent for Germany and Denmark respectively.[10] Overall, while immigrants in Denmark have more frequently arrived as refugees, they manage to fare better than immigrants in Germany with regard to labor force participation, earnings, spatial integration, and pre- and post-migration education. The statistics for our sample of 18- to 59-year-old workers indicate that immigrant groups in Denmark earn more money than the equivalent immigrant groups in Germany, though they have fewer years of labor market experience.

In Table 6.2 we present the earnings dispersion by nationality and gender. We also disaggregate the immigrant samples by ethnicity and German/Danish citizenship. We present the wages and years of work experience in the host country of the wage earners in our bi-national sample for all six nationalities. To gain more insight we present these statistics by gender. The statistics in this table are based on workers with valid values of wages and years of work experience. The table illustrates four points: (1) earnings vary widely among the six nationalities within each country, with citizens of the host country being at the top; (2) there is a strong wage disparity between German and Danish immigrants, with each nationality earning more in Denmark than in Germany, for both sexes; (3) there are pronounced wage differences between the sexes, with men earning more than women; and (4) the relationship between wages and years of experience in the host country is spurious, both within and across countries.

For immigrant men in Germany and Denmark, we find naturalized citizens at the top of the earnings distribution. In Germany, Lebanese nationals are at the bottom of the earnings distribution; Lebanese immigrant men earn 47 percent less than the German citizens and 41 percent less than the Poles, the next highest earning group. In Denmark, we also find Polish immigrant men earning the highest wages after the naturalized citizens. Iranian men are at the bottom, earning 26 percent less than the Danish citizens and 19 percent less than the Poles.

Furthermore, we find that men from the former Yugoslavia and German citizens have the longest years of work experience in Germany. Except in the case of the naturalized citizens, there is no relationship between additional years of experience and earnings. For example, the Poles, who have fewer years of work experience in Germany than the Turks and the citizens of the former Yugoslavia, earn a lot more than either of those groups. In Denmark, the Turks have the longest labor market tenure and the Lebanese have the shortest. Once again, we cannot establish a clear relationship between labor market experience and wages. The Poles, for example, who have fewer years of experience than the Turks, earn almost €100 more per week than them.

---

10 The greater proportion with host-country citizenship in Denmark could be a reflection of the sampling design of our surveys; see the Appendix to this volume for a detailed discussion.

A similar pattern pertains to the wages of immigrant women. In both countries, immigrant workers who have a German/Danish passport rank higher and fare better than other nationalities. Among immigrant women in Germany, Turkish women are at the bottom of the distribution (just below the Lebanese) and women from the former Yugoslavia are at the top (competing with the German citizens). In Denmark, we find the Polish women at the top of the earnings distribution, although still behind the immigrant citizens, and the Lebanese women at the bottom.

Table 6.2. Immigrant wages and years of experience in the host country by nationality and gender.

	Turkish	From Former Yugoslavia	Polish	Iranian	Lebanese	Citizens
			Men			
Weekly Wages in Germany (Euro)	455.45	468.34	513.71	468.53	304.08	578.54
Work Experience in Germany (years)	11.81	12.25	9.70	8.80	6.06	12.01
Number of Observations	308	213	196	180	161	65
As percent of Total Observations	27	19	17	16	14	5
Weekly Wages in Denmark (Euro)	557.48	552.65	630.90	511.06	529.70	694.64
Work Experience in Denmark (years)	6.78	3.00	4.95	1.70	0.95	5.80
Number of Observations	82	109	21	17	10	261
As percent of Total Observations	16	22	4	3	2	52
			Women			
Weekly Wages in Germany (Euro)	237.99	314.86	273.16	294.06	249.15	386.08
Work Experience in Germany (years)	9.26	11.27	6.99	6.57	4.94	10.99
Number of Observations	202	144	319	109	50	73
As percent of Total Observations	22	16	35	12	5	8
Weekly Wages in Denmark (Euro)	423.03	429.20	495.32	405.57	351.67	557.20
Work Experience in Denmark (years)	3.38	2.44	3.78	0.41	0	6.87
Number of Observations	61	54	72	14	3	182
As percent of Total Observations	16	14	19	4	1	47

Table 6.2 reveals not only ethnic differences but a pronounced gender difference as well. On average, every immigrant woman earns less than her male counterpart in each country. In addition, although immigrant women in Denmark earn more than immigrant women in Germany, they still earn less than comparable immigrant men in Germany. An exception is the Lebanese women, who earn more than the Lebanese men in Germany. However, due to the very small sample size of the female Lebanese workers in Denmark, this finding should be seen with caution. Women from the former Yugoslavia and naturalized citizens have the longest years of work experience in Germany. In Denmark, it is the women who have obtained citizenship and Polish women who have the longest years of work experience.

In sum, these statistics reveal pronounced ethnic and gender differences within each country, and in a bi-national comparison. For both sexes and in both countries, the immigrants who have taken German/Danish citizenship earn the highest wages. This could be because these immigrants are positively selected, or that citizenship helps immigrants to fare better monetarily in the labor market, or both. For the remaining five nationalities, the Poles stand out with high earnings, although they do not have as many years of work experience. Among immigrants in Germany, Polish men and women from the former Yugoslavia earn the highest wages. In Denmark, it is the Polish men and women who earn the highest wages. At the bottom, we find Lebanese men in Germany, in Denmark Iranian men. Turkish women and women from Lebanon are at the bottom of the distribution for Germany and Denmark respectively.

6.5 Empirical Results

6.5.1 Selection-Adjusted Earnings Profiles

In this section we present the results for the earnings of immigrant workers in Germany and Denmark aged 18 to 59. In Table 6.3 we report the coefficients and standard errors of the selection-adjusted earnings regression, after we have applied the Heckman two-stage technique and controlled for labor force participation selection. The asterisk denotes the statistical significance level at 5 percent in a two-tailed test. In the discussion that follows we will concentrate on the significant results. The first two columns of Table 6.3 pertain to the immigrant sample in Germany and the last two columns to the immigrant sample in Denmark. The dependent variable is the natural logarithm of the gross weekly earnings.

The larger estimated intercept indicates higher starting wages for immigrants in Denmark. From the first two rows in Table 6.3 we see that, for immigrants in both countries, earnings increase at a decreasing rate with age. The coefficients for age and age squared are significant and support the expected inverted U-shape. Figure 6.1 (p. 204) depicts the estimated average age-earnings profile of German and Danish immigrants for the relevant age range. The estimated profiles have been calculated at the means of all variables for each country. This figure reveals that the age-earnings profile of the Danish immigrants lies entirely above that of German immigrants, and that the gap widens with increasing age. The earnings of the immigrants in Denmark increase at an increasing rate, peaking at around 43 years of age, and decline slightly after that. German immigrants' earnings increase steadily and slowly at an increasing rate, reach a maximum much earlier (at 37 years of age), and decline faster thereafter.

To find the effect of age on the earnings of German and Danish immigrants, we calculated the partial effect of age at 20 and 40 years of age. Holding other variables

Table 6.3. Selection-adjusted earnings equation.

Variable	Germany Coeff.	St. Error	Denmark Coeff.	St. Error
Age	0.063*	0.012	0.050*	0.009
Age Squared	-0.001*	0.0002	-0.001*	0.0001
Age at Entry	0.01	0.008	0.005	0.005
Age at Entry Squared	-0.00003	0.0002	-0.0001	0.0001
Years of Experience in Host Country Linear	-0.007*	0.001	0.142*	0.024
Years of Experience in Host Country Squared	0.008*	0.001	-0.026*	0.006
Years of Experience in Host Country Cubic	-0.0004*	0.0001	0.002*	0.001
Years of Experience in Host Country Quatric	0.00001*	0.000001	-0.00005*	0.00001
Male	0.438*	0.035	0.122*	0.024
Primary/Secondary School in Host Country	0.145*	0.068	-0.030	0.034
Abitur/University in Host Country	0.274*	0.066	0.185*	0.034
Vocational Training in Host Country	0.272*	0.040	0.056	0.028
Speak Host Country Language Well	0.079*	0.035	0.064*	0.030
Disability	-0.153*	0.046	0.009	0.075
Pre-Migration Schooling	0.009	0.053	-0.026	0.041
Pre-Migration Employment	0.051	0.038	-0.028	0.029
Hours of Work per Week	0.001*	0.0001	0.024*	0.002
Working in a Small Company	-0.101*	0.032	-0.098*	0.026
Working in Commerce industry	0.081	0.044	-0.031	0.045
Working in Government or Non-Profit Industry	0.228*	0.047	-0.066*	0.031
Working in Manufacturing	0.320*	0.041	-0.011	0.032
Working in Construction or Mining	0.320*	0.055	0.030	0.069
Working in Other Industries	0.053	0.068	-0.036	0.037
Born in the Host Country	0.235*	0.082	0.092	0.061
Host Country Citizen	0.227*	0.060	0.058	0.035
From Former Yugoslavia	0.136*	0.045	0.073	0.042
Polish	0.096*	0.043	0.061	0.036
Iranian	0.108*	0.055	-0.047	0.068
Lebanese	-0.117*	0.056	0.107	0.094
Lambda Selection Term	-0.055	0.345	-0.051	0.098
Intercept	3.553*	0.23	4.129*	0.172
Log Gross Weekly Wage (Mean, Std. Dev.)	5.708	0.779	6.264	0.428
Number of Observations	1,998		879	
R^2	0.38		0.48	
Log likelihood value	-1,839.86		-194.81	
F	39.15		26.34	

Notes: 1) Results are adjusted for heteroscedasticity. 2) Comparison group: female, no school in host country, not disabled, no pre-migration schooling or pre-migration employment, working in a bigger company in the service industry, born in home country, have Turkish citizenship. * indicates significance at the 5 percent level in a two-tailed test ($p < 0.05$).

constant, the earnings of Danish immigrants at ages 20 and 40 increase by 2.6 percent and 0.3 percent respectively. The earnings of German immigrants at ages 20 and 40 increase by 2.9 percent and 0.5 percent respectively. While the earnings of German immigrants increase a little faster, this is not enough for them to approach the earnings of Danish immigrants.

The coefficients for all four powers of work experience in the host country are significant for both countries. However, earnings as a function of work experience exhibit a different pattern in Germany than in Denmark. In Figure 6.2 (p. 207 we plot these profiles evaluated at the means of all other variables for 0 to 25 years of work experience in the host country. Overall, the earnings profile of the German immigrants is upward-sloping, indicating that additional years of work experience pay off in the German labor market. After the first 5 years of experience (where their earnings increase at an increasing rate) the earnings increase at a decreasing rate and reach a maximum at 22 years of experience in Germany. After that, earnings start decreasing at a very slow rate.

The earnings-experience profile of the Danish immigrants is rather flat, indicating that their earnings do not increase with experience. The earnings of immigrants in Denmark start higher than those of the German immigrants at zero years of labor market experience in the host country. They reach a local maximum at 5 years of experience in Denmark, dip slightly after that, and increase slowly thereafter to reach another maximum at 18 years of experience. The earnings of the Danish immigrants decrease precipitously after 18 years of experience. This steep drop in immigrant earnings beyond 18 years of labor market experience is in fact a statistical artifact. The number of observations with experience greater than 18 years is very small, and we find practically no observations with more than 20 years of experience.

Comparing the two profiles in Figure 6.2, we see that Danish immigrants have higher earnings than German immigrants at every year of experience. When immigrants first enter the labor market, immigrants in Germany start with lower earnings and stay entirely below the Danes for a good part of their working lives. This indicates that there are disparate wage structures and no prospect that the German immigrants will achieve the higher earnings level of the Danish immigrants. While Figure 6.2 shows that after 22 years of experience German immigrants appear to be able to catch up with the Danish immigrants, this crossover occurs because the earnings of Danish immigrants start decreasing after 18 years of experience. While there are sufficient observations for German immigrants with more than 20 years of labor market experience (maximum of 40 years), there are no observations with more than 20 years of experience in Denmark.

The rest of the earnings determinants in Table 6.3 show that male immigrants earn more than female immigrants. The gender wage disparity is larger in Germany than in Denmark, with men earning 44 percent more than women in Germany but only 12 percent more in Denmark. Post-migration human capital is rewarded in general in Germany, but in Denmark only for those who have finished high school or university. Compared to those immigrants who have no education in Germany or Denmark, immigrants with Abitur/University earn 27 percent and 19 percent more respectively. Completion of vocational training is rewarded only in Germany, with immigrants earning 27 percent more than those who do not have a vocational training qualification. This indicates that vocational training is a powerful asset in the German labor market, and the immigrants who acquire it are better off.

Speaking the host country's language well is a plus in the labor market for both countries. Immigrant workers who speak German well earn 8 percent more than those who do not speak German well. In Denmark, immigrants who speak Danish well earn 6 percent more than those who do not speak Danish well. As expected, immigrants with disabilities earn 15 percent less than immigrants with no disabilities in Germany. The disability variable is not a significant determinant of the earnings of Danish immigrants.

With regard to labor market determinants, we find that immigrants who work more hours per week earn higher wages. However, earnings increase more with hours of work in Denmark than in Germany. As predicted, we find that employment in a small firm has a negative impact on the earnings of immigrants in both countries. Being employed in a small company lowers earnings by 10 percent relative to employment in a large company in both Germany and Denmark.

Immigrants in Germany who work in construction and mining as well as those working in manufacturing earn 32 percent more than immigrants in service industries. The differences between these industrial sectors are not statistically significant for the earnings of Danish immigrants. Working in the government or non-profit sectors (relative to service industries, which is the omitted category) has a significant effect on the earnings of immigrants in both countries. While this effect is positive in Germany and immigrant earnings are 23 percent higher for those in this sector, the effect is negative in Denmark. In fact, there is a penalty of 7 percent for employment in the government sector relative to the service sector. While we acknowledge that in this analysis we do not control for the distribution of jobs, a possible explanation for the case of Germany could be that jobs in the public sector pay extra because of strongly enforced labor union contracts and less discrimination. In the case of Denmark, the slightly lower wages in the public sector could be related to the fact that the public sector in general pays less, but instead offers more security in the job and better maternity or vacation packages. At the same time, it could be that because more immigrants in Denmark are citizens and thus have access to the government jobs, and since they are in general working in clerical jobs, they earn less.

Controlling for everything else, the estimated results for the nationality variables show differences between Germany and Denmark. Among the immigrants in Germany, those who were born in Germany and have acquired German citizenship are significantly rewarded in the labor market, earning about 23 percent more than the foreign-born and the non-citizens (the reference groups). Interestingly, these variables are not statistically significant for the earnings of Danish immigrants. For the remaining nationalities we find that all four groups, except the Lebanese, earn significantly more than the Turks, who are the reference group. Immigrants from the former Yugoslavia earn 14 percent more than Turks, followed by the Iranians with 11 percent more than Turks, and the Poles with 10 percent more than Turks. Lebanese immigrants in Germany, however, earn 10 percent less than Turks. Results for Denmark show that, once we separate the naturalized immigrants from their respective nationalities, none of the foreign nationals are significantly different than the Turks, the reference group.

Taken as a whole, these results from Table 6.3 and Figures 6.1 and 6.2 indicate that immigrants in Denmark fare better in terms of earnings than comparable immigrants in Germany. Not only do they earn more on average (5.7 versus 6.3 in log wages) but they earn more throughout their working lives and their labor market experience. Comparing Figure 6.1 to Figure 6.2 we see that the earnings-experience profiles lie above those of age in both countries. Our explanation is that quatric specification of experience could be a better representation, or that years of labor market experience are better rewarded, or both.

The question we pose next is whether this wage disparity between immigrants in the two countries is due to the specific country structures or to the characteristics of the immigrants themselves. In the next section we apply a counterfactual analysis and try to address this question.

6.5.2 Counterfactual Analysis of the Immigrant Earnings Profiles

The rationale behind this analysis is that we might be able to explain with more certainty whether immigrants in Denmark fare better because of the conditions in Denmark or because of the quality of immigrants to Denmark if we could exchange the immigrant populations of the two countries. To that end we undertake a counterfactual analysis where we take the immigrants from Denmark and place them in Germany. Similarly, we take the German immigrants and place them in Denmark, and we then compare their earnings.

Figures 6.3, 6.4, 6.5, 6.6, and 6.7 illustrate this counterfactual analysis based on the age-earnings profiles. Figure 6.1 is the reference figure. These profiles are calculated at the means of all other variables. First we perform a complete swap of the immigrant populations. In Figure 6.3 we compare the German immigrants' earnings, when they are transplanted into Denmark, to Danish immigrants' earnings, when they are transplanted into Germany.[11] On the basis of this figure, it is clear

---

11 Specifically we use the coefficients from the Danish wage equation on the German immigrants, and we use the coefficients from the German wage equation on the Danish immigrant population.

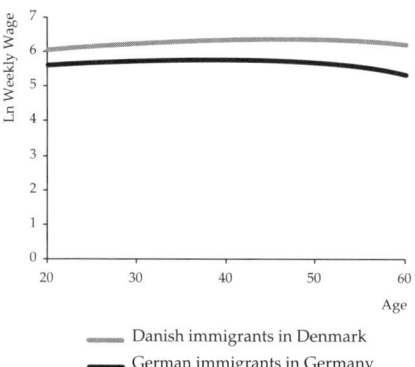

Figure 6.1. Earnings-age profiles

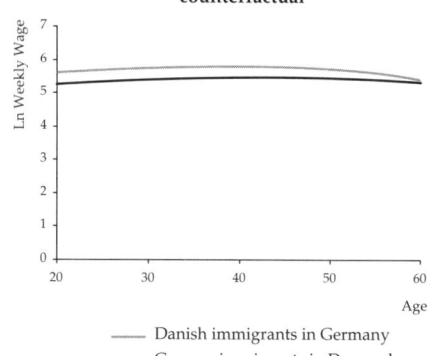

Figure 6.3. Earnings-age profiles; counterfactual

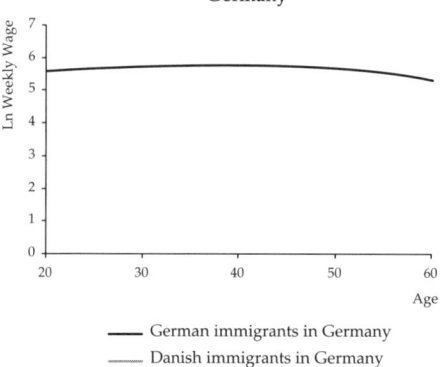

Figure 6.4. Earnings-age profiles; German and Danish immigrants in Germany

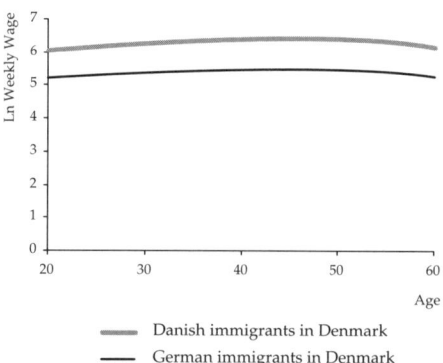

Figures 6.5. Earnings-age profiles; German and Danish immigrants in Denmark

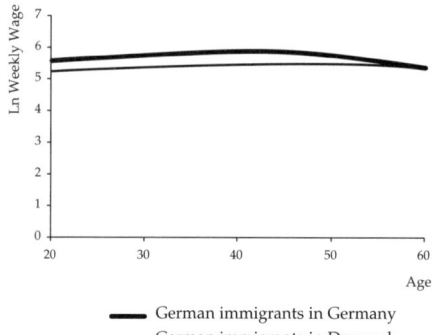

Figure 6.6. Earnings-age profiles; German immigrants in Germany and Denmark

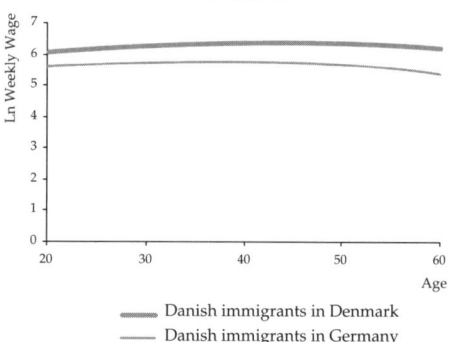

Figure 6.7. Earnings-age profiles; Danish immigrants in Germany and Denmark

that Danish immigrants in Germany would fare better than German immigrants in Denmark. Their earnings-age profile lies entirely above that of German immigrants in Denmark during their entire working lives. At first sight this pure swapping of the populations might lead us to conclude that it is the quality of immigrants to Denmark that makes a difference in the labor market. Not only do Danish immigrants excel in Denmark (Figure 6.1), but they also excel, comparatively, when they are moved to Germany.

Next, we investigate this finding further by exchanging the two immigrant populations and keeping the economic systems the same. In other words, we experiment by bringing both the German and Danish immigrant groups into the same country. First we place both the Danish and German immigrants in Germany and compare their earnings-age profiles. Figure 6.4 shows that the earnings-age profile of the Danish immigrants entirely overlaps with that of the German immigrants. This occurs because the Danish profile shifts down (in comparison to Figure 6.1), indicating that the Danish immigrants suffer a great financial loss when they are moved to Germany. Their earnings drop at every age, showing that Germany does not offer the right environment for these immigrant workers and Danish immigrants cannot cope well in the new environment.

Second, we compare the earnings of the Danish and the German immigrants when they are both in Denmark. That is, keeping the Danish immigrants where they are, we bring the German immigrants to Denmark. We find that the Danish immigrants fare better than the German immigrants. Figure 6.5 illustrates that when German immigrants go to Denmark they lose, and their earnings will never catch up with the earnings of the Danish immigrants. The wage disparity is, in fact, larger than in Figure 6.1, and there are no prospects for convergence. This disparity is larger because the German immigrants who are moved to Denmark perform worse than if they had remained in Germany. On the basis of this figure, we cannot confirm that it is a country effect that makes a difference in the earnings of immigrants. Figures 6.4 and 6.5 illustrate that the hypothetical swapping of the immigrant populations is detrimental to both the German and the Danish immigrants.

We proceed with the counterfactual analysis by comparing the earnings of the same immigrant groups in the two different countries. That is, we study the earnings profile of the immigrants in Germany compared to the profile they would have if they were to live in Denmark. Figure 6.6 depicts the results of this exercise. Clearly, when the German immigrants are transferred to Denmark they earn less than if they had stayed in Germany. German immigrants suffer a loss when they are moved to Denmark, throughout their entire lives. However, the wage gap decreases with age and there is some prospect of convergence close to retirement age.

Likewise, in Figure 6.7 we experiment by comparing Danish immigrants in Denmark to the same Danish immigrants if they were to move to Germany. This transplant seems to be even more detrimental. The immigrants who are moved from Denmark to Germany sustain a bigger loss than the German immigrants who move to Denmark. The earnings profiles of Figure 6.7 show an indisputable widening. The earnings of the immigrants who are moved from Denmark to Germany are a lot lower than the earnings of these same immigrants if they were to stay in Denmark; they reach a maximum much earlier, and decrease much faster afterwards. These pictures illustrate that the immigrant groups under study are better off staying in the country where they are.

From the last five figures we see that it is probably not the quality of people that makes the difference (as was initially inferred from Figure 6.3) but neither is it the country. Taken together, these experimental exercises seem to suggest that some invisible hand has managed to make the right allocation of people to the respective countries. Although German immigrants in Germany fare worse than Danish immigrants in Denmark, they would fare even worse if they were to move to Denmark. However, there is something in Denmark that can partly alleviate the detrimental effect of the move (better labor market conditions). Similarly, we find that the Danish immigrants would perform a lot worse if they were to move to Germany. In that case, Danish immigrants would suffer a great loss. The German labor market is not the right place for these immigrant workers.

We repeat this counterfactual analysis on the basis of the work experience earnings profiles. Figure 6.2 is now the reference figure. Figures 6.8, 6.9, 6.10, 6.11, and 6.12 show a similar story to that told in the previous experiments. Figure 6.8 shows that if German immigrants were to go to Denmark and Danish immigrants were to go to Germany, the former would be gainers and the latter losers. Thus, it might appear that there is something in Denmark that can provide an earnings advantage to the German immigrant workers. German immigrants in Denmark would increase their earnings. The earnings of German immigrant workers who go to Denmark fit a flat line until 18 years of labor market experience. Their drop after that is probably a statistical artifact due to the small number of observations at the tail. Danish immigrants in Germany lose in that they experience lower earnings in relation to labor market experience. There is, however, some convergence after 15 years of experience.

In Figures 6.9 and 6.10 we experiment with placing the two different immigrant populations in the same countries. First we compare the earnings of the Danish immigrants to the German immigrants when they are both in Germany (Figure 6.9). This exercise shows that the Danish immigrants fare better, since their earnings-experience profile lies entirely above that of the German immigrants in Germany. This figure might lead us to believe that Germany is a better place for the Danish immigrants. However, if we compare the earnings of the German immigrants to the Danish immigrants when they are both in Denmark, the German immigrants fare worse (Figure 6.10). This leads us to suspect that this is not a country effect.

In the last step we keep the immigrant populations constant and we place them in the different countries. In Figure 6.11 we look at the earnings of German immigrants in Germany and the earnings of the same German immigrants if we place

Immigrant Selection and Earnings

Figure 6.2. Earnings-experience profiles

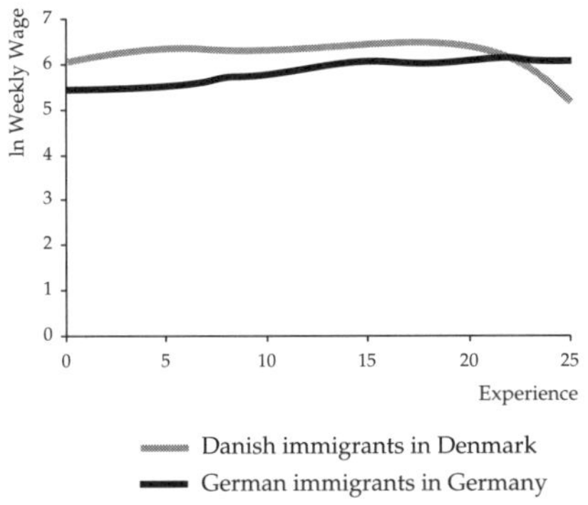

Figure 6.8. Earnings-experience profiles; counterfactual

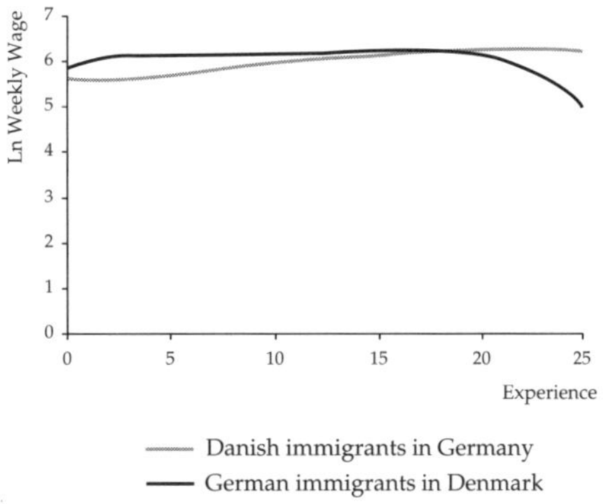

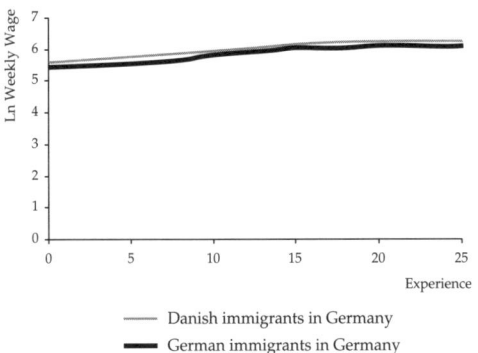

Figure 6.9. Earnings-experience profiles; German and Danish immigrants in Germany

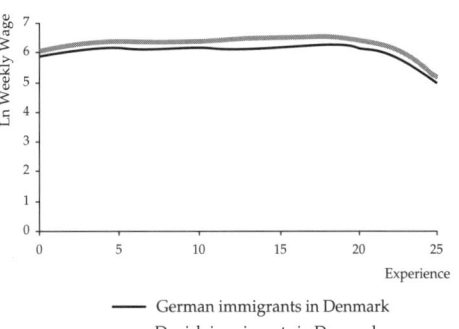

Figure 6.10. Earnings-experience profiles; German and Danish immigrants in Denmark

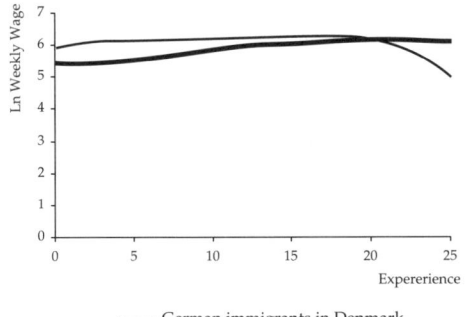

Figure 6.11. Earnings-experience profiles; German immigrants in Germany and Denmark

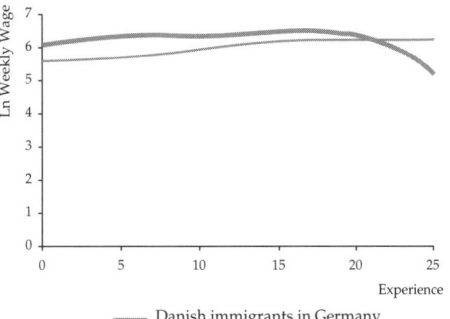

Figure 6.12. Earnings-experience profiles; Danish immigrants in Germany and Denmark

them in Denmark. Here we observe a clear gain from the move. German immigrant workers who move to Denmark start with an earnings advantage which continues until 20 years of experience. Although the earnings advantage decreases with additional years of experience, German immigrants benefit from a move to Denmark. Once again, the earnings-experience profile of the immigrants in Denmark is rather flat until 20 years of experience, indicating that additional years of labor market experience are not rewarded in Denmark.

In the last figure we compare the same Danish immigrants in Denmark and in Germany (Figure 6.12). When Danish immigrants join the German labor market they suffer an earnings loss that is sustained throughout their working lives. While the profile is upward-sloping and there is a crossover at 22 years of experience, the earnings of the Danish immigrants in Germany never reach the level of the higher earnings that they could have had if they had stayed in Denmark.

In sum, Danish immigrants in Denmark fare better than German immigrants in Germany, better than German immigrants in Denmark, and better than Danish immigrants in Germany, for both the age and experience analysis. Danish immigrants would suffer an earnings loss if they were to move to Germany. The Danish labor market works well for these immigrants. While the labor market conditions might be better in Denmark, it could also be that the immigrants who go to Denmark and decide to work are more productive people and are rewarded accordingly.

German immigrants in Germany, on the other hand, fare worse than Danish immigrants in Denmark, worse than the Danish immigrants in Germany, and in the experience analysis even worse than they themselves would do in Denmark. Based on this sample of immigrant workers and their earnings-experience profile, we see that German immigrants who moved to Denmark would see an improvement in their earnings compared to their earnings in Germany. This earnings advantage is especially large in the beginning of their careers and lasts for 20 years. It could be, therefore, that the Danish labor market can offer an earnings-experience advantage to its immigrants who are willing to work in paid employment.

6.6 Recapitulation and Concluding Remarks

In this chapter we study the earnings of immigrants in paid employment in Germany and Denmark. Specifically, we estimate earnings dispersion among immigrant groups both within a country and across countries in a bi-national comparison based on our surveys, the RFMS-G and RFMS-D. Our analysis focuses on the same five immigrant groups in both countries. Our surveys give us the opportunity to introduce the following fresh contributions in the earnings literature: (1) We employ the actual years of labor market experience in the host country, along with age, and age at entry. The years of labor market experience is specified as a 4th degree polynomial and better captures the change in earnings. (2) We employ an objective measure of host country language proficiency. (3) We create a "pure" nationality variable by extracting the immigrants who acquire host-country citizenship from their corresponding national groups. We thus end up with six national groups.

Our brief overview of the migration framework in both countries shows that there are some commonalities. Both countries initiated guest worker migration, but in both cases this was abandoned in the early 1970s and has been followed by kinship migration ever since. Many of these guest workers are still living in Germany and Denmark with their families. At the same time, international political instabilities and generous asylum laws in both countries have resulted in considerable inflows of refugees. While since the late 1990s both countries have been trying to devise laws to curb the influx of asylum seekers, both countries are characterized by high percentages of immigrants in their populations.

Our descriptive analysis shows that the earnings of immigrants vary widely among the six nationalities within each country. We consistently find that naturalized citizens (for both sexes and in both countries) are at the top of the earnings distribution. Immigrants in Denmark earn more than immigrants in Germany both on average and by each respective nationality. There are pronounced wage differences between the sexes, with men earning more than women.

Taken as a whole, the results from the econometric analysis indicate that immigrants in Denmark fare better financially than comparable immigrants in Germany, and earn higher wages throughout their working lives. The quatric experience approximation shows that years of work experience are not as well rewarded in the Danish labor market, but that immigrants in Denmark start with an earnings advantage that is sustained throughout their labor market tenure. Human capital invested in the host country offers immigrants an undeniable earnings premium in both countries. While earnings increase with additional hours of work, there is a penalty in earnings for working in a small company. Lastly, while there are significant differences among the nationalities in Germany, there are none in Denmark. Keeping all else constant, once we isolate the naturalized immigrants from their respective national groups, the earnings of all other groups in Denmark are not significantly different from those of the Turks.

Several exercises in a counterfactual analysis framework show that Denmark may be more effective in enhancing the immigrants' capacity to succeed in the labor market when it comes to earnings. Danish immigrants in Denmark fare better than German immigrants in Germany, better than German immigrants in Denmark, and better than Danish immigrants in Germany for both the age-earnings and experience-earnings analyses. If Danish immigrants were to move to Germany, they would suffer an earnings loss.

On the other hand, we find that German immigrants in Germany fare worse than Danish immigrants in Denmark, worse than Danish immigrants in Germany, and in the experience analysis even worse than German immigrants in Denmark.

Based on their earnings-experience profile, if German immigrants were to move to Denmark they would experience an improvement in their earnings compared to their earnings in Germany. This earnings advantage is especially large at the beginning of their careers and lasts for 20 years. It could be, therefore, that the Danish labor market can offer an earnings-experience advantage to its immigrants who are willing to work in paid employment.

References

Borjas, George. 1985. "Assimilation, Changes in Cohort Quality, and the Earnings of Immigrants," *Journal of Labor Economics*, 3 (4), 463-489.

Chiswick, Barry R. 1978. "The Effect of Americanization on the Earnings of Foreign-Born Men," *Journal of Political Economy*, 86 (5), 897-922.

Constant, Amelie. 1998. *The Earnings of Male and Female Guestworkers and Their Assimilation into the German Labor Market: A Panel Study 1984-1993*. Ph.D. Dissertation, Vanderbilt University.

Eurostat, the Statistical Office of the European Communities (ed.) 2003: Labour Costs Survey 2000. *Statistics in Focus.* Theme 3-7.

Heckman, James J. 1979. "Sample Selection Bias as a Specification Error," *Econometrica*, 47 (1), 153-161.

Husted, Leif, Helena Skyt Nielsen, Michael Rosholm and Nina Smith. 2001. "Employment and Wage Assimilation of Male First Generation Immigrants in Denmark," *International Journal of Manpower*, 22 (1/2), 39-68.

Licht, Georg and Viktor Steiner. 1994. "Assimilation, Labour Market Expencence and Earnings Profiles of Temporary and Perment Immigrant Workers in Germany". *International Review of Applied Economic,* 8 (2), 130-156.

Mincer, Jacob. 1974 *Schooling, Experiences, and Earnings*. New York: National Bureau of Economic Research.

Murphy, Kevin M., and Finis Welch. 1990. "Empirical Age-Earnings Profiles," *Journal of Labor Economics* 8 (21), 202-229.

Nielsen Helena Skyt, Leif Husted, Michael Rosholm and Nina Smith. 2001. "Qualifications, Discrimination, or Assimilation? An Extended Framework for Analysing Immigrant Wage Gaps." *IZA Discussion Paper* No. 365.

OECD. 2003. *Taxing wages 2001-02*. Paris.

OECD. 2004. *Main Economic Indicators.* March 2004. 257. Paris.

Pedersen Peder J., and Nina Smith. 2001. "International Migration and Migration Policy in Denmark." Working Paper 01-05. Centre for Labour Market and Social Research.

Piore, Michael J. 1979. *Birds of Passage: Migrant Labor and Industrial Societies*. Cambridge University Press.

Schmidt, Christoph M., and Klaus F. Zimmermann. 1991. "Work Characteristics, Firm Size and Wages," *The Review of Economics and Statistics*, 73 (4), 705-710.

Wilkins, Roger. 2003. "Immigrant Earnings Adjustment: The Impact of Age at Migration," *Australian Economic Papers* 42 (3), 292-315.

Zimmermann, Klaus F. 1995. "Tackling the European Migration Problem," *Journal of Economic Perspectives* 9 (2), 45-62.

CHAPTER 7

Immigrant Self-Employment and Economic Performance*

By Amelie Constant and Marie Louise Schultz-Nielsen

7.1 Introduction

The recent emergence of research into self-employment only partially reflects the importance of this invigorating sector of the economy. Self-employment, whether in an incorporated business or not, whether in agriculture or not, creates dynamism on the labor market. It spans a broad spectrum of different types of work. It can range from small businesses – traditional "mom and pop" or retail stores – to hi-tech companies and electronic commerce. Self-employment contributes to innovation of technology, job creation, economic growth, personal financial independence, higher socio-economic standing, and personal self-worth, while it alleviates the welfare burden.

While the prevalence of self-employment among both immigrants and natives in the labor market has been researched and documented by many studies in the US, research on immigrant entrepreneurship in Germany and Denmark has been scant. Empirical research on immigrant assimilation has typically found an entry wage disadvantage for immigrants, which narrows over time as immigrants "assimilate" into the host country's labor market. The rate of convergence varies among the different immigrant groups. Borjas' (1986) study on the self-employment experience of immigrants in the US shows that not only do they have higher annual incomes than salaried workers, they also have higher incomes than comparable self-employed natives. Likewise, the sociological literature has demonstrated that immigrants who become self-employed are able to climb the ladder of economic success. Other studies find that the incidence of self-employment is higher for older workers and creates greater feelings of job satisfaction (Blanchflower et al., 2001).

Germany is known to have a comparatively low rate of self-employment, and immigrants exhibit an even lower rate. This is in spite of the fact that the self-

---

* Constant has immensely benefited from Constantine Katsinis stimulating questions that have shaped this chapter. Pascal Arnds offered able student assistance.

employed immigrants reach earnings parity with self-employed natives and earn a premium of 30 percent over immigrant workers in the blue collar category (Constant, 1998). Comparing immigrant men to native German men on the basis of the German Socio-Economic Panel (GSOEP), Constant and Shachmurove (2003) find that immigrant men have lower self-employment rates than natives, but fare well in the German labor market. This study finds that the guest workers manage to reach earnings parity with the native West Germans, while East Germans perform more poorly than either of the other two groups. The earnings of other self-employed ethnic immigrants can even surpass the earnings of native West Germans. Self-employed immigrants also earn 22 percent more than salaried workers, and the guest workers as a group are twice as likely to become self-employed as the other immigrant groups. Turks are twice as likely as any other immigrant group to choose self-employment (Constant et al., 2003).

The rate of self-employment in Denmark is on the same level as in Germany (Hancock and Bager, 2003). Among the employed, immigrants in Denmark have higher rates of self-employment than natives. This is in spite of the fact that, according to official tax registers,[1] self-employed immigrants earn less than immigrants in paid employment (OECD, 2003). A study by Blume et al. (2001), analyzing transitions in and out of self-employment for males in Denmark, also shows that the self-employment rate for immigrants is higher than that for comparable native Danes, but that the self-employment rate of native Danes is falling. Based on data from Danish administrative registers they ascertain that self-employment rates among the immigrant groups vary by nationality; while self-employment is a positive development for most immigrant groups, it is a continuing tradition for the Iranians and an option of last resort for Turks and Pakistanis.

Wadensjö and Orrje's (2002) study concludes that, depending on whether one uses a broad or a narrow definition of self-employment, immigrants may be found to be under- or over-represented in that sector. Compared to Danes, immigrants are more likely to become self-employed, but their earnings are lower or at best about the same as those of the Danes. Schultz-Nielsen (2001) documents that among self-employed immigrants, the chief reasons for becoming self-employed are professional independence and higher earnings than for wage earners. One fifth of the self-employed respondents also stated that they chose self-employment because they were unable to find jobs as wage earners.

In this chapter we focus on identifying the self-employed and understanding their socioeconomic characteristics. On the basis of our own immigrant surveys (RFMS-G and RFMS-D) we conduct a bi-national analysis of the same immigrant groups, investigating the factors that determine whether individuals become self-

---

1 These figures must be interpreted with some caution, as the possibilities of achieving non-registrered income is higher for self-employed than for salary earners.

employed. We further look into the monetary success of self-employed immigrants. We address the following questions: who are the self-employed, what are their characteristics, and are they a self-selected group among all workers? Are some immigrant groups more prone to self-employment than others, and what characteristics can make a difference in their earnings once they are self-employed? Do self-employed immigrants in Germany fare better than, equally well as, or worse than self-employed immigrants in Denmark?

To answer these questions we employ reduced form models, and analyze the economic and social determinants of the probability of becoming an entrepreneur. We control for the standard human capital variables, and we augment the analysis to account for labor market characteristics, demographics, and family background. We also employ a log-wage regression with similar determinants to those above, but fine-tuned to explain wage differences. In this exercise we also include labor market characteristics such as the size of the business and the number of years one has been in business. Through a counterfactual analysis, we also seek to evaluate the self-employment performance of immigrants in the two countries, and to disentangle individual from country effects.

The rest of the chapter is structured as follows. In Section 7.2 we describe and compare the labor market institutions, policies, and cyclical dynamics in Germany and Denmark. In Section 7.3 we present the model of the self-employment choice, the earnings model, the hypotheses, the variables employed, and our sample. In Section 7.4 we discuss the characteristics of the immigrant populations under study. Here we juxtapose the self-employed with salaried workers and illustrate ethnic differences among the self-employed. In Section 7.5 we present and discuss the results of our analyses. We summarize and conclude in Section 7.6.

7.2 Labor Market Institutions, Policies, and Cyclical Dynamics

Entrepreneurs can be encumbered or empowered by the institutional settings within which they work in a country. In this section we present the national self-employment statistics and a brief overview of the self-employment sectors in Germany and Denmark.

7.2.1 The German Realities: Emphasis on Immigrants

In general, compared both to the US and to other countries that are less industrialized, Germany is characterized by a low level of entrepreneurial activity. However, in 2000 the self-employed made up 9.8 percent of the total labor force, with 12.6 percent of the male labor force and 6.2 percent of the female labor force being self-employed. Of the German self-employed, 27.1 percent work in knowledge intensive services. Overall, close to 3 million small or medium-size enterprises (SMEs), involved in crafts, industry, trade, tourism, service, and the liberal professions, create nearly 70 percent of all jobs and account for 46 percent of gross investment in Germany.

The self-employment structure of the immigrant workforce in Germany has changed significantly since the mid-1970s, when almost all guest workers[2] were in paid employment. For example, in the early 1970s only 40,000 immigrants were registered as self-employed, and their businesses were either restaurants or linked to catering to the needs of their compatriots. Since then, more and more foreigners have become self-employed. Since the mid-1980s the number of business start-ups by foreigners has increased rapidly. By April 2001, 257,000 out of the 3.1 million foreigners in the workforce – or 8.4 percent of the immigrant workforce – were self-employed. Over the last decade, the absolute number of self-employed foreigners has increased faster than the number of self-employed Germans. For example, the number of self-employed foreigners rose by 23.6 percent between 1992 and 2001, while the increase in the share of self-employed Germans was only 17 percent (*Mikrozensus*). The Institut für Mittelstandsforschung in Mannheim reports that the shares of self-employed immigrants in 2001 were 16 percent for Turks and Italians and 9 percent for Greeks. While the overwhelming majority of self-employed Greeks and Italians are in the restaurant and hotel business, the majority of Turks are in the wholesale/retail business.

The institutional and legal conditions for foreigners planning to become self-employed have improved over the recent decades. The Aliens Act of 1965 explicitly prohibited immigrants to engage in business (Kanein, 1988). EU nationals and immigrants with certain residence permits were exempted from this law, however. Now immigrants from EU countries have basically the same legal rights as German entrepreneurs. Immigrants from non-EU countries are subject to the Aliens Act and require an unlimited residence permit, or have to apply for permission to found a business if they have a limited residence permit. In practice, the approval of such applications has been liberalized over the last years.

Within Germany, many individual states and cities are seriously taking actions to promote self-employment. In the city of Berlin, for example, the "Consulting Centre for Self-Employment" caters to the needs of immigrants in general, and especially Turks. This center is funded by the German Government. Among other things, it provides training in accounting and marketing, advises on business opportunities in Berlin, and enhances cooperation between business associations (IOM, 2003). The federal government itself actively seeks to encourage, foster and strengthen the performance and competitiveness of SMEs and offer them new growth development possibilities. In June 2002, the German government started assisting the development of a private risk capital market in Germany by making available in considerable

---

2 In general, the term guestworkers denotes recruited immigrants from the following countries: Turkey, Greece, Spain, Italy, and former Yugoslavia.

quantities venture capital for young technology companies, especially via the VTC scheme – Venture Capital for Small Technology Companies.

Nonetheless, immigrants face various hurdles if they choose self-employment, such as difficulty in raising capital or securing loans, lack of managerial skills, and difficulties in taking advantage of market opportunities. One of the most significant hurdles is difficulty in obtaining credit or limited availability of capital for business start-up. Most newly founded businesses in Germany are financed with the entrepreneur's own capital in combination with outside capital provided by credit institutes. Venture capital, private investors, or business "angels" play a role in only a few cases. In the case of immigrants, family and friends are usually the business angels. Another hurdle is the lack of knowledge about the support programs that are available to encourage and promote self-employment, and about the existing consulting centers.

Still, even if immigrants are informed about business opportunities and encouraged to open their own businesses, the next hurdles to overcome concern regulations and bureaucracy. Experts are critical of the fact that there are too many regulations that hinder entrepreneurial activities, and advocate the abolition of unreasonable paperwork. Further, the complicated German tax system can also deter many potential founders of businesses. In recent years many changes have been made regarding the tax laws, often making it impossible for businesses to get an overview of the system.

Another impediment to self-employment is the alleged German "welfare culture." This culture has at least two dimensions. On the one hand, less privileged workers need to be protected from unemployment or from precarious, risky employment. This is one reason why the German labor market legislation has focused on paid employment rather than self-employment. Labor unions have also encouraged paid employment, since independent trades do not fall under their umbrella. On the other hand, unwritten rules (that emphasize collective behavior) deter individuals from choosing the entrepreneurial avenue and making high profits.

7.2.2 The Danish Realities: Emphasis on Immigrants

Like Germany, Denmark is characterized by a relatively low level of entrepreneurial activities. Among the adult population 5.9 percent are classified as entreprenuers, and 1.7 percent as nascent entrepreneurs (Hancock and Bager, 2003). Until 1997 there was a substantial and direct subsidy to entrepreneurs. Currently, the focus of the Danish government is to help entrepreneurs in the start-up phase through personal guidance and consultancy, provision of innovative environments, and removing obstacles to business start-ups.

In principle, all Danish residents aged 18 and older can open their own businesses. Certain craft professions, real estate agents, etc, require authorization. Others (taxi drivers, restaurateurs, and pharmacists) require a license. While Scandinavians have the same privileges as native Danes, EU citizens have to have a residence permit before they can open a business. Non-EU citizens who wish to open a business in Denmark are required to have obtained a one-year permit both for residence and work in order to be registrered as self-employed. Normally, applicants from abroad are not given permits to open retail businesses and restaurants. For immigrants, therefore, it is easier to go into self-employment after they have been in Denmark for at least a year.

In general, self-employment rates among natives have become lower in Denmark over time. In 1998 the self-employed made up 7.7 percent of the employed, compared to 11.3 percent in 1985. Ten percent of the employed men in 1998 were self-employed, as were 5.0 percent of the women (see Schultz-Nielsen, 2001). Those who are in self-employment earn, according to registers, 18 percent more than those in paid employment (OECD, 2003). Danish entrepreneurs tend to be better educated than the rest of the workforce, and less likely to be employed in low value-added business sectors (OECD, 2003).

One reason for the moderate self-employment rate might be found in the Danish entrepreneurial culture, which some believe to be influenced by the Danish concept of *"Janteloven"*. *Janteloven*, sometimes described as the Dane's "Just who do you think you are?" attitude, can discourage income spread and conspicuous consumption, and thus hinder entrepreneurship. Another reason might be that Danes are more risk averse than most other nationalities. Most of the enterprises in Denmark are established within business services and retail. The largest increase in start-ups has been in the IT sector in recent years. *Intrapreneurship* (i.e. start-ups within the framework of an existing organisaton) is the entrepreneurial way of the Danes, meaning that "Danes enjoy the challenging nature of the work involved in starting a business, but do not want to take the risks associated with owning and managing such an enterprise" (Hancock and Bager, 2001). There are still very few female entrepreneurs in Denmark.

As in Germany, tax and administration burdens constitute the biggest obstacles to flourishing entrepreneurship in Denmark (Hancock and Bager, 2001). Administrative technicalities are even more problematic for those immigrants who have language problems. The government's latest plan of action to assist entrepreneurs contains a number of suggestions for political initiatives. Among these suggestions are actions on reducing the risks to entrepreneurship, on improving consultancy, and on changing the *Janteloven* culture in the new generation through involvement of teachers and students. The Danish Government has already taken some initiatives to improve entrepreneurial activities among the immigrants, such as making entrepreneurial activities a theme in the courses for asylum seekers and in the introduction programs for aliens (OECD, 2003).

Immigrants in Denmark are characterized by high self-employment rates compared to native Danes. Figures from 2002 show that of all non-Western immigrants in the labor force, 10 percent are self-employed, as against 7 percent of natives. Interestingly, the self-employment rate varies substantially among immigrant nationalities. While 16 percent of the Lebanese and Iranians and 13 percent of the Turks in Denmark are in self-employment, only 8 percent and 3 percent respectively of the immigrants from Poland and the former Yugoslavia are self-employed. However, self-employed immigrants achieve very low income levels, and have a negative wage gap in comparison to their salaried counterparts (OECD, 2003). These low wages, coupled by long hours of work, could indicate that immigrants go into self-employment out of necessity. That is, if they were able to find jobs as salaried workers, they probably would.

The Danish government has announced three initiatives to improve and broaden the self-employment activities of immigrants: (1) giving them proper guidance and developing local networks, (2) emphasizing the importance of self-employment in the courses that refugees receive and in other programs for all aliens, and (3) seriously investigating the financial barriers that immigrants face in opening a business (OECD, 2003).

In sum, both countries are making serious efforts to encourage and ensure the viability of business enterprises, placing special emphasis on the needs of immigrant entrepreneurs. In addition to the initiatives being made by the German and Danish governments, the European Union also actively encourages entrepreneurship in all its national members. Special funds are earmarked for both Germany and Denmark for the encouragement of entrepreneurship. Small and medium businesses are the first priority, and aid for them is co-financed by the European Fund for Regional Development and the European Social Fund.

7.3 Modeling of Self-employment: Methods and Hypotheses

7.3.1 Self-Employment probabilities

To model the self-employment choice we estimate reduced form models. Empirically, the unit of the analysis is the individual. A self-employed individual is one who works for him-/herself, or one who also has employees. We model the self-employment choice behavior of individuals who are in the labor force. That is, given that individuals are in the labor force, we study their occupational choice between self-employment and paid employment. In the paid employment choice we include individuals who are registered as unemployed. We assume that individual agents in the host country have two alternatives: the option of becoming self-employed versus the option of being a wage or salary worker. Individual agents maximize utility gained from the attributes of that choice. Such behavior is described in probabilistic terms. This probability is not directly observed.

We employ a binomial logit to estimate the probability of choosing self-employment as opposed to choosing salaried work. Our dependent variable is thus, dichotomous, and takes the value of one if an individual is self-employed and the value of zero if an individual is an employee or registered as unemployed. The results from this exercise will give us insights into the self-selection process and the role of various characteristics in choosing the entrepreneurial avenue versus seeking paid employment (working for somebody else or being registered as unemployed).

The human capital paradigm implies that the well-educated will more often go into self-employment, because self-employment offers opportunities for considerable economic success. At the same time, self-employment also implies greater risks. Well-educated and able individuals will be able to successfully face the challenges of self-employment. In addition to the drive for financial rewards, individuals might choose self-employment as a corrective measure to job mismatch or as an option for economic independence and a psychological boost to self-worth (Constant and Shachmurove, 2003). More important is entrepreneurial talent, which often cannot be taught. In this study, we only measure formal training and educational qualifications. Abilities may be correlated with measured human capital, and the relationship with self-employment may be clouded in practice due to measurement problems. Formal educational levels often guarantee success in employment, and hence, people with entrepreneurial abilities and no formal educational qualifications are more likely to be self-employed.

The choice of the independent variables in our analysis draws from research in sociology and the neoclassical theory of economics. The variables we employ are expected to have a differential impact on the individual's probability of becoming an entrepreneur. The explanatory variables used in this paper include human capital variables (education and health), variables that show socioeconomic attachments to Germany and Denmark (citizenship, owning a house in Germany or Denmark), family background variables, enclaves, and other control variables (marital status, ethnicity, and gender).

We measure separately the effects of schooling in the home country and schooling and vocational training in the host country. In this way we control for differences in the initial stock of human capital (education before migration). Completed schooling in Germany or Denmark is indicated by dummy variables on the following educational levels: primary/lower secondary education and high school diploma or university degree. Acquiring no educational qualification in Germany/Denmark is the reference category. Vocational training is kept as a separate dummy variable to be able to differentiate this branch of education from the more academic orientated line. In theory, better educated individuals are more likely to choose self-employment because schooling enhances one's knowledge and sharpens intelligence and other abilities. The health status of an individual is another facet of human capital. The prediction is that more healthy individuals will be more likely to go into self-employment. We construct a disability variable on the basis of the RFMS-G and RFMS-D questionnaires. We expect to find a negative coefficient on the disability variable.

Pre-migration human capital is also included in the model. The literature has established that the endowments immigrants bring with them are to a large extent crucial in their labor market integration. Schooling[3] and work experience in the

---

3 Schooling in home country is measured by a dummy variable that takes the value one if the respondent has attended school in the home country, otherwise the variable is zero.

home country are two important variables. We expect that pre-migration schooling and experience will positively affect the individuals' labor force participation in the host country, and prompt them to choose self-employment. There are some factors that may lessen the impact of pre-migration human capital. The imperfect transferability of qualifications is one. However, difficulty in getting recognition of educational qualifications might make self-employment an attractive choice for immigrants.

The chief variable for immigrant assimilation is the years-since-migration variable. This variable measures the time and quality of exposure to the host country environment. It measures labor market experience and human capital accumulated in Germany or Denmark. It also denotes knowledge about the local labor market and culture. Potentially, much like the age variable, this duration variable also measures access to financial capital and compliance with legal restrictions. We, thus, expect that the more years-since-migration individuals have accumulated, the greater will be the probability of entering self-employment. The age variable suggests that the older one becomes, the more knowledge one acquires and the more financially independent one becomes. An older and more mature person might also have better judgment, and make the correct moves and decisions for business success. We expect that as age increases, the probability of choosing self-employment will increase, albeit at a decreasing rate.

In our attempt to delineate a more comprehensive model of the self-employment choice, we include a number of additional regressors.

Father's occupation is entered as another explanatory variable to capture the individual's family background. This variable is coded one if the father is in self-employment and zero otherwise. A father who is in the self-employment sector, besides providing life-experiences and know-how to his children, can also provide free on-the-job training and learning by doing. It is also more likely that a self-employed father will be able to financially support his children's start-up business and properly guide them in their decision. Lastly, children of self-employed fathers are more likely to inherit the business and go straight into self-employment. The father's self-employment status should thus, have a positive effect on the probability of choosing self-employment.

Next, we control for unemployment in the region and marital status. In general, the higher the unemployment rate is in a region, the less likely individuals are to find a job. Especially in Germany, where inter-regional mobility is low, high unemployment can make labor force participation impossible for individuals. In that case, self-employment can be an attractive route out of unemployment (if one finds it difficult to move to another city). We conjecture that a high unemployment rate will increase the chances of choosing self-employment. Marital status and young children in the household are additional determinants of self-employment, since they directly affect the preferences and motives of the individuals. In principle, men who are married and have children will increase their work efforts and choose a job that can increase their chances of meeting their family obligations. Attracted by the higher financial rewards of entrepreneurship, married men who have children may choose self-employment because they feel responsible for providing for their family.

However, marital status plays a role in self-employment from two conflicting directions. On the one hand, married men are able to be more productive, by means of the division of labor and household production. Self-employment can be a very attractive choice for married individuals because it can offer flexibility in the allocation of time between family and work. Married men can benefit from their wives' support and can count on their spouses helping with their businesses as well. Self-employed married men can also count on the stable incomes of their wives, if they are working. The additional income from the spouse is viewed as a strategy of income smoothing to get through rough times, in the event that the business is not going well. This is a more plausible scenario for immigrants and certain occupations. On the other hand, self-employment is considered to be a risky venture, and as such married men might not opt for this choice, especially when their households depend on their incomes.

Home ownership is another variable that captures the individual's financial resources. In the event of liquidity constraints, one can always put the house up as collateral for a loan, and thus be able to pursue the entrepreneurial avenue. Individuals who own their homes will have a higher probability of choosing self-employment. Ethnic enclaves are viewed as an essential determinant of the probability of self-employment, especially in the sociology literature. Living in an ethnic neighborhood renders immigrants more prone to create their own business. One reason is that immigrants in an enclave can identify a niche more easily, and cater to an established clientele. Furthermore, the poverty of an enclave environment can also be a push factor into self-employment, especially if self-employment is viewed as an escape from unemployment and a chance to make it in life. One could therefore, expect this variable to have a positive impact on the probability of self-employment.

An alternative expectation could be that as the immigrant becomes successful as an entrepreneur, his/her economic situation will become better and he/she will move out of the enclave. In that case there would be a negative correlation between living in an enclave and probability of self-employment. We construct an enclave variable on the basis of our questionnaires that takes the value of one if the respondent lives in a neighborhood where people with a different ethnic background make up more than half the population.

We expect significant differences between men and women, with men being more likely to choose self-employment, just as we also expect significant differences among the different nationalities of immigrants. Besides the five nationalities in our sample, we control for German and Danish citizenship. Immigrants in Germany, even those who are born in Germany, are not automatically German citizens. Although the laws on acquiring citizenship have become less stringent in the recent years, many immigrants choose not to become German citizens. In Denmark, it is easier to become a citizen, and many immigrants choose to do so.

We construct the citizenship variable on the basis of the respondents' answers. It includes people of all immigrant nationalities who have acquired the host country's passport. Citizenship is thought of as testimony to full integration. It may facilitate access to government jobs, and can also signal stability and willingness to embrace the country's values and ideals to employers. We expect this variable to have a negative effect on the probability of self-employment, because citizens have more secure alternative options in the labor market.

7.3.2 Economic Returns to Self-employment

We investigate the monetary well-being of self-employed immigrants deriving from this occupational status. The estimation of earnings is made through a standard Mincerian wage equation augmented with labor market and individual characteristics. The dependent variable is the natural logarithm of gross weekly earnings.

The vector of independent variables includes socioeconomic characteristics similar to those specified in the logistic analysis but fine tuned to identify earnings. Here we include actual weekly working hours, the size of the business, and the number of years the owner has been in business. Age and years-since-migration are entered with their quadratic specifications to capture any diminishing returns on earnings. Following the literature, we expect the earnings profiles with respect to age and years-since-migration to have an inverted U-shape.

Following the premises of the neoclassical human capital theory, we expect that the healthier and better educated individuals will have higher earnings. If self-employed workers are positively self-selected for their inner drive to be independently successful and to climb the socioeconomic ladder, they should also earn significantly higher wages, all other things being equal. We also predict that individuals who work longer hours per week, and have longer tenure in their business, will have higher earnings. From the questionnaire, we construct a variable pertaining to the size of the business one has. The small size variable takes the value of one when the individual employs 0 to 4 persons, and zero otherwise. We expect that individuals owning smaller businesses will have lower earnings than those owning larger businesses.

7.3.3 Data

For the empirical analyses, our data are drawn from the Surveys about Immigrants in Germany and Denmark (RFMS-G and RFMS-D). These surveys give us the opportunity to assess immigrant differences within each country and to assess cross-national differences. From these surveys we choose the same five immigrant groups that are present in both countries.[4] Thus, we look at both men and women

---

4 The Danish survey contains more immigrant nationalities, but to make the samples as comparable as possible between the 2 countries we concentrate on these 5 nationalities.

from the following countries of origin: Turkey, former Yugoslavia, Poland, Iran, and Lebanon. The samples we select for our analyses exclude those individuals who are enrolled in school.

In our German sample there are 300 self-employed immigrants and 3,093 immigrants in paid employment or registered as unemployed. Self-employed immigrants constitute 9 percent of our German sample. Out of the 300 self-employed foreign nationals, 50 are Turks, 40 are from the former Yugoslavia, 36 are Polish, 130 are from Iran, and 44 are from Lebanon. The Danish sample contains 128 self-employed immigrants and 1,137 immigrants in paid employment, including those registered as unemployed. Self-employed immigrants constitute 10 percent of our Danish sample. Disaggregated by nationality, we find 36 Turks, 6 people from the former Yugoslavia, 22 Poles, 49 Iranians, and 15 Lebanese.

For the analysis of earnings, we consider only those self-employed immigrants who have reported valid wages, hours of work, and years in business. Omitting outliers, our samples are further reduced to 177 self-employed immigrants in Germany, and 81 in Denmark. While we are aware of the fact that the sample sizes are small for some of the ethnic groups, we are confident that the self-employment decision of all German and Danish migrants can be usefully analyzed on the basis of these two data sets.

7.4 Characteristics of the Sample Populations

7.4.1 Self-Employed Versus Salaried Workers

This section pertains to selected labor market and human capital characteristics of the same five groups of self-employed immigrants in Germany and Denmark, based on raw data from the RFMS-G and RFMS-D. More precisely, we first contrast differences in immigrant characteristics between the self-employed and those in paid employment. The latter group includes those currently employed and those who are seeking employment but are registered as unemployed. In Table 7.1 we illustrate the means and standard deviations for the self-employed and the salaried immigrants in Germany, and in Table 7.2 we illustrate the corresponding statistics for Denmark. Second, we look at the self-employed alone, and we juxtapose the differences in their characteristics by nationality within a country and across countries. Tables 7.3 and 7.4 refer to these statistics for Germany and Denmark respectively.

Table 7.1. Selected summary statistics for self-employed and salaried immigrant workers in Germany.

Variables	Self-employed		In the Labor Force[2]	
	Mean	St. deviation	Mean	St. deviation
Age	42.72	10.97	37.93	10.69
Working Hours per Week[1]	54.34	15.71	34.69	12.24
Wage per Week (Euro)[1]	768.31	496.55	385.66	239.32
Employed	-	-	0.75	0.43
Self-Employed	1.00	0.00	-	-
Registered as Unemployed	-	-	0.22	0.42
No Education in Germany	0.66	0.47	0.72	0.45
Primary/Lower Secondary School in Germany	0.17	0.38	0.22	0.41
Abitur/University in Germany	0.16	0.37	0.06	0.24
Vocational Training in Germany	0.14	0.35	0.16	0.37
Years Since Migration	20.34	10.16	16.88	9.92
School Attendance in Home Country	0.83	0.37	0.76	0.43
Worked in Home Country	0.53	0.50	0.52	0.50
Turkish	0.17	0.37	0.26	0.43
From Former Yugoslavia	0.13	0.34	0.18	0.38
Polish	0.12	0.33	0.25	0.42
Iranian	0.43	0.50	0.16	0.35
Lebanese	0.15	0.35	0.14	0.34
German Citizens	0.06	0.24	0.06	0.24
Born in Germany	0.07	0.26	0.11	0.31
Own Dwelling in Germany	0.25	0.44	0.08	0.27
Live in Enclaves	0.26	0.44	0.42	0.49
Residential Status: Employment	0.18	0.39	0.16	0.37
Residential Status: Family Reunification	0.20	0.40	0.32	0.47
Residential Status: Refugee	0.30	0.46	0.28	0.45
Male	0.82	0.39	0.60	0.49
Married	0.73	0.45	0.72	0.45
Children under 14 in Household	0.41	0.49	0.44	0.50
Disability	0.09	0.29	0.14	0.34
Father Self-Employed	0.42	0.49	0.22	0.41
Number of Observations		300		3,093
Number of Observations with > 0 wages		183		2,051

Notes: 1) Number of observations with wages greater than zero. 2) In the labor force: includes those in paid employment and those who are registered as unemployed.

Table 7.1 shows that there are clear differences between the self-employed and immigrants in the salaried sector in Germany. Note that the group of salaried workers includes those registered as unemployed. On average, self-employed immigrants are older than the salaried workers, work substantially more hours per week, and earn more than the salaried workers. Indeed, self-employed immigrants in Germany earn almost twice as much as their salaried counterparts. While 100 percent of the self-employed are working, only 75 percent of the salaried group are in employment.

With respect to human capital acquired in Germany, the self-employed are more educated than their salaried counterparts. A smaller percentage of the self-employed have no schooling in Germany and a much larger percentage of them have acquired higher levels of schooling while in Germany. While 16 percent of the self-employed have Abitur/University degrees, only 6 percent of the salaried workers do. The self-employed immigrants have also been in Germany for a longer time, and a larger percentage of them have pre-migration schooling.

The Iranians dominate among the self-employed immigrants and the Turks (together with the Poles) among the salaried immigrants. The proportions of naturalized immigrants are a low 6 percent in both groups. Other noticeable differences between the self-employed and salaried workers relate to their ways of life in Germany. For example, self-employed immigrants have a higher standing with regards to wealth. One fourth of the self-employed immigrants own their dwellings, as opposed to only 8 percent of the salaried immigrants.

Another striking difference between the self-employed and the salaried immigrants in our sample concerns their residential neighborhood and whether they were born in Germany. The self-employed manage to live outside the enclaves and be more spatially integrated, although a much smaller percentage of them were born in Germany. Many of the self-employed have gained their residence permits from refugee status, while more of the salaried workers have gained their permits from family reunification. Lastly, a larger share of the self-employed have gained residence permits through employment than the salaried immigrants.

The overwhelming majority among the self-employed in Germany are males in good health. Finally, 42 percent of the self-employed reported that their fathers are also self-employed, as opposed to only 22 percent among the salaried workers, pointing to a continuation in the family business. All in all, Table 7.1 provides evidence that the self-employed immigrants in our German sample are self-selected with respect to age, education, health, work experience, years-since-migration, home ownership, spatial integration, and family background. They are also predominantly males from Iran. Clearly, all the self-employed immigrant nationalities in Germany display the image of being a well-adjusted and integrated group, faring better than the salaried immigrants.

In Table 7.2 we present comparable summary statistics for immigrants in Denmark. This immigrant self-employed sample shares some common characteristics with the German sample. For example, compared to salaried workers, self-employed immigrants in Denmark are also older and work more hours per week. When it comes to their weekly wages, however, we see that self-employment in Denmark yields almost the same returns as paid employment. To be precise, self-employed immigrants earn slightly less than salaried immigrants in Denmark. This is in sharp contrast to the German case. More importantly, comparing Danish and German self-employed immigrants, we find that the former earn a lot less than the latter.

Regarding labor force participation rates, we find that – as in Germany – all self-employed immigrants in Denmark are working. In comparison to the salaried immigrant workers in Germany, a higher percentage of the Danish migrants in the salaried category are employed, and a lower percentage of them are registered as unemployed.

On average, the self-employed immigrants have lower post-migration human capital, compared to the salaried immigrants. Specifically, a larger percentage of them have acquired no schooling in Denmark, and a lower percentage of them have basic schooling or Gymnasium/University from Denmark. However, they display a higher level of achievement in vocational training acquired in Denmark. This is almost the opposite of the portrait of the self-employed in Germany. The average self-employed immigrant in Denmark has also been in the country for almost the same number of years-since-migration as the salaried average person. Overall, the self-employed have more pre-migration education and more pre-migration working experience.

The Iranians, once again, dominate the self-employed group of immigrants. This indicates that this ethnic group has an innate entrepreneurial trait that is not affected by the situation in the host country. Among the salaried immigrants, Turks and Poles are the largest groups. In sharp contrast to the German sample, a high percentage of the Danish sample have become Danish citizens. Within this category, a larger share of the self-employed are naturalized than their salaried counterparts, but when it comes to being born in Denmark, we find that none among the self-employed were born in Denmark. Another difference from the German self-employed sample lies in the proportion who own their own homes. In Denmark, we find fewer self-employed immigrants owning their houses compared to the salaried immigrants. Yet home ownership among immigrants in Denmark is a lot higher than in Germany.

A quarter of the immigrants in Denmark – whether self-employed or salaried – live in enclaves. This is a much lower proportion than in Germany where especially salaried workers live in enclaves. As in Germany, many of the self-employed immigrants have gained their residence permits on the basis of refugee status, while the largest proportion of the salaried immigrants have gained residence permits on the basis of family reunification. In contrast to Germany, Denmark has a much higher percentage of refugee immigrants.

Table 7.2. Selected summary statistics for self-employed and salaried immigrant workers in Denmark.

Variables	Self-Employed		In the Labor Force[2]	
	Mean	St. deviation	Mean	St. deviation
Age	38.27	8.85	35.83	10.13
Working Hours per Week[1]	51.11	16.02	35.12	8.46
Wage per Week (Euro)[1]	624.28	349.60	630.22	1,519.89
Employed	-	-	0.87	0.34
Self-Employed	1.00	0.00	-	-
Registered as Unemployed	-	-	0.13	0.34
No Education in Denmark	0.72	0.45	0.62	0.49
Primary/Lower Secondary School in Denmark	0.16	0.36	0.22	0.41
Gymnasium/University in Denmark	0.13	0.33	0.16	0.37
Vocational Training in Denmark	0.19	0.39	0.17	0.38
Years Since Migration	16.73	7.10	15.95	8.11
School Attendance in Home Country	0.91	0.29	0.81	0.40
Worked in Home Country	0.52	0.50	0.45	0.50
Turkish	0.28	0.45	0.26	0.44
From Former Yugoslavia	0.05	0.21	0.23	0.42
Polish	0.17	0.38	0.26	0.44
Iranian	0.38	0.49	0.17	0.38
Lebanese	0.12	0.32	0.08	0.27
Danish Citizens	0.60	0.49	0.51	0.50
Born in Denmark	0.00	0.00	0.10	0.30
Own Dwelling in Denmark	0.27	0.44	0.29	0.46
Live in Enclaves	0.25	0.43	0.25	0.43
Residential Status: Employment	0.05	0.23	0.06	0.24
Residential Status: Family Reunification	0.39	0.49	0.38	0.49
Residential Status: Refugee	0.45	0.50	0.36	0.48
Male	0.77	0.42	0.55	0.50
Married	0.73	0.44	0.72	0.45
Children under 14 in Household	0.55	0.50	0.54	0.50
Disability	0.11	0.31	0.06	0.24
Father Self-Employed	0.07	0.26	0.05	0.23
Number of Observations	128		1,137	
Number of Observations with > 0 wages	91		843	

Notes: 1) Number of observations with wages greater than zero. 2) In the labor force: includes those in paid employment and those who are registered as unemployed.

We find consistently that there are more men than women in self-employment. The percentages with regard to the disability status of the immigrants in Denmark are almost the complete reverse of the German case. A larger percentage among the self-employed have disability problems than either the salaried workers in Denmark or the self-employed in Germany. Lastly, more of the self-employed have fathers who are in self-employment than the salaried workers do. In sum, there are clear differences between the self-employed and salaried workers in Denmark, notably with regards to human capital. Comparing the self-employed in the two countries, we also find some differences, the most important one being the low returns to self-employment in Denmark.

7.4.2 Self-Employed Ethnic Groups

In Table 7.3 we present the summary statistics for the German self-employed immigrants disaggregated by ethnicity. Clearly, these ethnic groups are different with respect to certain characteristics. On average, the oldest ethnic group is the Iranians, while Turks and Lebanese are the youngest. Looking at their weekly wages, we see that they vary widely among the nationalities. The Poles earn the highest wages and the Lebanese the lowest. The Iranians display the greatest longevity in business, with the average Iranian being in business for 9 years. The Poles have the fewest years in business, even less than the Lebanese, who have the fewest years-since-migration to Germany. Overall, the vast majority across all nationalities owns a small size business, comprising 0 to 4 employees.

These five nationalities also differ with respect to human capital acquired in Germany. More Turks have finished primary/lower secondary schooling, but more Iranians have finished higher education (28 percent have finished Abitur/University). Self-employed immigrants from the former Yugoslavia form the largest group with vocational training. While all ethnic groups have a high percentage of members with pre-migration schooling, the Turks are the least likely to have pre-migration education.

The Iranian self-employed immigrants are the group with the highest home ownership share and the lowest share living in enclaves. An impressive 37 percent of Iranian self-employed immigrants own their dwellings in Germany, and only 16 percent of Iranians live in enclaves. At the other end of the spectrum we find the Lebanese. Only 5 percent of the Lebanese own their dwellings and 46 percent of them live in enclaves. It seems that even 15 years after immigration to Germany, the Lebanese are not well integrated. Among the Lebanese in the survey, none were born in Germany. In contrast, 18 percent of the Turks were born in Germany.

The people from the former Yugoslavia stand out with respect to having acquired a residence permit through their employment status. The majority of Poles have acquired residency through family reunification, and the majority of Lebanese have acquired residency through refugee status. The majority of the Lebanese are also males, and married with small children. The self-employment family succession is displayed to a great extent by the Iranians; 40 percent of Iranians have a father who is also self-employed. The next most entrepreneurial group is the Lebanese. The Poles have the lowest percentage with self-employed fathers.

Table 7.3. Average characteristics of self-employed immigrants in Germany by ethnicity.

Variables	Turkish	From Former Yugoslavia	Polish	Iranian	Lebanese
Age	38.72	43.7	40.39	46.14	38.16
Wage per Week (Euro)[1]	625.00	780.95	971.86	821.18	585.58
Number of Years in Business[1]	7.27	6.81	4.56	9.22	5.23
Small Size Business[1] (0-4 Employees)	0.73	0.76	0.83	0.77	0.89
No Education in Germany	0.54	0.78	0.78	0.62	0.73
Primary/Lower Secondary School in Germany	0.36	0.15	0.20	0.10	0.18
Abitur/University	0.10	0.08	0.03	0.28	0.09
Vocational Training	0.18	0.23	0.11	0.12	0.11
Education in Home Country	0.64	0.80	0.89	0.89	0.89
Years Since Migration	22.6	23.38	16.28	21.49	14.93
Own Dwelling in Germany	0.22	0.15	0.25	0.37	0.05
Live in Enclave	0.34	0.28	0.25	0.16	0.46
Born in Germany	0.18	0.13	0.08	0.03	0.00
German Citizenship	0.02	0.00	0.14	0.07	0.07
Residential Status: Employment	0.16	0.43	0.19	0.14	0.09
Residential Status: Family Reunification	0.40	0.25	0.42	0.09	0.11
Residential Status: Refugee	0.18	0.13	0.08	0.32	0.68
Male	0.84	0.73	0.69	0.83	0.96
Married	0.80	0.65	0.67	0.72	0.77
Children under 14 in Household	0.58	0.23	0.28	0.39	0.57
Disability	0.04	0.13	0.06	0.12	0.07
Worked in Home Country	0.34	0.53	0.69	0.52	0.66
Father Self-Employed	0.12	0.13	0.03	0.40	0.32
Number of Observations	50	40	36	130	44
Number of Observations with > 0 Wages	26	21	18	86	26

Note: 1) Number of observations with wages greater than zero.

To sum up, among the self-employed, the Poles and the Iranians fare best financially. This is especially interesting, for the Poles, who have lived on average fewer years in Germany, were not usually born into self-employed households, have a lower average level of education than the other ethnicities, and most frequently moved to Germany through family reunification. Yet they earn the highest wages of any group. The Iranians display the most intergenerational transmission of self-employment status, have the highest average level of education, have higher homeownership rates than other groups, and are the most spatially integrated.

Parallel characteristics among the self-employed ethnic groups in Denmark are presented in Table 7.4. As the number of observations is limited, especially among the self-employed from the former Yugoslavia and Lebanon, we have checked whether the findings in Table 7.4 are in accordance with register infor-

Table 7.4. Average characteristics of self-employed immigrants in Denmark by ethnicity.

Variables	Turkish	From Former Yugoslavia	Polish	Iranian	Lebanese
Age	33.77	42.67	44.27	39.61	34.07
Wage per Week (Euro)[1]	559.47	886.53	739.94	611.03	490.81
Number of Years in Business[1]	3.04	8.33	7.71	4.22	1.75
Small Size Business[1] (0-4 Employees)	0.71	0.00	0.25	0.49	0.66
No Education in Denmark	0.69	0.50	0.59	0.82	0.87
Primary/Lower Secondary School in Denmark	0.33	0.17	0.14	0.06	0.07
Gymnasium/University	0.03	0.33	0.27	0.12	0.07
Vocational Training	0.03	0.33	0.18	0.29	0.20
School attendance in Home Country	0.83	1.00	0.96	0.96	0.80
Years Since Migration	18.83	23.33	20.05	14.02	13.06
Own Dwelling in Denmark	0.17	0.50	0.59	0.22	0.07
Live in Enclaves	0.58	0.00	0.09	0.08	0.33
Born in Denmark	0.00	0.00	0.00	0.00	0.00
Danish Citizenship	0.36	0.33	0.64	0.73	0.80
Residential Status: Employment	0.11	0.50	0.00	0.00	0.00
Residential Status: Family reunification	0.86	0.17	0.32	0.16	0.20
Residential Status: Refugee	0.00	0.33	0.32	0.80	0.67
Male	0.89	0.83	0.50	0.73	1.00
Married	0.78	0.83	0.73	0.67	0.80
Children under 14 in Household	0.61	0.67	0.32	0.55	0.73
Disability	0.00	0.17	0.23	0.16	0.00
Worked in Home Country	0.25	0.67	0.59	0.69	0.47
Father Self-Employed	0.03	0.17	0.00	0.16	0.00
Number of Observations	36	6	22	49	15
Number of Observations with > 0 Wages	24	4	16	41	6

Note: 1) Number of observations with wages greater than zero.

mation for all self-employed immigrants from the five countries. We add similarities and differences with the registers as we present the statistics based on our survey.

While we find considerable differences by nationality among the self-employed in Denmark, we also find differences between the self-employed in Denmark and the self-employed in Germany. Here, it is the Poles who are the oldest group on average, while Turks (and the Lebanese) are the youngest. Our small sample of immigrants from the former Yugoslavia shows that they have the highest weekly wages, while immigrants from Lebanon have the lowest. The people from former Yugoslavia have also been in business for the longest time on average, and the Lebanese for the shortest. While the Turks almost exclusively own small businesses, the people from former Yugoslavia do not.

Immigrants from the former Yugoslavia have acquired the most human capital in Denmark. Not only have 33 percent of them finished Gymnasium/University, but 33 percent of them also have vocational training. According to the register information covering all self-employed immigrants in Denmark, the self-employed from the former Yugoslavia, Poland, and Iran have acquired much more human capital than the Turks and Lebanese. Overall, self-employed from all nationalities have a fairly high proportion of people with some education from their home country. Practically all the immigrants from the former Yugoslavia, Poland and Iran have attended school in the home country, but this could be because of the greater average age of the group. On average, people from former Yugoslavia, Poland and Turkey have been in Denmark for more than 18 years. In contrast, the Iranians and the Lebanese have only been in the host country for an average of 13 years.[5] Almost two thirds of the people from former Yugoslavia, Poland and Iran had pre-migration work experience.

Remarkably, more than half of the Poles own their dwelling in Denmark, none from the small group of people from the former Yugoslavia lives in enclaves; the group that mostly lives in enclaves is the Turks (58 percent). The people from former Yugoslavia stand out because of their employment status. Half of the self-employed people from former Yugoslavia gain their right of residence in Denmark through employment, but none of the Poles, the Iranians, or the Lebanese do. Instead, they take the refugee route. This is not the case in Germany, where there seems to be more of a balance among the different categories of residence status. For example, while some of the Poles in Germany also arrived as refugees, there are many of them who migrated through employment. In Denmark, 80 percent of the Iranians arrived as refugees. In contrast, 86 percent of the Turks arrived through family reunification.

Another difference among the self-employed immigrants in Denmark lies in their citizenship status. In our small sample, none of the self-employed immigrants in Denmark were born in the country.[6] Yet they all have high rates of naturalization, especially the Poles and Iranians, where more than 60 percent of them have been granted Danish citizenship. A remarkable 80 percent of the Lebanese are Danish citizens. All of the self-employed Lebanese in our survey are males, and they all have excellent health. The people from former Yugoslavia display the highest percentage of intergenerational self-employment, even surpassing (and followed by) the Iranians.

Overall, this section shows that the self-employed are faring better than the salaried workers in Germany, but not in Denmark. The wage disparity between

---

5 Our statistics are diverging from register information with regards to people from former Yugoslavia. Among all 448 self-employed Yugoslavs only 8 percent have Gymnasium/University, and they have been in Denmark for about 13 years on average.
6 Register information shows that 5-7 percent of the Turks, people from former Yugoslavia and Poles were born in Denmark.

self-employed and salaried workers is much more pronounced in Germany, where self-employed immigrants earn twice as much as the salaried immigrants. This indicates that self-employment is a better choice in Germany than in Denmark. Among the self-employed, however, some nationalities are faring a lot better than others. While the Poles achieve the highest wages in Germany, it is the people from former Yugoslavia who do best financially in Denmark. Except for the people from former Yugoslavia, each nationality earns more per week in Germany than in Denmark. The Lebanese earn the least among all the self-employed immigrants in both countries. Caution should be taken, though, as the numbers of observations are very small for some of the groups. Nevertheless, it is safe to say that there are noticeable differences in the self-employed immigrant groups in the two countries.

7.5 Estimation Results

In this section we will examine the role of these characteristics on the proclivity for self-employment through a multivariate analysis.

7.5.1 Proclivity for Self-Employment. Binomial Logit Results

In Table 7.5 we present the results of the binomial logit estimation on the probability of choosing self-employment versus being in paid employment or being registered as unemployed. The first three columns pertain to Germany and the last three to Denmark. We present the coefficient estimates, the standard errors, and the odds ratios, evaluated at the means of all covariates; the asterisk denotes the significance level at 5 percent. The discussion focuses mainly on the determinants that are significant at the 5 percent level in a two-tailed test.

Starting with the results for Germany, we see that age is a significant determinant of the proclivity for self-employment for our immigrant groups. As immigrants age, they have a higher probability of choosing self-employment as opposed to paid employment, and this probability increases at a decreasing rate. Similarly, we find that for each additional year an immigrant resides in Germany, his/her chances of choosing self-employment versus paid employment increase, albeit in a non-linear way. While the quadratic coefficient is not statistically significant, the pair of this variable indicates that with more years in Germany, immigrants master cultural challenges, accumulate social capital, and become more labor market aware. We also find that the odds of choosing self-employment versus paid employment more than double for men, controlling for everything else.

The results for the human capital variables are as expected. Schooling acquired in Germany strongly increases the odds of becoming an entrepreneur. Immigrants who finish primary/lower secondary or Gymnasium/University are 1.5 times as likely to choose self-employment as opposed to paid employment compared to those

Table 7.5. Binomial logit results on immigrant self-employment probabilities.

Variables	Germany			Denmark		
	Coefficient	St. Error	Odds Ratio	Coefficient	St. Error	Odds Ratio
Age	0.098*	0.046	1.103	0.102	0.093	1.107
Age^2	-0.001	0.001	0.999	-0.0012	0.0015	0.999
Years Since Migration	0.054*	0.026	1.055	-0.013	0.064	1.013
Years Since Migration^2	-0.001	0.001	0.999	0.0003	0.002	1.000
Male	0.982*	0.166	2.668	0.900*	0.244	2.460
Primary/Lower Secondary Education	0.467*	0.237	1.596	-0.124	0.345	0.883
Gymnasium/University	0.440*	0.222	1.552	-0.550	0.328	0.577
Vocational Training	-0.153	0.196	0.858	-0.207	0.271	0.813
Education in Home Country	0.299	0.219	1.348	0.510	0.378	1.664
Disability	-0.790*	0.220	0.454	0.714*	0.349	2.042
Worked at Home	-0.051	0.173	0.95	-0.040	0.248	0.961
Unemployment in Region	0.024	0.022	1.024	0.160	0.098	1.173
Father Self-Employed	0.438*	0.145	1.55	-0.480	0.383	0.619
Married	-0.179	0.175	0.837	-0.083	0.282	0.921
Children under 14 at Home	-0.085	0.161	0.918	-0.017	0.243	0.983
Own Dwelling	0.995*	0.178	2.703	0.048	0.252	1.050
Live in Enclaves	-0.419*	0.147	0.658	0.110	0.244	1.117
From Former Yugoslavia	0.189	0.233	1.208	-1.794*	0.522	0.166
Polish	0.043	0.247	1.044	-0.289	0.364	0.749
Iranian	1.147*	0.211	3.149	0.722*	0.358	2.059
Lebanese	0.713*	0.237	2.04	0.264	0.392	1.302
Citizen of Host Country	-0.412	0.280	0.663	-0.116	0.253	0.890
Intercept	-7.042*	0.954	-	-6.113*	1.736	-
AIC (Intercept and covariates)		312.565			777.288	
Likelihood Ratio		1,761.504			95.171	
Number of Observations		3,393			1,253	

Note: * indicates significance at the 5 percent level in a two-tail test.

who have obtained no educational qualification in Germany. Surprisingly, vocational training is not a statistically significant determinant of self-employment for the immigrant groups in our sample. The odds of choosing self-employment decrease by 55 percent for those immigrants in poor health.

The coefficient from the father's occupation clearly indicates strong intergenerational occupational choices. As predicted, when an immigrant's father is in self-employment, we find that the individual is 1.5 times more likely to choose self-employment. This could indicate that immigrants rely on kinship and familial support when they open a business. Home ownership is also a strong determinant of self-employment choices. The chances of being self-employment almost triple for those immigrants who own their own homes in Germany.

With regards to enclaves, we find that the immigrants who live in enclaves exhibit a negative proclivity to self-employment. Contrary to predictions and the results from other sociological studies, we find that immigrants in Germany who are living in a heavily ethnic neighborhood are less likely to choose self-employment by 34 percent. We suspect that living in an ethnically segregated neighborhood can isolate immigrants from the rest of society and act as a trap into cultural prejudices and a different mentality. Our results show clearly that ethnic enclaves in Germany act as a barrier to entrepreneurship. Immigrants who want to succeed in the self-employment sector have to go out of the enclave and do business with the native population. An alternative interpretation is that as one becomes successful as an entrepreneur, one can afford to live outside the enclave and therefore moves out.

With respect to ethnicity, we find that there are significant differences among the various nationalities. The odds of choosing self-employment triple for the Iranians compared to Turks, who are the reference group. The next most entrepreneurially active national group are the Lebanese, who are twice as likely as the Turks to choose self-employment. The results from our analysis point to the fact that the Iranians and Lebanese are truly entrepreneurial. These results for ethnicity are of particular interest, because other studies have shown that Turks in Germany are also entrepreneurial. For example, Constant et al. (2003) find that Turks are more likely to choose self-employment than other immigrant groups. However, that study does not include Iranians and Lebanese. Finally, Table 7.3 shows that the German passport is not a significant determinant of self-employment choice for immigrants.

In sum, for immigrants in Germany, we find that education acquired in Germany plays a vital role in the odds of choosing self-employment. Older, more seasoned migrants whose fathers are also self-employed, and who own their homes, tend to go into self-employment. The Iranians and Lebanese are found to be more entrepreneurial than the Turks in our sample.

The corresponding analysis for immigrants in Denmark shows that very few factors determine proclivity for self-employment there. Age and years-since-migration are not significant determinants of self-employment in Denmark. As expected, males are 2.5 times more likely than females to choose self-employment. The coefficients on school qualifications acquired in Denmark are negative, albeit non-significant. In contrast to Germany, where the educated immigrants had higher probabilities to choose self-employment, it seems that in Denmark education does not have a significant impact on self-employment choices. Disability status, however significantly determines self-employment choices. Unlike the German case, immigrants with disabilities in Denmark are twice as likely to chose self-employment as the healthy ones.

Turning to the ethnicity variables, we see that the coefficients for the people from former Yugoslavia and Iran are significant. And while the odds of choosing self-employment are 83 percent lower for immigrants from the former Yugoslavia than for Turks, the odds for Iranians are two times higher than for Turks. The analysis for the Danish sample points to the possibility that self-employed immigrants in

Denmark are not self-selected to the same degree. Very few of the characteristics have a differential impact on self-employment probabilities. Overall, conditional on being in the labor force, the probabilities of choosing self-employment are higher in Germany than in Denmark, but this tendency is not systematically driven by our variables. In the next section we will study the earnings of the self-employed immigrants in the two countries.

7.5.2 The Returns to Self-Employment

Table 7.6 shows the wage regression results for self-employed immigrants in Germany and Denmark. We present the coefficient estimates and the standard errors. The asterisk denotes a significance level at 5 percent in a two-tail test. In general, we concentrate our discussion on the statistically significant variables. For Germany, the results show that age is a significant determinant of earnings for self-employed immigrants. In fact, we confirm the expected concave shape of the age/earnings profile. Just as for salaried workers, earnings increase with age at a decreasing rate for the self-employed; in fact, earnings eventually even seem to decrease as age increases.

In Figure 7.1 we plot the age-earnings profile of the self-employed immigrants in Germany, and we juxtapose it to the Danish profile. These plots have been calculated at the means of all other characteristics. Figure 7.1 illustrates that the earnings of self-employed immigrants in Germany slowly increase (at a decreasing rate) until 40 years of age, where they reach a maximum, and slowly decrease after that. Overall, this is a rather flat profile that could indicate less skilled workers.[7] The human capital variables are not statistically significant for the earnings of the self-employed immigrants. Our results are consistent with other studies of self-employed immigrants in Germany where education is again found to be irrelevant for their earnings (Constant and Shachmurove, 2003).

Labor market aspects of self-employment are the only determinants of earnings in Germany. Self-employed immigrants in Germany who have a small business of 0 to 4 employees earn 41 percent less than the self-employed who have larger companies. It is very interesting that length of time in the business is highly significant. The more years immigrants are in business, the higher their earnings are from that business. Actually, each additional year they are in business increases their earnings by 2 percent. We also find that there is a penalty for those self-employed immigrants who live in enclaves; they earn 22 percent less than the self-employed who do not live in enclaves. Finally, our results show that once immigrants are self-selected into self-employment, nationality is not a statistically significant determinant of their earnings. All immigrant nationalities are indistinguishable from the Turks – the reference category – with regard to their earnings.

---

7 We are aware that cohort effects might bias our conclusions. It is not possible from a cross-section to disentangle these effects.

Table 7.6. Wage regression results on self-employed immigrants.

Variables	Germany		Denmark	
	Coefficient	St. Error	Coefficient	St.Error
Age	0.046	0.027	0.096	0.058
Age^2	-0.0006*	0.0003	-0.001	0.001
Years Since Migration	-0.007	0.019	-0.038	0.060
Years Since Migration^2	0.0004	0.0004	0.001	0.002
Male	0.199	0.118	0.082	0.176
Primary/Lower Secondary Education	-0.240	0.157	-0.122	0.221
Gymnasium/University	-0.069	0.124	0.084	0.248
Vocational Training	-0.095	0.125	-0.002	0.174
Education in Home Country	-0.102	0.147	0.016	0.189
Worked at Home	-0.046	0.112	-0.061	0.540
Disability	-0.026	0.182	-0.548*	0.200
Weekly Working Hours	0.004	0.003	0.004	0.005
Firm of Small Size	-0.410*	0.105	-0.104	0.185
Years in Business	0.020*	0.010	0.014	0.030
Live in Enclaves	-0.222*	0.106	-0.017	0.190
From Former Yugoslavia	0.113	0.169	-	-
Polish	0.339	0.182	0.062	0.247
Iranian	0.098	0.139	-0.072	0.240
Lebanese	-0.136	0.163	-0.378	0.353
Citizen of Host Country	0.404	0.224	0.227	0.154
Intercept	5.496*	0.613	4.523*	1.132
Dependent Mean	6.459		6.310	
F Value	4.08		1.75	
R^2	0.344		0.353	
Number of Observations	177		81	

Note: * indicates significance at the 5 percent level in a two-tail test.

The last 2 columns of Table 7.6 depict the earnings results for self-employed immigrants in Denmark. This is a much smaller sample than the one for Germany. The self-employed sample with valid wages and hours is reduced to 81 observations; in fact, the sample for people from former Yugoslavia is reduced to a non-estimable level. We therefore had to omit this ethnicity variable from the earnings regression. The wage regression results show that there are not many characteristics that differentially affect the earnings of self-employed immigrants in Denmark. While the age variables are at the border of statistical significance, we nevertheless decided to plot the age-earnings profile of self-employed immigrants in Denmark because of its economic significance. As in the German case, this profile is calculated at the means of all other variables.

Figure 7.1 shows that that the earnings of self-employed immigrants in Denmark increase quite fast, reach a maximum at 35 years of age, and decrease faster thereafter. The Danish profile lies at a lower level than that for Germany throughout.

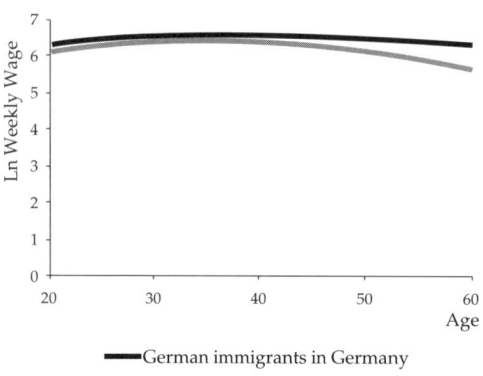

Figure 7.1. Earnings-age profiles of self-employed immigrants.

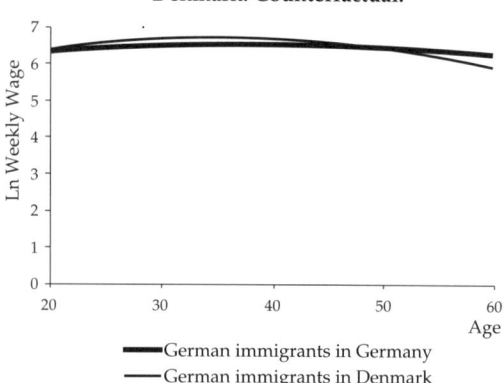

Figure 7.2. Earnings-age profiles; German immigrants in Germany and Denmark. Counterfactual.

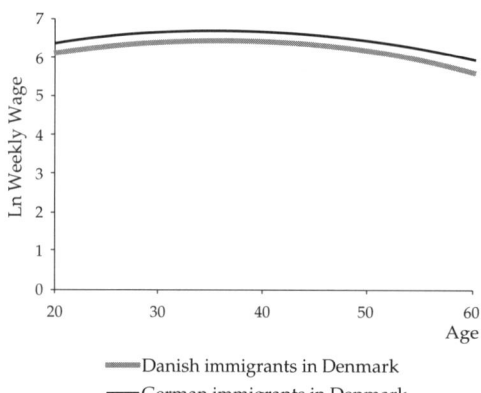

Figure 7.3. Earnings-age profiles; Germans and Danes in Denmark. Counterfactual.

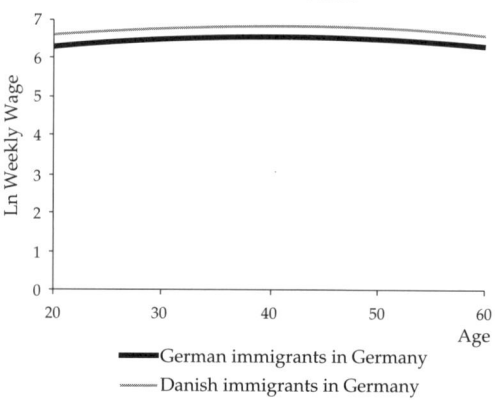

Figure 7.4. Earnings-age profiles; Germans and Danes in Germany. Counterfactual.

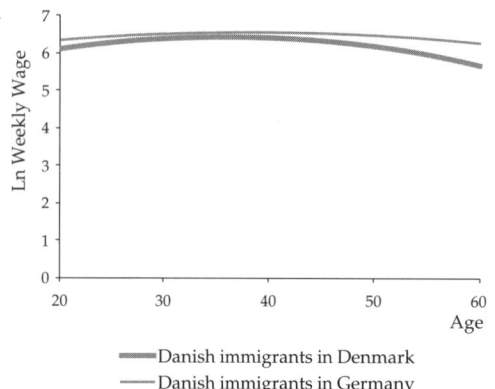

Figure 7.5. Earnings-age profiles; Danish immigrants in Germany and Denmark. Counterfactual.

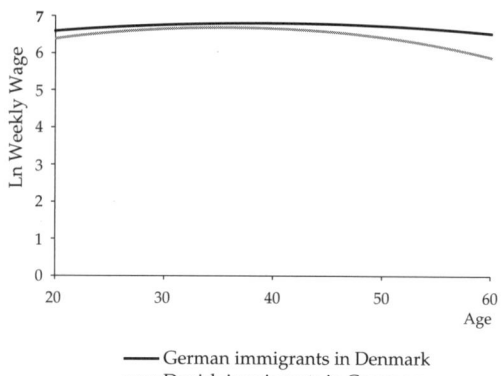

Figure 7.6. Earnings-age profiles; Complete swapping. Counterfactual.

While the profiles come close to convergence at their maxima, they diverge again after that, and the gap widens as age increases. This picture shows that while the earnings of Danish self-employed immigrants increase faster in the beginning, they reach a maximum earlier in life and decrease faster afterwards.

For the rest of determinants in Table 7.6 we see that the only statistically significant variables for the Danish sample is disability. Self-employed immigrants with disabilities suffer an earnings decrease (by 55 percent) compared to healthy self-employed immigrants. In Denmark, being self-employed seems to require only non-measurable talents; handicapped people have a chance, but have to suffer a negative wage premium.

To sum up, the only important positive determinants of the earnings of the self-employed immigrants in Germany are age and length of time in business. For self-employed immigrants, earnings increase significantly the longer they are in business, indicating a powerful effect through the stability and longevity of their business. Our results show that the typical human capital model, where the returns to education are high for those in paid-employment, does not apply to the self-employment sector in either country. Once immigrants have chosen the self-employment avenue, other characteristics cannot improve their earnings by much.

For Germany, having a business of small size (0 to 4 employees) and living in an enclave are detrimental to the earnings of the self-employed. For Denmark, our results show that there are not many characteristics that differentially affect the earnings of the self-employed immigrants. But self-employed handicapped immigrants are penalized in the labor market. A comparison of the age-earnings profiles of the self-employed immigrants in the two countries shows that immigrants in Germany earn more than those in Denmark at every age. The mean log weekly wage for German self-employed immigrants is 6.459 and the mean log weekly wage for Danish self-employed immigrants is 6.310.

7.5.3 A Country or an Immigrant Effect?

The conclusion from Figure 7.1 is that the self-employed immigrants in Germany fare better than the immigrants in Denmark, in all age groups. The question we pose next is whether this finding is due to the better quality of the immigrants in Germany or due to the better labor market conditions in Germany. In Figures 7.2-7.6 we undertake a counterfactual analysis, and try to arrive at an answer to this question. The age-earnings profiles are calculated at the means of all other variables.

First, we ask if the German immigrants would fare better if they were to move to Denmark. In Figure 7.2 we place the German immigrants in Denmark, that is, we use the coefficients from the Danish equation on the German immigrants, and compare the results with the German immigrants in Germany. This figure shows that German immigrants who moved to Denmark would experience a boost in their earnings up until they were 48 years old, compared to the German immigrants who stayed in Germany. After 48 years of age, however, their earnings would decrease to a level below that of the German earnings. While it appears that this move would benefit the younger self-employed immigrants, it would be detrimental to the older ones. The overall effect seems to be marginal, however. A conclusion at first sight is that German self-employed immigrants might slightly benefit from moving to Denmark.

Once the German immigrants have been moved to Denmark, we are tempted to compare them to the Danish immigrants in Denmark. In Figure 7.3 we see that the German self-employed immigrants who moved to Denmark would fare better than the Danish immigrants in Denmark at every age. Their profile lies above that of the Danes and there is a steady gap throughout their working lives. Figures 7.2 and 7.3 appear to suggest that German self-employed immigrants might be better off if they were to move to Denmark. At the very least, compared to Danish immigrants, German immigrants would fare better. Furthermore, it could be that it is not only the people, but also the country that makes a difference to their earnings.

Next we apply the same counterfactual analysis to the Danish immigrants. Figure 7.1 illustrated that the Danish self-employed immigrants fare worse than the German self-employed immigrants. If this is a country effect, then the Danish immigrants who moved to Germany should fare better. In Figure 7.4 we illustrate this exercise. Indeed, the Danish immigrants who moved to Germany would fare even better than the German immigrants in Germany throughout their lives. A move to Germany appears to be highly beneficial to the Danish self-employed immigrants. Since both populations are in the same constant environment, this might indicate that this is because of a more compatible quality of the Danish self-employed immigrants.

In the last step, we compare the Danish immigrants who are moved to Germany to the Danish immigrants who stay in Denmark to see whether there is a country effect. Figure 7.5 illustrates that the Danish self-employed immigrants who moved to Germany would experience a dramatic improvement in their earnings. Not only would they enjoy higher earnings, but this earnings advantage would also be long lasting. This indicates a country effect on top of the people effect, and suggests that the Danish self-employed immigrants would be better off with the German set-up.

Putting all figures together, in Figure 7.6 we compare the self-employed immigrants in a complete swapping of the populations. That is, we place the Danish immigrants in Germany and the German immigrants in Denmark and we compare their age-earnings profiles. Danish immigrants in Germany compared to German immigrants in Denmark would enjoy higher earnings throughout their working lives, reach a maximum later in life, and would be able to maintain higher earnings even towards the end of their working lives. Figure 7.6 illustrates a strong country effect, whereby self-employment in Germany is rewarded more than in Denmark.

The analysis in this section shows that the German self-employed immigrants fare better than their Danish counterparts, and that Danish self-employed immigrants would fare a lot better in the German labor market, if they were to change countries. Germany is more conducive to self-employment (especially for more mature immigrants). While German immigrants who move to Denmark might fare better relative to the Danish immigrants, on average they slightly lose.

7.6 Conclusions

In this chapter we examine the immigrants in the self-employment sector in Germany and Denmark. In particular, we study the self-employment choice and economic success of the same immigrant groups in Germany and Denmark. Focusing on the immigrants who are in the labor force, we address the following empirical questions: (1) what are the probabilities that immigrants in the labor force choose self-employment versus paid employment, and (2) once immigrants are in self-employment, what are their earnings?

According to Hancock and Bager (2003), entrepreneurial activities in Denmark are on the same relatively low level as in Germany. However, our sample of immigrants in these two countries shows significant entrepreneurial activity. In this chapter we are able to establish that 9 percent of our immigrant sample in Germany and 10 percent of our immigrant sample in Denmark are in the self-employment sector. The raw characteristics of immigrants presented in this chapter suggest that there are clear differences between the self-employed and the salaried workers within a country, just as there are differences between the self-employed in Germany and Denmark. In Germany, self-employed immigrants are clearly self-selected with respect to human capital, age, years-since-migration, and family background characteristics. They have a larger share of home ownership and a lower share of living in an ethnic neighborhood. For Denmark, the self-selection of the self-employed is not as prominent, especially with respect to human capital.

Self-employment seems to be a lucrative choice for immigrants in Germany. Self-employed immigrants rival other immigrants who are in paid employment in terms of financial success. In fact, our sample of self-employed immigrants in Germany earn twice as much as the group of the salaried workers that includes those registered as unemployed. This is not the case in Denmark, where self-employed immigrants earn slightly less than the salaried group. Immigrants who go into self-employment in Denmark generally do not do so for the higher earnings.

Overall, the immigrant workers who choose self-employment have distinct characteristics. Among all ethnic groups, on average, the Iranians stand out as being the most entrepreneurial in both countries. Many of the self-employed immigrants are from refugee status in both countries. But a relatively larger share of the self-employed in Germany have gained their residence characteristics on the basis of their employment status. Self-employed in Denmark are characterized by higher ownership rates and lower rates in enclave living, compared to German self-employed immigrants. The raw statistics show clearly that the self-employment status of the father is a considerable factor in the self-employment status of the children.

The empirical results of our multivariate analysis confirm that the self-employed fare better in the labor market than paid workers – at least in financial terms. In the German analysis, we find that educated healthy men from Iran and Lebanon are the most likely to choose self-employment over salaried employment. Older and more seasoned migrants who own their own homes also tend to be found in self-employment. The figures for the father's self-employment suggest a positive spillover to the self-employment of children, and a strong intergenerational effect. Living in enclaves acts as a deterrent to self-employent proclivity.

A parallel analysis on the Danish sample shows that the choice to go into self-employment is not significantly affected by pre- or post-migration human capital. The incentives to become self-employed in Denmark are very low, at least in financial terms. Immigrants in Denmark have higher reservation wages than immigrants in Germany because the welfare system is more generous. If the remuneration is high enough, then, they would probably rather join the salaried sector than the self-employment sector. Overall, there is a strong probability that male immigrants and immigrants with disabilities will go into self-employment. Among the different nationalities in Denmark, the people from former Yugoslavia are the least entrepreneurial and Iranians the most entrepreneurial, compared to Turks.

Finally, with regards to self-employment returns, we find that only age and length of time in business are strong and positive determinants of earnings for immigrants in Germany. However, once immigrants are in the self-employment sector, education is not a significant determinant of their earnings. Self-employed immigrants who live in enclaves and own small businesses are penalized in the German labor market. Lastly, we are not able to confirm any nationality effects on the earnings of the self-employed in Germany.

For Denmark, the earnings regression could not confirm any strong effects besides disability. Overall, we find that the average German self-employed immigrant who lives in Germany fares better than the average Danish self-employed immigrant who lives in Denmark.

A counterfactual analysis shows that self-employed immigrants would find a better match for their talents if they could operate within the general conditions of the other country. Specifically, we find a country effect whereby Germany could offer a better environment to the self-employed Danish immigrants, and the effect of this would be long lasting. However, we cannot rule out the possibility that Danish self-employed immigrants may be more entrepreneurial than their German counterparts. While it appears that Denmark could accommodate the entrepreneurial skills of the German self-employed immigrants in the short term, over the course of a working life it seems to cancel out.

References

Blanchflower, David G., Andrew Oswald & Alois Stutzer. 2001. "Latent Entrepreneurship Across Nations," *European Economic Review* 45, 680-691.

Borjas, George J. 1986. "The Self-Employment Experience of Immigrants," *The Journal of Human Resources*, 21 (4), 485-506.

Blume Jensen, Kræn, Mette Ejrnæs, Helena Skyt Nielsen and Allan Würtz. 2003. "Self-Employment for Immigrants: A Last Resort?" *CAM Working Paper* 2003-08. University of Copenhagen.

Constant, Amelie. 1998. *The Earnings of Male and Female Guestworkers and Their Assimilation into the German Labor Market: A Panel Study 1984-1993*. Ph.D. Dissertation, Vanderbilt University.

Constant, Amelie and Yochanan Shachmurove. 2003. "Entrepreneurial Ventures and Wage Differentials between Germans and Immigrants." *IZA Discussion Paper* No. 879. Bonn: IZA.

Constant, Amelie, Yochanan Shachmurove and Klaus F. Zimmermann. 2003. "What Makes an Entrepreneur and Does it Pay? Native Men, Turks, and other Immigrants in Germany." *IZA Discussion Paper* No. 940. Bonn: IZA.

Hancock, Mick and Torben Bager. 2001. *Global Entrepreneurship Monitor: Danish National Report – 2001*. Odense: Odense University Press.

Hancock, Mick and Torben Bager. 2003. *Global Entrepreneurship Monitor Denmark 2003*. Copenhagen.

IOM (International Organization for Migration). 2003. *World Migration 2003: Managing Migration – Challenges and Responses for People on the Move*. Geneva: IOM.

Kanein, Werner. 1988. *Ausländerrecht*. C. H. Beck: München.

OECD (Organization for Economic Cooperation & Development). 2003. *Economic Surveys: Denmark*. Paris: OECD.

Schultz-Nielsen, Marie Louise. 2001. *The Integration of Non-Western Immigrants in a Scandinavian Labour Market: The Danish Experience*. Copenhagen.

Wadensjö, Eskil and Helena Orrje. 2002. "Immigrants and Self-Employment in Denmark." Mimeo.

CHAPTER 8

Social Transfers to Immigrants in Germany and Denmark*

By Niels-Kenneth Nielsen

8.1 Introduction

Both Germany and Denmark have in the last half century evolved into societies with highly developed welfare states that acknowledge an obligation to support those who are unable to support themselves, whether this is because of age, unemployment, or sickness or for some other reason. During this period the welfare states in Western Europe have faced serious challenges. In the 1970s the oil crises caused high unemployment rates, and in the 1990s the aging population meant increasing costs for pensions and care of the elderly. At the same time as the problem of the ageing population a third challenge appeared, namely the increasing immigration from less developed countries. People migrating from such countries often have a low level of education and poor skills in the languages of the host countries, which means they will have difficulties in gaining a foothold on the labor market in highly developed economies like those of Germany and Denmark. The alternative means of getting an income will then often be the social benefits system. As a part of the general description of migrants' living conditions in Germany and Denmark, this chapter will give an overview of the two social systems, describe how many immigrants are covered by the respective systems, and what characterizes those who receive benefits.

The chapter will focus especially on foreign citizens from non-Western countries. There are two main reasons for this. First, there is a lack of information on immigrants from Western countries living in Germany in the data material used for this project. Second, for Denmark, where there is excellent data for the Western group of immigrants, previous analyses have shown that immigrants from Western countries receive social benefits to about the same extent as Danes (see for example Nielsen,

---

* The author would like to thank Regina T. Riphahn, Associate Professor at the Department of Economics at University of Basel and Eskil Wadensjö, Professor at the Swedish Institute for Social Research (SOFI) for very helpful comments on earlier drafts of this chapter.

2002). There are no obvious reasons to assume that this should be essentially different in Germany.

The chapter is divided into three main parts. The first part describes the formal requirements for access to the social benefits systems in each country, with a special focus on the access rules for foreigners, including refugees. This part includes the main social security benefits such as unemployment benefit and social assistance. This section will also compare the access conditions in the two countries, and point out differences and similarities. The second part compares the non-Western foreigners' use of social security benefits in Germany and Denmark. The figures are also compared to nationals in the respective countries; this is done separately for each benefit. While this part is more descriptive in nature, the third and final part is more analytical. This section attempts to determine the factors that affect the probability of receiving social security benefits and the importance of each factor.

8.2 Formal Access Condition to Social Security Benefits in Germany and Denmark

This sub-section describes the formal requirements for access to the social security systems in Germany and Denmark and compares the two systems with a special focus on the access rules for foreigners. First, it must be said that this description is not a complete coverage of the social security systems in Germany and Denmark. The chapter will in general concentrate on the benefits related to the labor market. First and foremost, this means benefits like unemployment insurance and social assistance, but the analysis will also include a wider range of benefits such as old age pension, disability pension, child benefit and housing benefit, since these are relevant for the conditions of life for foreign citizens.

A comparison of the Danish and the German social security systems has been done before, in Hansen et al. (2002), for the year 2000. This chapter will refer to the access conditions for 2002, but no radical changes have occurred in the two intervening years. Hansen (2002) compares the social security systems of 8 countries – including Denmark and Germany – and is therefore not as detailed as Hansen et al. (2002). The comparison in Hansen (2002) is for the year 1999.

There will – as mentioned above – be a special focus on foreigners' access to social security benefits compared with access conditions for nationals. As the description below will show, the access rules for foreigners and nationals are quite similar in each country. To put it in another way: if a foreigner is staying legally in one of the two countries and fulfils the relevant general requirements for eligibility, this person will receive benefits on equal terms with nationals (this does not include asylum seekers). There are of course some exceptions, but if nothing else is mentioned in the following sub-sections, it means that the rules are identical for foreigners and nationals.

The description of access rules is given in rather general terms to make it easier to compare the two countries and to get an overview. Some topics have been excluded, e.g. portability of benefits, that is, the possibility of taking benefits to another country. Finally it is necessary to mention that the benefits are compared one by one. No accumulation effects that may exist will be covered; accumulation effects are the possibilities existing in the welfare systems of receiving more than one benefit at the time.

8.2.1 Unemployment Insurance

Membership of the unemployment insurance scheme in Germany is mandatory and financed by contributions from employer and employee, while membership of unemployment insurance is voluntary in Denmark and financed by general taxes and membership fees. The fee varies depending on which unemployment insurance fund one is a member of, because of differing administration expenses. The size of the fee is in the range of EUR 400-540 per year.

The Danish unemployment insurance scheme (*Arbejdsløshedsforsikring*) provides up to 90 percent of the previous gross salary. The benefit is taxable income. The relatively low maximum benefit (EUR 1,761/month before tax, 2002 level[1]) means that a considerable share of the unemployed in Denmark receive compensation at a rate that is lower than 90 percent of their salary when last employed. To be eligible for support one must have been member of a government approved unemployment insurance fund[2] for 1 year and must have been employed for at least 1 year within the last 3 years (Forsikringsoplysningen, 2002). The maximum benefit period is 4 years for everybody, irrespective of how long the person was employed before the period of unemployment, although an unemployed person can be expected to be engaged in workfare programs after 1 year. If the benefit period has ended and a person is no longer entitled to support, the alternative in Denmark is social assistance (see section 8.2.2).

The German unemployment insurance (*Arbeitslosenversicherung*) is a two-component system consisting of unemployment benefit (*Arbeitslosengeld*) and unemployment assistance (*Arbeitslosenhilfe*). The first component, unemployment benefit, is the main benefit, and the compensation rate is 67 percent of the previous salary for persons providing for children and 60 percent for other people. In contrast to the system in Denmark, this percentage is calculated on the basis of the net salary, and the compensation rates are therefore not directly comparable to those in Den-

---

1 Throughout the chapter, all amounts are stated in Euro (EUR). The Danish currency is Danish Kroner (DKK). All amounts for Denmark have been converted into EUR using the average rate of exchange for 2002, which was DKK 7.43 to EUR 1.
2 77.6 percent of the Danish labor force were members of unemployment insurance funds in 2002 (Statistics Denmark, 2002).

mark. As in Denmark, there is a maximum level of benefit, although it is difficult to specify an exact amount for this maximum because it depends on which tax class one is placed in. But for monthly gross incomes larger than the maximum contribution assessment limit the level of unemployment benefit becomes independent of the former income (Lampert, 1998). The limit in 2002 was EUR 4,500 (per month) in Western Germany and EUR 3,750 in Eastern Germany.

The qualifying period is the same as in Denmark, but the benefit period depends on work history before the spell of unemployment and on age. For example, the maximum benefit period is 2⅔ years, but this is only possible with a minimum age of 57 years and a work history before unemployment of at least 64 months (BGSS, 2002). If a person has only worked 12 months before unemployment, the benefit period is 6 months, regardless of age.

If a person has been receiving unemployment benefit and is no longer entitled to it, the exit scheme is not social assistance as in Denmark. Instead the second component of the scheme, unemployment assistance, is invoked[3]. The compensation rate is lower than with unemployment benefit – 57 percent of the net earnings if providing for children and 53 percent otherwise. Unlike unemployment benefit, unemployment assistance is means tested, and there is no limit on the benefit period.

In the German insurance system there are also other transfer schemes such as compensation for reduced employment hours (*Kurzarbeitergeld*) and bad weather compensation (*Winterausfallgeld*), but these benefits will not be described here.

The concept of net replacement rates will be used here in order to illustrate the differences between the unemployment insurance systems in Germany and Denmark. This illustrates the impact on net income on becoming unemployed or retiring. This is done for several income levels in relation to the income level of the OECD average production worker (APW). Table 8.1 shows the net replacement rate for a single insured worker who becomes unemployed for 1 year with former labor income levels ranging from 75 percent to 200 percent of the APW income level. As mentioned previously, the calculation does not include any accumulation effects, which of course means that one must be careful when interpreting the table.

The table shows that the replacement rates are highest in Denmark for lower incomes, and in Germany for higher incomes. The German replacement rates are constant up to quite a high income level – somewhere between 150 and 175 percent of the APW level. This is not the case in Denmark because of the relatively low cap on benefits. Here the replacement rates begin to fall at between 75 and 100 percent of the APW level.

---

3 Before January 1 2000, it was actually possible to enter the unemployment assistance scheme directly if one had worked 5 months within the previous year. As described above, unemployment assistance is now available only as an exit scheme for unemployment benefit.

Table 8.1. Net replacement rates for a single insured worker when unemployed for one year. 1999 level. Percent.

	Former income in percentages of the APW-level ranging from 75 to 200 percent					
	75	100	125	150	175	200
	Net replacement rates					
Germany	59	58	58	58	55	49
Denmark	79	61	52	46	41	37

Source: Hansen (2002).

8.2.2 Social Assistance

Social assistance is in both countries the benefit of last resort, i.e. an individual is only entitled to social assistance if he or she is not eligible for any other benefit and is unable to support him or herself in any other way. In both countries this means, for example, that one will receive social assistance if one becomes unemployed and does not fulfil the eligibility criteria for unemployment benefit/assistance.

The German social assistance system (*Sozialhilfe*) is basically divided into two main components, namely income support (*Hilfe zum Lebensunterhalt*) and support for special circumstances (*Hilfe in besonderen Lebenslagen*). The purpose of income support is to ensure that the individual is able to lead a 'dignified' life based on a socio-culturally determined minimum income (Riphahn, 2001). This minimum income is determined by the sum of an income threshold, rent, heating costs, and possible extra needs. If the income is below this level, one is eligible for income support. The amount of social assistance is tapered against other income (defined above) in such a way that the amount received is the difference between the minimum income and the actual income of the household. Support in special circumstances is intended for persons with special needs.[4] This type of support is also tapered against other income, but the requirements are less stringent (Riphahn, 2001).

In 2002, the threshold (*Eckregelsatz*) for income support was EUR 286[5] per month for a one-person household. In addition, social assistance will also cover housing costs, first and foremost rent and heating, if they are "reasonable" (BGSS, 2002). The benefits from support in special circumstances are more individualised, as they try

---

4 The most frequently occurring special benefits are support for illness (*Krankenhilfe*), integration assistance for people with disabilities (*Eingliederungshilfe für Behinderte*) and care assistance (*Hilfe zur Plege*) (Haustein, 2002).
5 The amount varies between the different German Länder. The amount stated is an average, including both new and old Länder.

to cover more individual needs, such as medical expenditures during illness and care for elderly (Hansen et al., 2002). It is possible to receive both income support and support in special circumstances at the same time. As mentioned above, the threshold at which tapering against other income begins is higher for support in special circumstances, being EUR 551 per month. As in the case of income support, the threshold is increased with each household member. For both schemes there is a limit on how much wealth one may have. While the two schemes treat income somewhat differently, this is not the case for wealth. For income support the limit is EUR 1,279 for single persons, which can be increased by EUR 614 for any spouse and EUR 256 for each child.

The benefits are typically given on the basis of the needs of the household, at least in the case of income support. This is in contrast to the Danish social assistance system, where the assessment of need is made on an individual basis. In Germany the head of the household will receive the standard rate of EUR 286. The payment for any spouse will be 80 percent of that amount, while for children living in the household a further 50 to 90 percent of the standard payment to the head of the household will be paid, depending on the age of the children. In certain cases where the household has additional needs there is a possibility of supplementary payments (*Mehrbedarfzuschlag*) (BGSS, 2002).

'Topping up' is possible in the German social assistance system. If one is receiving another benefit that does not provide adequate means to cover living expenses, it is possible to receive social assistance up to the minimum income level. Likewise it is possible to receive social assistance even if one is employed, if the income from employment is very low.

The Danish social assistance (*Kontanthjælp*) is triggered by a 'social event', which means that a person for some reason (social event) becomes incapable of supporting himself or herself. Examples of this social event could be unemployment (if the person is not eligible for unemployment benefit), pregnancy or sickness. In the Danish social assistance system one will normally receive standard payments. As with the German system, there are also possibilities to receive more individualized payments in special situations. Examples of such payments include assistance with debt restructuring and payment of expenses for furniture (Forsikringsoplysningen, 2002). Housing costs such as rent can also be covered by social assistance. In 2002, the standard payment (*Hjælp til forsørgelse*) was EUR 1,416 per month[6] for persons aged 25 or over providing for children and EUR 1,066 for other persons aged 25 or over. For persons under 25 the payments were somewhat lower. Other income is deducted from the benefit. It is usually a condition of receiving social assistance that one does not have any wealth, but the authorities will usually ignore amounts up to EUR 1,346 for single persons.

---

6 The benefits are taxable income.

As mentioned above, in the Danish social assistance system the payments are given on an individual basis, i.e. in households with married couples, both spouses will have the opportunity to receive social assistance only if they apply separately and each fulfils the normal rules for eligibility.[7] However, in the case of married couples, if one spouse is working and the other spouse is receiving social assistance, the amount received will be adjusted downwards depending on the labor income earned by the spouse. Unlike in the German system, there is no "topping up" in the Danish system.

In the Danish system there are special rules for newcomers, including foreigners. Newcomers are entitled to a so-called introduction benefit during the first three years in Denmark. The access rules for introduction benefit are exactly the same as for social assistance, and the benefit level is also the same. However, in the social assistance scheme there is a qualifying period, which means that to receive benefit one must have resided in Denmark for at least 7 years during the previous 8. If this requirement is not fulfilled, one will receive lower benefits. This holds for all, including Danish citizens who have been living abroad for a period, but it is clear that it is mostly immigrants who are affected by this requirement.

8.2.3 Old-age Pension

In both countries old-age pensions represent a large expenditure in the government budgets. This has become more obvious in recent years, because the population in both countries is generally aging. As a consequence, the German government has passed various pension reforms – one of the latest being the 2001 pension reform. Elements of this reform included a modification of the pension formula in order to restrict the growth in pension benefits and the introduction of voluntary private pension accounts (Bonin, 2002).

The official retirement age is 65 years in both Denmark[8] and Germany. The pension systems in Germany and Denmark are very different. The German old-age pension is a part of the *Rentenversicherung* (RV), an insurance system mandatory for all non-civil-servant employees in Germany[9] (disability pension is also a part of RV, see

---

7 There are special rules that apply to married couples where the spouse has chosen to work at home (e.g. a housewife). In this case the male spouse receiving social assistance can get an increased amount, see Forsikringsoplysningen, 2002.
8 In Denmark, the official retirement age was recently lowered from 67 to 65 years, but only for persons who reached their 60th birthday on July 1, 1999 or later. This means that this reform will take effect from 2004. The lowering of the personable age is remarkable, as many European countries have raised or are considering raising the personable age due to their ageing populations.
9 In Germany, the pension system differentiates between blue collar and white collar workers (*Rentenversicherung der Arbeiter/Rentenversichrrung der Angestellten*). In Germany there is also a pension system for public servants (*Beamtenpension*). This system is more or less independent of the pension system described above.

Sub-section 8.2.4). In order to obtain pension rights one must have been a member of the insurance system for at least five years. This does not necessarily mean that one must have paid contributions[10] in all five years. Time spent on child raising and education can also be included as insurance time, however only in connection with a work period. Refugees are permitted to register work time in the home country. This rule is exclusively for refugees (Hansen et al., 2002).

The amount of a German pension is determined by a pension formula. This is basically the product of the number of pension points, a pension type factor, an age factor (*Zugangsfaktor*) and the current pension value. The pension points are calculated on an annual basis. They are determined by the actual wage received in relation to the average wage for all insured persons in the current year. This means, for example, that if the salary is 20 percent over the average, an individual will earn 1.2 pension points that year. The pension points are further adjusted by an age factor. If the retirement time is prolonged beyond the age of 65 the pension points will be adjusted upwards, and vice versa if one retires before the age of 65.

The pension type factor reflects what kind of pension one receives. The factor will be one if it is a standard old-age pension, but will in some cases be less than one if one receives disability pension; see Sub-section 8.2.4.

The current pension value reflects the monthly amount that is ascribed to each pension point. It is determined by several factors, among them the average rate of increase in wages and demographic factors. This part of the pension formula has been the subject of reforms in recent years, e.g. the 1995 and the 2001 pension reforms aimed at moderating pension expenditure growth.[11] The standard German old-age pension is not tapered against other income, except if one begins receiving old-age pension before the age of 65.

The description of the German system has concentrated on the standard old-age pension (*Regelaltersrente*). There are other types of retirement benefit, such as long service pensions (*Altersrente für langjährig Versicherte*) and old-age pension after unemployment or partial retirement (*Altersrente wegen Arbeitslosigkeit oder nach Altersteilzeitarbeit*), but the rules for eligibility are basically the same, with some exceptions. If one is not entitled to an old-age pension in Germany, the alternative is social assistance.

The Danish pension system is very different from the German system, as it is almost independent of former income. Danish old-age pension is instead residence based, though there exists a supplementary work-related pension scheme (ATP). Nationals must have resided in the country for at least three years between their 15th

---

10 In 2002 the contribution was 19.1 percent of the gross wage, divided equally between employer and employee.
11 The objective was to stabilize contribution rates and ensure that they do not exceed 22 percent in 2030 (BGSS, 2002). The current pension value in 2002 was 25.31 percent in Western Germany and 22.06 percent in Eastern Germany.

and 66th birthdays to be eligible for pension. For foreign citizens the rule is ten years, except for refugees who do not have any requirement for a minimum stay; so as in Germany, refugees are better off than other foreigners. There are also some exceptions for guest workers from Turkey and the former Yugoslavia. In order to receive an old-age pension they must have worked at least one year in Denmark and must have been in the country for at least five years.[12]

Two points should be noted here. First, the Danish pension system is universal in its character, with relatively low uniform benefits for everybody, but with some tapering against other income. It is therefore common that employees have private pension arrangements individually agreed upon with employers. This type of pension is exclusively dependent on the work record. This chapter will concentrate only on the public pension. Second, as described above, the official retirement age in Denmark is 65 years. However, there are some other possibilities for withdrawing from the labor market before that. A person who has been member of an unemployment insurance fund for at least 25 years has the possibility of receiving early retirement benefit (*Efterløn*) on reaching his or her 60th birthday, provided that the person has paid contributions. The benefit is calculated as for unemployment benefit.

In order to receive a full pension a person must have lived in Denmark for 40 years. For example, if a person has been resident in Denmark for 20 years, this person will receive half the normal pension on retirement.[13] Refugees are allowed to include time spent in their home country when calculating their period of residence in Denmark. As in Germany, if one is not eligible for any pension, one may receive social assistance instead.

A Danish pension consists of a basic amount and a supplementary amount. The basic amount in 2002 was EUR 7,069 per year for both married and single persons. The supplementary amount was EUR 7,116 for single persons and 3,320 for married persons. In contrast to the German pension system, a Danish pension is generally tapered against other income. The basic amount is tapered against labor income, but not against other types of income, while the supplementary amount is tapered against all other income, including income of a spouse. The income limit before the basic amount is tapered is EUR 30,040 per year for both single and married persons. For every EUR 13.46 by which the labor income exceeds the maximum limit, the pension is reduced by EUR 4.04. The tapering of the supplementary amount is more complicated, depending on marital status and all types of income.

As with unemployment insurance, the differences between the German and Danish pension systems will be illustrated by calculating the net replacement rates. As the earnings principles are very different, two cases are shown in Table 8.2, namely

---

12 Denmark has bilateral agreements with a number of countries outside the EU, but here we have only mentioned those of interest for this study.
13 On the assumption that the pension is not tapered against any other income.

Table 8.2. Net replacement rates for a single pensioner with and without former work record. 1998 level. Percent.

	Former income in percentages of the APW-level ranging from 75 to 200 percent				
	75	100	150	175	200
			Net replacement rate		
Germany					
With former work	70	75	83	81	71
Denmark					
With former work	70	55	41	36	32
Without former work	62	48	36	32	29

Source: Hansen et al. (2002).

Note: Housing benefit is not included. For persons without a former work record the net replacement rate means persion level relative to a non-earned annual disposable income of APW(r), for r= 75,100,..., 200, see Hansen (2002).

those of a pensioner with a former work record and a pensioner without a former work record, though only for Denmark. The design of the German pension system means that if one has no work record there will be no pension payments. The calculation is for a person with a work record of 45 years, so it can be said to be a kind of maximum pension (Hansen et al., 2002). In the case without a work record it is assumed that the pensioner has stayed in the country for 40 years.

It can be seen from Table 8.2 that while in Denmark it is not crucial to have a work record, this is much more decisive in Germany. For a person in Germany with a former income of 100 percent of the APW level, the net replacement rate is 75 percent with a work record, while such a person would not receive any pension without a work record. For Denmark the corresponding percentages are 55 and 48.

8.2.4 Disability Pension

Access to disability pensions is closely linked to the access rules for old-age pensions in both countries. In Germany the disability pension is – as mentioned above – part of the *Rentenversicherung* (RV). Eligibility for a German disability pension requires five years of membership, with at least three years of contributions from work in those five years.

The German disability pension scheme was altered with the 1999 pension reform. Before this reform disability pension was divided into two main schemes, namely occupational disability pension (*Berufsunfähigkeitsrente*) for those who had lost at least half of their earnings capacity, and invalidity pension (*Erwerbsunfähigkeitsrente*) for those for whom the earnings capacity was almost completely lost.

On January 1, 2001 these two schemes were replaced by a two-level reduced earnings capacity pension (*Rente wegen verminderter Erwerbsfähigkeit*). Full-rate reduced earnings capacity pension is paid to persons with a working capacity of less than 3 hours a day on the general labor market. The other possibility is a half rate reduced earnings capacity pension for persons with a working capacity of less than 6 hours per day.[14]

With some exceptions, disability pension in Germany is calculated in a similar way to old-age pension. The exceptions arise from the fact that one will typically begin receiving disability pension before reaching the age of 65, which means that some of the insurance period is anticipated (from the point where disability pension is needed and onwards until the age of 65). Moreover, with a half rate pension the pension type factor will be a half, so the size of the pension will equal half an old-age pension. For a full rate disability pension the pension type factor is one.

The rules of access for the Danish disability scheme are similar to those current in the Danish old-age pension scheme. Furthermore, like the old-age pension, the Danish scheme is residence based, though with some differences. The size of a Danish disability pension depends on the ratio between actual time of stay and 4/5 of the "theoretical" time of stay. The theoretical time of stay is the length of time from the age of 15 to the date when the disability pension is granted. This can best be illustrated by an example (Forsikringsoplysningen, 2002): A 40-year-old person is granted a disability pension. He has lived in Denmark for 10 years. The theoretical time of stay is 40-15=25 years. The size of the disability pension is then 10/(4/5*25) = 50 percent. In addition to this, it should be noted that there are four different levels of disability pension, depending on the degree of loss of work capability. They all consist of a combination of a basic and a supplementary benefit, as with the old-age pension system. In severe cases where almost all ability to work is lost there exist additional supplements.

8.2.5 Housing Benefit

The rules determining who is eligible for housing benefit are quite complicated in both countries, except insofar as the most fundamental regulations are concerned. Basically, housing benefit depends on family income, family size and housing costs. While the Danish scheme (*Boligstøtte*) only grants support to tenants,[15] the German scheme (*Wohngeld*) grants support to both tenants (*Mietzuschuss*) and home owners (*Lastenzuschuss*).

---

14 Persons who were receiving disability pension before January 1, 2001 remain subject to the prior law.
15 Home owners who are old-age pensioners are entitled to housing benefits if they fulfil the general rules for eligibility.

In Germany it is the total income of the family which primarily decides eligibility. The income limits and maximum housing costs are determined on the basis of the number of persons in the household, the year of construction of the home, and the rent level (*Mietenstufe*) under which the home is categorized. Each dwelling in Germany is categorized into one of six rent levels, which are related to the overall level of rent in the area. For a five-person household living in a dwelling with a rent level of *Mietenstufe VI* the monthly income limit is EUR 2,100, while the income limit for a one-person household with the same rent level is EUR 830. The maximum housing benefit available for a single provider was EUR 321 per month in 2002 (BGSS, 2002a); but this would only apply if the income was very low and the rent very high.

The total household income is calculated as the sum of the gross incomes of each household member, minus deductions (e.g. a flat-rate deduction for each child). There are also deductions for contributions to social security and/or taxes.

The Danish system is somewhat different. The maximum housing cost included in the eligibility calculation varies with the number of children in the household. The family income is based on personal income as recorded on the income tax declaration, and only income over a certain level counts. The income limits are increased with the number of children in the household. The Danish scheme operates on the basis of a concept of an "own payment", an amount of rent which the householder can reasonably be expected to pay and which depends on the family income. The housing benefits are calculated as the difference between the actual housing costs and this "own payment". The maximum housing cost that can enter the benefit calculation for a single provider with one child was EUR 712 per month in 2002. The maximum housing benefit for the same type of household was EUR 358 per month. The scheme is more generous to pensioners than to other people.

8.2.6 Child Benefit

Both countries have schemes that support families with children. In Germany, the allowance can be given as a tax credit or a cash payment, while in Denmark it is only given as a cash payment. To be eligible, the general rule in both countries is that the person taking care of the child is subject to income tax in that country and that the child is not living abroad. There are some exceptions for children living in other EEA countries or countries where bilateral agreements exist.

The German system is actually a two-component system consisting of child benefit (*Kindergeld*) and child deduction (*Kinderfreibetrag*). The family will receive whatever is the most advantageous. If a family is eligible for support, they will receive child benefit as a cash payment during the year, and at the end of the year the taxation authorities will determine whether the child deduction would be better for the family (BGSS, 2002). The benefit is independent of parents' income.

Child benefit/deduction can normally be received until the child reaches the age of 18, but children up to the age of 27 can receive child benefit if they are still in education and do not earn more than EUR 7,188 per year. Under special circumstances children older than 27 can also receive child benefit. In 2002 the child benefit rates were EUR 154 per month for the first three children, and EUR 179 for the fourth and each further child (non-taxable income). The amount of the child deduction was EUR 3,534.

The Danish system is also a two-component system. Child family benefit (*børnefamilieydelse*) can be received regardless of the size of the parents' income and is calculated for each child. Depending on the age of each child, the rates are EUR 1,682 per year for each child under the age of 2, EUR 1,521 for children between 3 and 6 years, and EUR 1,198 for children between 7 and 17 years. In addition, it is possible under certain circumstances to receive child supplement (*Børnetilskud*). Ordinary child supplement (*Ordinært børnetilskud*) is payable only if the child has a single parent, or if both parents are receiving old-age pensions or disability pensions. This amount is EUR 527 per child per year and is independent of parents' income. Other types of child supplement are dependent on family income; see Forsikringsoplysningen (2002). All benefits are non-taxable.

8.2.7 Rules of Access to Social Security Systems: Summary

When the selected social benefits are examined, it is clear that in general terms, the two systems are very different. The German benefits are typically work-related and dependent on former income up to a relatively high income level. The APW calculations showed that the net replacement rate is constant over a wide income span. Hansen et al. (2002) call this an 'insurance-like' approach.

The Danish benefits are dependent on former income to a much lesser extent and are typically residence based, which means that it is less important in Denmark than in Germany to have a stable work record. Hansen et al. (2002) describe the Danish system as "schemes of solidarity". The benefit schemes are relatively universal, as most recipients receive almost the same amounts. Together with progressive income taxes, this contributes to a more equal income distribution in Denmark.

It can generally be said that access rules are the same for newcomers, including foreigners, and nationals in both countries, but with some exceptions. For the pension systems in particular there are different rules for refugees. In this respect, foreigners with refugee status have easier access to the pension systems in both countries.

The question is, then, to determine in which country it is easiest to access the social benefit system. Hansen et al. (2002) conclude that the social security schemes in Germany seem more difficult for foreign citizens to access, in the sense that a work record is usually required. Our description has not revealed anything that contradicts this conclusion. One could add that the Danish social security system favors low income groups to a greater extent than the German system, and a considerable number of non-Western immigrants belong to low income groups.

8.3 Who Receives Benefits in Denmark and Germany?

This sub-section will describe the shares of the different population groups that receive transfer benefits in each country. In the light of the previous section, it is already possible to point out a couple of interesting questions. For example, it will be interesting to see how the different approaches in the pension systems affect the possibilities for receiving pensions, especially for refugees. In the unemployment insurance systems it will also be interesting to see what it means that unemployment insurance in Denmark is voluntary. As mentioned previously, this section will be of a rather descriptive nature in order to give an overview of immigrants' use of social security benefits.

In this specific area the German literature mainly concentrates on social assistance and especially on what factors affect the probability of receiving social assistance (see Sub-section 8.4.1). Studies that describe the use of a wider range of social benefits in summary form are more scarce. The main source is the official statistics (*Statistisches Bundesamt*). Examples of studies that give a brief overview of the use of social assistance in Germany are Haustein (2002) and Bauer (2002). One result found in Haustein (2002) is that in 2000 the foreign households in Germany, which comprised around 7 percent of all households, received around 22 percent of the total social assistance paid out (income support only). For Denmark, the literature on this field is a little more extensive – probably, among other things, because of the good opportunities for obtaining data. Studies like Pedersen (2000), Nielsen (2002), The Think Tank on Integration in Denmark (2001) and Poulsen and Lange (1998) give an overview of the use of social benefits by immigrants in Denmark. One result found in Nielsen (2002) is that in 2000 non-Western immigrants, who comprise about 5 percent of the population in Denmark, received around 35 percent of the social assistance. These figures are not directly comparable with the German figures mentioned above, as the German figures include all immigrants (and not only non-Western immigrants), only income support is included, and the figures are given on the household level, while the Danish figures are on the individual level.

The analysis will concentrate on selected benefits, the selection being mainly determined by the limited data possibilities for Germany. While Danish data originate from administrative registers, where the data available are quite comprehensive, information on transfer income in Germany originates from survey data. Our German survey (*Rockwool Foundation Migration Survey – Germany*, RFMS-G) was carried out in 2002 specially for this project among 5,669 foreigners living in Germany and originating from the former Yugoslavia, Iran, Lebanon, Poland and Turkey. In face-to-face interviews the respondents were asked about a variety of socio-economic questions, including questions on whether they had received transfer income in the previous month. The survey is described in more detail in the appendix. Data on German nationals are based on information from Statistisches Bundesamt and the GSOEP.

The Danish data originate from administrative registers for 2001. There is detailed information on the type of benefit received, the amount received and duration of the benefit. This information has been linked with two samples drawn from the Danish population register. The first sample consists of all non-Western immigrants and descendants living in Denmark, and the second sample consists of 2 percent of the Danish population (randomly drawn). These samples are described in more detail in the appendix.

The German data are recorded on a monthly basis, while the Danish register data is usually listed on a yearly basis; see for example Statistics Denmark (2002). Fortunately it is possible to find sufficient information in the registers to enable information for both countries to be shown on a monthly basis in order to compare the results.[16] In order to make the Danish figures as comparable as possible, only statistics for foreign citizens living in Denmark are included in the study. But as a considerable share of the immigrants living in Denmark have acquired Danish citizenship, figures for all immigrants and descendants living in Denmark have also been given as a comparison.

8.3.1 Unemployment Insurance

Table 8.3 shows the shares that receive unemployment benefit/assistance, distributed by the five foreign nationalities in each country plus German and Danish nationals. For Germany it can be seen from the table that among the 5 immigrant countries the share that receives unemployment benefit (UB) or unemployment assistance (UA) is generally higher than for German nationals, and most significantly for men. 15 percent of the immigrant men in Germany receive UB or UA, while the corresponding figure for German nationals is less than half that level. This is of course no surprise, as official statistics show that the unemployment rates generally are higher for foreigners than for German nationals (see for example Statistisches Bundesamt, 2001).

---

16 In the German survey the respondents were asked if they received benefits "last month". As the interview period lasted from April 2002 to August 2002, the respondents were referring to different months within that period. Therefore, the Danish figures are an average of the months March to July.

Table 8.3. The share of the population who received unemployment benefit/assistance in Germany (2002) and Denmark (2001), distributed by population groups (citizenship). Percent.

	Germany, 18-64 years, 2002						Denmark, 18-66 yers, 2001	
	Unemployment benefit		Unemployment assistance		Total		Unemployment benefit	
	Men	Women	Men	Women	Men	Women	Men	Women
Former Yugoslavia	6	4	5	2	11	6	8	7
Iran	7	4	5	4	12	8	6	4
Lebanon	11	2	16	3	27	6	6	3
Poland	6	3	5	4	11	7	7	9
Turkey	10	4	8	4	18	8	15	13
All five countries	8	4	7	4	15	7	11	9
All five countries[1]	*	*	*	*	*	*	10	9
Germans[2]	4	3	2	2	6	5	-	-
Danes	-	-	-	-	-	-	4	6

Notes: 1) Including naturalized persons. 2) Figures apply to a whole year (2001). "-" = Not applicable. "*" = Information not available. The number of observations is given in Appendix Table 1.

Sources: RFMS-G (Figures for Germany, except for German nationals), Danish Register for Social Statistics (Figures for Denmark), GSOEP 2001 (Figures for German nationals), own calculations.

Within the 5 groups there is considerable variation. The highest figures are those for Lebanese men. 11 percent receive UB and 16 percent receive UA; that is to say, 27 percent of Lebanese men receive some kind of unemployment insurance. The share of Turkish men is somewhat lower; 18 percent receive either UB or UA. The lowest percentages are observed for men from the former Yugoslavia and Poland, 11 percent in both cases.

It is interesting to note the differences between men and women. For the immigrant men the shares that receive unemployment insurance are often 2 or 3 times larger than the corresponding shares for women. For German nationals the shares for men and women are more equal, with a slightly higher percentage for men. The reason for this is obviously not that the foreign women are more frequently employed than foreign men (see Chapter 4).

In the RFMS-G the respondents were asked about their labor market status in the week before the interview. One answer possibility was "Housewife/Houseman" and while very few immigrant men describe themselves as a "Houseman", a considerable share of the immigrant women reported themselves as being housewives. Roughly 65 percent of the Lebanese women answered that they were housewives. For Turkish women the percentage is 40, while the percentage among

Polish women is about 21. This is very different from the Danish figures, where many fewer immigrant women report themselves as housewives. The Danish figures lie in the range of 1 to 5 percent, and this probably reflects the structure of Danish society, since Danish women have a level of labor market activity that is almost as high as for men. In the case of Denmark, Table 8.3 shows that the shares for men and women are not that different. The share for foreign men is 11 percent, whereas the percentage for foreign women is 9. Among Danish nationals the percentage is higher for women.

The largest share of any group receiving unemployment benefit in Denmark is to be found among the Turks. 15 percent of Turkish men and 13 percent of Turkish women receive unemployment benefits. The remaining groups vary relatively little, especially in the case of the men, with shares receiving unemployment benefits of around 6 to 8 percent for men and between 3 to 9 percent for the women. The difference between men and women is not particularly marked, and the shares for men are generally larger than those for women except in the case of Poles.

Table 8.3 reveals many differences between Germany and Denmark. If UB and UA are considered together for Germany and compared with UB in Denmark, it seems clear that the shares of immigrant men receiving benefit are somewhat larger in Germany, especially in the case of Lebanese men. The picture for the immigrant women is more mixed, as the percentages for some groups are higher in Germany and for other groups they are higher in Denmark, but if we consider the total for female immigrants from all the five countries of origin then the share receiving benefit is larger in Denmark. The percentages of German men and women receiving benefit are on the same level as for Danish men and women. In considering explanations for the differences between Germany and Denmark there are some obvious factors to be taken into account. The labor market attachment of the immigrants is better in Germany, see Chapter 4 of this volume. This should tend to reduce the shares of immigrants receiving benefit in Germany. As this is not the case (for men), there must be other factors pulling in the opposite direction. One factor is differences in the regulations for access to unemployment insurance. As mentioned in sub-section 8.2.1, unemployment insurance in Denmark is voluntary. Parsons et al. (2001) point out that many low-waged workers in Denmark are not insured, because it is more advantageous to receive social assistance instead (given the amount of the contributions to the unemployment insurance fund). As a considerable share of immigrants are expected to be in low-wage jobs, this factor could certainly explain some of the differences between Germany and Denmark. To illustrate this, consider the figures in Table 8.4. This table shows the shares that receive unemployment insurance or social assistance transfers for the same groups. Of course, one has to be careful when interpreting Table 8.4, as some people receive social assistance for reasons other than unemployment, but the table can still illustrate how the access conditions to unemployment insurance have a different impact in the two countries.

From Table 8.4 it can be seen that for immigrant men the shares are more alike

Table 8.4. The share of the population who received unemployment benefit/assistance or social assistance in Germany (2002) and Denmark (2001), distributed by different population groups (citizenship). Percent.

	Germany, 2002		Denmark, 2001	
	Unemployment benefit or unemployment assistance or social assistance, 18-64 years		Unemployment benefit or social assistance, 18-66 years	
	Men	Women	Men	Women
Former Yugoslavia	25	20	25	29
Iran	24	22	35	38
Lebanon	53	45	46	57
Poland	16	13	15	21
Turkey	22	13	25	29
All five countries	23	16	26	29
All five countries[1]	*	*	23	27
Germans[2]	7	7	-	-
Danes	-	-	6	8

Notes: 1) Including naturalized persons. 2) Figures apply to a whole year (2001). "-" = Not applicable. "*" = Information not available. The number of observations is given in Appendix Table 1.

Sources: RFMS-G (figures for Germany, except German nationals), Danish Register for Social Statistics (figures for Denmark), GSOEP 2001 (figures for German nationals), own calculations.

for Denmark and Germany than was the case in Table 8.3. 23 percent of immigrant men in Germany receive unemployment insurance or social assistance, while the figure in Denmark is 26 percent. The picture seems to be that more immigrants in Germany receive unemployment benefit/assistance than social assistance, while the opposite is the case in Denmark.

As mentioned before, the labor market performance of the immigrants is somewhat better in Germany than in Denmark. This means – all other things being equal – that it will be easier for immigrants in Germany to fulfil the work history condition in the unemployment insurance system if they become unemployed.

Table 8.4 also shows that immigrant women in Denmark more frequently receive unemployment insurance or social assistance than immigrant women in Germany. This means that while immigrant women in Germany receive support less often than immigrant men (in Germany), the situation is the opposite in Denmark. The explanation for this probably lies in the differences in availability for the labor market of the immigrant women in Germany and Denmark, and this topic will be discussed further in the next section.

8.3.2 Social Assistance

After having covered unemployment benefit/assistance and social assistance in part, we now turn to a more thorough description of the receipt of social assistance, in both countries the "last resort" benefit. In our RFMS-G survey the respondents were asked if their household or/and they themselves had received social assistance during the previous month, but no distinction was made between income support and support in special circumstances, which means that the figures include transfers under both schemes. In most of the German literature on this topic, especially on the take-up of social assistance, the focus is concentrated on income support; see for example Riphahn (1998) and Bird et al. (2001). One reason for this is that it is possible to determine from the data who is eligible or not eligible for income support, while this is more difficult for support in special circumstances. Other studies, such as Riphahn (2001) and Fertig & Schmidt (2001), also use data where it is not possible to differentiate between the two schemes. The main point being made here is that as this chapter is trying to describe the living conditions of immigrants in Germany and Denmark in general terms, it seems most reasonable to include both schemes. It should be noted that the German figures will probably be somewhat underestimated. The reason for this is that many of the benefits in special circumstances scheme are non-cash benefits, such as home help for disabled persons. As the benefit is non-cash one cannot be sure that the respondent will regard this as social assistance. But the problem is probably manageable, as the Danish registers do not include services such as home help for disabled persons either.

Table 8.5 shows the shares of the population that receive social assistance, distributed by gender and different population groups. Two columns have been added to those in the previous table, showing the shares in each country receiving social assistance on the household level. This is done in order to make comparisons easier, cf. the description of formal rules of access to social assistance in Germany and Denmark in Sub-section 8.2.2.

The general picture revealed in Table 8.5 is that the shares of the various groups receiving social assistance are generally higher for Denmark, but besides that there are some structural similarities. The share of Lebanese citizens that receive social assistance is considerably higher compared to all other groups in both countries. 45 percent of the Lebanese households living in Germany receive social assistance, while the corresponding figure for Denmark is 56. The level for German and Danish nationals is around 2 to 4 percent. If one looks at the five countries of origin together, the table shows that the share for immigrant men is 9 percent in Germany against 15 percent in Denmark. For women and for households the share in Denmark is almost twice as high as in Germany. This picture can be compared to the fact that the shares of native Germans receiving social assistance in Germany are on the same level as the corresponding shares for native Danes in Denmark. The higher share for immigrants in Denmark is probably – cf. the previous sub-section – caused by

Table 8.5. The share of population that receives social assistance distributed by different population groups (citizenship). Percent.

	Germany, 2002			Denmark, 2001		
	Social assistance, respondent, 18-59 years			Social assistance, respondent, 18-66 years		
	Men	Women	Social assistance, household	Men	Women	Social assistance, household
Former Yugoslavia	15	15	18	16	22	23
Iran	14	15	18	29	35	36
Lebanon	33	41	45	40	54	56
Poland	5	7	7	7	12	12
Turkey	5	7	9	10	15	18
All five countries	9	10	13	15	20	22
All five countries[1]	*	*	*	13	18	21
Germans[2]	2	4	2	-	-	-
Danes	-	-	-	2	2	3

Notes: 1) Including naturalized persons. 2) Figures apply to the whole year (2001). "-" = Not applicable. "*" = Information not available. The number of observations is given in Appendix Table 1.

Sources: RFMS-G (figures for Germany, except German nationals), Danish Register for Social Statistics (figures for Denmark), GSOEP 2001 (figures for German nationals), own calculations.

their poor labor market affiliation and by the fact that they receive unemployment insurance to a lesser extent.

It can be seen from Table 8.5 that while the differences between immigrant men and women in Germany – except in the case of Lebanese citizens – are moderate, the differences between male and female immigrants in Denmark are somewhat greater. In the previous section, it was noted that the proportion of immigrant women who describe themselves as housewives is considerably higher in Germany than in Denmark. The question is, though, whether this is the complete picture of the situation in the two countries. ILO calculations presented in Chapter 5 of this volume show that immigrant women in Denmark are available for the labor market (according to the ILO definitions) to a much lesser extent than immigrant women in Germany. Furthermore, it is also clear that a rather small proportion of the immigrant social assistance recipients are available for the labor market, according to the ILO definitions. This could indicate that some immigrant women living in Denmark report themselves as being unemployed or receiving social assistance even though they are in reality not available for the labor market, and are thus in a similar situation to housewives. If this is the case, it could explain some of the differences between the figures for German and Danish immigrant women.

8.3.3 Old-age and Disability Pension

This subsection moves on to giving an overview of which groups receive old-age and disability pensions in Denmark and Germany. As mentioned earlier in Sub-section 8.2.3, the official retirement age is 65 years in Germany, but given the possibilities for retiring before the age of 65 (with a reduced pension), the retirement age will typically be around 60 years. This can be confirmed by official statistics which show that the majority of those who retire because of age actually retire between the ages of 60 and 65 years (Statistisches Bundesamt, 2002). This is important from a data point of view, because in the RFMS-G only one question has been asked concerning pension payments, which means that it is not possible to tell immediately if the respondent receives a pension because of age or because of disability. But by dividing the respondents into two age groups, namely 18-59 years and 60 years and more, it should be possible to determine who is receiving what to within an acceptable margin of error.[17] Table 8.6 shows the recipients of pension in Germany, distributed by the age groups described above and by country of origin. The table also shows the percentage of old-age pensioners (those aged 60 and over) who receive social assistance, and their average length of stay and work history in years. Finally, the figures for those aged 65 years and over have been added in parentheses. These figures will be commented on later in this section.

If the first column in Table 8.6 is regarded as an indicator of how many people receive old-age pension, two groups stand out as different from the others. Immigrants from Iran and Lebanon do not receive old-age pension as often as immigrants from Turkey, the former Yugoslavia and Poland. Only a little more than 25 percent of Lebanese aged 60 or over receive pensions, whereas the shares of Turks and persons from the former Yugoslavia that receive pension are around 60 percent. To explain these differences we will have to examine how long each group has worked and stayed in Germany, recalling from Sub-section 8.2.3 that a minimum work history of 5 years is a condition for receiving old-age pension in Germany. This can explain why the share of Lebanese is rather small. The table shows that the average length of work history for Lebanese citizens is somewhat less than for other groups, and it is therefore more difficult for them to fulfil the access requirements for an old-age pension. The question is of course whether they then receive any other social benefit instead. As can be seen from column two in Table 8.6, the Lebanese receive social assistance instead to a large extent. The picture is less clear for the Iranians. While they have an average length of work history on a level with the Poles, only 29 percent of Iranians over 60 receive a pension, while the corresponding percentage for the Poles is 80. The table shows that only some Iranians receive social assistance transfers instead of pension. The explanation for this is that a much larger share of the Iranians aged 60 years or more is still active on the labor market.

---

17 It is not possible to identify those receiving widow's or widower's pension (Witwenrente), but this is a fact that will have to be ignored.

Table 8.6. Shares receiving pensions in Germany, distributed by country of origin (citizenship) and different age groups. 2002. Percent.

	Germany, 2002					
	Pension, persons aged 60 and over (65 and over)	Social assistance, persons aged 60 and over (65 and over)	Average length of stay, persons aged 60 and over (years)	Average length of work history, persons aged 60 and over (years)	Percentage with residence permit as refugee	Pension, persons aged 18-59 years
Former Yugoslavia	61 (86)	16 (20)	29	22	14	4
Iran	29 (47)	28 (36)	26	17	33	2
Lebanon	26 (...)	57 (...)	18	9	68	<1
Poland	82 (93)	6 (5)	27	16	22	2
Turkey	62 (81)	7 (9)	30	20	7	4
All five countries	62 (82)	10 (12)	29	14	11	4
Germans[1]	86 (*)	1 (*)	-	*	-	4

Notes: 1) Figures apply to a whole year (2001). "-" = Not applicable. "*" = Information not available. "..." = Too few observations. The number of observations is given in Appendix Table 1.

Sources: RFMS-G (figures for Germany, except German nationals), GSOEP 2001 (figures for German nationals), own calculations.

As mentioned above, 80 percent of the Poles receive a pension, which is the highest share among the foreign groups; only Germans receive a pension more often (86 percent). This is probably because the labor market activity rate is higher among Polish women, while women from Turkey or Lebanon more frequently live in more traditional family circumstances, as housewives provided for by their husbands. It should be noted here that it is of some importance what age groups one considers. A special data run on RFMS-G shows that a considerable percentage of the Iranians in Germany aged between 60 and 65 are still active on the labor market. If only persons over the age of 65 are considered, one can observe that the shares receiving a pension become somewhat higher. The share of persons from the former Yugoslavia rises to 86 percent, and of Poles, to 92 percent. For all five countries of origin together, the share becomes 82 percent. The relative levels of the shares for the five countries are not altered, but except for Lebanon, the shares all become somewhat greater.

It is remarkable that the two groups where only a minority receives pensions are those two groups with the largest percentages holding residence permits as refugees, see column 5 in Table 8.6. It was noted in Sub-section 8.2.3 that – all other things being equal – it is easier for a refugee to obtain pension rights compared to other foreigners. The figures seem to indicate, however, that this is not a direct advantage for refugees in Germany, at least not for the Lebanese. With respect to the amounts received, in the RFMS-G the respondents were asked what amount they received the previous month, but the number of observations is quite low for some groups, so it is necessary to be careful about drawing strong conclusions. The responses show that persons from the former Yugoslavia, Turkey and Poland receive on average a monthly pension of around EUR 700-800. There are too few observations for Lebanon to say anything definite, but the Iranians receive on average EUR 1,300. This could indicate that some Iranians have had the advantage of being refugees, but it could also be a result of the apparently high level of labor market activity of the Iranians.

There is little variation among the shares that receive disability pension (pension, 18-59 years). The shares for all groups lie within the range of 1 to 4 percent, which makes it difficult to say anything definite about this benefit.

Turning to Denmark, it should first be noted that as with the previous tables, the Danish figures are based on information from administrative registers, which means that it is possible to distinguish accurately between old-age pension and disability pension. The shares that receive old-age pension, disability pension, early retirement benefit (*Efterløn*) and social assistance are showed in Table 8.7. Early retirement benefit has been included in the analysis because it resembles a kind of pension in that it can be received without having any disability. In comparison with the corresponding table for Germany one column has been omitted, namely that for average work history. Average work history is less relevant for Denmark, as pension rights are primarily earned through length of stay.

Table 8.7 shows that a considerable share of foreign citizens from the five countries receive old-age pension: 80 percent, to be more exact. This is smaller than the share for Danes, which is almost 100 percent.[18] The smallest share is observed among Iranians, where 41 percent receive old-age pension. Turks are the immigrant group where the largest proportion receive a pension, and they are also the group with the longest average duration of stay. More generally, it seems that duration of stay can explain some of the variation in the shares that receive a pension. One example is the immigrants from Poland, for whom the duration of stay is shorter and the share that receive old-age pensions is consequently also smaller. But it is also obvious that this does not hold for all groups. 80 percent of the citizens from the former Yugoslavia receive old-age pensions, but their average duration of stay is shorter than that of the Poles. In this case it seems that persons from the former Yugoslavia have benefited from the fact that around 73 percent of them hold residence permits as refugees – mainly those who came to Denmark because of the civil war in Yugoslavia. The situation looks more curious for the Iranians. The average duration of stay is low, but around two-thirds arrived in Denmark as refugees, so one would expect the share receiving old-age pension to be greater than 41 percent. One possible explanation for this could be, as suggested by Pedersen (2000) and Nielsen (2002), that some of

---

18 The reason why it is not 100 percent is among other things that some persons aged 67 or more are still active on the labor market and that their income exceeds the income limit in the Danish pension system.

Table 8.7. The population shares receiving old-age and disability pensions and early retirement benefit in Denmark, distributed by different population groups. (Citizenship). 2001. Percent.

	Denmark, 2001					
	Old-age pension, persons aged 67-70 years	Social assistance, persons aged 67-70 years	Early retirement benefit or disability pension or social assistance, persons aged 60-66 years	Average length of stay (years)	Share with residence permits as refugees[2]	Disability pension, persons aged 18-66 years
Former Yugoslavia	80	14	89	9	73	11
Iran	41	29	57	7	66	9
Lebanon	47	36	72	8	45	5
Poland	58	18	75	12	3	4
Turkey	95	1	85	19	1	7
All five countries	80	11	85	13	40	8
All five countries[1]	82	9	82	13	45	8
Danes	97	0	65	-	-	8

Notes: 1) Including naturalized persons. 2) Figures based on RFMS-D. "-" = Not applicable. The number of observations is given in Appendix Table 1.

Sources: Danish Register for Social Statistics, own calculations.

the older Iranians have left Denmark to spend their retirement in the home country without notifying the Danish authorities.

Among those aged from 60 to 66, the table shows the shares that receive early retirement benefit, disability pension, or social assistance, in order to get an indication of how many in this age group have retired. Social assistance has been included in the analysis even though some will be receiving this benefit because of unemployment, but a considerable number of those who receive social assistance in this age group have in reality relatively small chances of being employed again. 85 percent of the immigrants receive one of these three benefits, which is on level with the shares among the 67 to 70 year-olds that receive old-age pension or social assistance. The picture is different for Danes, as 65 percent receive one of the three benefits, compared to almost 100 percent receiving old-age pension (or social assistance) in the 67 to 70 age group.

The share that receives disability pensions in Denmark seems to be on the same level for Danes and immigrants. The highest share is 11 percent and is observed among citizens from the former Yugoslavia.

The share of the immigrant population receiving old-age pensions seems to be smaller in Germany than in Denmark. 62 percent of the five immigrant nationalities receive pensions in Germany, compared to 80 percent among immigrants in

Denmark. The differences can mostly be explained by differences in labor market attachment. As mentioned earlier, the shares receiving pensions among people aged 65 or over are also shown in Table 8.6. If these figures are compared with those for Denmark, there are no major differences between the shares for the two countries. Therefore it is difficult to tell whether either one of the pension systems is easier to access compared to the other. The shares receiving disability pension are higher in Denmark, but the difference is not that great. As can be seen from Table 8.7, the share who receive old-age pensions among the Lebanese is higher in Denmark than in Germany, and this difference cannot be explained by labor market differences. An explanation could be that the Lebanese in Denmark have actually benefited from being refugees, while this not the case in Germany to the same extent. One has though to be careful not to draw firm conclusions, as the number of observations is relatively low, but a possible explanation could then be that it is more difficult to fulfil the German work requirement than the Danish residence requirement.

8.4 Probability of Receiving Benefits

This section presents an analysis of how the probability of receiving social transfers is correlated with various social and economic factors. In the previous paragraphs some factors have been mentioned that are likely to statistically affect the probability of receiving benefits: factors such as labor market attachment, gender, and age. In this analysis a wider range of factors will be included in a logistic regression model to see which factors matter and how much effect they each have. In Section 8.3 it was observed that foreign citizens in both countries generally receive benefits more often than natives. One important explanation mentioned in the same sub-section was of course labor market attachment, which is generally lower for immigrants in both countries, see Chapter 4 of this volume. This analysis will also include foreigner-specific factors such as duration of stay and type of residence permit. It is important to emphasize that this analysis includes only immigrant groups and no natives, and that it will concentrate on what factors characterize recipients of social assistance transfers among immigrant groups.

As this section will show, it is not that straightforward to perform comparable analyses for Germany and Denmark. As described in Sub-section 8.2.2, there are some similarities in the German and Danish social assistance systems, but one main difference remains, namely that German social assistance is allocated on a household basis, while Danish social assistance is allocated on an individual basis. Furthermore, in Denmark social assistance is a substitute for a labor market income, whereas in Germany it can to some extent also be a supplement to a low wage. In spite of these differences, the next two sections will attempt to compare the probability of receiving social assistance benefits in Denmark and Germany by means of analyses on both the household and individual levels.

8.4.1 Germany

Before starting the analysis, we will give an overview of some of the existing literature on Germany. Riphahn (1998) and Riphahn (1999) estimate a logit model on the German Socio-Economic Panel (GSOEP), with some focus on panel attrition. The dependent variable is whether a household receives social assistance or not.[19] A main question is whether the share of immigrants receiving social assistance is explained by household characteristics or by behavioral characteristics, such as take-up. The result found is that immigrant households do not have a higher probability of receiving welfare than German households if all the household characteristics (and panel attrition) are accounted for. As a matter of fact, when household characteristics are taken into account, the foreign households are actually less likely to receive social assistance. Among the household characteristics that explain some of the differences between natives and immigrants, the labor market status of the head of the household is the primary factor. It seems that if the head of the household is outside the labor force, this has a much greater effect on welfare dependence for foreign households than for national households.

Similar results are found by Bird et al. (2001), who estimate a probit model on GSOEP data for 1996. Eligible immigrants are not more likely to claim benefit than similar eligible natives. The more extended use of welfare benefits among immigrants can be explained by differences in patterns of income, household structure, and age between immigrants and natives.

Voges et el. (1998) estimate a logistic regression model, where the dependent variable is whether the household receives social assistance or not. The data source is, as in the previously mentioned studies, the GSOEP; but this time the data are for the year 1995. This study shows that foreign immigrants arriving in the previous 10 years have a higher probability of receiving social assistance compared to nationals, even when exogenous characteristics are taken into account. Foreign immigrants arriving before 1984 have no significantly higher probability of receiving welfare compared to nationals.

Studies like Kayser and Frick (2000) and Riphahn (2001) mainly concentrate on the take-up aspect and have less focus on foreigners. Both studies show that a remarkably large share of all households in Germany actually do not claim benefits, even though they are entitled to. Finally there is Fertig and Schmidt (2001), who estimate a probit model on the German Mikrozensus.[20] Fertig and Schmidt focus especially on differences in the use of social assistance between first- and second-generation immigrants and people with different durations of stay, educations and ages.

---

19 This includes only the income support scheme. The same is true for most of the other studies mentioned, except Fertig and Schmidt (2001), which also includes support in special circumstances.
20 See the appendix chapter for references to a more detailed description of the German Mikrozensus.

Table 8.8 shows four logistic regressions of the probability of receiving social assistance in Germany, with the dependent variable including both income support and support in special circumstances.[21] The analysis is made on our own RFMS-G, so only foreign citizens are included. Second generation foreigners are excluded from the analysis. As the table shows, two regressions are at the household level and two at the individual level. This is to take into account the differences between the German and Danish social assistance systems, see Table 8.5. Most of the German literature on the subject considers the household level; one exception is Fertig and Schmidt (2001), which uses an individual approach. So in the regressions for Germany and Denmark both approaches will be used. Furthermore, two regressions are made for each level, one with variables that indicate labor market attachment and one without. The analysis will show that this factor has a very large impact on the probability of receiving social assistance, and by running a regression without this factor it will be possible to see if it represses the explanatory power of other variables. But the regression including the labor market attachment variables will be the starting point.

The dependent variable is one if the household or respondent received social assistance in the previous month and zero otherwise. The background variables are divided into three groups, namely respondent, head of household and household characteristics. The respondent characteristic is naturally most relevant in the individual regression, but country of origin and language abilities for the respondent have also been included in the household regression as proxies for nationality and language abilities of the head of household.[22] The respondent variables include, in addition to the most common demographic variables, factors such as age, gender, health, employment status (included in regressions 1 and 3 and excluded in regressions 2 and 4) and foreigner-specific variables such as type of residence permit and duration of stay.

The table shows that country of origin has a significant impact on the probability even if all other variables are accounted for. The Lebanese have a significantly higher probability of receiving social assistance than people from the former Yugoslavia, while a lower probability is observed for Turks. Language abilities are also a significant factor; it can be seen that very poor German abilities increase the probability of receiving social assistance, and that the opposite is the case if the person has very good or good language abilities.

---

21 As mentioned before, in the RFMS-G it is not possible to determine whether the respondent has received income support or support in special circumstances. Furthermore, we also note that some of the benefits in the scheme for support in special circumstances might not be included, cf. Section 8.3.2.
22 As the RFMS-G is an individual-based questionnaire there is limited information on the head of household. With a simple set of rules based on the existing household information, it is determined who the head of household is (typically a male). Because of this no information on the education of the head of household is available.

Table 8.8. Logistic regression of the probability of receiving social assistance in Germany. Foreign citizens. 2002.

	Household level		Individual level, persons aged 18-59 years	
	1	2	3	4
	Coeff. (std. err.)	Coeff. (std. err.)	Coeff. (std. err.)	Coeff. (std. err.)
Constant	***-1.710 (0.489)	***-1.442 (0.430)	**-1.728 (0.771)	-0.496 (0.710)
Respondent				
Age/10			-0.268 (0.387)	***-1.187 (0.366)
Age squared/100			0.034 (0.051)	**0.156 (0.048)
Female (0/1)			***-0.592 (0.129)	-0.023 (0.110)
Former Yugoslavia	Reference	Reference	Reference	Reference
Iran	**0.347 (0.139)	0.188 (0.126)	*-0.282 (0.173)	*-0.278 (0.161)
Lebanon	***0.915 (0.134)	***0.931 (0.120)	**0.316 (0.161)	**0.365 (0.151)
Poland	***-0.661 (0.158)	***-0.949 (0.146)	-0.145 (0.213)	*-0.358 (0.200)
Turkey	***-0.804 (0.139)	***-0.918 (0.130)	***-0.759 (0.200)	***-0.780 (0.192)
Very good German	***-0.569 (0.128)	***-0.713 (0.117)	*-0.335 (0.177)	***-0.535 (0.165)
Good German	***-0.474 (0.125)	***-0.553 (0.114)	-0.172 (0.147)	***-0.358 (0.138)
Average German	Reference	Reference	Reference	Reference
Poor German	***0.413 (0.129)	***0.548 (0.119)	**0.296 (0.147)	***0.500 (0.138)
Very poor German	***0.940 (0.157)	***1.059 (0.140)	***0.806 (0.177)	***0.993 (0.166)
Duration of stay/10			**-0.218 (0.095)	***-0.318 (0.092)
Bad health (0/1)			**0.415 (0.175)	***0.859 (0.168)
German education (0/1)			-0.171 (0.229)	**-0.490 (0.219)
Refugee (0/1)			***1.041 (0.125)	***1.073 (0.119)
Employed			***-2.088 (0.173)	
Out of labor force			***0.429 (0.142)	
Unemployed			Reference	
Employed in home country			*0.255 (0.132)	0.175 (0.125)
Student in home country			0.330 (0.242)	0.286 (0.233)

Other activity in home country		Reference	Reference
Family at arrival (0/1)		-0.066 (0.110)	-0.107 (0.103)
Islam (0/1)		***0.467 (0.140)	***0.459 (0.133)
Head of household			
Female (0/1)	***0.905 (0.122)		
Age/10	**-0.400 (0.183)		
Age squared/100	**0.047 (0.019)		
Employed	***-2.257 (0.115)		
Out of labor force	**0.235 (0.116)		
Unemployed	Reference		
Household			
No. children <16 yrs	***0.266 (0.037)	***0.244 (0.033)	***0.202 (0.039)
No. persons > 16 yrs	***0.180 (0.052)	***0.216 (0.048)	*0.084 (0.060)
Owns home	***-1.954 (0.394)	***-2.338 (0.391)	***-1.882 (0.517)
Single person	-0.099 (0.156)	0.165 (0.148)	**0.364 (0.176)
Single parent	***1.172 (0.255)	***1.044 (0.225)	***2.280 (0.226)
Other type of family	Reference	Reference	Reference
Log Likelihood	-1749.9	-2090.3	-1289.9	-1460.6
No. of observations	5,614	5,614	4,542[1]	4,542[1]

Notes: *** = significant at 1 percent level, ** = significant at 5 percent level, * = significant at 10 percent level. [1] The difference between the numbers of observations is due to the age constraint in regressions 3 and 4.

Sources: RFMS-G, own calculations.

Although a labor market variable is included in the analysis, this effect can most probably be explained from a labor market perspective; good language abilities increase the opportunities on the labor market and the possibility of supporting oneself. One could also have made a take-up interpretation of the language variable: better German language skills will make it easier to approach the authorities and to understand the social assistance system. However, this interpretation seems less likely to be relevant. This is confirmed in the regressions where the labor market attachment variables are excluded. The coefficients of the language variables become both numerically larger and more significant. Regression 3 also seems to indicate that when labor market attachment is included, what matters is to be at least average in the German language – better language abilities will not reduce the use of social assistance.

If a person is resident in Germany as a refugee, the likelihood of receiving social assistance is much greater. The reason for this could be that refugees might have mental or physical problems because of persecution or civil war in the home country, but it could also be that they do not bring the same amount of human capital as other types of immigrants.

The most important factor seems to be labor market attachment. Not surprisingly, being employed reduces the likelihood of the respondent receiving welfare benefits considerably compared to the case where the respondent is out of the labor force. This is not only true for the individual regression; a household has a much smaller probability of receiving social assistance if the head of the household is employed. Employment of course gives the respondent or head of household a much better possibility of supporting himself/herself or the household.

There are some differences between the household regressions and the individual regressions concerning the basic demographic variables like age and gender. At the household level, it seems that the age of the head of the household is less important, while if the head of the household is a woman this increases the probability of receiving social assistance. This can be explained by considering the household characteristics. Here it can be seen that it is much more likely that a single provider receives social assistance compared to other household types. The gender variable could include some unexplained variance from this variable, as the majority of single providers are women. Regression 3 shows that women have a significantly lower probability of receiving social assistance. Excluding the labor market variable in regression 4 shows that gender is then without importance. In other words, this means that when labor market attachment is taken into account, women are less likely to receive social assistance, probably because they are typically supported by their husbands. Among the other household characteristics, it is noticeable that home ownership has a large negative impact on the probability of receiving social assistance, probably because there is a wealth constraint in the eligibility rules (see Sub-section 8.2.2).

The individual regression shows that as expected, bad health increases the risk of being on welfare. Sickness will make it harder for a person to perform well on the labor market and therefore increases the probability of receiving social assistance. Also, as expected, a longer period of residence makes social assistance less likely, because a longer period of residence means that an immigrant has better opportunities on the labor market, as shown in Chapter 5. There might also be a cohort effect from this variable, because the type of immigration varies with the time of arrival, i.e. in the seventies Germany mainly experienced labor immigration, while in the nineties most immigration was related to giving asylum to refugees and family reunification.

8.4.2 Denmark

The Danish literature on this particular subject is rather limited. One reason could be that it is very difficult – if not impossible – to include the take-up aspect in an analysis of the Danish social assistance system. Unlike the German, the Danish system does not have an income limit under which one is entitled to benefits, but eligibility is instead determined by a 'social event', see Sub-section 8.2.2. It is obvious that such an event is hard to identify in ordinary survey data. Some studies on the probability of receiving social assistance in Denmark do exist, though. Pedersen (2000) shows that the probability of receiving social assistance increases with age (until the age of 35) and also with poor knowledge of Danish. Nielsen (2002) estimates a similar model on data from 2000. Some of the main results are that immigrants from Lebanon and Somalia have a significantly higher probability of receiving social assistance than immigrants from Turkey, even though a number of background variables are accounted for. As in Pedersen, the analysis shows that poor Danish language skills mean an increased risk of being dependent on social assistance. The same is the case if one has a bad health.

Table 8.9 shows the four regressions of the probability of receiving social assistance in Denmark. The sample is based on our RFMS-D survey and, unlike the German sample, it includes naturalized foreigners, but second generation immigrants are excluded. The regressions correspond, with some exceptions, to the regressions for Germany in Table 8.8. Most importantly, there are some differences for the variable indicating labor market attachment. We have not included a variable indicating whether the respondent or head of household is employed, because it is very unlikely that an employed person can receive social assistance in Denmark. Therefore a dummy variable indicating whether the respondent or head of household is in or out of the labor force is included instead. The dependent variable is also a little different. In this case it is one if the household or respondent received social assistance in the period March-July 2001, and zero otherwise. The latter difference is due to data differences.

Table 8.9. Logistic regressions of the probability of receiving social assistance in Denmark. Foreign citizens and naturalized immigrants. 2001.

	Household level		Individual level, persons aged 18-59 years	
	1	2	3	4
	Coeff. (std. err.)	Coeff. (std. err.)	Coeff. (std. err.)	Coeff. (Std. Err.)
Constant	***-3.743 (0.765)	***-2.217 (0.720)	***-2.996 (1.124)	***-1.868 (1.062)
Respondent				
Female (0/1)	**0.423 (0.177)	***0.446 (2.277)	0.099 (0.159)	***0.424 (0.148)
Age/10	***1.078 (0.191)	***1.313 (0.180)	0.680 (0.561)	0.208 (0.533)
Age squared/100	**-0.576 (0.235)	***-0.765 (0.227)	-0.099 (0.074)	-0.020 (0.071)
Former Yugoslavia	Reference	Reference	Reference	Reference
Iran	*-0.348 (0.182)	***-0.493 (0.175)	0.107 (0.245)	0.366 (0.232)
Lebanon	**-0.385 (0.176)	**-0.370 (0.168)	*0.500 (0.263)	***1.029 (0.249)
Poland	-0.059 (0.158)	-0.131 (0.150)	*-0.594 (0.345)	-0.485 (0.334)
Turkey	Reference	Reference	*-0.584 (0.337)	-0.308 (0.321)
Very good Danish	0.251 (0.202)	**0.399 (0.192)	***-0.742 (0.282)	***-0.758 (0.269)
Good Danish	0.429 (0.272)	**0.659 (0.263)	-0.202 (0.185)	-0.196 (0.174)
Average Danish			Reference	Reference
Poor Danish			0.141 (0.226)	0.262 (0.215)
Very poor Danish			0.183 (0.331)	0.242 (0.312)
Duration of stay/10			-0.152 (0.162)	**-0.322 (0.158)
Bad health (0/1)			**0.438 (0.212)	***0.870 (0.204)
Danish education (0/1)			**-0.616 (0.249)	***-0.694 (0.234)
Refugee (0/1)			0.214 (0.192)	0.227 (0.182)
Out of lab. force (0/1)			***1.517 (0.164)	
Employed in home country			*-0.763 (0.452)	*-0.786 (0.430)
Student in home country			-0.023 (0.186)	0.041 (0.176)
Other activity in home country			Reference	Reference
Metropolitan area	-0.198 (0.167)	**-0.341 (0.159)	-0.056 (0.211)	-0.095 (0.199)
Jutland	0.148 (0.169)	0.128 (0.168)	0.108 (0.208)	0.129 (0.196)

	(1)	(2)	(3)	(4)
Rest of the islands	Reference	Reference	Reference	Reference
Family at arrival (0/1)			0.203 (0.168)	0.104 (0.160)
Religion (0/1)			0.171 (0.220)	0.244 (0.209)
Head of household				
Female (0/1)	-0.275 (0.183)	-0.011 (0.173)		
Age/10	***0.998 (0.354)	0.413 (0.338)		
Age squared/100	***-0.124 (0.040)	-0.043 (0.038)		
Out of lab. force (0/1)	***1.460 (0.129)			
Household				
No. children <16 yrs	***0.204 (0.059)	***0.199 (0.056)	0.084 (0.071)	*0.118 (0.066)
No. persons >16 yrs	0.076 (0.084)	*0.132 (0.080)	-0.095 (0.113)	-0.111 (0.109)
Owns home (0/1)	***-1.266 (0.214)	***-1.533 (0.206)	***-1.268 (0.303)	***-1.519 (0.296)
Single person	***-0.678 (0.245)	***-0.640 (0.237)	-0.464 (0.303)	-0.360 (0.289)
Single parent	-0.096 (0.307)	0.045 (0.293)	0.348 (0.339)	0.385 (0.323)
Other family type	Reference	Reference	Reference	Reference
Log Likelihood	-918.6	-991.1	-630.3	-696.9
No. of observations	2,167[1]	2,173[1]	1,795[1]	1,823

Notes: *** = significant at 1 percent level, ** = significant at 5 percent level, * = significant at 10 percent level. [1] The differences between the numbers of observation are due to the age constraint in regressions 3 and 4 and to missing values.

Sources: RFMS-D, own calculations.

The regressions in Table 8.9 show that the labor market variable has a large impact on the likelihood of receiving social assistance, with the largest effect at the individual level. The regressions generally show that compared to the German regression there are fewer significant variables, and those which are significant, are more seldom significant at the one percent level, because there are much fewer observations available.

In all regressions, except for regression 4, there are no significant differences between men and women, while age has some impact at the household level. At the household level, the probability of receiving social assistance increases with age, but only until around the age of 37. After that the probability decreases, probably because of the increased likelihood of receiving a disability pension instead (Nielsen, 2002).

Table 8.9 shows that even when all important background variables are accounted for, country of origin still has a significant effect. The former Yugoslavia is again taken as the baseline for comparison. Turks and Poles have a somewhat lower probability of receiving social assistance than persons from the former Yugoslavia, mainly because their labor market attachment is better, and when unemployed they receive unemployment benefit instead of social assistance, see Tables 8.3 and 8.4. On the other hand it is clear that people from Lebanon have a greater probability of receiving social assistance.

All the regressions in the table show that very good language skills reduce the risk of being dependent on social assistance. Having some language skills does not change the likelihood of receiving social assistance. It seems to be the situation that either you are perfect in Danish or your language skills are of no use. Poor Danish skills are estimated with a positive coefficient, but are not significant. Concerning household characteristics, it seems very clear that households owning their home have a much lower likelihood of receiving social assistance, most likely because home owners, all other things being equal, have relatively higher incomes. But it should be noted that owning a house can also strengthen participation incentives, as average taxation is lowered because mortgage interest is deductible. It was noted above that labor market attachment is quite important. It is also of some importance what activities one has been doing in one's home country before arriving. Having been employed in the home country decreases the risk of being dependent on social assistance by some margin.

The individual regression shows that bad health increases the probability of receiving social assistance. The interpretation is most likely the same as for Germany: bad health decreases the opportunities on the labor market and consequently the chances of being able to support oneself. Having children under 16 slightly increases the probability of receiving social assistance, mainly because children constitute an increased need for support.

8.4.3 Comparison of Germany and Denmark

As Tables 8.8 and 8.9 have shown, there are as expected many differences, but also some similarities in what characterizes the receipt of social assistance among the same immigrant groups in German and Denmark. This paragraph will concentrate on the main differences and similarities.

To begin with the similarities, it goes for both countries that country of origin has a significant influence on the probability of receiving social assistance, even when all other background variables are accounted for. People from Lebanon have a higher likelihood of receiving social assistance. The analyses also show that language abilities seem to be very important in both countries, in the sense that good language abilities reduce the probability of receiving social assistance.

Whether or not the household owns their home has a large impact in both countries. Owners have a much smaller probability of receiving social assistance, most likely because home owners have a high income and consequently less need for social assistance, but there could also be indirect incentive effects from owning a house.

Finally, labor market attachment has a major effect as expected. In both countries we have seen that if one is unemployed or outside the labor force this has a large impact on the likelihood of receiving social assistance.

As for differences, we have observed that gender is of some importance in Germany, but not in Denmark. This result seems to confirm what was indicated in Subsection 8.3.2, namely that there are some behavioral differences between immigrant women in Germany and in Denmark. Immigrant women in Germany often report themselves as being housewives and are thus supported by their spouses. They are therefore less likely to receive social assistance than immigrant men. In Denmark, immigrant women very seldom report themselves as housewives, but instead as unemployed or social assistance recipients. In Denmark, the behavior in this respect is not that different from that of immigrant men.

It has been noted that duration of stay has some effect in Germany, while surprisingly no effect is registered for Denmark. It is clear that, at least for Denmark, this variable interacts with labor market attachment. When the labor market dummy variable is excluded, there is a significant negative coefficient of duration for Denmark, although it is numerically smaller than for Germany.

An interesting difference exists for the variable that indicates whether a person holds a residence permit as a refugee or not. In Germany, it greatly increases the likelihood of receiving social assistance if a person is a refugee, while it has no importance in Denmark. The reason is probably that refugees in Denmark generally have easier access to the labor market compared to refugees in Germany who, according to analyses in Chapter 5, have significantly lower employment chances than non-refugee immigrants. Another explanation could be that this variable includes some unexplained variance from the human capital variables (education, employment in home country), and that there is a larger difference between refugees and other types of immigrants in Germany than in Denmark as regards human capital.

Another interesting difference seems to be the effects from language skills. In Denmark it seems that one has to have perfect skills in the language of the country to reduce the probability of receiving social assistance; not even good language skills are enough. In Germany the relationship is monotonic and both average and good language skills are sufficient to reduce the risk of being dependent on social assistance.

8.5 Summary and Conclusions

This chapter has described the access to the social security systems in Germany and Denmark as well as the use of benefits among immigrants and nationals in the two countries, and it has investigated what factors influence the likelihood of receiving benefits.

In Section 8.2 *formal rules of access* to the social security systems in Germany and Denmark were described, including the rules for unemployment insurance, social assistance, old-age pension, disability pension, housing benefits and child benefit, with a special focus on access rules for foreigners and refugees. For both Germany and Denmark it can generally be said that eligibility rules for foreigners are the same as for nationals, though there are some exceptions. For pensioners in particular there are special rules for foreigners, in that the principles for earning pension rights are different. Refugees are generally better off than other foreigners in this area with regard to the formal rules for eligibility.

The German benefits are typically related to work and income, and the replacement rate is constant over a relatively wide income span – an insurance-like approach. The Danish benefits are primarily residence based, and the benefits are more flat rate. This means that the benefit profile in Denmark favors low-income groups more than that in Germany. Hansen et al. (2002) describe the Danish social security system as "schemes of solidarity".

Section 8.3 describes the *actual use* of unemployment insurance, social assistance, old-age pension and disability pension among immigrants and natives in Germany and Denmark. For unemployment insurance the comparison between Germany and Denmark shows that the share that receives unemployment insurance benefits is higher for immigrant men in Germany than in Denmark, while the opposite is the case for immigrant women. In Germany, 15 percent of the immigrant men and 7 percent of the immigrant women receive unemployment insurance benefits, while the corresponding figures for Denmark are 11 and 9 percent respectively.

For immigrant men the difference can be explained by differences in the access conditions to unemployment insurance, which is voluntary in Denmark. This has the effect that many low-wage workers are better off by not being insured and receiving social assistance instead. When unemployment insurance and social assistance are combined, one can see that the differences for immigrants narrow between Germany and Denmark (for immigrant men). The story is somewhat different for immigrant women, as the immigrant women living in Denmark receive social assistance to a greater extent than their German counterparts. 20 percent of the immigrant women in Denmark receive social assistance, 15 percent of the male immigrants. The figures for Germany are 9 and 10 percent. Some immigrant groups have relatively high shares receiving social assistance; 45 percent of the Lebanese households in Germany receive social assistance, while the figure for Denmark is 56 percent.

The differences for women seem to be explained by behavioral differences. The share of immigrant women that report themselves as housewives in Germany is much larger than the corresponding share in Denmark, indicating that many immigrant women in Germany are supported by their spouses, but also that many immigrant women in Denmark receive social assistance, even though they may in reality not be available to the labor market. Calculations based on ILO definitions seem to confirm this. Immigrant social assistance recipients in Germany are available for the labor market to a greater degree than immigrant social assistance recipients in Denmark. All in all it seems clear that the interaction between unemployment insurance and social assistance is different in the two countries. In Denmark, immigrants more often receive social assistance compared to immigrants in Germany.

The comparison of old-age pension and disability pension shows that the shares of immigrants that receive a pension in Denmark are in general terms on the same level as in Germany. It is the case that 61 percent receive old-age pension in Germany, while the percentage in Denmark is as high as 81, but the difference can be explained by the greater labor market attachment of German immigrants in that age group. If for Germany we only consider persons aged 65 or more, the share is on level with that in Denmark. It seems that Lebanese refugees in Denmark actually benefit from the positive treatment with respect to formal access requirements, while this is not the case to the same extent in Germany. A possible explanation could be that it is more difficult to fulfil the German work requirement than the Danish residence requirement.

The last section contains an analysis using a logistic regression model of what characterizes the receipt of social assistance. The regressions are made at both the individual and household levels. Among other things, the analysis seems to confirm what was indicated above, namely that there are some behavioral differences between immigrant women in Germany and in Denmark. The German analysis shows that when labor market attachment is accounted for, women actually have a lower probability of receiving social assistance, while in Denmark, gender is without importance.

The factors that have most influence in both countries are factors like labor market attachment, language skills and home ownership. Good labor market performance and home ownership reduce the probability of receiving social assistance substantially. In both countries, it can also be seen that good language skills reduce the risk of being dependent on social assistance, although the impact profile seems somewhat different. To reduce the probability of receiving social assistance in Denmark requires perfect language skills, while in Germany average and good skills in the language of the host country can reduce the risk of being dependent on social assistance.

Finally it was observed that being a refugee in Germany increases the probability of receiving social assistance compared to other foreigners, while this is not the case in Denmark. An explanation could be the institutional differences that exist; it is easier for refugees in Denmark to access the labor market than refugees residing in Germany. Some of the difference could perhaps also be explained by human capital differences between refugees in Germany and refugees in Denmark.

References

Bauer, Thomas. 2002. "Migration, Sozialstaat und Zuwanderungspolitik," *DIW-Vierteljahrshefte zur Wirtschaftsforschung – Quarterly Journal of Economic Research*, 71 (2), 249-271.

Bird, Edward J., Hilke Kayser, Joachim R. Frick and Gert G. Wagner. 2001. "The immigrant welfare effect. Take-up or eligibility?" *International Migration Review* 35, 726-748.

Bonin, Holger. 2002. "Will it last? An Assessment of the 2001 German Pension Reform," *The Geneva Papers on Risk and Insurance* 24 (4), 547-564.

BGSS (Bundesministerium für Gesundheit und Soziale Sicherung). 2002. *Social Security at a Glance*. Bonn.

BGSS (Bundesministerium für Gesundheit und Soziale Sicherung). 2002a. *Soziale Sicherung im Überblick*. Bonn.

Fertig, Michael and Christoph M. Schmidt. 2001. "First and Second-generation Migrants in Germany: What Do We Know and What Do People Think?" in Ralph Rotte and Peter Stein (eds): *Migration Policy and the Economy: International Perspectives*. Munich.

Forsikringsoplysningen. 2002. *Sociale ydelser 2002*. Copenhagen.

Hansen, Hans, Helle Cwarzko Jensen, Claus Larsen and Niels-Kenneth Nielsen. 2002. "Social Security Benefits in Denmark and Germany – with a Focus on Access Conditions for Refugees and Immigrants. A Comparative Study." Study No. 9. Copenhagen: The Rockwool Foundation Research Unit.

Hansen, Hans. 2002. *Elements of Social Security*. Copenhagen: The Danish National Institute of Social Research.

Haustein, Thomas. 2002. "Ergebnisse der Sozial- und Asylbewerberleistungsstatistik 2000." *Wirtschaft und Statistik*, Nr. 2. Wiesbaden: Statistisches Bundesamt.

Kayser, Hilke and Joachim R. Frick. 2000. "Take It or Leave It: (Non-) Take-up Behaviour of Social Assistance in Germany," *DIW Discussion Paper* No. 210. Berlin: DIW.

Lampert, Heinz. 1998. *Lehrbuch der Sozialpolitik*. Berlin: Springer.

Nielsen, Niels-Kenneth. 2002. "Overførselsindkomster til indvandrere," in Gunnar Viby Mogensen & Poul Chr. Matthiessen (eds): *Indvandrerne og arbejdsmarkedet. Mødet med det danske velfærdssamfund*. Copenhagen: Spektrum, 198-258.

Parsons, Donald O., Torben Tranæs and Helene Bie Lilleør. 2001. *Voluntary Public Unemployment Insurance*. Copenhagen: EPRU.

Pedersen, Søren. 2000. "Overførselsindkomster til indvandrere," in Gunnar Viby Mogensen and Poul Chr. Matthiessen (eds): *Integration i Danmark omkring årtusindskiftet. Indvandrernes møde med arbejdsmarkedet og velfærdssamfundet*. Aarhus: Aarhus University Press, 160-207.

Poulsen, Marius Ejby and Anita Lange. 1998. *Indvandrere i Danmark*. Copenhagen: Statistics Denmark.

Riphahn, Regina. 1998. "Immigrant Participation in Social Assistance Programs," *IZA Discussion Paper* No. 15. Bonn.

Riphahn, Regina. 1999. "Immigrant Participation in Social Assistance Programs: Evidence from German Guest workers," *CEPR Discussion Paper* No. 2318. London.

Riphahn, Regina. 2001. "Rational Poverty or Poor Rationality? The Take-up of Social Assistance Benefits," *Review of Income and Wealth* 47 (3), 379-398.

Statistics Denmark. 2002. *Statistisk Tiårsoversigt*. Copenhagen.

Statistisches Bundesamt. 2001. "Ausländische Bevölkerung in Deutschland", *Im Blickpunkt*. Wiesbaden.

Statistisches Bundesamt. 2002. *Statistisches Jahrbuch 2002*. Wiesbaden.

Think Tank on Integration in Denmark, The. 2001. *Udlændinges integration i det danske samfund*. Copenhagen.

Voges, Wolfgang, Joachim Frick and Felix Blüchel. 1998. "The Integration of Immigrants Into West German Society: The Impact of Social Assistance," in Hermann Kurthen, Jürgen Fijalkowski and Gert G. Wagner: *Immigration, Citizenship and the Welfare State in Germany and the United States*. London: JAI Press.

Appendix Table 1. Number of observations behind the figures in Tables 8.3-8.7.

	Germany						Denmark			
	Persons aged 18-64 years		Persons aged 18-59 years		Persons aged 60- years	Persons aged 65- years	Persons aged 18-66 years		Persons aged 67-70 years	Persons aged 60-66 years
	Men	*Women*	*Men*	*Women*	*All*	*All*	*Men*	*Women*	*All*	*All*
Former Yugoslavia	525	433	475	406	113	36	11,679	11,036	639	1,547
Iran	530	419	493	407	97	47	1,837	1,637	128	169
Lebanon	502	419	495	413	23	10	581	988	37	52
Poland	408	745	394	725	90	55	1,123	3,273	40	119
Turkey	697	672	647	639	153	69	10,981	10,507	470	876
All five countries	2,662	2,688	2,504	2,590	476	217	26,201	27,441	1,314	2,763
All five countries[1]	*	*	*	*	*	*	44,561	41,669	1,634	3,686
Germans	7,636	8,071	6,770	7,145	5,395	*	-	-	-	-
Danes	-	-	-	-	-	-	32,174	31,311	3,152	6,905

Notes: See Table 8.3.

Sources: See Table 8.3.

CHAPTER 9

Immigration and Crime in Germany and Denmark*

By Horst Entorf and Claus Larsen

9.1 Introduction

Immigrants and crime are often linked in the public debate, and the topic is of a controversial nature, but crime is also an aspect of living conditions in the same way as education, work, and social and economic conditions, all of which are dealt with in other chapters of this book. Criminal behavior is linked in important ways to the main topic of this book, the employment situation of immigrants. A person may commit a crime because he cannot get a job or an education, but the reverse can also be true, namely that it is difficult to get a job if you have committed a crime. Job applicants are required to have specific job qualifications, but having no criminal record is just as important. The aim of the following sections is to evaluate the level and pattern of crime among foreigners living in Denmark and Germany in comparison with that of native Danes and Germans.

Criminologists agree upon a certain number of factors that are correlated with crime. In general, criminals are relatively young, most of them are male, they are less educated, they more probably grew up in disrupted families, and they often face problems resulting from a lack of integration into society. The simultaneous existence of multiple risk factors seems to influence the criminal behavior of immigrants and descendants, at least when they come from non-Western countries. The disadvantaged backgrounds of immigrants – and the fact that foreign-looking people are more often subject to police checks than others – need to be kept in mind when we look at the relatively high crime rates among foreigners in Germany and in Denmark. However, since immigrants of working age are seen by many as one of the solutions to the problems caused by aging Western nations, ignoring the problem of immigration and crime, for example, because of its controversial and difficult nature is counter-productive and could lead to xenophobic myths and sentiments as well as to costly social exclusion.

---

* We wish to thank Phil Savage, Institut für Volkswirtschaft, Technische Universität Darmstadt, for helpful assistance and proof-reading.

Our results confirm the importance of taking differences in age and sex distribution into account, but even when controlling for such differences as well as for education, citizens with a foreign background are still over-represented in crime statistics. These results challenge future research to focus on issues of integration and social networks.

Section 9.2 of this chapter presents existing descriptive evidence about "crime and national origins" in the case of Germany, while descriptive evidence for Denmark is presented in Section 9.3. The presentations are made to be as comparable as possible, but differences in concepts and definitions still exist and have to be taken into consideration. Similarities and differences between the two countries are summarized in Section 9.4, while Section 9.5 deals with the question of crime prevention based on the existing literature on causes of immigrant crime, with a special emphasis on the importance of education. Section 9.6 sums up and concludes, and points to the need for further research.

9.2 Immigration and Crime in Germany: Descriptive Evidence

Providing hard statistical facts about crime and immigration is a challenging task. Preliminary (and misleading) figures give the impression that offense rates among immigrants are about three times as high as those for German citizens: population statistics reveal that by the end of the year 2000 (31 Dec., 2000) the share of non-German citizens in the population was 8.8 percent (Statistisches Bundesamt, 2002a), whereas the ratio of non-German crime suspects among all crime suspects arrested by the police was 24.9 percent (see Table 9.1). However, it is difficult to attribute crimes to immigrants, as non-German crime suspects might be tourists or illegal migrants without (legal) residence in Germany. The proportion of crimes committed by immigrants can thus only be estimated (see Table 9.4). Official statistics (PKS, 2001) published by the German Federal Police Office ("Bundeskriminalamt") avoid this delicate task by only differentiating between "German" and "non-German" crime suspects. In the present chapter on crime and immigration in Germany, crime by "immigrants" refers to immigrants with legal residency status but without a German passport, a definition that includes asylum seekers, and which corresponds to the definition of the "Foreign Population" in official population statistics of the German Statistical Office ("Statistisches Bundesamt"). Ethnic Germans from abroad (so-called "Aussiedler" from historic German settlement areas, mainly from Russia, Ukraine, Romania, and Poland), that is, "immigrants with a German passport", as they are called according to PRC (2001: 26) are not considered here, because this German experience does not have counterparts in other international statistics, although these persons seem to face similar problems of illegal behavior and integration as do immigrants without a German passport (see PRC, 2001: 26 and PSB, 2001: Chapter 2.11.2 for details).

"Crimes" are defined as (illegal) activities of people who are deemed to be "criminals" by society because of their deviant activities. A definition of this kind seems to be superfluous, but it hints at the fact that legal norms differ between societies and that migration leads to problems when a clash of cultures creates a problem of integration of immigrants.

Most statistics used in this chapter are based on official statistics, so-called "reported" or "documented" crime, published by the German Federal Office, in particular PKS (2001). Thus, what becomes defined as crime depends on the reporting behavior of the population and on the administrative efforts and capacities of the police. "More crimes", therefore, might simply reflect a more effective and complete administration of criminal "cases". It should be noted that immigrants are more often subject to police control activities, so that the probability of getting away with a crime might be lower for immigrants than for natives.[1] Moreover, since we are interested in the residency status of criminals, we are restricted to the use of "solved" criminal cases, where "solved" means that a crime suspect has been arrested (which does not necessarily imply that a later conviction or punishment ensues; see PKS (2001: 12) for the official definition of clear-up rates used in German crime statistics). As usual in criminological research, road traffic offenses are excluded from the analysis.

Table 9.1 shows the trends in crime and crime suspects in Germany. Crime rates were in a state of permanent increase until 1993, when the maximum was reached at the level of 8,337 cases per 100,000 inhabitants (8.3 percent). Since then the burden of crime has remained at almost the same level (it was 7.7 percent in 2001), which is much higher than it was in the 1960s and 1970s (it was 3.0 percent in 1965). The number of (potentially) identified criminals (crime suspects) is not perfectly parallel to the number of cases, which shows that the clear-up rate was higher in the late 1990s and in the most recent years than before. The clear-up rate was 53.1 percent in 2001 compared to 43.8 percent in 1993 (PKS, 2001: 65). The proportion of non-German suspects among all suspects known to the police increased after the 1980s, and reached its maximum in 1993 when the share amounted to 33.6 percent. Since then we observe a steady downward movement to 24.9 percent in 2001.

The very high number in 1993 and adjacent years is affected by the high inflow of asylum seekers, which was highest in 1992/1993 (1992: 1.5 million, 1993: 1.3 million; PSB (2001: 307)). According to PKS (2001: 119), 33.2 percent of all non-German crime suspects belonged to the group of asylum seekers in the year 1993, but a substantial share of the criminal cases involving asylum seekers had simply to do with their unclear residency status as "non-Germans". The same is the case with respect to illegal migrants who are detected by the police; their breaches of the residency laws are also included in the crime statistics. Therefore, Table 9.1 includes a column

---

1 On the other hand, the higher control density among immigrants might be a rational strategy since the share of undetected crimes is possibly higher among immigrants than among natives.

Table 9.1. Crime and crime suspects in Germany, 1984-2001[1].

Year	Crime rate[2] (percent)	Total number of crime suspects	Proportion of non-German crime suspects (percent)	Adjusted[3] proportion of non-German crime suspects (percent)
1984	6.7	1,254,213	16.6	13.7
1989	7.0	1,370,962	24.5	19.8
1993	8.3	2,051,775	33.6	26.7
1995	8.2	2,118,104	28.5	21.9
1997	8.0	2,273,560	27.9	21.7
1999	7.7	2,263,140	26.6	20.4
2000	7.6	2,286,372	25.8	20.0
2001	7.7	2,280,611	24.9	19.3

Notes: 1) 1984-1989: West Germany, 1993-2001: Germany; 2) Number of reported cases/100 inhabitants; 3) Non-German crime suspects excluding those suspected of violations of the Asylum Procedure Act ("Asylverfahrensgesetz") and violations of the Aliens Act ("Ausländergesetz").

Sources: Crime rates: PKS (2001: 26); Crime suspects: PKS (2001: 107).

showing an adjusted share of non-German crime suspects which is corrected for violations of the German Asylum Procedure Act ("Asylverfahrensgesetz") and of the Aliens Act ("Ausländergesetz"). Ever since 1995 the corrected share has been quite stable at about one fifth of all crime suspects.

Table 9.2 takes a closer look at non-Germans in the German crime statistics. Compared to 1984, the importance of illegal immigrants (21.6 percent in 2001) and asylum seekers (14.4 percent in 2001) has increased, though the contribution of asylum seekers to the overall non-German crime figures has decreased substantially following restrictions in the German asylum law and after the Schengen Agreement of 1995. A large and growing group is characterized as "others" in official statistics. It consists mainly of unemployed immigrants, asylum seekers who have not been granted asylum and who are still awaiting a decision, and refugees.

Criminal behavior is mainly observed for younger people (men), whose crime-prone age is between 18 and 21 years. The distribution of German crime suspects by age groups is shown in Table 9.3. Moreover, the table gives information about the proportions of non-German crime suspects among all suspects of the age groups considered. Since 1993 these proportions have been falling across more or less all age groups, but non-Germans are highly over-represented in the age groups 18-21 and 21-25, particularly during the years 1993-1997, that is, during the period of high influx of asylum seekers.

Table 9.2. "Non-Germans" in German crime statistics, 1984-2001.

	1984	1998	2001
Number of non-German crime suspects (100 percent)	207,610	628,477	568,384
Illegal immigrants (percent)	13.6	22.4	21.6
Persons staying legally (percent)	86.4	77.6	78.4
Thereof (percent):			
- Asylum seekers	7.7	17.8	14.3
- Employees	32.6	16.1	17.5
- Tourists	6.7	6.9	7.0
- Students, school pupils	14.7	7.6	7.6
- Self-employed, employers	3.6	2.7	2.8
- Armed forces and relatives	4.5	0.5	0.6
- Others[1]	16.6	25.9	28.6

Note: 1) "Others" refers to a heterogeneous group consisting mainly of unemployed people, asylum seekers who have not been granted asylum and who are still awaiting an official notice, and refugees.

Source: PKS (2001: 118).

Table 9.3. Age-crime profile of all crime suspects/ percentage shares of non-German crime suspects in various age groups, 1984-2001.

	Age group (… to under … years of age; percent)				
	8-14	14-18	18-21	21-25	≥ 21
1984	5.3/ 22.4	12.5/ 14.9	11.9/ 15.7	12.9/ 18.5	70.3/ 16.6
1989	4.1/ 30.9	9.1/ 27.9	10.3/ 26.5	13.8/ 28.4	76.5/ 23.5
1993	4.3/ 24.7	10.1/ 27.6	10.1/ 42.1	14.5/ 47.7	75.4/ 33.8
1995	5.5/ 19.2	12.0/ 21.7	9.8/ 33.5	12.1/ 41.7	72.7/ 29.6
1997	6.3/ 18.7	12.9/ 21.2	10.0/ 29.7	11.1/ 42.2	70.8/ 29.6
1999	6.7/ 18.1	13.1/ 19.8	10.6/ 27.6	11.1/ 38.5	70.2/ 28.5
2000	6.4/ 18.2	12.9/ 18.8	10.8/ 25.5	11.2/ 36.0	69.9/ 27.8
2001	6.3/ 17.3	13.1/ 17.8	10.8/ 23.7	11.3/ 33.4	69.8/ 27.1

Notes: Distribution of crime suspects by age groups/ share of non-German suspects out of all crime suspects in each age group.

Sources: PKS (2001), Tables 34, 36, 38, 40, 42.

It seems to be obvious that the reason behind the high proportion of non-German offenders presented in Table 9.1 is the relatively high ratio of immigrants to Germans among the young cohorts. It is higher than the comparable proportions in other (older) age groups. The proof of this is presented in Table 9.4, which shows the proportions of the total number of crime suspects among the number of inhabitants by age groups. These figures are arrived at by combining information from German police statistics and resident population statistics. Starting with the native population first, we see that the proportion of German crime suspects among the overall age group of 8 years and older is 2.5 percent. A naive and preliminary estimate for the comparable proportion among immigrants would amount to 8.7 percent. However, since the intention of this work is to compare the number of arrests of Germans and legal immigrants, we have to subtract illegal immigrants,[2] transients, tourists and asylum seekers accused of violating the German Asylum Procedure Act or the Aliens Act from the number of non-German crime suspects. The adjusted ratio is then reduced to 5.9 percent, which is 2.4 times the German rate. Compared to the figure for the total population, it is not true that young immigrants are involved in criminal activities to a much greater extent than their German counterparts: the proportion of suspects within the German age group 14 to under 18 years of age is 7.4 percent, whereas it is 10.4 percent for the corresponding group of immigrants. This gives a ratio of 1.4 (and for the group aged 18-21 years, the ratio is 7.4 percent to 12.2 percent, or 1.6).

The results presented in Table 9.4 are indirect estimates that must be interpreted with caution. However, they correspond surprisingly well with the more direct results of a special survey carried out by Bavarian police statisticians which is based on Bavarian raw data and was made in 1999 (see PSB (2001: 313) for details). According to this source, the (unadjusted) ratio "non-German crime suspects/immigrant residents above 8 years of age" is 4.9 times the corresponding ratio of German (Bavarian) crime suspects to German (Bavarian) citizens above 8 years of age. In Table 9.4 the analogous overall German ratio is 3.5. The Bavarian ratio is reduced to 2.4 when offenses that could only be committed by non-Germans as a consequence of their illegal residency status are ignored (that is, prosecutions for offenses against the Aliens Act and the Asylum Procedure Act). Almost the same ratio (2.46) is reached from the data in Table 9.4.

Which crimes are committed by immigrants? With the exception of some crime categories, there are no significant differences compared to crimes committed by Germans. Non-Germans make up larger percentages of the total number of crime suspects accused of murder and manslaughter (30.4 percent), rape and sexual constraint (30.9 percent), pickpocketing (55.3 percent), illegal trade and smuggling of heroin (37.3 percent) and cocaine (60.6 percent) as well as for document forgery (52.2 percent). For more details, see PKS (2001: 120).

---

2 According to PKS (2001: 118), 92 percent of all persons belonging to the group of suspected illegal immigrants are accused because of violations of the German Asylum Procedure Act or violations of the German Aliens Act.

Table 9.4. Rates of German crime suspects by age group, 2001.

	Age group (... to under ... years of age; percent) In parentheses: percentage of males out of all crime suspects				
	Total[1] (≥ 8 years)	8-14[1]	14-18	18-21	≥ 21
Germans	2.5 (75.9)	2.3 (71.1)	7.4 (74.3)	7.4 (80.9)	2.0 (76.0)
Immigrants, unadjusted[2]	8.7 (79.4)	4.6 (73.5)	15.4 (79.6)	18.1 (80.9)	8.1 (79.5)
Immigrants, adjusted[3]	5.9 (79.4)	3.1 (73.5)	10.4 (79.6)	12.2 (80.9)	5.5 (79.5)

Notes: 1) In German crime statistics, offenses committed by children are counted for children from 8 to under 14 years of age. Since statistics of the non-German population are available only for the age group 6-14, 5/7 of the latter population group was assigned to the offense group of interest, that is, to the group of 8-14 years. Analogous calculations have been made to determine the number of all immigrants above 8 years of age living in Germany. 2) "Unadjusted values" are calculated as "number of non-German crime suspects in a well-defined age group" divided by "number of non-German inhabitants in the corresponding age group". 3) "Adjusted values" are calculated by subtracting all accused illegal immigrants, transients and tourists (PKS, 2001: 118) and the subset of 13.9 percent of all arrested asylum seekers who are accused of violating the German Asylum Procedure Act or the Aliens Act (PKS, 2001: 119, 120) from the number of all non-German crime suspects. The allocation of this number (185,010) to different age groups has been made under the assumption that the age-crime profile of illegal migrants, tourists, transients and asylum seekers does not differ from that of other non-German crime suspects.

Sources: (Absolute) Numbers of German and non-German crime suspects: PKS (2001: 73); percentages of German crime suspects: PKS (2001: 73); resident population of immigrants: German Statistical Office (Statistisches Bundesamt, 2002a); own calculation of rates among immigrants.

The largest proportion among all non-German crime suspects is of Turkish nationality (see Table 9.5). If we correct national shares for distortions arising from violations of the Asylum Procedure and Aliens Acts, which only applies in the cases of 13.7 percent of accused Turks (PKS, 2001: 115), the Turkish fraction among all non-German arrests was 24.8 percent in 2001. This high portion is not surprising: it is even somewhat below the proportion of Turks among the non-German resident population (26.7 percent). The second largest group comes from the former Yugoslavia (10.9 percent in 2001), followed by Polish (6.6 percent) and Italian (6.4 percent) crime suspects (all figures refer to adjusted ratios for the year 2001). 12.4 percent of all crime suspects have their origin in EU member states, which is well below their representation in the overall non-German resident population (25.5 percent).

Table 9.5. Non-German crime suspects by national origin (percent of all non-German suspects), 1997-2001.

	1997	1999	2000	2001	2001[1]
Turkey	20.0	20.4	20.4	20.5	24.8
Former Yugoslavia	12.3	16.0	13.3	10.5	10.9
Poland	9.5	7.5	7.5	7.6	6.6
Italy	4.3	4.5	4.6	4.7	6.4
Russia and Ukraine[2]	3.8	4.1	4.4	5.7	3.7
Greece	1.7	1.8	1.9	1.9	2.6
EU Member states	11.2	11.7	12.1	12.4	n.a.

Notes: 1) Crime suspects excluding those accused of violations of the Asylum Procedure Act and the Aliens Act; 2) According to PKS (2001: 114) there might be inconsistencies in classifying offenders from the former Soviet Union.
For comparison purposes: Proportions (percent) of immigrants living in Germany (as of 31 Dec., 2001; source: Statistisches Bundesamt, (2002b): Turkey: 26.7, former Yugoslavia: 8.6, Poland: 4.2, Italy: 8.4, Russia and Ukraine: 3.3, Greece: 5.0, EU member states: 25.5.

Sources: PKS (2001), Tables 71, 72, 74.

The discrepancy between offender rates among citizens from EU member states and among immigrants from non-member states reveals the much more advantaged socio-economic background of citizens coming from Western industrialized countries. The simultaneous existence of many confounding risk factors seems to influence crimes committed by those groups of immigrants who to a large extent left their home countries for economic reasons. Some figures presented in "The First Periodical Report on Crime and Crime Control in Germany" (PSB, 2001; PRC, 2001) illustrate the unequal situations of native Germans and labor migrants (PSB, 2001: 310-311). Immigrants in Germany are, on average, younger, and the proportion of males in the population of immigrants is higher than the respective proportion in the German population (figures as of 1999): for Germans, the proportion of the total population of the age group of 8 to 30 years is 23.1 percent, whereas it is 36.6 percent for non-Germans. For Germans, the proportion of males in the population is 48 percent; among foreigners it is 54 percent. Moreover, the majority of immigrants face a higher risk of unemployment, and they have lower social status: the unemployment rate among non-Germans was 19.2 percent in 1998, which is almost twice the rate of that for Germans. The proportion of Germans who are entitled to social assistance transfers is about 3 percent, whereas it is 9 percent for foreigners living in Germany. It is important to note that almost 50 percent of young immigrants of the age group 20 to 30 have not finished any vocational training or higher education. Moreover, 48 percent of all immigrants, but only 29 percent of all Germans, live in cities with more than 100,000 inhabitants (PSB, 2001: 313), which might be a relevant observation, since crime problems are more likely associated within urban areas.[3]

Immigrants are more often victims of crime than German residents, though only local evidence on this different view of criminality is available (unfortunately, Germany does not participate in the regular International Crime Victimisation Survey (ICVS); see van Kesteren (2001) for the results of the most recent survey in 17 industrialized countries). According to the special survey by the Bavarian police referred to above, in 1999, there were 11 percent of non-Germans among all victims of crime, whereas the proportion of immigrants in the Bavarian population was only 8.4 percent (PSB, 2001: 311). The proportion of unreported crimes is possibly higher among immigrants, in particular in the group of asylum seekers who are exposed to the risk of expulsion. Immigrants are more often victims of violent crimes; in the majority of cases (where suspects were identified) the attackers were immigrants themselves (PSB, 2001: 311).

It is very difficult to consider all the social factors that distinguish immigrants from non-immigrants, and only some of the factors suspected of increasing the probability of committing crimes have been controlled for above. Family background, however, is one of the most relevant factors for crime (see, for instance, empirical evidence collected by Entorf and Spengler, 2002). Since criminal behavior often arises in disrupted families and as a consequence of violence experienced in childhood, a survey conducted by "Kriminologisches Forschungsinstitut Niedersachsen" among school pupils (juveniles) in the German cities Hamburg, Hanover, Munich and Leipzig during the year 2000 deserves special attention. According to this source, 19.0 percent among all German juveniles, but actually 34.5 percent of all Turkish and 29.7 percent of all juveniles from former Yugoslavia reported that they had experienced severe violence and maltreatment during their childhood (PSB, 2001: 505).

9.3 Immigration and Crime in Denmark: Descriptive Evidence

The aim of this section is to present a short overview of the results of Danish register-based descriptive analyses of "crime and national origin". Such analyses have been carried out by Statistics Denmark (1998, 2002a) and the Ministry of Justice (Kyvsgaard, 2000) covering the years 1995, 1998, and 2000, and by the Rockwool Foundation Research Unit (Larsen, 2000) covering the years 1993-1998.[4]

These analyses compare crime rates among "immigrants" (persons born abroad to parents who are both either non-Danish citizens or born abroad), 'descendants'

---

3 It is not clear, however, whether crime arises because of the particular climate of cities, or whether it is urbanity that attracts criminals.
4 The source is Statistics Denmark's statistical register of crime based on reports from the police.

(persons born in Denmark to parents neither of whom are Danish citizens born in Denmark), and "Others". Here the expression "Danes" has been used for the latter group, which comprises more than 90 percent of the total population. These definitions (see also Appendix Figure 2.1 of Chapter 2), based primarily on the nationality and place of birth of the parents of the person in question, are now predominant in official Danish statistics rather than definitions based on citizenship, as they are considered more appropriate for the purposes of analysis. Neither tourists nor asylum seekers nor persons staying illegally in Denmark are included in the definitions, as such people do not have civil registration numbers, which is the key to the population register. A few summary statistics based on citizenship, and thus more comparable with those of other countries, have been published and are presented in Section 9.3.2.

The criminality rate is defined as the number of persons found guilty of one or more offenses as a percentage of the total number of persons in the group in question (immigrants, descendants, Danes, the total population, etc.). Less emphasis has been placed on people charged with crimes (crime suspects). Persons registered are those who have been found guilty according to criminal law of one or more violations of the Penal Code (that is, sexual offences, crimes of violence, offenses against property, and "other offenses", for example, crimes against the state and drug trafficking), the Road Traffic Act or special laws. Special laws are laws not falling under the terms of the Penal Code, but nevertheless being within the criminal law system, which means that violations may be punished with fines or imprisonment. In that sense of the word the Road Traffic Act is also a special law, but violations are – due to their large number and special character – always mentioned separately. Examples of what is included under the heading "special laws" are the Euphoriants Act, the Aliens Act, the Firearms Act and the Income Tax and Fiscal Acts (termed "fiscal legislation" below). Of the special laws, the Euphoriants Act, which prohibits the buying and selling as well as the possession and making of euphoriants, is the one with the highest number of reported violations (Statistics Denmark, 2002d: 14). Violations of the Euphoriants Act can be punished with up to 2 years imprisonment but may be termed "small-scale" compared with the more serious, large-scale cases of trafficking and smuggling of drugs, which come under the Penal Code.

The calculation of the criminality rate is based on court decisions and decisions made by the prosecution or the police leading to unsuspended or suspended imprisonment, fine, withdrawal of charges, "no charge" in cases where the difficulties, expenses, or time spent in connection with the prosecution of the case can be expected to be out of proportion to the importance of the case and, as a consequence, with the sanction,[5] and other decisions (except acquittal) (Statistics Denmark, 2002a:

---

5 Left out of account in the analyses by the Rockwool Foundation Research Unit.

2). The statistics include all decisions on violations of the Penal Code and the Euphoriants Act, while for other laws, minor fines and the like are usually not included (Statistics Denmark, 2001: 29). 'Decisions' is the term used in Danish crime statistics but here, to emphasize that the person has been found guilty of an offense, irrespective of the sanction and though the decision has not necessarily been made by a judge, all decisions included will be referred to as "convictions".

9.3.1 Criminality Rates Among Immigrants, Descendants, and Danes – Convictions

As was noted above, younger persons and men are more likely to be registered in the crime statistics than older persons and women. Of those in the age group 15 (the age of criminal responsibility) to 64 inclusive, in 2000, 60 percent of immigrants and 86 percent of descendants were between 15 and 39 years old, as compared to only 51 percent of Danes. Additionally, 32 percent of descendants were between 15 and 19 years old, this being the case for less than 8 percent of immigrants and Danes (Statistics Denmark, 2002a: 2-3).[6]

The figures in Table 9.6 confirm the importance of taking these differences in age and sex distributions into account. But even when this is done, men as well as women with a foreign background are still over-represented in the crime statistics – and this tendency seems to have increased from 1995 to 2000. For instance, in 1995, 10.0 percent of 15-19-year-old male immigrants received a conviction for violation of the Penal Code, Road Traffic Act, or special laws, but the figure was 11.3 percent in 2000, while the corresponding figures for the total population were 6.6 percent and 6.5 percent.

Table 9.7 divides immigrants and descendants by national origin into either Western or non-Western countries – the overall grouping used in this book – resulting in two different pictures of the crime level compared with Danes. "Western" countries are the 15 EU countries before the enlargement in 2004, Iceland, Liechtenstein, Norway, Switzerland, USA, Canada, Australia, and New Zealand. All other countries are termed "non-Western".

Immigrants and descendants from non-Western countries – with the exception of male descendants in the age group 30-39 years – have an above-average risk of being convicted of a crime. The younger the age group in question, the more pronounced this general picture becomes. Immigrants and descendants from Western countries are closer to the average, with male immigrants being below the average up until the age of 40, and female immigrants until the age of 30, after which the proportions are slightly higher than among Danes. Male descendants from Western countries lie, for the most part, above Danes of the same age, the exception being the age group 20-29

---

6 See Chapter 2 for the sex and age distribution of foreign citizens living in Denmark and Germany.

Table 9.6. Criminality rates[1] in Denmark by sex, age and immigrant status[2], 1995 and 2000. Percent.

Age	Men				Women			
	Immigrants	Descendants	Total population	Others	Immigrants	Descendants	Total population	Others
1995								
15-19	10.0	11.9	6.6	...	2.0	1.9	1.0	...
20-29	9.5	15.1	8.3	...	1.8	2.5	1.2	...
30-39	7.5	7.9	6.5	...	1.8	..	1.3	...
40-49	5.9	4.8	4.5	...	1.4	..	1.0	...
50-59	3.8	..	3.1	...	1.1	..	0.7	...
60-64	1.8	..	1.7	...	0.8	..	0.4	...
2000								
15-19	11.3	11.9	6.5	6.0	2.0	1.7	1.1	1.0
20-29	10.9	18.5	8.3	8.0	1.7	3.0	1.5	1.5
30-39	8.5	8.1	6.7	6.5	1.8	..	1.7	1.7
40-49	6.5	5.2	4.7	4.6	1.7	..	1.3	1.2
50-59	4.0	..	3.2	3.1	1.1	..	0.8	0.8
60-64	2.1	..	2.0	2.0	1.0	..	0.5	0.5

Notes: ... Information not conclusive (too few observations) ... Not published. 1) Proportion in the group with a conviction for violation of the Penal Code, Road Traffic Act, or special laws. 2) As defined in the text.

Sources: Statistics Denmark (1998: 9) and (2002a: 4).

years, while there are too few female descendants registered in the crime statistics in the sample underlying the table[7] to say anything conclusive about their behavior as far as crime is concerned.

The figures in Tables 9.6 and 9.7 may be compared with the evidence for Germany in Table 9.4, which revealed that the German rate of crime suspects among the groups of young immigrants (males as well as females) aged 14-18 and 18-21 was 10.4 percent and 12.2 percent in 2001, whereas it was 7.4 percent among both age groups of German nationality in that year. The criminality rates (males) in 2000 shown in Table 9.6 were 11.9 percent and 18.5 percent among descendants aged 15-19 and 20-29 respectively as compared to 11.3 percent and 10.9 percent among immigrants from

---

7 While the tables from Statistics Denmark are based on the total population – aged 15-64 years – the tables from Larsen (2000) are based on total counts of non-Western immigrants and descendants, a 25 percent sample of Western immigrants and descendants, and a 2 percent sample of the total population aged 16-70 years.

Table 9.7. Criminality rates[1] in Denmark by sex, age, immigrant status[2] and national origin[2], average 1993-1998. Percent.

Age	Immigrants		Descendants		Danes	Immigrants		Descendants		Danes
	Non-Western	Western	Non-Western	Western		Non-Western	Western	Non-Western	Western	
	---------- Men ----------					---------- Women ----------				
16-19	13.9	6.7	17.3	11.2	7.6	2.2	..	2.3	..	1.2
20-29	11.7	3.9	18.5	7.6	8.0	2.0	1.1	3.0	..	1.4
30-39	9.1	5.1	6.4	7.4	6.4	2.0	1.7	..	..	1.4
40-49	6.8	4.6	..	5.2	4.1	1.6	1.4	..	..	0.9
50-59	4.0	3.4	..	..	3.0	1.3	0.9	..	..	0.7
60-70	1.7	1.4	..	..	1.3	0.8	0.5	..	..	0.3

Notes: See Table 9.6.

Source: Larsen (2000: 268).

the same countries and 6.0 percent and 8.0 percent among Danes. If we consider only immigrants and descendants from non-Western countries, as shown in Table 9.7, on average for the years 1993-1998 the corresponding proportions were 17.3 percent and 18.5 percent among descendants aged 16-19 and 20-29 respectively, as compared to 13.9 percent and 11.7 percent among immigrants from the same countries and 7.6 percent and 8.0 percent among Danes.

Calculating ratios of "criminality rates of immigrants"/"criminality rates of Danes" based on Table 9.6 we find 11.3/6.0 = 1.9 for young males aged 15-19, 10.9/8.0 = 1.4 for males aged 20-29, and 8.5/6.5 = 1.3 for the corresponding age group 30-39. Such ratios are higher for descendants/Danes, amounting to 2.0, 2.3, and 1.2 for corresponding groups of males aged 15-19, 20-29 and 30-39 respectively.

Considering the fact that descendants were born and grew up in Denmark, these findings may seem surprising, as the immediate expectation would be lower crime rates in that section of the population than among immigrants. A number of background variables may contribute to the explanation of this, and it must be remembered that only the most obvious ones – age and sex – have been controlled for here.

The calculation of identical ratios on the basis of individual register data to those for Denmark is impossible for German statistics. If we look instead at proportions of crime suspects in the respective age groups, the criminality rate was 2.5 percent among all Germans aged 8 years or older in 2001, while it was 5.9 percent among non-nationals – that is, 2.4 times the German rate. Among the 14 to under 18 years age group the figures are 7.4 percent and 10.4 percent respectively (1.4 times higher), and in the group 18 to under 21 years 7.4 percent and 12.2 percent respectively (1.6 times higher). Finally, in the age group 21 years and over the figures are 2.0 percent and 5.5 percent respectively (2.8 times higher).

Thus, the general impression is that the ratios do not differ much between the two countries, but in Germany young immigrants (aged 14-18) seem to be somewhat "less deviant" relative to "national" German juveniles than Danish immigrants and descendants are relative to Danes of the (almost) corresponding age group 15-19.

Note that in spite of the resemblance found between Germany and Denmark, a direct comparison is not possible because of the differences in statistical presentation. The Danish percentages are based on convictions, whereas German percentages are calculated using charges. Moreover, data from the Danish population are here limited to males and do not include asylum seekers or others without a formal residence permit. Also Danish data only include persons 15 years old and over and are based on violations of the Penal Code as well as of the Road Traffic Act and (other) special laws, whereas 8 years is the lower age limit in the German data, which, furthermore, omit violations of the Road Traffic Act and offenses against the German Asylum Procedure Act and the Aliens Act (see the "adjusted" ratio described in Section 9.2).

The most detailed overview of criminality rates by national origin has been published by Statistics Denmark (2002a) using the United Nations' definition of more developed and less developed countries. Table 9.8 shows the figures for the years 1995, 1998 and 2000. Calculations are standardized by age – that is, they are made as if all the groups had the same age distribution – in order to compensate for the differences in age distribution mentioned above. The over-representation of immigrants and descendants shown in Table 9.6 can be quantified to 33 percent and 90 percent for male immigrants and descendants respectively, and 23 percent and 70 percent for women. The highest criminality rates are, thus, found among descendants – for 20- to 29-year-old male descendants, more than twice the average level of the total population (not shown in the table).

The different pictures wich were outlined in Table 9.7 of the risk of being involved in crime depending on national origin in either a Western or a non-Western country are also further illustrated in Table 9.8. Note that the group of more developed countries comprises all the countries which are here termed Western, plus a number of others – especially Eastern and Central European. Men from less developed countries lie about two thirds above the average, women from more and less developed countries 25 percent and 29 percent above respectively. Of single groups of countries Africa, especially, along with Europe outside the EU, and Asia show high levels among men as well as women. The figures for men from more developed countries lie near the average level of the total population, while those for men and – less markedly – women from EU countries and America lie below the average level. Immigrants and descendants of Turkish origin make up 17.0 percent of the convicted with a foreign background (and 11.8 percent of all 15- to 64-year-old immigrants and descendants living in Denmark), followed by the present Federal Republic of Yugo-

---

8 Bosnia-Herzegovina (4.1 percent and 5.1 percent) and other parts of former Yugoslavia are calculated separately.

Table 9.8. Index for criminality rates[1] in Denmark by sex, national origin[2] and immigrant status[2], 1995, 1998, and 2000. Index, 100 = the total population.

Year	More developed countries	Less	Europe			Africa	America	Asia	Foreign background		
			EU	Other	Total				Immigrants	Descendants	Total
Men, 15-64 years											
2000	101	167	73	157	126	157	73	161	133	190	138
1998	102	160	77	151	122	159	71	156	129	186	134
1995	102	143	92	136	119	152	73	134	121	164	124
Women, 15-64 years											
2000	125	129	96	127	117	239	85	304	123	170	127
1998	142	141	114	149	137	284	101	352	140	167	142
1995	142	149	127	145	138	208	121	152	143	180	146

Notes: See Table 9.6.

Source: Statistics Denmark (2002a: 15).

slavia at 7.5 percent (4.5 percent)[8], Pakistan 7.5 percent (4.5 percent), and Lebanon 6.7 percent (3.8 percent). The figure for immigrants and descendants from EU member states is 11.2 percent (21.1 percent) (Statistics Denmark, 2002a: 5, 8-9).

Like Table 9.6, Table 9.8 shows the changes in criminality rates from 1995 to 2000, and shows that there has been an increase in the over-representation of men – especially descendants – with a foreign background, while for women with a foreign background the index is lower in 2000 than in 1995. Note that such an increase or decrease in an index only tells us how the criminality rates of different groups change in relation to each other, not whether there has been an increase or a decrease in the shares registered. Information about the actual shares is presented in Tables 9.6 and 9.7. The figures in Table 9.8 also show that while the increase among men can be attributed to those from less developed countries, the decrease among women is more evenly distributed.

The findings in Table 9.8, that criminality rates among persons from EU member states are similar to criminality rates of Danes, while higher rates are found among citizens from parts of the world other than the Western industrialized countries, correspond to what was found for Germany (see Table 9.5). The largest groups among non-German crime suspects are Turks, people from the former Yugoslavia, Poles, Italians, Russians and Ukrainians, and Greeks, which to a large extent also reflects the respective groups' relative proportional size in the total foreign resident population.

So far in this section, violations of the Penal Code, the Road Traffic Act, and special laws have been treated together, but obviously the seriousness of these violations – in the general public opinion as well as measured by the sentencing – is not the same, and in analyses of the causes of crime, as well as in international comparisons, violations of the Road Traffic Act are normally omitted. Table 9.9 shows the changes in the distribution on different types of offenses among those convicted.

While in Denmark there are certain offenses against property and crimes of violence and other crime categories where immigrants and descendants differ from Danes, it was the general impression that in Germany there were no significant differences except for some crime categories such as murder and manslaughter, rape and sexual constraint, pickpocketing, illegal trade and smuggling of heroin and document forgery.

Generally, as shown in Table 9.9, in Denmark, measured as a percentage of the total number of persons with a conviction, the proportion registered for violations of the Penal Code has decreased for all groups, but is still markedly higher among immigrants and descendants registered in the crime statistics with a conviction than the average for the total population – primarily due to the large proportions with convictions for offences against property. This is especially so among women of foreign origin. In 2000, theft alone constituted about 50 percent of all violations of the Penal Code among immigrant women, about one third among descendants, and 16 percent among Danes (details are not shown in Table 9.9, and neither are figures for Danes). As far as men are concerned, convictions for crimes of violence constituted 8.5 percent among immigrants, 11.1 percent among descendants, and 4.7 percent among Danes with convictions for violations of the Penal Code in 2000.

On the other hand, among immigrants and descendants with a conviction, violations of the Road Traffic Act make up a much smaller proportion than among Danes, especially with respect to violations involving alcohol. Violations of the Road Traffic Act made up 54.4 percent among all male immigrants registered, 45.8 percent among descendants, and no less than 68.9 percent among Danes. The total number of criminal law convictions has increased for both immigrants and descendants from 1995 to 2000 while it remained constant for the total population, implying a decrease among Danes (Statistics Denmark, 2002a: 4-5, 15-16). Note that the share of immigrants and descendants in the total population has also increased during the period: from 5.3 percent in 1995 to 7.1 percent in 2000 (Larsen and Matthiessen, 2002: 37).

Fines are the most common sanction in all three groups, but there has been a particular increase in the number of descendants, male as well as female, who are sentenced to imprisonment. In 2000, the shares were 27.1 percent of male and 13.1 percent of female descendants registered, as compared to 19.6 percent and 8.7 percent among immigrants and 15.4 percent and 8.3 percent among Danes (Statistics Denmark, 2002a: 5-6, 16).

Table 9.9. Persons with a conviction for a violation of the Penal Code, Road Traffic Act, or special laws by type of offense[1] sex, age and immigrant status[2], Denmark, 1995, 1998, and 2000.

	Immigrants			Descendants			Total population		
	1995	1998	2000	1995	1998	2000	1995	1998	2000
Men, no. of persons	7,202	8,937	9,905	927	1,228	1,478	99,444	99,137	99,486
					Percent				
Total	100.0	100.0	100.0	100.0	100.0	100.0	100.0	100.0	100.0
Penal code	44.5	38.0	34.7	57.4	47.2	42.7	28.3	25.3	23.6
– Sexual offenses	0.6	0.6	0.8	1.0	0.3	0.5	0.4	0.4	0.5
– Crimes of violence	7.7	7.7	8.5	9.7	10.4	11.1	4.8	4.6	5.2
– Offenses against property	33.8	27.6	23.1	44.2	34.1	27.5	21.5	18.7	16.3
– Other offenses	2.5	2.1	2.2	2.5	2.4	3.6	1.6	1.5	1.6
Road Traffic Act	41.2	50.0	54.4	31.3	40.1	45.8	60.8	64.5	67.1
Special laws	14.2	12.1	10.9	11.3	12.6	11.5	10.9	10.2	9.2
Women, no. of persons	1,507	1,776	2,035	156	179	235	18,382	18,476	21,711
					Percent				
Total	100.0	100.0	100.0	100.0	100.0	100.0	100.0	100.0	100.0
Penal code	66.7	65.3	57.9	52.6	62.0	46.0	52.6	37.6	28.6
– Sexual offenses	..	..	..	..	..	..	..	..	..
– Crimes of violence	2.0	2.0	2.5	1.9	3.9	2.6	1.9	1.6	1.7
– Offenses against property	63.1	61.8	53.7	48.7	54.7	41.7	48.7	34.4	25.6
– Other offenses	1.5	1.5	1.6	1.9	3.3	1.7	1.9	1.5	1.2
Road Traffic Act	22.2	28.7	35.7	30.8	31.8	48.9	30.8	56.5	66.2
Special laws	11.1	6.0	6.4	16.7	6.1	5.1	16.7	6.0	5.2

Note: 1) If more than one type of offense, the most serious one has been chosen. 2) As defined in the text.

Source: Statistics Denmark (2002a: 15).

9.3.2 Trends in Crime Levels Measured with Danish Data Adjusted to German Statistics

The above-mentioned statistics, analyses and reports all use the definitions of immigrants, descendants, and Others (Danes), which are now predominant in the publications of Statistics Denmark, but internationally only a few countries (Norway, Sweden, and the Netherlands) use similar, though not identical, definitions. It is common practice to distinguish between nationals and non-nationals. Furthermore, crime rates in the Danish statistics are now calculated on the basis of convictions rather than charges, but international comparisons would in most cases require the latter.

In this subsection an attempt will be made to present statistics which are as comparable as possible with the German crime statistics. An overall measure of the level of crime is reported offenses, that is, offenses which have come to the attention of the police. Ignoring violations of the Road Traffic Act, Table 9.10 shows the changes in crime levels since the mid-1980s measured as the number of reported violations of the Penal Code and of special laws per 100 inhabitants (per 100 inhabitants aged 15 years – the age of criminal responsibility – and over in parentheses). For the years 1985-1989 the number of foreign citizens with a conviction as well as the number of foreign citizens charged have been published by Statistics Denmark. Since then, such statistics of charges by nationality have only been published once – by the Commissioner of Police (1995) for the year 1994. Statistics of convictions by nationality have not been published for the period 1990-1996, but are available again as from 1997. Statistics of convictions and charges in Table 9.10 refer to violations of the Penal Code and the most important special laws other than the Road Traffic Act: the Euphoriants Act, the Firearms Act and fiscal legislation.

Two principal findings may be obtained from Table 9.10. First, there were more or less steady increases in reported violations of the Penal Code and especially of special laws until 1993, when the number of cases per 100 inhabitants reached 10.56 and 1.55 respectively. After 1993 decreases set in. The 2001 level for violations of the Penal Code is lower, while violations of special laws remain at a higher level than in 1985. However, the number of reported violations of the Penal Code per 100 inhabitants in 2001 is still about twice as high as in the 1960s and about 40 percent higher than in the 1970s. Secondly, the table shows an increasing share of foreign citizens in the crime statistics like in the total population.

This is parallel to the long-term trend in Germany, where the incidence of crime has also fallen slightly since 1993, but where current rates are much higher than in the 1960s and 1970s. In Germany, the number of reported crimes per 100 inhabitants has fallen from 8.3 in 1993 to 7.7 in the year 2001 (see Table 9.1).

The right-hand column of Table 9.10 represents an attempt to construct what in the German section was referred to as the "adjusted" share of (non-German) suspects among all persons charged – that is, ignoring violations of the Asylum Procedure Act and the Aliens Act. Compared with Table 9.1, the proportions of foreign citizens of the total number of persons charged seem to have been almost twice as high in Germany as in Denmark in the years for which (approximately) comparable data exist: 13.7 percent and 26.7 percent in Germany in 1984 and 1993, compared with 8.9 percent in 1984 and 13.3 percent in 1994 in Denmark. Since 1995, however, the adjusted share has remained quite stable at about one fifth of all crime suspects in Germany, which is a little higher than the reported – also rather stable – level of 17 percent in Denmark. The latter, however, refers to convictions, as statistics based on charges have not been published since 1994, and the level could therefore be expected to be somewhat higher if it was based on charges like in Germany, as persons of foreign origin are charged without this leading to a conviction more often than is the case for native Danes.

Table 9.10. Reported violations of the Penal Code and of the Euphoriants Act, the Firearms Act, and fiscal legislation in Denmark, and the share of foreign citizens of the total number of persons with convictions and charges, 1985-2001.

Year	Reported violations per 100 inhabitants (per 100 inhabitants 15 years and over) of:		Violations of the Penal Code, the Euphoriants Act, the Firearms Act, and of fiscal legislation. Share of foreign citizens of total number of persons:	
	the Penal Code	all special laws, approx	with a conviction	charged
1985	9.34 (11.4)	1.00 (1.2)	7.7	8.9
1986	10.02 (12.2)	1.03 (1.3)	9.1	9.5
1987	10.23 (12.4)	1.12 (1.4)	10.3	10.0
1988	10.47 (12.7)	1.23 (1.5)	10.1	10.2
1989	10.46 (12.6)	1.31 (1.6)	10.6	10.8
1990	10.27 (12.4)	1.25 (1.5)	...	...
1991	10.10 (12.1)	1.39 (1.7)	...	...
1992	10.40 (12.5)	1.51 (1.8)	...	...
1993	10.56 (12.7)	1.55 (1.9)	...	...
1994	10.53 (12.7)	1.39 (1.7)	...	[1,2]13.3
1995	10.33 (12.5)	1.31 (1.6)	...	...
1996	10.06 (12.2)	1.27 (1.5)	...	...
1997	10.07 (12.2)	1.21 (1.5)	[1]17.1	...
1998	9.43 (11.5)	1.17 (1.4)	[1]16.5	...
1999	9.30 (11.4)	1.20 (1.5)	16.7	...
2000	9.46 (11.6)	1.24 (1.5)	17.2	...
2001	8.85 (10.8)	1.24 (1.5)	17.1	...

Notes: 1) Weighted average of shares with a conviction/ charged for violation of the Penal Code and of one of the special laws, as the same persons may appear in both statistics for 1997 and 1998, unlike other years. 2) Fiscal legislation not included.

Sources: Statistics Denmark: 'Kriminalstatistik', 'Kriminalitet' (various years) and the Commissioner of Police (1995: 31).

When comparing figures for the two countries, it must be taken into account that while the foreign resident population in Denmark (asylum seekers excluded) made up 2 percent of the population in the mid-1980s, the corresponding German figure (asylum seekers included) was more than 2.5 times higher. In 1993, the proportions had increased to 3.5 and 8.5 percent respectively, and in 2001 to about 5 and 9 percent (see Chapter 2).

As mentioned above, asylum seekers, tourists, and others without a civil registration number are not included in Statistics Denmark's population register, and normally not in publications based on the statistical register of crime either. The figures in Tables 9.10 and 9.11 are exceptions. The latter shows the shares made up of, on the one hand, Danish nationals and, on the other, of foreign citizens with and without a

Table 9.11. Danes and non-Danes in Danish crime statistics with convictions for violations of the Penal Code, the Euphoriants Act, the Firearms Act, or fiscal legislation, 1997-2001. Percent.

	Danes	Asylum seekers	Illegal immigrants	Foreign citizens with a residence permit	Tourists and foreign citizens with a visa	Not stated	Total
1997	¹83,2	¹1,6	¹0,6	¹12,2	¹2,2	¹0,1	100
1998	¹83,3	¹1,7	¹0,8	¹11,6	¹2,6	¹0,1	100
1999	82,8	2,2	0,9	11,3	2,7	0,1	100
2000	82,6	2,8	0,9	11,1	2,5	0,1	100
2001	82,8	2,5	0,8	11,4	2,4	0,1	100

Notes: 1) Weighted average of shares with a conviction for violation of the Penal Code or of one of the three special laws, as the same person may appear in both parts of the statistics for 1997 and 1998, unlike other years.

Sources: Statistics Denmark: "Kriminalstatistik", "Kriminalitet" (various years).

residence permit in Denmark. The share of Danish nationals is rather stable at about 83 percent over the 5-year period, while the share of asylum seekers seems to have increased, and the share of foreign citizens with a residence permit to have decreased. The register data available to this project do not offer the possibility of including asylum seekers and others without a residence permit, as such people do not have a civil registration number.

Compared with the structure of non-nationals in German crime statistics – again based on charges or crime suspects – first of all, the share of illegal immigrants in the number of foreign crime suspects amounts to more than one fifth in Germany, but to just under 5 percent in Denmark in 1998 and 2001. The proportions made up by "asylum seekers" in Germany are 17.8 percent (1998) and 14.3 percent (2001) respectively. This group comprises for instance persons with a "Duldung", while those whose cases are still being processed are included in the group "Others". Foreigners "with a residence permit" in Denmark make up three quarters of non-Danes in the crime statistics in 1997 and two thirds in 2001. Not included in these figures are those defined as asylum seekers in a Danish context – 10.2 percent in 1998 and 14.5 percent in 2001 (calculated on the basis of Table 9.11 as the percentage share of non-Danes the various years). Unlike Germany, in Denmark only persons who are still awaiting official notice (or have been denied asylum) are defined as asylum seekers. In the German statistics tourists have made up about 7 percent of the crime suspects over the whole period since 1984, while in Denmark the percentage made up of "tourists/foreign citizens with a visa" is about twice as high (only 1997-2001).

The last table to be presented in this Danish section is Table 9.12, which shows the change in the proportions of crime suspects among Danish nationals and non-

Table 9.12. Crime suspects[1] by age and nationality[2], men, Denmark, 1993-2001. Percent.

	16-19			20-24			25-29			30+		
	Danes	Western	Non-West.	Danes	Western	Non-West.	Danes	Western	Non-West.	Danes	Western	Non-West.
1993	5.7	5.5	14.2	4.2	4.8	10.6	3.7	3.0	8.7	1.5	2.8	6.2
1994	5.2	7.2	14.4	4.1	3.3	11.5	3.5	3.2	9.0	1.4	2.6	6.2
1995	4.6	7.3	14.4	4.1	3.0	11.2	3.1	2.3	8.6	1.4	2.3	6.1
1996	5.5	7.7	15.5	4.3	3.7	11.0	3.0	3.1	9.3	1.4	2.3	6.1
1997	4.9	12.9	15.4	4.0	2.8	10.8	2.7	2.6	8.2	1.4	1.9	5.4
1998	4.6	10.2	15.1	4.2	3.6	11.4	2.8	1.8	8.6	1.3	2.1	5.2
1999	4.6	7.6	14.9	3.5	3.6	10.5	2.5	1.8	8.0	1.2	1.7	5.2
2000	6.6	8.4	17.0	4.1	3.5	10.4	2.9	1.1	8.0	1.2	1.5	5.1
2001	5.3	10.1	16.4	3.9	3.9	11.0	3.0	1.8	7.6	1.1	1.7	5.2

Notes: 1) Shares charged with violations of the Penal Code and/or special laws (except the Road Traffic Act and the Aliens Act). 2) As explained in the text.

Source: Own calculations based on register data from Statistics Denmark's statistical register of crime.

nationals from Western and non-Western countries, respectively, during the period 1993-2001. Only men are included in the table. By using these definitions based on citizenship of subgroups of the population in Denmark, and by using charges as a measure of crime, two of the main problems of comparability between the statistics of the two countries are accounted for.

It should be emphasized that as Statistics Denmark does not publish figures based on charges any more, the data behind Table 9.12 (and Table 9.14) have not been checked as thoroughly as the data behind the tables based on decisions. The following should be read with that reservation in mind.

Table 9.12 indicates either an overall downward tendency or an unchanged level during the period from 1993, which might be expected on the basis of the statistics for convictions and reported crime, but with an upward movement from 1999 to 2001 for some groups. The highest criminality rates are still found among foreign citizens from non-Western countries, though the levels decrease somewhat in the age groups 25 years and over. Criminality rates are in the interval 4-6 percent for the youngest Danes in the age group 16-19 years, and 3-4 percent in the 20-24 years age group. The corresponding figures among non-nationals from non-Western countries are – on average – about two and a half to three times higher. Relatively large differences – up to just over four times higher among non-Western immigrants than among Danish nationals – remain in the older age groups, but at lower levels. In general, comparing the adjusted Danish ratios from Table 9.12 to German evidence based on Table 9.4 confirms the above-mentioned conclusions based on convictions, though the use of charges instead of convictions reveals that also in Denmark ratios for "foreign citizens/nationals" are higher for older age groups than for younger age groups (in Germany, the crime ratio "immigrants/nationals" for the group older than 21 was 2.8). Again, the tables are not directly comparable, mainly because Danish data refer to male immigrants by nationality in either Western or non-Western countries, whereas German data are based on males and females for the group of all (Western and non-Western) immigrants. The corresponding figures for Western nationals in most cases lie around or even below the level for Danish nationals.

9.4 Comparison of Descriptive Evidence from Germany and Denmark

In the previous sections descriptive evidence was presented concerning the levels and trends in criminality in Denmark and Germany, with special reference to the question of "crime and national origin". Despite differences in statistical presentation, the general impression is an over-representation of foreign citizens as compared to nationals in the crime statistics in both countries. However, as was also noted, pointing out or establishing apparent differences in criminality rates between foreigners or immigrants and descendants on the one hand, and nationals on the other, may lead to premature conclusions. For instance, sex and age distributions among nationals and non-nationals are not the same, and as, in general, the highest crime rates are found among young men, this makes it obvious that differences in demographic structures must be taken into account. Otherwise, the mere fact that the group of foreign nationals or, depending on the definitions used, immigrants and descendants are, on average, younger than the national population would lead to an exaggeration of the level of crime among persons of foreign origin.

In Denmark, it is common practice to use a broader definition than just citizenship to define the section of the population which may be of interest as far as the question of integration of immigrants and descendants into the economy or society is concerned. In Germany and in most other countries, crime statistics distinguish between persons with and without national passports, that is, between nationals versus non-nationals, whereas definitions such as the above-mentioned in respect of immigrants, descendants, and "Others" are specific to Denmark and a few other countries. Moreover, Danish statistics are based on convictions, whereas internationally – and in Germany – statistics are normally based on charges, that is, crime suspects. Because of these and other differences, direct comparisons between Danish and German data are difficult to make.

With these potential problems in mind, we still observe similar age-crime profiles in both countries. When differences in age and sex distribution are taken into account, men as well as women with a foreign background are over-represented in the crime statistics. In particular, fairly high criminality rates are found among young men from what are here called non-Western countries.

Generally, the incidence of crime as measured by reported crimes per 100 inhabitants has fallen slightly since 1993 in both countries, but current rates are much higher than in the 1960s and 1970s.

Looking at different age groups in 2000, and calculating ratios of "crime rates of immigrants"/"crime rates of Danes" and similarly of descendants/Danes, we find levels of between 1.2 and 2.3, the highest being among the youngest groups below the age of 30, and the ratios being higher for descendants/Danes than for immigrants/Danes. Considering the fact that descendants were born and grew up in Denmark, this latter finding may seem surprising, as the immediate expectation might be lower crime rates in that section of the population than among immigrants.

If we compare the Danish figures with the German proportions of crime suspects in the same age groups and concentrate on the "adjusted" ratio, then we see that although the data are not directly comparable, ratios do not seem to differ much between the two countries. One thing to note, though, is that in Germany, young immigrants (aged 14-18) seem to be somewhat "less deviant" relative to "national" German juveniles than Danish immigrants and descendants are relative to Danes of the (almost) corresponding age group 15-19.

As mentioned above, in spite of the resemblance between the above results for Denmark and Germany, the data are not directly comparable. To provide Danish data which are as comparable as possible with the available German statistics for the period after the mid-1990s as well, calculations were made based on information about nationality and charges in Statistics Denmark's registers of population and crime. Concentrating on male crime suspects and violations of the Penal Code and special laws (except the Aliens Act) and omitting violations of the Road Traffic Act, these calculations indicate an overall downward trend or an unchanged level during the period from 1993, which might be expected based on statistics of convictions and reported crime, but with an upward movement from 1999 to 2001 for some groups. In general, when we compare the adjusted Danish ratios with German evidence, though the latter is based on females as well as males and, unlike the Danish data, includes asylum seekers and tourists, etc., the conclusions based on convictions outlined above are confirmed, though the use of charges instead of convictions reveals that in Denmark ratios for "foreign citizens/nationals" are also higher for older age groups than for younger age groups.

Going a step further as far as comparability is concerned and looking at the "adjusted" share of non-national suspects among all persons charged in those relatively few years for which (approximately) comparable Danish data have been published – that is, data based on charges, ignoring violations of the Asylum Procedure Act and the Aliens Act and including asylum seekers and tourists, etc. in both countries – the share seems to have been almost twice as high in Germany as in Denmark, and about twice as high at the beginning of the 1990s as in the mid-1980s.

After it reached its peak at 26.7 percent in 1993, the adjusted share decreased and has remained quite stable at about one fifth of all crime suspects in Germany. In Denmark, only data based on convictions have been published after 1994 and the share of foreign citizens has increased to a rather stable level of 17 percent in 1997-2001.

These proportions are higher than the shares of foreign citizens of the total populations in both countries, but the difference between Denmark and Germany in the 1980s and the beginning of the 1990s, and the increases during the period, mirror the relative sizes and changes of the resident foreign populations, while the developments from the mid-1990s can only partly be explained by demographic changes.

A description of the structure of non-nationals in the crime statistics – but now again based on convictions in the case of Denmark and on charges, or crime suspects, in the case of Germany – reveals some striking differences. First of all, the share of illegal immigrants in the number of non-German crime suspects amounts to more than one fifth in Germany, but just under 5 percent in Denmark in 1998-2001. The share of asylum seekers in all non-German crime suspects has also increased significantly, while such data are not available for Denmark for the 1980s, and in general the term "asylum seeker" does not mean exactly the same in the two countries.

As far as national origin is concerned, crime rates among persons from EU member states are similar to crime rates of nationals in both countries, while higher rates are found among citizens from parts of the world other than the Western industrialized countries. Certain offences against property and crimes of violence are crime categories where immigrants and descendants in Denmark differ from the Danish nationals, while in Germany it is the general impression that there are no significant differences except for some crime categories.

It should be stressed again, as in the previous sections, that apart from age and sex controlled for here, place of residence and a number of other – primarily socio-economic – factors not controlled for also affect the probability of being involved in crime. Such factors are the topic of the next section.

9.5 Prevention of Immigrant Crime: Education and Other Factors

Criminologists agree upon a certain number of high-risk characteristics that increase the probability of getting involved with criminal behavior and even result in some citizens becoming chronic offenders with multiple delinquency referrals. In general, criminals are relatively young, most of them are male, and they are poorly educated, which leads to low occupational status, unemployment, and low socio-economic status. They more probably grew up in disrupted families, a factor which is often associated with lack of family stability, including poor parental control and lack of parenting skills. Such problems are accompanied and even caused by problems stemming from a lack of integration into society, reinforced by bad (urban) neighborhoods and having family members involved in crime. Evidently, the living conditions of many immigrants in European countries make them more likely to belong to the high-risk group. The simultaneous existence of multiple risks mentioned above affects the criminal behavior of immigrants and descendants, at least when they come from non-Western countries.

A Danish register-based study (Christoffersen et al., 2003) investigates the underlying factors of violent criminal behavior among young men and points to the importance of family structure for whether or not boys develop into troublesome youths with convictions for crimes of violence. It is concluded "that violent adolescents or young men are more often coming from families suffering from the following disadvantages: 1) disturbance of family unit (teenage parenthood, family break-up, and children's placement outside the home); 2) violence in the family and paternal criminality; 3) a mother's alcohol abuse; 4) a father's lack of vocational training" (p. 377). In addition to such poor family conditions, the study also points to much more widespread structural factors such as, first of all, unemployment but also poor educational achievement in terms of completed upper secondary school and vocational training or higher education to be the most significant characteristics to reinforce the violent criminal behavior.

Another possible explanation is discrimination in the sense of being subject to special attention by the police and to false accusations, an issue which has been addressed by Kyvsgaard (2001: 363, translation by CL):

"It is a well-known fact that persons of foreign ethnic origin are over-represented in the crime statistics … It can be debated whether this over-representation is due to circumstances within the group or rather to mechanisms in the system of justice which mean that persons belonging to ethnic minorities are particularly at risk of being registered as criminals."

As to mechanisms in the system of justice, Kyvsgaard (2001: 373) concludes on the basis of data from 1998 (see also Kyvsgaard, 2000) that persons of foreign origin more often than is the case for persons of Danish origin are charged, arrested, or arrested in connection with a charge without this leading to a conviction at a later stage. Though a number of possible explanations are mentioned, her conclusion is that the law-enforcing authorities seem to take tougher action against certain ethnic minorities than against other groups in society. Apart from this possible bias in the attitude of the authorities towards ethnic minorities, there may be other reasons why young men of foreign ethnic origin attract the attention of the police and the system of justice to a larger extent than other groups, implying a higher risk of being detected. If, for instance, they belong to a group where the police expects violation of the law to take place, the police will be more likely to look for offenders there than elsewhere. As already mentioned, this may be considered a rational strategy, since the share of undetected crimes is possibly relatively high, too. On the other hand, many charges not leading to a conviction could be an argument against such a strategy if the aim is to maximize the clear-up or detection rate.

No overall analysis exists which can explain the differences in crime rates which appear from the descriptive statistics presented above. However, Statistics Denmark (1998, 2002a) has carried out partial analyses including possible explanatory background variables such as urbanization, income, and education. These three variables appeared to have the expected effect on the general risk of being involved in crime, but they did not contribute – or only contributed marginally – to the explanation of the differences in criminality rates described above. The total index values remained roughly the same as in Table 9.8, where only age differences were accounted for: namely 138 for men and 127 for women of foreign origin. Three variables which – with certain qualifications – did appear to contribute to the explanation of the differences were (1) receipt or not of social transfer payments and (2) the level of gross income which, when controlled for, reduced the over-representation among men as well as women of foreign origin, and (3) occupational status, which may explain part of the over-representation among men of foreign origin.

These results confirm the economic theory of crime which predicts that good opportunities for legal income might prevent crime. As pointed out in Becker's (1968) seminal article, national and non-national citizens try to make the best of their lives, given their personal capabilities and resources. Obviously, a high stock of human and social capital (in the sense of "good" social networks; see Coleman, 1988) helps a person to live a law-abiding life without any harmful incentive to take the risk of criminal behavior. Thus, since access to education is the key to economic and social success, a high level of education should also be the key to crime prevention.

As far as education in the OECD countries is concerned, there are two main different models of schooling system, and the matter of which is in use may have a great impact on integration and criminality prospects of immigrants: early differentiation and ability grouping between different schools as in Germany, where children are allocated to Gymnasium, Realschule, or Hauptschule after four years of primary school, or late differentiation and ability tracking by course systems within schools or even within classes, as in the Scandinavian countries. In Sweden, Olof Palme's ideas for reforming compulsory and upper secondary schooling were aimed at reducing early differentiation, and in this way counteracting the social bias of recruitment for higher education and employment. Denmark has retained a system of late differentiation between different schools in post-16 education, with the *Gymnasium* providing general and academic schooling, while technical schools, commercial schools and some more specialized schools offer vocational education.

Which schooling system is best suited to the school performance and reducing the probability of immigrants getting involved with criminal behavior? Based on the distribution of children across Hauptschule, Realschule, and Gymnasium, it seems as if the system of early differentiation (as it is applied in Germany) has a negative impact on the school performance of socially disadvantaged juveniles, a high proportion of whom come from families with a migration background. The average share of children coming from families of foreign-born or first-generation

Table 9.13. Correlation coefficients for immigration, schooling systems, and PISA scores.

	Size of risk group	National score of foreign-born	National score of first generation	National score of natives	Within-school variation	Between-school variation
Size of risk group	1	-0.823	-0.795	-0.934	-0.520	0.330
National score of foreign-born		1	0.857	0.747	0.588	-0.474
National score of first generation			1	0.752	0.594	-0.502
National score of natives				1	0.548	-0.188
Within-school variation					1	-0.755
Between-school variation						1

Note: Correlation coefficients based on data from N = 27 OECD countries.

Sources: PISA (2001), "within-school variation", "between-school variation": www.pisa.oecd.org/knowledge/summary/h.htm, Table 2.4 (6 Jan., 2003). National averages of foreign-born and first-generation immigrants and of natives: www.pisa.oecd.org/knowledge/summary/g.htm, Table 6.10 (6 Jan., 2003). Percentage at proficiency level 1 and below ("risk group"): www.pisa.oecd.org/knowledge/summary/a.htm, Table 2.1.a (6 Jan., 2003).

immigrants in the top-level secondary school *(Gymnasium)* is 14 percent, whereas it is 40 percent at the lowest-level secondary school *(Hauptschule,* see PISA (2001: 462)), and it is even above 50 percent in many urban areas.

Is there more international evidence on the performance of immigrants under these two competing schooling systems? Indeed there is. The "Programme for International Student Assessment" (PISA, OECD, 2001) provided evidence in favor of the hypothesis that high between-school variation in cognitive abilities leads to higher social segregation than high within-school variation and prevents integration of immigrants into societies of OECD countries. In order to show some background information for this conclusion, we will look at some published data from the PISA study. The OECD countries' average national PISA scores are based on 15-year-old students' performance at reading/retrieving information. Skills are categorized into 5 different levels, where 5 represents the highest and 1 the lowest proficiency level. As regards opportunities for legal future work and incomes, the students at level 1 or below can be characterized as a "risk group". OECD (2001: Table 2.4) decomposes the total variation of scores into the two shares of variance that arise between schools and within schools. Those countries with the greatest differences between schools (such as Germany) tend to be those that send students to different kinds of secondary school, often at an early stage of life on the basis of prior performance in the first four to six years of school. In Nordic countries the differences are mainly within schools (OECD, 2001: Table 2.4).

Table 9.13 reveals that school systems with high between-school variation are positively correlated with the national size of this risk group (r = 0.33), whereas school systems with high within-school variation seem to reduce the number of students at risk (r = − 0.52). Table 9.13 also includes national PISA scores (averages)

Table 9.14. Highest completed Danish or foreign education or training and shares with charges for violation of the Penal Code and/or special laws[1] in the respective groups, by age and nationality, men, 1999. Percent.

	No schooling/ not stated		Basic school		Upper secondary school		Vocational training		Tertiary education		Total educ./ train.
		- charged		- charged		- charged		- charged		- charged	
16-19 years											
Danes	1.2	..	94.6	4.4	4.2	3.2	0.1	..	0.0	..	100
Western	23.0	9.2	69.1	7.5	7.0	..	0.9	..	0.0	..	100
Non-Western	14.1	14.2	82.3	15.3	1.6	6.5	1.8	9.9	0.2	..	100
20-24 years											
Danes	0.9	..	33.7	8.4	33.2	0.5	29.2	1.8	3.1	1.0	100
Western	34.9	1.3	19.4	12.7	21.5	1.6	17.1	2.0	7.1	0.0	100
Non-Western	16.1	8.4	53.7	14.0	11.8	3.8	15.7	6.6	2.7	7.0	100
25-29 years											
Danes	1.0	13.9	23.4	6.0	14.4	0.2	41.2	2.1	20.0	0.3	100
Western	26.3	2.6	11.2	5.4	9.9	0.0	24.8	1.5	27.7	0.5	100
Non-Western	16.9	7.8	31.4	10.1	13.7	8.5	24.6	6.3	13.4	5.9	100
30-70 years											
Danes	1.9	2.7	30.0	2.0	3.8	0.8	43.1	0.9	21.3	0.5	100
Western	16.2	1.5	12.9	3.1	7.0	3.1	31.2	1.0	32.7	1.4	100
Non-Western	17.8	6.3	29.3	4.8	8.5	6.0	24.4	5.0	20.1	4.7	100

Notes: ... Less than a total of 30 persons in the group. 1) Except the Road Traffic Act and the Aliens Act. Background information: Information about foreign education and training is based on a questionnaire survey carried out by Statistics Denmark in 1999 among immigrants without a Danish vocational or higher education. The response rate was 50 percent. Information for the 50 percent who did not return the questionnaire is based on imputation. New immigrants to Denmark are systematically asked about foreign education, so the percentage of the information which is based on imputation will gradually decrease. For information about Danish education and training see Appendix Table 9.1 and Chapter 3.
The table should be read as in the following example: 27.7 percent of all men in the age group 25-29 years from Western countries had a tertiary education. Taking these 27.7 percent as 100 percent, 0.5 percent of this particular group have been charged with a crime.

Source: Own calculations based on Statistics Denmark's statistical registers of crime and of education.

of first-generation immigrants (born in the country of assessment, but whose parents are foreign born) and foreign-born immigrants (foreign born, also parents are foreign born). Both variables are negatively correlated with between-school variation (correlation coefficients are -0.47 for foreign-born and -0.50 for first-generation immigrants), whereas immigrants seem to benefit from schooling systems with high variation within schools. Both correlation coefficients are positive and high (0.59).

Given this tentative evidence (which would certainly benefit from some more profound econometric analysis), it might not be surprising that high between-school variation leads to social segregation and prevents integration of immigrants into the German society. As regards German PISA results, not only the performance of immigrants but also Germany's average score for the group of all students participating in PISA gave rise to serious concerns. Germany ranked only 21st among 27 participating OECD countries. Denmark ranked 16th (national score: 497, German score: 484, OECD average: 500). A striking feature of the German results was the very high variation in student performance. The difference between the score of the 5 percent percentile – 284 – and the score of the 95 percent percentile – 650 – was the highest among all participating nations. Education in Denmark is more equally distributed: the 5 percent percentile and 95 percent percentile were 326 and 645 respectively (PISA, 2001: 107, Table 2.5).

To prevent criminal behavior among immigrants, it seems advisable to improve their integration into society, but since so many immigrants remain disintegrated among other immigrants within *Hauptschulen*, that is, the lowest level of Germany's secondary schools, in Germany there is an ongoing discussion as to whether, at least from the viewpoint of crime prevention, the German system of very early school differentiation after only 4 years of school needs to be reformed.

Unfortunately, preliminary evidence gathered in Table 9.14 based on Statistics Denmark's statistical registers of crime and education suggests that the mere presence of higher education among immigrants seems to be insufficient alone to bring crime rates among immigrants down to those among Danes, although it becomes clear that for foreigners as well as for nationals completion of higher education makes people less exposed to the risk of crime, at least for younger people. To illustrate this point more clearly, the following figures are extracted from Table 9.14:

Crime rates (charges) among Danes and immigrants, and highest completed education:

	Basic School	Vocational Training age 20 – 24	Tertiary Education
Danes	8.4	1.8	1.0
Non-Western	14.0	6.6	7.0
		age 30 – 70	
Danes	2.0	0.9	0.5
Non-Western	4.8	5.0	4.7

Thus, when education level is taken into account, rates of criminality among immigrants from non-Western countries remain above those of nationals. Table 9.14 shows that this observation does hold for all age groups. It is quite surprising that for the group of non-Western middle-aged and mature adults (aged 30-70), criminality rates do not go down with higher education. However, it should be noted that criminality rates for Western immigrants in most age groups are below even those of Danes.

The observations presented here, which are based on simple descriptive evidence, show that more research is necessary to understand the differences in delinquent behavior among citizens with and without national passports. More multivariate investigations are needed to understand the complex interaction between the socio-economic conditions of immigrants and their potential illegal behavior.

9.6 Conclusions, Future Research

The purpose of this chapter is to present an overview of mainly descriptive evidence on the very complex interactions between "crime and national origin". International comparisons are very difficult, as definitions and counting rules differ between countries. Not surprisingly, this was also the case for statistics from Denmark and Germany. Nevertheless, the study of joint similarities and differences between the two countries has opened new horizons for future research into both immigration and criminology. In total, there are many more similarities than differences. Although we did not perform any sophisticated econometric analyses at this stage, our results confirm the importance of taking differences in age and sex distribution into account. However, even when such differences are controlled for, citizens with a foreign background are still over-represented in the crime statistics. Evidence available only from the Danish register data shows that criminality rates for immigrants remain relatively high even when education is taken into consideration. It needs to be added, however, that this conclusion only holds for immigrants from non-Western countries, whereas crime rates among immigrants from industrialized Western countries are within the range of Danes and Germans, or below.

Our results show that we are still at the beginning of understanding statistical differences based on national origins. Of course, the true reason cannot be found in less law-abiding attitudes within specific nations or even in ethnic backgrounds. Although this was not the main purpose of our work, we have mentioned some potentially relevant issues that are worth more detailed consideration in future research. For instance, immigrants bear multiple risk-factors such as crime-prone neighborhoods, lack of knowledge of the national languages, lack of education and lack of integration, all of which might interact in a potentially hazardous way. Moreover, higher attention given to foreign-looking people and more frequent police checks might cause higher clear-up ratios among immigrants from non-Western countries than among national citizens and immigrants of European appearance.

Summing up, it seems that not only is human capital the key to successful prevention of immigrant crime, but that the missing link to successful crime prevention is also higher accumulation of social capital. A high stock of both human and social capital (in the sense of "good" social networks; see Coleman, 1988) helps people to live law-abiding lives without any harmful incentives to take the risk of criminal behavior.

References

Becker, G. S. 1968. "Crime and Punishment: An Economic Approach," *Journal of Political Economy* 76, 169-217.

Christoffersen, Mogens Nygaard, Brian Francis, and Keith Soothill. 2003. "An Upbringing to Violence? Identifying the Likelihood of Violent Crime among the 1966 Birth Cohort in Denmark," *The Journal of Forensic Psychiatry & Psychology* 14 (2), September 2003, 367-381.

Coleman, J. S. 1988. "Social Capital in the Creation of Human Capital," *American Journal of Sociology* 94, 95-120.

Commissioner of Police. 1995. *Sammenlignende analyse af kriminalitet begået i Danmark af danske og udenlandske statsborgere 1994*. Copenhagen.

Entorf, H. and H. Spengler. 2002. *Crime in Europe: Causes and Consequences*. Heidelberg and New York: Springer Science.

Kyvsgaard, B. 2000. "Kriminalitet og national oprindelse 1998," Annex 3, in Ekspertgruppen om ungdomskriminalitet: *Rapport om ungdomskriminalitet*. Ministry of Justice and Commissioner of Police: Copenhagen, 173-184

Kyvsgaard, B. 2001. "Kriminalitet, retshåndhævelse og etniske minoriteter," *Juristen* No. 9, 363-373.

Larsen, C. 2000. "Kriminalitet," in Gunnar Viby Mogensen and Poul Chr. Matthiessen (eds): *Integration i Danmark omkring årtusindskiftet*. Aarhus: Aarhus University Press, 252-278.

Larsen, C. and P. C. Matthiessen. 2002. "Indvandrerbefolkningens sammensætning og udvikling i Danmark," in Gunnar Viby Mogensen and Poul Chr. Matthiessen (eds): *Indvandrerne og arbejdsmarkedet*. Copenhagen: Spektrum, 25-79.

OECD. 2001. *The OECD Programme for International Student Assessment*, www.pisa.oecd.org (10 Jan., 2003).

PISA. 2001. *PISA 2000. Basiskompetenzen von Schülerinnen und Schülern im internationalen Vergleich*, edited by German PISA-Konsortium, Opladen: Leske and Budrich.

PKS. 2001. *Polizeiliche Kriminalstatistik – Bundesrepublik Deutschland – Berichtsjahr 2001*. Wiesbaden, www.bka.de/pks/pks2001/index.html (6 Jan., 2003).

PRC. 2001. *First Periodical Report on Crime and Crime Control in Germany, English summary of PSB (2001)*, edited by the German Federal Ministry of the Interior and Federal Ministry of Justice, Berlin, www.eng.bmi.bund.de/Annex/en_ 23474/ Download_Abridged_Version.pdf (10 Jan., 2003).

PSB. 2001. *Erster Periodischer Sicherheitsbericht*, edited by Federal Ministry of the Interior and Federal Ministry of Justice (Bundesministerium des Inneren, Bundesministerium der Justiz), Berlin, www.bmi.bund.de/frame/dokumente/ Artikel/ix_49371.htm (10 Jan., 2003).

Statistisches Bundesamt. 2002a. *Ausländische Bevölkerung nach Altersgruppen* (Foreign Population by Age Group), http://www.destatis.de/themen/d/ thm_bevoelk.htm (Excel file, downloadable, 10 Jan., 2003).

Statistisches Bundesamt. 2002b. *Ausländische Bevölkerung nach Geburtsland* (Foreign Population by Country of Birth), http://www.destatis.de/basis/d/bevoe/ bevoetab10.htm (10 Jan., 2003).

Statistics Denmark. 1986-1990, 1998-1999. *Kriminalstatistik* 1985, 1986, 1987, 1988, 1989, 1997, 1998. Copenhagen.

Statistics Denmark. 1998. "Kriminalitet og national oprindelse 1995", *Statistiske Efterretninger. Social sikring og retsvæsen* 1998:2. Copenhagen.

Statistics Denmark. 2000. *Kriminalitet 1999*. Copenhagen.

Statistics Denmark. 2001. *Kriminalitet 2000*. Copenhagen.

Statistics Denmark. 2002a. "Kriminalitet og national oprindelse 2000," *Statistiske Efterretninger. Sociale forhold, sundhed og retsvæsen* 2002:9. Copenhagen.

Statistics Denmark. 2002b. *Børns levevilkår*. Copenhagen.

Statistics Denmark. 2002c. *Befolkningens bevægelser 2001*. Copenhagen.

Statistics Denmark. 2002d. *Kriminalitet 2001*. Copenhagen.

Van Kesteren, J. N. van, Mayhew, P., and Nieuwbeerta, P. 2000. "Criminal Victimisation in Seventeen Industrialized Countries: Key-findings from the 2000 International Crime Victims Survey," *Onderzoek en beleid* No. 187. The Hague: Ministry of Justice, WODC.

Appendix Table 9.1. Information about Danish education and training.

Basic school	*Primary and lower secondary education.* 9 years of compulsory schooling, with an optional 10th year. Teaching in the Danish *Folkeskole* takes place in classes and (since 1975) the students remain together for the entire period of compulsory school. Differentiation takes place within the framework of the class.
Upper secondary school	3-year programs. *General upper secondary school* is academically oriented and qualifies students for higher education. *Technical and commercial upper secondary education* are offered at technical and business colleges respectively and qualify students for employment in trade and industry – usually in training positions – as well as for higher education.
Vocational training (VET)	2-5-year programs (3½-4 years are normally required to receive a certificate of completed apprenticeship) offered at technical (trades, industries, service trades) and business (commerce, administration) schools or colleges and qualify students to enter the labor market as skilled workers and in some cases also for higher education. The programs are made up of periods of practical, most often on-the-job training, alternating with courses at school or college. Examples: carpenter, electrician, mechanic.
Higher education	*Short-cycle* (13-14 years of education in total). Examples: laboratory technician and policeman. *Medium-cycle* (15-16 years of education in total). Examples: teacher in the Folkeskole (basic school, see above), nurse, librarian. The *Bachelor's degree* is at the same level, while the highest level of education comprises *Master's, Ph.D.* and the traditional doctoral degrees.

Source: See Chapter 3.

CHAPTER 10

Immigrants and the Public Sector in Denmark and Germany*

By Eskil Wadensjö and Christer Gerdes

10.1 Immigration, the Public Sector and the Economy – the Starting Point

Whatever the cause of international migration, the phenomenon produces economic effects in the host country and elsewhere. Immigration influences the economy of the host country in several ways. Among the effects of immigration are those which influence the public sector and economic policy. These effects can be divided into two groups. The first group results from the fact that the public sector redistributes resources among individuals and groups of individuals on the basis of factors such as family status, age, and labor market circumstances. The immigration of a group involves a transfer to and from the public sector, via taxes, transfers, and public consumption. This can result in net transfers to and from the rest of the population. The second group of factors that affect public policy results from the fact that immigration can influence a country's economy and, thereby, also indirectly influence the circumstances on which economic policy is based, as well as the policy itself.

In this chapter we deal with the fiscal impact of immigration in Denmark and Germany. In Chapter 11 we analyze the effects on wages and unemployment and also present some information on the income distribution of immigrants and natives.

10.2 Immigration and its Fiscal Impact: Theory[1]

Individuals are consumers throughout their entire lives, but are only active in production for part of this time. Children are not allowed to take employment, and after a period of employment individuals typically spend a number of years as pensioners.

---

* The data on Denmark used in Chapters 10 and 11 are from the Law model which is based in the Ministry of Finance. We wish to express gratitude to the Ministry for its very positive attitude to independent research based on their data. We especially thank Frederik Hansen for assistance with the data and for many helpful comments. We would also like to thank Jan Ekberg and Peder Pedersen for helpful comments on an earlier version.
1 See Wadensjö and Orrje (2002) for a survey of the theory and empirical studies. A recent survey, Leibfritz, O'Brien and Dumont (2003), contains some additional recent references.

What they produce during their "active" lives must not only meet the needs of their own consumption in that period, but also cover consumption expenses for people of a "passive" age, i.e. children and the elderly. This is made possible by means of a process of redistribution between the generations. This process takes place mainly in three different ways: via the family (for example, parents who provide for their children), via the market (for example, working individuals who invest in pension insurance) and via the public sector (two examples are publicly financed schools and a pension system funded by tax revenues). Redistribution between the generations via the public sector has come to be ever more important.

The redistribution of resources is carried out not only between generations, but also between individuals of "active" age. An important form of this type of redistribution is that which takes place between those who are employed and those who are not employed or who hold a job but cannot work due to illness. Resources are also redistributed from people with high incomes to those with low incomes. This is done in part via a tax system in which the amount of tax paid increases along with an increase in income, and in part via the transfer system. On the other hand, individual-oriented public consumption is generally not dependent upon the individual's wage or income, but mainly on other attributes such as age, while other types of public consumption and investment are mainly related to the size of the population.

Immigration can influence redistribution via the public sector in different ways. In most societies, immigrants are over-represented among those of active age. This implies that resources are transferred from them to the rest of society, provided that all factors other than age are equal for both groups. On the other hand, in Denmark, Germany and most other European countries, employment and wages are lower among non-Western immigrants than among natives, which would suggest a transfer to the immigrants. The matter of the direction in which resources are actually transferred is an empirical question, and the answer varies from country to country and within a given country over time.

The public sector obtains revenues from taxes and contributions and has expenditures for transfer payments and for public consumption and investment. Both revenues and expenditures are influenced by immigration. We will treat these different items in turn.

Immigrants contribute to public sector finances by paying taxes and various special contributions, such as those paid for unemployment insurance and pensions. One problem in relating taxes to individuals and groups is that it is not always clear who actually pays the taxes. It is easy to determine who pays some taxes. Income tax, for example, can be attributed to the person who formally pays the tax. A fairly easy solution can also be found for some other taxes. Value-added tax and selective purchase tax can be allocated in proportion to the consumption level of different individuals and households, and payroll taxes can be distributed in proportion to wages. The most difficult taxes to distribute are business taxes (taxes on profits, environment taxes, etc.). The degree of uncertainty surrounding this point, as well as many others, means that the type of calculations in which we are engaged should be interpreted with caution.

Transfer payments intended for specific individuals are easy to distribute. They are simply traced to the individual in question. It is more difficult, however, to find an appropriate principle for the granting of subsidies to businesses (in many cases it might not be appropriate to distribute them on individuals). Each of these transfers must be examined separately to see what the relevant principle of distribution is.

Public sector consumption can be divided into several different parts: 1) a part which is independent of the size of the population (public good), 2) a part where the extent of public sector activity depends upon the size and composition of the population, but where it is not possible to tie a particular unit to a particular person, and 3) a part which can be viewed as publicly financed private goods. It is also possible to distinguish a part 4) consisting of public sector activities directly connected to immigrants.

As regards the discussion of the various revenues and expenditure items within the public sector, it is clear that the most important principle is that expenditure should be tied to specific individuals if the expenditures vary with individual participation. This is easy in the case of transfer payments, since a direct connection can most often be made. This is also possible to do for some types of public consumption – for instance, when information is available about who attends a particular school, who has been admitted to a hospital, and so on. Sometimes this information is lacking, even in cases where individual-oriented public consumption is involved, and then it becomes necessary to work with general patterns, for example, to distribute expenditure evenly for all individuals in a particular age group. Certain kinds of expenditure cannot, as previously mentioned, even theoretically be related to specific individuals, even if the expenditure varies in accordance with the number of individuals in the economy. In such cases, general patterns and averages are the only way forward.

The way in which an analysis is carried out should depend upon the questions to be answered. The questions raised in much of the discussion are: "What effect does a marginal increase (or a non-marginal increase) in the number of immigrants moving to Denmark or Germany have on public sector finances?" and "What does the redistribution pattern between natives and immigrants look like in a given year?" – In this chapter, we try to answer the second question.

Cross-sectional studies are the most common in studies of the fiscal effects of immigration. Such studies examine the occurrence of redistribution over the course of a year (or more) between immigrants and the native population. It is important to include the children of immigrants. If they are not included, only a portion of the effects of the increase in population enters into the calculations. Data problems associated with this can arise in connection with the descendants of earlier groups of immigrants. A possible solution is to limit the investigation to a group of immigrants who arrived in the country after a particular year. The problem then is that one can generally see whatever redistribution occurs during the first decades after immigration, but not after that.

10.3 Data

10.3.1 Denmark[2]

The study of Denmark presented in this and the next chapter is based on data from the Ministry of Economic Affairs' Law Model.[3] The database contains detailed information on income, taxes, transfers, and public consumption for 1/30 (3.3 percent) of the population living in Denmark. A new model population is created every year.[4] There is also information regarding demographic variables, including whether a person is an immigrant or has a parent who is. The database also has information on employment status.

This study builds on detailed information from the Law Model covering average values for many different items for seven years – 1991 and 1995-2000 – for various groups (including groups of immigrants). For six years, 1995-2000, information covering the net transfer on the individual level combined with some other variables has been used for the analysis. For five years – 1996-2000 – data on individuals aged 18 years and older, with information for the children included as part of the net transfer for their parents, has been used. For 1995, 1998, 1999 and 2000 information on the net transfer for all, independent of age – not only those 18 years and older – has also been available, which makes it easier to see how net transfer varies over the life cycle. There is information on demographic variables – age, gender, family type, immigration status (classified by country of birth and country of birth of the parents, and year of arrival) – for net transfers between the individual and the public sector and for the individual employment rate. Information on the country of origin is divided into two categories, Western and non-Western countries. We also have separate information for the year 2000 for the same (non-Western) groups as are included in the German studies.

The major part of the public sector's costs and revenues are distributed across individuals in the Law Model.[5] The direct personal income taxes are ascribed to the individuals who pay them, and the indirect taxes are distributed across individuals in proportion to their disposable incomes.[6] Income transfers are referred to those individuals who receive them. The main part of public consumption is either dis-

---

2 See Wadensjö and Orrje (2002) for a detailed presentation of the data used.
3 See Hansen, Nicolaisen, Dehlbæck and Schnor (1991), Ministry of Economic Affairs (2000) and Ministry of Finance (2003) for presentations of the database. The Law Model is now administered by the Ministry of Finance. Knudsen, Larsen and Pedersen (1998) and Linderoth (1999) give detailed presentations of the structure of the public sector and of the tax system in Denmark.
4 The design of the Law Model has recently been changed to a panel, which means that it will be possible to follow individuals from year to year.
5 See Ministry of Economic Affairs (1997: 188-200) for a presentation of how the different items are assigned to individuals.
6 We have not taken into account the fact that the part of the income saved may vary between groups, including variation between immigrants and natives.

tributed according to information on actual use (for example school, health care and old age care) or evenly divided over the population. Public investment (for example road investments) is also evenly distributed across the whole population (both native Danes and immigrants). The public sector costs, which are not distributed across individuals and therefore not included in the Law Model, are such costs that are assumed to be independent of the size of the population. Some examples are central state administration, defence, and some subsidies to the private sector (especially agriculture).[7]

The variable net transfer to the public sector is calculated for each individual as the difference between the taxes ascribed to the individual and the sum of income transfers and public consumption and investment ascribed to the same individual. Compared to an analysis by the Ministry of Economic Affairs[8] in 1995 there is one important difference as regards the items included in the calculation. In the analysis presented here, the costs for refugees in the period before they know if they will obtain refugee status or not are excluded. We consider those costs to be a part of the regulation of immigration and as such part of the border control costs.

The basic principles for the Law Model have been the same for all of the years covered by this study. However, there are some variations as to the extent to which it has been possible to attribute the transfers and other public expenditure to individuals.

The Law Model contains many observations covering almost 140,000 people aged 18 or over for every year. The large sample means that quite a few immigrants are included in the database – almost 3,000 from Western countries and more than 5,000 from non-Western countries. The groups who have foreign backgrounds are considerably larger in 2000 than in 1991.[9] This is especially so for first and second generation immigrants from non-Western countries. In spite of the large total number of immigrants the number of observations is rather small for studying certain groups of immigrants, for example immigrants belonging to a certain age group.

The employment rate is an important variable in many of the analyses. An individual's employment rate varies between 0 and 100 per cent. In order to be counted as having an employment rate of 100 per cent, a person must have worked full-time during the entire year. There are some problems regarding the definition of full-time. The working hours are calculated by using contributions to the ATP pension scheme. Since 1993, a person who has 27 or more working hours a week has had to pay a full contribution and is counted as working full-time in the Law Model.[10] A person who

---

7 See le Maire and Scheuer (2001) for a detailed presentation of what is and what is not distributed across individuals in the 1998 Law Model.
8 See Ministry of Economic Affairs (1997) and Indenrigsministeriet (1999).
9 See Chapter 2 in this book for more details.
10 The ATP contribution is also paid if a person is unemployed or on sick leave, but such periods are not included in the calculation of the employment rate.

works at least 18 hours, but less than 27 hours, pays two-thirds of the full contribution and is counted as having an employment rate of two-thirds (of course given that the person works throughout the entire year). Those who work at least 9 hours but less than 18 hours pay one-third of the full contribution and are counted as working one-third of full-time.[11] Those working less than 9 hours a week on a regular basis do not pay any ATP contribution and are not counted as employed.

Those who are self-employed, and the wives or husbands who work in their family businesses are counted as having an employment rate of 100 per cent if the income is the same or higher than the maximum benefit level in the unemployment insurance. If the income for the self-employed is below that level and non-negative, the employment rate is proportionally reduced. For the self-employed with a negative income from that activity, the employment rate is set at zero. For those who are part-time self-employed and part-time in someone else's employ, the two employment rates are added, but the employment rate is never set higher than 100.

This method of calculation of working hours means that the rate of employment will not be correctly estimated for a number of people. For quite a few there will be an overestimation. People with long part-time work (for example 30 hours a week) will be counted as working full-time. Most likely more women than men will be wrongly classified in this way. The lower limit of 9 hours probably means that young people who are combining high school or university studies with odd jobs are wrongly counted as having an employment rate of 0. It is also not possible to see if people are working more than the full-time rate of 37 hours a week with this method. Another problem is that those aged 67 or older do not pay an ATP contribution and therefore we do not know their employment rate.

The uncertainties in the calculations of the working week and the resulting uncertainties in calculations of the employment rate also mean that the calculation of the hourly wage by using information on the earnings and employment rate will be uncertain, but the method is fairly robust building on experiences with other micro-data sets.

10.3.2 Germany

For Germany, an interview survey (the RFMS-D data) has been the starting point for the calculation of the individual net transfers to the public sector. For the estimation we need information on taxes, income transfers, public consumption and public investments related to individuals or population size. Various types of information have been used, both information from the interviews and aggregated data from various elements of the public sector. This means that the income transfer informa-

---

11 Full-time work in Denmark is 37 hours a week. Working full time and for a full year, excluding the vacation period and public holidays, entails 1,692.5 hours a year. This figure is used in the calculation of the hourly wage rate.

tion created is a mixture of individual information and the average situation for an individual of given age and gender in Germany. The aim has not been to get an exact estimate of the net transfer for each individual interviewed. If this had been done, there would have been information missing; for example, we would not have taken into account the costs for institutional care, as everyone who was interviewed was living in their own home. The procedure for ensuring that these costs were also distributed across the individuals interviewed may be seen as a way of taking into account the probability of being placed in an institution for a person of the relevant type (in terms of age and gender). Of course, it would have been better if those who are placed in institutions had also been interviewed and thus included as individual observations; but given the focus of this study, the method is reasonable. In our case the focus is on the total net transfers for the groups included in the study and the importance of individual characteristics. There exist calculations of a similar type in other studies (for example Bonin 2002), but in those studies the starting point has been to study the total effects for the public sector, both for the present and for the future. The focus in those studies has been on the long-run viability of the present obligations of the public sector.[12] The approach has been to distribute *all* taxes, income transfers and other public expenditure across individuals. This means for example that taxes that cannot be related to specific individuals such as company taxes are also distributed across individuals.

The starting point is the information given by the persons interviewed. The calculations are more individual and less schematic with regard to incomes, taxes and income transfers received when it is based on the interviews. The method used makes it possible to take into account the facts that the income tax is progressive and that married couples are taxed together.[13] Then it is feasible to investigate to what extent year of arrival, education and demographic variables influence the individual net transfer to the public sector. With respect to the distribution of aggregate data, we distribute revenues and costs which are related to individuals. In some cases the distinction is difficult to make; for example, investments in infrastructure such as road investments are related both to individuals and to firms.

To estimate the net transfer profiles we build on earlier studies made within the tradition of "generational accounting".[14] These studies provide information about the availability of aggregated data for Germany and methods of data handling. The studies by Holger Bonin (2001) and Stephan Boll (1994) have been of particular value

---

12 This type of accounting is called "generational accounting" in Anglo-Saxon literature.
13 In earlier generational accounting studies in Germany, the distribution across individuals of taxes on labor income has been based on information from the individuals included in the German Socio-economic Panel (GSOEP). This information has been applied to all the population (see Boll 1994). Such information on income taxes on the individual level is not available in our interview material but has been estimated with the use of information regarding the individual's income (labor income and other income) and the income of the spouse.
14 We have tried to follow the principles of the Danish Law Model as closely as possible.

for the calculations made for this study. In some cases we have not had access to the same information, but we believe that the data is of high enough quality to satisfactorily perform the analyses. In the distribution of aggregate data it has not been possible in most cases to make a distinction between natives and immigrants. This is particularly the case with regard to public consumption, for example expenditure for public investments, public administration etc. Where the costs are distributed across individuals, they are distributed with a few exceptions by an equal amount for each individual, the same for natives and immigrants.[15]

The costs for social insurances (of those types not covered by the interviews) are ascribed to individuals according to age and gender. This means that natives and immigrants have been assumed to have the same costs if they are of the same age and gender. Those costs for social insurances which has not been possible to allocate using information from the interviews or according to age and gender are distributed equally on all residents, natives or immigrants. This is the same method as used by Boll (1994).

It could be argued that it is unsatisfactory that not more of the costs and the incomes for the public sector were distributed by explicitly taking into account immigrant status, but the statistical sources only allowed us to do this to a limited extent. It is also uncommon to make a distinction between Western and non-Western immigrants in the official statistics regarding public sector incomes and costs, which would have been of interest for the present study.

This means that the variations in net transfer to the public sector beside those related to gender and age are mainly explained by variations in the answers of the people interviewed regarding income and income transfers, and the variations in tax payments and contributions to the social insurance schemes calculated on the basis of that information. It is difficult to say if this results in overestimates or underestimates of the figures that would have been produced if we had had access to more detailed data. For older people it is most likely that we overestimate the costs as immigrants more often receive care by relatives in the home instead of in institutions than is the case for natives. On the other hand, the expenses for education could be underestimated for immigrants as their children go to *Sonderschulen*, which are more expensive than other primary schools, more often than natives of the same age.[16]

As explained earlier, we will not go into detail here about the data we used for the calculations. For such a presentation see Gerdes (2004).

---

15 The methods used are described below and in much more detail in Gerdes (2004). According to Bonin (2002) the immigrants enhance the costs for the public sector with the marginal cost, the value of which, however, is difficult to determine. A uniform distribution on all individuals with the average cost is, however, an acceptable approximation according to Bonin. An exception is the costs for schools and universities. We have distributed those costs on the basis of average costs from Statistisches Bundesamt, and the answers from the interviewed individuals (if the individual attends an institution of education or not).
16 See Chapter 3 in this book for more details on the educational system in Germany.

10.4 The Fiscal Impact of Immigration in Denmark, 1991-2000[17]

We will start by studying the fiscal impact of immigration in Denmark on the aggregate level. In Table 10.1 the calculations for 1991 and 1995-2000 regarding the average net transfer per person of 18 years and older to the public sector are given for various groups (the transfers to and from children of 17 years or younger are added to those of their parents).[18]

From the last line in the table we can see that the average amount for all residents in Denmark is positive and increasing over time. This is not to be seen as indicating that Denmark has a large and increasing budget surplus. Rather it can be explained by the fact that a larger part of the revenues of the public sector (taxes and contributions) than of the costs for public consumption and investments are distributed across individuals. The reason that a large part of the public sector expenditure has not been distributed is that it is assumed that it is not sensitive to (marginal) changes in the size of the population. It is possible that it would have been better if a larger part had been distributed.[19] The immigration to Denmark (and Germany) is hardly a marginal phenomenon any more, which means that most types of public expenditure, also for roads, central governmental administration, and defense, vary to some extent with the population. We have made the choice here, however, to continue to follow the same procedure as in earlier studies based on the Law Model.

For immigrants from Western countries the net transfer to the public sector is positive all the time. It declined between 1991 and 1995, which can be ascribed to the decline in activity in the Danish economy, and gradually increased in the second half of the 1990s. The figures are even higher for second generation immigrants from Western countries. The figures are also positive for native Danes and increase from year to year.

For immigrants from non-Western countries the amounts are strongly negative the entire time. There is always a net transfer from the public sector to this group of immigrants. These net transfers increase markedly – more was transferred per person – from 1991 to 1995, and the trend continued in the same direction in 1996, though to a lesser degree. The public sector transfers in 1996 were EUR 8,900 per non-Western immigrant of 18 years and older. The net transfers declined markedly between 1996 and 1998 when the economic and labor-market situation improved. As business activity continued to improve in 1999 and 2000 there were reasons to

---

17 See Ministry of Economic Affairs (1997), Wadensjö (2000, 2000a, 2002), Wadensjö and Orrje (2002) and le Maire and Scheuer (2003) for earlier studies.
18 We also have information for 1995, 1998, 1999 and 2000 for all individuals separately. The net transfers of the children are in this case ascribed to themselves. We will also use that data in this chapter.
19 For a discussion of this issue see, for example, Ekberg (1999) and Gott and Johnston (2002).

Table 10.1. Net transfers to the public sector (in Euro)[20] for different groups in 1991 and 1995-2000, per individual 18 years and older. The amounts in 1997 prices are shown in parentheses.

Group	1991	1995	1996	1997	1998	1999	2000
Danish population (excluding those who have one immigrant parent)	1,800 (2,000)	2,100 (2,200)	2,500 (2,600)	3,100	3,400 (3,300)	3,700 (3,500)	4,000 (3,700)
Second generation – two parents from Western countries	2,600 (2,900)	2,500 (2,700)	3,700 (3,800)	4,600	2,600 (2,600)	5,400 (5,200)	6,800 (6,300)
Immigrants from Western countries	2,000 (2,100)	1,300 (1,300)	1,500 (1,500)	1,800	3,200 (3,200)	3,400 (3,200)	5,300 (5,000)
Immigrants from Western countries (first and second generation)	2,000 (2,200)	1,400 (1,500)	1,700 (1,700)	2,000	3,200 (3,100)	3,600 (3,500)	5,500 (5,100)
Second generation – two parents from non-Western countries	90 (100)	-4,400 (-4,500)	-1,600 (-1,600)	-1,800	300 (300)	-2,100 (-2,000)	-1,700 (-1,600)
Immigrants from non-Western countries	-6,600 (-7,200)	-8,600 (-9,000)	-8,900 (-9,100)	-8,100	-7,300 (-7,100)	-7,500 (-7,200)	-7,900 (-7,400)
Immigrants from non-Western countries (first and second generation)	-6,500 (-7,100)	-8,400 (-8,800)	-8,600 (-8,800)	-7,800	-6,900 (-6,800)	-7,200 (-6,900)	-7,500 (-7,000)
Total	1,600 (1,800)	1,700 (1,800)	2,000 (2,100)	2,600	2,900 (2,900)	3,200 (3,100)	3,500 (3,200)

Note: Western countries are the EU countries, Norway, Switzerland, Iceland, North America, Australia and New Zealand; non-Western countries are all other countries.

expect a continued decline in the net transfers to the non-Western immigrants in those years.[21] That did not happen, however; to the contrary, the net transfer was slightly higher in 2000 than in 1998 in real terms. This development differs markedly from that for Danes and Western immigrants, for whom the net transfers *to* the public sector increased between 1998 and 2000.

We have also studied the question of whether the net transfers to the public sector from non-Western immigrants vary with the length of stay in Denmark.[22] There are some differences, but they are not as large as we would have expected from the experiences of the U.K. and the U.S., for example. The net transfers to the immigrants are largest to those who have been in the country for 3-5 years.

20 We have in Chapters 10 and 11 in all calculations converted Danish *kroner* to Euro at the rate 1 EUR =7.424 DKK.
21 See Wadensjö and Orrje (2002).
22 For more details on how immigrants gradually establish themselves on the Danish labor market see Chapter 4 in this book. See especially Figure 4.3.

There are some variations between the years of study in the pattern according to length of stay, but the general pattern is the same. Even for those who have lived in Denmark for a long period the net transfers go from the public sector to individuals. A contributing factor may be that a gradually better labor market situation with longer stay in Denmark may be countervailed by changes in the household composition.

Table 10.1 shows that there are large variations between the years in the net transfer for the second generation immigrants, both Western and non-Western. A contributing factor to the large variations in the net transfers from and to second generation immigrants, especially those from non-Western countries, is that there are large changes in the size and composition of these groups. The majority are of the age when many are entering the labor market (which generally means going from negative to positive net transfers to the public sector). A small change in the age composition may lead to large changes in the size of the net transfers. Another explanation for the large variations is that the groups are small, which means that the inclusion of a person with very high positive net transfers one year but not another year may strongly influence the results.

In the public debate it is not the net transfers per person that have been of most interest, but figures for the total net transfers from the immigrants to the public sector. The total net transfers are also those which are of most interest in discussing the total economic effects of immigration. The total transfers from a group depend on the transfers per person and the number of persons in the group. Information on the total net transfers is presented in Table 10.2.

For the Western immigrants there exists a substantial net transfer *to* the public sector in all the years for which we have information. The net transfer declined somewhat in the first half of the 1990s and has gradually increased since then. The amount was EUR 521 million in the year 2000.

The pattern is quite different for immigrants from non-Western countries. The net transfers to these immigrants were already large in the early 1990s and they increased twofold by 1996. The net transfers declined in two years, 1997 and 1998, but increased again in 1999 and 2000 (mainly due to an increase in the size of the group, less due to an increase in the amount per person).

Another measure of the size of the transfers is given by comparing them with Denmark's GDP in the same years. In 1991, the total net transfers to immigrants, Western and non-Western, corresponded to 0.41 percent of the GDP. This amount increased to 0.81 percent in 1996. Between 1996 and 1998, it declined to 0.56 percent and was 0.54 percent of the GDP in 2000. If we only consider the net transfers to the non-Western immigrants the corresponding figures were 0.54 percent in 1991, 0.91 percent in 1996, 0.75 percent in 1998 and 0.84 percent in the year 2000.

One of the main results shown in Tables 10.1 and 10.2 is that the figures are very different for the different groups of immigrants. There is a net transfer from the Western immigrants to the public sector, and a net transfer to the non-Western

Table 10.2. Total net transfers to the public sector (in million Euro) for different groups in 1991 and 1995-2000. The amounts in 1997 prices are shown in parentheses.

Group	1991	1995	1996	1997	1998	1999	2000
Second generation – parents from Western countries	17 (18)	17 (17)	28 (28)	34	19 (18)	41 (39)	54 (51)
Immigrants from Western countries	141 (155)	109 (113)	123 (125)	142	284 (278)	297 (285)	466 (434)
Immigrants from Western countries (first and second generation)	158 (173)	125 (131)	150 (154)	176	302 (297)	338 (324)	521 (485)
Second generation – parents from non-Western countries	0.1 (0.1)	-20 (-21)	-9 (-9)	-12	2 (2)	-20 (19)	-19 (-18)
Immigrants from non-Western countries	-654 (-719)	-1,134 (-1,182)	-1,303 (-1,330)	-1,242	-1,184 (-1,162)	-1,271 (-1,218)	-1,433 (-1,334)
Immigrants from non-Western countries (first and second generation)	-645 (-719)	-1,154 (-1,203)	-1,312 (-1,340)	-1,254	-1,182 (-1,160)	-1,290 (-1,237)	-1,452 (-1,352)
All immigrants (first and second generation)	-496 (-545)	-1,029 (-1,072)	-1,162 (-1,186)	-1,079	-880 (-864)	-952 (-913)	-931 (-867)
Immigrants from Western countries (first and second generation) as percent of GDP	+0.13	+0.09	+0.10	+0.12	+0.19	+0.21	+0.30
Immigrants from non-Western countries (first and second generation) as percent of GDP	-0.54	-0.85	-0.91	-0.84	-0.75	-0.79	-0.84
All immigrants as percent of GDP	-0.41	-0.76	-0.81	-0.72	-0.56	-0.58	-0.54

Note: Western countries are the EU countries, Norway, Switzerland, Iceland, North America, Australia and New Zealand; non-Western countries are all other countries.

immigrants from the public sector. Another result that can be seen is that in total, net transfers go to the immigrants from the public sector. The same pattern of net transfers is found in Norway and Sweden and also in some other Western European countries, but not for all immigration countries. According to a recent study, total net transfers in the U.K. go from the immigrants to the public sector.[23]

---

23 See Gott and Johnston (2002). For a comprehensive survey of studies in the field, see Chapter 3 in Wadensjö and Orrje (2002).

Table 10.3. Net transfers to the public sector in Germany in 2002 for different groups of immigrants (foreign citizens) per individual (aged 17 and older); children's net transfers added to those of their parents.

Group	Amounts in Euro		
	First generation	Second generation	First and second generation
Iran	-2,254	-2,903	-2,274
Lebanon	-11,831	-8,115	-11,698
Poland	-2,423	1,199	-2,095
Turkey	-5,962	-2,546	-5,213
Former Yugoslavia	-3,575	622	-3,161
All	-5,107	-1,668	-4,744

10.5 The Fiscal Impact of Immigration in Germany 2002

For Germany we have data for one year, 2002, and not for natives and Western immigrants but only for immigrants (foreign citizens) from five non-Western countries – Iran, Lebanon, Poland, Turkey and the former Yugoslavia. This means that our results are only partly comparable with those from Denmark.

Table 10.3 gives information on net transfers for the five different groups separately and for them all taken together. Like Denmark, the net transfers in Germany go from the public sector to the first generation of immigrants. The amounts are lower than those for first generation non-Western immigrants in Denmark. There could be many factors contributing to this difference between Denmark and Germany: differences in the countries of origin, differences in the periods of stay, differences in the functioning of labor markets in the two countries, differences in the tax, income transfer and public consumption systems, and of course differences in the data sources used. Even if there is a clear difference in the size of the average individual net transfer between the two host countries it should be underlined that the main result is the same – the net transfer goes to the immigrants from the public sector.

It is of interest to note the large differences between the five different groups of immigrants. The net transfers are largest to the group from Lebanon and lowest to the groups from Iran and Poland. The groups from Turkey and the former Yugoslavia have values in between. These differences should be seen in the light of the differences in labor market integration shown in other chapters in this book.

The transfers to the second generation immigrants are much lower on average, just as in Denmark. There is one exception to that general pattern – second generation immigrants from Iran receive slightly larger net transfers than first generation immigrants from the same country. It should also be noted that the net transfer for

Table 10.4. Net transfers to the public sector in Denmark in 2000 for different groups of first generation immigrants per individual (aged 17 and older); children's net transfers added to those of their parents.

Group	Amounts in Euro
Iran	-5,381
Lebanon	-17,974
Poland	-2,098
Turkey	-9,181
Former Yugoslavia	-6,167
All	-8,179

the second generation immigrants from Poland and the former Yugoslavia goes from the immigrants to the public sector. The high net transfers to the second generation immigrants from Lebanon are especially remarkable, underlining the fact that this group is less integrated in the economy than the other four groups included in the study.

The information presented in Table 10.3 can be compared with the corresponding figures for the same immigrant groups in Denmark. Note that we only have information for first generation immigrants in Denmark when we present information for separate countries of origin. See Table 10.4.

If we compare the figures in the two tables we find that the patterns are similar in the two countries but that the net transfers from the public sector are larger in Denmark than in Germany with the exception of immigrants from Poland. For the four other groups the net transfer from the public sector is about 50 percent higher in Denmark than in Germany.

10.6 Which Factors Influence the Individual Net Transfers to the Public Sector in Denmark and in Germany?

10.6.1 Denmark

Up to now we have considered the net transfers per person and aggregated for various groups. We will now examine how different factors influence the individual net transfers and we will start with Denmark.

In all societies transfers go from those of active to those of passive age. It is typical for welfare societies like Denmark that these transfers go through the public sector to a very large extent. This means that the size of the average net transfer for a group largely depends on the age composition of the group. Among immigrants few are old and many are children or young people. The fact that few immigrants are old is a factor leading to low net transfers to the group, and the fact that many are children is a factor leading in the opposite direction. It is an empirical question to determine which effects are the most important. There is also a net transfer between men and women through the public sector, and a corresponding unregistered transfer in the form of unpaid household work in the other direction within households. Since women work less in the market economy (and more in households), they pay less tax. This will be of importance in the individual analysis, but less so when studying aggregate figures, as the gender composition is more or less the same in all groups.[24]

We will illustrate the importance of the age composition by showing how the net transfers vary with age for natives, Western immigrants and non-Western immigrants. Here children are considered separately; the net transfers for them are not added to those of their parents.

Figure 10.1 shows that there is a net transfer to children and young people in all three groups. In the same way there is a net transfer to older people. For natives and Western immigrants the net transfer to the public sector changes to a net transfer from the public sector at around the age of 60. From that age the net transfers from the public sector gradually increase with age. It is the costs for health and nursing care that especially increase with age. There are few immigrants who are 68 years old and over and therefore we have used the figures for natives to represent immigrants who are of that age; otherwise outliers would have had too large an influence. In the figure we have also smoothed the variations by showing the average for three years of age (for example, the value for 42 years stands for an average of the values of those who are 41, 42 and 43 years old).

If we study those who are 20 to 60 years old, there are both similarities and dissimilarities between the groups. For native Danes and Western immigrants the pattern is more or less the same. Among young adults the net transfers are lower among Western immigrants, which may be explained by the fact that they study to a greater extent. Some of them have also come to Denmark to study. The students have low or no incomes and therefore pay less in taxes. However, the large difference is between non-Western immigrants on the one hand and natives and Western immigrants on the other. For non-Western immigrants the net transfer in almost all one-year age groups, even among those of active age, goes in the direction from the public sector to the immigrants. The reason for this is of course that this group is poorly integrated into the Danish labor market. We will return later to the importance of the relation between employment and net transfers.

It is particularly interesting to see if the development of the net transfers from the second generation of immigrants is more like that of the natives. In Figure 10.2 we compare the net transfer from the second generation of Western and non-Western

---

24 See Chapter 2 for more information on this issue.

Figure 10.1. Net transfers to the public sector per person (three-year average) in 2000

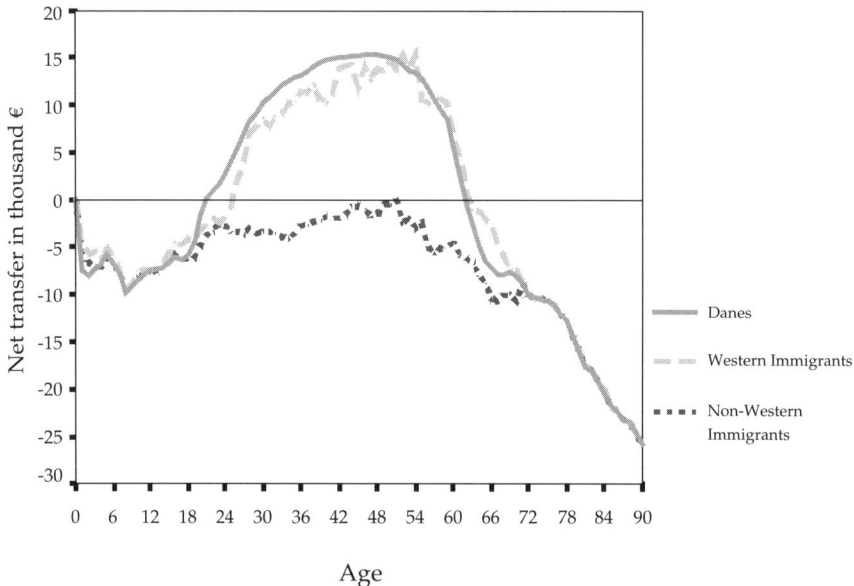

Note. The actual average values have been used for those aged 0-70 years. For those aged 71 and older the values for natives have been used for all three groups as there are so few observations for older immigrants.

Figure 10.2. Net transfers to the public sector per person (three-year average) in 2000; Danes and second generation Western and non-Western immigrants

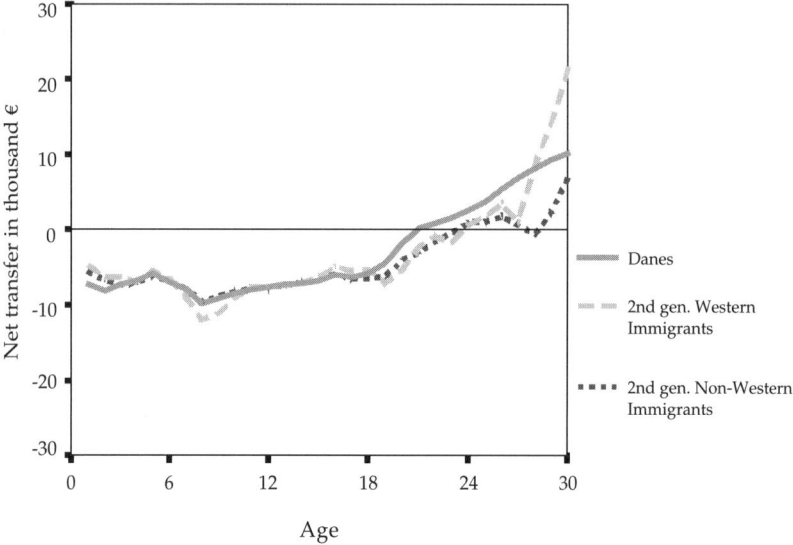

Figure 10.3. Tax payments (three-year average) in 2000

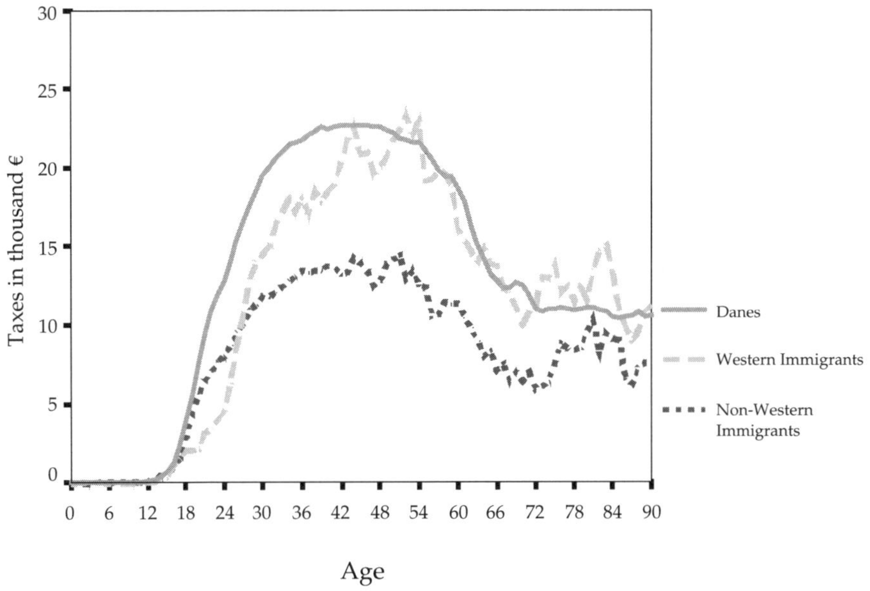

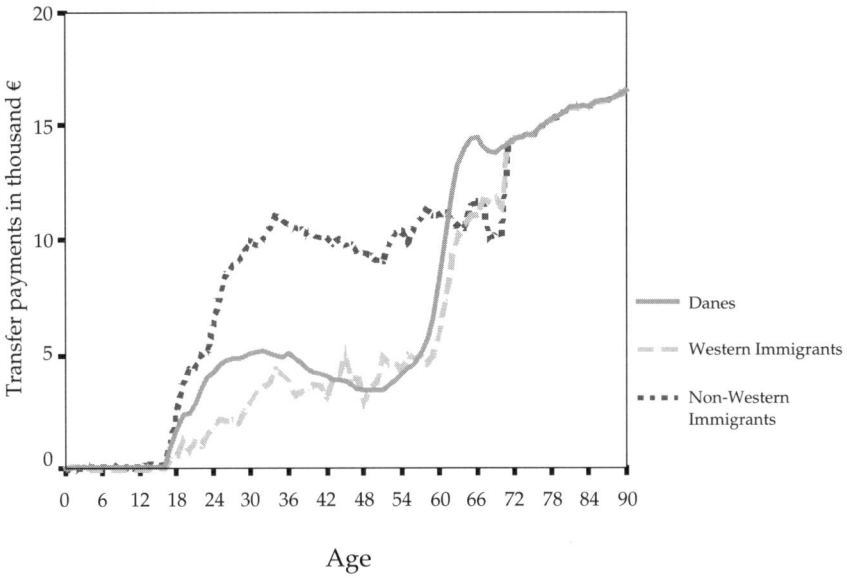

Note: Those under the age of 18 are also included with data of their own.

Figure 10.4. Transfer payments from the public sector according to age (three-year average) in 2000

Note: Those under the age of 18 are also included with data of their own. The actual average values have been used for those aged 0-70 years. For those aged 71 and older the values for natives have been used for all three groups as there are so few observations for older immigrants.

Figure 10.5. Public consumption according to age (three-year average) in 2000

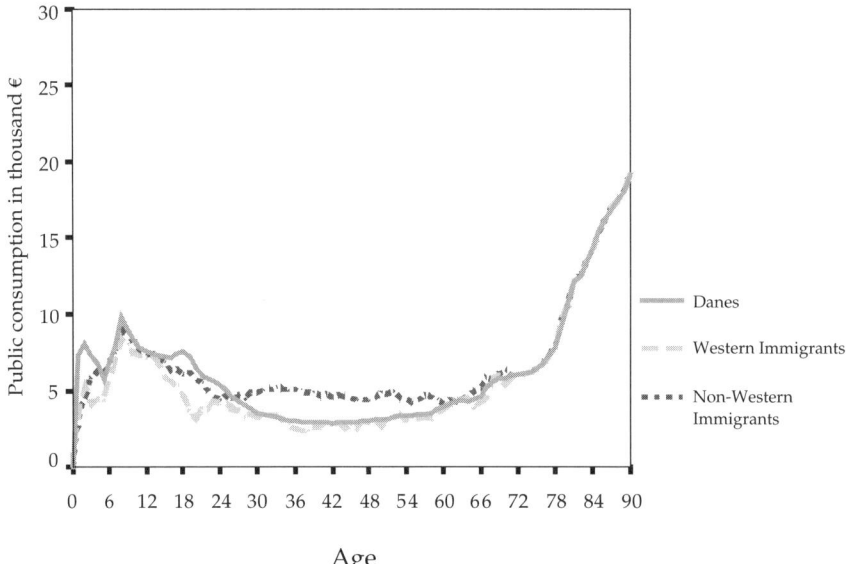

Note: Those under the age of 18 are also included with data of their own. The actual average values have been used for those aged 0-70 years. For those aged 71 and older the values for natives have been used for all three groups, as there are so few observations for older immigrants.

immigrants with that of natives. As there are only a few second-generation non-Western immigrants aged 30 and over we restrict the age interval to up to 30 years. The figure shows that the net transfer to the public sector is lower than for the native population of the same age for second generation non-Western immigrants. But the age profile of the net transfer for the two groups are much more similar than for natives and first generation non-Western immigrants; for the second generation net transfers even are very positive. The second generation Western immigrants have a pattern of net transfers which is more like that of the natives than that of the non-Western immigrants.

We will now turn to the three main components of the net transfers: taxes, income transfers and public consumption. Figure 10.3 shows how tax payments vary with age for the three groups: natives, immigrants from Western countries and immigrants from non-Western countries. Figures 10.4 and 10.5 show the corresponding pattern for transfer payments and public consumption. Large differences between the non-Western group and the other two groups can be seen with respect to taxes and transfer payments. The non-Western immigrants are in employment less often than the other groups, and therefore pay less in taxes and receive more in transfer payments (unemployment benefits, social welfare payments).

We will now continue by examining how much of the difference between immigrants and natives in net transfers to the public sector is possible to explain by demographic factors such as age, gender and family status, by education, and by variables representing integration on the labor market and the economy such as employment, earnings, and labor income (earnings plus income from self-employment). The analysis is based on a regression analysis with net transfer as the dependent variable, where we gradually include new independent variables to see how the differences in the coefficients representing various groups of immigrants change. The native Danish group is the reference group at all times. See Table 10.5. The net transfers to children below 18 years of age are added to those of their parents.

Table 10.5. Difference in net transfer to the public sector per person aged 18 years and older in 2000 (in thousand Euro) according to regression estimates between those who are first and second generation immigrants and Danes (both parents born in Denmark).

Group	Controls for other variables than country of origin					
	no controls	age, gender, family status	as (2) and education	as (3) and employment rate	as (3) and earnings	as (3) and labor income
	(1)	(2)	(3)	(4)	(5)	(6)
Born in Denmark						
One parent born in Denmark, one in a Western country	1.9***	0.4	-0.6	0.6	-0.1	0.1
One parent born in Denmark, one in a non-Western country	-0.4	-0.2	-1.0	1.0	0.6	0.7
Both parents born in a Western country	3.0**	-1.7	0.3	2.8***	1.6*	1.2
Both parents born in a non-Western country	-5.7***	-2.5***	-1.1***	2.6***	1.5*	0.9
Born outside Denmark						
Born in a Western country	0.7	0.6	-1.5***	3.1***	2.1***	2.2***
Born in a non-Western country	-11.7***	-12.3***	-12.3***	-1.5***	-1.7***	-0.6***

Notes: *** = significant difference between the cross-section and panel estimates on the 1 percent level; ** = significant difference on the 5 percent level; * = significant difference on the 10 percent level. Calculation based on 10 family status groups: single or cohabiting, and with 0, 1, 2, 3, or 4 or more children. Age is represented with one linear and one quadratic term. Eight educational groups. Net transfers to children under 18 are added to those of their parents.

In the first column no other variables than those representing immigrant groups have been included in the estimation. The differences between the groups are in accordance with those in Table 10.1.[25] Note that the comparison is with the reference group (the Danes) in Table 10.4 (and not as in Table 10.1 with zero). Table 10.5 shows that net transfer to the public sector is about the same for first generation Western immigrants and native Danes (the difference is not statistically significant), positive for the second generation immigrants from the same countries, large and negative for the second generation non-Western immigrant group (5,700 EUR), and even more so for the first generation from the same countries (11,700 EUR).

In the second column age, gender and family status are included among the independent variables. For most immigrant groups the coefficients are small and close to zero – i.e. close to the values of Danes. There are two exceptions: first and second generation immigrants from non-Western countries. The value of the coefficient for the first generation is close to that shown in column 1, and the value of the coefficient for the second generation is lower than in column 2 (the net transfer from the public sector is smaller).

If we include variables representing education (column 3), the value of the coefficient for the first generation does not change, but the value of the coefficient for the second generation immigrants declines. We now also get a significant negative effect for the group of first generation Western immigrants.

The next step is to control for the individual labor market situation. This is done in columns 4, 5 and 6. In column 4 the employment rate is included. The net transfer from the public sector is markedly reduced for non-Western immigrants – from 12,300 to 1,500 Euro (column 4). It shows that the low employment rate explains the major part of the difference in net transfer between that group and Danes. For the other groups the coefficient value becomes positive and significantly different from zero in some of the cases.

The employment rate is not the only factor that determines labor income. It also depends on the wage rate for employees and the income from self-employment for those employed in that way. In column 5 the employment rate is replaced by earnings and in column 6 with labor income (earnings plus income from self-employment). The results change somewhat, but not very much. The demographic and the education variables probably took care of much of the variation in the wage rate in the earlier estimations.

There is an implicit assumption in Table 10.5 that the labor market variables have the same effects for the different groups. We test that assumption by making

---

25 The division in groups is different than in Table 10.1. Another difference is that a small group of young people who left home before the age of 18 is not included.

Table 10.6. Effect on net transfers according to regression estimates (in thousand Euro in current prices) if a person instead of being non-employed had been employed full-time and all year; for different groups.

Group	Effect on net transfer in thousand Euro if a person instead of being non-employed had been employed full-time, all-year				
	1996	1997	1998	1999	2000
Born in Denmark					
Both parents born in Denmark	26	27	28	29	31
Both parents born in Western countries	27	29	27	31	37
Both parents born in non-Western countries	17	20	25	21	25
Born outside Denmark					
Born in a Western country	23	23	23	24	26
Born in a non-Western country	26	25	25	27	29

Note: The other independent variables included in the regressions, but for which estimates are not shown here, are age, age-squared, female, and the family status variables (four categories).

separate estimates for each group and looking at the coefficients for the employment rate, earnings and labor income. These estimates are shown in Tables 10.6, 10.7 and 10.8. In all estimations the net transfers to children below 18 are added to the net transfers of their parents.

The coefficients for the employment rate are shown in Table 10.6. We show how much greater a net transfer a person would have had if the employment rate was 100 instead of 0. We see that there are some variations over time (partly explained by inflation) and between different groups. The most remarkable thing, however, is that the effects are rather similar in size for native Danes, Western immigrants and non-Western immigrants. This underlines the importance of employment for the net transfer to the public sector.

The estimates contained in Table 10.6 do not show from which value the net transfer starts when the employment rate changes from 0 to 100. This value can be calculated by using the same regression equations. We have calculated the initial values by using the average values of both continuous and dummy variables, and the value of zero for the employment rate. The results, the initial values, are given in Table 10.6.a.

The figures are all negative but the estimates differ due to differences in the age, gender and family status composition of the various groups. Note also that the values in Table 10.6 in all cases are larger than the initial values in Table 10.6.a. Full employment means a net transfer to the public sector for all groups.

Table 10.6.a. Initial values of net transfers (in thousand Euro in current prices) calculated by using the same regression equation as in Table 10.6, assuming that the employment rate is zero and that all other variables are at average values

	Initial values (i.e., for a non-employed individual) in thousand Euro				
Group	1996	1997	1998	1999	2000
Born in Denmark					
Both parents born in Denmark	-12	-12	-13	-13	-13
Both parents born in Western countries	-11	-13	-11	-11	-14
Both parents born in non-Western countries	-10	-10	-10	-11	-12
Born outside Denmark					
Born in a Western country	-9	-8	-7	-7	-7
Born in a non-Western country	-15	-15	-15	-16	-17

Note: In addition to the employment rate, the independent variables included in the regressions are age, age-squared, female, and the family status variables (four categories).

In the next step, Table 10.7, we study the effects of a change in earnings. It can be seen as the marginal "net tax" effect: How much of each extra earned Danish *krone* goes to strengthening the public finances? We see that the marginal effect is higher for those from non-Western countries than for natives. This can be explained by the importance of the transfer payments for those with low incomes and by the fact that these payments are reduced with increased earnings. As the immigrants are lower paid, they more often receive reduced transfer payments when their earnings increase.

In Table 10.8 the corresponding estimates for labor income are shown. The incomes from self-employment are also included. The pattern is the same, with the greatest marginal effects for non-Western immigrants. The large marginal effects show that measures which lead to employment for immigrants may have positive effects on public finances even if the initial costs are high. A requisite is of course that the measures actually lead to a higher employment rate and higher incomes from labor.

The main conclusion of this analysis is that net transfers are influenced by several different types of variables. Both demographic variables and education are of importance. However, if we study the differences in net transfers to the public sector between natives and first generation immigrants from non-Western countries, those variables are not very important. The main part of the differences in net transfer to the public sector is explained instead by the fact that, given those variables, non-Western immigrants have a lower employment rate and thus lower incomes from labor.

Table 10.7. Effect on net transfers according to regression estimates as percent of a change of earnings for different groups

Group	Effect on net transfers as percent of a change in earnings			
	1996	1998	1999	2000
Born in Denmark				
Both parents born in Denmark	69.6	69.8	70.8	72.8
Both parents born in Western countries	69.0	66.5	67.8	76.6
Both parents born in non-Western countries	71.8	53.2	82.2	76.4
Born outside Denmark				
Born in a Western country	66.0	65.0	67.1	74.3
Born in a non-Western country	88.8	77.9	83.2	81.8

Note: The other independent variables included in the regressions, but for which estimates are not shown here, are age, age-squared, female, and the family status variables (four categories).

Table 10.8. Effect on net transfers according to regression estimates as percent of a change of labor income for different groups

Group	Effect on net transfers as percent of a change in labor income			
	1996	1998	1999	2000
Born in Denmark				
Both parents born in Denmark	68.6	68.1	70.3	73.0
Both parents born in Western countries	42.4	72.4	66.8	68.4
Both parents born in non-Western countries	79.4	70.9	84.7	82.7
Born outside Denmark				
Born in a Western country	67.7	64.8	73.1	61.9
Born in a non-Western country	88.3	80.3	81.4	81.8

Note: The other independent variables included in the regressions, but for which estimates are not shown here, are age, age-squared, female, and the family status variables (four categories).

Figure 10.6. Net transfer to the public sector from the immigrants in Germany (three-year average) in 2002 (net transfers for children are not added to those of their parents). Each group of immigrants is weighted with a factor that corresponds to its size

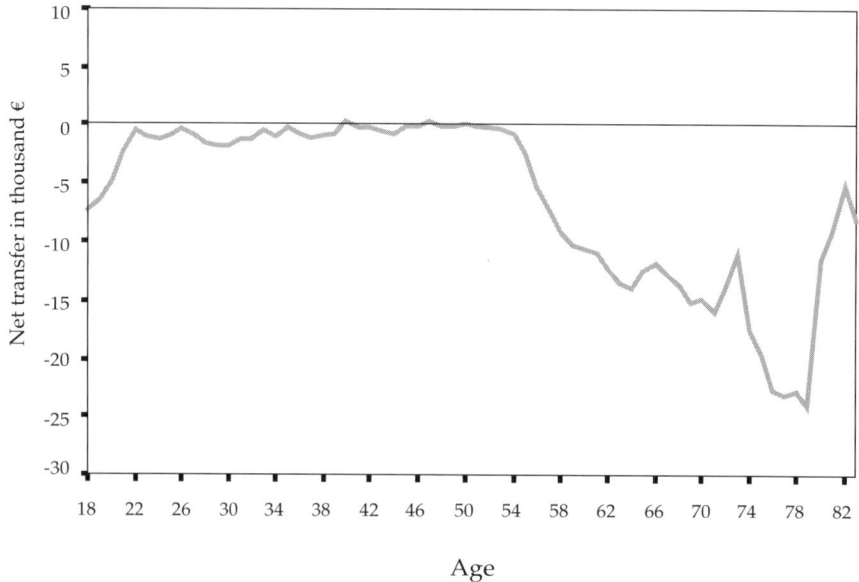

10.6.2 Germany

We will now turn to Germany and start by showing how the net transfer to the public sector varies with age for the immigrants included in the study. See Figure 10.6. In this figure the individuals are given different weights depending on the respective sizes of the immigrant groups. The transfers to children are not added to those of their parents in this figure. The main result is that the net transfers are going in the direction from the public sector for all age groups, but the values are close to zero for those aged from 22 to 54. The net transfers from the public sector to immigrants are large from around 55 years of age. This is explained by the fact that many people of that age or over are not employed.

Of special interest is to study the development of the net transfers from the second generation of immigrants. In Figure 10.7 we compare the net transfer from the first and the second generations of non-Western immigrants. As there are only a few non-Western immigrants aged over 36 years we restrict the age interval to up to 36 years. The figure shows that the net transfer from second generation non-Western immigrants is larger than for the first generation.

Figure 10.7. Net transfers to the public sector per person in 2002 (three-year average); first and second generations of non-Western immigrants

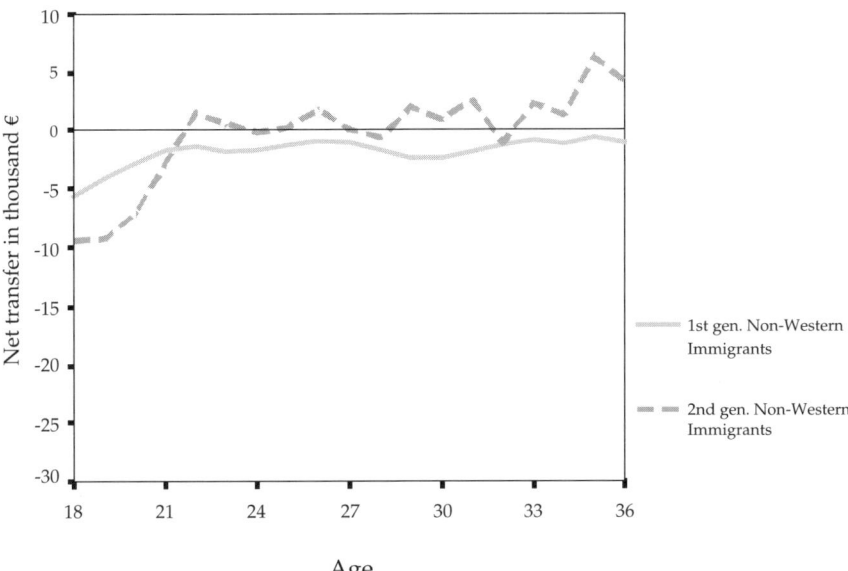

Figure 10.8. Net transfer to the public sector from the immigrants in Germany in 2002 (three-year average) (net transfers for children added to those of their parents). Each group of immigrants is weighted with a factor that corresponds to its size

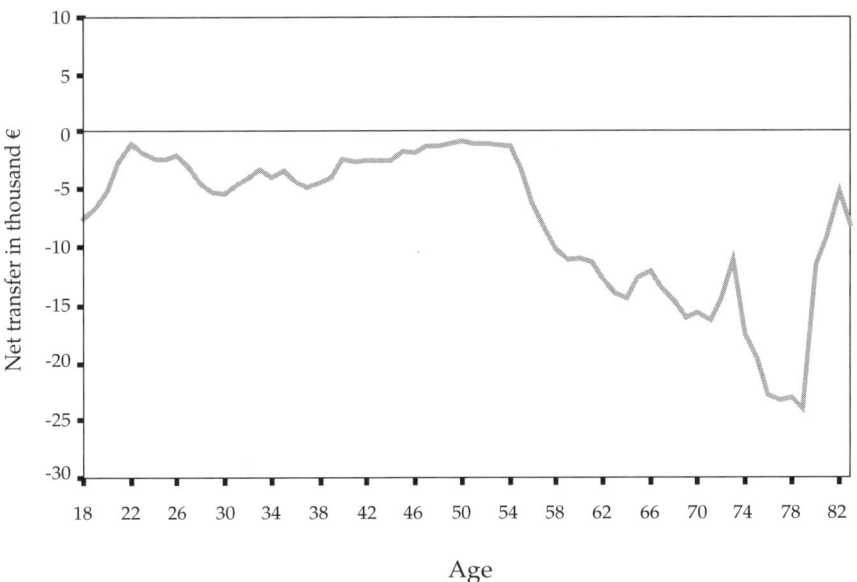

Figure 10.9. Net transfers to the first and second generation of non-Western immigrants (children not included) in Germany in 2002 (three-year average); non-weighted values

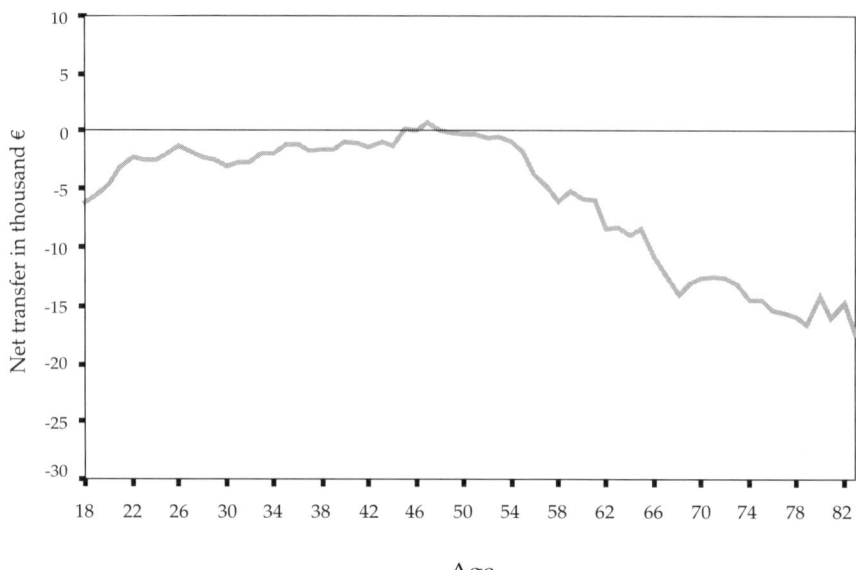

In Figure 10.8 the net transfers to children are added to those of their parents. The main change is that the net transfers for those aged 25 to 45 years, which in Figure 10.6 were close to zero, are now negative.

The variations in net transfers between different age groups are large among those who are 70 years and older. This is because the number of observations in that age interval is small, not least among those who belong to the largest of the five immigrant groups. Outliers are important, especially those who belong to the largest group. The importance of that is shown in Figure 10.9, where each observation is given the same weight, independent of the size of the group. The variations are much smaller among the elderly in this case.

The next step is to examine separately the net transfer for the five immigrant groups included in the study. In Figure 10.10 the values are calculated without adding the net transfers to children to those of their parents. The figure shows that the immigrants from Lebanon receive more in net transfers than those from other countries, irrespective of age. It also shows that immigrants from Poland of active age are net contributors to the public sector. The other three groups have values in between those of immigrants from Poland and Lebanon. In Figure 10.11 the net transfers to the children are added to those of their parents. The order among the countries does not change, but the differences are larger – the immigrants from Lebanon have larger families.

Figure 10.10. Net transfers to the public sector for each immigrant group in Germany in 2002 (three-year average) (net transfers for children are not added to those of their parents)

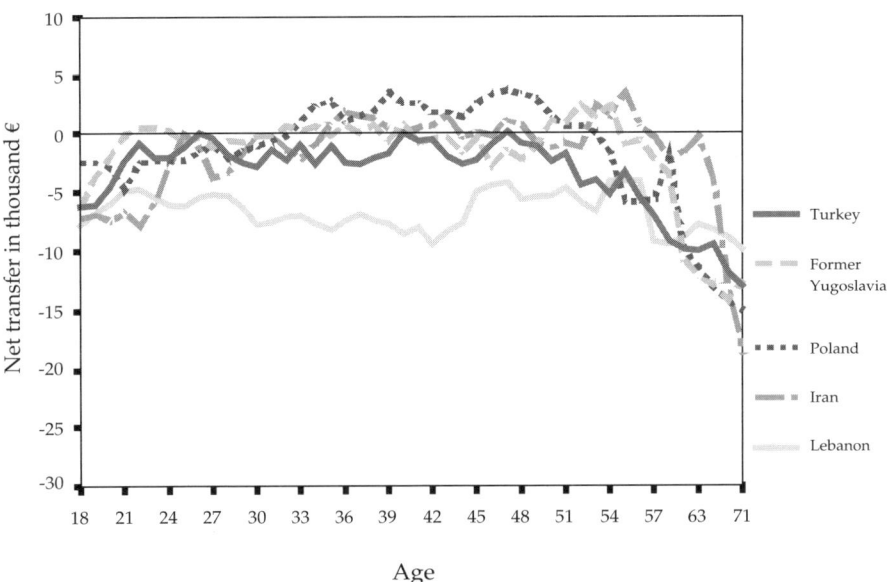

Figure 10.11. Net transfers to the public sector from each immigrant group in Germany in 2002 (three-year average) (net transfers for children are added to those of their parents)

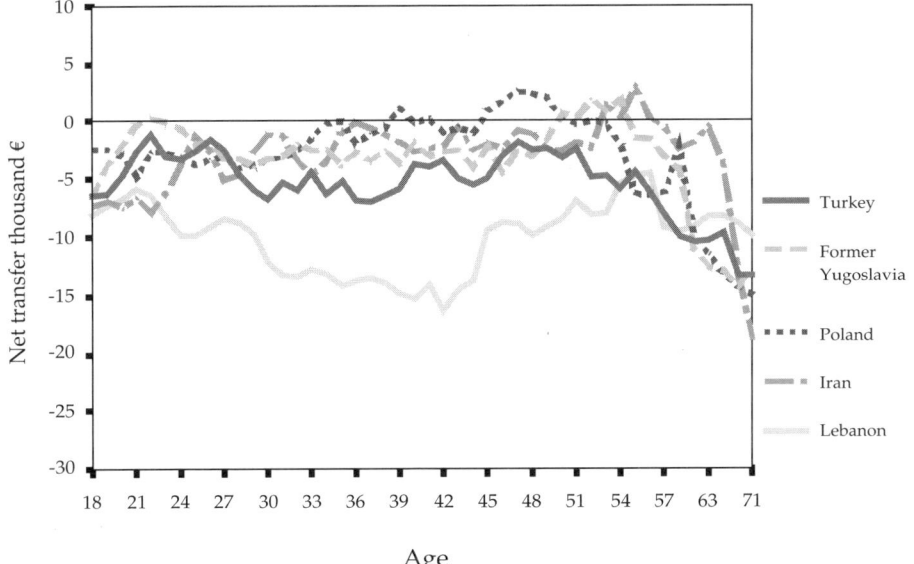

Figure 10.12. Tax payments including social security contributions by the first generation of non-Western immigrants in Germany in 2002 (three-year average); non-weighted values

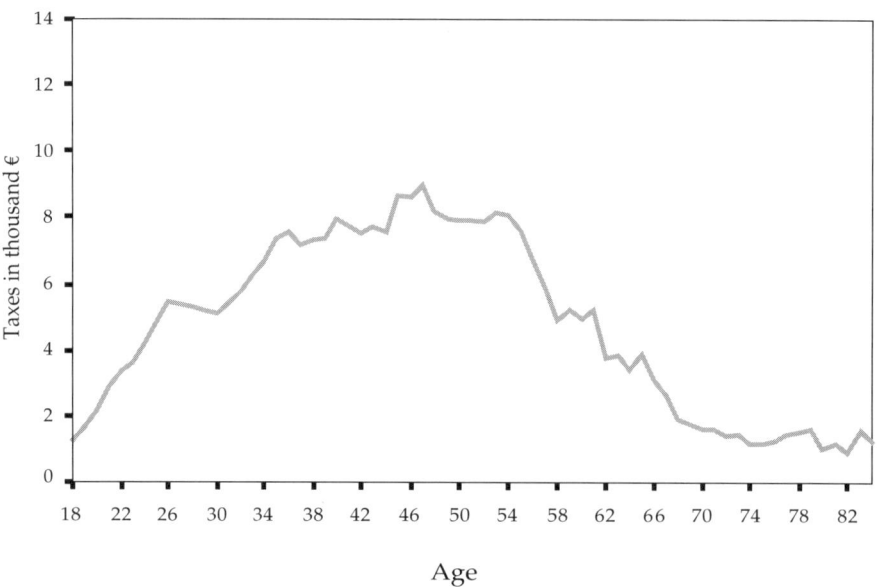

Figure 10.13. Transfer payments to the first generation of non-Western immigrants in Germany in 2002 (three-year average); non-weighted values

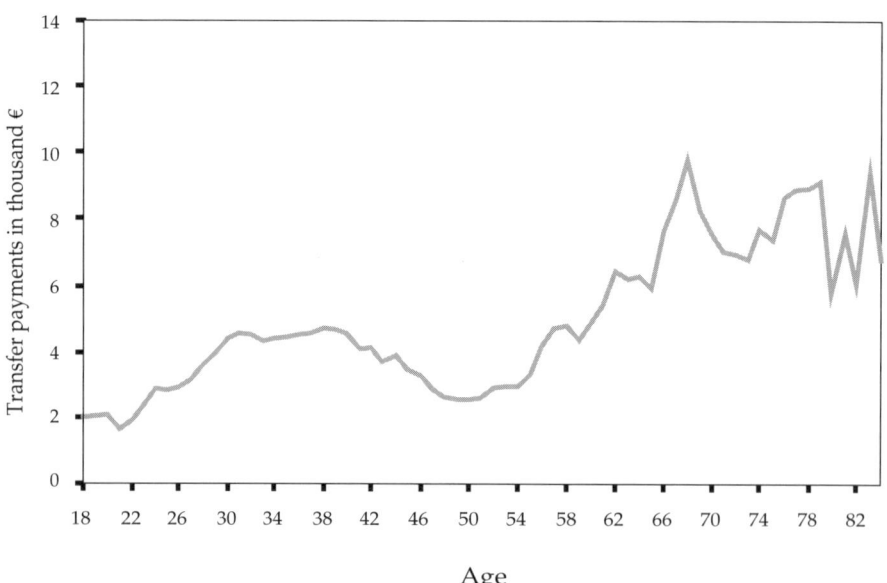

Figure 10.14. Individualized public consumption of the first generation of non-Western immigrants in Germany in 2002 (three-year average); non-weighted values

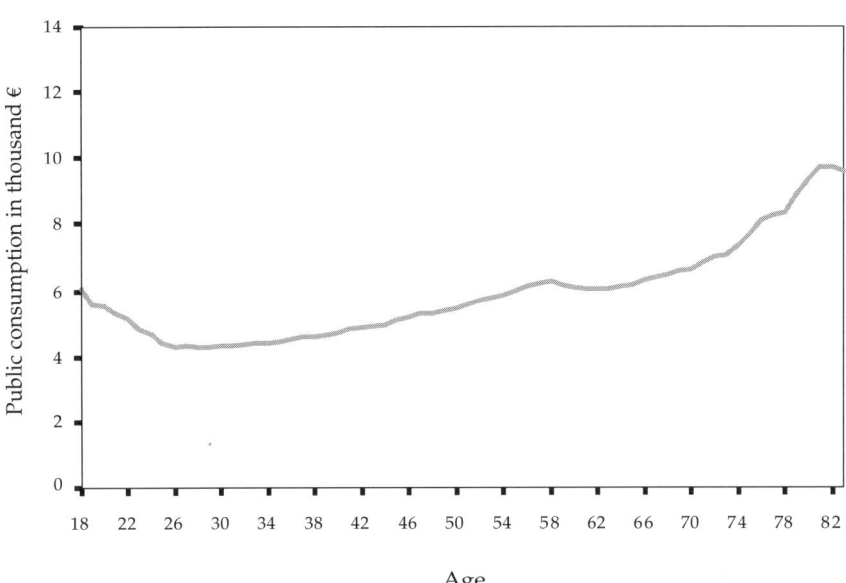

Next we will see how the three main components in the net transfers – tax payments, transfer payments and individualized public consumption – vary with age. Figure 10.12 shows, not surprisingly, that tax payments are highest in those age groups that have the largest employment rate, and Figure 10.13 that the transfer payments are largest for older people (pensions).

The pattern of variation over age for the costs for public consumption is very dependent on whether the costs relating to children are added to those for their parents or not. We therefore show both alternatives – Figure 10.14 without these costs added and Figure 10.15 with the costs added. In the first figure the costs gradually increase with age (except for those up to age 25). In the second figure the pattern is quite different with a maximum at those ages when many people have children living at home.

The next step is to examine the effects of variables representing the individual employment rate, earnings or labor income. As in the Danish case, we will show the effects for the first and the second generation separately, and not show the coefficients for the other variables included in the estimations.

In Table 10.9 the effects on the net transfer of a change in the employment rate from 0 to 100 percent are shown. There are some variations between the different immigrant groups, but they are not very large. For the first generation the estimates are highest for immigrants from Iran and lowest for those from Lebanon. Compared

Figure 10.15. Individualized public consumption of the first generation of non-Western immigrants in Germany in 2002 (three-year average), with costs for children included; non-weighted values

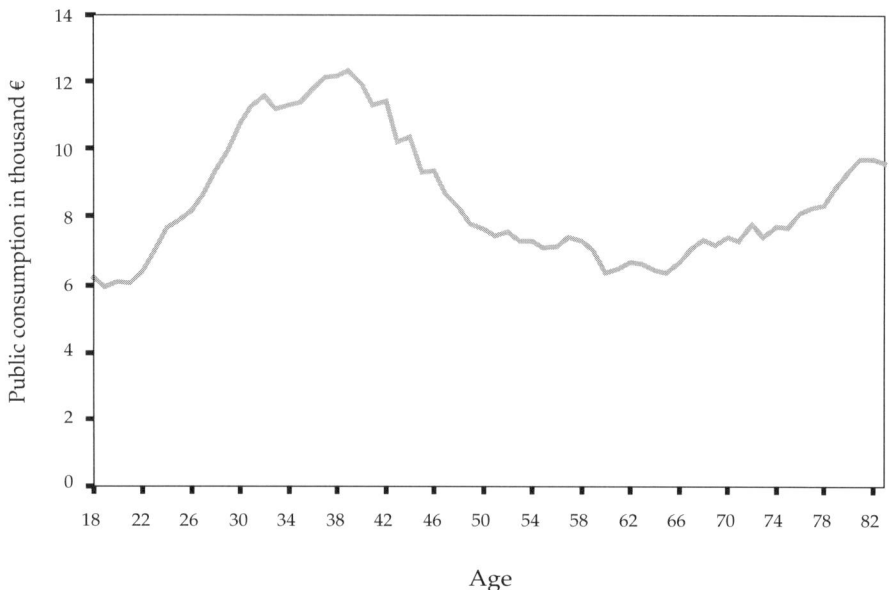

to the corresponding results for non-Western immigrants in Denmark, the values are lower. To some extent, that difference could be a result of differences in the wage rates, but most of the difference is probably explained by differences in the system for organizing and financing the public sector.

The estimates shown in Table 10.9 do not show from which value the net transfer starts when the employment rate changes from 0 to 100. This value can be calculated by using the same regression equations. We have calculated the initial values by using the average values of both continuous and dummy variables, and the value of zero for the employment rate. The results, the initial values, are given in Table 10.9.a.

The figures are all negative and lower than the corresponding values for non-Western immigrants in Denmark (see Table 10.6.a). The estimates differ between the groups due to differences in the age, gender and family status composition, but not very much. Note also that the values in Table 10.9 in all cases except one (first generation immigrants from Lebanon), are larger than the initial values in Table 10.9.a. Full employment entails a net transfer to the public sector for all groups.

The effects on net transfers of a change in the earnings are shown in Table 10.10. The values can be interpreted as a form of "marginal net tax rate" – the percentage of the increased earnings which would go back to the public sector by higher tax payments or reduced expenditure. There are some variations: a lower value for those

Table 10.9. Effect on net transfers according to regression estimates in thousand Euro if a person instead of being non-employed had been employed full-time and all year in 2002, for different groups in Germany.

Group	Effect on net transfer in thousand Euro if a person instead of being non-employed had been employed full-time, all year	
	First generation	Second generation
Iran	19.7	15.8
Lebanon	15.7	17.6
Poland	18.0	18.8
Turkey	18.1	14.8
Former Yugoslavia	17.5	18.1
All	18.8	17.0

Note: The other independent variables included in the regressions, but for which estimates are not shown here, are age, age-squared, female, and the family status variables (four categories).

Table 10.9.a. Initial values of net transfers in thousand Euro calculated by using the same regression equation as in Table 10.9, assuming that the employment rate is zero and that all other variables are at their average values.

Group	Initial values (i.e., for a non-employed individual) in thousand Euro	
	First generation	Second generation
Iran	-11.1	-10.6
Lebanon	-16.0	-13.5
Poland	-10.7	-8.5
Turkey	-12.8	-10.0
Former Yugoslavia	-11.0	-9.5
All	-12.6	-10.2

Note: In addition to the employment rate, the independent variables included in the regressions are age, age-squared, female, and the family status variables (four categories).

from Iran and higher for those from Lebanon. The immigrants from Lebanon have lower incomes and lose more in transfer payments when their incomes increase. If we compare Denmark and Germany we find that the values are lower than for non-Western immigrants in Denmark.

Table 10.11 gives the corresponding estimates for labor income. The estimates are higher in almost all cases than the coefficient for earnings. Again the coefficients are lower than in the corresponding estimations for non-Western immigrants in Denmark.

Table 10.10. Effect on net transfers according to regression estimates as percent of a change of earnings in 2002 for different groups in Germany.

Group	Effect on net transfers as percent of a change in earnings	
	First generation	Second generation
Iran	51.9	52.6
Lebanon	65.7	78.8
Poland	59.2	51.4
Turkey	61.9	61.2
Former Yugoslavia	58.0	59.4
All	60.4	60.4

Note: The other independent variables included in the regressions, but for which estimates are not shown here, are age, age-squared, female, and the family status variables (four categories).

Table 10.11. Effect on net transfers according to regression estimates as percent of a change of labor income in 2002, for different groups in Germany.

Group	Effect on net transfers as percent of a change in labor income	
	First generation	Second generation
Iran	57.3	58.5
Lebanon	66.3	78.8
Poland	60.4	56.4
Turkey	64.3	65.1
Former Yugoslavia	60.2	59.2
All	62.7	62.5

Note: The other independent variables included in the regressions, but for which estimates are not shown here, are age, age-squared, female, and the family status variables (four categories).

10.6.3 A Comparison

In presenting the results we have already made various comparisons between Denmark and Germany. In this section we will compare the results in two fields: the tax system, and the effects of some of the characteristics studied.

The income taxes for non-Western immigrants in the two countries are shown in Figure 10.16. The values in almost all groups are higher in Denmark than in Germany. The difference is largest for older people, which reflects differences in pension systems and rules for taxation of pensions. The differences between the two countries are much larger, however, when we compare the indirect taxes paid. See Figure 10.17. Immigrants pay much more in indirect taxes in Denmark than in Germany. The indirect tax rates are higher in Denmark, both as regards the Value Added Tax and other indirect taxes. The higher tax rates in Denmark also contribute to explaining the larger effects on net transfers of increases in earnings (and labor incomes) in that country. When people earn more they pay more in indirect taxes, which adds to the marginal effect – and more so in Denmark than in Germany.

The next step is to compare the regression estimates. In Tables 10.12 and 10.13 we do so in a simplified manner by including just demographic variables (gender, age and family status) and variables representing employment or income from employment (earnings, labor income).

We find some similarities and some dissimilarities. In both countries the net transfer to the public sector depends on the individual's labor market situation – a higher employment rate, higher earnings, and higher labor income mean a larger net transfer to the public sector. The effects are greater in Denmark than in Germany. Another similarity is that married people with children, and to an even greater extent those who are single with children, receive a large net transfer from the pub-

Figure 10.16. Income taxes including social security contributions for the first generation of non-Western immigrants in Denmark (year 2000) and Germany (year 2002) (three-year average)

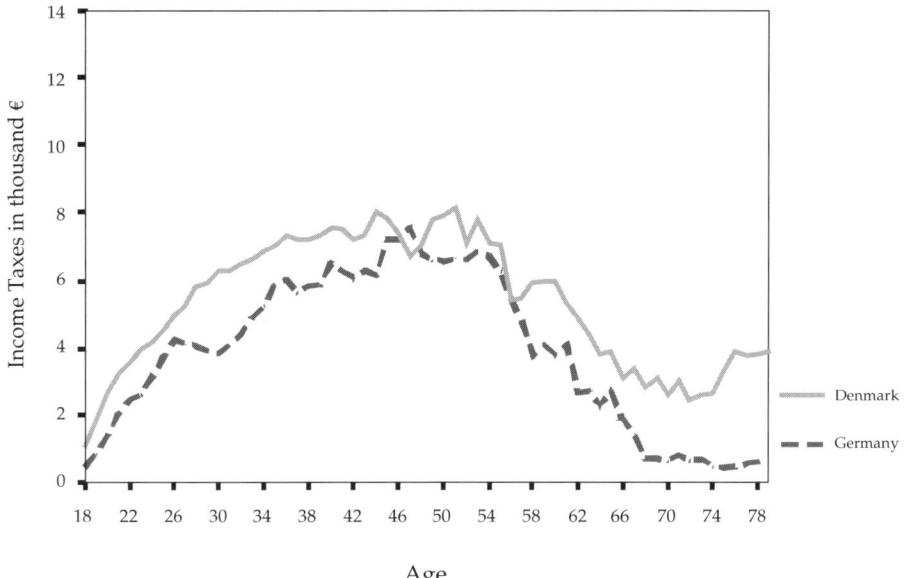

Notes: The data for Denmark are based on all non-Western immigrants, not only those from the five countries included in the German data set. The data are from different years from the two countries. The change in the price level in Denmark from 2000 to 2002 is 4.9 percent.

Figure 10.17. Indirect taxes for the first generation of non-Western immigrants in Denmark (year 2000) and Germany (year 2002). For both countries the calculations are based on the incomes of households (three-year average)

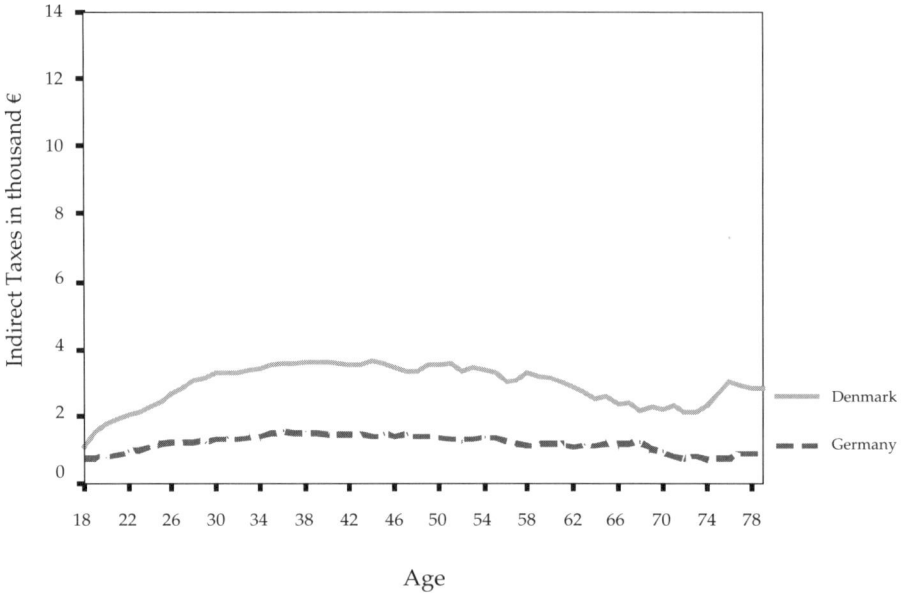

Notes: The data for Denmark is based on all non-Western immigrants, not only those from the five countries included in the German data set. The change in the price level in Denmark from 2000 to 2002 is 4.9 percent.

lic sector compared to those who are single and without children. This effect too, is greater in Denmark than in Germany.

One dissimilarity is that the coefficient for females is negative in the estimations for Denmark and positive in the estimations for Germany.[26] This is probably mainly due to two factors. First, there are differences between the two countries in their income tax systems. Denmark has an individual-based system and Germany a system in which the incomes of both spouses are added together, leading to a higher taxation of the incomes of married women in Germany. Second, there are differences between the social insurance systems in the two countries. Germany's system is more of the Bismarck type and Denmark's more of the Beveridge type. This means that transfer payments in Germany go to men to a greater extent than in Denmark, since men more often than women have a history of employment.

---

26 Note that this difference is dependent on the inclusion of variables representing the individual employment situation or income from employment. If such variables are not included the coefficient for females in both countries is strongly negative, because women are less often employed (but the absolute value is larger for Denmark, i.e. the coefficient is more negative).

Table 10.12. Regression estimates (Ordinary Least Squares) with net transfer to the public sector in 2000 for first generation non-Western immigrants living in Denmark (from the same countries included in the German survey) (in thousand Euro) as the dependent variable

Variables	(1)	(2)	(3)
Constant	-9.544 (1.376) ***	-6.857 (1.342) ***	-5.960 (1.229) ***
Female	-3.230 (0.366) ***	-3.313 (0.357) ***	-2.341 (0.329) ***
Age	-0.054 (0.069)	-0.122 (0.067) *	-0.201 (0.062) ***
Age²	0.0003 (0.0008)	0.0008 (0.0008)	0.0016 (0.0007) **
Family status			
Single, no children	*reference*	*reference*	*reference*
Single with children	-19.965 (0.960) ***	-19.053 (0.935) ***	-19.754 (0.857) ***
Married/cohabiting, no children	1.674 (0.531) ***	1.800 (0.517) ***	1.611 (0.474) ***
Married/cohabiting with children	-9.455 (0.474) ***	-8.674 (0.461) ***	-9.125 (0.423) ***
Employment rate	0.288 (0.004) ***		
Earnings		0.832 (0.012) ***	
Total labor income			0.831 (0.011) ***
Number of observations	2739	2739	2739
R²(adj)	0.690	0.706	0.753

Note: Standard errors in parentheses. "Married" means living together, irrespective of whether a couple is formally married or not.

The coefficients for the age variables also differ between the two countries. Again, the difference is dependent on the inclusion of variables representing the individual employment situation or income from employment. If such variables are not included the coefficients have the same sign in the estimations for both countries.

10.7 Summary and Conclusions

Immigration has consequences for public sector finances. In this chapter we have dealt with one of those consequences, the net transfers to the public sector from immigrants in Denmark and Germany. We have done so by looking at the effects of a number of variables by using information on cross-sections of the population. It would have been of great interest to use a longitudinal approach as well, but that has not been possible due to lack of data.

For Denmark it has been possible to study more issues because the data covers several years (1991, 1995-2000), and also samples of all the population (natives and immigrants) in those years. For Germany we have information on five (major) immigrant groups from non-Western countries for one year (2002).

The Danish data make it possible to follow the development over time. The data

Table 10.13. Regression estimates (Ordinary Least Squares) with net transfer to the public sector in 2002 for first generation non-Western immigrants living in Germany (in thousand Euro) as the dependent variable

Variables	(1)	(2)	(3)
Constant	-15.892 (1.107) ***	-11.675 (1.051) ***	-9.733 (0.830) ***
Female	1.857 (0.239) ***	1.608 (0.225) ***	2.896 (0.179) ***
Age	0.328 (0.056) ***	0.279 (0.053) ***	0.105 (0.042) **
Age^2	-0.0042 (0.0006) ***	-0.0043 (0.0006) ***	-0.0024 (0.0005) ***
Family status			
Single, no children	*reference*	*reference*	*reference*
Single with children	-15.431 (0.644) ***	-15.612 (0.607) ***	-15.405 (0.479) ***
Married/cohabiting, no children	0.470 (0.340)	0.514 (0.321)	0.419 (0.253) *
Married/cohabiting with children	-6.267 (0.312) ***	-7.277 (0.294) ***	-6.985 (0.232) ***
Employment rate	0.188 (0.003) ***		
Earnings		0.604 (0.008) ***	
Total labor income			0.627 (0.006) ***
Number of observations	3927	3952	3952
R^2(adj)	0.639	0.675	0.798

Note: Standard errors in parentheses.

show that the net transfer in all years studied goes from Western immigrants to the public sector, and from the public sector to immigrants from non-Western countries. The amounts are considerable. The size per person varies with the business cycle (and the employment rate), and the total amount also varies with the size of the immigrant population. It is a little surprising that the reduction in amounts for both individuals and in total which took place between 1996 and 1998 did not continue in 1998-2000 in spite of an improvement in the labor market situation. The study of Germany shows that the net transfer goes from the public sector to the immigrants, i.e. in the same direction as in Denmark for non-Western immigrants. The net transfers per person are smaller on average in Germany than in Denmark and vary considerably between different non-Western immigrant groups.

For both countries it has been possible to study the effects of individual characteristics and the employment situation (and income from employment) on the individual net transfer to the public sector. In both countries, if the employment/income variables are left out, the net transfers from the public sector are greater to women than to men, and greater to those who are young and especially to those who are old, and to those who have children (especially single parents). Some of these effects disappear when variables representing employment/income are included, but the effect of having children is still very strong. For other variables the effects become smaller and to some extent change signs for the two countries, a result which may be explained by differences in the tax and transfer systems. The employment/income variables are highly significant with large effects. The effects are larger in Denmark than in Germany. These differences may be explained by differences in the tax systems and in the public sector expenditure.

References

Boll, Stephan. 1994. "Intergenerationale Umverteilungswirkungen der Fiskalpolitik in der Bundesrepublik Deutschland, Ein Ansatz mit Hilfe des Generational Accounting," *Finanzwissenschaftliche Schriften*, Band 66, Frankfurt am Main: Peter Lang GmbH.

Bonin, Holger. 2001. *Generational Accounting, Theory and Application*. Berlin: Springer-Verlag.

Bonin, Holger. 2002. "Eine fiskalische Gesamtbilanz der Zuwanderung nach Deutschland," *Quarterly Journal of Economic Research* 71, 215-229.

Ekberg, Jan. 1999. "Immigration and the Public Sector: Income Effects for the Native Population in Sweden," *Journal of Population Ecconomics* 12, 411-430.

Gerdes, Christer. 2004. "Beräkning av nettobidrag av invandringen för den offentliga sektorn i Tyskland," Swedish Institute for Social Research, Stockholm University.

Gott, Ceri and Karl Johnston. 2002. "The Migrant Population in the UK: Fiscal Effects," RDS Occasional Paper No 77, Home Office, London.

Hansen, Frederik, Sten Nicolaisen, Finn Dehlbæck and Ole Schnor. 1991. *Lovmodel*, September 1991. Copenhagen: Ministry of Economic Affairs.

Indenrigsministeriet. 1999. *Udlændinge og kommunerne – Opgaver, udgifter og finansiering*, November 1999. Copenhagen: Indenrigsministeriet.

Knudsen, Lars Kirk, Thomas Larsen and Niels Jørgen Mau Pedersen. 1998. *Den offentlige sektor* (4th edition), Copenhagen: Copenhagen Business School Press.

Leibfritz, Willi, Paul O'Brien and Jean-Christophe Dumont. 2003. "Effects of Immigration on Labor Markets and Government Budgets – An Overview," CESifo Working Paper No. 874.

Linderoth, Hans. 1999. "Offentlig sektor," in Torben M. Andersen et al., *Beskrivende Økonomi* (6th edition). Copenhagen: Jurist- og Økonomforbundets Forlag.

le Maire, Daniel and Christian Scheuer. 2001. "Langsigtet finanspolitik og immigrationen – en generationsregnskabsbaseret tilgang," Økonomisk Institut, Københavns universitet.

le Maire, Daniel and Christian Scheuer. 2003. "Indvandringens betydning for den finanspolitiske holdbarhed," Økonomisk Institut, Københavns universitet.

Ministry of Economic Affairs. 1997. *Økonomisk oversigt. December 1997.* Copenhagen: Ministry of Economic Affairs.

Ministry of Economic Affairs. 2000. *The Law Model*. Copenhagen: Ministry of Economic Affairs.

Ministry of Finance. 2003. *Lovmodellen*. Copenhagen: Ministry of Finance.
Wadensjö, Eskil. 2000. "Immigration, the Labor Market, and Public Finances in Denmark," *Swedish Economic Policy Review* 7, 59-84.
Wadensjö, Eskil. 2000a."Omfördelning via offentlig sektor: en fördjupad analys" in Gunnar Viby Mogensen and Poul Chr. Matthiessen (eds): *Integration i Danmark omkring årtusindskiftet*, Aarhus: Aarhus University Press.
Wadensjö, Eskil. 2002. "Ekonomiska effekter av invandringen" in Gunnar Viby Mogensen and Poul Chr. Matthiessen (eds): *Indvandrerne og arbejdsmarkedet*, Copenhagen: Spektrum.
Wadensjö, Eskil and Helena Orrje. 2002. *Immigration and the Public Sector in Denmark*, Aarhus: Aarhus Universitetsforlag.

CHAPTER 11

Some Socioeconomic Consequences of Immigration[1]

By Eskil Wadensjö and Christer Gerdes

11.1. Immigration, Wages and Unemployment

In Chapter 10 we analysed the net transfers to the public sector. In this chapter we will follow up that study with a number of issues related to the discussion and the results of the analyses in that chapter. One of the results that emerged in Chapter 10 is the crucial importance of employment and labor income for the size of the net transfer to the public sector. In this chapter more detailed information on employment, incomes and wages is provided and analysed. In Section 11.2 we focus on average labor income and the composition of that income. Wage equations are estimated, and the differences between the wage rates of natives and immigrants are analysed. Income from labor can be divided into wage income and income from self-employment. In Section 11.4 this second element of labor income, income from self-employment, is analysed.

In the analysis of the net transfer from immigrants to the public sector in Chapter 10, we showed how the net transfer from natives to the public sector could change as a result of immigration influencing the labor market. In Section 11.3 the effects of immigration on the native wage rate is analysed, while Section 11.5 considers the effects of immigration on native unemployment.

The net transfers to and from the public sector analysed in Chapter 10 are to a high extent intended to redistribute incomes. The pattern of income distribution before taxes and income transfers differs from that after taxes and transfers. Section 11.6 presents and analyzes information on net incomes per equivalent household member after taxes and income transfers.

---

1 This chapter is mainly on Denmark because the data bases we use contain more information for Denmark than for Germany. The main difference is that the Law Model contains information not only on non-Western immigrants but also on Western immigrants and native Danes. We would like to thank Jan Ekberg and Peder Pedersen for helpful comments on an earlier version.

11.2. Immigration, Employment and Incomes in Denmark[2]

The employment rate differs greatly between different groups. We will now continue by studying the relation between employment and incomes. We will start by looking at the total income from labor regardless of whether it comes from being an employee or being self-employed. Table 11.1 shows the average income from employment for all individuals aged 18 years and over. Even those who are not employed are included in calculating the average values.

The table shows that there are large differences between the groups. Second-generation immigrants from Western countries have the highest incomes from labor in 1996, 1999 and 2000 and relatively high incomes in 1995 and 1998 as well. It is a group consisting of many people of active age (few young people and few aged 65 years or over), and the employment rate is relatively high even if the age structure is taken into consideration. The second-generation immigrants from non-Western countries have much lower incomes on average. This is a young group and the employment rate is low, even if we take age structure into account.

Among the other three groups, native Danes have the highest income from labor and the non-Western immigrants the lowest. The Western immigrants have incomes in between the other two groups, but much closer to those of the natives. The low income for non-Western immigrants is a consequence of the low employment rate which was discussed in Chapter 10.

We will now look at the incomes for those with a positive income from labor. Table 11.2 shows considerably smaller differences between the groups. The order of the groups is also different to some extent. First- and second-generation immigrants from Western countries have had the highest incomes in recent years and first- and second-generation immigrants from non-Western countries the lowest. When comparing the groups we should be aware that the average individual employment rate could differ between those who were employed in the groups. Part-time and part-year employment could be more frequent in some groups than in others. There may also be a difference regarding the extent to which people in different groups are employees or self-employed, and this may affect income. We will therefore continue by studying the composition of the labor income with respect to wage income and income from self-employment for the different groups.

---

2 The results in this section should be compared with those on non-Western immigrants in Chapter 6. As we also have information on Western immigrants and native Danes we are able to study the wages of non-Western immigrants compared to those of the other two groups.

Table 11.1. Average annual labor income (wages and income from self-employment) among all aged 18 or over; thousand Euro[3].

Group	1995	1996	1998	1999	2000
Native Danish population (including those who have one immigrant parent)	17.9	18.5	20.6	21.1	22.1
Second generation – parents from Western countries	17.1	21.3	19.4	22.9	25.6
Immigrants from Western countries	15.7	15.2	17.5	17.9	20.0
Second generation – parents from non-Western countries	8.7	11.0	11.3	11.9	13.3
Immigrants from non-Western countries	7.2	7.3	9.1	10.2	10.3
Total	17.5	18.0	20.0	20.6	21.6

Notes: Western countries are the EU countries, Norway, Switzerland, Iceland, North America, Australia and New Zealand; non-Western countries are all other countries. Also those with none or negative labor income are included.

Table 11.2. Average annual labor income (wages and income from self-employment) for those with positive labor income among all aged 18 and over; thousand Euro.

Group	1995	1996	1998	1999	2000
Native Danish population (including those who have one immigrant parent)	25.5	26.1	28.8	29.6	30.9
Second-generation – parents from Western countries	23.7	29.0	27.1	32.9	34.2
Immigrants from Western countries	25.9	25.2	28.7	29.6	32.1
Second-generation – parents from non-Western countries	11.7	13.9	14.7	14.5	16.2
Immigrants from non-Western countries	16.9	17.5	18.8	20.4	20.9
Total	25.4	25.9	28.5	29.3	30.6

Note: Western countries are the EU countries, Norway, Switzerland, Iceland, North America, Australia and New Zealand; non-Western countries are all other countries.

Before studying wage income and income from self-employment in more detail we will present some information on the relative importance for the two types of income for the different groups. Table 11.3 shows that wage income dominates for all groups. For the total population, income from self-employment comprises around 10 percent of the total income from labor. The pattern is very consistent for the five years on which we have information.

3 In Chapter 10 and 11 we have converted Danish *kroner* to Euro at the rate 1 EUR =7.424 DKK.

Table 11.3. Average percentage of labor income (wage income and income from self-employment) from self-employment among all aged 18 and over.

Group	1995	1996	1998	1999	2000
Native Danish population (including those who have one immigrant parent)	8.2	8.5	7.9	8.5	8.2
Second-generation – parents from Western countries	2.2	12.5	5.1	9.6	7.8
Immigrants from Western countries	10.2	11.3	8.7	7.4	9.6
Second-generation – parents from non-Western countries	4.9	3.2	5.8	2.7	2.0
Immigrants from non-Western countries	9.0	11.7	9.1	9.6	8.7
Total	8.2	8.6	7.9	8.5	8.2

Note: Western countries are the EU countries, Norway, Switzerland, Iceland, North America, Australia and New Zealand; non-Western countries are all other countries.

There are some differences between the groups. The proportion of income from self-employment is lowest among second-generation immigrants from non-Western immigrants. Few are self-employed in this group, which can be explained by the fact that this is a young group and that it takes time to establish an own business. The differences are small between the other four groups.

Most people who have a labor income, both natives and immigrants, earn that income as employees. Even if self-employment is important, wages and not incomes from self-employment constitute the major part of labor income. Table 11.4 shows the average wage income for the various groups among those who have a positive income from wages.[4]

The table shows that there are considerable differences between the groups. Second generation immigrants from non-Western countries have had the lowest wage incomes, and second-generation immigrants from Western countries have had the highest during the last two years of observation. In addition to differences in the employment rate, age differences may be an important cause of the pattern found. Second-generation immigrants from Western countries are considerably older than second-generation immigrants from non-Western countries. The large variations between the years may be explained by the fact that the number of observations is

---

[4] There are few people with negative wage incomes. The amounts are small in most cases. The explanation for the negative amounts is probably that some people were paid too much in one year and paid it back in the beginning of the next year and did not have other wage income in that second year.

Table 11.4. Average annual wage incomes for those with wage incomes among all aged 18 and over; thousand Euro in current prices.

Group	1995	1996	1998	1999	2000
Native Danish population (including those who have one immigrant parent)	24.1	24.8	27.1	28.3	29.5
Second-generation – parents from Western countries	23.2	23.6	26.0	31.1	32.4
Immigrants from Western countries	25.1	24.5	27.7	28.5	30.7
Second-generation – parents from non-Western countries	11.7	14.0	14.0	14.5	15.5
Immigrants from non-Western countries	16.5	17.3	18.6	20.0	20.4
Total	23.9	24.6	26.9	28.1	29.2

Note: Western countries are the EU countries, Norway, Switzerland, Iceland, North America, Australia and New Zealand; non-Western countries are all other countries.

small for these groups, so that outliers included in one year but not in another may have large effects. When studying the figures we should also remember that the employment rate varies greatly between groups.

The most interesting comparison is between native Danes and first-generation immigrants from Western and non-Western countries. It shows that natives and Western immigrants have considerably larger wage incomes than non-Western immigrants. The Western immigrants have even larger wage incomes than natives in four of the five years of study. Note that the comparison only includes those who have wages. The native Danes have higher wage incomes per person if all people of active age are included, also those who do not have any wage income. The explanation for this difference is that the native Danes have a higher rate of employment than Western immigrants. Note also that the wage incomes of every group increase over the period studied, as expected, since income is not deflated.

The next step is to study the hourly wages to see if they differ among the various groups.[5] Among all three groups shown in Table 11.5 – native Danes, Western, and non-Western immigrants – men have higher wages on average than women. We also see that there are large differences between the groups. Immigrants from Western countries have the highest wages and non-Western immigrants the lowest.

---

5 We have excluded those who have an employment rate of 0.05 and lower. The calculated hourly wages are uncertain for those with very low employment rates. See Wadensjö and Orrje (2002).

Table 11.5. Average hourly wage in Euro.

Group		1995	1996	1998	1999	2000
Native Danish population (excluding those who have one immigrant parent)	Men	19.96	20.69	22.12	23.19	24.19
	Women	16.45	17.08	18.24	18.81	19.60
	All	18.21	18.88	20.18	20.99	21.87
Immigrants from Western countries	Men	21.90	22.11	23.80	24.62	25.54
	Women	18.06	18.73	19.62	22.05	21.72
	All	20.10	20.47	21.87	23.39	23.76
Immigrants from non-Western countries	Men	17.46	18.07	18.21	19.18	20.45
	Women	14.64	15.74	16.41	17.07	17.86
	All	16.33	17.12	17.47	18.25	19.31
Total	Men	19.91	20.63	22.02	23.06	24.05
	Women	16.44	17.09	18.22	18.83	19.59
	All	18.19	18.86	20.13	20.95	21.81

Notes: Western countries are the EU countries, Norway, Switzerland, Iceland, North America, Australia and New Zealand; non-Western countries are all other countries. Only those who have a positive wage rate, are aged 18 to 65, have an hourly wage rate less than EUR 1,346.98 (=DKK 10,000), no income from self-employment and an employment rate greater than 0.05 are included.

A lower hourly wage means lower wage income and taxes and larger transfer payments. This is one of several reasons to study the wage differences in more detail. We will do this by first estimating wage equations.[6] These equations are shown in Table 11.6. The wage equations are estimated with the logarithm of the hourly wage in 2000 as the dependent variable. In the first of the columns, age, education, gender and family status are included as independent variables together with those variables representing the groups (native Danes, Western immigrants, non-Western immigrants). Age may be seen as an indirect measure of experience in the labor market and may therefore be seen, like education, as a variable representing human capital investment.

---

6 The equations are of Mincer type. A problem with estimations of this type of equations is that observations are missing on hourly wages for those who are not employed. In the Law Model information on the hourly wage is also missing for those who besides being employed also have income as self-employed. Of special importance in our case is that we lack information on hourly wages for many non-Western immigrants. If those who are not employed (and for whom we do not have information on the hourly wage) differ from those who are employed with regard to unobserved characteristics influencing the wage, we have a problem of selectivity. It may be the case that immigrants with a specific education who are employed have a generally higher competence than those with the same education who are not employed. If that is the case we may over-estimate the effects of education.

As the hourly wage calculated using the data available in the Law Model is uncertain, especially for people who work few hours, we have made calculations for different definitions of the population studied. In the first estimates all individuals with positive hourly wage rates are included; in the next, we exclude those with (unrealistically) low wage rates; and in the third, we only include those who are working full time and all year. Another problem is that we do not have information on the education of all immigrants – not every immigrant answers the questionnaire that Statistics Denmark sends out and which asks about the individual's educational level upon arrival to Denmark. In most such cases Statistics Denmark has imputed an educational level. In the fourth estimation we have excluded those who have an imputed education. The values of the coefficients for most variables are more or less the same in all estimations independent of which of the four methods is used to define the population. We have therefore decided to include only the estimates using the widest definition.[7]

The results for the group representing the different immigration groups show that the coefficient is negative for non-Western immigrants. It is about -0.10, which means that this group of immigrants have about 10 percent lower wages, given the characteristics we have included.[8] For the other groups the coefficients are small and in most cases not significantly different from that of the native Danes.

In columns 2 and 3 we present separate wage equations for men and women. For immigrants from non-Western countries the coefficients are negative for both men and women, but the size of the coefficient is much larger for men than for women. There is a larger negative effect for male immigrants from non-Western countries than for female immigrants from the same countries; this is not explained by the variables included. We now also get significant values for the coefficients for Western immigrants for men. The signs of the coefficients are different for men and women, however. Women from Western countries have a higher wage than native Danish women with the same characteristics. On the other hand, men from Western countries have lower wages than natives with the same characteristics. These effects are smaller in absolute terms than those for non-Western immigrants, which suggests that the main point of interest is the more detailed study of the wages of the non-Western immigrants.

---

7 Estimations with other definitions of the population studied are available from the authors.
8 The coefficient estimates for low values may be directly translated to percentages (0.05 to 5 percent etc.). For higher values this approximation is too crude.

Table 11.6. Regression estimates (OLS) with hourly wage (log) in the year 2000 as the dependent variable.

Variables	All	Men	Women
Constant	2.388 (0.019)***	2.164 (0.026)***	2.442 (0.028)***
One parent born in Denmark, one in a Western country	0.028 (0.012)**	0.025 (0.016)	0.031 (0.018)*
One parent born in Denmark, one in a non-Western country	0.003 (0.033)	0.031 (0.033)	-0.035 (0.034)
Both parents born in a Western country	0.032 (0.033)	0.037 (0.045)	0.028 (0.048)
Both parents born in a non-Western country	0.042 (0.026)	0.030 (0.038)	0.030 (0.034)
Born in a Western country	-0.005 (0.012)	-0.034 (0.016)**	0.020 (0.017)
Born in a non-Western country	-0.101 (0.009)***	-0.131 (0.012)***	-0.066 (0.014)***
Female	-0.189 (0.003)***		
Age	0.025 (0.001)***	0.034 (0.001)***	0.017 (0.001)***
Age^2	-0.00024 (0.00001)***	-0.00035 (0.00002)***	-0.00014 (0.00002)***
Vocational education	0.096 (0.004)***	0.112 (0.006)***	0.072 (0.006)***
High school	0.198 (0.007)***	0.209 (0.010)***	0.171 (0.010)***
Short higher education	0.216 (0.008)***	0.218 (0.011)***	0.205 (0.011)***
Medium-length higher education	0.265 (0.005)***	0.317 (0.008)***	0.231 (0.007)***
Long higher education	0.464 (0.007)***	0.496 (0.009)***	0.475 (0.011)***
In education	0.027 (0.006)***	-0.019 (0.009)**	0.051 (0.009)***
Education not reported	0.081 (0.013)***	0.092 (0.017)***	0.068 (0.021)***
Single with children	-0.009 (0.009)	-0.005 (0.022)	-0.063 (0.010)***
Married/cohabiting, no children	0.022 (0.004)***	0.084 (0.006)***	-0.057 (0.006)***
Married/cohabiting with children	0.031 (0.004)***	0.107 (0.006)***	-0.070 (0.007)***
Number of observations	78518	39075	39443
R^2(adj)	0.165	0.202	0.091

Notes: *** significant at the 1 percent level, ** significant at the 5 percent level, * significant at the 10 percent level. Comparison group: Danes, men, primary education (9 years or less), single without children. Standard errors in parentheses. All individuals aged 18 years and over are included. Those with an hourly wage of EUR 1,346.98 (=DKK 10,000) or over are excluded.

We will now try to see if the wage differences we have found between natives and non-Western immigrants can be explained by their different characteristics, for example different educations. We do this by using the wage equation estimated for natives and calculate the expected wage rate for immigrants given their age, educa-

Table 11.7. Explained and unexplained wage differences in the year 2000 between Danes and non-Western immigrants (Blinder-Oaxaca decomposition).

	All
All	
Wage difference	0.115
Explained part (%)	16.7
Unexplained part (%)	83.3
Men	
Wage difference	0.148
Explained part (%)	14.9
Unexplained part (%)	85.1
Women	
Wage difference	0.102
Explained part (%)	41.3
Unexplained part (%)	58.7

tion, etc. In the next step we compare the calculated wage with the actual wage. This method – the Blinder-Oaxaca decomposition – is shown in Table 11.7.

The table shows that the wage difference is larger between native and non-Western men than between native and non-Western women. It also shows that for men almost no part of the wage differential between natives and non-Western immigrants is explained by differences in characteristics (age, education, etc.) but almost everything by differences in return on characteristics. There may be several explanations for this. Important variables for which we do not have information may be missing, the individuals' education may be measured in an unsatisfactory way, experience may be measured too crudely by using age, and the non-Western immigrants may be discriminated against in the Danish labor market.

To investigate the question a little more fully, we show separate estimates in Table 11.8 for native Danes, Western immigrants, and non-Western immigrants. There are two main differences in the estimation for native Danes and non-Western immigrants.

One of the differences is that the return to education is lower for non-Western immigrants.[9] The coefficients for short, medium-length, and long higher education are 0.079, 0.165, and 0.284 for non-Western immigrants compared to 0.224, 0.271, and 0.510 for natives. For both groups the comparison is made with those who have only

---

9 The results for non-Western immigrants here are in line with those shown in Chapter 6.

Table 11.8. Regression estimates (OLS) with hourly wage in Euro (log) in the year 2000 as the dependent variable.

Variables	Danes	Western immigrants	Non-Western immigrants
Constant	2.377 (0.020)***	2.673 (0.192)***	2.520 (0.102)***
Female	-0.193 (0.003)***	-0.143 (0.026)***	-0.129 (0.007)***
Age	0.025 (0.001)***	0.015 (0.009)*	0.018 (0.007)***
Age^2	-0.00024 (0.00001)***	-0.00013 (0.00011)	-0.00016 (0.00008)**
Vocational education	0.098 (0.004)***	0.046 (0.047)	0.057 (0.027**)
High school	0.213 (0.007)***	0.055 (0.068)	0.039 (0.037)
Short higher education	0.224 (0.008)***	0.074 (0.066)	0.079 (0.046)**
Medium-length higher education	0.271 (0.005)***	0.149 (0.053)***	0.165 (0.038)***
Long higher education	0.510 (0.007)***	0.281 (0.054)***	0.284 (0.043)***
In education	0.032 (0.006)***	-0.056 (0.064)	-0.079 (0.034)**
Education not reported	0.043 (0.017)***	0.035 (0.054)	0.049 (0.030)
Single with children	-0.004 (0.009)	0.003 (0.068)	-0.026 (0.044)
Married/cohabiting, no children	0.024 (0.004)***	-0.020 (0.033)	-0.043 (0.028)
Married/cohabiting with children	0.036 (0.004)***	0.005 (0.035)	-0.078 (0.026)***
Number of observations	72,786	1,384	2,375
R^2(adj)	0.171	0.071	0.078

Notes: *** significant at the 1 percent level, ** significant at the 5 percent level, * significant at the 10 percent level. Comparison group: men, primary education (9 years or less), single without children. Standard errors in parentheses. All individuals aged 18 years and over are included. Those with an hourly wage of EUR 1,346.98 (=DKK 10,000) or over are excluded.

primary education (9 years or less). The natives' return to education is twice that of the non-Western immigrants. Here some caution is recommended in interpreting the results due to the uncertainty in the quality of the information regarding education for the immigrants. The results are similar for Western and non-Western immigrants. The results indicate that it is of interest to study the situation of immigrants with higher education in more detail.

The second difference is that wages increase at different rates with age for different groups. Wages increase less with age for immigrants, both from Western and non-Western countries, than for native Danes. This suggests that immigrants often have jobs where experience is rewarded less, or by age being less good as a proxy for work experience for the immigrants, as they have more and longer periods out of work.

11.3. The Impact of Immigration on the Native Wage Rate

Immigration means that economic production capacity increases. Since remuneration falls when the size of the labor force grows, the wages earned by immigrants do not entirely match the increase in production that immigration creates, given that wages are equal to the value of the marginal contribution.[10] This means that the existing population in the host country will reap an economic gain from immigration. While it is true that the native labor force will see a decrease in wages, this decrease will be more than compensated by an increase in returns on capital. The way in which this affects individual members of the society depends on how capital is distributed. If one imagines that capital is distributed equally among the entire native labor force, then the result would be that everyone wins. A more realistic picture is that capital is distributed in such a way that some segments of the labor force win while others lose.

Probably more important than the fact that immigration influences capital intensity is the fact that it also influences the composition of the labor force. This influence is important, as research on the demand for labor shows that a simplified analysis using only a single type of labor fails to reveal significant relationships. One result is that different types of labor are not, in many cases, substitutes, but complements in the production process. If a certain part of the labor force grows because of immigration, and wages then fall for this group, it may also imply an increase in demand and higher wages for other groups that complement the first group in the production process.[11]

In general, immigrants are also highly over-represented in certain regions. In most countries, immigrants are primarily over-represented in large cities. In Denmark an average of 7.1 percent of the population consisted in the year 2000 of immigrants and their children.[12] In the Danish capital, Copenhagen, and the surrounding areas, this percentage was significantly larger (13.9) and in some municipalities within this area – for instance in the Municipality of Copenhagen (17.6), and suburbs such as Ishøj (24.2), Brøndby (21.1) and Albertslund (20.0) – it was even larger. Outside the Copenhagen region, the percentage is especially high in larger cities such as Aarhus and Odense, and in some of the municipalities along the border to Germany. The percentages are much larger in some areas of these municipalities.[13]

The effects on wages can be greater for some occupations, educational groups

---

10 This is the standard result of the analysis. See, however, Lundborg and Segerstrom (1998) for an analysis of a model (with endogenous economic growth) where the result is a fall in the return on capital.
11 See, for example, Bauer (1998) for a study of the effects in Germany.
12 Figures taken from Statistics Denmark, Statistikbanken.
13 See Hummelgaard et al. (1995) for a discussion of the concentration of immigrants within certain residential areas.

and regions than for the labor force as a whole, due to the selectivity of immigration. The wage effect depends, among other things, on the degree of geographic and job-related mobility among the native labor force. Increased movement away from regional labor markets with a high density of immigrants and decreased settlement in such markets can thus reduce the effect on wages.[14] The mobility among the immigrants and the selectivity as regards region, occupation and education among those of the immigrants leaving the country can also influence the wage effect.

There are two basic types of studies of the effects of immigration on wages.[15] The first type is based on differences between the percentages of immigrants living in various regions or in different occupations. This type of study generally shows only a minimal effect on wages.[16] One explanation why the expected effects do not appear might be that a movement of immigrants to an area is entirely or partly countered by changes of the settlement patterns of the native population, and by a movement of capital to the area to which the immigrants have moved. The other type of study is based on a view of the country as a single economic entity. The study of this entity is then based on the fact that variations in the composition of production factors can be traced over time. In this type of study, immigration appears to have a considerably greater effect on wages.

There are a number of studies of the effects on the native wage rate in Germany, see Bauer et al. (forthcoming) for a survey. The main results are that the "effects are small or insignificant, or even positive which can be interpreted in the sense that migrants are complements to natives". On the other hand, there are no such studies available on Denmark. We will show results from such a study below.

To study the effects of immigration on the native wage rate we have re-estimated the wage equations presented in section 11.3, adding variables representing the proportion of immigrants in the population of the municipality – non-Western and Western – and the unemployment rate in the municipality (the unemployment variable is added to control for co-variation between the labor market situation and the inflow of immigrants). The estimations are presented in detail in the appendices to this chapter, but the main results are contained in Table 11.9. The table shows that the effect of the percentage of immigrants (both Western and non-Western) on the

---

14 Card and DiNardo (2001) did not find any selective out-migration of natives as a response to immigration in local labor markets in the U.S.
15 See Borjas, Freeman and Katz (1996) for a discussion of both types of studies.
16 See Leibfritz et al. (2003) for a recent survey and Bauer et al. (forthcoming) for a comprehensive survey of studies on Germany. Both surveys show that according to most studies there are no or small effects of immigration on wages. See also Addison and Worswick (2002) for a recent study of Australia, with references to earlier studies of that country. They did not find any impacts on the native wage from immigration to Australia. However, there are studies with differing results. A study of the United States, Enchautegui (1997), indicates that immigration accounts for only a small part of the decrease in wages for high-school dropouts nationally, but that it has a larger effect on areas where large numbers of immigrants live. See also a recent paper by Borjas (2002) which shows large negative effects of immigration on the native wage rate.

Table 11.9. Regression estimates (OLS) with hourly wage (log) in the year 2000 as the dependent variable and with age, gender, family status, country of origin, education, and municipality characteristics as explanatory variables.

Variables	All	Men	Women
Percentage of immigrants from Western countries in the municipality	0.023 (0.002)***	0.023 (0.002)***	0.021 (0.002)***
Percentage of immigrants from non-Western countries in the municipality	0.007 (0.0004)***	0.006 (0.0006)***	0.007 (0.0006)***
Unemployment rate in the municipality	-0.018 (0.001)***	-0.023 (0.001)***	-0.013 (0.001)***
Number of observations	78516	39075	39441
R^2(adj)	0.178	0.215	0.102

Notes: *** significant at the 1 percent level, ** significant at the 5 percent level, * significant at the 10 percent level. The coefficients of the other variables are shown in the appendices. Standard errors in parentheses. All with an hourly wage below EUR 1,346.98 (=DKK 10,000) are included.

wage rate is positive. A larger proportion of immigrants means a higher wage rate. The sign of the unemployment variable, is as expected, negative. The explanation for the positive effect on the wage rate of the proportion of immigrants could be that unemployment is not good enough as a control for the labor market situation or that natives and immigrants are complements (and not substitutes) in the production function. It would also have been of interest to make a fixed effect estimation, but this has not been possible to do in this case.

Differences in urbanization may have an influence but we have not controlled for that. To remedy this we have re-estimated the regressions shown in Table 11.9 adding dummy variables for different degrees of urbanization (according to a classification developed by Statistics Denmark; the higher the number the less urbanised is the municipality).

The coefficients of the urbanization dummies show that the wages are higher in more urbanised municipalities than in less urbanized municipalities. Of special interest in this connection are the variables representing the immigrant shares in the municipality. The coefficient for the percentage of immigrants from Western countries in the municipality is only significant for men (and all) and is smaller than in the estimations that do not include the urbanization variables. The coefficient for the percentage of immigrants from non-Western immigrants in the municipality is also smaller and has, which is more important, changed sign. A larger percentage of non-Western immigrants leads to a lower wage. The effect is small, however. The coefficient for the unemployment rate in the municipality is still negative and significant but smaller than in the estimations that do not include the urbanization variables.

We have also made regressions where we include the change in percentage units of the immigrant percentage between 1995 and 2000 instead of the percentage of

Table 11.10. Regression estimates (OLS) with hourly wage (log) in the year 2000 as the dependent variable and with age, gender, family status, country of origin, education and municipality characteristics as explanatory variables

Variables	All	Men	Women
Percentage of immigrants from Western countries in the municipality	0.004 (0.002)*	0.007 (0.003)**	-0.0002 (0.003)
Percentage of immigrants from non-Western countries in the municipality	-0.004 (0.0007)***	-0.004 (0.0009)***	-0.004 (0.001)***
Unemployment rate in the municipality	-0.008 (0.001)***	-0.013 (0.002)***	-0.003 (0.002)
Urbanization category 2	-0.029 (0.007)***	-0.019 (0.010)*	-0.030 (0.010)***
Urbanization category 3	-0.082 (0.010)***	-0.083 (0.014)***	-0.077 (0.014)***
Urbanization category 4	-0.106 (0.012)***	-0.088 (0.017)***	-0.116 (0.018)***
Urbanization category 5	-0.087 (0.009)***	-0.076 (0.012)***	-0.095 (0.012)***
Urbanization category 6	-0.139 (0.011)***	-0.116 (0.015)***	-0.159 (0.015)***
Urbanization category 7	-0.148 (0.010)***	-0.133 (0.014)***	-0.157 (0.015)***
Urbanization category 8	-0.151 (0.011)***	-0.141 (0.015)***	-0.152 (0.016)***
Urbanization category 9	-0.185 (0.011)***	-0.167 (0.015)***	-0.193 (0.016)***
Urbanization category 10	-0.194 (0.011)***	-0.186 (0.015)***	-0.190 (0.016)***
Urbanization category 11	-0.186 (0.013)***	-0.177 (0.017)***	-0.182 (0.018)***
Urbanization category 12	-0.200 (0.012)***	-0.177 (0.017)***	-0.209 (0.018)***
Number of observations	78,516	39,075	39,441
R^2(adj)	0.183	0.220	0.108

Notes: *** significant on the 1 percent level, ** significant on the 5 percent level, * significant on the 10 percent level. The coefficients of the other variables are shown in the appendices. Standard errors in parentheses. All with an hourly wage below EUR 1,346.98 (=DKK 10,000) are included. Urbanization category 1 – the reference category – is the capital (Copenhagen and Frederiksberg).

immigrants in the population in the municipality in the year 2000. We get a significant and positive sign for the change in the non-Western immigrant percentage, but insignificant results for the change in the percentage of Western immigrants (these results are not shown in the table).

We make a further check by estimating separate wage equations for natives and non-Western immigrants. The wage equation for natives gives the same results as the wage equation for the whole population, which is not very surprising as the natives constitute the large majority of the population. For the wage equation for non-Western immigrants we get a significant effect on the wage rate for the percentage of Western immigrants but not for the percentage of non-Western immigrants. This lends some support to the hypothesis that the Western and non-Western immigrants are not substitutes in the production function but are complements. If dummies representing

Table 11.11. Regression estimates (OLS) with hourly wage (log) in the year 2000 as the dependent variable and with age, gender, family status, country of origin, education, and municipality characteristics as explanatory variables.

Variables	Danes	Non-Western immigrants
Percentage of immigrants from Western countries in the municipality	0.023 (0.002)***	0.015 (0.008)*
Percentage of immigrants from non-Western countries in the municipality	0.007 (0.0005)***	0.001 (0.002)
Unemployment rate in the municipality	-0.017 (0.001)***	-0.015 (0.007)**
Number of observations	72784	2375
R²(adj)	0.184	0.080

Notes: *** significant at the 1 percent level, ** significant at the 5 percent level, * significant at the 10 percent level. The coefficients of the other variables are shown in the appendices. Standard errors in parentheses. All with an hourly wage below EUR 1,346.98 (=DKK 10,000) are included

urbanization are included in the regressions, the results change to some extent. The changes are the same for Danes in Table 11.11 as for the group "all" in Table 11.9 as is to be expected since the Danes constitute the vast majority of the population in Denmark. For the group non-Western immigrants the coefficient for the variables representing the percentage of non-Western immigrants in the municipality becomes insignificant.

We have also made regressions where we include the change in percentage units of the immigrant population between 1995 and 2000 instead of the percentage of immigrants in the population in the municipality in the year 2000. The signs of the coefficients are the same as for the regressions shown in Table 11.11 (these results are not shown in the table). Also in this case the coefficient for non-Western immigrants (change in the percentage between 1995 and 2000 in the municipality) changes sign if the urbanization dummies are included in the regression.

11.4. Self-employed Immigrants in Denmark[17,18]

Table 11.3 showed that first-generation immigrants from non-Western countries had a slightly higher proportion of their labor income from self-employment than other

---

17 For a more detailed analysis of self-employment among immigrants based on the same data see Wadensjö and Orrje (2002a). For surveys of current research on self-employment among immigrants in Denmark see Bager (2002) and Rezaei (2002).
18 The results in this section should be compared with those in Chapter 7. The main addition to the results in Chapter 7 is that here we are able to compare the self-employed non-Western immigrants with self-employed native Danes and self-employed immigrants from Western countries.

Table 11.12. Percentage of people with income from self-employment among all the employed (employees and self-employed) aged 18-64.

	Danes			Western immigrants			Non-Western immigrants			All		
	1998	1999	2000	1998	1999	2000	1998	1999	2000	1998	1999	2000
All with a positive income from self-employment	11.8	11.6	11.6	11.8	11.1	13.0	10.1	11.4	9.9	11.7	11.5	11.6
All with income from self-employment larger than that from wages	6.3	6.3	6.2	7.3	7.0	8.1	7.9	9.3	7.9	6.4	6.3	6.2
All with a positive income from self-employment who have no wage income	4.8	4.7	4.6	5.8	5.3	6.4	6.7	7.9	6.5	4.9	4.8	4.6

groups. We will now study the self-employed immigrants and their income situation in more detail.

In many cases it is not self-evident whether a person should be classified as self-employed or as an employee. One of the problems is that many people have income from both self-employment and as an employee. Another problem is that the incomes, especially for those who are self-employed, can vary greatly over the years, in some years even resulting in a negative income. Should those with negative income from self-employment be classified as self-employed? Table 11.12 shows the proportion who are self-employed according to three different definitions.

The non-Western immigrants are not overrepresented among the self-employed if we include all who are self-employed (all with a positive income from self-employment). They are overrepresented, however, if we define the self-employed as all who have an income from self-employment that is higher than their wage income or who have an income from self-employment but no wage income. The reason for the discrepancy between the results according to the three definitions is that many native Danes with wage incomes also have income from self-employment, including those with high wage incomes. Such combinations are less common among non-Western immigrants. For them the income from self-employment is more often the only or the main income.

The proportion that are self-employed may be of importance for the net transfer to the public sector, if the average income from self-employment differs from the average wage income and if the tax rates for the two types of wage income differ. The incomes that are relevant are the incomes declared to the tax authorities, as these are the basis for income taxation.[19] If the average income from self-

---

19 It is therefore not important in this context that the proportions of the incomes that are registered differ between incomes from self-employment and wage incomes. See Bager (2002) for a discussion of this question.

Table 11.13. Average annual income from self-employment among all aged 18-64 with a positive income from self-employment; thousand Euro.

	Danes			Western immigrants			Non-Western immigrants			All		
	1998	1999	2000	1998	1999	2000	1998	1999	2000	1998	1999	2000
All with a positive income from self-employment	25	26	27	22	26	30	15	18	20	25	25	27
All with income from self-employment larger than that from wages	48	49	47	38	44	46	17	23	23	46	47	46
All with a positive income from self-employment who have no wage income	41	42	44	35	34	42	18	20	23	40	40	43

employment and the average wage income are the same, and the average tax rate is the same for the two types of incomes, the distribution and changes in distribution of form of employment should be without effect on the net transfers. Otherwise, there are effects. Hence, there are good arguments for investigating the incomes from self-employment. Table 11.13 presents some relevant information.

The table shows that the incomes from self-employment vary greatly according to the definition used. They are lowest if we look at the incomes for all who have an income from self-employment. Many have an income from self-employment as a supplement to wage income from a full-time job. This is especially so for native Danes and Western immigrants. However, regardless of the definition chosen, non-Western immigrants on average have lower incomes from self-employment than the other two groups. There are many factors behind this difference. One of them is that self-employed non-Western immigrants work in other sectors, especially in retailing and restaurants, than those worked in by native Danes and Western immigrants.

It is of special interest to study those who have income from self-employment but no wage income. The non-Western immigrants have much lower incomes than the other two groups. Their incomes have increased considerably between 1998 and 2000, but, nevertheless, these incomes are still much lower than for the other two groups, and they are also lower than for those who only have wage income, which is not the case for the other two groups.[20] A greater proportion of self-employed in this group means a lower average labor income and therefore a lower base for tax payments. Another issue is that the effect on net transfer may differ between

---

20 This information is not included in the table.

incomes from self-employment and wages (the average and the marginal net transfer rate may differ). We have studied this by estimating regressions with net transfer to the public sector as the dependent variable and income from self-employment and from wages as two independent variables (besides the demographic variables). The result is that the (marginal) effect is much higher for wages (80 percent in 2000) than for incomes from self-employment (57 percent in 2000). It increases the negative effects of the high proportion of self-employed among the non-Western immigrants. We have also made the same type of estimation for the separate groups. The results for the native Danes are 80 percent for wages and 58 percent for income from self-employment, for first-generation immigrants from Western countries 76 and 27 percent, for second-generation immigrants from Western countries 78 and 33 percent, for first-generation immigrants from non-Western countries 84 and 67 percent, and for second-generation immigrants from Western countries 86 and 71 percent. The levels vary but the coefficient for wages is larger for all groups than that for income from self-employment. We have also made the corresponding estimations for the non-Western immigrants in Germany who are included in the study. The results are 66 percent for wages and 53 percent for income from self-employment for the first-generation of immigrants, and 65 and 48 percent for second-generation immigrants.

11.5. Immigration and Unemployment among Native Workers in Denmark[21]

If immigration influences native unemployment, it could influence the net transfer from natives to the public sector. The effect of immigration on native unemployment is interesting because of this, but also for other reasons. The exact nature of this influence, however, is not clear. It depends upon the way in which the structure of labor demand and labor supply is influenced by the immigration. One case that has been dealt with in various studies is the way in which immigration influences the state of the economy, or more generally whether immigration helps to exaggerate swings in the economy, or contributes to promoting stability. How do investments (private and public), consumption (private and public) and production look in the period immediately following a wave of immigration? Immigration can lead, for example, to investment in jobs (companies see a chance to expand), residential property, and infrastructure, so that the total level of demand rises.

Does a large wave of immigration and thus an increase in the immigrant population lead to greater unemployment? A superficial investigation does not support

---

21 For a survey of studies of the German experiences see Bauer et al. (forthcoming). The results differ between studies but the main conclusion is that the effects are small, if any. We have not found any study of this type for Denmark. Pedersen's (forthcoming) recent survey of Danish economic immigration research does not contain any references to such studies.

this hypothesis. It seems as if unemployment levels are determined by other factors, for example by a political desire to keep inflation at bay. Lower unemployment levels lead to higher inflation. In a way, one could say that the contribution that unemployment makes to the economy is to fight inflation, and that the unemployed are, in part, compensated for their efforts and, in part, contribute themselves to the control of inflation by having a lower standard of living.[22] The question is whether an unemployed immigrant contributes as much to holding inflation down as an unemployed native Dane. If the immigrant does contribute as much, one could say that the Danish population has managed to attain a certain given (low) inflation level along with lower unemployment for them by allowing the immigrants to "take over" a part of the unemployment that is needed to fight inflation. Results in Section 11.3, "The Impact of Immigrantion on the Native Wage Rate", give some indication that the influence from the unemployment of non-Western immigrants on wages is not significant.

It might also be the case that immigration leads to an increase in structural unemployment. Immigration leads to a larger increase in the labor supply in certain occupations and local labor markets than in others. This can, at least in the short term, lead to imbalances in the labor market if no adjustment of relative wages occurs, or if the imbalances are not removed via mobility between different occupations and mobility or commuting between different municipalities. Without an adjustment, the total level of unemployment may increase at any given level of inflation.

Another way to test the effects of immigrants and immigration on unemployment is to use observations on the municipal level. In Table 11.14 the municipal unemployment rate for native Danes is the dependent variable and the immigrant proportion of the population or change in the immigrant proportion of the population are independent variables with or without controls for the native unemployment rate five years earlier. The main result is that the signs for the coefficients for non-Western proportion of the population and the change in that proportion are negative and significant (but small). The higher the proportion of non-Western immigrants (or change in that proportion), the lower is the municipal unemployment rate for native Danes. On the other hand, the coefficient for change of the proportion of immigrants from Western countries in the population is significant and positive. One possible explanation is that the Western immigrants and native Danes are substitutes and native Danes and non-Western immigrants are complements in the production process.

In Table 11.15 we estimate an equation with the municipal unemployment rate for non-Western immigrants as the dependent variable. The main result, as expected, is that the coefficient for the non-Western proportion of the population is positive. The

---

22 For an analysis in this line of thought that relies on the efficiency wages theory, see Epstein & Hillman (2000).

Table 11.14. Regression estimates (OLS) with unemployment rate (%) for native Danes in the municipalities in the year 2000 as the dependent variable.

	(1)	(2)	(3)
Proportion of the population of the municipality from non-Western countries	-0.0010 (0.0003)***	-0.0013 (0.0002)***	
Proportion of the population of the municipality from Western countries	0.0006 (0.0010)	0.0006 (0.0006)	
Change in the proportion of the population of the municipality from non-Western countries between 1995 and 2000			-0.0017 (0.0007)**
Change in the proportion of the population of the municipality from Western countries between 1995 and 2000			0.0067 (0.0024)***
Municipal unemployment rate for native Danes in 1995		0.4900 (0.0197)***	0.4823 (0.0208)***
Constant	0.0428 (0.0020)***	0.0003 (0.0020)	-0.0009 (0.0020)
R^2 (adj)	0.0231	0.7020	0.6735
Number of observations	275	275	275

Notes: *** significant at the 1 percent level, ** significant at the 5 percent level, * significant at the 10 percent level. The coefficients of the other variables are shown in the appendices. Standard errors in parentheses. All with an hourly wage below EUR 1,346.98 (=DKK 10,000) are included.

Table 11.15. Unemployment rate for non-Western immigrants in the municipalities in the year 2000; OLS estimates.

Municipal unemployment rate for Danes in 2000	2.9949 (0.3124)***
Proportion of the population of the municipality from non-Western countries	0.0052 (0.0019)***
Constant	0.0066 (0.0.154)
R^2 (adj)	0.2500
Number of observations	275

Notes: *** significant at the 1 percent level, ** significant at the 5 percent level, * significant at the 10 percent level. The coefficients of the other variables are shown in the appendices. Standard errors in parentheses. All with an hourly wage below EUR 1,346.98 (=DKK 10,000) are included.

value of the coefficient for the municipal unemployment rate for Danes is around three. It means that a change in the unemployment rate for native Danes leads to a three times higher change in the unemployment rate among non-Western immigrants. This underlines the fact that the immigrants' labor market situation very much depends on the general labor market situation, as suggested in Chapter 4 based on the aggregated time series.

11.6. Income Distribution among Immigrants and Natives[23]

In earlier sections of this chapter we dealt with income from labor. To that could be added other forms of incomes from the market, for example income from capital. The disposable incomes available to households, however, are determined not only by the market but also by redistribution through the public sector. The public sector makes income distribution more equal by making taxes lower and transfers higher for those with low incomes. In Chapter 10, in studying the net transfer to and from the public sector, we also included individualized public consumption (and to some extent public investments). Here we will only take account of the redistribution through direct taxes and transfer payments to individuals. We will compare the disposable incomes of immigrants and natives in Denmark and study the disposable incomes of immigrants in Germany.

We will start by making a comparison of the net incomes per equivalent household member according to age for the groups in Denmark (native Danes, Western immigrants, non-Western immigrants) and non-Western immigrants in Germany. Table 11.16 shows average net household income according to age.

We will comment on the figures for Denmark first. The average income for immigrants is also related to the incomes of the natives in Denmark. As the table shows, the levels and the patterns differ among the groups. It is common for all groups, however, that the age group 55-59 years has the highest income, even if the levels differ. It is highest for immigrants from Western countries and lowest for those from non-Western countries. The native group have incomes in between the values of the other two.

The non-Western immigrants have considerably lower incomes than the natives in all age groups except the oldest one. The explanations for this are mainly differences in the age structures within the age group, and the fact that older non-Western immigrants more often live in the same household as their children. The average age among those who are 67 years and over is 76.4 years among native Danes, 76.8 years among Western immigrants, and 74.3 years among non-Western immigrants. The households of native Danes aged 67 and over consist to 49 percent of one person, 48 percent of two persons, and 3 percent of three persons or more. The corresponding percentages for Western immigrant households are 51, 44 and 5 and for non-Western immigrant households 29, 41 and 31.[24]

---

[23] Büchel and Frick (2003) study the incomes before and after government redistribution among natives and immigants in eight countries including Denmark and Germany. The redistribution to immigrants is much larger in Denmark than in Germany and the other countries included in their study.

[24] One remaining puzzle is that non-Western immigrant households aged 67 and over with two members have higher disposable income than native Danish households in the same age group and of the same size.

Table 11.16. Disposable income per equivalent household member in Denmark in the year 2000 and Germany in 2002 according to country of origin and age; all amounts in Euro.

Age	Danes	Western immigrants		Non-Western immigrants		Non-Western immigrants in Germany (Euro)
	Euro	Euro	% of the incomes of native Danes	Euro	% of the incomes of native Danes	
18-24	20,427	11,320	55.4	17,612	86.2	10,890
25-29	20,850	17,283	82.9	16,864	80.9	11,277
30-39	21,546	20,821	96.6	16,763	77.8	11,697
40-49	24,131	23,896	99.0	18,067	74.9	12,778
50-59	25,835	28,084	108.7	20,743	80.3	13,334
60-66	22,504	23,777	105.7	19,044	84.6	12,090
67-	17,455	20,024	114.7	19,747	113.1	11,792
All	22,011	21,696	98.6	17,670	80.3	11,992

Notes: Disposable income is calculated per equivalent household member. The square root of number of members of the household is used as the equivalence scale. A few people under 18 years of age constitute separate households in the Law model. They are not included in this table. The values for Denmark are converted to year 2002 by using the Harmonised Indices of Consumer Prices (HICPs).

Among those aged 30-59, an age group with few people engaged in studies or retired, the average income of the non-Western immigrants is about three fourths of the incomes of Danes of the same age. For the Western immigrants the average income is lower than for native Danes up to the age of 50 and higher above that age.

The net incomes of non-Western immigrants in Germany are much lower than those of non-Western immigrants in Denmark. The difference is more or less of the same size in all age groups. There may be several explanations for this difference; these include generally higher incomes in Denmark than in Germany, different compositions of the groups of non-Western immigrants in the two countries, and higher compensation levels in the income transfer programs in Denmark.

Table 11.16 gives a picture of the averages for the different groups according to age but does not give information on the variation of incomes within the groups. We will now study the variations of incomes in different ways and start by seeing how the incomes for the three different groups are distributed across deciles in Denmark (we do not have information for the income distribution for natives in Germany). This information is given in Table 11.17.

Table 11.17. The composition of the income deciles in Denmark in the year 2000.

Decile	Danes	Western Immigrants	Non-Western Immigrants	All
1	87.3	4.1	8.6	100
2	89.1	2.1	8.8	100
3	90.7	2.2	7.1	100
4	92.9	2.0	5.1	100
5	93.9	1.8	4.3	100
6	94.9	1.5	3.6	100
7	95.0	1.8	3.2	100
8	95.7	1.8	2.5	100
9	95.9	1.9	2.2	100
10	95.3	2.8	1.9	100
All	93.1	2.2	5.1	100

Notes: The placement in deciles is made according to disposable income per equivalent household member. The square root of the number of members of the household is used as the equivalence scale.

The table shows that the natives are the largest group in all deciles – they constitute the great majority, 87 percent, even in the first decile (that with the lowest incomes). Most people with low incomes are native Danes even if non-Western immigrants are over-represented in that group.

The immigrants from Western countries, which constitute 2.2 percent of the population covered by the study, are over-represented both among those with the lowest incomes and among those with the highest incomes. The over-representation among those with low incomes may be due to the low household incomes among guest students. The income pattern for the non-Western immigrants, who constitute 5.2 percent of the population, is unambiguous. The higher the decile, the lower is the proportion of non-Western immigrants in the group. In the first two deciles the proportions are 8.6 and 8.8 percent respectively, and in the highest decile it is 1.9 percent.

The next step is to study the distribution across socio-economic groups in the various deciles for the three groups in Denmark and for non-Western immigrants in Germany. The socioeconomic groups are the self-employed, wage earners, disability pensioners, old-age pensioners, special early retirement pensioners (only for Denmark), students and "others". A person's main activity during the year determines the classification.

Table 11.18. Socio-economic groups distributed by deciles in the year 2000; native Danes; percentage distribution within each decile.

Decile	Socio-economic status							
	Self-employed	Wage earners	Disability pensioners	Old age pensioners	Early retirees	In education	Other	All
1	9.2	28.3	2.9	33.8	3.7	7.7	14.4	100
2	4.3	25.1	7.6	44.4	5.7	2.6	10.4	100
3	4.3	41.4	11.9	26.3	6.1	1.8	8.2	100
4	3.9	56.3	10.0	14.1	6.6	2.0	7.1	100
5	3.7	64.1	6.6	11.7	5.7	1.8	6.5	100
6	4.1	70.7	5.2	8.4	4.7	1.6	5.3	100
7	4.3	75.5	3.6	6.0	4.0	1.5	5.0	100
8	4.5	78.2	2.9	4.9	3.4	1.7	4.4	100
9	4.7	81.0	2.1	4.5	2.2	1.4	4.0	100
10	8.8	76.7	1.7	5.5	2.1	1.2	4.2	100
All	5.2	59.7	5.4	15.9	4.4	2.3	6.9	100

Note: All individuals aged 18 years and over, distributed according to decile and socio-economic status.

We will study the distribution in Denmark first (see Tables 11.18-11.20).[25] Two socio-economic groups make up an equal proportion of all three groups: disability pensioners (5.4 percent among Danes, 4.4 percent among Western immigrants, and 5.6 percent among non-Western immigrants) and the self-employed (5.2, 5.9 and 4.4 pecent). If we only look at those with incomes from employment (wage earners and the self-employed), the self-employed constitute a larger proportion of immigrants from non-Western countries than of Western immigrants and native Danes.

Wage earners are the largest group among native Danes (59.7 percent) and Western immigrants (50.0 percent). Among the non-Western immigrants, wage earners and "others" are of the same size, 38.3 percent. The category "others" includes those who received their main income during the year from unemployment benefits or welfare payments, and housewives. "Others" make up only 6.9 percent of the native Danes and 18.7 percent of the Western immigrants. The old age pensioners are a larger group among natives and Western immigrants than among non-Western immigrants, which is explained by the fact that few non-

---

25 The distribution by deciles is made for the separate groups in question and not according to the total distribution.

Table 11.19. Socio-economic groups distributed by deciles in the year 2000; Western immigrants in Denmark; percentage distribution within each decile.

Decile	Socio-economic status							
	Self-employed	Wage earners	Disability pensioners	Old age pensioners	Early retirees	In education	Other	All
1	7.9	26.7	1.6	1.3	0.0	1.7	45.6	100
2	10.4	28.6	3.5	22.0	6.0	5.0	24.5	100
3	6.0	28.0	7.9	32.4	3.8	5.3	16.7	100
4	4.1	39.7	8.8	21.4	3.5	1.9	20.5	100
5	4.1	52.8	5.7	14.2	4.7	2.2	16.4	100
6	4.7	55.7	5.7	15.4	2.5	1.6	14.5	100
7	5.0	63.7	4.7	9.8	4.1	1.2	11.4	100
8	5.7	70.8	2.2	6.9	4.7	0.6	9.1	100
9	4.1	69.8	2.5	9.1	1.9	0.3	12.2	100
10	7.6	63.7	1.9	7.3	3.5	0.3	15.8	100
All	5.9	50.0	4.4	14.0	3.5	3.6	18.7	100

Note: All individuals aged 18 years and over, distributed according to decile and socio-economic status.

Western immigrants are aged 65 or older. The proportion with an early retirement pension is higher among natives, due to the fact that this group is more established in the Danish labor market (one condition for being able to get this type of benefit). The proportion in education is largest among the non-Western immigrants. They are younger. The fact that studying the Danish language and other types of education is used as a measure for integration and as a labor market program may also explain the high percentage among non-Western immigrants who are in education.

We will now continue with the immigrants from Western countries and compare them with the natives. With some minor exceptions the proportion who are wage earners increases with the decile number. However, with one exception the level is lower than among the native Danes. The proportion for 'other' is higher among Western immigrants than among native Danes – part of the explanation is that there are a greater proportion of housewives in the population. The self-employed are over-represented in the lowest two deciles and in the highest decile for both groups. In both groups there is a non-negligible number of self-employed.[26]

---

26 Part of the explanation for this may be under-reporting of incomes and the fact that incomes can be moved between years.

Table 11.20. Socio-economic groups distributed by deciles in the year 2000; non-Western immigrants in Denmark; percentage distribution within each decile.

	Socio-economic status							
Decile	Self-employed	Wage earners	Disability pensioners	Old age pensioners	Early retirees	In education	Other	All
1	8.9	15.1	1.4	2.3	0.2	17.3	54.9	100
2	6.5	19.6	3.6	7.0	0.9	10.4	51.9	100
3	4.7	15.2	4.2	4.8	1.6	9.9	59.6	100
4	3.0	19.8	7.2	5.1	1.4	8.1	55.4	100
5	2.6	33.1	9.5	3.3	1.7	7.6	42.1	100
6	2.4	45.6	10.1	2.2	1.6	7.2	30.8	100
7	4.5	51.5	6.5	3.1	2.0	6.2	26.1	100
8	3.3	57.2	5.6	2.6	3.0	6.4	22.0	100
9	2.5	63.3	3.7	2.5	2.3	4.8	20.8	100
10	5.5	62.5	4.0	3.4	1.6	4.0	19.0	100
All	4.4	38.3	5.6	3.6	1.6	8.2	38.3	100

Note: All individuals aged 18 years and over, distributed according to decile and socio-economic status.

Table 11.21. The socio-economic groups distributed by deciles in the year 2002; non-Western immigrants in Germany; percentage distribution within each decile.

	Socio-economic status						
Decile	Self-employed	Wage earners	Disability pensioners	Old age pensioners	In education	Other	All
1	0.5	10.9	0.7	2.3	30.2	55.3	100
2	0.1	16.7	0.7	5.2	17.1	59.0	100
3	1.7	24.0	1.2	5.6	10.4	57.1	100
4	2.3	33.4	1.2	6.4	8.5	48.1	100
5	2.4	43.8	2.1	8.7	5.9	37.1	100
6	6.2	47.0	2.2	7.4	4.2	33.0	100
7	4.0	58.1	1.3	5.9	2.6	28.0	100
8	5.5	60.6	1.5	4.7	3.1	24.4	100
9	7.8	70.7	0.9	2.7	2.7	15.1	100
10	21.5	60.0	0.0	3.8	3.1	11.6	100
All	5.2	42.5	1.2	5.3	8.8	37.0	100

Note: All individuals aged 18 years and over, distributed according to decile and socio-economic status.

The most characteristic feature of the non-Western group is the high proportion of people who are classified as "other". In the first four deciles they are the majority, and as previously noted they make up 38.3 percent of all non-Western immigrants. Wage earners are in the majority only in the four highest deciles. The self-employed are present in the lowest deciles to a greater extent than is the case for the other two groups. An explanation for the high levels of self-employment among non-Western immigrants may be that it is not a preferred choice for many of them, but rather the last resort when they have not been able to find a job. One indication that the opportunities on the labor market are small is the fact that those who have incomes mainly in the form of transfer payments are in higher deciles than those in other groups with the same types of income.

We will now turn to the non-Western immigrants in Germany and compare them especially with non-Western immigrants in Denmark. Compared to Denmark, more of the group are employed in Germany (the self-employed and wage earners taken together), fewer are in income transfer programs and fewer in education or in the "other" category. The differences are not very large, however. The distribution by socio-economic categories is much more similar for the groups of non-Western immigrants in the two countries than it is for different groups in Denmark when they are compared with each other. A large difference is that the proportion of self-employed increases rapidly and consistently with the decile number in Germany, which contrasts strongly with the situation in Denmark.

Another method of studying the income distribution is to use a more comprehensive measure. We will do so here by calculating the Gini coefficient for the various groups. It shows how large a part of the incomes has to be redistributed to make all incomes equal. Table 11.22 shows the Gini coefficient for the three groups in Denmark, for non-Western immigrants in Germany and separately according to the five different countries of origin in Germany.

The table shows that the native Danes have a slightly more equal distribution than the total population in Denmark. The immigrants from non-Western countries have almost the same Gini coefficient value as the native Danes. Many of the non-Western immigrants have no incomes from employment, but the welfare state works towards an equalized income structure after taxes and transfers. On the other hand, the value of the Gini coefficient is much higher for Western immigrants. One explanation is that there are relatively many students with low incomes in this group, at the same time as there are relatively many with high incomes from employment.

The Gini coefficient value for non-Western immigrants in Germany is higher than the corresponding value for non-Western immigrants in Denmark. The differences can probably be ascribed mainly to differences in the tax and income transfer

Table 11.22. **Income equality measured with the Gini coefficient for groups in Denmark in the year 2000 and in Germany in 2002.**

Group	Gini coefficient (%)
Danes	22.84
Immigrants from Western countries	33.29
Immigrants from non-Western countries	23.15
All in Denmark	23.22
Non-Western immigrants in Germany	29.32
of whom from	
Turkey	24.12
former Yugoslavia	30.30
Poland	25.53
Iran	33.28
Lebanon	27.73

Note. The placement in deciles is made according to disposable income per equivalent household member. The square root of the number of household members is used as the equivalence scale.

system between the two countries. A comparison of the Gini coefficients for the five immigrant groups shows that it is highest for immigrants from former Yugoslavia and Iran, and lowest for immigrants from Turkey and Poland.

11.7. Summary and Conclusions

Some questions raised in Chapter 10 are dealt with in more depth in this chapter. The first concerns the labor incomes of immigrants. It is shown that both labor income in total and the wage income are much lower among non-Western immigrants than among native Danes and Western immigrants in Denmark. The wage rate determination is studied in more detail. The wage rate of non-Western immigrants is lower and the difference is not explained by the characteristics (age, education, etc.) that we are able to observe. The incomes of the self-employed are also studied. These incomes are also lower for non-Western immigrants.

Other issues dealt with in the chapter are the effects of immigrants and immigration on the wages and the unemployment for natives. It is difficult to control for all other variables that may be of importance so the results should be interpreted with care. The results indicate that a larger proportion of immigrants in the population of a municipality does not lower the wages of the natives. The estimates indicate the opposite effect. One explanation for this result may be that the groups are complements and not substitutes in the production process. Another explanation may be that we have not included a variable which is important for the wage determination and which is correlated with the share of non-Western immigrants in the municipality. Such a variable may be the degree of urbanisation of the municipality. We have tested that by re-estimations including dummies for the degree of urbanisation. The coefficient for the percentage of non-Western immigrants changes sign and becomes negative. It should be noted that the size of the coefficient is small.

The results of the attempts to estimate the effects of the proportion of immigrants on the unemployment among natives show that the proportion of non-Western immigrants in the population has a negative effect – the higher the proportion of immigrants the lower the native unemployment rate. This is consistent with the hypothesis that non-Western immigrants and natives are complements in the production function, and also with the results from the wage equation estimates. On the other hand, the sign of the coefficient for a change of the proportion of Western immigrants is positive. This is not in accordance with the results reached in the wage estimations; further research is needed. Differences in urbanization is a factor which may have an influence but for which we have not controlled.

Also studied in Chapter 11 are net incomes after taxes and transfers per equivalent household member. There are large differences between the average income of natives and immigrants in Denmark in spite of the large amount of redistribution. It is also shown that there are substantial differences between the net incomes of non-Western immigrants in Denmark and Germany. Another result found is that the incomes of non-Western immigrants are also more equally distributed in Denmark than in Germany.

References

Addison, Thomas and Christopher Worswick 2002. "The Impact of Immigration on the Earnings of Natives: Evidence from Australian Micro Data," *The Economic Record* 78, 68-78.

Bager, Torben. 2002. "Indvandrervirksomheder i Danmark – med vægt på perioden siden 1980", in *Erhvervshistorisk Årbog 2002*, Meddelser fra Erhvervsarkivet, No. 51.

Bauer, Thomas. 1998. *Arbeitsmarkteffekte der Migration und Einwanderungspolitik: Eine Analyse für die Bundesrepublik Deutschland*. Heidelberg: Physica-Verlag.

Bauer, Thomas, Barbara Dietz, Klaus F. Zimmermann and Erik Zwintz. Forthcoming 2004. "German Migration: Development, Assimilation and Labour Market Effects," in Klaus F. Zimmermann (ed.): *European Migration: What Do We Know?* Oxford: Oxford University Press.

Borjas, George J., Richard B. Freeman and Lawrence Katz. 1996. "Searching for the Effect of Immigration on the Labor Market." *American Economic Review* 86, Papers and Proceedings, May, 246-51.

Borjas, George J. 2002. "The Labour Demand Curve *Is* Downward Sloping: Reexamining the Impact of the Immigration on the Labour Market," EALE conference in Paris.

Büchel, Felix and Joachim R. Frick. 2003. "Immigrants' Economic Performance Across Europe – Does Immigration Policy Matter?" EPAG Working Paper No. 42.

Card, David and John E. DiNardo. 2000. "Do Immigrant Inflows Lead to Native Outflows?" *American Economic Review* 90, Papers and Proceedings, May, 360-367.

Enchautegui, Maria E. 1997. "Immigration and wage changes of high school dropouts," *Monthly Labor Review* 120 (10), 3-9.

Epstein, Gil S. and Arye L. Hillman. 2000. "Social Harmony at the Boundaries of the Welfare State: Immigrants and Social Transfers". IZA Discussion Paper No. 168.

Hummelgaard, Hans, Leif Husted, Anders Holm, Mikkel Baadsgaard and Benedicte Olrik 1995. *Etniske minoriteter, integration og mobilitet*. Copenhagen: AKF Forlaget.

Leibfritz, Willi, Paul O'Brien and Jean-Christophe Dumont. 2003. "Effects of Immigration on Labour Markets and Government Budgets – An Overview," CESifo Working Paper No. 874.

Lundborg, Per and Paul P. Segerstrom. 2002. "The Growth and Welfare Effects of International Mass Migration." *Journal of International Economics* 56, 177-204.

Pedersen, Peder. Forthcoming. "Immigration in a Scandinavian Welfare State: The Recent Danish Experience," in Klaus F. Zimmermann (ed.): *European Migration: What Do We Know?* Oxford: Oxford University Press.

Rezaei, Shahamak. 2002. "Indvandrerejede virksomheder," AMID Working Paper Series 8/2002.

Wadensjö, Eskil and Helena Orrje. 2002. *Immigration and the Public Sector in Denmark*. Aarhus Universitetsforlag, Aarhus.

Wadensjö, Eskil and Helena Orrje. 2002a. "Immigrants and self-employment in Denmark," mimeo, The Swedish Institute for Social Research, Stockholm University.

Appendix tables

Table A11.1. Regression estimates (OLS) with hourly wage (log) in the year 2000 as the dependent variable.

Variables	(1)	(2)	(3)	(4)
Constant	2.335 (0.019)***	2.471 (0.020)***	2.425 (0.020)***	2.479 (0.020)***
One parent born in Denmark, one in a Western country	0.011 (0.012)	0.026 (0.012)**	0.009 (0.012)	0.025 (0.012)**
One parent born in Denmark, one in a non-Western country	-0.028 (0.024)	0.002 (0.024)	-0.029 (0.024)	-0.002 (0.024)
Both parents born in a Western country	0.009 (0.033)	0.034 (0.033)	0.011 (0.033)	0.032 (0.033)
Both parents born in a non-Western country	0.050 (0.026)	0.040 (0.026)	-0.001 (0.026)	0.033 (0.026)
Born in a Western country	-0.027 (0.012)**	-0.005 (0.012)	-0.027 (0.012)**	-0.006 (0.012)
Born in a non-Western country	-0.128 (0.009)***	-0.100 (0.009)***	-0.129 (0.009)***	-0.105 (0.009)***
Female	-0.190 (0.003)***	-0.189 (0.003)***	-0.190 (0.003)***	-0.189 (0.003)***
Age	0.023 (0.001)***	0.025 (0.001)***	0.024 (0.001)***	0.025 (0.001)***
Age^2	-0.00021 (0.00001)***	-0.00024 (0.00001)***	-0.00022 (0.00001)***	-0.00024 (0.00001)***
Vocational education	0.094 (0.004)***	0.095 (0.004)***	0.093 (0.004)***	0.094 (0.004)***
High school	0.180 (0.007)***	0.196 (0.007)***	0.178 (0.007)***	0.194 (0.007)***
Short higher education	0.206 (0.008)***	0.213 (0.008)***	0.203 (0.008)***	0.212 (0.008)***
Medium-length higher education	0.254 (0.005)***	0.264 (0.005)***	0.253 (0.005)***	0.263 (0.005)***
Long higher education	0.460 (0.007)***	0.489 (0.007)***	0.455 (0.007)***	0.485 (0.007)***
In education	0.011 (0.006)*	0.029 (0.006)***	0.012 (0.006)**	0.027 (0.006)***
Education not reported	0.070 (0.013)***	0.081 (0.013)***	0.069 (0.013)***	0.079 (0.013)***
Single with children	-0.001 (0.009)	-0.010 (0.009)	-0.002 (0.009)	-0.010 (0.009)
Married/cohabiting, no children	0.031 (0.004)***	0.022 (0.004)***	0.031 (0.004)***	0.023 (0.004)***
Married/cohabiting with children	0.050 (0.004)***	0.027 (0.004)***	0.047 (0.004)***	0.030 (0.004)***
Percentage of immigrants from Western countries in the municipality	0.026 (0.001)***		0.023 (0.002)***	
Percentage of immigrants from non-Western countries in the municipality	0.005 (0.0004)***		0.007 (0.0004)***	
Unemployment rate in the municipality		-0.016 (0.001)***	-0.018 (0.001)***	
Unemployment rate among native Danes in the municipality				-0.028 (0.002)***
Unemployment rate among Western immigrants in the municipality				0.002 (0.0007)**
Unemployment rate among non-Western immigrants in the municipality				0.0002 (0.0002)
Number of observations	78,516	78,516	78,516	78,516
R^2(adj)	0.174	0.168	0.178	0.170

Notes: *** significant at the 1 percent level, ** significant at the 5 percent level, * significant at the 10 percent level. Comparison group: Danes, men, primary education (9 years or less), single without children. Standard errors in parentheses. All 18 years and over with an hourly wage less than EUR 1,346.98 (=DKK 10,000) are included.

Table A11.2. Regression estimates (OLS) with hourly wage (log) in the year 2000 as the dependent variable. Men.

Variables	(1)	(2)	(3)	(4)
Constant	2.126 (0.026)***	2.273 (0.027)***	2.243 (0.027)***	2.277 (0.027)***
One parent born in Denmark, one in a Western country	0.010 (0.016)	0.022 (0.016)	0.007 (0.016)	0.021 (0.016)
One parent born in Denmark, one in a non-Western country	0.003 (0.033)	0.029 (0.033)	0.001 (0.032)	0.024 (0.033)
Both parents born in a Western country	0.019 (0.044)	0.045 (0.045)	0.025 (0.044)	0.041 (0.044)
Both parents born in a non-Western country	-0.008 (0.038)	0.029 (0.037)	-0.014 (0.037)	0.019 (0.037)
Born in a Western country	-0.054 (0.016)***	-0.034 (0.016)**	-0.054 (0.016)***	-0.036 (0.016)**
Born in a non-Western country	-0.155 (0.012)***	-0.130 (0.012)***	-0.158 (0.012)***	-0.137 (0.012)***
Age	0.032 (0.001)***	0.035 (0.001)***	0.033 (0.001)***	0.035 (0.001)***
Age^2	-0.00033 (0.00002)***	-0.00036 (0.00002)***	-0.00034 (0.00002)***	-0.00036 (0.00002)***
Vocational education	0.112 (0.006)***	0.112 (0.006)***	0.111 (0.005)***	0.112 (0.006)***
High school	0.187 (0.010)***	0.206 (0.010)***	0.183 (0.010)***	0.203 (0.010)***
Short higher education	0.209 (0.011)***	0.216 (0.011)***	0.207 (0.011)***	0.215 (0.011)***
Medium-length higher education	0.304 (0.008)***	0.315 (0.008)***	0.303 (0.008)***	0.314 (0.008)***
Long higher education	0.465 (0.009)***	0.490 (0.009)***	0.458 (0.009)***	0.485 (0.009)***
In education	-0.036 (0.009)**	-0.017 (0.009)*	-0.034 (0.009)***	-0.019 (0.008)**
Education not reported	0.081 (0.017)***	0.092 (0.017)***	0.081 (0.017)***	0.091 (0.017)***
Single with children	0.006 (0.022)	-0.006 (0.022)	0.005 (0.022)	-0.006 (0.022)
Married/cohabiting, no children	0.088 (0.006)***	0.084 (0.006)***	0.088 (0.006)***	0.084 (0.006)***
Married/cohabiting with children	0.121 (0.006)***	0.103 (0.006)***	0.118 (0.006)***	0.105 (0.006)***
Percentage of immigrants from Western countries in the municipality	0.028 (0.002)***		0.023 (0.002)***	
Percentage of immigrants from non-Western countries in the municipality	0.004 (0.0006)***		0.006 (0.0006)***	
Unemployment rate in the municipality		-0.021 (0.001)***	-0.023 (0.001)***	
Unemployment rate among native Danes in the municipality				-0.034 (0.001) ***
Unemployment rate among Western immigrants in the municipality				0.002 (0.001)**
Unemployment rate among non-Western immigrants in the municipality				0.0002 (0.0003)
Number of observations	39,075	39,075	39,075	39,075
R^2(adj)	0.210	0.207	0.215	0.208

Notes: *** significant at the 1 percent level, ** significant at the 5 percent level, * significant at the 10 percent level. Comparison group: Danes, men, primary education (9 years or less), single without children. Standard errors in parentheses. All 18 years and over with an hourly wage less than EUR 1,346.98 (=DKK 10,000) are included.

Table A11.3. Regression estimates (OLS) with hourly wage (log) in the year 2000 as the dependent variable. Women.

Variables	(1)	(2)	(3)	(4)
Constant	2.376 (0.028)***	2.502 (0.029)***	2.443 (0.029)***	2.510 (0.029)***
One parent born in Denmark, one in a Western country	0.014 (0.018)	0.030 (0.018)*	0.013 (0.018)	0.029 (0.018)
One parent born in Denmark, one in a non-Western country	-0.064 (0.034)*	-0.036 (0.034)	-0.064 (0.034)*	-0.038 (0.034)
Both parents born in a Western country	0.004 (0.048)	0.027 (0.048)	0.003 (0.048)	0.025 (0.048)
Both parents born in a non-Western country	-0.002 (0.035)	0.027 (0.035)	-0.007 (0.035)	0.023 (0.035)
Born in a Western country	-0.002 (0.017)	0.020 (0.017)	-0.002 (0.017)	0.018 (0.017)
Born in a non-Western country	-0.090 (0.014)***	-0.065 (0.014)***	-0.090 (0.014)***	-0.068 (0.014)***
Age	0.016 (0.001)***	0.017 (0.002)***	0.016 (0.002)***	0.017 (0.002)***
Age^2	-0.00013 (0.00002)***	-0.00015 (0.00002)***	-0.00013 (0.00002)***	-0.00015 (0.00002)***
Vocational education	0.069 (0.006)***	0.071 (0.006)***	0.068 (0.006)***	0.070 (0.006)***
High school	0.159 (0.010)***	0.169 (0.010)***	0.157 (0.010)***	0.168 (0.010)***
Short higher education	0.195 (0.011)***	0.202 (0.011)***	0.191 (0.011)***	0.201 (0.011)***
Medium-length higher education	0.222 (0.007)***	0.231 (0.007)***	0.222 (0.007)***	0.230 (0.007)***
Long higher education	0.444 (0.011)***	0.472 (0.011)***	0.441 (0.011)***	0.469 (0.011)***
In education	0.039 (0.009)***	0.052 (0.009)***	0.039 (0.009)***	0.050 (0.009)***
Education not reported	0.059 (0.021)***	0.067 (0.021)***	0.058 (0.021)***	0.066 (0.021)***
Single with children	-0.053 (0.010)***	-0.064 (0.010)***	-0.054 (0.010)***	-0.063 (0.010)***
Married/cohabiting, no children	-0.044 (0.006)***	-0.058 (0.006)***	-0.044 (0.006)***	-0.057 (0.006)***
Married/cohabiting with children	-0.046 (0.007)***	-0.073 (0.007)***	-0.049 (0.007)***	-0.071 (0.007)***
Percentage of immigrants from Western countries in the municipality	0.024 (0.002)***		0.021 (0.002)***	
Percentage of immigrants from non-Western countries in the municipality	0.006 (0.0006)***		0.007 (0.0006)***	
Unemployment rate in the municipality		-0.011 (0.001)***	-0.013 (0.001)***	
Unemployment rate among native Danes in the municipality				-0.020 (0.002)***
Unemployment rate among Western immigrants in the municipality				0.001 (0.001)
Unemployment rate among non-Western immigrants in the municipality				0.00006 (0.0003)
Number of observations	39,441	39,441	39,441	39,441
R^2(adj)	0.100	0.092	0.102	0.094

Notes: *** significant at the 1 percent level, ** significant at the 5 percent level, * significant at the 10 percent level. Comparison group: Danes, men, primary education (9 years or less), single without children. Standard errors in parentheses. All 18 years and over with an hourly wage less than EUR 1,346.98 (=DKK 10,000) are included.

Table A11.4. Regression estimates (OLS) with hourly wage (log) in the year 2000 as the dependent variable.

Variables	Danes	Danes	Non-Western immigrants	Non-Western immigrants
Constant	2.323 (0.020)***	2.413 (0.021)***	2.483 (0.118)***	2.550 (0.122)***
Female	-0.194 (0.003)***	-0.195 (0.003)***	-0.128 (0.007)***	-0.127 (0.019)***
Age	0.023 (0.001)***	0.024 (0.001)***	0.018 (0.007)***	0.019 (0.007)***
Age^2	-0.00021 (0.00001)***	-0.00022 (0.00001)***	-0.00016 (0.00008)*	-0.00017 (0.00008)**
Vocational education	0.096 (0.004)***	0.095 (0.004)***	0.055 (0.027)**	0.055 (0.027)**
High school	0.194 (0.007)***	0.191 (0.007)***	0.033 (0.037)	0.035 (0.037)
Short higher education	0.213 (0.008)***	0.210 (0.008)***	0.073 (0.046)	0.074 (0.046)
Medium-length higher education	0.259 (0.005)***	0.259 (0.005)***	0.160 (0.038)***	0.162 (0.038)***
Long higher education	0.474 (0.007)***	0.470 (0.007)***	0.278 (0.044)***	0.274 (0.044)***
In education	0.015 (0.006)**	0.016 (0.006)**	-0.081 (0.034)**	-0.079 (0.034)**
Education not reported	0.033 (0.018)*	0.034 (0.018)*	0.046 (0.031)	0.046 (0.031)
Single with children	0.003 (0.009)	0.002 (0.009)	-0.028 (0.053)	-0.032 (0.053)
Married/cohabiting, no children	0.034 (0.004)***	0.034 (0.004)***	-0.042 (0.028)	-0.043 (0.028)
Married/cohabiting with children	0.056 (0.004)***	0.053 (0.005)***	-0.073 (0.026)***	-0.076 (0.026)***
Percentage of immigrants from Western countries in the municipality	0.027 (0.002)***	0.023 (0.002)***	0.016 (0.008)*	0.015 (0.008)*
Percentage of immigrants from non-Western countries in the municipality	0.006 (0.0005)***	0.007 (0.0005)***	0.0003 (0.002)	0.001 (0.002)
Unemployment rate in the municipality		-0.017 (0.001)***		-0.015 (0.007)**
Number of observations	72,784	72,784	2,375	2,375
R^2(adj)	0.181	0.184	0.079	0.080

Notes: *** significant at the 1 percent level, ** significant at the 5 percent level, * significant at the 10 percent level. Comparison group: Danes, men, primary education (9 years or less), single without children. Standard errors in parentheses. All 18 years and over with an hourly wage less than EUR 1,346.98 (=DKK 10,000) are included.

CHAPTER 12

Migrants, Work, and the Welfare State: Summary and Conclusions

By Torben Tranæs and Klaus F. Zimmermann

This final chapter reviews the general findings of our investigations and provides an overview and assessment of the potential lessons for researchers, the public, and the policy-making community. What are the experiences of immigrants in Germany and Denmark, and how different are they? What have been the consequences of different migration and social policies and of differences in the needs of the respective economies? Are there differences between Germany and Denmark in attracting high-skilled and low-skilled immigrants, and how do immigrants adjust their skills when they enter the respective labor markets? What is the level of attachment of immigrants to the labor market, and how is it affected by social and labor market policies? How do immigrants fare with respect to earnings, employment, unemployment, self-employment, welfare take-up, and crime? And how do they impact on public sector finances? What do migrants do that is to the advantage or disadvantage of the natives? The book has covered this broad range of questions, struggling to provide lucid and coherent answers. This chapter summarizes the core findings and provides some clear-cut conclusions.

12.1 Migration and the Policy Stand

The historical development of migration and the evolution of migration policies are studied for the period since World War II for both Denmark and Germany. Germany has always taken much higher numbers of migrants than Denmark, something which is reflected in the much larger proportion of migrants in its population. However, Chapter 2 documents the fact that both countries are now rather similar in their current legislation regulating entry into the country and access to the labor market. The remaining differences have historical roots. Denmark has traditionally followed a more liberal policy towards immigrants from the Nordic countries and potential asylum seekers. In Germany, Turks are much more dominant than they are among Danish immigrants. Furthermore, EU nationals comprise a much larger share of immigrants in Germany than they do in Denmark, while Pakistanis are more heavily represented in Denmark than among the German immigrants.

Like other Western European countries, both Denmark and Germany recruited foreign guest workers in the 1960s – Germany particularly intensively – in order to satisfy a pressing need for labor, until both countries halted recruitment in 1973 in the face of a deep pan-European recession. After that, immigration continued at a high level, but mainly by the family members of the guest workers. In the late 1980s both countries saw a heavy increase in the inflow of asylum seekers and refugees. Since the mid-1990s, this has caused the passing of more restrictive asylum legislation. Since the early 1990s Germany, unlike Denmark, has allowed the inflow of temporary workers from eastern European countries on the basis of special treaties, although at a low level. While migrants in both countries typically live in urban areas, immigrants in Denmark are even more likely to be settled in cities and larger towns than is the case in Germany.

The core innovation of this project is the production of a comparative data set about the Danish and German migrants, the *Rockwool Foundation Migration Survey – Denmark* (RFMS-D) and the *Rockwool Foundation Migration Survey – Germany* (RFMS-G). Both surveys are based on similar questionnaires, a fact which made it possible to carry out comparative analyses of the socio-economic characteristics and of the living and working conditions of immigrants in both countries.[1] The Danish survey (RFMS-D) involved 3,615 individuals in 1999 and 3,262 in 2001. Eight countries of origin were selected from among the largest groups of immigrants and their descendants in Denmark (both naturalized and foreign citizens), including individuals from the former Yugoslavia, Iran, Lebanon, Pakistan, Poland, Somalia, Turkey, and Vietnam. First- and second-generation immigrants from these countries account for approximately two thirds of all non-Western immigrants in Denmark. The German counterpart (RFMS-G) was collected in 2002 involving 5,569 foreign citizens from Turkey, the former Yugoslavia, Poland, Iran, and Lebanon living in Germany. These five nationalities represented approximately 60 percent of the foreign non-Western population living in Germany in 2001. Therefore, it was possible to directly compare the performance of these five groups across both countries.

12.2 Educational Attainment and Training

Human capital is of paramount importance for enhancing economic performance. While most studies in the literature so far have concentrated on the labor market outcomes of immigrant education, Chapter 3 investigates the post-migration human capital investment of immigrants. Starting with a thorough review of the educational systems in Denmark and Germany, the chapter finds many similarities between the

---

1 See the Appendix chapter for more details.

two educational systems with regard to structure, years of education, and length of various programmes. Major differences are the early differentiation of pupils in the German school system, as opposed to the comprehensive principle applied in Denmark, and the extension in Germany of compulsory education beyond primary and lower secondary school to include an introduction into vocational training.

Immigrants in Denmark are on average less well educated upon arrival, but they acquire more schooling once they are in Denmark than do immigrants in Germany. This fact could be related to a more intensively applied integration policy in Denmark. Second-generation immigrants fare better than the first generation in both countries. Especially with regard to primary and secondary schooling choices, the second generation has managed to narrow the educational gap between them and the total population. More immigrants in Germany finish vocational training than in Denmark, indicating the importance of vocational training in Germany. However, these accomplishments are not sufficient, given the well-known difficulties of German migrants, for them to perform well on the labor markets. There are also significant differences in the educational achievement among the five nationalities: Poles and Iranians acquire more human capital in Denmark than other groups, while Lebanese and Turks rank the lowest. Iranians also stand out for their high level of schooling achievement in Germany, while the Turks are again at the bottom. This is particularly worrying, as the Turks are by far the largest immigrant group in Germany and one of the largest groups in Denmark.

A careful econometric analysis in Chapter 3 investigated the determinants of educational attainment and vocational training, and identified the nature of the observed differences in both countries. The analysis of the educational levels in Denmark showed that younger, healthier males from Poland and Iran, those who have acquired a Danish passport, or those who have better educated fathers have greater chances of finishing *Folkeskole* or *Gymnasium*/university as opposed to not finishing school in Denmark. Pre-migration work experience, religiosity, and growing up in a small town act as barriers to finishing schooling. Apparently the incentive structure in Denmark does not seem to encourage those with low skills to take advantage of the Danish educational system.

The analysis of the educational levels in Germany indicated that those male immigrants who are healthier, arrive in Germany at a younger age, live in Germany for a long time, have no pre-migration schooling, and have educated fathers have a higher probability of completing *Haupt-/Realschule* or *Gymnasium*/university as opposed to the option of not going to school in Germany. Most importantly, Chapter 3 shows that there is intergenerational transmission of human capital. Nevertheless, the educational attainment of immigrants in Germany is dependent on gender and ethnicity. While it is not surprising that German citizens have higher probabilities of finishing schooling in Germany than do immigrants on average, it is of concern that immigrants who are born in Germany have a smaller likelihood of finishing schooling in Germany than immigrants born abroad.

The following conclusions were reached concerning vocational training. In Denmark, it was found that the older immigrants with pre-migration education who have acquired a Danish passport, or foreign nationals who come from Poland or Iran, or immigrants whose fathers are in upper white collar-jobs, all have greater chances of finishing vocational training, irrespective of gender. In Germany, younger age at entrance to the country, more years since migration, upper secondary pre-migration education, no pre-migration education, family background, and citizenship are all significant positive determinants of finishing vocational training. Immigrant women and second-generation immigrants born in Germany invariably have smaller chances of completing vocational training. Gender differences in the vocational training system in Germany may be the putative cause for the differences in career paths and the occupational sex segregation of women. We cannot explain why immigrants born in Denmark and Germany have the same and lower chances respectively of completing vocational training than immigrants born abroad, but it certainly suggests that integration problems lie ahead. One reason, however, could be the less satisfying return to vocational training for immigrants, which is also one of our findings (see below).

Making a comparison across the two countries, there are greater ethnic differences in Germany than in Denmark for both educational attainment and vocational training. However, the Iranians fare consistently better than the Turks in educational attainment, and the Lebanese fare worse than the Turks. Compared to Turks, Poles have greater chances of finishing vocational training, while the Lebanese do worse.

12.3 Employment Trends

An important measure of attachment to the economy is the employment rate. Chapter 4 shows a severe level of under-employment among immigrants in both countries. Recently, only 54 percent of immigrants from non-Western countries in Germany were in employment, as opposed to 67 percent of native Germans. In Denmark, 46 percent from the same non-Western countries were in employment, compared to 76 percent of native Danes. The employment rate for non-Western foreigners is lower in Denmark than it is in Germany, although natives are more attached to the labor force in Denmark than in Germany. The employment of immigrants has quite simply been much more successful in Germany than in Denmark.

The fact that Germany is more successful than Denmark in employment participation does not indicate that this country has no problem with low employment rates for immigrants. Germany has experienced a downward trend in employment rates, documented in Chapter 4, since the mid-1980s, a phenomenon that can be traced back to the beginning of the 1970s. This fall in employment has had a clear parallel in Denmark. However, Danish migrants have been substantially less employed, especially in the early 1990s.

Despite the difference in employment levels for foreign citizens in Germany and Denmark, the pattern of employment for the various nationalities is fairly similar across the two countries. Poles exhibit the highest level of employment in both countries, while employment levels are the lowest for migrants from Lebanon. The relative employment rates for male and female immigrants are also more or less the same in Denmark and Germany. Thus, the generally higher employment rate among women in Denmark does not seem to have influenced the employment behavior of immigrants in Denmark.

12.4 Employment Incentives

Chapter 5 goes a step further, studying and identifying the culprits of why immigrants generally have a lower labor market attachment than natives, especially in Denmark. A potentially important cause of low employment rates is that financial incentives to work are low: the proportion of immigrants in the labor force between 25-55 years of age who gain less than € 100 extra per month from working was between 17 and 18 percent in Germany and between 35 and 41 percent in Denmark. The financial incentives to work are lower in Denmark primarily because the unemployment benefit system pays a higher replacement rate to the low-paid groups, which include many immigrants. In Germany, the lowest paid workers receive relatively lower benefits than in Denmark, and the middle- and high-income earners receive relatively higher benefits. Hence, it is not surprising that large shares of the immigrants in Denmark who are unemployed are unavailable to the Danish labor market. It is striking that the proportion of unemployed immigrants who meet the ILO's availability criteria is 60 percent in Germany and 51 percent in Denmark, compared to 66 percent of unemployed workers in general in Denmark in 2002.

On the basis of econometric investigations, this chapter shows that female immigrants are relatively less likely to be in the labor force in Germany than in Denmark. However, once they participate in the labor force, they have a relatively better chance of being employed in Germany than men, indicating a serious commitment to the labor force. The analyses also showed that human capital factors are important for immigrants' labor market attachment in both Denmark and Germany. The likelihood both of participating in the labor force and of being employed is positively related to good health, good language skills, and a good educational background, either from the home countries or, even better, from the host countries. Educational qualifications acquired in the home country play a greater role in immigrants' labor market attachment in Germany than in Denmark.

Vocational training exerts a positive effect on the labor market attachment and employment chances in both countries. Yet we find, as mentioned above, that relatively few second-generation immigrants finish vocational training. The labor market benefits from having a university degree are less clear-cut. Employment seems to be higher for immigrants with a university degree solely because it increases their labor force participation, while the employment chances for these immigrants are not better than those for immigrants with no education. In fact, the unemployment risk for vocationally-educated immigrants is lower than for immigrants with a university degree in both countries.

The analyses also showed strong ethnic disparities whereby Polish immigrants have the highest likelihood of participating in the labor force and of being employed in both Denmark and Germany. On the other hand, Lebanese immigrants have the lowest likelihood of participating in the labor market in Germany. In Denmark, while Lebanese immigrants are particularly poorly represented among the employed, Iranians have the lowest likelihood of participating in the labor force.

12.5 Earnings Dispersion

Once immigrants are working, one objectively-measurable key indicator of their successful labor market integration and performance is earnings. Chapter 6 investigates the monetary dispersion of paid employment using the *Rockwool Foundation Migration Survey* for Denmark (RFMS-D) and Germany (RFMS-G) and focusing on the same five common immigrant groups in both countries. Innovations to the literature made possible by the data set include the use of a direct measure of the labor market experience in the host country and an objective measure of language proficiency. Migrants who have become citizens of the host country were treated as a separate group. The earnings data exhibit a large variation in both countries among people from the former Yugoslavia, Poles, Iranians, Lebanese, Turks, and the naturalized immigrants. Naturalized citizens of both sexes in both countries have the highest earnings. In both countries males earn more than females. More remarkable, immigrants in Denmark earn more than immigrants in Germany, both on a general level and for each single migrant group.

Utilization of multivariate analyses led to deeper structural results: Danish immigrants earn more throughout their working lives than comparable immigrants in Germany. Although experience is not as well rewarded in Denmark as in Germany, an initial earnings advantage upon arrival is sustained. Human capital acquired in the host country generates an earnings premium in both Denmark and Germany. But education after arrival is not rewarded as much as expected; in particular when it comes to vocational training, which is rewarded only modestly in Germany and not at all in Denmark. This may help explain why second-generation immigrants in both countries stay away from vocational training. After the inclusion of the individual characteristics the differences across the nationalities disappear among the Danish immigrants. They remain, however, among the German immigrants: compared to Turks, all groups earn more except the Lebanese, who earn less on average, even though few of them work.

The econometric models were further used to execute a counterfactual analysis, where German immigrants were moved to Denmark and Danish immigrants were assumed to be in Germany. Such experiments show that Danish immigrants in Denmark fare better than German immigrants in Germany, better than German immigrants in Denmark, and better than Danish immigrants in Germany for both the age and experience profiles at all levels. If employed Danish immigrants were to move to Germany, they would suffer an earnings loss. German immigrants in Germany fare worse than Danish immigrants in Denmark, worse than the Danish immigrants in Germany, and worse than the German immigrants in Denmark. Based on their earnings-experience profile, if German immigrants were to move to Denmark they would experience an improvement in their earnings compared to their earnings in Germany. This earnings advantage is especially large at the beginning of their careers, and lasts for 20 years. This suggests that the Danish labor market can offer an earnings-experience advantage to any immigrant in paid employment. Denmark seems to be more effective in enhancing the employed immigrants' capacity to succeed in the labor market. For the many immigrants in Denmark without a job, the high immigrant wages might represent a barrier to entry.

12.6 Immigrant Self-employment

Chapter 7 uses the *Rockwool Foundation Migration Survey* to examine a special group of immigrant workers in both countries: the self-employed. The issues investigated are the decision to take up the self-employment route as opposed to the paid-employment option, and the determinants of the earnings of the self-employed. At first sight, both countries seem to attract immigrants with similar levels of entrepreneurial spirit: 9 percent of the German and 10 percent of the Danish immigrants in the samples are self-employed. Among all ethnic groups in Denmark and Germany, the Iranians stand out as being the most entrepreneurial. It is also important to note that the majority of the self-employed immigrants in both counties have had refugee status.

Nevertheless, there are distinct differences between the self-employed migrants in both countries and between the self-employed and the salaried workers within the countries. Among these differences are the following. Self-employed immigrants in Germany are clearly self-selected with respect to human capital, age, years since migration, and family background characteristics. A larger proportion of the self-employed are home-owners, and a smaller proportion live in ethnic neighbourhoods, in comparison with those immigrants who are not self-employed. The self-selection of the self-employed Danish immigrants is much less marked, especially with respect to human capital. Self-employed immigrants in Germany earn twice as much as their salaried counterparts in the labor force. However, this is not true for the Danish self-employed immigrants, who earn slightly less than the salaried group. On average, self-employed migrants in Germany earn much more than in Denmark.

With respect to the self-employment choice, the only similarities between the two countries are the following. Male immigrants are about 2.5 times more likely to be self-employed than females. Iranians have an entrepreneurial spirit, and are more likely to be self-employed than all other ethnic groups. However, individuals in poor health are less likely to be self-employed in Germany, and more likely to be self-employed in Denmark. A further major difference is that the self-employment choice in Denmark does not depend on many other individual characteristics, especially age, time spent in the host country, education, economic conditions and the like, while the reverse is the case in Germany. Education, age, years since migration, father being self-employed, and home ownership all exhibit a positive impact on the self-employment choice, while living in an ethnic enclave has a negative impact on being self-employed in Germany. Hence, self-employment is a selective process in Germany, while it seems more random in Denmark.

Danish self-employed immigrants are, on average, a group with lower quality characteristics. This is consistent with the fact that they have lower earnings when compared to immigrant entrepreneurs in Germany and other immigrants in the Danish labor force. Consequently, the earnings of the Danish self-employed immigrants are hardly affected by measurable individual characteristics. An exception is poor health, which depresses earnings. However, in Germany, migrant entrepreneurs of younger age and with larger firms, more business experience and a home outside ethnic enclaves have higher earnings.

In a counterfactual simulation analysis, Chapter 7 also compares the earnings potentials that both the Danish and German migrant entrepreneurial groups have in both countries, using the estimated earnings regressions. The reference case is the observation in the two samples that self-employed immigrants in Germany have higher earnings across all ages if compared with self-employed immigrants in Denmark. According to the simulations, the self-employed Danish immigrants would fare better in Germany than the self-employed German immigrants in Denmark, and much better than if they had stayed in Denmark. Immigrants to Germany would not really gain by moving to Denmark.

While these hypothetical computations suggest that Germany provides a somewhat better environment for entrepreneurial activities, the analyses give no clear-cut evidence that the immigrants attracted to self-employment in Germany are actually a higher quality group than the equivalent group of immigrant entrepreneurs in Denmark. While German immigrants would do better as entrepreneurs in Denmark than the actual Danish immigrants, Danish immigrants would do better in Germany than the actual German immigrants. This suggests that a reallocation of the migrants would create an overall welfare improvement, because it would maintain the income status of the German immigrants, increase the income of the Danish migrants, and leave both countries with higher total earnings.

12.7 Welfare take-up

It is frequently hypothesized that immigrants make heavy use of the welfare system. Chapter 8 describes the access to the social security systems in Denmark and Germany, and their use by immigrants. The determinants of their take-up decisions are also studied. A first investigation outlines in detail the formal rules of access to the social security systems in both countries, including the rules for unemployment insurance, social assistance, old-age pension, disability pension, housing benefits and child benefits. In general, eligibility rules for foreigners are the same as for nationals, while they are typically easier for refugees. The German benefit system typically relates benefits to work and income, and the replacement rate is constant over a relatively wide income span. The Danish benefits are primarily residence-based, and the benefits provided follow more of a flat rate. This means that low income groups are better compensated in Denmark than in Germany.

When it comes to the take-up data, it is found that the proportion of immigrants over the official retirement age who receive pensions is about 80 percent in both countries. In Denmark, however, immigrants receive social assistance more often than in Germany. Social assistance and the take-up of unemployment benefits interact in a complex way that is different in the two countries. There are also clear-cut gender differences within and across the countries. In Germany, 15 percent of immigrant men and 7 percent of immigrant women receive unemployment insurance benefits, while the corresponding figures for Denmark are 11 percent and 9 percent. In Denmark, 15 percent of male immigrants and 20 percent of female immigrants receive social assistance, while in Germany the figures are 10 percent for males and 9 percent for females. For men, the differences in both countries can be explained by the fact that unemployment insurance in Denmark is voluntary, and many low-wage workers find themselves better off not being insured in order to receive social assistance. More female migrants in Germany report themselves as housewives than in Denmark, and are therefore supported by their husbands, which may explain why their level of take-up for social assistance is much lower in Germany than in Denmark.

An econometric analysis investigating the determinants of welfare take-up completes the study. A core issue is social assistance: it is found that good labor market performance, language skills and home-ownership reduce the probability of receiving social assistance in both countries considerably. But there are also cross-country differences: the analysis for Germany shows that when labor market attachment is accounted for, women actually have a lower probability of receiving social assistance, while in Denmark, gender plays no particular role. In addition, refugees in Germany have a higher probability of receiving social assistance compared to other foreigners, while this is not the case in Denmark. A possible explanation is that it is easier for refugees in Denmark to access the labor market than for refugees in Germany, who have significantly lower chances of being in employment than non-refugee immigrants. There are also significant human capital differences between refugees in the two countries. It should be noted, though, that asylum seekers are not included in the Danish sample, whereas they are in the German sample.

12.8 Crime

It is often suggested that migrants have higher crime rates than natives, but reliable data sources on the issue are scarce. International comparisons, in particular, are very difficult, because definitions and counting rules differ between countries. This is also the case for statistics from Denmark and Germany. Nevertheless, the study of joint similarities and differences in immigrant crime rates between the two countries that is described in Chapter 9 has opened new horizons for future research into the link between immigration and crime.

All in all, many more similarities than differences were found for Denmark and Germany. Although no sophisticated econometric analyses could be undertaken, the results confirm the importance of accounting for differences in the age and sex distribution. However, even when such differences are taken into accout, citizens with a foreign background are still over-represented in the crime statistics. Evidence available only from the Danish register data shows that the crime rates of immigrants from non-Western countries remain relatively high even when education is taken into account in the analysis.

The results show that research is still at the beginning of understanding statistical differences based on national origins. Potential relevant issues that are worth more detailed consideration in future research include the multiple risk factors related to immigrants, such as crime-prone neighbourhoods, lack of knowledge of the national languages, lack of education, and lack of socio-economic integration, all of which might interact in a potentially hazardous way. Moreover, as a word of caution, greater attention paid to foreign-looking people and more frequent police checks might cause higher clear-up rates among immigrants from non-Western countries than among national citizens and immigrants of European appearance.

12.9 The Public Coffers

Chapter 10 studied the consequences of immigration for the public sector finances. Ideally, one would wish to study this issue in a life-cycle framework, which would require the availability of longitudinal data. Due to the lack of such data, the chapter is based on cross-sectional data, and is able to use more detailed information for Denmark than for Germany. For Denmark, a series of cross-sectional data sets from the 1990s were used, while for Germany one cross-section data set from 2002 was used.

The evidence for Denmark is that the net transfers in public contributions are from Western immigrants to the public sector, and then from the public sector to immigrants from non-Western countries. This implies that immigrants from Western countries produce a net surplus, while immigrants from non-Western countries represent a net deficit, which was found to be of considerable size. The size of the net transfer per person varies across the business cycle and with the employment rate, and the total amount of the net transfer was found to vary also with the size of the immigrant population. It is a little surprising that the reduction in the net transfer amounts which took place between 1996 and 1998, for both individuals and in total, did not continue in the 1998-2000 period despite an improvement in labor market conditions. In Germany, a net transfer from the public sector to the non-Western immigrants was also observed. As expected given the differences in employment attainment and in the levels of social benefits, the net transfers per person were smaller on average in Germany than in Denmark, and varied considerably among different non-Western immigrant groups. Due to lack of data, the net transfer by Western immigrants in Germany was not calculated.

For both countries, it was also investigated how the individual net transfers to the public sector vary when the econometric analysis controls for differences in individual characteristics, personal employment situation, and labor income. The individual characteristics were less relevant when work-related variables were taken into account. The employment and labor income variables exhibited very strong effects, although stronger in Denmark than in Germany. These differences may be explained by differences in the tax and transfer systems and in the public sector expenditures. In the German set-up, with more weight placed on experience-related social benefits and with fewer tax-financed public services, the employment rate of a population group seems to impact less on the public purse: you cannot receive before you have paid in, and therefore the German system seems more self-regulating.

12.10 Socio-economic Consequences

The findings in Chapter 10 point to the crucial importance of employment and labor income of immigrants for the size and the direction of the net transfer to the public sector. Hence, Chapter 11 investigates in more detail what determines wages and employment across immigrant groups, and compares the results with those for the natives. The first part of the analysis deals with the determination of wages; differences between the Danish population, the immigrants from Western countries and the immigrants from non-Western countries were studied, with controls for a large number of individual characteristics such as education, training, family characteristics, age and country of origin. It was found that the immigrants born in non-Western countries have significantly lower wages than natives, whereas females do somewhat better in comparison than males. Foreign-born men have 13 percent lower wages than native male Danes, while foreign-born females have only 7 percent lower wages than native female Danes. Immigrants born in a Western country do better, though whereas females are not different from their Danish counterparts, males still experience a small wage disadvantage of 3 percent. These differences cannot be explained by the differences in individual characteristics measured in the data.

The second part of the analysis deals with the effects of immigration on native Danish wages and unemployment. The results indicate that the existence of a larger proportion of immigrants in the population of a municipality does only have a marginal effect on the wages of the natives and it does not increase their unemployment rates. In fact, a larger presence of migrants in the local labor market is associated with lower unemployment rates. These results are consistent with the findings in other European countries (including Germany) and suggest that immigrants are complements to natives in the production process. The presence of non-Western-born immigrants is not necessarily beneficial as is the presence of Western-born immigrant men. A larger presence of immigrants born in non-Western countries is associated with lower unemployment rates among native Danes, while immigrants from Western countries have no significant effect.

The final analysis described in this chapter was an attempt to investigate the amount and direction of redistribution and the degree of inequality among immigrants. For this purpose the disposable incomes of immigrants and natives in Germany and Denmark were studied. In comparison to native Danes, the average disposable income of Danish Western immigrants is about the same, that of Danish non-Western immigrants is 80 percent, and that of the German non-Western immigrants is 57 percent. Obviously, immigrants to Denmark do much better than immigrants to Germany, in net terms as well, which is consistent with the investigations in previous chapters. Native Danes have a slightly more equal income distribution than the total population in Denmark. Immigrants from non-Western countries have almost the same distribution as the native Danes. Many of the non-Western immigrants have no income from employment, but the welfare state works towards an equalized income structure after taxes and transfers. In comparison, non-Western immigrants in Germany exhibit a much more unequal distribution of disposable income.

12.11 The Findings in Brief

This study is largely based on a rich representative data set collected specifically for the purpose, the *Rockwool Foundation Migration Survey*, which relates to the same groups of immigrants (Turks, people from the former Yugoslavia, Poles, Iranians, and Lebanese) in Denmark and Germany. Most chapters made intensive use of this data source, while some also added knowledge from other data sets. The analyses are based on descriptive statistics and in-depth econometric investigations used to generate reliable scientific conclusions. The project has met the challenge of providing innovative and coherent findings on an important area of social and economic life in both societies that was not sufficiently studied before.

Both countries share a similar history of immigration and migration policies over the last decades. They are fairly similar in their current legislation regulating entry into the countries and access to the respective labor markets. Denmark follows a more liberal immigration policy towards the Nordic countries and has done so towards asylum seekers in the past, while Germany has always received much higher numbers of migrants, who consequently make up a much larger proportion of its population. Both countries had guest worker programmes which were largely stopped after 1973, as in many Western European countries.

There are greater ethnic differences in Germany than in Denmark with respect to both educational attainment and vocational training. Immigrants in Denmark are less well educated upon arrival, but they acquire more schooling once they are in the country than immigrants in Germany. Apart from the early differentiation in the German school system, education and training systems are similar in the two countries, but the Danish system does not encourage those with low skills to acquire further education. In comparison to natives, there is severe under-employment of immigrants in both countries. The employment rate is lower for non-Western immigrants in Denmark than it is in Germany, although natives are more attached to the labor force in Denmark than in Germany. Immigrants have a larger presence in the German labor market than in Denmark. Probable reasons for this difference are that immigrants in Denmark are less educated upon arrival, and that financial incentives to work are low in Denmark, primarily because the unemployment benefit system pays a higher replacement rate to the low-paid income groups. Education and vocational attainment are powerful determinants of labor market attachment in both countries.

Whereas immigrants in Denmark are less financially motivated to seek employment than their counterparts in Germany, once at work, they earn more throughout their working lives than comparable immigrants in Germany. Although experience is not as well rewarded in Denmark, an initial earnings advantage upon arrival is sustained. Human capital acquired in the host country generates an earnings premium in both Denmark and Germany. If Danish immigrant workers were to move to Germany, they would suffer a financial loss. However, if German immigrant workers were to move to Denmark they would experience an improvement in their earnings compared to their earnings in Germany.

While Denmark seems to be a more attractive country for employed immigrant workers, Germany was found to offer better opportunities for entrepreneurs. Although the self-employment rates are similar, self-employed immigrants in Germany are clearly positively self-selected, while those in Denmark seem to be more randomly allocated. Consequently, self-employed immigrants earn much more in Germany than in Denmark, and also more than regular migrant workers in Germany. The Danish self-employed migrants earn less than the salaried group. The analysis demonstrated that self-employed immigrants from Germany would not really gain by moving to Denmark, while the Danes would do much better in Germany than in their actual host country.

The last part of the book deals with the idleness of immigrants and their alleged over-representation in welfare take-up, crime, and the direction of the redistribution of public sector finances. While a sizable level of welfare take-up by immigrants is documented, especially in Denmark, it is also found that good labor market performance, language skills, and home ownership considerably reduce the probability of receiving social assistance in both countries. The analysis of crime rates makes the case that even when differences in age, gender, and educational distributions are controlled for, individuals with foreign backgrounds exhibit a greater presence in the crime statistics. This presence, however, could also be a statistical artifact due to measurement problems, as a large number of issues were not taken into account. Immigrants induce a redistribution through public sector finances whereby the net transfers in public contributions go from Western immigrants to the public sector, and from the public sector to immigrants from non-Western countries. These redistribution efforts bring the average disposable income of Danish non-Western immigrants much closer to the disposable income of native Danes, which is much higher than that of German non-Western immigrants. These immigrants have almost the same distribution as native Danes, while these migrant groups exhibit a much more unequal distribution of disposable income in Germany.

It can be concluded that Germany is able to attract more able immigrants, get them into employment, and offer more to people with entrepreneurial talents. Denmark keeps more immigrants in the welfare system, but offers better remuneration to regular workers and some incentives for immigrants to educate themselves to higher levels – but not to undertake vocational training. The findings reported here also suggest that both countries could benefit quite considerably by executing more pro-active labor market recruitment and integration measures.

APPENDIX

Data Description

By Thomas Bauer and Niels-Kenneth Nielsen

A.1 Introduction

This appendix extends the general description of the data used for this project. It provides a detailed description of the process of data collection, the sampling design, and a comprehensive analysis of the representativeness of the data.

The main part of the data for this project consists of the results of two surveys carried out among the same groups of immigrants and descendants in Denmark and Germany. In the following, these surveys are referred to as the *Rockwool Foundation Migration Survey – Denmark* (RFMS-D) and the *Rockwool Foundation Migration Survey – Germany* (RFMS-G). Both surveys were based on a similar questionnaire, enabling us to perform comparative analyses of the socioeconomic characteristics and the living and working conditions of immigrants in Germany and Denmark.[1] The interviews for the Danish survey were carried out by Statistics Denmark in Copenhagen; Infratest Sozialforschung in Munich collected the German data.

Section A.2 of this appendix describes the RFMS-D; the corresponding German data is described in Section A.3. Both sections are subsequently divided into subsections describing the arrangement of the surveys, the sampling design, an analysis of the effects of non-response on the representativeness of the two surveys, and the weighting procedure used for the empirical analysis in this book.

A.2 Data Sources for Denmark

A.2.1 The Rockwool Foundation Migration Survey – Denmark (RFMS-D)

The main source of information for the Danish part of this project was two surveys involving 3,615 and 3,262 completed interviews with non-Western immigrants and their descendants from eight countries. The interviewing took place in 1999 and 2001

---

1 The questionnaires are available on request.

respectively.[2] Eight nationalities were selected among the largest groups of immigrants and their descendants in Denmark, including individuals from the former Yugoslavia, Iran, Lebanon, Pakistan, Poland, Somalia, Turkey, and Vietnam. First and second generation immigrants from these countries account for approximately two thirds of all non-Western immigrants in Denmark.

The survey was mainly carried out by computer assisted telephone interviews (CATI).[3] The computer controlled the filters in the questionnaire and showed the questions on the screen in the relevant language. For technical reasons it was only possible to show the questions in Turkish, Serbo-Croat, Urdu/Punjabi, Polish and Somali, but not in Arabic, Farsi or Vietnamese. In these three cases the computer only controlled the filters, while the interviewer used a hard copy of the questionnaire.

For Denmark, it was possible to merge the RFMS-D with administrative register data available at Statistics Denmark. Therefore, the persons interviewed in the RFMS-D were not asked about background variables such as age, duration of stay,[4] marital status, personal income, household income, and other types of income, because this information could be drawn from the administrative registers.

A.2.2 Sample Design

The Danish sample was randomly drawn from the Danish Central Person Register (CPR). Every person residing legally in Denmark obtains a social security number and is registered in the CPR. Asylum seekers staying legally in the country, however, are not registered in the CPR. Therefore, this group of immigrants is not included in the Danish sample. The sample was further limited to persons between 16 and 70 years of age and persons who had lived for at least 2 years in Denmark. The latter condition was applied to ensure that only persons with a certain potential labor market attachment and proficiency in Danish were included in the sample. Because the CPR is known to be quite reliable, the quality of the sample can be expected to be relatively good, as will be discussed in further detail in the sub-section on the representativeness of the RFMS-D.

Unlike the German data, the RFMS-D also includes persons with foreign background who have acquired Danish citizenship, because such persons can be identified through the CPR. The RFMS-D consists of a representative sample of both naturalized and non-naturalized foreigners with residence in Denmark. In the 1999

---

2 The interviews for the two surveys actually took place from November 1998 to July 1999 and from December 2000 to July 2001. For the sake of convenience the text will refer to these surveys in the following as the 1999 sample and the 2001 sample.

3 In order to obtain an acceptable response rate, face-to-face interviews were conducted with some of those who could not be contacted by telephone.

4 For some participants in the survey, duration of stay in Denmark was not available in the administrative registers. For these people, the information on duration of stay was collected in the interviews for the RFMS-D.

sample of the RFMS-D, 67.2 percent are foreign nationals; the corresponding figure for the 2001 sample is 54.2 percent.

For a sub-sample of individuals, the RFMS-D provides longitudinal information, because 2,348 of the respondents in the 1999 sample were interviewed for a second time in 2001 (see figure A.1). In 1999, the respondents were asked if they were willing to be re-interviewed at a later time. The 3,307 individuals who gave an affirmative answer to this question formed the basis for the 2001 sample. Some of these individuals had died or emigrated between the first and the second surveys, leading to a potential gross sample of 3,161 persons, of which 2,348 could be contacted in 2001. To compensate for the non-response, the 2001 sample was supplemented with "new" persons.

Two circumstances had to be taken into account for the sampling scheme of the new sample. The 1999 sample had been restricted to persons who had lived in the country for at least two years and were between 16 and 70 years old. Hence, in 2001 these persons had stayed in the country for at least four years and were between 18 and 72 years old. To compensate for the panel attrition from the 1999 sample, 18- to 70-year-old persons with a minimum of 4 years of stay were added to the 2001 sample. In addition, the 2001 refreshment sample was supplemented with 16- to 17-year-old persons with at least two years of stay, and 18- to 70-year-old persons with 2-3 years of stay (see figure A.1).

Figure A.1. Outline of the Danish sample 1999 and 2001. (Number of respondents).

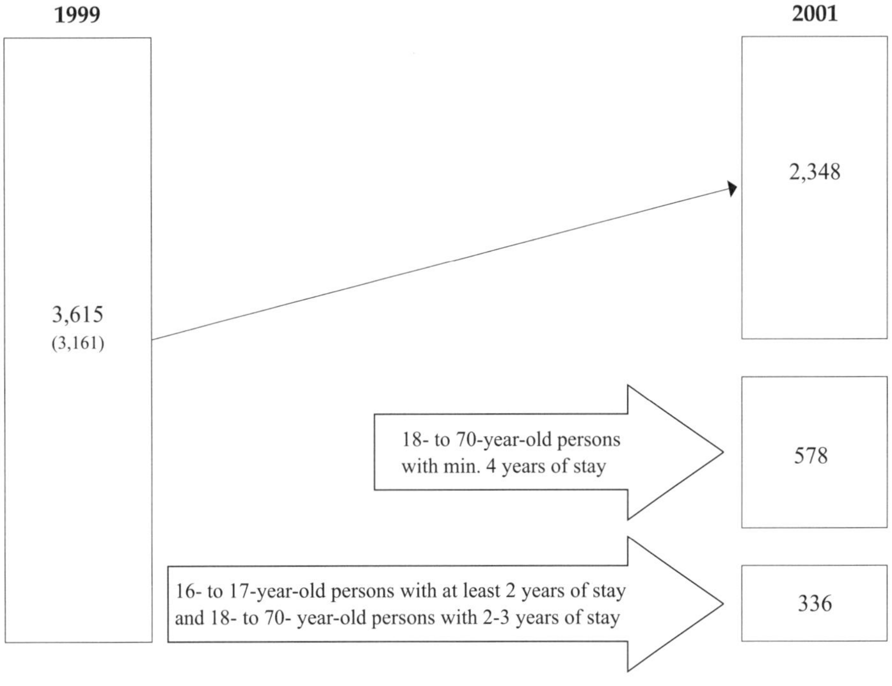

1999: 3,615 (3,161)

2001:
- 2,348 (re-interviewed from 1999)
- 578 (18- to 70-year-old persons with min. 4 years of stay)
- 336 (16- to 17-year-old persons with at least 2 years of stay and 18- to 70-year-old persons with 2-3 years of stay)

Source: Nielsen (2002)

Table A.1. Summary of persons interviewed and non-response in the Danish (panel) survey, distributed by age in July, 2001.

	Total	16-17 years	18-70 years	71-72 years
1999 sample				
Interviewed	3,615			
Non-response	2,642			
Response rate (percent)	57.8			
2001 sample				
Interviewed	3,262	155	3,089	18
Repetitions from 1999	2,348	0	2,330	18
New respondents	914	155	759	0
Non-response	1,406	64	1,336	6
Non-response among resp. from 1999	813	0	807	6
Non-response among new sample	593	64	529	0
Response rate (percent)	69.9	70.8	69.8	75.0
Repetitions from 1999	74.3	-	74.3	75.0
New sample	60.7	70.8	58.9	-

Sources: RFMS-D, own calculations.

A.2.3 Response Rate

The response and non-response rates for the two samples of the RFMS-D are shown in Table A.1. For the 2001 survey, these rates are also shown by the age of the persons in July. The response rate in the 1999 sample was 57.8 percent; in the 2001 sample a response rate of 69.9 percent was achieved.

Compared to other Danish migration studies that also use survey data, these response rates are acceptable. For instance, Togeby and Møller (1999) achieved a response rate of 48.2 percent among immigrants from Bosnia-Herzegovina, Lebanon, Somalia and Turkey. The relatively high response rate in the 2001 sample can partly be explained by the fact that the vast majority of the respondents were being interviewed for the second time. Among those interviewed in both years, the response rate was 74.3 percent, while the response rate among the new respondents was 60.7 percent.

Table A.2. Respondents in the Danish survey and the whole population of non-Western immigrants and descendants from the eight survey countries, distributed by age and sex. Percent.

	Respondents in Danish survey			The whole population with minimum 2 years of residence 1.7.2000		
	Men	Women	Total	Men	Women	Total
16-17 years	4.7	4.8	4.8	4.9	4.9	4.9
18-24 years	16.9	18.8	17.8	17.0	18.2	17.5
25-29 years	11.2	14.0	12.6	12.3	15.2	13.7
30-39 years	30.9	27.7	29.4	30.9	27.8	29.4
40-49 years	21.8	20.8	21.3	19.3	18.3	18.8
50-59 years	10.4	9.8	10.1	10.2	10.0	10.1
60-70 years	4.1	4.1	4.1	5.5	5.7	5.6
Total	100.0	100.0	100.0	100.0	100.0	100.0
Percent	51.5	48.5	100.0	52.2	47.8	100.0
No. of Observations	1,672	1,572	3,244[1]	58,016	53,096	111,112

Note: 1) 18 persons aged 71 and 72 have been excluded.

Sources: RFMS-D, register for population statistics, own calculations.

A.2.4 Representativeness in the Danish Survey

The following analysis examines the representativeness of the RFMS-D in relation to the whole population of immigrants and descendants from the former Yugoslavia, Iran, Lebanon, Pakistan, Poland, Somalia, Turkey and Vietnam, in the following just referred to as the "whole population".

In principle, we want to determine whether the distribution of answers to the questions (the dependent variables) in the survey is the same as the distribution we would have obtained if we had asked everybody in the whole population. Since this obviously is not possible, we examine instead the distribution of respondents in the Danish survey by central background variables (the independent variables), such as sex, age and geography. If these distributions coincide with those for the whole population, then it is reasonable to assume that the respondents did not answer the questions very differently from the way the whole population would have done.

Table A.2 provides a comparison of the respondents of the RFMS-D with the whole population by sex and age. Overall, there are no obvious differences between the age-sex-distribution of the respondents of the RFMS-D and that of the whole population.

The biggest deviation can be observed among 40- to 49-year-olds, who seem to be slightly over-represented in the RFMS-D; whereas 21.3 percent of the respondents in

Table A.3. Respondents in the Danish survey and the whole population of non-Western immigrants and descendants from the eight survey countries, distributed by age and region. Percent.

	Respondents in Danish survey				The whole population with minimum 2 years of residence 1.7.2000			
	Metropolitan area	The rest of the islands	Jutland	Total	Metropolitan area	The rest of the islands	Jutland	Total
16-17 years	3.8	5.6	5.8	4.8	4.5	5.3	5.3	4.8
18-24 years	19.4	18.7	15.1	17.8	18.3	17.1	17.1	18.7
25-29 years	13.4	10.9	12.2	12.6	14.4	13.0	13.0	14.4
30-39 years	27.0	30.9	32.0	29.4	28.4	29.6	29.6	29.0
40-49 years	20.6	20.0	23.0	21.3	17.5	19.9	19.9	18.1
50-59 years	11.9	9.3	7.8	10.1	11.2	9.4	9.4	9.7
60-70 years	4.0	4.7	4.0	4.1	5.7	5.8	5.8	5.4
Total	100.0	100.0	100.0	100.0	100.0	100.0	100.0	100.0
Percent	49.1	17.0	33.9	100.0	54.8	15.5	29.8	100.0
No. of Observations	1,594	551	1,099	3,244[1]	64,848	17,166	33,098	111,112

Note: 1) 18 persons aged 71 and 72 have been excluded.

Sources: RFMS-D, register for population statistics, own calculations.

the RFMS-D are aged between 40 and 49, only 18.8 percent of the whole population fall into this age group. Overall, however, the RFMS-D appears to be representative with respect to the age and sex distribution.

The same conclusion holds when the RFMS-D is compared to the whole population by age and region. Table A.3 shows the distribution of the respondents of the RFMS-D and the whole population by age and three regions, namely the Metropolitan area, the rest of the islands, and Jutland, illustrated in Figure A.2 (at the end of the chapter). The discrepancies between the RFMS-D and the whole distribution are minor – not more than two or three percentage points.

Table A.4 compares the RFMS-D and the whole population by sex and labor market status. Note that the information on labor market status in the RFMS-D has been obtained from the administrative labor market registers. Table A.4 shows that employed people are over-represented among the respondents of the RFMS-D: 49.9 percent of the sample is either employed or self-employed, compared to 45 percent in the whole population. Accordingly, the unemployed and individuals not in the labor force are under-represented in the RFMS-D. These differences

Table A.4. Respondents in the Danish survey and the whole population of non-Western immigrants and descendants from the eight survey countries, distributed by sex and labor market status. Percent.

	Respondents in Danish survey			The whole population with minimum 2 years of residence 1.7.2000		
	Men	Women	Total	Men	Women	Total
Self-employed	9.1	3.0	6.1	8.6	2.8	5.8
Wage earner	49.6	37.6	43.8	44.1	33.9	39.2
Unemployed	7.1	6.3	6.7	8.9	7.4	8.2
Not in labor force	34.2	53.2	43.4	38.5	55.9	46.8
Total	100.0	100.0	100.0	100.0	100.0	100.0
Percent	51.6	48.4	100.0	52.2	47.8	100.0
No. of Observations	1,672	1,569	3,241[1]	57,819	52,962	110,781[2]

Notes: 1) 18 persons aged 71 and 72 have been excluded. Furthermore, three persons could not be found in the register for labor force statistics. 2) 331 persons could not be found in the register for labor force statistics.

Sources: RFMS-D, register for population statistics, register for labor force statistics, own calculations.

can be explained by the experience that "well-performing" immigrants are more willing to report on their labor market status and other personal information. This effect could have been intensified by the fact that most of the respondents were interviewed twice.

Overall, this sub-section has shown that the RFMS-D appears to be quite representative. Only with regard to labor market status some differences are found, and these will be taken into account in the empirical analysis of the project by using an appropriate weighting procedure, which is described in more detail in the next sub-section.

A.2.5 Weighting of the Danish Data

This sub-section provides a detailed description of the weighting procedures for the RFMS-D. As already mentioned above, it seems to be necessary to consider the labor market status in the weighting procedure. In addition, the weighting procedure considers the age of the respondents in order to account for the supplement of 16- to 17-year-old persons, and duration of residence in Denmark in order to weight for the supplement of persons with 2-3 years of stay in the 2001 sample. These considerations lead to the 32-4=28 strata shown in Table A.5.

Table A.5. Respondents in the Danish survey distributed by strata. Number of persons.

	16- to 17-year-olds and immigrants with 2-3 years of residence (18- to 70-year-olds)	18- to 70-year-old non-employed immigrants with min. 4 years of residence	18- to 70-year-old employed immigrants with min. 4 years of residence	18- to 70-year-old descendants	Total
F. Yugoslavia	50	211	189	33	483
Iran	40	167	213	...	420
Lebanon	34	224	88	...	346
Pakistan	21	112	116	91	340
Poland	30	106	255	49	440
Somalia	110	164	51	...	325
Turkey	22	176	230	80	508
Vietnam	29	140	213	...	382
Total	336	1,300	1,355	253	3,244

Note: "..." means too few observations.

Sources: RFMS-D, own calculations.

Because there were too few descendants from Iran, Lebanon, Somalia and Vietnam interviewed, these groups are placed according to their labor market status among the 18- to 70-year-old immigrants with at least 4 years of residence. Even though it might seem to make no sense to speak of duration of residence for a descendant, this group fulfils the condition of at least of 4 years of stay in Denmark. Likewise the Iranian, Lebanese, Somali and Vietnamese descendants are put in a category that only includes first generation immigrants. This procedure is necessary because there are too few descendants from these 4 countries to construct reasonable weights.

The weights used in the empirical analysis (only the descriptive parts) of this project are constructed by proportioning the figure in each cell to the corresponding number for the whole population. This procedure leads to the weights listed in Table A.6.

A.2.6 Survey among Danes

In order to enable comparative analyses between the first and second generation immigrants covered by the RFMS-D and the native Danish population, selected questions from the RFMS-D were repeated in two omnibus surveys to native Danes. The first survey was carried out as a computer-assisted telephone interview (CATI) in February 1999 and provided information for 961 respondents. The original sample

Table A.6. Weights for the Danish survey.

	16- to 17-year-olds and immigrants with 2-3 years of residence (18- to 70-year-olds)	18- to 70-year-old non-employed immigrants with min. 4 years of residence	18- to 70-year-old employed immigrants with min. 4 years of residence	18- to 70-year-old descendants
F. Yugoslavia	83.760	55.853	52.249	47.818
Iran	23.050	25.760	19.634	…
Lebanon	26.618	29.076	24.772	…
Pakistan	54.810	38.062	30.741	25.846
Poland	22.767	29.698	18.227	12.633
Somalia	21.118	23.945	16.059	…
Turkey	146.273	68.528	50.204	39.263
Vietnam	23.966	21.237	17.141	…

Note: "…" means too few observations.

Sources: RFMS-D, own calculations.

for this omnibus survey included 1,499 persons selected randomly from the general population (i.e. including immigrants and descendants), giving a response rate of 64.1 percent. The second survey covering native Danes is obtained by merging three omnibus surveys which were carried out in February, March and July of 2001 respectively. This second survey contains information on 2,712 native Danes, which corresponds to an average response rate of 61.1 percent. For neither the 1999 nor the 2001 omnibus surveys of native Danes has it been necessary to apply a weighting procedure.

A.3 Danish Register Data

In the case of Denmark, it was possible to use information from administrative register data. This section gives a brief description of these data. A more detailed description is given by Nielsen and Pedersen (2001). Note that it has not been possible to use comparable data for Germany.

For the empirical analysis of this project, three samples were drawn from the administrative records. The first two samples consisted of the whole population of *non-Western* immigrants and their descendants who were resident in Denmark and were between 16 and 70 years of age on at least one of the following dates: 01.01.1984, 01.01.1985,…, 01.01.1998, 01.07.1998, 01.01.1999, 01.01.2000, 01.07.2000, 01.01.2001 and 01.01.2002. Altogether this sample consisted of 267,354 persons.

The second sample was a 25 percent sample of the population of *Western* immigrants and their descendants who had been registered as legal Danish residents (and were between 16 and 70 years of age) on at least one of the following dates: 01.01.1984, 01.01.1985,…, 01.01.1998, 01.07.1998, 01.01.1999, 01.01.2000, 01.07.2000, 01.01.2001 and 01.01.2002. In total, this sample covers 49,468 persons.

In order to compare the above two samples to the whole Danish population, a two percent sample of the whole Danish population (including immigrants and descendants) was drawn from the administrative register data, applying the same exclusion criteria used for sampling the two other samples. This third sample comprised 99,404 persons.

Finally, the administrative samples were supplemented with information about the family members of the persons included in the three register samples. The family members had to be resident in Denmark on the 01.07.1998 and the 01.07.2000. In total, this supplementary data covered 110,500 persons.

A considerable amount of data from different administrative registers available at Statistics Denmark has been merged with these three samples, including demographic variables, education variables, information about employment, income and a number of other variables.

A.4 German Data

The data used for the German part of the analyses is almost entirely based on a survey collected in 2002 among 5,569 foreign citizens from Turkey, the former Yugoslavia, Poland, Iran, and Lebanon living in Germany. These five nationalities represent approximately 66 percent of the foreign *non-Western* population living in Germany in 2001. This survey will be referred to as the *Rockwool Foundation Migration Survey – Germany (RFMS-G)*. In some parts of this project the analyses also use data from the *German Socioeconomic Panel Survey (GSOEP)*, the *German Microcensus*, and the *Allgemeine Bevölkerungsumfrage der Sozialwissenschaften (ALLBUS)*. This appendix will refrain from giving a description of these data sets, because detailed documentation is available elsewhere. A description of the ALLBUS is provided by Koch et al. (2001); the GSOEP has been described in detail by Haisken-DeNew et al. (2002) and Burkhauser et al. (1993); and a recent description of the German Microzensus can be found in Schwarz (2001).

Although the RFMS-G was inspired by the Danish survey, it differs from the RFMS-D survey in some important ways that will be described below. The remainder of this section is structured in a similar way to the description of the Danish survey in Section A.2 and includes a description of the questionnaire and the sampling design of the survey, an analysis of the representativeness of the data, a description of the weighting procedure, and a discussion of problems arising through item non-response and possible solutions to these problems.

A.4.1 Arrangement of the German Survey

The questionnaire for the RFMS-G was based on the RFMS-D. In collaboration with Infratest Sozialforschung, the Danish questionnaire was translated into German. Mainly because of institutional differences between Denmark and Germany, it was not possible to translate all questions directly. In particular, it was necessary to adjust the German questionnaire for questions on educational attainment and labor market conditions. For other types of questions, such as personal attitudes, it was possible to use a direct translation of the Danish questionnaire.

As described earlier, some information on the Danish respondents could be gathered through administrative registers. Therefore, it was not necessary to ask the respondents in Denmark about income and other information covered by these registers. Even though administrative registers do exist in Germany as well, the information covered by these registers is rather limited compared to that in the Danish counterparts. In addition, there are severe data access restrictions in Germany which would not allow us to merge administrative data with the survey data. For these reasons it was necessary to add some new questions to the RFMS-G, most significantly a large block of questions concerning the income of the respondents and their households. Because this is indeed more sensitive information, a considerable share of the respondents refused to answer these questions. Subsection A.4.4 will discuss this problem in more depth.

The RFMS-G was carried out between April 2002 and August 2002 as face-to-face interviews in the respondents' homes using computer-assisted personal interviews (CAPI). The interviewer used a laptop that contained a programmed German version of the questionnaire. The answers were typed directly into the laptop. As a starting point, the interviewers tried to carry out the interview in German, in order to evaluate the language skills of the respondent. If the respondents had difficulties in understanding German, the interviewers could use hard copies of the questionnaire in Turkish, Serbo-Croatian, Polish, Farsi, and Arabic. Hence, the interviewers were able to show the questions and, if necessary, possible answers in the native language of the respondents. In addition, the interviewers could use the help of an interpreter to overcome language difficulties.

Before the main fieldwork took place, the questionnaire was tested in a pilot study by conducting 108 interviews, see Bielenski and Fischer (2002a). Because the pilot study showed that the questionnaire generally worked well, only minor changes were necessary before the start of the main field work phase.

A.4.2 Sample Design

The German sample was designed to take several factors into account. Each legal resident in Germany has to register with the local *Einwohnermeldeamt*. In a first step, Infratest Sozialforschung contacted the *Einwohnermeldeämter* in the 100 largest communities and cities in former West Germany and the 3 largest cities in former East

Table A.7. **Proportions of foreign citizens who acquired German and Danish citizenship respectively in 2000. Percent.**

	German citizenship	Danish citizenship
Turkey	4.0	7.6
Former Yugoslavia	2.0	4.3
Poland	1.9	3.6
Iran	13.3	19.4
Lebanon	10.5	32.2

Sources: Beauftragte der Bundesregierung für Migration, Flüchtlinge und Integration (2002) and Statistics Denmark (2001).

Germany in order to acquire information concerning the number of foreigners and their nationalities in each community. Using this information, it was decided to use 500 sample points selected randomly among the 103 cities that conformed to the universe of the sample (but not necessarily in all 103 cities). By using these 500 sample points it was planned to obtain about 5,500 interviews, that is, 1,100 interviews from each nationality and 11 interviews in each sample point. In order to reduce the cost of the samples obtained from the *Einwohnermeldeämter*, the sample points were allotted to a limited number of communities.

Because of the random process of selecting sampling points among the cities, only 72 communities were included in the final sample. In some cities like Hamburg or West Berlin the random sampling process resulted in a very high concentration of sampling points. In order to avoid clustering effects and to consider to some extent the size of the local interviewer staff, some sampling points were removed and placed in other cities.

Unlike the Danish sample, the RFMS-G only contains foreign citizens, because it is impossible to identify naturalised foreigners from the register data at the *Einwohnermeldeämter*. Hence, the Danish and the German surveys are not completely comparable, since the former also includes a representative sample of naturalised foreigners. This difference, however, seems to create only minor problems with regard to the comparability of the two surveys. In the past, the rules on obtaining citizenship have generally been more restrictive in Germany than in Denmark. In recent years the Danish rules have been made stricter, while the German rules have been made less restrictive (see chapter 2). Nevertheless, because of the institutional differences between Germany and Denmark, the proportion of naturalized foreigners is much smaller in Germany.

Table A.7 confirms that the naturalization rates are substantially higher in Denmark if compared to Germany for all five nationalities covered by the two surveys. Ethnic differences in the naturalization rates are, however, very similar in Germany and Denmark, indicating that the different sampling procedures in the two coun-

Table A.8. Response and non-response in the German survey, distributed by country.

	Turkey	Former Yugoslavia	Poland	Iran	Lebanon	Total
Gross sample	3,789	3,427	4,239	3,330	2,422	17,207
Wrong address, address does not exist (percent)	4.9	8.3	12.8	13.1	8.3	9.6
Respondent is dead (percent)	0.1	0.2	0.2	0.1	0.1	0.2
Resp. does not live at given address (percent)	9.9	12.2	20.1	14.3	13.8	14.3
Addresses used (=100 percent)	3,225	2,715	2,835	2,413	1,883	13,071
No contact possible with household (percent)	15.2	16.5	18.3	20.3	15.5	17.1
No contact with respondent (percent)	5.7	6.1	6.0	6.5	4.2	5.8
Respondent travelling or on holidays (percent)	7.3	7.1	4.6	3.4	3.2	5.4
Respondent refuses because of (percent)						
Illness	0.9	1.5	0.8	1.2	0.8	1.0
Time reasons	2.9	4.5	4.4	4.8	3.0	3.9
General refusal	15.6	20.6	14.6	15.0	15.7	16.3
Language problems (percent)	2.0	1.5	1.2	1.9	1.9	1.7
Other non-response (percent)	4.5	4.9	6.7	5.1	4.7	5.2
Completed interviews (percent)	45.9	37.3	43.4	41.6	51.0	43.5
Interview too late (percent)	0.1	0.2	0.0	0.0	0.0	0.1
Interview not accepted (percent)	0.2	0.0	0.1	0.1	0.1	0.1
Valid interviews	1,473	1,008	1,228	1,001	959	5,669

Source: Bielenski and Fischer (2002).

tries resulted mainly in a level effect but did not necessarily affect the structure of naturalizations across the different home countries of the immigrants.

An alternative solution to this problem would have been to exclude naturalized immigrants from the Danish sample. This procedure, however, would have resulted in a considerable reduction of the Danish sample size. For this reason, it was decided against excluding naturalized immigrants from the Danish sample.

A.4.3 Response Rate

With 5,669 completed and valid interviews, the response rate in the German survey is 43.5 percent (see Table A.8). For each country the response rates range from a low of 37.3 percent to a high of 51.0 percent for the former Yugoslavia and Lebanon respectively. Compared to other German surveys, the overall response rate of 43.5 percent seems to be reasonable. In the year 2000 for example, the German ALLBUS (Allgemeinen Bevölkerungsumfrage der Sozialwissenschaften), a survey that covered only German nationals, achieved a response rate of about 47 percent for persons living in the western parts of Germany. The response rate in the ALLBUS was somewhat higher among persons living in East Germany, but this is less relevant in this case, since there are only a few observations in that region.

The response rate for the *German Socioeconomic Panel* (GSOEP) may serve as another comparison for the RFMS-G. In 2000, a new sample, called *Sample F*, was added to the GSOEP in order to diminish problems arising through panel attrition and to allow a more representative treatment of small sub-groups of the German population. The gross sample of Sample F consisted of 11,879 households, of which 6,060 households participated in the interviews, see von Rosenbladt (2001). This corresponds to a response rate of 51 percent.

Table A.8 also reports different reasons for non-response. For the persons where a usable address could be found, one major reason for non-response was that it was not possible to establish any contact with the target person or the household of the target person. This accounts for 22.9 percent of the usable addresses. More than 16 percent of the persons contacted by the interviewers refused to answer the questionnaire at all. Another 4 percent refused survey participation for time reasons.

A.4.4 Item Non-response

Among the completed interviews, a considerable number of persons refused to answer specific questions, in particular questions about their income. In the RFMS-G, the respondents were asked about what kind of income they received in the month before the interview. The questions covered both personal income and income of the household or of a possible spouse. With regard to these questions, the item non-response rate in the RFMS-G was quite significant. For the question on gross household income asked to persons living in households with more than one person, for example, the item non-response rate was 34 percent.

This number is considerably higher than those in the GSOEP for the year 2000. About 11 percent of Germans and 8.5 percent of the foreigners interviewed in the GSOEP refused to answer the question on gross income in the previous month. 5 percent of all households with at least one foreigner and 10 percent of all other households refused to answer questions on net household income in the previous month.

Several reasons may be responsible for this high non-response on the income questions. First, income is often seen as a very personal type of information and the respondent will therefore be less willing to give this information to a stranger (the interviewer). Second, some respondents may simply not remember their precise income of the last month (see Schräpler, 2003, on this issue). Third, since the RFMS-G was being collected for the first time, there was no possibility of creating a long-lasting and trustful relationship between the respondent and the interviewer, a factor that has been found by Hill and Willis (2001) to be very important in reducing item non-response. This may also explain the large difference in the non-response rates on income questions in the RFMS-G and the GSOEP. Fourth, non-response rates on income questions have been found to be concentrated in the tails of the income distribution, especially in the lower tails. Hence, the focus of the RFMS-G on foreigners, who are in general more concentrated on the lower end of the German income distribution, may be an explanation for the high non-response rates.

Unfortunately, there is rather little hard evidence on the question of whether high non-response rates on the income question lead to biased estimates in wage regressions. Existing studies on this issue have mixed results (see, among others Biewen, 2001, and the survey provided by Riphahn and Serfling, 2002). Some authors conclude that selection bias due to item non-response is non-negligible, while others suggest that there is only a little systematic variation in item non-response behavior and considerable randomness.

A.4.5 Representativeness of the RFMS-G

As in the last section describing the Danish survey, the representativeness of the RFMS-G is investigated by comparing the distribution of central variables such as sex, age, region, and country of origin between the RFMS-G and the whole population of foreign citizens from Turkey, the former Yugoslavia, Poland, Iran and Lebanon living in Germany. In the following, these groups are referred to as the "whole population". The data for the whole population were obtained from the *Ausländerzentralregister* (AZR), an administrative register that covers all foreigners living in Germany legally. For the following analysis, only foreigners registered in the AZR being older than 14 years are considered.

The information in the AZR is not fully reliable, mainly because some foreigners do not de-register when they leave Germany permanently. This seems to be especially problematic in the case of Polish foreigners as they often stay only a relatively short period in Germany. During the fieldwork phase, interviewers often reported that the respondent had left for his or her home country when they tried to establish contact with a Pole.

It might be argued, though, that this problem mainly affects the total number of foreigners registered in the AZR, and to a lesser extent the distribution of persons by different background variables such as sex and age. This argument holds if one assumes that the persons who do not de-register when they leave Germany permanently are randomly distributed over the background variables used in the following analysis of the representativeness of the RFMS-G. This assumption may be violated in reality, but it is the best one can do with the administrative data at hand.

Table A.9 shows the distribution of the persons registered in the AZR and the respondents of the RFMS-G by sex and country of origin. The distribution of immigrants from Turkey and the former Yugoslavia in the RFMS-G is very similar to

Table A.9. Respondents in the German survey and the whole population, distributed by sex and country of origin. Percent.

	Turkey		Poland		Lebanon		Iran		F. Yugoslavia	
	AZR	RFMS-G	AZR	RFMS-G	AZR	RFMS-G	AZR	RFMS-G	AZR	RFMS-G
Male	54.1	51.2	50.3	36.4	58.8	54.6	58.9	55.9	53.7	53.9
Female	45.9	48.8	49.7	63.6	41.2	45.4	41.1	44.1	46.3	46.1
Total	100.0	100.0	100.0	100.0	100.0	100.0	100.0	100.0	100.0	100.0
No. of Obs.	1,947,938	1,472	310,432	1,221	49,109	953	98,555	1,010	1,029,779	1,013

Sources: RFMS-G and Bielenski & Fischer (2002).

the shares of these nationalities in the AZR. In the RFMS-G males from Lebanon, and especially Poland appear to be under-represented. The significant difference for Polish males may be explained by the fact that they typically stay in Germany for short periods of time, and thus were more difficult to reach by the interviewers, while Polish women typically stay permanently in Germany, for example because of marriage to a German. It is hard to disentangle whether the differences between the RFMS-G and the whole population are a result of inaccurate register figures or whether the short duration of stays for Poles is responsible for a biased sample. Overall, however, one has to conclude that the RFMS-G is less representative than the corresponding Danish survey.

To investigate this issue further, Table A.10 shows the distribution of the respondents of the RFMS-G and the foreigners registered in the AZR by nationality and length of stay. The table shows that respondents with a shorter duration of residence are generally under-represented. This is not surprising, as one would expect that people who have had some time to settle in the new country would be easier to reach for an interview. Conversely, persons who have resided in Germany for some time are over-represented. This is especially evident for persons with more than 30 years of residence.

Remarkably, the RFMS-G seems to be most representative with respect to length of stay for immigrants from Poland, except that there are very few respondents with less than one year of residence. The distribution of immigrants from Turkey also looks quite representative, while the distributions for the other three countries do not tally in the same way, especially for persons with 10-20 years of residence.

Table A.11 compares the RFMS-G with the whole population using age and country

Table A.10. Respondents in the German survey and the whole population, distributed by period of residence and country of origin. Percent.

	Turkey		Poland		Lebanon		Iran		Former Yugoslavia	
	AZR	RFMS-G	AZR	RFMS-G	AZR	RFMS-G	AZR	RFMS-G	AZR	RFMS-G
< 1 year	1.7	0.1	7.2	0.3	4.3	0.3	5.6	0.0	2.8	0.1
1-4 years	9.4	5.3	16.0	14.4	11.5	7.5	11.9	8.9	10.8	8.0
4-6 years	7.5	3.3	11.0	10.2	7.6	6.2	9.0	6.8	6.7	6.8
6-8 years	6.9	5.1	8.8	9.7	8.0	7.0	6.6	11.9	12.5	6.9
8-10 years	7.6	6.0	11.4	7.5	10.7	4.3	6.6	7.9	18.0	10.2
10-15 years	15.4	13.8	29.7	28.0	43.6	39.7	33.1	20.2	8.7	22.6
15-20 years	8.6	10.7	9.7	13.7	7.8	24.9	13.0	24.7	4.2	5.9
20-25 years	15.9	16.8	2.6	7.3	5.3	7.5	7.2	8.4	6.6	6.3
25-30 years	17.4	17.3	1.0	1.9	0.8	1.9	2.5	3.5	13.2	7.1
30 years and more	9.5	21.7	2.7	7.2	0.6	0.8	4.5	7.7	16.4	26.1
Total	100.0	100.0	100.0	100.0	100.0	100.0	100.0	100.0	100.0	100.0
No. of Obs.	1,998,500	1,472	301,400	1,221	51,400	953	107,900	1,010	1,106,200	1,013

Sources: RFMS-G and Beauftragte der Bundesregierung für Migration, Flüchtlinge und Integration (2002), own calculations.

of origin. The table suggests that the RFMS-G appears to be fairly representative with regard to the age of the respondents. The largest difference between the RFMS-G and the whole population is for 18 to 29 year old persons from Lebanon, who appear to be somewhat under-represented. According to the AZR, 35 percent of the Lebanese are aged between 18 and 29 years, while the corresponding figure in the RFMS-G is 28 percent. The group from 30 to 39 years of age is on the other hand over-represented, as 40 percent in the data set are placed in this age group against 31 percent in the whole population. But as these are the largest differences, there is no reason to expect that the quality of the analyses will deteriorate because of such discrepancies.

Finally, Table A.12 shows the distribution of the whole population and the respondents of the RFMS-G by region and country of origin. For all nationalities sampled, respondents from North Rhine-Westphalia are over-represented. This holds in particular for migrants from Lebanon, where 50 percent of the respondents of the RFMS-G live in North Rhine-Westphalia, while only 30 percent of the whole population live in this region.

This is, however, not surprising, given the sampling program for the RFMS-G, which considered only individuals living in the 100 biggest German cities, and the

Table A.11. Respondents in the German survey and the whole population, distributed by age and country of origin. Percent.

	Turkey		Poland		Lebanon		Iran		Former Yugoslavia	
	AZR	RFMS-G	AZR	RFMS-G	AZR	RFMS-G	AZR	RFMS-G	AZR	RFMS-G
15-17 years	5.7	1.9	2.8	0.6	9.0	2.1	5.0	0.9	4.5	1.8
18-29 years	32.8	30.9	28.3	24.1	34.8	28.3	20.0	17.7	27.6	24.2
30-39 years	25.8	27.9	25.1	28.5	31.1	39.4	27.1	27.6	20.5	24.0
40-49 years	11.4	15.5	26.1	26.6	15.9	20.6	26.6	31.1	15.1	18.3
50-59 years	13.6	13.4	11.2	12.7	5.7	7.2	11.9	13.0	20.2	20.6
60-65 years	6.1	5.7	1.9	2.8	1.5	1.4	3.4	4.9	6.1	7.6
66 years or more	4.7	4.8	4.6	4.6	2.0	1.1	6.1	4.8	6.1	3.6
Total	100.0	100.0	100.0	100.0	100.0	100.0	100.0	100.0	100.0	100.0
No. of Obs.	1,464,922	1,472	287,428	1,221	32,779	953	85,104	1,010	843,066	1,013

Sources: RFMS-G and Bielenski & Fischer (2002).

fact that North Rhine-Westphalia is quite an urbanized area. When analyzing the data, it should of course be remembered that the sample consists mainly of persons living in cities.

To summarize, the RFMS-G appears not to be fully representative for the whole population of the five immigrants groups covered by the sample. The sample of Polish migrants in particular seems to be biased with regard to the sex distribution. Overall, however, the differences documented in this sub-section seem to be in an acceptable range.

A.4.6 Weighting in the German Data Set

This sub-section provides a detailed description of the weighting procedure used for the RFMS-G in the empirical analysis of this project. Compared to the weighting procedure in the Danish sample, this one relies on a relatively simple procedure. The procedure basically only takes the country of origin of the respondents into consideration, even though the last sub-section has shown that the data do not seem to be representative for all important background variables. The analysis in the last sub-section indicates that it might be reasonable to include other variables in the weighting procedure as well, such as, for example, the age of the respondents. In a different procedure, which is not shown here, a weighting procedure that considers both country of origin and age was applied. The use of this alternative procedure,

Table A.12. Respondents in the German survey and the whole population, distributed by region and country of origin. Percent.

	Turkey		Poland		Lebanon		Iran		Former Yugoslavia	
	AZR	RFMS-G	AZR	RFMS-G	AZR	RFMS-G	AZR	RFMS-G	AZR	RFMS-G
Berlin	6.5	6.4	9.6	6.6	15.7	21.1	7.1	4.8	5.4	3.2
Schleswig-Holstein	2.1	1.4	3.2	2.8	2.2	1.4	2.5	5.3	1.2	0.5
Hamburg	3.3	4.9	6.5	14.0	2.0	0.0	11.6	17.3	3.1	5.0
Lower Saxony	6.5	6.4	8.5	12.4	20.1	7.8	8.7	8.5	5.7	5.7
Bremen	1.6	6.4	1.2	2.4	3.0	6.5	2.7	0.6	0.7	4.2
North Rhine-Westphalia	33.8	42.3	27.8	32.7	30.8	50.2	28.8	32.3	23.1	36.3
Hesse	10.7	10.2	9.9	8.6	3.7	0.2	15.8	14.7	11.4	10.9
Rhineland-Palatinate	4.0	5.1	4.4	2.1	4.3	0.8	3.5	1.6	3.8	1.8
Baden-Württemberg	17.1	5.4	9.3	5.7	10.9	8.6	8.3	4.2	23.9	13.6
Bavaria	12.9	9.2	12.3	8.9	3.5	1.8	7.6	10.8	19.2	14.2
Saarland	0.8	0.0	0.8	0.0	1.8	1.7	0.8	0.0	0.8	0.0
East Germany	0.7	2.5	6.5	3.7	2.1	0.0	2.5	0.0	1.8	4.5
Total	100.0	100.0	100.0	100.0	100.0	100.0	100.0	100.0	100.0	100.0
No. of Obs.	1,925,123	1,472	304,317	1,221	47,426	953	96,011	1,010	1,017,532	1,013

Sources: RFMS-G and Bielenski & Fischer (2002).

however, only led to minor changes in the results. For this reason it was decided to stick with the simple weighting procedure.

As described in Section A.4.2 the sample was designed so that the total number of interviews should end up being distributed equally (or nearly equally) across the five countries, so that it would be possible to perform separate analyses for each country. The figures reported in Table A.13 confirm that the distribution of the respondents in the RFMS-G by country of origin is fairly even, though the share of Turkish respondents is somewhat larger than the share of Lebanese respondents (26 percent against 17 percent).

As a result of this sampling scheme, the RFMS-G does not reflect the actual composition of nationalities in the whole population. Table A.13 shows that foreigners from Turkey and the former Yugoslavia make up around 85 percent of the whole population, whereas the shares of these two ethnic groups account for only 44 percent of the RFMS-G. In order to make the RFMS-G representative of the whole population, at least with regard to distribution by the country of origin, it is necessary

Table A.13. Distribution of nationalities in the German data set and in the whole population. Age 15 years and up. Percent.

	RFMS-G.	AZR
Turkey	26.0	54.0
Former Yugoslavia	17.9	31.1
Poland	21.5	10.6
Iran	17.8	3.1
Lebanon	16.8	1.2
Total	100.0	100.0
Number of Observations	5,669	2,713,299

Note: The distribution is calculated on the basis of persons older than 14 years. In this it differs from the figures in Bielenski & Fisher (2002), as persons below 15 are included there.

Sources: RFMS-G and Ausländerzentralregister (AZR), own calculations.

to apply a weighting scheme that gives respondents from Turkey and the former Yugoslavia a relatively large weight and respondents from Poland, Iran, and Lebanon a relatively smaller weight. The construction of such weights has been achieved by applying the following formula:

$$\text{weight}_i = \frac{\text{no. of persons in the whole population from country i}}{\text{no. of persons in the data set from country i}} \times \frac{5{,}669}{2{,}713{,}299}$$

By multiplying by 5,669 (the total number of respondents in the RFMS-G) and dividing by 2,713,299 (the number of persons in the whole foreign population) it is ensured that the total number of observations still amounts to 5,669 persons when using the weights. Based on the above formula, the following weights are obtained for the different countries:

Table A.14. Weights in the RFMS-G

Country	Weight
Turkey	2.08
Former Yugoslavia	1.74
Poland	0.49
Iran	0.18
Lebanon	0.07

Table A.15 shows the effects of the weights on the distribution of some central variables (age, sex, region, and length of residence). Unlike the previous sub-section, this section only shows the distribution of these variables for the whole sample of the RFMS-G (without differentiating by country of origin). The effect of weighting the data on the regional distribution of the respondents is limited. The figures, however, change in the right direction, resulting in a weighted distribution that is more consistent with the regional distribution of the whole population. A similar effect of the weighting procedure can be observed for the gender distribution. With regard to length of residence, the use of the weights leads to a significant improvement in the representativeness of the RFMS-G, especially for the categories with 10-15 years and 15-20 years of residence. Overall, the weighting procedure improves the representativeness of the total sample of the RFMS-G with regard to all variables depicted in Table A.15. Note, however, that this conclusion does not hold when differentiating by country of origin.

Table A.15. Effects of the German weights. Percent.

	RFMS-G Un-weighted	RFMS-G Weighted	AZR		RFMS-G Un-weighted	RFMS-G Weighted	AZR
Berlin	8.0	5.5	6.6	< 1 year	0.2	0.1	2.6
Schleswig-Holstein	2.2	1.4	1.9	1-4 years	8.7	7.4	10.5
Hamburg	8.3	6.2	3.7	4-6 years	6.6	5.4	7.6
Lower Saxony	8.2	6.9	6.7	6-8 years	8.1	6.5	8.8
Bremen	4.1	5.1	1.3	8-10 years	7.1	7.6	11.4
North Rhine-Westphalia	38.7	39.2	29.9	10-15 years	24.4	18.9	15.5
Hesse	9.1	10.3	10.9	15-20 years	15.8	10.1	7.6
Rheinland-Palatinate	2.5	3.6	3.9	20-25 years	9.5	11.8	11.5
Baden-Württemberg	7.3	8.0	18.1	25-30 years	6.6	11.4	14.1
Bavaria	9.1	10.7	14.5	>30 years	12.8	20.7	10.8
Saarland	0.3	0.0	0.8				
East Germany	2.3	3.2	1.6	15-18 years	1.5	1.7	5.0
				18-30 years	25.4	27.6	30.3
Male	49.8	50.6	53.8	30-40 years	29.2	26.7	24.2
Female	50.2	49.4	46.2	40-50 years	22.1	18.1	14.6
				50-60 years	13.4	15.5	15.2
				60-65 years	5.1	6.7	5.5
				65 years or more	3.3	3.5	5.1

Sources: RFMS-G, AZR and Beauftragte der Bundesregierung für Migration, Flüchtlinge und Integration (2002), own calculations.

Figure A.2. Geographical division of Denmark

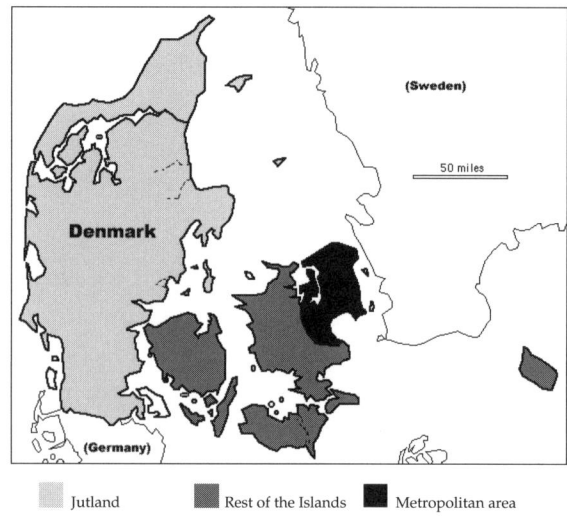

Jutland   Rest of the Islands   Metropolitan area

Source: EnchantedLearning.com

A.5 References

Beauftragte der Bundesregierung für Migration, Flüchtlinge und Integration. 2002. *Daten und Fakten zur Ausländersituation.* Berlin.

Bielenski, Harald and Gabriele Fischer. 2002. *Survey about Immigrants in Germany.* Unpublished note. Munich.

Bielenski, Harald and Gabriele Fischer. 2002a. *Survey among Immigrants in Germany. Report about the Pretest in February 2002.* Unpublished note. Munich.

Biewen, Martin. 2001. "Item Non-response and Inequality Measurement: Evidence from the German Earnings Distribution," *Allgemeines Statistisches Archiv* 85, 409-425.

Burkhauser, Richard and Friederike Behringer and Gert Wagner. 1993. "The English Language Public Use File of the German Socio-Economic Panel," *The Journal of Human Resources* 28 (2), 429-433.

Haisken-DeNew, John P. and Joachim R. Frick (eds.). 2002. *Desktop Companion to the German Socio-Economic Panel Study (GSOEP).* Berlin: DIW.

Hill, Daniel and Robert J. Willis. 2001. "Reducing Panel Attrition: A Search for Effective Policy Instruments," *Journal of Human Resources* 36 (3), 416-438.

Koch, Achim, Martina Wasmer, Janet Harkness and Evi Scholz. 2001. "Konzeption und Durchführung der ‚Allgemeinen Bevölkerungsumfrage der Sozialwissenschaften' (ALLBUS) 2000." *ZUMA-Methodenbericht* 2001/05. Mannheim.

Nielsen, Niels-Kenneth. 2002. "Databeskrivelse," in Gunnar Viby Mogensen and Poul Chr. Matthiessen (eds): *Indvandrerne og arbejdsmarkedet. Mødet med det danske velfærdssamfund.* Copenhagen: Spektrum, 327-348.

Nielsen, Niels-Kenneth and Søren Pedersen. 2001. "Data description," in Marie Louise Schultz-Nielsen with contributions from Olaf Ingerslev, Claus Larsen, Gunnar Viby Mogensen, Niels-Kenneth Nielsen, Søren Pedersen and Eskil Wadensjö: *The Integration of non-Western Immigrants in a Scandinavian Labour market: The Danish Experience.* Copenhagen: Rockwool Foundation Research Unit, 91-108.

Riphahn, Regina T. and Oliver Serfling. 2002. "Item Non-response on Income and Wealth Questions," *IZA Discussion Paper* No. 573. Bonn

Rosenbladt, Bernhard von. 2001. *Erprobung innovativer Erhebungskonzepte für Haushalts-Panel-Stichproben: Erstbefragung 2000 der SOEP-Stichprobe F – Methodenbericht.* Munich.

Schräpler, Jörg-Peter. 2003. "Gross Income Non-response in the German Socio-Economic Panel – Refusal or Don't Know?" *Schmollers Jahrbuch* 123 (1), 109-124.

Schwarz, Norbert. 2001. "The German Microzensus," *Schmollers Jahrbuch* 121 (4), 649-654.

Statistics Denmark. 2001. *Statistiske Efterretninger, Befolkning og Valg 2001:4.* Copenhagen.

Statistisches Bundesamt. 2000. *Statistisches Jahrbuch 2000.* Wiesbaden.

Togeby, Lise and Birgit Møller (1999). *Oplevet diskrimination.* Copenhagen: Nævnet for Etnisk Ligestilling.

Index

Act of Parliament 36
Act on Benefits for Asylum Seekers 38
Act on Repatriation 34
Act on the Central Aliens Register 38
Act to Amend the Basic Law 123
Adjustment effect 131-132, 134
Afghanistan 52, 123
Aging of the population 17
Aliens Act 32-35, 38, 45, 52, 290-294, 302, 305, 307, 312
Amin, Idi 48
Asylum Procedure Act 38, 123, 288, 290-292, 298, 302, 307
Asylum seekers 31-43, 45-52, 57, 62, 190, 286-291, 293-294, 303-304, 307-308,
ATP pension scheme 252, 323
"attachment requirement" 35
Auslaenderzentralregister, AZR 25
Austria 58
Availability 35, 148, 155-158, 174, 182, 217, 262, 325, 395, 400
Average labor income 357, 373
Average production worker (APW) 248, 254, 257

Bauer, Thomas 5, 10, 12, 26, 31, 75, 405, 436
Benefit period 247-248
Berlin Wall 41
Between-school variation 311-313
Bilateral agreements 36-38, 53-54, 56, 73, 253, 256
Blinder-Oaxaca decomposition 365
Blue-collar 78, 103-104, 107
Boll, Stephan 325
Bonin, Holger 75, 147, 282, 325
Borjas, G. 131, 151, 213, 268
Bulgarians 50

Bundesamt für Migration 51-52
Bundesamt für Migration und Flüchtlinge 51-52
Bundesanstalt für Arbeit 55, 76, 117
Business cycle sensitivity 136, 140

CEEC 38, 53-54, 64, 73
Central Office for Foreign Education 82
Chile 29, 48, 123
Chiswick, B.R. 96, 102, 131, 159
Clear-up rate 287
Clustering 62, 64, 416
Cohort effects 118, 131, 188, 193, 236
Coleman, David 123, 171, 310, 315
Commissioner of Police 33, 302-303, 315
Communication on Immigration, Integration, and Employment 17
Communism 41
Compensation rate 130, 149, 247-248
Composition effect 131, 134
Constant, Amelie 5-7, 12, 26-27, 75, 119, 147, 187, 213, 436
Consulting Centre for Self-Employment 216
Contract workers 37
Country effect 105, 181, 205-206, 240, 242
Counterfactual analysis 189, 203, 205-206, 209, 215, 239-242, 397-398
Country hopping 17
CRAM 124
Crimes committed 286, 290, 292
Criminal record 35-36, 285
Criminality rates 8, 295-299, 305-307, 310, 314
Cross-sectional studies 131, 321
Czech Republic 38, 54

Danish Immigration Service 33, 44-45, 51-52, 56, 66
Danish Integration Act 31
Danish Ministry of Education 76
Danish Ministry of Finance 13, 26
Danish Ministry of Foreign Affairs 34, 66
Danish Ministry of Justice 36, 66
Danish Ministry of Refugee, Immigration, and Integration Affairs 35-36, 66
Danish Ministry of the Interior 35, 49, 66
Danish referenda 34
Danish Refugee Council 33-34
Danish Register for Social Statistics 260, 262, 264, 268
De facto refugees 33
Demographic changes 17, 308
Discrimination 22, 29, 131, 136, 143, 148, 166, 181, 202, 210, 309
Dublin Accord 41
Dublin Convention 34

Early retirement benefit 253, 267-268
Earnings assimilation 131, 159, 188
Earnings distribution 197-198, 209, 427
Earnings profile 201, 205, 236
Eastern enlargement 16-17
EC 56
Educational level 5, 76, 81, 103, 134, 139, 363
EEA 56, 256
EEC 34, 38
EEC Residence Act 38
Ekberg, Jan 134, 319, 327, 357
Eligibility rules 251-252, 255, 274, 280, 399
Employment rate 17-19, 119-129, 134-135, 143-144, 149, 154, 322-324, 338-340, 347-351, 354, 358-362, 394-395
Entorf, Horst 8, 12, 27, 285, 436

Entrepreneurial activities 217-218, 241, 398
Ethnic differences 97, 113, 116, 198, 215, 394, 403, 416
Euphoriants Act 294-295, 302-304
European Commission 17
European Council 17
European Fund for Regional Development 219
European Social Fund 219
European Union 16-17, 19, 32, 37, 40, 65, 219
Eurostat 120, 123-124, 127, 129-130, 141-142, 145, 155, 188, 210
Eurostat Labour Force Survey 127, 130, 141-142

Family migrants 32, 37
Family migration 21, 107, 397
Family reunification 15, 31-35, 43-45, 66, 115, 131, 190-191, 196, 226-230, 232, 275
Federal Expellees Act 38
Federal Labour Institute (FLI) 189
Federal Statistical Office Germany 42, 47, 49, 58, 61, 66
Fertility rate 43
Financial incentives 37, 148-149, 151, 154-155, 157, 174, 181, 395, 403
Finland 42, 57-58
Firearms Act 294, 302-304
First oil crisis 32, 245
Fiscal impact of immigration 9, 319, 327, 331
Forced marriages 35
Fortress Europe 16
France 42

Gastarbeitnehmer 53-54
GDR 47, 62, 78
Gerdes, Christer 9, 12, 27, 319, 357, 436
German Federal Council 40
German Federal Police Office 286

German Labour Office 39, 54
German Minister for the Interior 40
German Supreme Court 40
Globalization 15, 21
Government Policies 20
Greece 36, 42, 59, 65, 189
Green Card 39-40, 53-55
Green Party 39
GSOEP 97, 214, 259, 270, 325, 414, 418-419
Guest worker 7, 31, 36, 42, 59, 62, 64, 115, 117, 129, 145, 184, 188-190, 209, 403
Guest worker program 36

Hate preachers 40
Hidden unemployment 120
High-skilled workers 15, 40
Human Capital 5-6, 15, 19, 26, 75-76, 82, 94-99, 102-103, 109, 113-118, 147, 160, 166, 176, 182-183, 188, 192-196, 201, 209, 215, 220-221, 223-224, 226-227, 229, 232-233, 236, 239, 241-242, 274, 279-282, 315, 362, 392-397, 400, 403
Hungary 48, 54

Iceland 23, 57, 295
Illegal migrants 15, 286, 291
ILO 148, 155-158, 174, 182, 264, 281, 395
Immigrant effect 7, 131, 239, 282
Immigrant-intensive 193
Immigration Act 190
Immigration Service 33, 44-45, 51-52, 56, 66
Income smoothing 222
Income support 249-250, 258, 263, 270-271
Income Tax and Fiscal Acts 294
India 55
Infratest Sozialforschung 13, 25, 405, 415
Institut für Mittelstandsforschung 216
Institute for the Study of Labor (IZA) 12, 13, 31

Integration Act 31, 132
Integration Affairs 35-36, 66
Integration strategies 17
Internet 16
Intrapreneurship 218
Introduction allowance 34
Introduction program 34-35
IOM 15, 28, 216, 243
Iran 50, 83-88, 113, 116, 166, 177, 181, 226, 232, 235, 242, 265, 384, 393-394
Iraq 49-50, 52
Iron Curtain 37, 45, 190
IT specialists 39, 54-55
Italy 36, 42, 59, 65, 121, 189, 216, 292

Job Card 32, 56
Job qualifications 285
Job-seeking foreigners 32

Know-how 221

Labor immigration policy 16
Labor market attachment 119, 129, 144, 147, 154, 159-162, 167, 181-182, 195, 261, 269, 271, 274-281, 395, 399, 403, 406
Labor market experience 98-99, 192-193, 195, 197, 201, 203, 206, 208, 221, 396
Labor market integration 19-21, 131, 148, 158-159, 220, 331, 396
Larsen, Claus 5, 8, 12, 26-29, 31, 66, 75, 118, 282, 285, 436
Law Model 13, 26, 319, 322-323, 325, 327, 355, 357, 362-363, 378
Lebanon 49, 83-84, 127, 144, 171, 175, 199, 231, 242, 265-267, 275, 278-279, 331-332, 344, 347, 395
Lisbon Agenda 16-17, 19
London Resolutions 34
Low-skilled workers 15, 19, 21, 36, 121

Maastricht Treaty 34, 41
Maintenance condition 33

Manifestly unfounded procedure 33-34
Manpower recruitment 41-42, 121
Marginal "net tax" effect 340
Matthiessen, Poul Chr. 5, 12, 26, 31, 184, 436
Metropolitan area 63, 101, 410
Mikrozensus 63, 97, 216, 270
Mincer, J. 118
Minimum wages 22, 131, 159
Mobility 20, 28, 37, 185, 221, 368, 375
Mogensen, Gunnar Viby 12, 435-436
Morocco 36, 42, 121
Municipal unemployment rate 375-376
Municipality of Copenhagen 63, 367

Nationality Law 32, 35, 38-39
Naturalization 18, 23-24, 31, 36, 47, 86, 232, 416
Net compensation rate 130
Net immigration 42-43, 45-46, 65
New economy 55
New Zealand 21, 23
Nielsen, Niels-Kenneth 8, 10, 12, 27, 245, 405, 436
Nordic countries 24, 32, 36, 56-58, 65, 122, 190, 311, 391, 403
Norway 22, 42, 301, 330

Occupational profile 141
OECD 21, 121, 248, 310, 313
Offender rates 292
Orrje, Helena 27, 214, 319, 436
Own payment 256

Pakistan 43-44, 59, 97, 127, 171
Palme, Olof 310
Parental capital 97
Participation rate 122, 124, 131-134, 138, 195
Pays to work 148
Penal Code 294-296, 298-305, 307, 312

Pension points 252
PISA 311-313, 315
Poland 38, 48, 88, 98, 113, 116, 166, 171, 175-176, 190, 218, 232, 265, 267, 331-332, 344, 384, 392-394, 406, 409, 424
Portugal 36, 42, 59, 121, 189
Positive list 56
Post-migration schooling 86, 88, 94-96, 98, 103
Prague Spring 48
Pre-migration experience 99, 104-105, 109, 116, 163, 192, 227, 232, 393
Pre-migration schooling 94, 102, 109, 113, 116, 196, 221, 226, 229, 393
Pro forma and forced marriages 35
Protective status 35
Pull migration 38, 53
Push factors 47

Recession 32, 37, 42-43, 392
Recognition rate 52
Recruitment policy 37, 42, 62
Refugee Board 33, 44
Refugee migration 21
Reservation wages 148-149, 170, 242
Residence permits 31-34, 37, 39, 44-46, 48-52, 55-57, 64, 69, 216, 226-227, 266-267
Residence requirement 269, 281
Residence rights 196
Retirement benefit 252-253, 267-268
Return migration 37, 43, 47, 122
Return to education 365
RFMS-D 10, 12, 24, 76, 81, 98, 120, 127, 149, 152, 155, 158-160, 188-189, 191, 208, 214, 220, 224, 275, 405-415
RFMS-G 10, 12, 25, 76, 81, 98, 120, 127, 149, 155, 159-160, 188-189, 191, 208, 214, 220, 224, 258, 260, 263, 266, 271, 405, 414-416, 418-426
Road Traffic Act 294-296, 298-302, 305, 307, 312

Rockwool Foundation Research Unit (RFF) 10, 12, 13, 22, 28, 293-294, 429
Rotationprinzip 189

Safe third country returns 34, 48-49
Schengen Accords 41
Schengen Convention 34
Schengen co-operation 34
Schultz-Nielsen, Marie Louise 6-7, 12, 27, 119, 147, 187, 213, 436
Seasonal workers 38, 53-54
Seizing the opportunity 109, 113
Selective immigration policy 21
Self-employment rate 213, 214, 218
Self-selected 130, 215, 223, 226, 236, 241, 397, 403
Single European Act 40
Social capital 96, 118, 233, 310, 315
Social Democrats 39
Social networks 286, 310, 315
Social security 8, 17, 23, 26, 28, 34-35, 53-54, 145, 184, 246, 256-258, 280, 282, 346, 351, 399, 406, 430
Social tensions 37, 43
Socio-economic characteristics 25, 192, 392
Somalia 49, 123, 127, 171, 175-177, 181, 190, 275
Soviet Union 50, 292
Spain 36, 42, 59, 189
Sri Lanka 48, 52, 123, 190
Statistics Denmark 13, 22, 25, 46, 63, 81, 101, 120, 124, 136, 259, 293, 298-301, 307, 310, 363, 369, 400, 405-406, 414
Stockholm European Council 17
Sweden 22, 57, 134-135, 301, 310, 330

Tamil 48
Technology 38-39, 56, 213, 217
Temporary workers 31, 38, 53, 56, 65, 392
Terror suspects 40

The Danish Centre for Assessment of Foreign Qualifications 76, 117
Think Tank on Integration in Denmark 67-68, 258, 283
Trade Unions 121
Transfer income 149-150, 158, 258-259, 324, 331, 378, 383
Transferability of skills 109
Trænæs, Torben 5, 9, 13, 15, 27, 283, 391, 436
Treaty of Amsterdam 41
Treaty of Rome 40
Tunisia 36, 42, 121
Turkey 36-37, 42-44, 48, 50, 57, 88, 97, 129, 166, 171, 232, 253, 265-267, 331

Uganda 48, 123
UN Refugee Convention 33
Unabhängige Kommission Zuwanderung 43-44, 67
Under-employment 121, 125, 143, 394, 403
Unemployment benefit 150, 152, 181, 246-250, 253, 259-263, 278, 395
Unemployment insurance (UI) 121, 150-153, 174, 181
Unemployment rate 19, 120, 124-126, 134, 136, 143, 147, 160, 167-169, 221, 292, 368-369, 375-376, 385
UNHCR 48, 50, 67
Unskilled labor 15, 130, 134
Urban areas 62, 64, 144, 293, 311, 392
Urbanization dummies 369-371
USA 42, 148, 295

Victims 293, 316
Vietnam 48, 127

Wadensjö, Eskil 9, 12, 27, 245, 319, 356, 357, 386, 435-436
Wage equations 357, 362-363, 368, 370
Wage floor 121, 130

War adjustment 41
Welfare benefits 26-27, 152, 170, 187, 191, 270, 274, 336, 380, 429
Welfare shopping 17
Well endowed 147
White-collar 77-78, 97, 103, 107, 110-111, 113, 116
Within-school variation 311-312
Work permits 32, 38-39, 53-55, 70
Work requirement 269, 281
World War II 31, 36, 41, 47, 62, 391

Yugoslavia 21, 34, 36-37, 42-46, 54-55, 83-88, 97, 107, 111, 113, 121-122, 166, 171, 190, 196-199, 203, 218, 229-233, 235, 242, 265-268, 271, 278, 291-293, 332

Zimmermann, Klaus F. 5, 9, 13, 15, 27, 391, 436

The Rockwool Foundation Research Unit: Publications in English

Time and consumption, *ed. by Gunnar Viby Mogensen. (Statistics Denmark. 1990).*

Solidarity or Egoism? *by Douglas A. Hibbs. (Aarhus University Press. 1993).*

Danes and Their Politicians, *by Gunnar Viby Mogensen. (Aarhus University Press. 1993).*

Welfare and Work Incentives. A North European Perspective, *ed. by A.B. Atkinson and Gunnar Viby Mogensen. (Oxford University Press. 1993).*

Unemployment and Flexibility on the Danish Labour Market, *by Gunnar Viby Mogensen. (Statistics Denmark. 1994).*

On the Measurement of a Welfare Indicator for Denmark 1970-1990, *by Peter Rørmose Jensen and Elisabeth Møllgaard. (Statistics Denmark. 1995).*

Work Incentives in the Danish Welfare State: New Empirical Evidence, *ed. by Gunnar Viby Mogensen. With contributions by Søren Brodersen, Lisbeth Pedersen, Peder J. Pedersen, Søren Pedersen and Nina Smith. (Aarhus University Press. 1995).*

The Shadow Economy in Denmark 1994. Measurement and Results, *by Gunnar Viby Mogensen, Hans Kurt Kvist, Eszter Körmendi and Søren Pedersen. (Statistics Denmark. 1995).*

Actual and Potential Recipients of Welfare Benefits with a Focus on Housing Benefits, 1987-1992, *by Hans Hansen and Marie Louise Hultin. (Statistics Denmark. 1997).*

The Shadow Economy in Western Europe. Measurement and Results for Selected Countries, *by Søren Pedersen. With contributions by Esben Dalgaard and Gunnar Viby Mogensen. (Statistics Denmark. 1998).*

Immigration to Denmark. International and National Perspectives, *by David Coleman and Eskil Wadensjö. With contributions by Bent Jensen and Søren Pedersen. (Aarhus University Press. 1999).*

Nature as a Political Issue in the Classical Industrial Society: The Environmental Debate in the Danish Press from the 1870s to the 1970s, *by Bent Jensen. (Statistics Denmark. 2000).*

The integration of non-Western immigrants in a Scandinavian labour market: The Danish experience, *by Marie Louise Schultz-Nielsen. With contributions by Olaf Ingerslev, Claus Larsen, Gunnar Viby Mogensen, Niels-Kenneth Nielsen, Søren Pedersen and Eskil Wadensjö. (Statistics Denmark. 2001).*

Foreigners in the Danish newspaper debate from the 1870s to the 1990s, *by Bent Jensen. (Statistics Denmark. 2001).*

Immigration and the public sector in Denmark, *by Eskil Wadensjö and Helena Orrje. (Aarhus University Press. 2002).*

Social security in Denmark and Germany – with a focus on access conditions for refugees and immigrants. A comparative study, *by Hans Hansen, Helle Cwarzko Jensen, Claus Larsen and Niels-Kenneth Nielsen. (Statistics Denmark. 2002).*

The Shadow Economy in Germany, Great Britain and Scandinavia. A measurement based on questionnaire surveys, *by Søren Pedersen. (Statistics Denmark. 2003).*

Do-it-yourself work in North-Western Europe. Maintenance and improvement of homes, *by Søren Brodersen. (Statistics Denmark. 2003).*

Migrants, Work, and the Welfare State, *ed. by Torben Tranæs and Klaus F. Zimmermann. With contributions by Thomas Bauer, Amelie Constant, Horst Entorf, Christer Gerdes, Claus Larsen, Niels-Kenneth Nielsen, Poul Chr. Matthiessen, Marie Louise Schultz-Nielsen, and Eskil Wadensjö. (University Press of Southern Denmark. 2004).*